lonely planet

New Zealand's
South Island
(Te Waipounamu)

D1423929

Nelson &
Marlborough
(p283)

The
West
Coast
(p248)

Christchurch
& Canterbury
(p64)

Queenstown
& Wānaka
(p204)

Dunedin
& Otago
(p133)

Fiordland &
Southland
(p172)

Brett Atkinson, Peter Dragicevich,
Monique Perrin, Tasmin Waby

Contents

LAKE TEKAPO, MACKENZIE
COUNTRY P122

QUEENSTOWN P210

SIMONBRADFIELD/GETTY IMAGES ©

KLANARONG CHITMUNG/SHUTTERSTOCK ©

Contents

COVID-19

We have re-checked every business in this book before publication to ensure that it is still open after 2020's COVID-19 outbreak. However, the economic and social impacts of COVID-19 will continue to be felt long after the outbreak has been contained, and many businesses, services and events referenced in this guide may experience ongoing restrictions. Some businesses may be temporarily closed, have changed their opening hours and services, or require bookings; some unfortunately could have closed permanently. We suggest you check with venues before visiting for the latest information.

Welcome to the South Island

From turquoise lakes and lush peninsulas to snow-capped mountains and sparkling glaciers, the South Island's majestic landscapes offer awe and adventure in equal measure.

Wandering Wild

You'll have no trouble finding your own slice of wilderness on New Zealand's 'mainland'. The only problem: choosing between the sublime forests, mountains, lakes, beaches and fiords that make this island one of the best outdoor destinations on the planet. Lace up your boots and tackle one of the Great Walks, or choose from short nature strolls. The Department of Conservation's track and hut network makes it easy to find a way in.

Adventure Ahoy

Hiking (or 'tramping' here) may be the South Island's quintessential activity, but there are racier ways to immerse yourself in its landscapes. Slip down the Buller or Rangitata Rivers in a raft, or paddle the glassy coves of the Marlborough Sounds, Abel Tasman National Park or Fiordland. In winter, slice up the slopes around Wānaka, Queenstown or Mt Hutt, while in warmer weather the Alps 2 Ocean Cycle Trail and Otago Central Rail Trail beckon to those on two wheels. For the hardcore thrill seekers, Queenstown's gravity-defying menu of bungy, paragliding or skydiving is sure to get your adrenalin pumping.

Meet the Locals

Prepare to meet the South Island's idiosyncratic wildlife. Whales, fur seals, dolphins and penguins all frequent the coastal waters around Kaikōura; endangered Hector's dolphins cavort alongside penguins in Akaroa Harbour and the Catlins; and the Otago Peninsula shelters penguins, sea lions and even a colony of royal albatrosses. Further south, remote Stewart Island/Rakiura is the perfect place to spot the iconic but shy kiwi.

Tantalise Your Taste Buds

Epicurious travellers will delight in the South Island's smorgasbord of seasonal produce, from luscious berries, stone fruit, asparagus and root vegetables to local seafood, lamb, beef and a plethora of artisanal dairy delights. Roadside kiosks sell everything from farm eggs to grandma's traditional tomato relish, while world-class regional restaurants skim the cream of local crops for innovative tasting menus. Add some of the world's best cool-climate wines, from Central Otago's superb pinot noir to Marlborough's renowned sauvignon blanc, as well as some of the most exciting craft breweries in the country, and you have a recipe for a foodies' paradise.

Why I Love the South Island

By Monique Perrin, Writer

Sometimes I just want to feel like a tiny speck in the face of the universe. The South Island is one of those rare places that reassure me of the splendour and endurance of the natural world. Far less populated than the North, Te Waipounamu admits us into her grand galleries – the vertical cliffs and mountain-fringed lakes of Fiordland, the majestic glaciers of the West Coast and the bird-filled, ferny valleys of Stewart Island/Rakiura. It's the perfect antidote to my busy urban life. I come here to lose myself, and my phone reception, in the wilderness.

For more about our writers, see p384.

Above: Milford Sound (Piopiotahi; p201), Fiordland

New Zealand's South Island

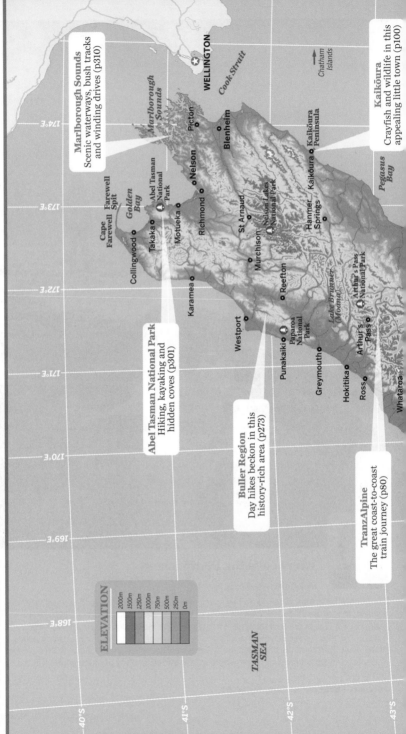

Marlborough Sounds
Scenic waterways, bush tracks and winding drives (p310)

Kaikōura
Crayfish and wildlife in this appealing little town (p100)

Abel Tasman National Park
Hiking, kayaking and hidden coves (p301)

Buller Region
Day hikes beckon in this history-rich area (p273)

TranzAlpine
The great coast-to-coast train journey (p80)

ELEVATION
2000m
1500m
1250m
1000m
750m
500m
250m
0m

0 — 200 km
0 — 100 miles

WELLINGTON

Cook Strait

Marlborough Sounds

Picton
Blenheim
Nelson
Richmond
Abel Tasman National Park
Golden Bay
Farewell Spit
Cape Farewell
Collingwood
Takaka
Motueka
St Arnaud
Nelson Lakes National Park
Murchison
Hanmer Springs
Kaikōura
Kaikōura Peninsula
Pegasus Bay
Karamea
Reefton
Westport
Punakaiki
Paparoa National Park
Lake Brunner (Moana)
Arthur's Pass National Park
Greymouth
Hokitika
Ross
Arthur's Pass
Whataroa

TASMAN SEA

Chatham Islands

Christchurch
Dynamic cityscape with world-class gardens (p65)

Banks Peninsula
French history and coastal landscapes (p94)

Mackenzie Country
Mountains tower above powder-blue lakes (p119)

Ōamaru
Victorian heritage and steampunk culture (p137)

Central Otago
History, cycling & summer fruit (p161)

Queenstown
New Zealand's snow (and après-ski) centre (p210)

Otago Peninsula
Meet the locals: penguins, seals and sea lions (p157)

The Catlins
Wildlife on the scenic route (p178)

Stewart Island/Rakiura
Kiwis and far-flung southern coastlines (p188)

Fox Glacier
Glacial thrills, lakes and rainforest (p254)

Milford Sound
Peaks soaring from indigo depths (p201)

SOUTH PACIFIC OCEAN

Bounty Islands;
Antipodes Islands

Campbell
Island

Snares Islands;
Auckland Islands

Christchurch
Lyttelton
Banks
Peninsula
Akaroa

Mt Hutt
Methven
Ashburton

Geraldine
Temuka
Timaru

Canterbury
Bight

Mt Aspiring (3781m)
Aoraki/Mt Cook (3724m)
Westland
Tai Poutini
National Park
Mt Cook Village
Aoraki/Mt Cook
National Park
Lake
Pūkaki

Fox Glacier
Haast
Jackson
Bay/Okahu

Twizel
Ōmārama
Waimate
Ōamaru

Palmerston

Otago
Peninsula
Dunedin

Mt Aspiring (3035m)
Fiordland
National Park
Milford
Sound
George
Sound

Wānaka
Arrowtown
Cromwell
Clyde
Alexandra
Queenstown

Lake
Wānaka
Lake
Wakatipu

Glenorchy
Te Anau
Manapōuri
Lake
Te Anau
Lake
Manapōuri

Lumsden

Gore

Lake
Mahinerangi

Milton
Balclutha

Catlins
Conservation
Park

Chaslands
Mistake

Doubtful
Sound

Dusky
Sound

West
Cape

Tuatapere
Winton
Invercargill
Bluff

Foveaux
Strait

Stewart
Island
(Rakiura)

Oban

45°S
46°S
47°S

The South Island's
Top 16

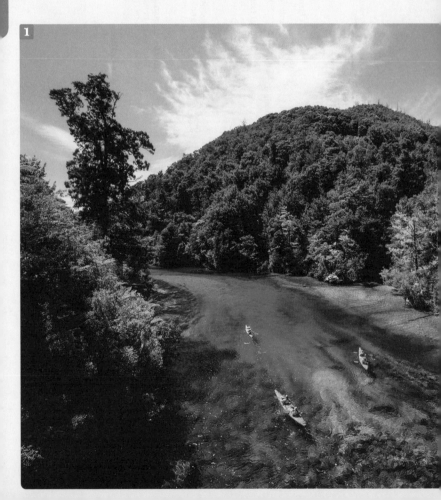

1

Abel Tasman National Park

1 This is New Zealand at its most glorious and seductive: lush green hills fringed with golden sandy coves, slipping gently into warm shallows before meeting a crystal-clear sea. Abel Tasman National Park (p301) is the quintessential postcard paradise and you can put yourself in the picture in an endless number of poses: kayaking, swimming, sunbathing and, of course, hiking the Abel Tasman Coast Track. This sweet corner of the South Island raises the bar and effortlessly keeps it there.

Milford Sound

2 Fingers crossed you'll be lucky enough to see Milford Sound (p201) on a clear, sunny day, when the world-renowned collage of waterfalls, verdant cliffs and peaks, and dark cobalt waters is at its best. More likely, though, is the classic Fiordland scenario of rain, with the landscape an arguably more dramatic scene of gushing waterfalls and Mitre Peak revealed slowly through swirling mist. It's awesome no matter what the weather, particularly when special inhabitants such as seals, dolphins and native birds show up alongside a boat cruise or sea-kayaking trip.

Below right: Stirling Falls, Milford Sound (p201)

Stewart Island/ Rakiura

3 Birdwatching, kayaking, hiking and cycling are some of the ways you can explore New Zealand's third island (p188), one where only 400 people live and 85% of the land is protected by Rakiura National Park. It's also your best opportunity to view kiwis in the wild. Seeing these small indigenous birds tramping along the beach in the dark under a dazzling Milky Way is worth the one-hour ferry ride from the historic port of Bluff. Above: Halfmoon Bay, Stewart Island/Rakiura (p188)

Queenstown

4 Queenstown (p210) may be known as the birthplace of bungy, but there's more to do in NZ's adventure capital than just leaping off a bridge tied to a giant rubber band. Amid the ridiculously beautiful scenery of Lake Wakatipu, the Shotover River and the Remarkables mountain range, travellers can spend their days hiking, mountain biking, paragliding, skydiving, rafting or heading cross-country on a 4WD tour. The lively hospitality hubs of Queenstown and nearby Wānaka are stimulating places to relive the adventures over a drink or dinner. Top right: Shotover River, Queenstown (p210)

Marlborough Sounds

5 Way more than just the place where the Interislander ferry docks, Picton is a vibrant hang-out and hub for adventure trips into the serpentine Marlborough Sounds (p310), four different waterways linked by bush tracks and winding drives. Boat trips allow the deepest penetration into the area's countless nooks and crannies. Hike or bike the Queen Charlotte Track, or paddle a kayak between back-to-nature campsites. A host of boat trips offer everything from activity combos to lunch cruises and trips to Motuara Island to meet precious rare birds. Bottom right: Queen Charlotte Sound (p310)

Christchurch

6 There's more to Christchurch (p65) than its colonial architecture suggests. Linger for a day or two and you'll discover a creative, cosmopolitan city full of culture and heart. After the devastation of the 2011 earthquakes, Christchurch's city centre has been transformed into an open, pedestrian-friendly space, with multiple green zones, public spaces to 'play' and walls of street art. A world-class art gallery, fascinating museums and blissful botanic gardens to go for a punt on the Avon River all combine to make Christchurch a must-see stop. Below: Transitional Cathedral (p70)

Ōamaru

7 A wonderfully restored Victorian townscape, a quirky celebration of steampunk culture and the nightly arrival of hundreds of little blue penguins: surprising Ōamaru (p137) has plenty of reasons for inclusion on your itinerary. Explore the town's historic harbourside precinct on a penny-farthing bicycle before adjourning for high tea in one of the charming cafes. At dusk, grab a grandstand seat to greet a parade of penguins returning home after a day's fishing, before toasting their ocean-going bravery with a beer at the nearby brewery.

CHRISADAM /GETTY IMAGES ©

VKF-AUSTRALIA /GETTY IMAGES ©

Kaikōura

8 First settled by Māori, with their appreciation for its abundant seafood, Kaikōura (p100) – meaning 'eat crayfish' – is also NZ's best spot for communing with marine life. Whale spotting is one of the primary draws either from land, a boat or from a seaplane. You can also take tours swimming with seals and dolphins (with licensed operators); and spot albatrosses, petrels and other seabirds. Along the Kaikōura coastline you'll see evidence of the complex 2016 earthquake that changed the landscape and lifted the seabed. Top right: Whale near Kaikōura

TranzAlpine

9 New Zealand's most scenic train route, the TranzAlpine (p80) is a five-hour journey from the Pacific to the Tasman Sea. After leaving Christchurch and speeding across the bucolic Canterbury Plains, it heads into the Southern Alps, negotiating tunnels and viaducts to reach the Waimakariri Valley. A stop within Arthur's Pass National Park is followed by the 8.5km-long Otira tunnel, burrowing through the bedrock of the South Island's alpine spine. Then downhill through the Taramakau Valley and into sleepy Greymouth. Unforgettable.

Akaroa & Banks Peninsula

10 Infused with a healthy dash of Gallic ambience, Francophile Akaroa village sits within one of the prettiest harbours on the Banks Peninsula (p94). Dainty dolphins and plump penguins inhabit clear waters that are perfect for sailing and exploring. Elsewhere on the peninsula, the spidery Summit Rd traces the rim of an ancient volcano, with winding offshoots that descend to hidden bays and coves. Spend your days hiking and kayaking amid the improbably beautiful land- and seascapes, unwinding at night in cosy town bistros or atmospheric rural B&Bs.

Mackenzie Country

11 Canterbury's Mackenzie Country (p119) is the star of scenic Hwy 8 between Christchurch and Queenstown, serving up icons such as Lake Tekapo and Aoraki/Mt Cook. Ringed by mountain ranges and infilled with golden tussock and surreal blue hydro lakes, this unique basin offers plenty of options for soaking up the scenery, from the gentle Alps 2 Ocean Cycle Trail to horse trekking, scenic flights and hiking. There are also stargazing tours that take advantage of the basin's status as the southern hemisphere's only International Dark Sky Reserve. Bottom right: Lake Tekapo (p122)

WILLGAOSILI/GETTY IMAGES ©

Otago Peninsula

12 Few cities anywhere have such remarkable wildlife on their doorstep as Dunedin. Only 15 minutes' drive from the city centre, the Otago Peninsula (p157) is a narrow strip of land lined with peaceful beaches, craggy coves and cliffs. It's a haven for seals and sea lions, but its seabirds – including rare yellow-eyed penguins (hoiho; pictured), and the world's most northerly royal albatross colony at Taiaroa Head – are what make it so special. Visit in January or February to see the huge albatrosses soaring above the cliffs and making clumsy landings.

Fox Glacier

13 Unusually close to both the Tasman Sea and the loftiest peaks of the Southern Alps, the twin glaciers of Franz Josef and Fox (p254) are a must-see for their crazy valleys and spectacular ice flows. Hiking on the ice is a great way to view them, as are scenic flights soaring over the glaciers and up to Aoraki/Mt Cook. Fox Glacier's amazing extras are Lake Matheson (pictured), the famous 'mirror' lake fringed with beautiful rainforest, and wild Gillespies Beach, with its rusting mining relics and walkway to a remote seal colony.

Central Otago

14 Here's your chance to balance virtue and vice. Take two wheels to negotiate the easygoing Otago Central Rail Trail (p162; pictured), cycling through some of NZ's most beautiful landscapes and the heritage streetscapes of former gold-mining towns. All the while, snack on the summer stone fruit for which the region is famous. Balance the ledger with well-earned beers at one of the numerous historic pubs. Alternatively, taste your way to viticultural ecstasy in the vineyards of one of the country's most acclaimed wine regions.

Buller Region

15 The vast majority of West Coast travellers turn south from Westport, missing the opportunity to explore the less-visited Buller Region (p273) to the north. An incredible array of sights and experiences are on offer: hike and cycle around ghostly Denniston Plateau, discover regional history at Charming Creek – one of NZ's best day walks – and gaze at the sublime limestone arches of Ōpārara Basin. Beyond the relaxed, estuary-side town of Karamea is the Kōhaihai end of the Heaphy Track, where there's a memorable half-day hike to raw, empty Scotts Beach. Left: Moria Gate Arch, Ōpārara Basin (p279)

The Catlins

16 Even for many New Zealanders, the rugged Catlins (p178) coast is unknown territory. Avoid the speedy but functional inland route linking Dunedin and Invercargill, and traverse the Catlins' more diverse and interesting procession of isolated bays and coves, dramatic landforms such as waterfalls and caves, and opportunities to chinwag with friendly locals and spot local wildlife. The Catlins' highlights include the quirky Lost Gypsy Gallery at Papatowai, swimming (or surfing) with dolphins at Curio Bay, and the walk to windswept Slope Point, the southernmost tip of the South Island.

Need to Know

For more information, see Survival Guide (p351)

Currency
New Zealand dollar ($)

Languages
English, Māori, NZ Sign Language

Visas
Visitors need an NZeTA (NZ$12 online). Also, tourists are expected to pay an International Visitor Conservation and Tourism Levy (IVL; $35).

Money
Bank cards are used for most purchases, and are accepted in most hotels and restaurants. ATMs are widely available in cities and larger towns.

Mobile Phones
It's simple to buy a local SIM card and prepaid account at outlets in airports and large towns (provided your mobile is unlocked).

Time
New Zealand time (GMT/UTC plus 12 hours)

When to Go

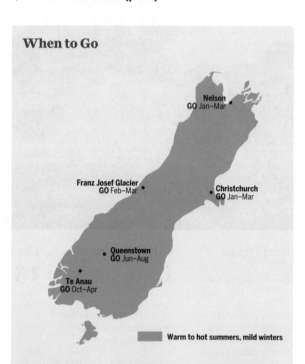

Nelson
GO Jan–Mar

Franz Josef Glacier
GO Feb–Mar

Christchurch
GO Jan–Mar

Queenstown
GO Jun–Aug

Te Anau
GO Oct–Apr

Warm to hot summers, mild winters

High Season
(Dec–Feb)

➡ Best weather and conditions for beachtime and outdoor adventures.

➡ Domestic holidaymakers fill up hot spots and keep roads busy.

➡ Major international tourist influx fills all available gaps.

Shoulder
(Mar–Apr & Sep–Nov)

➡ Generally settled weather; a great time to travel.

➡ Locals back to school and work.

➡ The south is cool from September to November, especially at night.

Low Season
(May–Aug)

➡ Unpredictable weather, ranging from glorious to ghastly.

➡ No crowds, easy bookings, but quiet towns go into hibernation.

➡ High season in the ski towns, especially around Queenstown.

Useful Websites

The Spinoff (www.thespinoff.co.nz) Latest culture, arts and politics.

100% Pure New Zealand (www.newzealand.com) Comprehensive government tourism site.

Department of Conservation (www.doc.govt.nz) DOC parks, trail and camping info.

Lonely Planet (www.lonelyplanet.com/new-zealand) Destination information, hotel bookings, traveller forum and more.

Te Ara (www.teara.govt.nz) Online encyclopedia of NZ.

Important Numbers

Regular numbers have a two-digit area code followed by a seven-digit number. When dialling within a region, the area code is required.

NZ's country code	64
International access code	00
Emergency (Ambulance, Fire, Police)	111
Directory Assistance (charges apply)	018

Exchange Rates

Australia	A$1	NZ$1.04
Canada	C$1	NZ$1.19
China	¥10	NZ$2.26
Euro zone	€1	NZ$1.73
Japan	¥100	NZ$1.44
Singapore	S$1	NZ$1.14
UK	UK£1	NZ$2.05
US	US$1	NZ$1.59

For current exchange rates, see www.xe.com.

Daily Costs

Budget: Less than $150

➡ Dorm beds or campsites: $15–45 per night

➡ Main course in a budget eatery: less than $20

➡ InterCity Flexipass: 30 hours, multiple trips $245

Midrange: $150–250

➡ Double room in a midrange hotel/motel: $130–200

➡ Main course in a midrange restaurant: $20–35

➡ Car rental: per day from $50

Top End: More than $250

➡ Double room in an upmarket hotel: $200–350

➡ Three-course meal in a classy restaurant: from $80

➡ Domestic flights: from $100

Opening Hours

Opening hours vary seasonally depending on where you are. Most places close on Christmas Day and Good Friday.

Banks 9am–4.30pm Monday to Friday, some also 9am–noon Saturday

Cafes 7am or 8am–3pm or 4pm

Post offices 8.30am–5pm Monday to Friday; larger branches also 9.30am–1pm Saturday

Pubs and bars noon–late ('late' varies by region, and by day)

Restaurants noon–2.30pm and 6pm–9pm

Shops and businesses 9am–5.30pm Monday to Friday and 9am–noon or 5pm Saturday

Supermarkets 7am–9pm

Arriving on the South Island

Christchurch Airport Christchurch Metro Purple Line runs into the city ($8.50 when paying in cash) regularly from around 7am to 11pm. Door-to-door shuttles run 24 hours (from $25). A taxi into the city costs around $50 to $65 (20 minutes).

Queenstown Airport Taxis charge around $50 for trips between the airport and town. Super Shuttle runs an airport service ($15 per person). Door-to-door shuttle costs vary by destination.

Wildlife Interactions

➡ New Zealand offers many opportunities to interact with wildlife, but ensure your life-changing experience is not life-changingly harmful to the unique animals that call the South Island home.

➡ Never feed wild animals. This includes birds.

➡ Accept nature's realities: if it's the wrong season to be spotting whales off Kaikōura, enjoy the seals instead.

➡ Stick to the track; take your litter with you (organic and inorganic); and travel sustainably.

➡ Tour operators that guarantee seeing animals in the wild may not be the best ones to go with. Do your due diligence. You don't want to be chasing down shy kiwis on Stewart Island/Rakiura to satisfy paying customers.

➡ Recognise that all your interactions with the environment affect the wildlife.

For much more on **getting around**, see p363

First Time South Island

For more information, see Survival Guide (p351)

Checklist

➡ Ensure your passport is valid for at least three months past your intended return date from New Zealand

➡ Book rental cars, campervans and train tickets well in advance, particularly for travel during summer

➡ Got travel insurance? Does it cover activities like bungy jumping?

➡ Read up on NZ's Māori culture; learn some phrases

What to Pack

➡ Sturdy walking shoes – visiting NZ without doing at least *some* hiking (tramping) is a crime!

➡ Small day pack

➡ NZ electrical adaptor

➡ Sunglasses for bright southern days

➡ Woolly hat for unexpectedly chilly evenings

➡ Reusable water bottle

➡ Earplugs for hostel dorms

Top Tips for Your Trip

➡ Allow more driving time than you think you need. Outside cities, roads are narrow, winding and slow with mountains and campervans to navigate. Don't try to see the whole island in two weeks.

➡ Booked activities and tours can be cancelled at the last minute due to weather. Build extra time into your itinerary in case your tour is bumped to the following day.

➡ Don't expect wi-fi to be free (or fast) outside cities. Where they do provide wi-fi, hotels and cafes may sometimes offer vouchers for a limited amount of data.

What to Wear

Given the locals' propensity for the outdoorsy life, dress norms in NZ are generally fairly practical and versatile. Dress up for a night out on the town in major cities (don't expect to get into a classy bar wearing shorts and flip-flops – or 'jandals' as the locals call them) – but elsewhere the key to comfort is to layer up.

The weather here can change in a blink, particularly around Fiordland and the West Coast

Etiquette

New Zealanders are a laid-back, modest bunch as a whole – exercising the usual good manners will help endear you to the locals.

Greetings Shake hands when meeting someone for the first time, and look people in the eye. Always say hello and shout a 'thanks' when getting on and off a bus.

Māori customs Adhere to strict Māori protocols (p340) if visiting *marae* (meeting-house complexes). Otherwise, respectful behaviour goes a long way, as always.

Invitations If you're invited to dinner or a barbecue at someone's house, bring some wine, beer, food or a bunch of flowers.

Expect the Unexpected

Sheep crossing – When you see a sign saying 'Sheep Crossing' there really will be sheep crossing the road.

No snakes – There are no venomous or dangerous animals.

Weather – The day may start with sunshine but it can turn torrential by lunchtime; prepare for all possible weather, especially if out walking.

Safety – People are genuinely friendly, but don't be lulled into thinking NZ is crime-free – normal precautions apply.

Paying the bill – While cafes may have table service it's normal to pay for your bill at the counter when you're ready to leave.

Bargaining

Haggling and bargaining aren't traditionally part of commercial culture in NZ. The only circumstances where you might have some luck are farmers markets at the end of the day or large private purchases (buying a local's car for a knock-down price). Otherwise, the price is the price.

Tipping

Tipping is completely optional in NZ.

Guides Your kayaking guide or tour-group leader would happily accept tips; and $10 is kind.

Restaurants The total on your bill is all you need to pay. If you like, reward good service with 5% to 10%.

Taxis If you round up your fare, don't be surprised if the driver hands back your change.

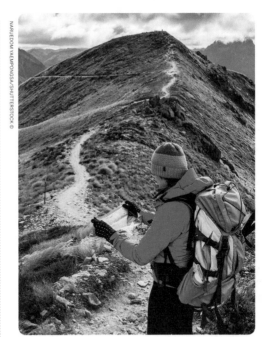

Hiker on Kepler Track (p175), Southland

Sleeping

Book well in advance in peak times: from Christmas to late January, at Easter, and during winter (June to September) in snowfield resort towns.

See Accommodation (p24) for more information.

Languages

English, te reo Māori and New Zealand Sign Language are NZ's official languages. These days Māori words cross over into daily parlance: you'll hear *kia ora* (hello) everywhere. Māori place names are now spelled correctly with macrons on most town signs. Online, www.maoridiction ary.co.nz has a handy translator. The app Kupu (kupu. co.nz) teaches Māori nouns for everyday objects, and popular language app Duolingo plans to include a te reo Māori course for beginners in 2020.

See Language (p369) for more.

What's New

Jacinda mania continues to sweep the world, with the PM's compassionate response to the Christchurch mosque attacks and White Island volcanic eruption in 2019 fuelling her global popularity. From its greenie consciousness to the decolonising of statues in Gisborne, New Zealand is as progressive today as it was when it first gave women the vote over a century ago.

Adventure Activities

The sheer range of adventure activities in Aotearoa (New Zealand) keeps expanding, with a slew of new options across both islands. The Paparoa Track and Pike29 Memorial Track are newcomers to the Great Walks (p43) of New Zealand fold (Hump Ridge Track is to be added next); stand-up paddleboarding (SUP) continues to conquer water sports; and the Nevis Catapult, the world's largest, slings thrill seekers 150m across the Nevis Valley, near Queenstown.

Waitaki Whitestone Geopark

Waitaki is shortlisted to be the first Unesco Global Geopark in Australasia.

Reaching from the Southern Alps to the sea, this collection of geological and cultural sites, dating from 60 million years ago to the present, includes the Moeraki Boulders, the spectacular sedimentary Clay Cliffs and the striking limestone Elephant Rocks.

Boutique Distilleries

Small-batch, artisanal distilleries have bloomed like mushrooms after rain in NZ in recent years. The likes of the Reefton Distilling Co (p280) join other South Island newbies such as the Cardrona Distillery (p242) and, in Takaka, Dancing Sands (p306). Expect distinctive whiskies, rums, vodkas and gins made from pure waters and high-quality grains and botanicals.

LOCAL KNOWLEDGE

WHAT'S HAPPENING ON THE SOUTH ISLAND

Tasmin Waby, Lonely Planet Writer

New Zealand is going green with gusto. Everyone brings their own bags to the store; solar panels are commonplace; e-campervans can be rented; and takeaway meals are delivered in eco-containers (when they're not, there's a heartfelt apology for using plastic).

Buzz concept 'overtourism' is nothing new in NZ where tourists sometimes outnumber locals, and visitor hot spots (made all the more famous by cinema screens and social media) can suffer from their popular appeal.

To ensure the environment is looked after, visitors are asked to take the Tiaki Promise, a modern-day enacting of the Māori *kaitiakitanga*. New Zealanders are also keen to encourage tourism dispersal, to less busy (and therefore more innately 'Kiwi') areas.

A new visitor visa and levy has also been introduced (catching some travellers unaware) to move some of the cost of tourism on to the people travelling in NZ rather than stretching the limited government budgets to build infrastructure like toilets and car parks at newly popular places.

Dunedin Street Art

Street art has blossomed all around Dunedin over the last couple of years as the warehouse precinct on the south side of the city centre has been redeveloped, filling up with restaurants, bars, shops and boutique hotels. In between are beautiful and unusual murals, paste-ups and colourful odes to Dunedin's creativity.

Kiwi Camp

New sites for 'freedom campers' are being developed by a group called Kiwi Camp (www.kiwicamp.nz), which provides basic pay-as-you-use facilities via an app and digital key fob. The company drops in a stand-alone container with showers, toilets and cooking hobs. Other benefits are parking and proper rubbish and recycling facilities. And with little staff or overheads, costs are low so travellers on a budget can afford to stay while ensuring their visit to New Zealand doesn't negatively impact the natural environment, which has been one of the key concerns with freedom campers in NZ to date.

Tasman's Great Taste Trail

At the end of 2019 a new section of track opened on the Great Taste Trail (p286) through Tasman Bay, rolling between Nelson, Wakefield, Richmond, Motueka and Kaiteriteri; another section to Tapawera is slated for 2020 with the ultimate goal to create a loop trail. Tasman's Great Taste Trail threads inland and along the coast for 174km, but most visitors do a section on a tailored day ride, allowing plenty of time for enjoying the sights and tastes of the region.

LISTEN, WATCH & FOLLOW

For inspiration and up-to-date news, visit www.lonelyplanet.com/new-zealand/articles.

Undertheradar (www.undertheradar.co.nz) Music news, gigs and ticket sales.

The Spinoff (www.thespinoff.co.nz) Culture and news.

All Blacks (www.allblacks.com) Follow the nation's unifying obsession.

Noted (www.noted.co.nz) The *Listener*, *Metro* and *North & South* magazines, plus Radio NZ.

FAST FACTS

Food trend Plant-based eating

Language Apps and emotikis in te reo Māori

Pop 4.69 million

Number of venomous snakes zero

= 3 people per sq km

Camp Glenorchy

New to the South Island, Camp Glenorchy (p229) near Queenstown is an excellent example of the next generation in sustainable tourism in NZ: an upmarket accommodation but with composting toilets. Digital controls cleverly allow guests to manage the water heating and ambient temperature, putting the power (and a green education) in the hands of travellers.

Accommodation

Find more accommodation reviews throughout the On the Road chapters (from p63)

Accommodation Types

Motels and Pubs Most towns have low-rise, midrange motels. Even small towns usually have a pub with rooms.

B&Bs In New Zealand B&Bs pop up in the middle of cities, in rural hamlets and on stretches of isolated coastline, with rooms offered in everything from bungalows to stately manors.

Holiday parks Ideal if you're camping or touring in a campervan. Choose from unpowered tent sites, simple cabins and en suite units.

Hostels Backpacker hostels include beery, party-prone joints and family-friendly 'flashpackers'.

Pods Small private spaces from airport hotels to glass pods in the forest.

Hotels From small-town pubs to slick global chain operations – with commensurate prices.

Lodges Luxurious in every sense, from the architecture to the locations, NZ has a stunning array of splash-out-worthy retreats.

Price Ranges

The following price ranges refer to a double room with bathroom during high season. Price ranges generally increase by 20% to 25% in Christchurch (as they do in Auckland and Wellington on the North Island). Here you can still find budget accommodation at up to $120 per double, but midrange stretches from $120 to $250, with top-end rooms more than $250.

$	less than $120
$$	$120–$200
$$$	more than $200

Best Places to Stay

Best for Families

Families are welcome at pretty much every holiday park and campsite across NZ. Kids are happier when they have playgrounds, swimming pools and nature to explore nearby. All that fresh air means bedtime is less likely to be a struggle – but don't expect them to stay asleep much past sunrise: you've been warned.

➡ Smiths Farm Holiday Park (p310), Queen Charlotte Track

➡ Old Bones Lodge (p143), Ōamaru

➡ Ross Beach Top 10 (p262), Ross

➡ Manapouri Motels & Holiday Park (p194), Manapōuri

➡ Curio Bay Accommodation (p182), Curio Bay

Best on a Budget

Sometimes the best places to stay in NZ are the budget options. You won't have your room serviced at these accommodations, and facilities might be shared so expect to do your own dishes. But you will meet other travellers, and staff and owners are that bit friendlier.

➡ Tasman Bay Backpackers (p290), Nelson

➡ Oamaru Backpackers (p143), Ōamaru

➡ Halfmoon Cottage (p96), Banks Peninsula

➡ Adventure Queenstown (p220), Queenstown

➡ Southern Comfort Backpackers (p183), Invercargill

➡ Hogwartz (p152), Dunedin

Best for Solo Travellers

No compromising on spending, no schedules and even a lie-in when you want one. The only downside of travelling solo is occasionally talking to yourself after you've been alone for days on end. That's why accommodation where it's easy to meet other travellers with whom to share stories, intel and meals can really make your trip.

➡ Tombstone Backpackers (p316), Picton
➡ Victoria Railway Hotel (p184), Invercargill
➡ Jailhouse (p85), Christchurch
➡ Majestic Mansions (p153), Dunedin
➡ Poshtel (p143), Ōamaru

Best Luxury Options

New Zealand's luxury lodges and accommodations are blessed not only with astonishing scenery, but also many are in remote locations offering guests privacy and seclusion as well as world-class facilities and unique Kiwi hospitality.

➡ Te Anau Lodge (p198), Te Anau
➡ Milford Sound Lodge (p203), Milford Sound
➡ Terminus Hotel (p152), Dunedin
➡ Pen-y-bryn Lodge (p143), Ōamaru
➡ Oliver's (p169), Clyde

Milford Sound Lodge (p203), Fiordland

Booking

Local visitor information centres are generally excellent for accommodation in the area; many can also make bookings on your behalf.

Lonely Planet (lonelyplanet.com/hotels) Find independent reviews, as well as recommendations on the best places to stay – and then book them online.

Automobile Association (www.aa.co.nz/travel) Online accommodation bookings (especially good for motels, B&Bs and holiday parks).

Bach Care (www.bachcare.co.nz) Rental listings for apartments of all sizes, including many beachfront options.

Book a Bach (www.bookabach.co.nz) Apartment and holiday-house bookings.

Holiday Houses (www.holidayhouses.co.nz) Holiday-house rentals NZ-wide.

Jasons (www.jasons.co.nz) Long-running travel service with myriad online booking options.

New Zealand Bed & Breakfast (www.bnb.co.nz) Great for all sorts of B&Bs.

Rural Holidays NZ (www.ruralholidays.co.nz) Farm and homestay listings across NZ.

Stay Native (https://explore.staynative.co.nz) Lists indigenous-run sustainable activities and hosts.

The Kiwi Bach

The basic Kiwi holiday home is called a 'bach' (short for 'bachelor', as they were historically used by single men as hunting and fishing hideouts); in Otago and Southland they're known as 'cribs'. These are simple self-contained cottages that can be rented in rural and coastal areas, often in isolated locations, and sometimes include surf, fishing or other outdoor gear hire in the cost. Prices are typically $150 to $250 per night, which isn't bad for a whole house or self-contained bungalow. For more upmarket holiday houses, expect to pay anything from $250 to $500 per double.

For more information on accommodation in South Island see p352.

Getting Around

For more information, see Transport (p362)

Travelling by Car or Campervan

Nothing beats the freedom that travelling around the South Island by car provides. You'll be able to access beautifully remote areas that are impractical to reach otherwise. Roads are mostly excellent, though a surprising number of tourists come unstuck while driving in New Zealand.

The major problems seem to be: drivers temporarily forgetting which side of the road to drive on (the left); fatigued drivers hiring cars after long flights and embarking on lengthy road journeys; and inexperience in driving on winding country roads, particularly in the South Island's famous mountainous terrain.

If you're hiring a campervan be aware that these are heavier to drive, and therefore not as easy to manoeuvre. Travel times will be even slower and remote unmade roads inaccessible in a large vehicle.

Note, if you're spotted driving erratically it's not unknown for locals to confiscate your keys and call the police; generally the police will contact the hire company who will cancel your contract, potentially leaving you stranded.

While driving in NZ isn't especially difficult, if you're inexperienced or your experience is limited to cities only, allow plenty of time or consider alternatives.

New Zealanders may come across as friendly and polite, but many seem to save their rage for the roads. Kiwi motorists are notoriously unaccommodating if you find you need to change lanes, although this is more pronounced in the bigger cities. If you're

RESOURCES

Automobile Association (www.aa.co.nz/travel) Emergency breakdown services, distance calculators, maps and accommodation guides. Has reciprocal arrangements with similar overseas organisations.

NZ Transport Agency (www.nzta.govt.nz) Real-time traffic reports, journey planner, and information on walking, cycling and public transport.

Nga Haerenga: The New Zealand Cycle Trail (www.nzcycletrail.com) Cycling information including suggested itineraries, track details, outlines of 23 'Great Rides', and cycling events.

driving a slower vehicle such as a campervan, pull over when you can do so safely to allow faster vehicles to overtake. Unfortunately tailgating is a dangerous behaviour some drivers in NZ indulge in.

If you're flying into Christchurch on a long flight, we highly recommend that you give yourself a day or two to recover, and see the sights (by public transport, taxi, rideshare or foot) before hiring a car.

Car Hire

It's easy to rent a car from any of the main centres, with the major international agencies having offices both at the airports and in the city centres. In most cases it's cheaper to hire from a local agency, where the cars may be a little older or slightly battered.

Driving Conditions

All major routes are well-maintained, but in more remote areas you may strike some unsealed roads. Many of the mountain roads, including some of the major routes out of Queenstown, are winding and narrow. Snow chains are required for a number of mountain routes in winter; if you're travelling without them, you'll be turned back.

No Car?
Bus

Buses connect all of the major towns, but services can be expensive, slow and infrequent. Various tour companies offer guided coach trips to the main destinations. The larger cities have extensive local bus networks.

Air

Aside from Christchurch and Queenstown, the main air-travel hubs, there are airports in Kaikōura, Blen-heim, Nelson, Hokitika, Westport, Timaru, Dunedin, Invercargill and Oban (Stewart Island/Rakiura). It's often possible to pick up a cheap domestic fare.

Train

The South Island's two train lines exist more as scenic journeys than as an effective transport mode. The Coastal Pacific connects Picton to Christchurch, while the TranzAlpine heads clear across the Southern Alps from Christchurch to Greymouth.

Bicycle

While plenty of people do it, New Zealand isn't the easiest country for cycle touring; the terrain is hilly and the traffic can be unforgiving and unaccommodating. The plains east of the Southern Alps are much easier going than the West Coast.

DRIVING FAST FACTS

➡ Drive on the left.

➡ All vehicle occupants must wear a seatbelt.

➡ Minimum age for a full licence is 18 years.

➡ Carry your licence at all times.

➡ Maximum speed 100km/h on motorways, 50km/h in built-up areas.

➡ Blood alcohol limit 50mg per 100mL (0.05).

ROAD DISTANCES (KM)

	Christchurch	Dunedin	Invercargill	Picton
Dunedin	360			
Invercargill	570	210		
Picton	340	690	900	
Queenstown	480	285	190	815

If You Like...

Hiking (Tramping)

Routeburn Track The Great Walk competing with the Milford as the best of the bunch. (p197)

Paparoa Track The newest of the Great Walks, opened in late 2019, cutting through alpine and limestone landscapes and thriving rainforests. (p250)

Mt Robert Circuit Nelson Lakes' premier day walk with stupendous views earned via the Pinchgut Track. (p295)

Old Ghost Road Built for bikers, this new multiday wilderness epic is also a hiker's delight. (p251)

Hump Ridge Track Traverse rugged tops and a remote coast in Tuatapere, in the deep south. (p188)

Abel Tasman Coast Track Stroll past sparkling seas, pristine beaches and coastal forests on this well-trodden track. (p287)

Māori Culture

Te Ana Māori Rock Art Centre Learn about traditional Māori rock art both in the museum and at nearby sites. (p117)

Okains Bay Māori & Colonial Museum View an outstanding array of heritage treasures including *waka taua* (war canoes). (p95)

Hokitika Watch the masters carve stone, bone, paua (shell) and *pounamu* (greenstone) in traditional Māori designs. (p262)

Ko Tane See a replica Māori village and an evening cultural show at Willowbank Wildlife Reserve. (p80)

Museums & Galleries

Christchurch Art Gallery Better than ever after post-quake restoration, with world-class permanent and temporary exhibitions. (p69)

Otago Museum Enlightening human stories and an introduction to the area's unique wildlife. (p147)

Canterbury Museum A wide-ranging collection of historical exhibits presented in a splendid earthquake survivor. (p70)

World of WearableArt Museum Home to the world-famous, wonderfully weird and wacky wearable-art show. (p285)

Eastern Southland Gallery Houses impressive works by iconic New Zealand artists Ralph Hotere and Rita Angus. (p182)

Shantytown Delve into the West Coast's flinty gold- and coal-mining past at this replica pioneer village. (p268)

Beaches

Wharariki No ice-cream van, no swimming. Just an enthralling, empty beach for wanderers and ponderers. (p308)

Kaka Point Sweeping surf beach on a coast home to seals, sea lions and myriad seabirds. (p178)

Colac Bay Top spot for surfing, but this far south be sure to pack a wetsuit. (p187)

Ōkārito Wild, empty West Coast gem backed by a bird-filled lagoon. (p260)

Wine Regions

Marlborough Superb sauvignon blanc and pretty winery restaurants are just the start of the story. (p320)

Nelson Marlborough's near neighbour is smaller in scale but equally scenic. (p285)

Waitaki Valley Truly boutique producers wrangle tricky terroir in NZ's edgiest wine region. (p136)

Central Otago Dozens of cellar doors nestle amid schist landscapes producing sublime pinot noir. (p161)

Waipara Valley North Canterbury's up-and-coming region produces spectacular pinot noir and riesling. (p110)

Extreme Activities

Queenstown Bungy, swing, or get flung with the original AJ Hackett's. (p212)

Skydive Franz Josef & Fox Glacier If you're going to do it, go for the highest – 20,000ft above alps and glaciers. (p257)

Abel Tasman Canyons Paddle, swim, slide and leap through a hidden gorge in the national park. (p301)

Raft the Buller Bounce through the thrilling rapids on this mighty West Coast river. (p282)

Skiing & Snowboarding

Treble Cone Challenging down-hill terrain within a stone's throw of Wānaka. (p235)

Canterbury Ski Mt Hutt, and stacks of smaller fields like Ohau, Roundhill, Porters and Broken River. (p111)

Coronet Peak Ski or snowboard Queenstown's oldest field then join the resort town's legendary après-ski scene. (p212)

Cardrona More great skiing in the Queenstown/Wānaka area, with slopes to suit all levels of experience. (p242)

Cities

Christchurch Cosmopolitan cafes, gorgeous gardens and surprising street art – post-quake Christchurch is brimming with activity. (p65)

Dunedin Gothic architecture, edgy arts, vibrant nightlife and wildlife on the doorstep. (p146)

Nelson Art, culture, cuisine and beaches – it's no wonder this is touted as the lifestyle capital of New Zealand. (p285)

Top: Hikers at Arthur's Pass (p112), Canterbury

Bottom: Snowboarder at Coronet Peak (p212), Queenstown

Invercargill Not rock and roll, but gloriously retro, friendly and full of neat old buildings. (p183)

Queenstown Petite but rollicking tourism centre with a sophisticated arts and dining scene. (p210)

Pubs, Bars & Beer

Nelson Tour pubs and breweries on a craft-beer trail throughout NZ's original home of hops. (p293)

Christchurch Pubs such as Pomeroy's and the Brewery show commitment to the craft cause. (p88)

Dunedin Home to lively student bars and two big-name breweries – Speight's and Emerson's. (p147)

Queenstown Quench your thirst after a day's mountain biking, bungy jumping or skiing. (p210)

History

Arrowtown Gold-rush-era town crammed with heritage buildings and the remains of one of NZ's earliest Chinese settlements. (p230)

Ōamaru Victorian Precinct Beautifully restored whitestone buildings and warehouses, now housing eclectic galleries, restaurants and artisan workshops. (p139)

Waiuta South of Reefton, explore the rusty relics of a ghost town, abandoned to nature in 1951. (p281)

Shantytown Embrace gold-rush nostalgia at this authentic re-creation of an 1860s mining town, south of Greymouth on the West Coast. (p268)

Toitū Otago Settlers Museum Human settlement on the South Island, told through interactive displays and a 100,000-object collection. (p146)

The Road Less Travelled

Stewart Island/Rakiura The end of the line! Catch the ferry to Oban and get lost for a few days. (p188)

Karamea Lesser-trodden marvels like the Ōpārara Arch and secluded Scotts Beach reward tramps on the northern West Coast. (p278)

Molesworth Station New Zealand's largest cattle farm traverses some seriously remote terrain – take a Molesworth tour. (p109)

Haast Chat to fisherfolk and drive to lonely Jackson Bay/ Okahu in the land of no phone signal. (p252)

Foodie Experiences

Central Otago vineyard restaurants Eye-popping scenery combined with the best of NZ food and wine. (p171)

Christchurch city scene Christchurch is excited about its new foodie and farmers market and its restaurant and bar scene is burgeoning. (p86)

Bluff oysters Guzzle silky, salty oysters between March and August; time your visit for May's oyster festival. (p186)

West Coast whitebait Whitebait fritters, bound in egg, are a South Island obsession. Try them on pizza, too. (p270)

Road Trips

Milford Highway Gasp at alpine peaks, sigh along thrilling forest-wrapped roads...the drive from Te Anau to Milford Sound is one of the world's finest. (p200)

Great Coast Road Overhanging cliffs and other-worldly rock formations feature on this route along the wild, windswept West Coast. (p274)

Arthur's Pass Between Canterbury and the West Coast, the Southern Alps' highest pass is a feat of daredevil engineering. (p112)

Southern Scenic Route Allow a week to do justice to this meandering route between Queenstown and Dunedin. (p195)

Month by Month

January

New Zealand peels its eyes open after New Year's Eve, gathers its wits and prepares for another year. Great weather, the cricket season is in full swing, and it's happy holidays for the locals.

☆ Nelson Jazz Festival

Get your jazz and blues groove on at rocking venues and ad hoc street corners. Acts range from Kiwi funkateers through to local hipsters, and Nelson's reputation for great wine and beer makes it very easy to enjoy the diverse beats. (p290)

☆ Bread & Circus World Buskers Festival

Christchurch throngs with jugglers, musicians, tricksters, puppeteers, mime artists and dancers. Shoulder into the crowd, watch the performances and leave a few dollars. Avoid if you're scared of audience participation. (p81)

☆ Soundsplash

The boutique mixed-genre music festival event Soundsplash (www.soundsplash.co.nz) has been running in Raglan for 15 years, and has now expanded to the South Island. Held at Caroline Bay in 2020, it's a family-friendly two-night festival across two stages, with camping available right by the beach.

February

The sun is shining, the days are long and the drinks are chillin' in the fridge: this is prime party time across New Zealand. Book your festival tickets – and accommodation – in advance.

🍷 Marlborough Wine & Food Festival

Revel in mandatory over-indulgence at NZ's biggest and best wine festival, featuring tastings from more than 40 Marlborough wineries, plus fine food and entertainment. (p320)

☆ TUKI

Wānaka's super-relaxed music festival offers a well-curated selection of NZ sounds with rock, roots, pop and electronica acts. (p238)

March

March brings a hint of autumn, along with harvest time in the vineyards of Marlborough and the orchards of Central Otago. Expect long dusky evenings and plenty of festivals to plan your visit around.

✖ Hokitika Wildfoods Festival

Chow down on worms, hare's testicles or stallion's semen at Hokitika's comfort-zone-challenging food fest. Not for the mild-mannered or weak-stomached... But even if you are, it's still fun to watch! There are plenty of quality NZ brews to cleanse the palate. (p265)

April

April is when canny travellers hit NZ: the ocean is warmish in northern parts of the South Island, the weather mild, and tours and accommodation plentiful. The exception is Easter, when locals are busy holidaying.

🍷 Clyde Wine & Food Festival

The main street of sleepy Clyde comes to life on Easter Sunday, as locals rub shoulders with foodie fanatics come to sample an abundance of local products, including renowned cool-climate pinot noir. (p170)

⊙ Warbirds Over Wanaka

Held every second Easter in even-numbered years, Warbirds Over Wanaka is an internationally renowned air show set against the rugged Central Otago landscape. Heritage and iconic aircraft pull crazy manoeuvres for up to 50,000 spectators. (p239)

May

Party nights are long gone and a chilly Kiwi winter beckons. Thank goodness for the Comedy Festival. May is also your last chance to explore Fiordland and Southland in reasonable weather.

🍴 Bluff Oyster & Food Festival

Bluff and oysters go together like, well, like a bivalve. Truck down to the deep south for some slippery, salty specimens at this local fest. It's chilly down here in May, but the live music and competitions warm everybody up. (p186)

☆ New Zealand International Comedy Festival

This three-week laughfest (www.comedyfestival.co.nz) kicks off on the North Island, but then hits the South Island with a travelling troupe of international and local comedic talent. Venues include Christchurch, Ōamaru and Invercargill.

June

Time to head south: it's ski season. Queenstown and Wānaka hit their strides, and international legions descend on Coronet Peak, the Remarkables, Treble Cone and Cardrona. On the coast some towns seem to take a winter hiatus.

☆ New Zealand Gold Guitar Awards

We like both kinds of music: country *and* western! These awards in Gore cap off a week of everlovin' country twang and bootscootin' good times, with plenty of concerts and buskers. (p182)

July

It's chilly all across the South Island, but the alps are still a hot ticket. Queenstown gets crazy with its annual winter festival. The less active can combine cinema, chocolate and craft beer in Dunedin.

☆ New Zealand International Film Festival

After seasons in Dunedin and Christchurch, this festival (www.nziff.co.nz) hits the road for screenings in regional towns from July to November, blessing film buffs from Greymouth to Invercargill.

⛷ Queenstown Winter Festival

This four-day snow fest attracts around 45,000 snow fans to Queenstown for fireworks, jazz, street parades, comedy, a Mardi Gras, a masquerade ball and lots of snow-centric activities on the slopes. Book accommodation in advance. (p220)

August

Winter is almost spent, but there's still not much happening outdoors: music, art and rugby games are your saviours.

☆ Christchurch Arts Festival

The South Island's biggest arts festival takes place in odd-numbered years. Celebrate with cultured Cantabrians at a wide array of venues right across the city. Music, theatre and dance all feature. (p81)

🏃 Snow Sports

Forget Europe or South America. Here's your chance to experience the widest range of snow-sports activities in the southern hemisphere. Focus on your downhill at Coronet Peak, achieve snowboarding nirvana at Cardrona, or go heliskiing at Mt Hutt.

Queenstown Winter Festival (p220)

September

Spring has sprung, blossoms burst across the South Island, and baby lambs are running amok. There are accommodation bargains to be had, but be ready for four seasons in one day. And the snow often lingers.

 ### Winter Pride

Officially kicking off in late August, but running through the first week of September, Winter Pride is a values-based festival celebrating LGBTIQ+ people in beautiful Queenstown: 'a small town with a bold heart'. (p220)

October

Post-rugby and pre-cricket sees sports fans twiddling their thumbs: a trip to Kaikōura, Akaroa or Nelson perhaps? October is 'shoulder season', with reasonable accommodation rates and smaller crowds. Weather can be changeable; pack your umbrella.

 ### French Fest

Allez à toute vitesse to Akaroa's French Fest, held in odd-numbered years in early October to celebrate the peninsula's Gallic heritage. Quirky events include a waiters' race and a French cricket tournament, as well as plenty of food and wine, of course. (p99)

☆ Otago Festival of the Arts

From 2000, this biennial arts festival has rallied Dunedin and Otago's performing artists, as well as bringing in acts from abroad. Expect to catch some intelligent and creative theatre, art, dance and spoken-word performances – plus cinema, virtual reality and other mediums.

November

Another NZ summer approaches as days lengthen following the introduction of daylight saving. Now's a good time to hike the Great Walks, but you'll need to book way ahead to get a place.

NZ Cup & Show Week

Christchurch's iconic annual NZ Cup & Show Week is a great opportunity for the good people of Christchurch to celebrate, with fashion shows, horse racing and the country-comes-to-town appeal of the A&P (agricultural and pastoral) Show. (p81)

Ōamaru Victorian Heritage Celebrations

Hark back to the good old days when Queen Vic sat on the throne, hems were low, collars high and civic decency was de rigueur. Ōamaru pays tongue-in-cheek homage to the past with dress-ups, penny-farthing races, performances and a grand fete. (p143)

December

Summertime! The crack of leather on willow echoes across the nation's cricket pitches and office workers surge towards the finish line. Everyone gears up for Christmas which means shopping will be hectic: steer clear!

Queen Charlotte Track

Beat the summer rush on the popular Queen Charlotte Track, either on two legs or two wheels, or even integrate a spot of sea kayaking into your journey. (p288)

Itineraries

 Southern Circuit

Begin in **Christchurch**: tour the city on the historic tram to get your bearings, then stroll through the pedestrian-friendly city centre to Christchurch Art Gallery and Canterbury Museum. Back in the fresh air, wander along the Avon River in the Botanic Gardens then board a gondola for a relaxing punt with water views.

City-saturated? Day trip to French quarter **Akaroa** on the Banks Peninsula, then head north for whale-watching and dolphin-spotting in **Kaikōura**. Continue through the **Marlborough wine region** and the harbour town of **Picton**, before whiling away a day or two in the **Marlborough Sounds**.

Detour west past artsy **Nelson** to eco-conscious **Golden Bay** before heading down the West Coast where **Punakaiki** and the glaciers – **Franz Josef** and **Fox** – will astound you. Get adventurous in **Queenstown** and **Wānaka**, be mesmerised by **Doubtful Sound** and chill out around the sleepy **Catlins**. Back up the East Coast, drop in to Scottish-flavoured **Dunedin**, then detour through the Waitaki Valley to the snowy heights of **Aoraki/Mt Cook** and the starry skies of **Lake Tekapo**, before rolling back into Christchurch.

Culinary Capers
Animal Planet

Nelson

Marlborough
Wine Region

Kaikōura

Waipara Valley

Christchurch

Akaroa

TASMAN
SEA

Oamaru

Moeraki

Taiaroa Head

Otago Peninsula

SOUTH
PACIFIC
OCEAN

Catlins
Conservation
Park

Dunedin

Bluff

Curio Bay

Stewart Island
(Rakiura)

 ## Culinary Capers

Hop into gear around **Nelson**, home to microbreweries such as Hop Federation and Townshend. Head over to **Marlborough,** NZ's best wine-touring territory, then down the South Island's rugged East Coast to **Kaikōura** for delicious seafood at rustic eateries. Graduate to classier dining at the vineyard restaurants of the **Waipara Valley** – Pegasus Bay and Black Estate are great for leisurely lunches.

Journey into **Christchurch** to sample the restaurant scenes around Victoria and New Regent Streets, and Lyttelton, and don't miss the excellent Christchurch Farmers Market on Saturday mornings. More craft-beer heaven awaits beer buffs at Pomeroy's Old Brewery Inn and the Brewery.

From Christchurch continue south to North Otago and award-winning eateries such as Riverstone Kitchen in **Ōamaru** and Fleur's Place in **Moeraki**. Emerson's and Speight's are the breweries to check out further south in **Dunedin** – before loading up the car with organic, free-range locavore goodies from Dunedin's Otago Farmers Market.

 ## Animal Planet

From **Christchurch**, travel to **Akaroa** to spot Hector's dolphins, New Zealand's smallest and rarest. Squeeze in a return trip up the coast to **Kaikōura** for whale-watching and swimming with NZ fur seals, before travelling south to **Ōamaru**. The historic precinct and steampunk subculture draws visitors, but nature buffs should make a beeline for the little blue penguin colony, which comes alive at dusk.

From Ōamaru continue south to the **Otago Peninsula** to spot more little blue penguins, as well as their extremely rare, shuffling cousin, the yellow-eyed penguin (hoiho). Join a tour to meet seals and sea lions before admiring the royal albatross colony on nearby **Taiaroa Head**. If time and weather allows book a seaborne tour too: another essential Otago Peninsula experience.

Continue south to the rugged and isolated **Catlins**, where penguins, Hector's dolphins and sea lions are all regular visitors at **Curio Bay**. Leave the South Island at **Bluff** for kiwi spotting on wild and idiosyncratic **Stewart Island/Rakiura**.

Top: Punting on the Avon River in Christchurch's Botanic Gardens (p72)

Bottom: Otago Peninsula (p157)

DELPIXEL/SHUTTERSTOCK ©

Off the Beaten Track

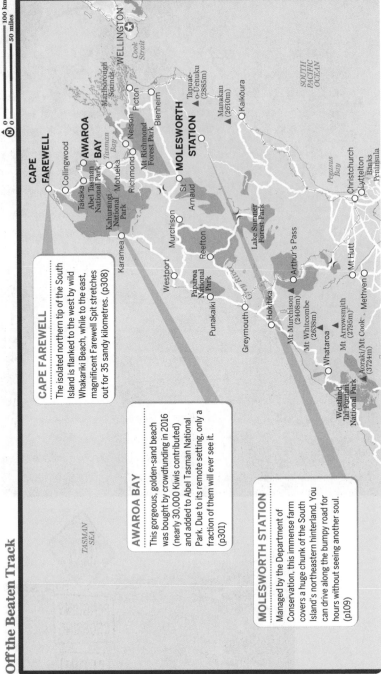

CAPE FAREWELL

The isolated northern tip of the South Island is flanked to the west by wild Whakariki Beach, while to the east, magnificent Farewell Spit stretches out for 35 sandy kilometres. (p308)

AWAROA BAY

This gorgeous, golden-sand beach was bought by crowdfunding in 2016 (nearly 30,000 Kiwis contributed) and added to Abel Tasman National Park. Due to its remote setting, only a fraction of them will ever see it. (p301)

MOLESWORTH STATION

Managed by the Department of Conservation, this immense farm covers a huge chunk of the South Island's northeastern hinterland. You can drive along the bumpy road for hours without seeing another soul. (p109)

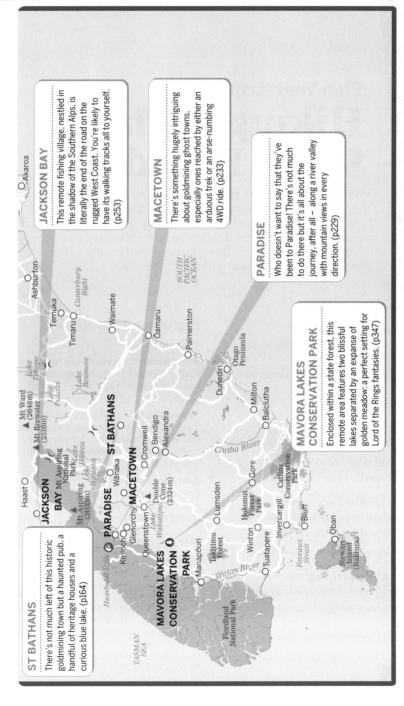

JACKSON BAY

This remote fishing village, nestled in the shadow of the Southern Alps, is literally the end of the road on the rugged West Coast. You're likely to have its walking tracks all to yourself. (p253)

MACETOWN

There's something hugely intriguing about goldmining ghost towns, especially ones reached by either an arduous trek or an arse-numbing 4WD ride. (p233)

PARADISE

Who doesn't want to say that they've been to Paradise! There's not much to do there but it's all about the journey, after all – along a river valley with mountain views in every direction. (p229)

MAVORA LAKES CONSERVATION PARK

Enclosed within a state forest, this remote area features two blissful lakes separated by an expanse of golden meadow: a perfect setting for Lord of the Rings fantasies. (p347)

ST BATHANS

There's not much left of this historic goldmining town but a haunted pub, a handful of heritage houses and a curious blue lake. (p164)

Plan Your Trip

Hiking on the South Island

Hiking (aka bushwalking, trekking or tramping, as Kiwis call it) is the perfect activity to really experience the South Island's natural beauty. There are thousands of kilometres of tracks here – some well marked (including the South Island's Great Walks), some barely a line on a map (don't head off on these without good preparation) – plus an excellent network of huts and campsites.

Best Walks

Top Multiday Hikes
Routeburn Track, Fiordland and Mt Aspiring National Parks

Abel Tasman Coast Track, Abel Tasman National Park

Heaphy Track, Kahurangi National Park

Top Day Hikes
Mt Robert Circuit, Nelson Lakes National Park

Avalanche Peak, Canterbury

Key Summit, Fiordland National Park

Top Wildlife Encounters
Bird life, St Arnaud Range Track, Nelson Lakes

Seals, Cape Foulwind Walkway, West Coast

Kiwi, Rakiura Track, Stewart Island/Rakiura

Best Hikes for Beginners
Queen Charlotte Track, Marlborough Sounds

Abel Tasman Coast Track, Abel Tasman National Park

Rob Roy Track, Mt Aspiring National Park

Planning Your Walk

When to Go

Mid-December–late January Hiking high season is during the school summer holidays, starting a couple of weeks before Christmas – avoid it if you can.

January–March The summer weather lingers into March: wait until February if possible, when tracks are (marginally) less crowded. Most non-alpine tracks can be walked enjoyably at any time from October to April.

June–August Winter is not the time to be out in the wild, especially at altitude – some paths close because of avalanche danger and reduced facilities and services.

What to Bring

Even on a day walk, your considerations are your feet and your shoulders. Make sure your footwear is as tough as old boots and that your pack isn't too heavy. If you're camping or staying in huts without stoves, bring a camping stove. Also bring insect repellent to keep sandflies away, and don't forget your 'scroggin' – a mixture of dried fruit and nuts (and sometimes chocolate) for munching en route.

Top: Hiker on the Routeburn Track (p206), Glenorchy

Bottom: Valley view from Roy's Peak (p209)

TOBIN AKEHURST/SHUTTERSTOCK©

TRACK SAFETY

Thousands of people hike across New Zealand without incident, but every year too many folks meet their maker in the mountains. Some trails are only for the experienced, fit and well equipped – don't attempt these if you don't fit the bill. Ensure you are healthy and used to walking for sustained periods.

The South Island's volatile climate subjects high-altitude walks to snow and ice, even in summer, and rivers can rise rapidly: always check weather and track conditions before setting off, and be prepared to change your plans or sit out bad weather. Resources include the following:

www.doc.govt.nz Track info, alerts and more from the Department of Conservation.

www.adventuresmart.org.nz Log your walk intentions online (and tell a friend or local!).

www.mountainsafety.org.nz Hiking safety tips.

www.metservice.co.nz Weather forecasts.

Maps

The topographical maps produced by Land Information New Zealand (www.linz.govt.nz) can be downloaded direct from the website as images, but take a paper printout because you'll lose battery power quickly if you're referring to it a lot. The LINZ map series includes park maps (national, state and forest), dedicated walking-track maps and detailed 'Topo50' maps (you may need two or three of these per track). Bookshops and outdoor gear stores have a limited selection of hard-copy maps for sale. Department of Conservation (DOC) offices often sell LINZ maps for local tracks.

Hiking Books

Department of Conservation – The DOC publishes detailed books on the flora and fauna, geology and history of NZ's national parks, plus leaflets detailing hundreds of New Zealand walking tracks.

Lonely Planet – *Hiking & Tramping in New Zealand* (2018) describes around 50 walks of various lengths and degrees of difficulty covering easy wilderness day walks as well as longer Great Walks.

Bird's Eye Guides – *Day Walks in New Zealand: 100 Great Tracks* (2016) has amazing topographical maps, as well as inspiring images from one of NZ's most respected hiking authors, Shaun Barnett.

Other Books – There are countless other books covering hikes, short urban walks and first-hand travelogues around NZ – scan the travel shelf of any local bookshop.

Useful Resources

www.freewalks.nz Descriptions, maps and photos of long and short hikes all over NZ.

www.tramper.co.nz Articles, photos, forums and excellent track and hut information.

www.trampingnz.com Region-by-region track info with readable trip reports.

www.peakbagging.org.nz Find a summit and get up on top of it.

Track Classification

Tracks in NZ are classified according to various features, including level of difficulty. We loosely refer to the level of difficulty as easy, medium, hard or difficult. The widely used track classification system is as follows:

Short Walk Well-formed; possibly allows for wheelchair access or constructed to 'shoe' standard (ie walking boots not required). Suitable for people of all ages and fitness levels.

Walking Track Easy and well-formed longer walks; constructed to 'shoe' standard. Suitable for most ages and fitness levels.

Easy Hiking Track Well formed; major water crossings have bridges and track junctions have signs. Light walking boots and decent fitness required.

Hiking Track Requires skill and experience; constructed to 'boot' standard. Suitable for people of good physical fitness. Water crossings may not have bridges!

Route Requires a high degree of skill, experience and navigation skills. Well-equipped, fit hikers only.

Responsible Hiking

If you went straight from the cradle into a pair of hiking boots, some of these hiking tips will seem *ridiculously* obvious. Nevertheless, they are worth emphasising:

➡ Time your hike to avoid peak season: fewer people equals less stress on the environment and fewer snorers in the huts.

➡ Carry out all your rubbish. Burying rubbish disturbs soil and vegetation, encourages erosion, and animals will probably dig it up.

➡ Don't use detergents, shampoo or toothpaste in or near watercourses (even if they're biodegradable).

➡ Use lightweight kerosene, alcohol or Shellite (white gas) stoves for cooking, not disposable butane gas canisters.

➡ Where there's a toilet, use it. Where there isn't one, dig a hole and bury your by-product (at least 15cm deep, 100m from any watercourse).

The DOC Freedom Camping site (http://freedomcamping.org) has plenty more responsible camping tips. For up-to-date advice ask DOC or i-SITE staff. Here are some you mightn't have considered:

➡ If a track passes through a muddy patch, plough straight on through – skirting around the outside increases the size of the bog.

➡ Wash dishes 50m from watercourses; use a scourer, sand or snow instead of detergent.

➡ If you really need to scrub your bod, use biodegradable soap and a bucket, at least 50m from any watercourse. Spread the waste water around widely to help the soil filter it.

➡ If open fires are allowed, use only dead, fallen wood in existing fireplaces. Leave any extra wood for the next happy camper.

➡ Keep food-storage bags out of reach of scavengers by tying them to rafters or trees.

➡ Feeding wildlife can lead to unbalanced populations, diseases and dependency on handouts. Keep your 'scroggin' to yourself.

Great Walks

New Zealand's 10 official Great Walks are the country's most popular tracks and need to be pre-booked online. Natural rugged beauty abounds here, but be prepared for busy tracks and huts over the peak summer period.

All of the South Island's Great Walks are described in Lonely Planet's *Hiking & Tramping in New Zealand* as well as shorter day walks if you're not up for multiday hikes. Local walks are also covered in pamphlets provided by DOC visitor centres and online at www.greatwalks.co.nz.

See p44 for more information on the Great Walks.

THE SOUTH ISLAND'S GREAT WALKS

WALK	DISTANCE (KM)	TIME (DAYS)	DIFFICULTY	DESCRIPTION
Abel Tasman Coast Track	60	5	Easy to intermediate	NZ's most popular walk (or sea kayak); beaches & bays in Abel Tasman NP
Heaphy Track	78	5	Intermediate	Forests, beaches & karst landscapes in Kahurangi NP
Kepler Track	60	3-4	Intermediate	Lakes, rivers, gorges, glacial valleys & beech forest in Fiordland NP
Milford Track	53.5	4	Easy to Intermediate	Rainforest, sheer valleys & peaks, & 580m-high Sutherland Falls in Fiordland NP
Paparoa Track & Pike29 Memorial Track	55	3	Intermediate	Limestone cliffs, mining history & majestic sunsets amid the Paparoa Range
Rakiura Track	39	2-3	Intermediate	Bird life (kiwi!), beaches & lush bush on remote Stewart Island/Rakiura
Routeburn Track	32	2-4	Intermediate	Eye-popping alpine scenery around Mt Aspiring & Fiordland NPs

Tickets & Bookings

To hike these tracks you'll need to book online or at DOC visitor centres and some i-SITEs before departing for NZ. These track-specific tickets cover hut accommodation ($130 per person per night; locals pay half that) and/or camping ($40 per adult per night). You can camp only at designated camping grounds; there's no camping on the Milford Track.

In the off-peak season (May to end of October) fees are substantially lower, but conditions are more challenging; only fit, well-prepared hikers should head out during these months. For more than one trek within a six- or 12-month period, a Backcountry Hut Pass will save you money.

You can book at DOC visitor centres using the online booking system on www.greatwalks.co.nz. Book in advance when bookings open in June if you're planning on walking during summer.

Backcountry Huts

The DOC maintains more than 950 backcountry huts in NZ's national and forest parks. Hut categories comprise:

Basic huts Just a shed!

Standard huts No cooking equipment and sometimes no heating, but mattresses, water supply and toilets.

Serviced huts Mattress-equipped bunks or sleeping platforms, water supply, heating, toilets and sometimes cooking facilities.

Details about the hut services can be found on the DOC website.

Conservation Campsites

The DOC also manages 200-plus 'Conservation Campsites' (often vehicle accessible) with different levels of comfort and costs to stay as follows:

Basic campsites Basic toilets and water; free and unbookable.

Backcountry campsites Basic toilets; water supply may be from a stream. Cooking shelters or fireplaces may be provided. Prices vary by location; see the DOC website.

Scenic campsites Toilets and water supply, cold showers, a wood barbecue and picnic tables usually provided; $15 to $18 per adult per night.

Serviced campsites Full facilities: flush toilets, tap water, hot showers and picnic tables. They may also have barbecues, an outdoor kitchen and laundry; $20 to $23 per adult per night; bookable via DOC visitor centres.

Infants under four stay for free; children five to 17 years are charged at half the price.

Trailhead Transport

Getting to and from trailheads can be problematic, except for popular trails serviced by public and dedicated hikers' transport. Having a vehicle only helps with getting to one end of the track (you still have to collect your car afterwards). If the track starts or ends down a dead-end road, hitching will be difficult and is never advisable.

Tracks accessible by public transport are also the most crowded. An alternative is to arrange private transport, either with a friend or by chartering a vehicle to drop you at one end, then pick you up at the other. If you leave a vehicle at a trailhead, don't leave anything valuable inside – theft from cars in isolated areas is a significant problem.

Cardrona Alpine Resort (p242), near Wanaka

Plan Your Trip
Skiing & Snowboarding

New Zealand's alpine region is loved by skiers and snowboarders with family-friendly ski areas, cross-country skiing and snowshoeing, daredevil snowboarding terrain and luxe-level heliskiing. The NZ ski season varies between regions, but it's generally mid-June through September, though it can run as late as mid-October on a good year.

Best Skiing & Snowboarding

Best for Beginners or with Kids

Mt Hutt, Central Canterbury

Cardrona, Queenstown

The Remarkables, Queenstown

Mt Dobson, South Canterbury

Roundhill, South Canterbury

Coronet Peak, Queenstown

Best Snowboarding

Mt Hutt, Central Canterbury

Treble Cone, Wānaka

Cardrona, Wānaka

Ohau, South Canterbury

Best Après-Ski Activities

Bar-hopping, Queenstown

Dining at Cardrona Hotel, Cardrona

Soaking in an outdoor onsen, Coronet Peak Ski Field

Indoor family climbing, Wānaka

Night luge at Skyline, Queenstown

Planning

Where to Go

The variety of locations and conditions makes it difficult to rate NZ's ski fields in any particular order. Some people like to be near Queenstown's party scene; others prefer the quality high-altitude runs on Mt Hutt, uncrowded Rainbow or less-stressed club skiing areas. Club areas are publicly accessible and usually less crowded and cheaper than commercial fields, even though nonmembers pay a higher fee.

Practicalities

New Zealand's commercial ski areas aren't generally set up as 'resorts' with ski-in

chalets or five-star hotels. Rather, visitor accommodation and après-ski carousing is usually in surrounding towns, which are then connected with the slopes via daily bus shuttles. This set-up is a bonus if you want to sample a few different ski areas, as you can base yourself in one town and day trip to a few different resorts. Many smaller 'club' ski fields have lodges where you *can* stay, subject to availability.

Visitor information centres in NZ, and Tourism New Zealand (www.newzealand.com) have information on the various ski areas and can make bookings and organise packages before you go. Lift passes are reasonably priced given the brevity of the ski season (and are usually half price for kids). Lesson-and-lift packages are available at most areas. Ski and snowboard gear and equipment rental is available in ski villages, and discounted for multiday hire.

Useful Resources

www.snow.co.nz Reports, webcams and ski info across the country.

www.nzski.com Reports, employment, passes and webcams for Mt Hutt, Coronet Peak and the Remarkables.

www.skiandride.nz Good all-round online portal for South Island ski areas with road conditions, school holiday dates and other practical info.

www.chillout.co.nz Portal to info on 13 ski areas and sales of ski passes that access them all. The 'Chill Travel Pass' areas are Broken River, Cheeseman, Craigieburn, Fox Peak, Hanmer Springs, Mt Dobson, Mt Lyford, Mt Olympus, Rainbow and Temple Basin (plus a couple of days on Treble Cone and Porters).

South Island Ski Regions

Queenstown & Wānaka

Coronet Peak (p212) At the Queenstown region's oldest commercial ski field, snow-making systems and treeless slopes provide excellent skiing and snowboarding for all levels, with plenty of family-friendly options. There's night skiing on Fridays and Saturdays (and on Wednesdays in July). Shuttles to the slopes run from Queenstown.

The Remarkables (p212) Visually remarkable, this ski field is near Queenstown – shuttle buses

Winter Sports Areas

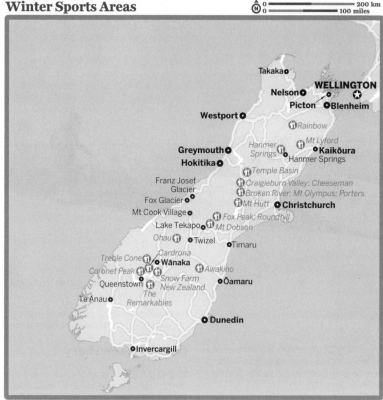

run during ski season. It has a good smattering of intermediate, advanced and beginner runs. Kids' club is on offer for five- to 15-year-old skiers.

Treble Cone (p235) The highest and largest of the southern lakes ski areas is in a spectacular location 26km from Wānaka, with steep slopes suitable for intermediate to advanced skiers (a rather professional vibe). There are also half-pipes and a terrain park for boarders.

Cardrona (p242) Around 34km from Wānaka, with several high-capacity chairlifts, beginners' tows and the southern hemisphere's biggest park and pipe playground for the freestylers. Buses run from Wānaka and Queenstown during ski season. A friendly scene with good services for skiers with disabilities, plus an on-mountain crèche for juniors if you need it.

Snow Farm New Zealand (p242) New Zealand's only commercial Nordic (cross-country) ski area is 33km from Wānaka on the Pisa Range, high above the Cardrona Valley. There are 55km of

groomed trails, huts with facilities and thousands of hectares of open snow.

South Canterbury

Mt Dobson (p122) The 3km-wide basin here, 26km from Fairlie, has a terrain park and famously dry powder. There's a huge learners' area and plenty for intermediates (and up high, dry powder and challenging terrain to suit more experienced skiers). On a clear day you can see Aoraki/Mt Cook and the Pacific Ocean from the summit.

Ohau (p126) This commercial ski area with a secluded feel is on Mt Sutton, 42km from Twizel. There are intermediate and advanced runs, excellent snowboarding, two terrain parks and sociable Lake Ohau Lodge, overlooking glorious views.

Fox Peak (p122) An affordable, uncrowded club ski area 40km from Fairlie in the Two Thumb Range. Expect rope tows, good cross-country skiing and dorm-style accommodation.

Skier at Coronet Peak (p212), Queenstown

Roundhill (p122) A small family-friendly ski area in Canterbury, accessible only by gravel roads, near the town of Lake Tekapo. Best for beginners and snow play.

HELISKIING

New Zealand's remote heights are tailor-made for heliskiing, with operators covering a wide off-piste area along the pristine slopes of the Southern Alps, including extreme skiing for the hardcore. Costs range from around $900 to $1450 for three to eight runs. Heliskiing is available at Coronet Peak, Treble Cone, Cardrona, Mt Hutt, Ohau and Hanmer Springs; independent operators include the following:

➡ Alpine Heliski (p213)

➡ Harris Mountains Heli-Ski (p213)

➡ Methven Heliski (p114)

➡ Over The Top (p218)

➡ Southern Lakes Heliski (p213)

Central Canterbury

Mt Hutt (p115) One of the highest ski areas in the southern hemisphere, as well as one of NZ's best. It's close to Methven; Christchurch is 118km to the east – ski shuttles service both towns. Road access is steep – be extremely cautious in lousy weather. The ski area is exposed to the mercy of the elements, but the snow is usually plentiful. Boasts beginner, intermediate and advanced slopes, with chairlifts, heliskiing and wide-open faces that are good for learning to snowboard.

Porters (p111) The closest commercial ski area to Christchurch (96km away on the Arthur's Pass road). The 'Big Mama' run boasts a 680m drop and gentler slopes, too. It also has a terrain park, good cross-country runs along the ridge, and lodge accommodation.

Temple Basin (p111) A club field with a cult following, 4km from Arthur's Pass. It's a 50-minute walk uphill from the car park to the ski-area lodges. It offers floodlit skiing at night and excellent backcountry runs for snowboarders.

Craigieburn Valley (p111) Centred on Hamilton Peak, Craigieburn Valley is no-frills backcountry heaven, 40km from Arthur's Pass. It's one of NZ's most challenging club areas, with upper

Skiers on a chairlift at The Remarkables (p212), Queenstown

intermediate and advanced runs (no beginners). Accommodation in lodges.

Broken River (p111) Not far from Craigieburn Valley, this club field is a 15- to 20-minute walk from the car park and has a real sense of isolation. Reliable snow, laid-back vibe and sheltered enough to minimise bad-weather closures. Catered or self-catered lodge accommodation available.

Cheeseman (p111) A club area in the Craigieburn Range, this smallish family-friendly operation is around 100km from Christchurch. Based on Mt Cockayne, it's a wide, sheltered basin with drive-to-the-snow road access. Lodge accommodation available.

Mt Olympus (p111) Difficult to find (but worth the search), 2096m Mt Olympus is 58km from

Methven and 12km from Lake Ida. This club area has intermediate and advanced runs, and solid cross-country trails to other areas. Access is sometimes 4WD-only, depending on conditions. Lodge accommodation available.

Northern South Island

Hanmer Springs (p108) A friendly commercial field based on Mt St Patrick, 17km from Hanmer Springs township (linked by shuttle buses), with mostly intermediate and advanced runs.

Mt Lyford (p107) Around 60km from Hanmer Springs and Kaikōura, and 4km from Mt Lyford village, this is more of a 'resort' than most NZ ski fields, with accommodation and eating options. It has a good mix of runs and a terrain park.

Plan Your Trip

Surfing, Cycling & Extreme Sports

From mid-air adventures to deep dives, New Zealand is pure adrenaline. Inspired by NZ's rugged landscape, even the meekest travellers muster the courage to launch from a hillside, skydive above mountains or thunder down river rapids. With their unique ingenuity New Zealanders have pioneered thrills like bungy jumping and jetboating, and their outdoorsy daredevil attitude can be infectious.

Top Adrenaline Rushes

Best Skydive Drop Zones

Queenstown

Fox & Franz Josef Glaciers

Top White-Water Rafting Trips

Shotover Canyon, Queenstown

Buller Gorge, Murchison

Top Mountain-Biking Tracks

Old Ghost Road, Westport

Queen Charlotte Track, Marlborough

West Coast Wilderness Trail, Hokitika

Alps 2 Ocean, South Canterbury

Top Surfing Spots

Kaikōura Peninsula

Taylors Mistake & New Brighton, Christchurch

St Clair Beach, Dunedin

Tauranga Bay, Westport

Colac Bay, Riverton

On the Water

Surfing

Big swells, golden sand, uncrowded beaches...are you scrambling for a surfboard yet? New Zealand's surf scene is world class, and the long coastline means there's heaps of variety for beginners and experienced surfers: point breaks, reefs, rocky shelves, hollow sandy beach breaks, and islands with swells from all points of the compass. If you're willing to travel off the beaten track, you can score waves all to yourself, though we don't recommend surfing completely alone obviously. A number of hostels and holiday parks double as surf schools and gear-rental outfits, making it easy to roll straight from bed to beach.

Regardless of the season, you'll need a wetsuit on the South Island, and do your weather research. Water temperatures and climate vary greatly from north to south. In summer on the South Island you can get away with a 2mm–3mm steamer wetsuit. In winter you'll need a 3mm–5mm with extras like a hood and booties. As all surfers know, you never fight strong currents sweeping you away from the shore. Swim parallel to the beach to get beyond the rip's reach before making your way back to land.

Surfing New Zealand (www.surfingnz. co.nz) has a list of approved surf schools where you can learn to catch waves, along with a calendar of competitions and events where you can go watch the pros.

Jetboating

The jetboat was invented in NZ by an engineer from Fairlie – Bill Hamilton (1899–1978) – who wanted a boat that could navigate shallow, local rivers. He credited his eventual success to Archimedes, but as most jetboat drivers will inevitably tell you, Kiwi Bill is the hero of the jetboat story.

River jetboat tours can be found throughout NZ, and while much is made of the hair-raising 360-degree spins that see passengers drenched and grinning from ear to ear, they are really just a sideshow. Just as Bill would have it, jetboat journeys take you deep into wilderness you could otherwise never see, and as such they offer one of NZ's most rewarding tour experiences. In Haast and Whataroa, jetboat tours plunge visitors into pristine wilderness, aflutter with birds.

Big-ticket trips such as Queenstown's Shotover, Kawarau and Dart all live up to the hype. But the quieter achievers will impress you just as much. Check out the Buller and Wilkin in Mt Aspiring National Park.

Parasailing & Kiteboarding

Parasailing (dangling from a modified parachute over the water, while being pulled along by a speedboat) is perhaps the easiest way for humans to achieve assisted flight. There are operators in Wānaka and Queenstown.

Kitesurfing, where a mini parachute drags you across the ocean on a mini surfboard, can be attempted (after some lessons if you need them!) at Nelson.

Sea Kayaking & SUPing

Sea kayaking offers a wonderful perspective of the coastline and gets you close to marine wildlife you may otherwise never see. Meanwhile tandem kayaks, aka 'divorce boats', present a different kind of challenge.

There are ample places to get paddling. Hot spots include the Marlborough Sounds (from Picton) and Abel Tasman National Park. Kaikōura is exceptional for wildlife spotting, and Fiordland for jaw-dropping scenery.

The Kiwi Association of Sea Kayakers (www.kask.org.nz) gives a good primer on paddling techniques, plus resources for kayakers with disabilities.

As is the case the world over, stand-up paddleboarding (SUP) is increasingly popular across NZ and another way to get out on the water.

Scuba Diving

New Zealand is just as enchanting under the waves, with warm waters in the north, interesting sea life all over and some impressive shipwrecks.

In the Marlborough Sounds, the MS *Mikhail Lermontov* is one of the world's largest diveable cruise-ship wrecks. In Fiordland, experienced divers can head for Dusky Sound, Milford Sound and Doubtful Sound, which have clear conditions and the occasional friendly fur seal or dolphin.

Expect to pay around $799 for a 3- to 4-day, PADI-approved, ocean-dive course. One-off organised boat- and land-based dives start at around $200.

New Zealand Underwater Association (www. nzunderwater.org.nz) Clean seas and diving-safety advocates whose website has safety info, diving tips, gear maintenance advice and more.

Dive New Zealand (www.divenewzealand.com) NZ's only dedicated dive magazine, plus safety info and listings of dive clubs and shops.

White-Water Rafting & Canoeing

Epic mountain ranges and associated rainfall mean there's no shortage of great rivers to raft, nor any shortage of operators ready to get you into the rapids. Rivers are graded from I to VI (VI meaning they can't be safely rafted), with operators often running a couple of different trips to suit ability and age (rougher stretches are usually limited to rafters aged 13 or above).

Queenstown's Shotover and Kawarau Rivers are deservedly popular, but the Rangitata (Geraldine), Buller (Murchison) and the Arnold and Waiho rate just as

PURIPAT LERTPUNYAROJ/SHUTTERSTOCK ©

Top: Jetboating on Shotover River (p216), Queenstown

Bottom: Paraglider over Lake Wakatipu (p217), Queenstown

highly. For a multiday epic, check out the Landsborough.

Kayaking and canoeing are rampant, particularly on friendly lake waters, although there are still plenty of places to paddle the rapids.

New Zealand Rafting Association (www.nz-rafting.co.nz) River conservation nonprofit; river gradings and listings of rafting operators.

New Zealand Kayak (www.kayaknz.co.nz) Community-based kayaking magazine.

On the Land
Bungy Jumping

Bungy jumping was made famous by Kiwi AJ Hackett's 1987 plunge from the Eiffel Tower, after which he teamed up with champion NZ skier Henry van Asch to turn the endeavour into an accessible pursuit for anyone.

Today their original home base of Queenstown is a spiderweb of bungy cords, including AJ Hackett's triad: the 134m Nevis Bungy (the highest in NZ); the 43m Kawarau Bungy (the original); and the Ledge Bungy (at the highest altitude – diving off a 400m-high platform). There's another scenic jump at Thrillseekers Canyon near Hanmer Springs. Huge rope swings offer variation on the theme; head to Queenstown's Shotover Canyon or Nevis Swing for that swooshy buzz.

Caving

Caving (aka spelunking) opportunities abound in NZ's honeycombed karst (limestone) regions. You'll find local clubs and organised tours around Charleston and Karamea. Golden Bay also has some mammoth caves.

For comprehensive information including details of specific areas and clubs, see the website of the New Zealand Speleological Society (www.caves.org.nz).

Paragliding & Hang Gliding

A surprisingly gentle but still thrilling way to take to the skies, paragliding involves setting sail from a hillside or clifftop under a parachute-like wing. Hang gliding is similar but with a smaller, rigid wing. Most flights are conducted in tandem with a master pilot, although it's also possible to get lessons to go it alone but you'll need to stick around for a while. For a taster tandem flight head to Queenstown, Wānaka, Nelson, Motueka or Christchurch. The New Zealand Hang Gliding and Paragliding Association (www.nzhgpa.org.nz) rules the roost.

Horse Trekking

Treks in NZ offer a chance to explore some remarkable landscapes – from farms to forests and along rivers and beaches. Rides range from one-hour jaunts (from around $60) to week-long, fully supported treks.

South Island options include beachy trips in Golden Bay and adventures around mountain foothills near Aoraki/Mt Cook, Lake Tekapo, Queenstown and Glenorchy – as a bonus, you can canter through several *Lord of the Rings* filming locations. Spectacular treks are offered from Punakaiki into Paparoa National Park. For info and operator listings, check out True NZ Horse Trekking (www.truenz.co.nz/horsetrekking).

Mountain Biking & Cycle Touring

Jaw-dropping mountains interlaced with farm tracks and old railway lines...it would be hard to design better mountain-biking terrain than NZ. The New Zealand Cycle Trail (www.nzcycletrail.com), some 2500km of tracks, helped mountain biking grow from a weekend sport to a national craze. Its popularity among outdoors enthusiasts of a certain age (and the potential for gear one-upmanship) has led biking to be dubbed 'the new golf'. But no age group is immune, and the variety of trails in NZ brings a choice of gentle pootles in meadows to multiday cycle tours, half-day downhill thrill rides to challenging week-long MTB adventures.

Mountain-bike parks – most with various trail grades and skills areas (and handy bike hire nearby) – are great for trying mountain biking NZ style. The South Island's most famous is Queenstown's downhill park, fed by the Skyline Gondola.

Classic trails include the Rameka on Takaka Hill and the trails around Christchurch's Port Hills – but this is just the tip of the iceberg. An increasing number of DOC hiking trails are being

NGĀ HAERENGA: THE NEW ZEALAND CYCLE TRAIL

The New Zealand Cycle Trail (www.nzcycletrail.com) – known in Māori as Ngā Haerenga, 'The Journeys' – is a 22-strong series of off-road trails also known as Great Rides. Spread from north to south, they are of diverse length, terrain and difficulty, with many following history-rich old railway lines and pioneer trails, while others are freshly cut adventures. Almost all penetrate remarkable landscapes.

There are plenty of options for beginner to intermediate cyclists, with several hardcore exceptions including the Old Ghost Road, which is growing to international renown. The majority are also well supported by handy bike hire, shuttles, and dining and accommodation options, making them a desirable way to explore NZ while minding your carbon footprint.

converted to dual use – such as the tricky but epic Heaphy Track and the challenging, history-rich Old Ghost Road – but mountain biking is often restricted to low season due to hiker numbers. Track damage is also an issue, so check with the DOC before starting out.

Your clue that there's some great biking around is the presence of bike-hire outfits. Bowl on up and pick their brains. Most likely cycle-obsessed themselves, they'll point you in the direction of a ride appropriate to your level. The go-to book is *Classic New Zealand Mountain Bike Rides* (2019; from bookshops, bike shops and www.kennett.co.nz).

If cycle touring is more your pace, check out the *Pedallers' Paradise* booklets by Nigel Rushton (www.paradise-press.co.nz). Changeable weather and road conditions mean cycle touring is less of a craze but there are remarkable road journeys, such as the Southern Scenic Route in the deep south.

Mountaineering

New Zealand has a proud mountaineering history – this was, after all, the home of Sir Edmund Hillary (1919–2008). Hillary and Tenzing Norgay, from Nepal, were the first two mountaineers confirmed to summit Mt Everest. When he came back down, Sir Ed famously uttered to friend George Lowe, 'Well, George, we knocked the bastard off!'

The Southern Alps are studded with amazing climbs. The Aoraki/Mt Cook region is outstanding, but there are other zones extending throughout the spine of the South Island from the Kaikōura Ranges and the Nelson Lakes peaks all the way through to the hotbeds of Mt Aspiring National Park and Fiordland. Be warned, though: this is rugged and often remote stuff, and climber deaths are a regular occurrence. Even confident climbers are strongly advised to seek out a local guide, whatever route you're planning to take.

Rock Climbing

Time to chalk up your fingers and don some natty little rubber shoes. Try the Port Hills area above Christchurch or Castle Hill on the road to Arthur's Pass. West of Nelson, the marble and limestone mountains of Golden Bay and Takaka Hill provide prime climbing. Other options are Long Beach (north of Dunedin), and Mihiwaka and Lovers Leap on the Otago Peninsula. Raining? You'll find an indoor climbing wall in Christchurch.

Climb New Zealand (www.climb.co.nz) has the low-down on the gnarliest overhangs around NZ, plus access and instruction info. Needless to say, instruction is a must for all but the most seasoned climbing pros.

Skydiving

With some of the most scenic jump zones in the world, NZ is a fantastic place to take a leap. First-time skydivers can knock off this bucket-list item with a tandem jump, strapped to a qualified instructor, experiencing up to 75 seconds of free fall before the chute opens. The thrill is worth every dollar, from $249 for a 9000ft jump to $559 for NZ's highest free-fall jump (a nerve-jangling 20,000ft, or 85 seconds, on offer over Franz Josef). Extra costs apply for a video recording or photographs capturing your mid-air terror/delight. Check out the New Zealand Parachute Federation (www.nzpf.org) for more info.

Plan Your Trip

Eat & Drink Like a Local

Travellers, start your appetites! Eating is a highlight of any visit to New Zealand, from fresh seafood and gourmet burgers to farmers market fruit-and-veg and crisp-linen fine dining. Drinking here, too, presents boundless opportunities to have a good time, with coffee, craft beer and wine of world renown.

Food Experiences

Meals of a Lifetime

5th Street (p88) Global influences marry perfectly with Kiwi produce at this sparkling Christchurch bistro.

Rātā (p223), Queenstown Food adventures and genuine hospitality at this uniquely Kiwi restaurant run by Michelin-starred chef Josh Emett in Queenstown.

Hokitika (p262) Get here in March to tantalise your taste buds at the Wildfoods Festival.

Bracken (p154) Delicately prepared seasonal tasting menus in this beautiful Dunedin dining room.

Cheap Treats

Fish and chips The UK may be the spiritual home of this beloved fast-food, but the Kiwis have raised it to an art form. Stop by Kaikōura for your fill at Cods & Crayfish (p105) with a view of the sea.

Pies Bakeries throughout NZ turn out golden-crusted delights filled with everything from beef to scallops and Thai vegetarian curry. The Fairlie Bakehouse (p122) produces superb examples.

Pineapple Lumps These chewy, tooth-gripping, chocolate-coated sweets have been a Kiwi favourite since the 1950s. Available everywhere.

The Year in Food

New Zealand's varied topography and bounteous maritime climate translates to great food and drink at any time of the year.

Summer (December to February)

Summer's bounty includes stone fruit, berries, flowering vegetables and even the first apples of the year.

Autumn (March to May)

Citrus and brassicas begin to replace late summer's fruit and vegetables, while Bluff oysters are celebrated in May's annual festival. It's also vintage time for Kiwi wines.

Winter (June to August)

Shellfish are at their best in the coldest months, when fennel, leeks and rhubarb are also in season.

Spring (September to November)

The return of the sun brings asparagus, artichokes and other tasty treats, plus Akaroa's French Festival celebrating all things Gallic.

Dare to Try

Kina New Zealand's native sea urchin, this spiky little echinoderm is harvested on both islands from August to January. It's much prized for its intensely flavoured roe: simply cut open to spoon the creamy, fishy goodness straight from the shell.

Pāua Harvested year-round from the Kaikōura and Southland coasts, and from islands such as Stewart and the Chathams, NZ's abalone are coveted by seafood lovers across the globe. The tough muscle of wild pāua often needs to be tenderised before eating, either raw, braised or flash-fried.

Whitebait fritters In NZ whitebait – the generic name for edible, immature sprats of schooling fish known as galaxids – is often served fried in a crispy, many-eyed fritter. The immature fish resemble translucent worms, posing a sensory challenge to some!

Local Specialities

Christchurch & Canterbury

Rock lobster Found in abundance along most of NZ's rocky coastline, these succulent crustaceans are most often associated with Kaikōura on the South Island.

Dunedin & Otago

Hokey Pokey ice cream Certain to rouse childhood nostalgia in Kiwis if you ask where to get the best Hokey Pokey ice cream (vanilla with chunks of honeycomb).

Fiordland & Southland

Bluff oysters Also known by the Māori name *tio paruparu*, these briny bivalves are endemic to NZ's coast. The eponymous South Island town of Bluff hosts a festival celebrating the catch every May.

Queenstown & Wānaka

Pavlova The queen of Kiwi desserts is a meringue base heaped with cream and berries, kiwifruit or passion fruit. Where else can you indulge guilt-free but in the adventure-sports capital?

Marlborough & Nelson

Sauvignon blanc Such is the world's thirst for NZ 'sav blanc' that the variety accounts for 73% of the nation's wine production, and an even higher proportion of its exports. The best examples, such as those from Marlborough, show characteristics of red pepper, passion fruit and gooseberry. Ideal with seafood, the style also matches tangy and astringent foods.

Eat & Drink Like a Local

While lacking the population centres of its northern counterpart, the South Island nonetheless offers abundant opportunity to dine well. From country pubs to chic restaurants, the emphasis is on home-grown ingredients like lamb, seafood and venison, with a thriving vegetarian and vegan food scene to please the plant-based.

When to Eat

Breakfast Kiwi cafes have raised the simple task of getting the day's digestion going to an art form. Good coffee is universally available while breakfast staples such as eggs, bacon or avocado on toast are steered in imaginative directions, particularly in urban joints aimed at the brunch crowd. And, of course, the simple staples of toast, waffles and granola have never disappeared.

Lunch Lunch, which can be either the day's primary or secondary meal, presents perhaps the widest palette of options. Casual ramen joints and gastropubs are joined by more high-flying restaurants and bistros, most of which open for lunch at least five days a week, in addition to traditional evening hours. With more than 10% of Kiwis adhering to vegetarian and vegan diets, plant-based options are increasingly available even in regional towns.

Dinner The day's concluding meal can be as casual or as fancy as you like (or can afford) in NZ, particularly in its cities. In order to wow the socks off increasingly demanding diners, restaurants must now succeed in fusing ingredients and traditions into ever more innovative fare. 'Modern NZ' has been coined to classify this approach: a melange of East and West, a swirl of Atlantic and Pacific Rim, with a dash of classical European technique and Mediterranean sensibility. Late opening is an urban affair; one-pub towns usually offer little after 8pm.

Where to Eat

New Zealand has undergone a dining revolution in the past few decades. The range of places to eat, from fish-and-chip shops to swanky cafes, ethnic restaurants,

Fresh New Zealand seafood

gastro-pubs and fine-dining establishments, has never been greater.

Once an occasional treat, eating out is now a commonplace undertaking for a multicultural country that is more food-literate than it has ever been. Principal cities like Auckland, Wellington and Christchurch offer plenty of options at most times of the day; in quieter, rural areas, you'll naturally find narrower options and opening hours. Most eating options are casual walk-ins (pubs, cafes and takeaways), but book top-end restaurants in advance.

Restaurants Open for dinner and lunch. 'Modern NZ' means locally sourced, top-quality fare with international influences.

Cafes Locally roasted beans, expert baristas, savvy breakfast-to-lunch food and usually family-friendly.

Takeaways Thai, Chinese, Indian...the big internationals are here, but the plastic-free revolution is creating a stir when it comes to eco-options.

Pubs and bars You can get a bite to eat at most Kiwi bars and pubs – from standard stodge to delicately wrought tapas and farmer-sized steaks.

Supermarkets In all sizeable towns and offering a huge variety of food, including healthy and gluten-free options. Open until 9pm; later in city centres.

Menu Decoder

Avo on toast Not your typical breakfast fare; expect creamy generous portions of smashed avocado.

Buddha bowl Colourful vegan or vegetarian single-bowl meals with small portions of several ingredients, served cold on a bed of rice or grains.

Hoki A popular and sustainably caught cod-like fish you could be eating with your chips.

Pipi A shellfish, like a mussel, but one that's found in sand not on rocks.

PRICE RANGES

The following price ranges refer to the average price of a main course.

$	less than $15
$$	$15–35
$$$	more than $35

Plan Your Trip
Family Travel

New Zealand's a dream for family travel: kid-centric activities, family-friendly accommodation, a moderate climate and very little danger. Unadventurous palates can always be accommodated and food servers are clued up on dietary requirements. Base yourself in a sizeable town for amenities galore and excursions within a short drive.

Keeping Costs Down

Accommodation

Campsites, holiday parks and kid-friendly motels are all great options for family travel on the cheap with shared kitchens to cook in. Coastal campsites are often located near beaches and may offer other free outdoor activities. Motels sometimes include a kitchenette.

Sightseeing

Most museums, galleries, entertainment parks, wildlife sanctuaries and similar attractions offer kids' concessions and/or family tickets that let the whole tribe in for less.

Eating

Most midrange restaurants and pubs will offer a kids' menu, with choices, portions and prices adapted to the needs of younger diners. When the weather's good, hit farmers markets for an alfresco picnic, where kids don't need to sit still.

Transport

Urban transport networks all offer discounts to children and students; infants usually travel for free. When weather, terrain and your plans allow, consider kitting the family out with rental bikes to take advantage of NZ's fantastic cycling infrastructure, or the flat topography of cities like Christchurch.

Children Will Love...

Wildlife Encounters

Kiwi Birdlife Park, Queenstown (p212) Spot a kiwi and myriad squawking birds.

Akaroa Dolphins (p98) Watch dolphins from a catamaran, in the company of a wildlife-spotting dog.

Orana Wildlife Park (p71) Open range zoo where African animals roam.

West Coast Wildlife Centre, Franz Josef (p256) Meet the tuatara (pint-sized dinosaurs).

Royal Albatross Centre (p158) Watch little penguins waddle ashore at dusk from Pilots Beach on the Otago Peninsula.

Stewart Island/Rakiura (p188) Chance to see the elusive kiwi in the wild.

Getting Active

Queenstown (p213) Everything from kids' rafting trips to paragliding, bungy jumping, zip lines, ice skating and (of course) skiing.

St Clair Beach (p150) Head to the heated salt-water pool if Dunedin's southern ocean beach is too chilly for little ones.

Abel Tasman Horse Trekking (p299) Paddock rides for little ones and beach horse treks for those aged 12 and up.

The Catlins (p178) Flat rambles a few minutes long, rewarded by waterfalls...no tired little legs here.

Baldwin Street (p149) Want to get those little legs moving, walk them up the world's (second) steepest street in Dunedin.

Food!

Kiwifruit (p297) Pick up a ripe bag at harvest time at the Sunday market in Motueka.

Sweet Alice's Fudge Kitchen (p266) Candies, ice cream and fudge on the West Coast in Hokitika.

Fish and chips (p105) For the best cod and crayfish on the beach head to Kaikōura.

Hokitika Wildfoods Festival (p265) One for kids unafraid to stretch their palates or laugh at mum having a go.

Mills Bay Mussels (p313) Kids will love the chance to eat with their hands here in Havelock.

History

Canterbury Museum, Christchurch (p70) A mummy, dinosaur bones and a cool Discovery Centre.

Shantytown, Greymouth (p268) All aboard a steam train for gold-panning in a re-created gold-rush town.

Toitū Otago Settlers Museum (p146) Dunedin's interactive history museum brings the story of the South Island to life.

Bluff Maritime Museum (p186) Learn the stories of the seafaring folk who came to Bluff.

National Transport & Toy Museum (p234) Eclectic collection in four huge hangars in Wānaka.

Region by Region
Christchurch & Canterbury

Urban and rural attractions alike lure families to this region, from Christchurch's magical Margaret Mahy Family Playground (p80) to the Orana Wildlife Park (p71), boating on the Avon River (p72) and horse trekking in Mackenzie Country (p123).

Dunedin & Otago

All kids will love the Otago Peninsula (p157) for wildlife, including penguins, fur seals, sea lions, albatrosses and whales. Elsewhere, there's the Otago Central Rail Trail (p162), the steampunk playground that is Ōamaru (p137) and winter sports in Naseby (p165).

Fiordland & Southland

This region is all about outdoor activities, from the all-ages splendour of Milford Sound (p201) to active farm holidays at Slope Point (p181) and the Te Anau Glowworm Caves (p196). Mechanically minded kids will love Invercargill for its two motor museums (p183) and the chance to operate huge diggers at Dig This (p183).

Queenstown & Wānaka

Queenstown (p210), the epicentre of skiing, bungy and general thrill-seeking in New Zealand, may be too extreme for some kids, but at Wānaka the over-nines can test their mettle on the much calmer via ferrata by Wild Wire (p236).

West Coast

While the wild West Coast is less populated and accessible than most parts of NZ, kids will love the re-created gold-rush-era Shantytown (p268), family-friendly rafting (p282) and the chance to net crayfish at the National Kiwi Centre (p263).

Nelson & Marlborough

More than just wineries and wilderness walks, this region offers plenty for families, including Nelson's Tahunanui Beach (p285), kayaking tours in Abel Tasman National Park (p302), and fishing and a petting zoo at the Anatoki Salmon (p304) hatchery.

Good to Know

Look out for the icon for family-friendly suggestions throughout this guide.

Babies and toddlers Attitudes to public breastfeeding are pretty enlightened throughout New Zealand, while infant formula, nappies and other essentials are readily available in supermarkets, pharmacies and smaller groceries.

Dining out The golden rule is 'be considerate': kids are welcome in most eating establishments, but their behaviour is your responsibility, and fine-dining patrons will expect to enjoy an adults-only environment. Generally, licensed establishments such as pubs welcome well-behaved kids, but not after dinner time.

Prams and pushchairs New Zealand's cities are well paved, well lit and easy to negotiate for parents pushing prams and pushchairs.

Seat belts Everyone must wear seat belts while in moving vehicles, with appropriately anchored chairs and capsules mandated by law for the very youngest.

Public transport Kids' discounts of different kinds exist for all mass-transit systems in New Zealand. Infants travel free.

Hire vehicles If your kids are little, check that your car-hire company can supply the right-sized car seat for your child, and that the seat will be properly fitted. Some companies legally require you to fit car seats yourself. Consider hiring a campervan. These formidable beasts are everywhere in NZ, kitted out with beds, kitchens, and even toilets and TVs.

Useful Resources

Lonely Planet Kids (www.lonelyplanetkids.com) Loads of activities and great family-travel blog content.

LetsGoKids (http://letsgokids.co.nz) Download the NZ edition for family travel inspiration and money-saving vouchers.

Kidspot (www.kidspot.co.nz) The 'Family Fun' section has suggestions for child-friendly activities, road trips and more.

Kids' Corner

Say What?

Hello.	Kia ora
Swimsuit.	Togs
Flip-flops/ thongs.	Jandals.
Good.	Sweet as

Did You Know?

- The smallest coin here is the copper 10c coin.

Have You Tried?

Lemon & Paeroa (L&P)
A sweet soft drink

Regions at a Glance

Get ready for an oft-changing selection of some of the planet's most surprising scenery. From the labyrinthine marine idylls of the Marlborough Sounds to the craggy volcanic hills of the Banks Peninsula, the South Island packs a stunning scenic punch. Kayak through the mist of Doubtful Sound, or test yourself on the Milford or Routeburn Tracks – often in the company of New Zealand's quirky wildlife – before strapping on some skis and hitting the world-renowned slopes around Queenstown and Wānaka. Spend some time strolling the newly restored pavements of creative Christchurch, or head back in time along the streets of historic Ōamaru and gothic Dunedin. Along the way, taste-test the best of the country's gourmet gastronomy at a profusion of regional restaurants, alongside world-class wineries and exciting breweries.

Christchurch & Canterbury

Architecture
Outdoor Activities
Wildlife

Christchurch & Akaroa

Post-earthquake Christchurch is an architectural mash-up of heritage buildings and creative modern design. Learn about the French and British colonial story in diminutive Akaroa.

Hiking & Kayaking

Explore alpine valleys around Arthur's Pass, kayak on Akaroa Harbour, or visit Aoraki/Mt Cook National Park for hiking and kayaking amid majestic glacial lakes.

Kaikōura

The South Island is home to a menagerie of creatures, both in the water and on the wing. There are myriad wildlife tours on water and wing too.

p64

Dunedin & Otago

Wildlife
Wineries
History

Birds, Seals & Sea Lions

Seals, sea lions and penguins patrol the Otago Peninsula, while rocky Taiaroa Head is the planet's only mainland breeding location for the magnificent royal albatross.

Bannockburn & Waitaki Valley

Barrel into the craggy valleys of Bannockburn for excellent vineyard restaurants or delve into the up-and-coming Waitaki Valley wine scene for riesling and pinot gris.

Victoriana

Explore the artsy and storied streets of Dunedin, or escape by foot or penny-farthing bicycle into the heritage ambience of Ōamaru's Victorian Precinct.

p133

Fiordland & Southland

Scenery
Outdoor Activities
Cruises & Coasts

Epic Landscapes

The star of the show is remarkable Milford Sound, but take time to explore the rugged Catlins coast or remote, end-of-the-world Stewart Island/Rakiura.

Hiking

Fiordland National Park comprises much of New Zealand's precious Te Wāhipounamu (Southwest New Zealand) World Heritage Area. Further south, Rakiura National Park showcases Stewart Island's beauty.

Watery Thrills

Cruise or kayak around glorious Doubtful Sound, test the surf in Curio Bay or get sprayed by waterfalls in the Catlins.

p172

Queenstown & Wānaka

Outdoor Activities
Scenery
Wineries

Queenstown Extreme

Few places on earth offer so many adventurous activities: bungy jumping, river rafting, skiing and mountain biking only scratch the adrenaline-fuelled surface.

Mountains & Lakes

Queenstown's combination of Lake Wakatipu and the soaring Remarkables is a real jaw-dropper. Or venture into prime NZ wilderness around Glenorchy and Mt Aspiring National Park.

Central Otago Wineries

Lunch at award-winning restaurants in Arrowtown, explore the unique terroir of the Gibbston Valley subregion and finish with a tasting at Rippon, overlooking gorgeous Lake Wānaka.

p204

The West Coast

Natural Wonders
Outdoor Activities
History

Crazy Rock Formations

This region is replete with prehistoric wonders: don't miss Ōpārara's famous arches, Punakaiki's Pancake Rocks and the sublime Hokitika Gorge.

Walking in Wilderness

Expect dramatic views along hour-long tracks and hardcore epics, like the wind-scoured, wildlife-rich Cape Foulwind Walkway.

Pioneer Tales

The West Coast's raffish pioneering heritage comes vividly to life in places like Reefton and Shantytown (Greymouth), and in ghost towns like Waiuta.

p248

Nelson & Marlborough

Wine
Arts
Wilderness

Marlborough Wine Touring

Bobbing in Marlborough's sea of sauvignon blanc, riesling, pinot noir and bubbly are barrel loads of quality cellar-door experiences and regional food.

Nelson

Nelson has an inordinate number of galleries; local artisans can be found at the Nelson Market on Saturdays. Add an excellent food and craft-beer scene, cycling tours and beautiful surroundings, and you have a perfect city to base yourself in.

National Parks

Not satisfied with just one national park, the Nelson region has three – Nelson Lakes, Kahurangi and Abel Tasman. You could hike all three in a week.

p283

On the Road

Christchurch & Canterbury

Best Places to Eat

➡ Pegasus Bay (p110)

➡ Earl (p86)

➡ Rona's (p100)

➡ Riverside Market (p86)

➡ 5th Street (p88)

Best Places to Stay

➡ Halfmoon Cottage (p96)

➡ Eco Villa (p81)

➡ Lakestone Lodge (p126)

➡ Woodbank Park Cottages (p108)

➡ Vicarage (p121)

Why Go?

Nowhere in New Zealand (NZ) is changing and developing as fast as post-quake Christchurch. The hospitality scene is flourishing and the central city is once again drawing visitors to its pedestrian-friendly streets.

A short drive from the city, Banks Peninsula conceals idyllic hidden bays and beaches that provide the perfect backdrop for wildlife cruises, with a sunset return to the attractions of pretty Akaroa. To the north is whale-watching at Kaikōura, the vineyards of the Waipara Valley and the relaxed ambience of Hanmer Springs, while westwards, the Canterbury Plains morph quickly into the dramatic wilderness of the Southern Alps.

Canterbury's attractions include hiking along alpine valleys and over passes around Arthur's Pass, and mountain biking around the turquoise lakes of Mackenzie Country. During winter (June to September), attention switches to the ski fields. Throughout the seasons, Aoraki/Mt Cook, the country's tallest peak, stands sentinel over this diverse region.

When to Go

➡ Look forward to hot and settled weather in January and March, with plenty of ways to get active amid the region's spectacular landscapes.

➡ From July to September hit the winter slopes at Mt Hutt or on one of Canterbury's smaller club ski fields.

➡ The shoulder season from October to November can be cool and dry, and blissfully uncrowded. Come prepared for all weather; snow is still possible on the mountains. March to May is also less busy.

ℹ️ Getting There & Away

AIR

Christchurch's international airport is the South Island's main hub with flights from Australia, Singapore, China, Dubai and Fiji. Air New Zealand flies here from 15 domestic destinations.

BUS

Christchurch is the hub for coaches and shuttles heading up the coast as far as Picton, down the coast to Dunedin (and on to Te Anau), over the Alps to Greymouth and inland down to Queenstown.

TRAIN

The year-round *TranzAlpine* service connects Christchurch and Greymouth, and the *Coastal Pacific* chugs north to Picton from late September to late April, with ferry connections across Cook Strait to the North Island.

CHRISTCHURCH

POP 388,000

Welcome to a vibrant city in transition, coping creatively with the aftermath of NZ's second-worst natural disaster. Traditionally the most English of NZ cities, Christchurch's heritage heart was all but hollowed out following the 2010 and 2011 earthquakes that left 186 people dead.

Today Christchurch is in the midst of an epic rebuild that has completely reconstructed the city centre, where over 80% of buildings needed to be demolished after the quake. Scaffolding and road cones will be part of the city's landscape for a while yet, but don't be deterred; exciting new buildings are opening at an astonishing pace, and sights are open for business.

Curious travellers will revel in this chaotic, crazy and colourful mix, full of surprises and inspiring in ways you can't even imagine. And despite all the hard work and heartache, the locals will be only too pleased to see you.

History

The first people to live in what is now Christchurch were moa (bird) hunters, who arrived around 1250. Immediately prior to colonisation, the Ngāi Tahu tribe had a small seasonal village on the banks of the Avon called Ōtautahi.

When British settlers arrived in 1850 it was an orderly Church of England project; the passengers on the 'First Four Ships' were dubbed 'the Canterbury Pilgrims' by the British press. Christchurch was meant to be a model of class-structured England in the South Pacific, not just another scruffy colonial outpost. Churches were built rather than pubs, the fertile farming land was deliberately placed in the hands of the gentry, and wool made the elite of Christchurch wealthy.

In 1856 Christchurch officially became NZ's first city, and a very English one at that. Town planning and architecture assumed a close affinity with the 'mother country' and English-style gardens were planted, earning *Continued on p69*

CHRISTCHURCH & CANTERBURY CHRISTCHURCH

CHRISTCHURCH IN...

Two Days

After breakfast at C1 Espresso (p86), take some time to walk around the regenerating city centre, visit Quake City (p69) and wander through Cathedral Sq (p70). Make your way to Christchurch Art Gallery (p69) and then visit the nearby Canterbury Museum (p70) and Botanic Gardens (p69). Return across the river for diverse lunch options at the Riverside Market (p86) before checking out the excellent street art (p80) around High St. That evening have a craft beer at the Institution (p89) in New Regent St before dinner at nearby Twenty Seven Steps (p87).

Start day two at Addington Coffee Co-op (p88) and then head up Mt Cavendish on the gondola (p70) for views and a walk at the top. Continue to Lyttelton for lunch at Civil & Naval (p93) before returning through the tunnel and around to Sumner for a late-afternoon swim or stroll. End the day with great pizza at The Brewery (p89) in Woolston followed by a live gig at nearby Blue Smoke (p90).

Four Days

On day three head to Akaroa (p97) to explore its wildlife-rich harbour and walk its pretty streets, enjoying stupendous views on the way there and back again. On day four, visit Orana Wildlife Park (p71) and Riccarton House & Bush (p71) before finishing the day with a drink at Not Without You (p89) and dinner at Little High Eatery (p87).

Christchurch & Canterbury Highlights

1 Christchurch
(p64) Experiencing the dynamic re-emergence of the city post-earthquake and exploring its serene Botanic Gardens.

2 Mt John (p122)
Marvelling at the other-worldly views of Mackenzie Country and the surreal azure blue of Lake Tekapo from the top.

3 Hanmer Springs
(p106) Soaking in the soothing waters at this famous hot spring.

4 Banks Peninsula
(p94) Admiring the surf-bitten edges from Summit Rd before descending to the quaint Gallic ambience of Akaroa.

5 Aoraki/Mt Cook National Park (p127) Gazing at the cloud-piercing silhouette of NZ's highest peak.

SOUTH PACIFIC OCEAN

50 km
25 miles

7 Kaikōura

6 Alps 2 Ocean Cycle Trail (p125) Cycling the best bits of the trail from unspoiled Twizel.

7 Kaikōura (p100) Getting up close to wildlife including whales, seals, dolphins and albatrosses.

TASMAN SEA

Lake Ellesmere (Te Waihora)

Dunsandel

Rakaia

Ashburton

Tinwald

Rangitata

Temuka

Pleasant Point

Timaru

Glentunnel

Windwhistle

Mt Hutt

Methven

Mayfield

Geraldine

Pass (945m)

Rakaia River

Rakaia Gorge

Mt Somers

Peel Forest

Lake Heron

Rangitata River

Ben McLeod (1952m)

Fox Peak (2331m)

Fairlie

Burkes Pass

Albury

Hunter Hills

Waimate

Glenavy

Pukeuri

Waitaki River

Forest Park

Lake Coleridge

Mt Bryce (2188m)

Mt Whitcombe (2638m)

Mt Arrowsmith (2795m)

Mesopotamia

The Thumbs (2545m)

Two Thumb Range

Lake Tekapo

Lake Tekapo

Mt John

Lake Benmore

Ross

Gorge

Mahinapua

Harihari

Lake Ianthe

Mt Tyndall (2524m)

Southern Alps

Mt D'Archiac (2865m)

Elie de Beaumont (3116m)

Westland Tai Poutini National Park

Mt Tasman (3498m)

MalteBrun (3154m)

Aoraki/Mt Cook (3724m)

Aoraki/Mt Cook National Park

Mt Cook Village

Lake Pukaki

Twizel

Lake Ohau

Ben Ohau Range

Ruataniwha Conservation Park

Glentanner

Whataroa

Okarito

Franz Josef

Fox Glacier

Mt Sefton (3151m)

Bruce Bay

Paringa

Haast

1

6

77

72

72

73

79

80

8

8

8

82

83

83

Christchurch

N   0 _____ 5 km
0 _____ 2.5 miles

Christchurch

◉ Sights
1 Christchurch Gondola C4
2 Pioneer Women's Memorial C4
3 Riccarton House & Bush A2

⌂ Sleeping
4 Christchurch Top 10 .... A1
5 Le Petit Hotel D3
6 Merivale Manor A1
7 Old Countryhouse B2

✕ Eating
8 Bohemian Bakery D3
Christchurch Farmers
  Market .... (see 3)
Civil & Naval .... (see 10)
9 Kinji A1
Lyttelton Coffee
  Company .... (see 10)
10 Lyttelton Farmers Market C4
11 Super D4
12 Under the Red Verandah B2

◖ Drinking & Nightlife
Eruption Brewing .... (see 10)
Spooky Boogie .... (see 10)
The Brewery .... (see 13)
Village Inn .... (see 8)
Wunderbar .... (see 10)

✿ Entertainment
13 Blue Smoke C3
14 Hollywood Cinema D3
15 Orangetheory Stadium A2

⌂ Shopping
Henry Trading .... (see 10)
London St Bookshop .... (see 10)
Tannery .... (see 13)

ℹ Information
Lyttelton Visitor Information
  Centre .... (see 10)

ℹ Transport
Black Cat .... (see 11)

Continued from p65

it the nickname, 'the Garden City'. To this day, Christchurch in spring is a glorious place to be.

Christchurch is also a city that has known great tragedy in recent years. Following earthquakes in 2010 and 2011, mass shootings at two mosques in the city in March 2019 killed 51 worshippers attending Friday prayers.

◉ Sights

The majority of Christchurch's key sights rebounded soon after the 2011 earthquakes. Today there is more to see than ever. The centre is graced by numerous notable arts institutions and museums, as well as the stunning Botanic Gardens and Hagley Park. Inner-city streets conceal art projects and pocket galleries, dotted among a thinned-out cityscape featuring remnant stone buildings and the sharp, shiny architecture of the new.

◉ City Centre

★ Christchurch Art Gallery   GALLERY
(Te Puna o Waiwhetu; Map p82; ☑ 03-941 7300; www.christchurchartgallery.org.nz; cnr Montreal St & Worcester Blvd; ⊙10am-5pm Thu-Tue, to 9pm Wed) FREE Damaged in the earthquakes, Christchurch's fantastic art gallery has reopened brighter and bolder, presenting a stimulating mix of local and international exhibitions. Collection items range from the traditional to the startlingly contemporary – think light installations and interactive sculptures. Highlights from New Zealand painters capturing the country's bold landscapes include works by Rita Angus and Colin McCahon. Free one-hour guided tours take place at 11am and 2pm daily.

★ Quake City   MUSEUM
(Map p82; ☑ 03-366 5000; www.canterburymuseum.com/quake-city; 299 Durham St N; adult $20, child accompanied/unaccompanied free/$8; ⊙10am-5pm) A must-visit for anyone interested in understanding the impact of the Canterbury earthquakes, this compact museum tells stories through photography, video footage and various artefacts, including the remnants of ChristChurch Cathedral's celebrated rose window and other similarly moving debris. There are exhibits aimed at engaging both adults and children. Most affecting of all is the film featuring survivors recounting their own experiences.

★ Botanic Gardens   GARDENS
(Map p82; www.ccc.govt.nz; Rolleston Ave; ⊙7am-9pm Nov-Feb, to 8.30pm Mar & Oct, to 6.30pm Apr-Sep) FREE Strolling through these 30 blissful riverside hectares of arboreal and floral splendour is a consummate Christchurch experience. Gorgeous at any time of the year, the gardens are particularly impressive in spring when the rhododendrons, azaleas and daffodil woodland are in riotous bloom. There are thematic gardens to explore, lawns to sprawl on, and a playground adjacent to the **Botanic Gardens Visitor Centre** (Map p82; ☑ 03-941 7590; ⊙9am-4pm), which also contains a lovely cafe and gift shop. Guided walks ($10, 1½ hours) depart at 1.30pm (October to May) from the gate near Canterbury Museum (p70), or hop aboard the Caterpillar (p80) electric shuttle.

Arts Centre   HISTORIC BUILDING
(Map p82; www.artscentre.org.nz; 2 Worcester Blvd; ⊙10am-5pm) FREE Dating from 1877, this enclave of Gothic Revival buildings was originally Canterbury College, the forerunner of Canterbury University. The buildings are now reopening to the public after extensive restoration work due to quake damage. Inside you'll find the visitor information centre i-SITE (p91), and shops, cafes, museums and galleries. Exhibition spaces play host to regular concerts, rehearsals, markets and events. Of the centre's 23 buildings, 21 are listed by Heritage New Zealand as category 1 Historic Place structures. If there's nothing on during your visit, you can still wander in and check out the North Quad and Great Hall in all their restored heritage splendour.

Canterbury Earthquake National Memorial   MEMORIAL
(Oi Manawa; Map p82; www.canterburyearthquakememorial.co.nz; Oxford Tce) Unveiled in 2017, this moving monument comprises a 100m-long memorial wall, curved along the south bank of the Avon and engraved with the names of the 185 people who died as a result of the 22 February 2011 earthquake. On the opposite bank, a shady park provides a space for reflection and remembrance. The memorial's Māori name, Oi Manawa, means 'tremor or quivering of the heart'.

Te Papa Ōtākaro/ Avon River Precinct   PUBLIC ART
(Map p82; www.otakaroltd.co.nz) One of the city's key post-earthquake redevelopment projects is reinvigorating the area around the Avon

(Ōtākaro) River. Running along the river as a self-guided walk, Ngā Whāriki Manaaki (Woven Mats of Welcome) is a series of 13 paved artworks welcoming visitors to the city. Look for them as you stroll along the riverside from the Canterbury Earthquake National Memorial (p69) to the Margaret Mahy Family Playground (p80).

Hagley Park   PARK

(Map p82; Riccarton Ave) Wrapped around the Botanic Gardens, Hagley Park is Christchurch's biggest green space, stretching for 165 hectares. Riccarton Ave splits it in two, while the Avon River snakes through the northern half. It's a great place to stroll, whether on a foggy autumn morning, or a warm spring day when the cherry trees lining Harper Ave are in flower. Joggers make the most of the tree-lined avenues year-round.

Transitional Cathedral   CHURCH

(Map p82; www.cardboardcathedral.org.nz; 234 Hereford St; entry by donation; ⊙9am-5pm Apr-Oct, to 7pm Nov-Mar) Universally known as the Cardboard Cathedral due to the 98 cardboard tubes used in its construction, this interesting structure serves as both the city's temporary Anglican cathedral and as a concert venue. Designed by Japanese 'disaster architect' Shigeru Ban, the entire building was constructed in 11 months.

Central Art Gallery   GALLERY

(Map p82; ☑03-366 3318; www.thecentral.co.nz; Arts Centre, 2 Worcester Blvd; ⊙10am-4pm Wed-Sun) FREE Housed in the Arts Centre's beautifully restored 1916 Library building, the Central Art Gallery exhibits contemporary works by established and emerging NZ artists.

> ### ⓘ CHRISTCHURCH ATTRACTIONS COMBO TICKETS
>
> Christchurch Attractions (www.christchurchattractions.nz) is the company that runs the punting (p72), tram (p80), gondola and botanic gardens tours (p80), as well as attractions in Hanmer Springs (p108). A baffling array of combo tickets are available, which will save you some money if you're considering doing more than one activity. All four Christchurch attractions are included on the five-hour **Grand Tour** (adult/child $129/69), as well as a stop in Sumner.

Rutherford's Den   MUSEUM

(Map p82; ☑03-363 2836; www.rutherfordsden.org.nz; Arts Centre, 2 Worcester Blvd; adult/child $20/10; ⊙10am-5pm) Canterbury College's most famous alumnus was the father of nuclear physics, Lord Ernest Rutherford, the NZ physicist who first split the atom in 1917 (that's him on the $100 bill). The rooms where Rutherford worked have now been turned into a small interactive science museum, with displays on the scientist's many important discoveries, as well as a room dedicated to renewable energy.

Canterbury Museum   MUSEUM

(Map p82; ☑03-366 5000; www.canterburymuseum.com; Rolleston Ave; ⊙9am-5.30pm Oct-Mar, to 5pm Apr-Sep; ⓐ) FREE Yes, there's a mummy and dinosaur bones, but the highlights of this museum are more local and more recent. The Māori galleries contain some beautiful *pounamu* (greenstone) pieces, while Christchurch Street is an atmospheric walk through the colonial past. The reproduction of Fred and Myrtle's gloriously kitsch Paua Shell House embraces Kiwiana at its best, and kids will enjoy the interactive displays in the Discovery Centre (admission $2). Free one-hour guided tours depart from the foyer daily at 2pm.

Christchurch Gondola   CABLE CAR

(Map p68; www.christchurchattractions.nz; 10 Bridle Path Rd; return adult/child $30/15; ⊙10am-5pm) Take a ride to the top of Mt Cavendish (500m) on this 862m cable car for wonderful views over the city, Lyttelton, Banks Peninsula and the Canterbury Plains. At the top there's a cafe and the child-focused Time Tunnel ride, which recounts the history of the area. You can also walk to Cavendish Bluff Lookout (30 minutes return) or the **Pioneer Women's Memorial** (Map p68; one hour return).

Cathedral Square   SQUARE

(Map p82; www.reinstate.org.nz) Christchurch's city square stands at the heart of the rebuilding efforts, with the remains of ChristChurch Cathedral emblematic of what has been lost. The February 2011 earthquake brought down the 63m-high spire, while subsequent earthquakes in June 2011 and December 2011 destroyed the prized stained-glass rose window. Other heritage buildings around the square were also badly damaged, but one modern landmark left unscathed is the 18m-high metal sculpture *Chalice*, de-

CHRISTCHURCH FOR CHILDREN

There's no shortage of kid-friendly sights and activities in Christchurch. If family fun is a priority, consider planning your travels around NZ's biggest children's festival, KidsFest (p81). It's held every July and is chock-full of shows, workshops and parties. The annual Bread & Circus (p81) buskers festival is also bound to be a hit with young 'uns.

The impressive Margaret Mahy Family Playground (p80) is a must for anyone with small people in tow. For picnics and open-air frolicking, visit the Botanic Gardens (p69); there's a playground beside the cafe, and little kids will love riding on the Caterpillar train. Extend your nature-based experience with a wildlife encounter at Orana Wildlife Park or the Willowbank Wildlife Reserve, or get them burning off excess energy in a rowing boat or kayak from the Antigua Boat Sheds (p72). Fun can be stealthily combined with education at the International Antarctic Centre, the Discovery Centre at Canterbury Museum and Quake City (p69).

If the weather's good, hit the beaches at Sumner or New Brighton.

signed by Neil Dawson. It was erected in 2001 to commemorate the new millennium.

The much-loved Gothic cathedral has been at the centre of a battle between those who seek to preserve what remains of Christchurch's heritage, the fiscal pragmatists, and those ideologically inclined to things new. In 2012 the Anglican Diocese announced that the cathedral was to be demolished, but work was stayed when heritage advocates launched court proceedings. Eventually, in September 2017, the church leadership voted to preserve the building after the government and Christchurch City Council banded together to offer significant financial support. It's thought that the rebuild could take up to 10 years, with an estimated cost of $104 million. Preliminary stabilisation work to make the building safe to enter for restorers began in early 2020. See www.reinstate.org.nz for updates on the project's progress.

◉ Other Suburbs

Riccarton House & Bush   HISTORIC BUILDING
(Map p68; www.riccartonhouse.co.nz; 16 Kahu Rd, Riccarton; ⊙9am-4pm Sun-Fri, to 1pm Sat) FREE Historic Riccarton House (1856) sits proudly amid 12 hectares of pretty parkland and forest beside the Avon River. The grounds host the popular Christchurch Farmers Market (p87) on Saturdays; the rest of the week you can visit the lovely restaurant on the ground floor.

The biggest draw, however, is the small patch of bush behind the house. Enclosed by a vermin-proof fence, this is the last stand of kahikatea floodplain forest in Canterbury.

Kahikatea is NZ's tallest native tree, growing to heights of 60m; the tallest trees here are a mere 30m and around 300 to 600

years old. A short loop track heads through the heart of the forest.

The majority of the house is only accessible on a guided tour, departing at 2pm Sunday to Friday (adult/child $18/5, one hour), as well as at 11am on Sundays only.

Orana Wildlife Park   ZOO
(☑03-359 7109; www.oranawildlifepark.co.nz; 793 McLeans Island Rd, McLeans Island; adult/child $36.50/9.50; ⊙10am-5pm; ⊕) Orana is an 'open range' zoo, and you'll know exactly what that means if you opt to jump in the cage on wheels for the lion encounter ($52.50 per person). There's an excellent walk-through native bird aviary, a nocturnal kiwi house, and a reptile exhibit featuring tuatara. Most of the 80-hectare grounds are devoted to Africana, including rhinos, giraffes, zebras, cheetahs and gorillas.

Willowbank Wildlife Reserve   ZOO
(☑03-359 6226; www.willowbank.co.nz; 60 Hussey Rd, Northwood; adult/child $32.50/12; ⊙9.30am-7pm Oct-Mar, to 5pm Apr-Sep; ⊕) 🖉 Willowbank focuses on native NZ critters (including kiwi), heritage farmyard animals and hands-on enclosures with wallabies, deer and lemurs. There's also a re-created Māori village, the setting for the evening Ko Tane (p80). It's 10km north of town, near the airport.

International Antarctic Centre   MUSEUM
(☑03-357 0519, 0508 736 4846; www.iceberg.co.nz; Christchurch Airport, 38 Orchard Rd; adult/child $59/29; ⊙9am-5.30pm; ⊕) As one of only five 'gateway cities' to Antarctica, Christchurch has played a special role in Antarctic exploration since expeditionary ships to the icy continent began departing from Lyttelton in the early 1900s. This huge complex, built for the administration of

the NZ, US and Italian Antarctic programs, gives visitors the opportunity to learn about Antarctica in a fun, interactive environment.

Attractions include the Antarctic Storm chamber (where you can get a taste of -18°C wind chill), face-to-face encounters with resident little blue penguins, and a meet-and-greet with rescue huskies. Entry also includes the '4D theatre' (a 3D film with moving seats and a water spray) and a joyride on a Hägglund all-terrain amphibious Antarctic vehicle. An optional extra is the Penguin Backstage Tour (adult/child $25/15), which allows visitors behind the scenes of the Penguin Encounter. A free shuttle to the centre departs from outside Canterbury Museum.

🏃 Activities

Boating

Antigua Boat Sheds   BOATING, KAYAKING
(Map p82; ☑ 03-366 5885; www.boatsheds.co.nz; 2 Cambridge Tce; ⊙ 9am-5pm; 🖼️) 🌿 Dating from 1882, the photogenic green-and-white Antigua Boat Sheds hires out rowing boats ($40), kayaks ($15), canoes ($40) and bikes (adult/child $10/5); all prices are per hour. There's also a good cafe and discounted combo deals when hiring a bike and a canoe.

Punting on the Avon   BOATING
(Map p82; www.punting.co.nz; 2 Cambridge Tce; adult/child $30/15; ⊙ 9am-6pm Oct-Mar, 10am-4pm Apr-Sep; 🖼️) 🌿 If rowing your own boat down the Avon sounds a bit too much like hard work, why not relax in a flat-bottomed

punt while a strapping lad in Edwardian clobber glides you peaceably through the Botanic Gardens? Tours depart year-round from the Antigua Boat Sheds; during the warmer months alternative trips run from sites at Mona Vale and Worcester Bridge.

Walking

The i-SITE (p91) provides information on walking tours as well as self-guided options, including the rewarding **Avon River Walk**, which takes in major city sights, and several excellent trails around the **Port Hills**.

For long-range city views, take the walkway from the **Sign of the Takahe** on Dyers Pass Rd, Cashmere. This walk leads up to the Sign of the Kiwi, through Victoria Park and then along the view-filled Summit Rd to Scotts Reserve. The various 'Sign of the...' places in this area were originally roadhouses built during the Depression as rest stops.

You can walk to Lyttelton on the **Bridle Path** (1½ hours), which starts at Heathcote Valley (take bus 28). The **Godley Head Walkway** (two hours return) begins at Taylors Mistake, crossing and recrossing Summit Rd, and offers beautiful views on a clear day.

Walks in Christchurch and throughout Canterbury are well detailed at www.christchurchnz.com.

Cycling

Being mostly flat and boasting more than 300km of cycle trails, Christchurch is a brilliant place to explore on two wheels. For evidence, look no further than the free *Christchurch City Cycle Map,* available around town or downloadable from www.ccc.govt.nz/transport/cycling. The i-SITE (p91) can advise on bicycle hire and guided tours. There's some great off-road riding around the Port Hills, while towards Banks Peninsula you'll find the best section of the Little River Trail (p96), one of NZ's Great Rides.

Chill   CYCLING
(Map p82; ☑ 03-365 6530; www.chillout.co.nz; 287 Durham St N; per day from $45; ⊙ 8.30am-5pm Mon-Fri, 9.30am-2.30pm Sat; 🖼️) 🌿 Bike hire and guided and self-guided cycling tours of the city. Helmets, locks and local knowledge are all supplied. Options include vintage-style bikes and e-bikes. Mountain-bike hire and advice on where to ride is also on offer.

City Cycle Hire   CYCLING
(☑ 0800 343 848; www.cyclehire-tours.co.nz; city bike half/full day from $25/35, touring bike per week from $200; 🖼️) 🌿 Offers door-to-door

THE CHRISTCHURCH EARTHQUAKES

Christchurch's seismic nightmare began at 4.35am on 4 September 2010. Centred 40km west of the city, a 40-second, 7.1-magnitude earthquake jolted Cantabrians from their sleep, and caused widespread damage to older buildings in the central city. Close to the quake's epicentre in rural Darfield, huge gashes erupted amid grassy pastures, and the South Island's main railway line was bent and buckled. Because the tremor struck in the early hours of the morning when most people were home in bed, there were no fatalities, and many Christchurch residents felt that the city had dodged a bullet.

Fast forward to 12.51pm on 22 February 2011, when central Christchurch was busy with shoppers and workers enjoying their lunch break. This time the 6.3-magnitude quake was much closer, centred just 10km southeast of the city and only 5km deep. The tremor was significantly greater, and many locals report being flung violently and almost vertically into the air. The peak ground acceleration exceeded 1.8, almost twice the acceleration of gravity.

When the dust settled after 24 traumatic seconds, New Zealand's second-largest city had changed forever. The towering spire of the iconic ChristChurch Cathedral lay in ruins; walls and verandas had cascaded down on shopping strips; and two multistorey buildings had pancaked. Of the 185 deaths (across 20 nationalities), 115 occurred in the six-storey Canterbury TV building, where many international students at a language school were killed. Elsewhere, the historic port town of Lyttelton was badly damaged; roads and bridges were crumpled; and residential suburbs in the east were inundated as a process of rapid liquefaction saw tons of oozy silt rise from the ground.

In the months that followed, hundreds of aftershocks rattled the city's traumatised residents (and claimed one more life), but the resilience and bravery of Cantabrians quickly became evident. From the region's rural heartland, the 'Farmy Army' descended on the city, armed with shovels and food hampers. Social media mobilised 10,000 students, and the Student Volunteer Army became a vital force for residential clean-ups in the city's beleaguered eastern suburbs. Heartfelt aid and support arrived from across NZ, and seven other nations sent specialised urban-search-and-rescue teams.

The impact of the events of a warm summer's day in early 2011 will take longer than a generation to resolve. Entire streets and neighbourhoods in the eastern suburbs have had to be abandoned, and Christchurch's heritage architecture is irrevocably damaged. Families in some parts of the city have been forced to live in substandard accommodation, waiting for insurance claims to be settled. Around 80% of the buildings within the city centre's famed four avenues have been demolished, and a few large damaged structures are also still standing due to the machinations of insurance claims. Amid the doomed, the saved, and the shiny new builds are construction sites and a few empty plots still strewn with rubble.

Plans for the next 20 years of the city's rebuild include a compact, low-rise city centre, large green spaces, and parks and cycleways along the Avon River. It's estimated that the total rebuild and repair bill could reach $40 or even $50 billion. See www.otakaroltd. co.nz for details of specific infrastructure projects set to transform the city.

To find out more about the effects of the quakes, and to hear survivors tell their experiences of that time in their own voices, visit the highly recommended Quake City (p69).

delivery of on- and off-road city bikes and touring bikes. Will also meet you with a bike at the top of the gondola if you fancy a 16km descent ($70 including gondola ride; 1½ hours).

Swimming & Surfing

Despite having separate names for different sections, it's one solid stretch of sandy beach that spreads north from the estuary of the Avon and Heathcote Rivers. Closest to the city centre is **New Brighton**, with a distinctive pier reaching 300m out to sea. On ei-

ther side, **South New Brighton** and **North Beach** are quieter options. **Waimairi**, a little further north, is our personal pick.

The superstar is **Sumner**, 12km from the city centre on the south side of the estuary. Its beachy vibe, eateries and art-house cinema make it a satisfying spot for a day trip.

Further east around the headland, isolated **Taylors Mistake** has the cleanest water of any Christchurch beach and some good surf breaks. Beginners should stick to Sumner or New Brighton.

DAY TRIPS FROM CHRISTCHURCH

LYTTELTON

Christchurch's historic port lies just over the prosaically named Port Hills from the city proper. Although it was badly hit during the earthquakes, it's well worth a trip through the 2km road tunnel during the day to explore its revitalised shopping strip, or at night to have a slap-up meal and catch a band.

☆ Best Things to See/Do/Eat

☉ Christchurch Gondola Stop before you reach the tunnel for an 862m ride on the cable car to the top of Mt Cavendish. The views over Christchurch, Lyttelton, Banks Peninsula and the Canterbury Plains are extraordinary. (p70)

🛍 London St Shopping Lyttelton has long had a bohemian edge. The best time to visit its compact shopping street is on a Saturday morning, when the farmers market is buzzing. (p93)

✗ London St Eating & Drinking Highlights include shared plates at Civil & Naval and craft beer at Eruption Brewing. (p93)

☆ How to Get There

Car From the city centre head southeast on Ferry Rd and veer onto Tunnel Rd (SH74). The journey takes around 20 minutes.
Bus Catch bus 28 or 535, which takes 30 minutes.

BANKS PENINSULA

You only need look at a map of this oddly shaped protuberance to realise what an absolutely unique place this is. Thumb shaped and with enough indents, whorls and contours to give it a fingerprint, this spectacular peninsula offsets rippling hills with sparkling waters. At its heart is an historic anomaly: the sweet little Frenchified village of Akaroa.

☆ Best Things to See/Do/Eat

☉ Giant's House Akaroa's most unusual attraction is this artsy garden, jam-packed with sculpture and mosaics made of broken china, mirrors and tiles. The pretty pink 1880 house at its centre is full of yet more of the owner's art. (p97)

🚶 Walk around Akaroa Pick up a pamphlet from the i-SITE and meander around Akaroa's heritage houses and churches. If you're after something more challenging, embark on the six-hour Skyline Circuit. (p95)

✗ Hilltop Tavern As you crest the hill and begin the descent to Akaroa Harbour, stop for a wood-fired pizza and craft beer at this historic pub. The views are spectacular. (p97)

☆ How to Get There

Car It takes less than 1½ hours to reach Akaroa from central Christchurch. The quickest route is to head southeast on Lincoln Rd and onto SH75. A more scenic route heads due south via Governors Bay. Alternatively, catch a shuttle.

WAIPARA VALLEY

The North Canterbury Wine Region is conveniently spread along either side of SH1, about an hour north of Christchurch. While it's one of New Zealand's smaller wine-producing areas, it's developing a reputation for cool-climate wines such as riesling, gewürztraminer and pinot noir.

☆ Best Things to See/Do/Eat

◉ **Willowbank Wildlife Reserve** As you're leaving the city, take a five-minute detour to the suburb of Northwood. This low-key zoo features a stellar roster of Kiwi critters and a re-created Māori village. (p71)

◉ **Wine Tasting** About a dozen of the region's wineries have public tasting rooms. Our favourite is pretty Pegasus Bay, set in verdant gardens and home to one of Canterbury's best restaurants. (p110)

✕ **Little Vintage Espresso** If you're in the mood for a more low-key lunch – or just a coffee to see you on your way – stop off at this whitewashed cottage as you pass through Amberley. (p110)

☆ How to Get There

Car Head north from the city centre on Sherborne St, Cranford St and Main Rd (SH74). If you're detouring to Willowbank, look for the signs to your left. SH74 joins SH1 at the northern edge of town. Buses aren't a viable option for visiting the wineries.

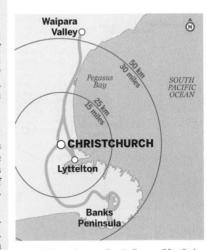

The South Island's big smoke is well positioned for day trips to beaches, mountains and wine regions. In winter you can even head out for a day's skiing on Mt Hutt.

HIKING IN CANTERBURY

BANKS PENINSULA

☆ Banks Track

START ONUKU FARM
END AKAROA
DURATION 3 DAYS
DISTANCE 29KM
DIFFICULTY EASY TO MODERATE

The first private walk established in NZ, the Banks Track takes you across private farmland and forest and along the peninsula's remote outer bays. The route takes in a spectacular volcanic coastline, native bush, waterfalls and sandy beaches, with two crossings of the crater rim high above Akaroa Harbour.

Other than two steep climbs of nearly 700m each, this is a relatively leisurely tramp, which allows plenty of time to take in the marvellous scenery. For the more energetic, cutting the tramp to two days is an option.

Bookings are essential and should be made through **Banks Peninsula Track** (p95).

Tramper numbers are limited to just 16 setting out each day, so book early for peak summer and NZ holiday periods. The three-day package ($330) includes transport from Akaroa to Onuku, three nights of accommodation, landowners' fees, track registration and a copy of *Banks Peninsula Track: A Guide to the Route, Natural Features and Human History*. The two-day package ($195) covers the same route, but just the one night on the track, staying at Stony Bay (plus the night before the tramp at Onuku).

LEWIS PASS

☆ St James Walkway

START LEWIS PASS
END BOYLE
DURATION 5 DAYS
DISTANCE 65KM
DIFFICULTY EASY TO MODERATE

Built in 1981, the St James Walkway begins in the Lewis Pass National Reserve, travers-

For heavy-duty hikers, Canterbury is all about the mountains, be it the tightly packed peaks of Arthur's Pass National Park or the valleys and view points that unveil Aoraki/Mt Cook.

es the western side of the St James Conservation Area, and ends in the Lake Sumner Forest Park. Despite taking in two mountain passes – Ada Pass (1008m) and Anne Saddle (1136m) – it's not particularly challenging, though there is one 17km day and some stream crossings. The climbs are not steep, and the rest of the walk is spent hiking through open valleys and beech forests.

The walkway follows historic pack tracks, is well benched and has an excellent series of serviced huts. The heart of the track, from Ada River along Anne River to upper Boyle River, runs through the St James Conservation Area. Vegetation within this area includes red, mountain and silver beech forests, manuka/kanuka and matagouri scrublands, numerous alpine species, at least five species of tussock and a vast expanse of valley-floor native grasslands. It is also home to around 430 indigenous species of flora and 30 native bird species.

ARTHUR'S PASS NATIONAL PARK

☆ Avalanche Peak
START/END ARTHUR'S PASS
DURATION 6–8 HOURS
DISTANCE 7KM
DIFFICULTY MODERATE

In this park of peaks, Avalanche Peak is without question the most popular one to climb and is the only mountain marked with a poled route to the summit. Its location is ideal, looming directly above Arthur's Pass village and just south of Mt Rolleston.

The alpine world experienced during this tramp is stunning on a clear day. Many experienced trampers will claim that this is in fact NZ's best day tramp, outshining the dramatic volcanic peaks and steamy vents of the Tongariro Alpine Crossing.

Unequivocal is the fact that Avalanche Peak is an alpine climb that should only be attempted by the fleet of foot in good conditions. The total climb and descent is 1100m, and although the route is clearly marked

and well trodden, it's still an arduous climb with a climax of 200m of narrow, crumbly ridge. People have died on Avalanche Peak when they failed to heed weather warnings.

Two routes, Avalanche Peak Track and Scotts Track, depart from SH73 and lead towards the peak, merging just before reaching it. Avalanche Peak Track is a much steeper climb, and at times you need to scramble up rock faces. Scotts Track is a more gradual and easier route. It's best to use Avalanche Peak Track to reach the summit and Scotts Track for the return, when your legs will be tired. Of course, the easiest return route to the peak is to simply use Scotts Track both ways, but that's not as much fun or as varied.

☆ Goat Pass Track
START GREYNEYS SHELTER
END MORRISON FOOTBRIDGE
DURATION 2 DAYS
DISTANCE 25KM
DIFFICULTY MODERATE

Goat Pass Track, also referred to as the Mingha-Deception Route (the two rivers the route follows), is an excellent introduction to hiking in Arthur's Pass. It is also one of the least complicated routes in the park, as long as the rivers run in your favour. Typical of the Southern Alps, the Bealey, Mingha and Deception Rivers can be very dangerous when in flood, and the Deception alone requires up to 30 compulsory crossings. This tramp should therefore not be attempted during periods of rain. Should the crossings start to look too difficult, backtrack or stay put – attempting a dicey crossing just isn't worth the risk.

This track forms the running leg of the Coast to Coast (www.coasttocoast.co.nz), NZ's most famous multisport race, which crosses the South Island from the Tasman Sea to the Pacific Ocean by a gruelling combination of cycling, kayaking and running. On your travels, you may come across some competitors training for the event. With luck you'll also encounter whio, the nationally vulnerable and very cute blue duck.

The Goat Pass Track can be tramped in either direction, but the Mingha-Deception direction allows for a shorter day first up.

☆ Harper Pass

START AICKENS CAR PARK
END WINDY POINT
DURATION 5 DAYS
DISTANCE 77KM
DIFFICULTY MODERATE

Māori often travelled over hhh as they crossed to the West Coast in search of *pounamu* (greenstone), and it was that knowledge and experience that would eventually see them lead the first Europeans through the area in 1857. Two guides, Wereta Tainui and Terapuhi, took Leonard Harper across the pass that now bears his name. By 1862, just three years after the first bridle paths were surveyed, the route was serving as the main gateway to the West Coast goldfields, with stores and liquor shops along the way. When the gold rush ended, however, the track fell into disrepair, until its reinvention as a hiking trail.

Today it is one of NZ's classic tramps, connecting Arthur's Pass to Lewis Pass, and is part of the country-length Te Araroa route (www.teararoa.org.nz), making it a particularly busy tramp during the summer months. The track crosses the Main Divide over Harper Pass, a low saddle at just 963m above sea level. The segment in Arthur's Pass National Park is a valley route along the Taramakau River, but in Lake Sumner Forest Park the track is well cut and marked.

Trampers need to be cautious with the Taramakau. It is a large and unruly river in a high-rainfall area, making it prone to sudden flooding. The track can be walked in either direction, but a west-to-east crossing is recommended as you can be surer of good conditions as you cross the Otira, Otehake and Taramakau Rivers, all of which are prone to flooding during rain. On the eastern side, the track is well defined along the Hurunui and Hope Rivers, and bridged at all major crossings.

☆ Bealey Spur

START/END CLOUDESLEY RD
DURATION 4–6 HOURS
DISTANCE 13.5KM
DIFFICULTY EASY TO MODERATE

To climb almost anything in Arthur's Pass National Park is to submit to steep ground. Bealey Spur is a rare exception, climbing

Hooker Valley Track

steadily but not steeply to a historic hut at around 1230m above sea level. Add to this the fact that the tramp doesn't climb above the bushline, and that it sits east of the Main Divide, making it often drier than other park tracks even when northwesterly winds are bringing rain to Arthur's Pass, and it's a comfort hike of sorts.

It's also a tramp where the rewards far exceed the effort, with expansive views over the national park and the valleys that cut so deeply into it. Though it's not steep, the tramp does climb around 600m from SH73 to Bealey Spur Hut.

AORAKI/MT COOK NATIONAL PARK

☆ Mueller Hut Route

START/END MT COOK VILLAGE
DURATION 2 DAYS
DISTANCE 10KM
DIFFICULTY DEMANDING

This route passes through a dynamic landscape, simultaneously uplifted and eroded in the never-ending battle between powerful natural forces. Rock beds of schist, sandstone, siltstone and greywacke have been

MATTEO COLOMBO/GETTY IMAGES ©

View across Hooker Lake to Aoraki/Mt Cook

carved out by glaciation, dramatically illustrated on the climb to Mueller Hut. Hanging glaciers, moraines and U-shaped valleys are all classic landmarks of icy geological transformation. Populating this inhospitable environment are alpine flowers and herb fields, of which there are many to see during the 1000m climb to the rocky ridge and hut atop it.

Mueller Glacier was named by Julius Haast in 1862, after the Danish explorer and writer Ferdinand von Mueller. A series of Mueller Huts have perched above it since the first one was built between 1914 and 1915.

☆ Hooker Valley Track
START/END WHITE HORSE HILL CAMPSITE
DURATION 3 HOURS
DISTANCE 10KM
DIFFICULTY EASY
....

Aoraki/Mt Cook National Park's signature tramp, the Hooker Valley Track, is a visual extravaganza to the base of NZ's highest mountain. A journey on foot into a glacial valley where moraines, glacial lakes and the glaciers themselves stand front and centre, it culminates just 10 straight-line kilometres from the summit of Aoraki/Mt Cook, on the shores of iceberg-laden Hooker Lake. And once you're standing beside the lake, the mountain actually looks even closer than that.

The tramp follows a wide and remarkably flat track (given its proximity to a 3724m-high mountain) through the stunning valley, making this a simple wander into mountain magnificence. All of which adds up to one small price to pay – popularity – with more than 80,000 people hiking through the Hooker Valley each year. Beat the crowds by setting out early in the blue light of dawn, or take the chance to spread out along the shore of Hooker Lake, claiming a private audience with the grandest NZ mountain of all.

Other Activities

Margaret Mahy Family Playground
PLAYGROUND

(Map p82; cnr Manchester & Armagh Sts) Named after beloved Kiwi children's author Margaret Mahy, this magical playground has four separate themed zones – peninsula, forest, wetlands and plains. From a splash park to a giant spiral slide, you'll find plenty to keep the kids (and kids at heart) entertained.

⚐ Tours

★ Tram
TRAM

(Map p82; ☑03-366 7830; www.christchurchattractions.co.nz; adult/child $25/free; ⊙9am-6pm Oct-Apr, 10am-5pm May-Sep) Excellent driver commentary makes this so much more than just a tram ride. The beautifully restored old dears trundle around a 17-stop loop, departing every 15 minutes, taking in a host of city highlights, including Cathedral Sq and New Regent St. The full circuit takes just under an hour, and you can hop on and off all day.

Also on offer is the evening Tramway Restaurant (four courses with/without wine matches $139/109) taking a leisurely two to three hours.

★ Watch This Space
CULTURAL

(www.watchthisspace.org.nz) With works enlivening post-earthquake derelict spaces and buildings, Christchurch is one of the world's best cities for street art, especially around the High St precinct. Check out this excellent website showcasing Christchurch street art, including a comprehensive map, photos and details of relevant artists. Guided tours of the city's street art scene are available by appointment ($30 per person).

See the website for details. Tours usually leave at 10am from outside the Canterbury Museum. Interviews with urban artists, reviews of new sites and previews of upcoming events are listed under Blogs on the website.

TranzAlpine
RAIL

(Map p82; ☑0800 872 467, 03-341 2588; www.greatjourneysofnz.co.nz; one way from $159) The *TranzAlpine* is one of the world's great train journeys, traversing the Southern Alps between Christchurch and Greymouth, from the Pacific Ocean to the Tasman Sea, passing through Arthur's Pass National Park. En route is a sequence of dramatic landscapes, from the flat, alluvial Canterbury Plains to narrow alpine gorges, an 8.5km tunnel, beech-forested river valleys, and a lake fringed with cabbage trees. The 4½-hour journey is unforgettable, even in bad weather (if it's raining

on one coast, it's probably fine on the other). The train departs Christchurch at 8.15am and Greymouth at 2.05pm.

Amiki Local Tours
FOOD & DRINK

(☑027 532 7248; www.hiddengemsnz.com; per person $65-225) Join passionate and in-the-know locals on walking tours combining the history and culture of the city – including indigenous Māori elements – with the best of eating and drinking around central Christchurch. Options include the one-hour Ōtautahi Hikoi culture walk, the two-hour food-focused City Meander, and a three-hour after-dark Kai Safari (Kai translates to 'food' in Māori).

Guided City Walks
WALKING

(Map p82; ☑0800 423 783; www.walkchristchurch.nz; Rolleston Ave; adult/teen/child $20/10/free; ⊙1pm daily, plus 10am Sep-May) Departing from the red kiosk outside Canterbury Museum, these tours offer a leisurely stroll around the city's main sights in the company of knowledgable guides. See website for booking details.

Hassle Free Tours
BUS

(Soaring Kiwis; Map p82; ☑03-385 5775; www.hasslefree.co.nz; Rolleston Ave) Explore Christchurch in an open-top red double-decker bus on a one-hour Central tour ($35) or two-hour Discover tour ($69). Tours depart outside Canterbury Museum. Regional options include a 4WD alpine safari, Kaikōura whale-watching, and visiting the location of Edoras from the *Lord of the Rings* trilogy.

Caterpillar Botanic Gardens Tour
OUTDOORS

(Map p82; ☑0800 88 22 23; www.christchurchattractions.nz/botanic-gardens-tours; adult/child $20/9; ⊙10am-3.30pm Oct-Mar, 11am-3pm Apr-Sep) Hop aboard the 'Caterpillar' electric shuttle for a tour of Christchurch's stunning Botanic Gardens (p69).

Garden City Helicopters
SCENIC FLIGHTS

(☑03-358 4360; www.helicopters.net.nz; 73-93 Grays Rd; 20min per person $1229) Scenic flights above the city and Lyttelton let you observe the impact of the earthquake and the rebuilding efforts.

Ko Tane
CULTURAL

(☑03-359 6226; www.kotane.co.nz; Willowbank Wildlife Reserve, 60 Hussey Rd, Northwood; adult/child $135/68; ⊙5.15pm) Rousing Māori cultural performance by members of the Ngāi Tahu tribe comprising a *pōwhiri* (welcome), the famous *haka,* a buffet *hāngi* (earth-oven) meal, and plenty of *waiata ā ringa* (singing and dancing). At Willowbank Wildlife Reserve (p71). There's also an option to include a kiwi tour kicking off 45 minutes earlier at 4.30pm.

Festivals & Events

Check www.ccc.govt.nz/events and www.christchurchnz.com/whats-on for comprehensive festival and event listings.

Bread & Circus
World Buskers Festival   PERFORMING ARTS
(World Buskers Festival; www.breadandcircus.co.nz; ⊙ Jan-Feb) National and international talent entertain passers-by for around three weeks from mid-January. Shows span stand-up comedy, burlesque, music and circus arts. Check the website for locations – and don't forget to throw money in the hat.

KidsFest   FAIR
(www.kidsfest.org.nz; ⊙ Jul) If family fun is a priority, consider planning your travels around NZ's biggest children's festival. KidsFest offers a smorgasbord of munchkin-friendly shows, workshops and parties, held during the winter school holidays.

Christchurch Arts Festival   PERFORMING ARTS
(www.artsfestival.co.nz;   ⊙ mid-Aug–mid-Sep) Month-long biennial arts extravaganza celebrating music, theatre and dance; the next festival will be held in 2021.

NZ Cup & Show Week   SPORTS
(www.nzcupandshow.co.nz;   ⊙ Nov)   Various horse races, fashion shows, fireworks and the centrepiece A&P Show, where the country comes to town. Held over a week in mid-November.

🛏 Sleeping

🛏 City Centre
All Stars Inn on Bealey   HOSTEL $
(Map p82; ☎ 03-366 6007; www.allstarsinn.com; 263 Bealey Ave; dm $35-39, d with/without bathroom $110/89; P @ 🛜) Large, well-designed rooms are the hallmark of this purpose-built complex on the city fringe. Dorms have fridges, USB points and individual lights; some have en suites, too. Private rooms are similarly well equipped. It's a 25-minute walk to the centre of town.

YHA Christchurch   HOSTEL $
(Map p82; ☎ 03-379 9536; www.yha.co.nz; 36 Hereford St; dm/s/d from $33/95/105; @ 🛜) Smart, well-run 100-plus-bed hostel conveniently located near Canterbury Museum and the Botanic Gardens. Dorms and doubles include many with en suite bathrooms. If it's full during summer, Christchurch's other YHA, Rolleston House, is one street away (5 Worcester Blvd) and used as an overflow facility from November to April only.

Around the World Backpackers   HOSTEL $
(Map p82; ☎ 03-365 4363; www.aroundtheworld.co.nz; 314 Barbadoes St; dm/d $29/79; P @ 🛜) Friendly, well-run hostel with good facilities, Kiwiana decor and sunny back garden (complete with hammock and barbecue). Rooms are small but clean; doubles have TVs and homey decorative touches.

Dorset House Backpackers   HOSTEL $
(Map p82; ☎ 03-366 8268; www.dorset.co.nz; 1 Dorset St; dm $29-37, s $89, d $89-94; P @ 🛜) 🐾 Built in 1871, this tranquil wooden villa has a sunny deck, a large regal lounge with a pool table, and great kitchen facilities. Dorms feature beds instead of bunks, and private rooms are small but spotless. It's a short stroll to Hagley Park and the Victoria St restaurant strip.

Chester Street Backpackers   HOSTEL $
(Map p82; ☎ 03-377 1897; www.chesterst.co.nz; 148 Chester St E; dm/s $32/67, d $70-96; @ 🛜) This relaxed wooden villa is painted in bright colours and has a sunny front room for reading. Rooms are cosy and colourful. Pipi the house cat is a regular guest at hostel barbecues in the peaceful wee garden.

Foley Towers   HOSTEL $
(Map p82; ☎ 03-366 9720; www.foleytowers.co.nz; 208 Kilmore St; dm $32-36, d with/without bathroom $88/78; P @ 🛜) Sheltered by well-established trees, Foley Towers provides a range of well-maintained rooms and dorms encircling a quiet, flower-filled garden. Friendly, helpful staff will provide the latest local info.

★ Eco Villa   GUESTHOUSE $$
(Map p82; ☎ 03-595 1364; www.ecovilla.co.nz; 251 Hereford St; d $145-230; P 🛜) 🐾 There are only eight rooms in this beautifully renovated villa, each individually decorated with luxe fittings and muted colours. The lovely shared lounge, kitchen and dining room all reflect the focus on sustainable, ecofriendly design, as does the lush edible garden (with twin outdoor bathtubs!). Be sure to try the delicious vegan breakfasts ($20 per person).

Central Christchurch

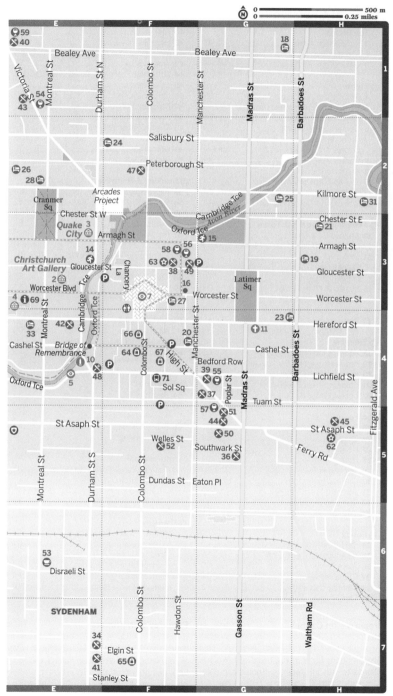

Central Christchurch

BreakFree on Cashel HOTEL **$$**
(Map p82; ☎03-360 1064; www.breakfreeoncashel.co.nz; 165 Cashel St; d $114-194; 🅿🛜) ♦ This large, modern hotel in the heart of town has options to suit all budgets. Rooms are compact, with smart TVs and pod bathrooms.

Pomeroy's on Kilmore B&B **$$**
(Map p82; ☎03-374 3532; www.pomeroysonkilmore.co.nz; 282 Kilmore St; r $155-205; 🅿🛜) Even if this cute wooden house wasn't the sister and neighbour of the city's best craft-beer pub, it would still be one of our favourites.

Three of the five elegant, en suite rooms open onto a sunny garden. Rates include breakfast at Little Pom's (p88) cafe next door.

Focus Motel   MOTEL **$$**
(Map p82; ☑03-943 0800; www.focusmotel.com; 344 Durham St N; studio $160,1-/2-bedroom ste from $180/250; ℗⊠) Sleek and centrally located, this friendly-vibe motel offers studio, one- and two-bedroom units with big-screen TVs, iPod docks, kitchenettes and super-modern decor. There's a guest barbecue and laundry, and pillow-top chocolates sweeten the deal.

★**George**   HOTEL **$$$**
(Map p82; ☑03-379 4560; www.thegeorge.com; 50 Park Tce; r $490-525, ste $795-1050; ℗⊠◎⊠) ✈
The George has 53 luxe rooms in a defiantly 1970s-looking building on the fringe of Hagley Park. Discreet staff attend to every whim, and ritzy extras include huge TVs, luxury toiletries and two highly rated in-house restaurants – Pescatore and 50 Bistro.

★**Hotel Montreal**   HOTEL **$$$**
(Map p82; ☑03-943 8547; www.hotelmontreal.co.nz; 363 Montreal St; d from $470; ℗⊠) Handy to all the city sights and Victoria St's restaurants, this upmarket hotel occupies a revamped apartment building. Swanky suites are boldly styled in black, grey and gold, with plush lounge areas, kitchenettes and balconies in all rooms. There's also a light-filled in-house restaurant and a gym. Good deals are available in the low season.

Heritage Christchurch   HOTEL **$$$**
(Map p82; ☑03-983 4800; www.heritagehotels.co.nz; 28-30 Cathedral Sq; ste $385-410; ℗⊠) ✈
Still standing grandly on Cathedral Sq, the 1909 Old Government Building owes its survival to a thorough strengthening when it was converted to a hotel in the 1990s. After a three-year post-earthquake restoration its spacious suites are more elegant than ever. All have separate bedrooms and full kitchens. Downstairs is the excellent OGB (p89) cafe and cocktail bar.

⌖ Merivale

Merivale Manor   MOTEL **$$**
(Map p68; ☑03-355 7731; www.merivalemanor.co.nz; 122 Papanui Rd; d $189-249, apt $320; ℗⊠)
A gracious 19th-century Victorian mansion is the hub of this elegant motel, with units both in the main house and in the more typical motel-style blocks lining the drive.

Accommodation ranges from studios to two-bedroom apartments.

⌖ Riccarton

Amber Kiwi Holiday Park   HOLIDAY PARK **$**
(☑0800 348 308, 03-348 3327; www.amberpark.co.nz; 308 Blenheim Rd, Riccarton; sites $49-55, cabins & units $75-135; ℗◎⊠⊠) Lovely gardens and close proximity to the city centre make this urban holiday park a great option for campervaners and campers. Tidy cabins and more spacious motel units are also available.

Lorenzo Motor Inn   MOTEL **$$**
(Map p82; ☑03-348 8074; www.lorenzomotor lodge.co.nz; 36 Riccarton Rd, Riccarton; d $160-175, apt $250; ℗✳⊠) There's a Mediterranean vibe to this trim two-storey motel – the best of many on the busy Riccarton Rd strip. There are a number of options available including studio and two-bedroom apartments; some have spa baths and little balconies, or sweet sitting areas.

Roma on Riccarton   MOTEL **$$**
(Map p82; ☑03-341 2100; www.romaonriccarton.co.nz; 38 Riccarton Rd, Riccarton; d $146-181, apt $246; ℗✳⊠) One of the many motels along the Riccarton Rd strip, this modern two-storey block offers clean, well-proportioned units ranging from studios to two-bedroom apartments.

⌖ Addington

★**Jailhouse**   HOSTEL **$**
(Map p82; ☑0800 524 546, 03-982 7777; www.jail.co.nz; 338 Lincoln Rd, Addington; dm $30-40, s/d $75/85; ◎⊠) From 1874 to 1999 this was Addington Prison; it's now one of Christchurch's most appealing and friendly hostels. Private rooms are a bit on the small side – they don't call them cells for nothing – but there are plenty of communal spaces to relax outside of your room. Perks include a TV room, unlimited free wi-fi and bikes for rent.

⌖ Sumner

Le Petit Hotel   B&B **$$**
(Map p68; ☑03-326 6675; www.lepetithotel.co.nz; 16 Marriner St, Sumner; d $159-179; ℗◎⊠)
Relaxed coffee-and-croissant breakfasts, friendly owners, elegant furnishings and close proximity to Sumner Beach make this charming B&B a definite *oui*. Request an upstairs room with a view.

🛏 Other Suburbs

Jucy Snooze Christchurch HOSTEL $

(📞 03-903 0070; www.jucysnooze.co.nz; 5 Peter Leeming Rd; dm/d $36/129; 🅿 ❄ 🛜) Only a 10-minute walk from the airport, this flash-packers offers Japanese-style capsule beds in place of traditional dorms. The 'pods' are cosy and private, with nice touches like USB-charge points and individual lights. There are also tiny but spotless double rooms, with surprisingly spacious en suites and flat-screen TVs. It's a 25-minute bus ride to the city centre.

Old Countryhouse HOSTEL $

(Map p68; 📞 03-381 5504; www.oldcountry housenz.com; 437 Gloucester St, Linwood; dm $38-47, d with/without bathroom $124/90; 🅿 @ 🛜 🏊) Spread between three separate villas, 2km east of Cathedral Sq, this chilled-out hostel has bright dorms, a reading lounge, and a lovely garden with native ferns and lavender. A spa pool and sauna heat things up.

Christchurch Top 10 HOLIDAY PARK $

(Map p68; 📞 03-352 9176; www.christchurchtop10. co.nz; 39 Meadow St, Papanui; sites $39-50, cabins & units $78-153; 🅿 @ 🛜 🏊) ✓ Family owned and operated for nearly 50 years, this large holiday park has a wide range of accommodation along with various campervan nooks and grassy tent sites. It has a raft of facilities, including a pool, games room and bike hire. Enthusiastic staff can help with travel advice and bookings.

🍴 Eating

🍴 City Centre

★ Riverside Market MARKET $

(Map p82; www.riverside.nz; 96 Oxford Tce; meals $10-20; ⏰ 9am-6pm Mon-Wed, to 9pm Thu-Sat, 10am-6pm Sun; 🦽) ✓ Central Christchurch's new essential destination for travelling foodies is this superb multi-level market combining fresh produce stalls with opportunities for eating and drinking. Many of Christchurch's most popular food trucks are represented, making the market a good one-stop option for great coffee, Greek souvlaki, Argentinean barbecue and Japanese ramen noodles. There's also a craft beer filling station and bar.

C1 Espresso CAFE $

(Map p82; www.c1espresso.co.nz; 185 High St; mains $10-22; ⏰ 7am-10pm; 🛜) ✓ C1 sits pretty in a grand former post office that somehow escaped the cataclysm. Recycled materials fill the interior (Victorian oak panelling, bulbous 1970s light fixtures) and tables spill onto a little square. Excellent coffee, eggy brekkies and bagels are available all day, while sliders (delivered via retro pneumatic tubes!) and burgers combine with craft beer later in the day.

Welder MARKET $

(Map p82; www.thewelder.nz; 22 Welles St; ⏰ 7am-late; 🚗) ✓ This health-and-wellbeing complex – occupying the repurposed industrial warehouses of the Welder – combines a yoga studio and plenty of opportunities for healthy eating and drinking. Options include an organic juicery, an artisan bakery and a traditional Japanese-style izakaya restaurant. The Welder had just opened at the time of writing, so check the website for what else is new.

Caffeine Laboratory CAFE $

(Map p82; www.caffeinelab.co.nz; 1 New Regent St; mains $11-23; ⏰ 7am-3pm Mon-Fri, from 8am Sat & Sun; 🚗) The small-scale, corner C-lab is hooked on coffee, but also cooks up delicious brunches like brioche French toast, house-smoked salmon or chipotle pulled pork. Around lunch, the menu switches to tasty hipster classics like fried chicken and mac 'n' cheese partnered with craft beer.

Utopia Ice ICE CREAM $

(Map p82; www.facebook.com/Utopiaice; 153 High St; from $5; ⏰ 11am-7pm Wed & Sun, to 10pm Thu-Sat; 🚗 🦽) ✓ Expanding into the central city from its farmers market and Sumner Beach roots, Utopia's thoroughly modern take on icy treats includes interesting flavours like walnut, raspberry and rhubarb. Vegan options are available and there's a strong emphasis on local and seasonal ingredients. Good coffee and waffles stuffed with fresh fruit and ice cream are other flavourful distractions.

★ Earl BISTRO $$

(Map p82; 📞 03-365 1147; www.earl.co.nz; 128 Lichfield St; mains $22-34; ⏰ noon-late Tue-Sun; 🚗) ✓ Mediterranean flavours are presented with flair in Earl's spacious dining room. Combine slow-cooked lamb and smoked yoghurt with a quinoa salad or mix it up from the shared plates menu including charcuterie, grilled octopus or fish crudo. The Eat like an Earl option ($60) presents the chef's favourites, while the concise wine list highlights a few different local producers each week.

Little High Eatery
FOOD HALL **$$**

(Map p82; www.littlehigh.co.nz; 255 St Asaph St; dishes $10-20; ⊘7.30am-10pm Mon-Wed, to midnight Thu & Fri, 8.30am-late Sat & Sun; 🖍🌶) Can't decide whether you want sushi, pizza or Thai for dinner? At Little High, you won't have to choose – this stylish and energetic food hall is home to eight different gourmet businesses, offering everything from dumplings to burgers. Stop in for your morning coffee or swing by for a late-night mojito in the beautifully outfitted space.

Unknown Chapter
CAFE **$$**

(Map p82; www.unknownchaptercoffee.co.nz; 254 St Asaph St; mains $14-22; ⊘6.30am-4pm; 🖍) Polished concrete, reclaimed timber tables, hanging plants and floor-to-ceiling windows give this cafe in the upcoming St Asaph/ Welles St precinct an urban hipster vibe. Drop in for your morning caffeine hit, or visit at lunchtime for gourmet sandwiches, tasty salads and an irresistible cake cabinet.

Black Betty
CAFE **$$**

(Map p82; 🖉03-365 8522; www.blackbetty.co.nz; 165 Madras St; mains $13-23; ⊘7.30am-4pm Mon-Fri, from 8am Sat & Sun; 📶) Black Betty's industrial-chic warehouse is a popular destination for students from the nearby college. Friendly service, great food and a laid-back atmosphere are all pluses, but the biggest attraction is the coffee from specialty roaster Switch Espresso – try pour-over, syphon, aeropress or traditional espresso brews.

Rangoon Ruby
BURMESE **$$**

(Map p82; 🖉022 028 0920; www.facebook.com/ RangoonRubyChch; 819 Colombo St; dishes $13-22; ⊘5.30-9.30pm Mon-Sat; 🖍) Rangoon Ruby is the latest iteration of longtime Christchurch fave Bodhi Tree, which has been wowing locals with the nuanced flavours of Burmese cuisine for more than a decade. Feel-good food comes in sharing-sized dishes and sings with zing. Standouts include *le pet thoke* (pickled tea-leaf salad) and *ameyda nut* (slow-cooked beef curry).

Lotus Heart
VEGETARIAN **$$**

(Map p82; 🖉03-377 2727; www.thelotusheart. co.nz; 363 St Asaph St; mains $11-28; ⊘7.30am-3pm Tue-Sun, 5-9pm Fri & Sat; 🖍) 🌶 Run by students of Indian spiritual leader Sri Chinmoy, this colourful vegetarian eatery serves a range of cuisines, from tasty curries and dosas to pizzas, nachos and burgers. Organic, vegan and gluten-free options abound, and you can quench your thirst with freshly squeezed juices, smoothies and a wide tea selection.

★ Inati
BISTRO **$$$**

(Map p82; 🖉03-390 1580; www.inati.nz; 48 Hereford St; shared plates $16-22, 4/6/8-course tasting menus $59/79/99; ⊘noon-2pm & 5pm-late Tue-Fri, from 5.30pm Sat; 🖍) 🌶 Shared plates enjoyed around an elegantly curved bar are divided into Earth, Land and Sea and include innovative and playful dishes harnessing ingredients like smoked mutton tartare, citrus-cured fish with fennel, and kiwifruit sorbet. Four- to eight-course tasting menus are a good way to explore the Inati ethos, and one of Christchurch's best wine lists featuring many South Island varietals.

★ Twenty Seven Steps
MODERN NZ **$$$**

(Map p82; 🖉03-366 2727; www.twentyseven steps.co.nz; 16 New Regent St; mains $33-42; ⊘5pm-late) 🌶 Overlooking the pastel-coloured New Regent St strip, this elegant restaurant showcases locally sourced seasonal ingredients. Mainstays include modern renditions of lamb, beef, venison and seafood, as well as outstanding risotto. Delectable desserts and friendly waitstaff seal the deal; reservations are advised.

King of Snake
ASIAN **$$$**

(Map p82; 🖉03-365 7363; www.kingofsnake.co. nz; 145 Victoria St; mains $27-43; ⊘4pm-late) Dark wood, gold tiles and purple skull-patterned wallpaper fill this hip restaurant and cocktail bar with just the right amount of sinister opulence. The interesting fusion menu gainfully plunders the cuisines of Asia – from India to Korea – to delicious, if pricey, effect.

✕ Merivale

Gatherings
MODERN NZ **$$$**

(Map p82; 🖉021 0293 5641; www.gatherings.co.nz; 2 Papanui Rd, Merivale; dinner 5-course tasting menu $65-80, with matched wines $120-135; ⊘6-11pm Wed-Sat; 🖍) 🌶 Thoughtful, seasonal vegetarian dishes are the focus at this petite restaurant on the edge of the Papanui Rd dining strip. The set five-course tasting menu changes regularly, with a focus on sustainable, local produce and unique flavour combinations.

✕ Riccarton

Christchurch Farmers Market
MARKET **$**

(Map p68; www.christchurchfarmersmarket.co. nz; 16 Kahu Rd, Riccarton; ⊘9am-1pm Sat; 🖿)

🥬 Held in the pretty grounds of Riccarton House (p71), this excellent farmers market offers a tasty array of organic fruit and veg, South Island cheeses and salmon, local craft beer and ethnic treats.

🍴 Addington

Addington Coffee Co-op
CAFE $

(Map p82; ☑ 03-943 1662; www.addingtoncoffee.org.nz; 297 Lincoln Rd, Addington; mains $9-29; ⏲ 7.30am-4pm Mon-Fri, from 9am Sat & Sun; 🛜🅿) You will find one of Christchurch's biggest and best cafes packed to the rafters most days. A compact shop selling fair-trade gifts jostles for attention with delicious cakes, gourmet pies, legendary breakfasts (until 2pm) and, of course, excellent coffee. An on-site laundry completes the deal for busy travellers.

Mosaic by Simo
MOROCCAN $

(Map p82; ☑ 03-338 2882; www.mosaicbysimo.co.nz; 300 Lincoln Rd, Addington; tapas & mains $8-19; ⏲ 9am-9pm; 🅿) This deli-cafe is popular for its takeaway *bocadillos* (toasted wraps filled with a huge selection of Middle Eastern- and African-inspired fillings, sauces and toppings). Other tasty offerings include super-generous platters, *merguez* sausages and tagines.

🍴 Sumner

Bohemian Bakery
BAKERY $

(Map p68; ☑ 021 070 6271; www.bohemianbakery.co.nz; 43 Nayland St, Sumner; pastries $4-6; ⏲ 7.30am-4pm Wed-Sun) The kitchen at this petite bakery is entirely open, so you can see the bakers at work crafting delicious yeasty treats all day long. Grab one of the famed cinnamon rolls and head to the beach.

🍴 Other Suburbs

★5th Street
BISTRO $$

(Map p82; ☑ 03-365 9667; www.5thstreet.co.nz; 5 Elgin St, Sydenham; shared plates $18-24; ⏲ 4.30-11pm; 🅿) Global influences punctuate the shared plates menu at his bespoke restuarant. The honey- and chipotle-fired chicken goes well with beers from Christchurch's Three Boys Brewery, while the pomegranate-glazed lamb shoulder partners with vegetables enlivened by hummus, garlic and feta. A serious approach to cocktails also makes 5th Street ideal for a drink and snacks.

Hello Sunday
CAFE $$

(Map p82; ☑ 03-260 1566; www.hellosunday-cafe.co.nz; 6 Elgin St, Sydenham; mains $13-24; ⏲ 7.30am-4.30pm Mon-Fri, from 8.30am Sat & Sun; 🛜🅿) Spread across two rooms of a restored old post office building, this popular cafe is a great spot for all-day brunches, spectacular salads and excellent coffee. The beef-cheek hash with poached eggs and the zing of kimchi and sriracha hot sauce is a good way to ease into another day.

Kinji
JAPANESE $$

(Map p68; ☑ 03-359 4697; www.kinjirestaurant.com; 279b Greers Rd, Bishopdale; mains $16-26; ⏲ 5.30-10pm Mon-Sat) Despite being hidden away in suburbia, this acclaimed Japanese restaurant has a loyal following, so it's wise to book. Tuck into the likes of sashimi, grilled ginger squid and venison *tataki,* but save room for the green-tea tiramisu, a surprising highlight.

Under the Red Verandah
CAFE $$

(Map p68; www.utrv.co.nz; 29 Tancred St, Linwood; mains $15-25; ⏲ 7.30am-3pm Mon-Fri, 8.30am-3pm Sat & Sun; 🅿) This lucky suburban backstreet boasts a lovely sunny cafe, beloved by locals and travellers alike. Take a seat under the namesake veranda and tuck into baked goodies, oaty pancakes, homemade pies and eggs multiple ways.

🍷 Drinking & Nightlife

🍷 City Centre

★Smash Palace
BAR

(Map p82; ☑ 03-366 5369; www.thesmashpalace.co.nz; 172 High St; ⏲ 3pm-late Mon-Thu, from noon Fri-Sun) Epitomising the spirit of transience, tenacity and resourcefulness that Christchurch is now known for, this deliberately downcycled and ramshackle beer garden is an intoxicating mix of grease-monkey garage, trailer-trash park and proto-hipster hang-out, complete with a psychedelic school bus, edible garden and blooming roses. There's craft beer, chips, Cheerios, and burgers made from scratch ($11 to $15).

★Pomeroy's Old Brewery Inn
PUB

(Map p82; ☑ 03-365 1523; www.pomspub.co.nz; 292 Kilmore St; ⏲ 3pm-late Tue-Thu, from noon Fri-Sun) With more than 30 taps featuring the best of NZ craft beers, Pomeroy's is an essential Christchurch destination. Among this cosy British-style pub's other endearing features are regular live music, a snug and sunny courtyard and **Victoria's Kitchen**, serving comforting pub food (mains $25 to $34). Also onsite, pretty **Little Pom's** cafe serves excellent brunch fare ($11 to $25) until mid-afternoon.

The Last Word COCKTAIL BAR

(Map p82; ☑ 022 094 7445; www.lastword.co.nz; 31 New Regent St; ⊙ 4pm-late Mon-Fri, 2pm-late Sat & Sun) This cosy spot amid the heritage Spanish Mission facades of New Regent St is a fine option any time of the evening. One of the city's best selections of whisky partners with good cocktails and a well-curated beer menu. Moreish bar snacks include platters and grilled-cheese sandwiches, and also on offer are special whisky and chocolate pairing menus.

Institution CRAFT BEER

(Map p82; www.theinstitution.co.nz; 28 New Regent St; ⊙ 4-11pm Tue-Fri, from 2pm Sat & Sun) The Institution may well be Christchurch's smallest bar – there's only room for around 20 punters upstairs – but there's no trade-off in the range of beers on offer. The taps often feature beers from smaller Canterbury breweries and there's a well-priced selection of interesting cans and bottles in the fridge. Service from the barstaff is chatty and friendly.

OGB COCKTAIL BAR

(Map p82; ☑ 03-377 4336; www.ogb.co.nz; Heritage Christchurch, 28 Cathedral Sq; ⊙ 11am-1am) Old-school speakeasy charm reigns at this versatile spot that's equally fine for a cocktail, craft beer or more substantial offering of a shared platter of cheese and charcuterie. In cooler weather sit in the supremely cosy interior, or on the hotel patio with views of Cathedral Sq during summer. If you're wondering, OGB stands for Old Government Building.

Dux Central BAR

(Map p82; ☑ 03-943 7830; www.duxcentral.co.nz; 6 Poplar St; ⊙ 11am-late) Pumping a whole lot of heart back into the flattened High St precinct, the epic Dux complex comprises a brew bar serving its own and other crafty drops, the Emerald Room wine bar, Upper Dux restaurant and the Poplar Social Club cocktail bar, all housed within the confines of a lovingly restored old building.

Boo Radley's BAR

(Map p82; ☑ 03-366 9906; www.booradleys.co.nz; 98 Victoria St; ⊙ 4pm-late) An intimate, speakeasy vibe makes Boo's an alluring late-night hang-out. Southern-style decor meshes with bourbons galore and American comfort food like sliders, fried chicken and curly fries (snacks $7 to $24). There's regular live music, too.

 Merivale

Vesuvio WINE BAR

(Map p82; ☑ 03-355 8530; www.vesuvio.co.nz; 4 Papanui Rd, Merivale; ⊙ 3pm-late) Half-hidden at the back of a busy cluster of eateries, this European-style wine bar is the perfect spot for a pre-dinner *aperitivo* – though the thoughtful selection of local and imported wines, excellent antipasti boards (from $19) and regular live jazz might mean you end up settling in for the night.

 Riccarton

Volstead
Trading Company BAR

(Map p82; www.volstead.co.nz; 55 Riccarton Rd, Riccarton; ⊙ 4-11pm Mon-Thu, from noon Fri-Sun) Concealed inside a suburban shopping strip, this cosy bar combines comfy old sofas from your last student flat with quirky murals and a wide range of craft beers on tap. The complementary beer-food menu features sliders, burritos and fried chicken. Volstead also makes its own craft brews in the onsite microbrewery. Try the American Amber Ale or hoppy US IPA.

 Sumner

Village Inn PUB

(Map p68; ☑ 03-326 6973; www.thevillageinnsumner.co.nz; 41b Nayland St, Sumner; ⊙ 11am-late Tue-Sun) This convivial spot on Sumner's main shopping strip has a sunny courtyard, good meals (mains $20 to $30) including pork souvlaki and rib eye steak, and live music on Sunday afternoons from 4pm. It's also popular for a lazy weekend brunch.

Other Suburbs

The Brewery CRAFT BEER

(Map p68; www.casselsbrewery.co.nz; 3 Garlands Rd, Woolston; ⊙ 8am-late) This is an essential destination for beer-loving travellers The

Cassels & Sons' brewery crafts beers using a wood-fired brew kettle, resulting in well-balanced ales and lagers. Tasting trays are available for the curious and the indecisive, live bands perform regularly, and the food – including wood-fired pizzas ($20 to $26) – is top-notch, too. Cassels' Milk Stout has deservedly won awards internationally.

Allpress Espresso
COFFEE

(Map p82; 110 Montreal St, Sydenham; ⊘7.30am-3.30pm Mon-Fri) Hidden behind a nondescript facade down the industrial end of Montreal St, the Christchurch branch of this famous Kiwi coffee roastery does a mean espresso – just as you'd expect. If you're feeling peckish, there are also fresh light lunch options and smoothies on offer.

☆ Entertainment

For live music and club listings, see www.undertheradar.co.nz and www.rdu.org.nz.

Isaac Theatre Royal
THEATRE

(Map p82; ☑03-366 6326; www.isaactheatreroyal.co.nz; 145 Gloucester St; ⊘box office 10am-5pm Mon-Fri) This century-old dear survived the quakes and emerged restored to full glory in 2014. Its heritage features are enjoyed by patrons venturing inside for everything from opera and ballet to contemporary theatre and rock concerts.

Blue Smoke
LIVE MUSIC

(Map p68; ☑03-288 0543; www.bluesmoke.co.nz; The Tannery, 3 Garlands Rd; variable; ⊘hours vary by event) Adjacent to the Brewery (p89) in Woolston, Blue Smoke is Christchurch's best small live-music venue. There's often a folk, roots music or Americana vibe to the acts, but rock, rap and spoken word also sometimes feature. Top local musicians to look out for include the Eastern, and Lyttelton's finest, Marlon Williams and Delaney Davidson.

Alice Cinema
CINEMA

(Map p82; ☑03-365 0615; www.alice.co.nz; 209 Tuam St; adult/child $17/12) This delightful two-screen art-house cinema can be found within the long-standing and excellent Alice In Videoland DVD library.

Court Theatre
THEATRE

(Map p82; ☑03-963 0870; www.courttheatre.org.nz; Bernard St, Addington; ⊘box office 9am-8.15pm Mon-Thu, to 10.15pm Fri, 10am-10.15pm Sat) Christchurch's original Court Theatre was an integral part of the city's Arts Centre, but it was forced to relocate to this warehouse after the earthquakes. The new premises are much more spacious; it's a great venue to see popular international plays and works by NZ playwrights.

Darkroom
LIVE MUSIC

(Map p82; www.darkroom.bar; 336 St Asaph St; ⊘7pm-late Thu-Sat) A hip combination of live-music venue and bar, Darkroom has lots of Kiwi beers and great cocktails. Live gigs are frequent – and frequently free.

Hollywood Cinema
CINEMA

(Map p68; www.hollywoodcinema.co.nz; 28 Marriner St, Sumner; adult/child $16/12) Screens art-house and blockbuster flicks in the seaside suburb of Sumner. Cheaper prices on Tuesdays.

Orangetheory Stadium
STADIUM

(Map p68; www.crfu.co.nz; 95 Jack Hinton Dr, Addington) After Lancaster Park was irreparably damaged during the 2011 earthquake, Canterbury Rugby Union shifted its home games to this smaller ground in Addington. The Crusaders play here from late February to July in the Super Rugby tournament, while from July to September, Canterbury plays in NZ's domestic rugby championship.

🛍 Shopping

★Tannery
SHOPPING CENTRE

(Map p68; www.thetannery.co.nz; 3 Garlands Rd, Woolston; ⊘10am-5pm) In a city mourning the loss of its heritage, this post-earthquake conversion of a 19th-century tannery couldn't be more welcome. The Victorian buildings have been beautifully restored, and are crammed with all manner of delightful boutiques selling everything from surfboards to vintage clothing to exquisite homewares.

When you're tired of shopping, stop by the Brewery (p89) for an afternoon pick-me-up. There are also several cafes, an art-house cinema and live music at Blue Smoke.

Scorpio Books
BOOKS

(Map p82; ☑03-379 2882; www.scorpiobooks.co.nz; BNZ Centre, 120 Hereford St; ⊘9am-6pm Mon-Fri, 10am-5pm Sat & Sun) A well-established Christchurch independent bookstore, Scorpio Books relocated after the earthquake to this modern central city location after several years in Riccarton. There's in-store seating and relaxed browsing is definitely encouraged.

New Regent St MALL

(Map p82; www.newregentstreet.co.nz) This pretty little stretch of pastel Spanish Mission–style shops was described as NZ's most beautiful street when it was completed in 1932. Fully restored post-earthquake, it's once again a delightful place to stroll, and has become something of a hub for quality cafes, bars and restaurants.

Ballantynes DEPARTMENT STORE

(Map p82; www.ballantynes.com; cnr Colombo & Cashel Sts; ⊙9am-5.30pm Mon-Fri, to 5pm Sat, 10am-5pm Sun) A venerable Christchurch department store selling men's and women's fashions, cosmetics, travel goods, stationery and speciality NZ gifts.

The Crossing SHOPPING CENTRE

(Map p82; ☑027 506 8149; www.thecrossing.co.nz; 166 Cashel St; ⊙9am-6pm Mon-Wed, to 8pm Thu, 10am-5pm Sat & Sun) Opened in 2017, this shiny complex fronting the Cashel St pedestrian mall is home to all manner of local and international retailers. There's also a good range of cafes and food outlets scattered through the Crossing's several floors.

Colombo Mall MALL

(Map p82; www.thecolombo.co.nz; 363 Colombo St, Sydenham; ⊙9am-5.30pm Mon-Sat, 10am-5pm Sun) Within walking distance of the CBD, this hip little mall is home to a few interesting, independent shops, an art-house cinema and a range of culinary delights – you'll find macarons, crêpes, dumplings, sushi, salads, craft beer and good coffee.

❶ Information

EMERGENCY & IMPORTANT NUMBERS

Emergency (police, fire, ambulance)	☑111
Country code	☑64
International access code	☑00

MEDICAL SERVICES

24-Hour Surgery (☑03-365 7777; www. 24hoursurgery.co.nz; 401 Madras St) No appointment necessary.

Christchurch Hospital (☑03-364 0640, emergency dept 03-364 0270; www.cdhb.govt. nz; 2 Riccarton Ave) Has a 24-hour emergency department.

TOURIST INFORMATION

Airport i-SITE (☑03-741 3980; www. christchurchnz.com; International Arrivals Hall; ⊙8am-6pm)

Christchurch i-SITE (Map p82; ☑03-379 9629; www.christchurchnz.com; Arts Centre, 28 Worcester Blvd; ⊙8.30am-5pm)

ChristchurchNZ (www.christchurchnz.com) Official tourism website for the city and region.

DOC Visitor Centre (Map p82; ☑03-379 4082; www.doc.govt.nz; Arts Centre, 28 Worcester Blvd; ⊙9am-4.45pm) Information on South Island national parks, including walk and hut bookings; located within the i-SITE.

❶ Getting There & Away

AIR

Christchurch Airport (CHC; ☑03-358 5029; www.christchurchairport.co.nz; 30 Durey Rd) The South Island's main international gateway, with regular flights to Australia, China, Dubai, Fiji, the USA and Singapore. Facilities include baggage storage, car-rental counters, ATMs, and foreign-exchange offices.

Air New Zealand (p363) Direct flights to/from Auckland, Wellington, Dunedin and Queenstown. Code-share flights with smaller regional airlines head to/from Blenheim, Hamilton, Hokitika, Invercargill, Napier, Nelson, New Plymouth, Palmerston North, Paraparaumu, Rotorua and Tauranga.

Jetstar (p363) Flies to/from Auckland and Wellington.

BUS

Tourist-oriented services generally stop outside the Canterbury Museum on Rolleston Ave; local and some long-distance services depart from the inner-city **Bus Interchange** (Map p82; cnr Lichfield & Colombo Sts).

Akaroa French Connection (Map p82; ☑0800 800 575; www.akaroabus.co.nz; Rolleston Ave; adult/child return $50/30) Daily service to Akaroa.

Akaroa Shuttle (Map p82; ☑0800 500 929; www.akaroashuttle.co.nz; Rolleston Ave; adult/child one way $36/31, return $6/41) Daily service to Akaroa.

Atomic Shuttles (Map p82; ☑03-349 0697; www.atomictravel.co.nz; Lichfield St) Destinations include Greymouth ($55, 3¾ hours), Timaru ($30, 2½ hours) and Dunedin ($40, 5¾ hours).

Budget Buses & Shuttles (Map p82; ☑03-615 5119; www.budgetshuttles.co.nz; Rolleston Ave; ⊙Mon-Sat) Offers a door-to-door shuttle to Geraldine ($65) and Timaru ($55).

East West Coaches Run between Christchurch and Westport via the Lewis Pass daily except Saturday (adult/child $60/45, five hours).

Hanmer Connection (Map p82; ☑0800 242 663; www.hanmerconnection.co.nz; Rolleston Ave; adult/child one way $30/20, return

$50/30) Daily coach to/from Hanmer Springs via Amberley and Waipara.

InterCity (Map p82; ☑ 03-365 1113; www.
intercity.co.nz; Lichfield St) New Zealand's widest and most reliable coach network. Coaches head to Timaru (from $31, 2½ hours), Dunedin (from $44, six hours), Queenstown (from $62, eight to 11 hours) and Picton (from $69, 5¼ hours) at least daily.

TRAIN

Christchurch Railway Station (www.greatjour neysofnz.co.nz; Troup Dr, Addington; ⊙ ticket office 6.30am-3pm) is the terminus for two highly scenic train journeys, the hero of which is the TranzAlpine (p80). The other, the **Coastal Pacific** (☑ 03-341 2588, 0800 872 467; www.
greatjourneysofnz.co.nz; from $59; ⊙ Oct-Apr), runs seasonally along the east coast from Christchurch to Picton, stopping at Waipara, Kaikōura and Blenheim.

ℹ Getting Around

TO/FROM THE AIRPORT

Christchurch Airport is located 10km from the city centre. A taxi to town costs $50 to $65. Alternatively, the airport is well served by public buses (www.metroinfo.co.nz). The Purple Line bus heads through Riccarton (20 minutes) to the central Bus Interchange (30 minutes) and on to Sumner (1¼ hours). Bus 29 heads through Fendalton (10 minutes) to the Bus Interchange (30 minutes). Both services cost $8.50 (pay the driver) and run every 30 minutes from approximately 7am to 11pm. Shuttle services are available for around $25 per person.

Ride-share services Uber, Ola and Zoomy all leave from the airport's Rideshare Pick-up Zone located outside of the main terminal behind the purple Express Car Park.

CAR & MOTORCYCLE

Most major car- and campervan-rental companies have offices in Christchurch, as do numerous smaller local companies. Operators with national networks often want cars from Christchurch to be returned to Auckland because most renters travel in the opposite direction, so you may find a cheaper price on a northbound route.

Local options include the following:

Ace Rental Cars (☑ 03-360 3270; www.ace rentalcars.co.nz; 166 Orchard Rd, Harewood)

Hitch Car Rental (☑ 03-974 4670; www.hitch carrentals.co.nz; 232 Roydvale Ave, Burnside; ⊙ 8am-6pm)

New Zealand Motorcycle Rentals & Tours (☑ 09-486 2472; www.nzbike.com)

New Zealand Rent a Car (☑ 03-961 5880; www.nzrentacar.co.nz; 26b Sheffield Cres, Burnside)

Omega Rental Cars (☑ 03-377 4558; www.
omegarentalcars.com; 158 Orchard Rd, Harewood; ⊙ 7.30am-6pm)

Pegasus Rental Cars (☑ 03-358 5890; www.
rentalcars.co.nz; 154 Orchard Rd, Harewood; ⊙ 8am-5pm)

E-SCOOTERS

Accessed via a smartphone app, e-scooters from Lime and Flamingo are both available in central Christchurch.

PUBLIC TRANSPORT

Christchurch's **Metro bus network** (☑ 03-366 8855; www.metroinfo.co.nz) is inexpensive, efficient and comprehensive. Most buses run from the inner-city Bus Interchange (p91).

Pick up timetables from the i-SITE (p91) or the Interchange. Tickets (adult/child $4.20/2.40) can be purchased on board and include one free transfer within two hours. Alternatively, Metro-cards allow unlimited zone one travel for two

MĀORI NZ: CHRISTCHURCH & CANTERBURY

Only 14% of New Zealand's Māori live on the South Island, and of those, half live in Canterbury. The first major tribe to become established here were Waitaha, who were subsequently conquered and assimilated into the Ngāti Māmoe tribe in the 16th century. In the following century, they in turn were conquered and subsumed by Ngāi Tahu (www.
ngaitahu.iwi.nz), a tribe that has its origins in the East Coast of the North Island. Today, Ngāi Tahu is considered to be one of Māoridom's great success stories, with a reputation for good financial management, sound cultural advice and a portfolio including property, forestry, fisheries and many high-profile tourism operations.

There are many ways to engage in Māori culture in Canterbury. Artefacts can be seen at Canterbury Museum (p70), Akaroa Museum (p97), Okains Bay Māori & Colonial Museum (p95) and South Canterbury Museum (p117). Willowbank Wildlife Reserve (p71) in Christchurch has a replica Māori village and an evening cultural show. Further south in Timaru, the Te Ana Māori Rock Art Centre (p117) has interactive displays and arranges tours to see centuries-old work in situ.

hours/one day/one week for $2.65/5.30/26.50. Cards are available from the Interchange; they cost $10 and must be loaded with a minimum of $10 additional credit.

TAXI

Ride-share apps including Uber, Ola and Zoomy all operate in Christchurch.

Blue Star (☑03-379 9799; www.bluestartaxis. org.nz)

First Direct (☑03-377 5555; www.firstdirect. net.nz)

Gold Band (☑03-379 5795; www.goldband taxis.co.nz)

AROUND CHRISTCHURCH

Lyttelton

POP 3100

Southeast of Christchurch, the prominent Port Hills slope down to the city's port on Lyttelton Harbour. Christchurch's first European settlers landed here in 1850 to embark on their historic trek over the hills. Nowadays a 2km road tunnel makes the journey considerably quicker.

Lyttelton was badly damaged during the 2010 and 2011 earthquakes, and many of the town's heritage buildings along London St were subsequently demolished. Today, however, Lyttelton has re-emerged as one of Christchurch's most interesting communities. The town's arty, independent and bohemian vibe is stronger than ever, and it is once again a hub for great bars, cafes and shops. It's well worth catching the bus from Christchurch and getting immersed in the local scene, especially on a sunny Saturday morning when the farmers market is buzzing.

Lyttelton's new passenger terminal will be completed by late 2020; the port should again be a favourite anchorage for cruise ships.

✖ Eating

Lyttelton Farmers Market MARKET $

(Map p68; www.lyttelton.net.nz; London St; ⊙10am-1pm Sat; 🚲🐾) 🍃 Every Saturday morning food stalls take the place of cars on Lyttelton's main street. Stock up alongside locals on fresh bread, baked goods, flowers, cheeses, local produce and good coffee.

Super ASIAN $$

(Map p68; ☑021 0862 2632; www.super.restaurant; 5 Norwich Quay; mains $22-28; ⊙9am-late Mon-Sat; 🅿) Pan-Asian flavours with a strong Japanese influence are the focus at Super, with the fun ambience further enhanced by bright and colourful *anime*-influenced decor. Standout small plates include the steamed bao buns with ginger beef and sriracha mayonnaise, and its take on ramen noodles is packed full of flavour. A concise drinks list showcases sake, wine and craft beer.

Civil & Naval TAPAS $$

(Map p68; ☑03-328 7206; www.civilandnaval. co.nz; 16 London St; shared plates $6-18; ⊙10am-11pm Sun-Thu, to 1am Fri & Sat) Steadfast staff at this compact, bijou bar serve a quality selection of cocktails, fine wines and craft beers, while the kitchen keeps patrons civil with an eclectic range of tapas. Try the tasty polenta-crumbed squid.

Lyttelton Coffee Company CAFE $$

(Map p68; ☑03-328 8096; www.facebook.com/lytteltoncoffeecompany; 29 London St; mains $13-20; ⊙7am-4pm Mon-Fri, 8am-4pm Sat & Sun; 🅿🐾) 🍃 Local institution Lyttelton Coffee Company has risen from the rubble and continues its role as a stalwart of the London St foodie scene, serving consistently great coffee and wholesome food in its cavernous, exposed-brick warehouse space.

🍷 Drinking & Nightlife

Eruption Brewing MICROBREWERY

(Map p68; ☑03-355 5632; www.eruptionbrewing. com; 26 London St; ⊙4-9pm Wed-Thu, to 11pm Fri, 10am-11pm Sat, to 8pm Sun) Every heritage port town needs a decent craft brewery and Eruption Brewing doesn't disappoint. It's a firm local favourite, especially on Friday and Saturday nights when the vintage 1970s furniture hosts punters enjoying decent brews like the Eruption IPA packed with citrusy NZ hops. Dining options include pizza, platters and gourmet burgers. Ask what other interesting seasonal beers are on offer.

Spooky Boogie COFFEE

(Map p68; www.facebook.com/spookyboogies; 54 London St; ⊙7am-4pm Mon-Fri, from 8.30am Sat & 9am Sun) More sweet than spooky, this hip coffee shop cum record store at the top end of London St does a roaring trade in silky coffee and smooth beats alike. There's lots of cool art and retro movie posters to check out too.

Governors Bay Hotel PUB

(☑03-329 9433; www.governorsbayhotel.co.nz; 52 Main Rd, Governors Bay; ⊙11am-late; 🛜) A scenic

9km drive southwest from Lyttelton is one of NZ's oldest operational pubs (1870). You couldn't ask for a more inviting deck and garden in which to quaff an afternoon tipple. The food is good, too, covering all the classic pub-grub bases (mains $22 to $36) with burgers, bangers and mash, and seafood. Upstairs are chicly renovated rooms with shared bathrooms (doubles $95 to $150).

Wunderbar BAR
(Map p68; ☑ 03-328 8818; www.wunderbar.co.nz; 19 London St; ⊙ 5pm-late Mon-Fri, 1pm-3am Sat & Sun) Wunderbar is a top spot to get down, with regular live music covering all spectra, and clientele to match. The kooky decor and decapitated dolls' heads alone are worth the trip. Enter via the stairs in the rear car park.

🛍 Shopping

London St Bookshop BOOKS
(Map p68; 48 London St; ⊙10am-4pm Tue-Sun) Dimly lit and crammed full of intriguing volumes, this charming secondhand bookshop is a bibliophile's dream.

Henry Trading HOMEWARES
(Map p68; ☑ 03-328 8088; www.henrytrading.co.nz; 33 London St; ⊙10am-4pm Tue-Sun) This tiny but perfectly curated store stocks a range of lovely homewares and gifts, many made by local producers, as well as a sweet line in artisanal Lyttelton souvenirs.

ℹ Information

Lyttelton Visitor Information Centre (Map p68; ☑ 03-328 9093; www.lytteltoninfocentre.nz; 20 Oxford St; ⊙10am-4pm Oct-Apr, 10.30am-2.30pm May-Sep) Friendly staff can provide information on accommodation, local walks and ferry departures.

ℹ Getting There & Away

Lyttelton is 15km from Christchurch CBD via the Lyttelton Tunnel. An alternative, more scenic road links Sumner Beach to Lyttelton (around 8km), which only reopened in mid-2019 after being closed following severe rock falls in the 2011 earthquake.
Bus No 28 runs from Christchurch to Lyttelton (adult/child $4.70/2.60, 30 minutes).
Ferry From Lyttelton, **Black Cat** (Map p68; ☑ 03-328 9078; www.blackcat.co.nz; 5 Norwich Quay) provides ferries to sheltered Quail Island (adult/child return $30/15, 10 minutes, once daily October to April only), as well as to sleepy Diamond Harbour (adult/child one way $6.50/3.20, 10 minutes, hourly).

Banks Peninsula
POP 4750

Gorgeous Banks Peninsula (Horomaka) was formed by two giant volcanic eruptions about eight million years ago. Harbours and bays radiate out from the peninsula's centre, giving it an unusual cogwheel shape. The historic town of **Akaroa**, 80km from Christchurch, is a highlight, as is the absurdly beautiful drive along Summit Rd around the edge of one of the original craters. It's also worth exploring the little bays that dot the peninsula's perimeter.

The waters around Banks Peninsula are home to the smallest and one of the rarest dolphin species, the Hector's dolphin, found only in NZ waters. A range of tours depart from Akaroa to spot these and other sealife, including white-flippered penguins, orcas and seals.

History

James Cook sighted the peninsula in 1770, believing it to be an island. He named it after the naturalist Sir Joseph Banks.

In 1831, Onawe *pā* (fortified village) was attacked by the Ngāti Toa chief Te Rauparaha and in the massacres that followed, the local Ngāi Tahu population was dramatically reduced. Seven years later, whaling captain Jean Langlois negotiated the purchase of Banks Peninsula from the survivors and returned to France to form a trading company. With French-government backing, 63 settlers headed for the peninsula in 1840, but only days before they arrived, panicked British officials sent their own ship to raise the flag at Akaroa, claiming British sovereignty under the Treaty of Waitangi. Had the settlers arrived two years earlier, the entire South Island could have become a French colony, and NZ's future might have been quite different.

The French did settle at Akaroa, but in 1849 their land claim was sold to the New Zealand Company, and in 1850 a large group of British settlers arrived. The heavily forested land was cleared and soon farming became the peninsula's main industry.

👁 Sights

Hinewai Reserve FOREST
(www.hinewai.org.nz; 632 Long Bay Rd) 🌿 Get a glimpse of what the peninsula once looked like with a stroll through this privately owned 1250-hectare nature reserve, which has been replanted with native forest. Pick up a map

Banks Peninsula

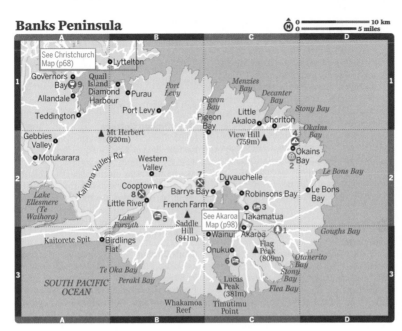

outlining the walking tracks at the visitor centre, a short walk from the main entrance.

Okains Bay Māori & Colonial Museum
MUSEUM

(www.okainsbaymuseum.co.nz; 1146 Okains Bay Rd, Okains Bay; adult/child $10/2; ⊙10am-5pm) Northeast of Akaroa, this museum has a respectable array of European pioneer artefacts, but it is the nationally significant Māori collection, featuring a replica *wharenui* (meeting house), *waka* (canoes), stone tools and personal adornments, that make this a worthwhile detour. Note the cute shop down the road.

🏃 Activities

Akaroa i-SITE (p100) stocks pamphlets on walks around Akaroa township, taking in the old cottages, churches and gardens that lend Akaroa its character. The six-hour Skyline Circuit also starts from town, and there are many more rewarding walks throughout the peninsula.

Banks Peninsula Track
HIKING

(☑03-304 7612; www.bankstrack.co.nz; 2-/3-days from $195/330; ⊙Oct-Apr) This privately owned and maintained 29km three-day tramp traverses farmland and forest along the dramatic coast east of Akaroa. Fees include transport

Banks Peninsula

from Akaroa and hut accommodation. The two-day option covers the same ground only faster, for experienced hikers.

Crater Rim Walks
WALKING

(www.craterrimwalks.co.nz; per person from $175; 🖥) 🞵 Stunning coastal scenery abounds during half- and full-day guided walks around the extinct volcanic landscapes of Banks Peninsula. Owner-guide Nicole Ellwood is a Christchurch local and very experienced in exploring the area.

LITTLE RIVER TRAIL

One of the Great Rides of the New Zealand Cycle Trail, this easy-graded, 49km cycle trail (www.littleriverrailtrail.co.nz) runs from Hornby, on the outskirts of Christchurch, to Little River at the base of Banks Peninsula. It rolls across rural plains, past weathered peaks and along the shores of Lake Ellesmere – home to NZ's most diverse bird population – and its smaller twin, Lake Forsyth. The best section of track can be enjoyed as a return ride from Little River, where there is a cafe (p97) and bike hire.

Courses

Bone Dude   ART
(☑03-329 0947; www.thebonedude.co.nz; 111 Poranui Beach Rd, Birdlings Flat; from $60; ☺1-4pm Fri, 10am-1pm Sat; 🖶) 🖉 Creative types should consider booking a session with the Bone Dude, who'll show you how to carve your own bone pendant (allow three hours). Sessions are limited to seven participants, so book ahead. Friendly owner John's always up for a good chat.

☞ Tours

Pohatu Plunge   WILDLIFE
(☑03-304 8542; www.pohatu.co.nz; adult/child tours $80/55, self-drive $50/30) 🖉 Runs three-hour evening tours from Akaroa to the Pohatu white-flippered penguin colony (a self-drive option is also available). The best time to see the penguins is during the breeding season from August to January, but it is possible throughout the year. Sea kayaking and 4WD nature tours are also available, as is the option of staying overnight in a secluded cottage.

Tuatara Tours   HIKING
(☑03-962 3280; www.tuataratours.co.nz; per person $1795; ☺Nov-Apr) 🖉 You'll only need to carry your day pack on the guided Akaroa Walk, a leisurely 39km, three-day guided tramp from Christchurch to Akaroa via the gorgeous Summit Ridge. Good accommodation and gourmet food are included.

Sleeping

★Onuku Farm Hostel   HOSTEL $
(☑03-304 7066; www.onuku.co.nz; Hamiltons Rd, Onuku; sites per person from $15, dm/d from $20/70; ☺Oct-Apr; ℗🐕🛜) 🖉 Set on a working farm 6km south of Akaroa, this blissfully isolated

backpackers has a grassy camping area, simple, tidy rooms in a farmhouse and 'stargazer' cabins with translucent roofing ($50 for two, BYO bedding). Tonga Hut affords more privacy and breathtaking sea views ($80). Ask about the swimming-with-dolphins tours (from $130), kayaking trips (from $40) and the Skytrack walk.

★Halfmoon Cottage   HOSTEL $
(☑03-304 5050; www.halfmoon.co.nz; SH75, Barrys Bay; dm/s/d $35/75/93; ☺closed Jun-Aug; ℗@🛜) This pretty 1896 cottage, 12km from Akaroa and right on the water, is a blissful place to spend a few days lazing on the big verandas or in the hammocks dotting the gardens. It offers proper home comforts and style, with the bonus of bicycles and kayaks to take exploring.

Okuti Garden   HOSTEL $
(☑03-325 1913; www.okuti.co.nz; 216 Okuti Valley Rd; adult/child $50/25; ☺Oct-Apr; ℗🛜) 🖉 Ecologically sound creds are just part of this delightfully eccentric package that includes a house truck and a series of romantic yurts dotted throughout colourful gardens. Freshly picked herbs, a pizza oven, a fire-warmed bath, hammocks and free-roaming chickens give this place some serious *Good Life* vibes.

Okains Bay
Camping Ground   CAMPGROUND $
(☑03-304 8789; www.okainsbaycamp.co.nz; 1357 Okains Bay Rd, Okains Bay; sites per adult/child $13/7; ℗🖶) This tidy camp sits on a pine-tree-peppered swathe of land right by a lovely beach and estuary. Facilities include kitchens, toilets and coin-operated hot showers, and the location is unbeatable. Laundry facilities are also available.

Coombe Farm   B&B $$
(☑03-304 7239; www.coombefarm.co.nz; 18 Old Le Bons Track, Takamatua Valley; d $180-220; ℗🛜) Choose between the private and romantic Shepherd's Hut – complete with outdoor bath – or the historic farmhouse lovingly restored in shades of Laura Ashley. After a luxe breakfast you can take a walk to the nearby waterfall, or drive the five minutes into Akaroa.

🍴 Eating

Barrys Bay Cheese   CHEESE $
(☑03-304 5809; www.barrysbaycheese.co.nz; 5807 Christchurch-Akaroa Rd; cheese $7-11; ☺9am-5pm; 🅿) 🖉 This award-winning cheese factory has a small store attached where you can taste its cheesy goodness and

pick up supplies for seaside picnics. Large windows give you a sneak peek into where the magic happens. It's 12km from Akaroa.

Little River Cafe & Gallery CAFE $$
(☑03-325 1944; www.littlerivergallery.com; SH75, Little River; mains $13-22; ⊙7.30am-4pm Mon-Fri, to 4.30pm Sat & Sun) On SH75 between Christchurch and Akaroa, the flourishing settlement of Little River is home to this fantastic combo of contemporary art gallery, shop and cafe. It's top-notch in all departments, with some particularly delectable home baking on offer as well as yummy deli goods to go.

Hilltop Tavern PUB FOOD $$
(☑03-325 1005; www.thehilltop.co.nz; 5207 Christchurch-Akaroa Rd; pizzas $26, mains $25-30; ⊙10am-late, reduced hours May-Sep) Craft beer, wood-fired pizzas, a pool table and occasional live bands seal the deal for locals and visitors alike at this historic pub. Enjoy stunning views of Akaroa harbour and the peninsula – especially at sunset.

❶ Getting There & Away

The daily Akaroa Shuttle (p100) runs from Christchurch to Akaroa, departing at 8.30am (hotel pick-ups available), returning to Christchurch at 3.45pm (late October to April). From May to late October, shuttles depart Christchurch at 9am and return at 4pm. Check the website for Christchurch pick-up options. Scenic tours from Christchurch exploring Banks Peninsula are also available.

French Connection (p100) has a year-round daily departure from Christchurch at 9am, returning from Akaroa at 4pm.

Akaroa

POP 625

Akaroa (Long Harbour) was the site of the country's first French settlement and descendants of the original French pioneers still reside here. It's a charming town that strives to recreate the feel of a French provincial village, down to the names of its streets and houses. Generally it's a sleepy place, but the peace is periodically shattered by hordes descending from gargantuan cruise ships. The ships used to dock in Lyttelton but since the earthquakes Akaroa has been a popular substitute. At the time of writing, Lyttelton's new cruise terminal was scheduled to open late 2020, but it is expected Akaroa's expansive and spectacular harbour will also remain a popular anchorage.

◉ Sights

★**Giant's House** GARDENS
(www.thegiantshouse.co.nz; 68 Rue Balguerie; adult/child $20/10; ⊙11am-4pm Oct-Apr, to 2pm May-Sep) An ongoing labour of love by local artist Josie Martin, this whimsical garden is really one giant artwork, a combination of sculpture and mosaics that cascades down a hillside above Akaroa. Echoes of Gaudí and Miró can be found in the intricate collages of mirrors, tiles and broken china, and there are many surprising nooks and crannies to discover. Martin also exhibits her paintings and sculptures in the lovely 1880 house, the former residence of Akaroa's first bank manager.

★**Akaroa Museum** MUSEUM
(www.akaroamuseum.org.nz; cnr Rues Lavaud & Balguerie; ⊙10.30am-4pm) **FREE** An arduous post-quake revamp has rewarded Akaroa with a smart, contemporary regional museum. Learn about the various phases of the peninsula's settlement, from the Māori to the French, and view interesting temporary exhibitions. The 20-minute historical film screening in the adjacent restored courthouse is worth a look, too. Note the donation box.

Old French Cemetery CEMETERY
The first consecrated burial ground in Canterbury, this hillside monument makes for a poignant wander. Follow the trail (up the hill) off Rue Brittan.

St Patrick's Catholic Church CHURCH
(www.akaroacatholicparish.co.nz; 29 Rue Lavaud; ⊙8am-7pm) Akaroa's Catholic church (1863) is a cute, frilly edged old dear, featuring richly coloured stained glass imported from Stuttgart.

St Peter's Anglican Church CHURCH
(46 Rue Balguerie) Graciously restored in 2015, this 1864 Anglican gem features extensive exposed timbers, stained glass and a historic organ. Well worth a peek whether you're godly or not.

🏃 Activities

Akaroa Adventure Centre OUTDOORS
(☑03-304 7784; www.akaroaadventurecentre.co.nz; 74a Rue Lavaud; ⊙9am-5pm; ⊞) Rents sea kayaks and stand-up paddleboards (per hour/day $25/70), paddle boats (per hour $25) and bikes (per hour/day $15/60). Based at the i-SITE (p100); open later in summer (December through March).

Akaroa

👉 Tours

Akaroa Guided
Sea Kayaking Safari
KAYAKING

(📞 021 156 4591; www.akaroakayaks.com; per person from $130; 👶) 🏄 Paddle serenely around the harbour on these guided kayaking tours, which cater for beginners and experienced paddlers alike. Slip into the water at 7.30am for a three-hour sunrise safari, or if early starts aren't your thing, try the 11.30am highlights tour.

Eastern Bays
Scenic Mail Run
DRIVING

(📞 03-304 7784; tours $80; ⊙ departs 9am Mon-Fri) Travel along with the ex-conservation-ranger postie to visit isolated communities and bays on this 120km, five-hour mail delivery service. Departs from the i-SITE (p100); bookings are essential as there are only eight seats available.

Black Cat Cruises
BOATING

(📞 03-304 7641; www.blackcat.co.nz; Main Wharf; nature cruises adult/child $90/35, dolphin swims $185/155; 👶) As well as a two-hour nature cruise, Black Cat offers a three-hour 'swimming with dolphins' experience. Wetsuits and snorkelling gear are provided, plus hot showers back on dry land. Observers can tag along (adult/child $95/55) but only 12 people can swim per trip, so book ahead. Cruises have a 98% success rate in seeing Akaroa's compact Hector's dolphins, and an 83% success rate in actually swimming with them (there's a 25% refund if there's no swim). Note that while concerns over the impact of swimming tours on the bottlenose dolphins in the Bay of Islands have caused such tours to be banned there, they are still allowed here in Akaroa.

Akaroa Dolphins
BOATING

(📞 03-304 7866; www.akaroadolphins.co.nz; 65 Beach Rd; adult/child $92/50; ⊙ 12.45pm year-

Akaroa

round, plus 10.15am & 3.15pm Oct-Apr; 📷) Two-hour wildlife cruises on a comfortable 50ft catamaran, complete with a complimentary drink, home baking and, most importantly, the company of an extraordinary wildlife-spotting dog.

Fox II Sailing — BOATING
(📞0800 369 7245; www.akaroafoxsail.co.nz; Daly's Wharf; adult/child $90/45; ⊙departs 10.30am & 1.30pm Jan-May) 🌊 Enjoy the scenery, observe the marine wildlife, learn some history and try your hand at sailing on *Fox II*, a gaff-rigged ketch built in 1922..

✨ Festivals & Events

French Fest — FOOD & DRINK
(www.akaroa.com/akaroa-frenchfest; ⊙Oct) This Gallic-inspired, two-day celebration features historical re-enactments, markets, activities and – *bien sûr* – plenty of food and wine. It's held biennially in odd-numbered years.

Sleeping

Akaroa Top 10 Holiday Park — HOLIDAY PARK $
(📞03-304 7471, 0800 727 525; www.akaroa-holidaypark.co.nz; 96 Morgans Rd; sites $44-47, cabins & units $72-125; 🅿@🛜♨📷) Grandstand views of the harbour and peninsula hills are the main drawcard at this basic holiday park. Cabins and motel units are dated but tidy, while the facilities blocks are due for an overhaul.

La Rochelle — MOTEL $$
(📞0800 452 762, 03-304 8762; www.larochellemotel.co.nz; 1 Rue Grehan; d/q $170/260; 🅿🛜) Tidy, modern and reasonably priced, La Rochelle has a range of excellent motel units within walking distance of the main village. Each room has a kitchenette and opens up onto a small private patio or balcony. The friendly family owners have lots of local advice on what to do and where to eat.

Akaroa Village Inn — APARTMENTS $$
(📞03-304 1111; www.akaroavillageinn.co.nz; 81 Beach Rd; units $139-299; 🅿🛜) Located right on the harbour front, this sprawling complex offers one- and two-bedroom units of varying levels of luxury. The water-view apartments are obviously the pick of the bunch, but ask to see a few, as they are individually owned, and furnishings vary widely.

Tresori Motor Lodge — MOTEL $$
(📞03-304 7500; www.tresori.co.nz; cnr Rue Jolie & Church St; d $135-205; 🛜) There are 12 tidy, modern units at the friendly Tresori Motor Lodge set one block back from the esplanade. All have kitchenettes, but given the proximity to Akaroa's cafe and restaurant strip, you needn't worry about having to use them.

★ Beaufort House — B&B $$$
(📞03-304 7517; www.beauforthouse.co.nz; 42 Rue Grehan; r $395; ⊙closed Jun-Aug; 🅿🛜) Tucked away on a quiet street behind gorgeous

gardens, this lovely 1878 house is adorned with covetable artwork and antiques. Of the five individually decorated rooms only one is without an en suite, compensated by a large private bathroom with a claw-foot tub just across the hall. A lovely breakfast is included.

Eating

Peninsula General Store   CAFE, DELI **$**
(☑ 03-304 8800; www.peninsulageneralstore.co.nz; 40 Rue Lavaud; ⊘ 9am-4pm Wed-Sat, to 2pm Sun) ✎ Not only does this darling little corner shop sell fresh bread, organic local produce and groceries, it also does the best espresso in the village.

Akaroa Boucherie & Deli   DELI **$**
(67 Rue Lavaud; ⊘ 10am-5.30pm Mon-Fri, 9am-4pm Sat) ✎ A dream scenario for picnickers and self-caterers, this sharp butcher's shop and deli peddles all manner of local produce from bread, salmon, cheese and pickles, to delicious pies, smallgoods and, of course, meat.

★ Rona's   CAFE **$$**
(☑ 03-304 8533; www.ronas.co.nz; 74 Rue Lavaud; mains $18-22; ⊘ 7am-3.30pm Thu-Tue; ☑) ✎ Rona's menu is divided neatly into 'On Toast' and 'In a Bowl'. The Turkish poached eggs on ciabatta with chilli and yoghurt is a hearty favourite, while açai and poke bowls hint at healthy Hawaiian influences. Good-value snack options include damn fine grilled cheese sandwiches ($11 to $14).

Little Bistro   FRENCH **$$$**
(☑ 03-304 7314; www.thelittlebistro.co.nz; 33 Rue Lavaud; mains $28-42; ⊘ 5.30-11pm Tue-Sat) A decent bet for refined food, this place serves a classic bistro-style menu featuring local seafood, South Island wines and New Zealand craft beers. The menu changes seasonally, but usually includes favourites such as crusted lamb or local salmon. Across the seasonal menu there's a strong commitment to harnessing ingredients from around Banks Peninsula.

Drinking & Nightlife

Harbar   BAR
(www.facebook.com/harbarakaroa; 83 Rue Jolie; ⊘ 5-9.30pm) Sporadic opening hours, sometimes dictated by the seasons, weather and demand, should not stop you from trying for a sundowner at Akaroa's favourite waterside bar. There's no better location for a harbour-front tipple. Gourmet burgers, fish tacos and local Canterbury craft beers are other essen-

tial attractions. Check the Facebook page for notice of occasional live music.

☆ Entertainment

Akaroa Cinema & Café   CINEMA
(☑ 03-304 8898; www.cinecafe.co.nz; cnr Rue Jolie & Selwyn Ave; adult/child $17/12) Grab a beer and settle in to watch an art-house, classic or foreign flick with high-quality sound and projection.

❶ Information

Akaroa i-SITE & Adventure Centre (☑ 03-304 7784; www.akaroa.com; 74a Rue Lavaud; ⊘ 9am-5pm) A helpful hub offering free maps, info and bookings for activities, transport etc. Doubles as the post office.

❶ Getting There & Away

Daily shuttles with **Akaroa Shuttle** (☑ 0800 500 929; www.akaroashuttle.co.nz; adult/child one way $36/31, return $46/41) from Christchurch to Akaroa depart at 8.30am (hotel pick-ups available), returning to Christchurch at 3.45pm (late October to April). From May to late October, shuttles depart Christchurch at 9am and return at 4pm.

French Connection (☑ 0800 800 575; www.akaroabus.co.nz; adult/child return $50/30) has a year-round daily departure from Christchurch at 9am, returning from Akaroa at 4pm.

NORTH CANTERBURY

South of Kaikōura, a popular destination for wildlife watching, SH1 crosses the Hundalee Hills and heads into Hurunui District, an area known for its wine and for the thermal resort of Hanmer Springs. It's also the start of the Canterbury Plains, a vast, flat, richly agricultural area partitioned by distinctive braided rivers. The region is bounded to the west by the Southern Alps. If you're crossing into Canterbury from either Westport or Nelson, the most direct route cuts through the Alps on the beautiful Lewis Pass Hwy (SH7).

Kaikōura

POP 1970

Kaikōura is a pretty peninsula town backed by the snow-capped Seaward Kaikōura Range, 180km north from Christchurch. Few places in the world are home to such a variety of easily spottable wildlife: whales, dolphins, NZ fur seals, penguins, shearwaters, petrels and several species of albatross live in or pass by the area.

Marine animals are abundant here due to ocean-current and continental-shelf conditions: the seabed gradually slopes away from the land before plunging to depths of 1200m where the southerly current hits the continental shelf. This creates an upwelling of nutrients from the ocean floor into the feeding zone.

In 2016, the Kaikōura region was struck by a severe magnitude 7.8 earthquake, but following the re-establishment of badly damaged transport links, the town is once again easily reached and an essential destination for anyone with an interest in wildlife.

History

The Kaikōura region was heavily settled by Māori, with excavations showing that the area was a moa-hunter settlement about 800 to 1000 years ago. The name Kaikōura comes from 'kai' (food/eat) and 'kōura' (crayfish).

James Cook sailed past the peninsula in 1770, but didn't land. His journal states that 57 Māori in four double-hulled canoes came towards the *Endeavour*, but 'would not be prevail'd upon to put along side'.

In 1828 Kaikōura's beachfront was the scene of a tremendous battle. A northern Ngāti Toa war party, led by chief Te Rauparaha, bore down on Kaikōura, killing or capturing several hundred of the local Ngāi Tahu tribe.

Europeans established a whaling station here in 1842 and in 1859 a dodgy land deal swindled local Māori out of most of their land. The town remained a whaling centre until 1922, after which time farming and fishing sustained the community. It was in the 1980s that wildlife tours began to transform Kaikōura into a lively tourist town.

The 7.8 magnitude earthquake that struck the Kaikōura region just after midnight on 14 November 2016 was one of the largest and longest quakes to strike the country since European settlement. Fatalities were mercifully limited to two deaths, but the damage done to the landscape was staggering. Huge gashes were torn through farmland, new lakes were formed overnight when rivers were dammed, sections of the coastline were lifted by 8m, and parts of NZ's South Island moved more than 5m closer to the North Island.

◉ Sights

Kaikoura Museum MUSEUM
(☑03-319 7440; www.kaikoura-museum.co.nz; 96 West End; adult/child $12/6; ⊙10am-5pm) Housed

in a modern building designed to resemble a crayfishing pot, this whizz-bang museum illuminates the region's geology and natural and social histories with well-curated exhibitions. Highlights include the fossilised remains of a plesiosaur and a mosasaur, a holographic prisoner in a padded cell, and poignant displays on the 2016 earthquake.

Fyffe House HISTORIC BUILDING
(☑03-319 5835; www.fyffehouse.co.nz; 62 Avoca St; adult/child $10/free; ⊙10am-5pm Oct-Apr, to 4pm Thu-Mon May-Sep) Kaikōura's oldest surviving building and the last remaining part of the Waiopuka whaling station, Fyffe House's whale-bone foundations were laid in 1844. Fronted with a colourful garden, the little two-storey cottage offers a fascinating insight into the lives of early British settlers. Interpretive displays are complemented by historic objects (including the biggest moa egg ever found), while peeling wallpaper and the odd cobweb lend authenticity. There's a cute heritage-themed shop, too.

Point Kean Seal Colony WILDLIFE RESERVE
New Zealand fur seals can usually be spotted lazing around on the rocks at the end of the peninsula. Give them a wide berth (10m), and never get between them and the sea – they will attack if they feel cornered and can move surprisingly fast. Since the uplift of the coastline during the 2016 earthquake, the seals have moved further from the road and car park, so keep a close eye on tides.

Emporium Brewing BREWERY
(☑03-319 5897; www.emporiumbrewing.co.nz; 57a Beach Rd; ⊙10am-7pm daily Dec-Apr, Wed-Mon May-Nov) Fill up a takeaway rigger or buy bottles of Emporium's tasty brews at this simple taproom. There are also escape rooms (two players $70; book ahead) and an on-site minigolf course (adult/child $10/5). Check out the hole featuring the 'earthquake cows', three bovine locals that were stranded on a tiny 'island' of farmland for three days following the 2016 earthquake.

Activities

There's a safe swimming **beach** on the Esplanade. Decent **surfing** can be found around the area, particularly at **Mangamaunu Beach** (15km north of town), where there's a 500m point break. **Fishing** is a common obsession in Kaikōura, with local boaties offering trips starting from around $70; the i-SITE (p105) has a full list of operators.

Kaikōura

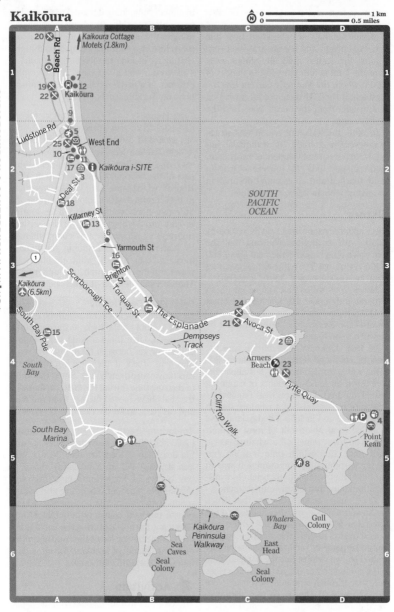

In 2019 the government announced funding of a 200km cycle route between Picton and Kaikōura to be known as the **Whale Trail** (www.thewhaletrail.nz); check the website for the most recent developments.

Kaikōura Peninsula Walkway WALKING

Starting from town, this must-do three- to four-hour loop heads out to Point Kean, along the cliffs to South Bay, then back to town over the isthmus (or in reverse, of course). En route you'll see fur seals and

Kaikōura

red-billed seagull and shearwater colonies. Lookouts and interesting interpretive panels abound. Collect a map at the i-SITE (p105) or follow your nose.

Kaikoura Coast Track HIKING
(☑03-319 2715; www.kaikouratrack.co.nz; 356 Conway Flat Rd, Ngaroma; adult/child $200/190) This easy two-day, 26km, self-guided hike across private farmland combines coastal and alpine views. The price includes two nights' cottage accommodation, including one night before actually beginning the walk, and pack transport; BYO sleeping bag and food, or pay extra for linen ($20), breakfast ($20), lunch ($20) and dinner ($50). It starts 45km south of Kaikōura.

Coastal Sports OUTDOORS
(☑03-319 5028; www.coastalsports.co.nz; 24 West End; ⊙9am-5.30pm Mon-Sat, 10am-4pm Sun, extended hours Oct–Easter) The friendly folk at this sports shop can hook you up with hire bikes (half/full day $30/40), surf gear (board and wetsuit $40 per day) and lots of local intel. There's also a good selection of hiking and outdoor gear to purchase.

☞ Tours

Wildlife tours are Kaikōura's speciality, particularly those involving whales (including sperm, pilot, killer, humpback and southern right), dolphins (Hector's, bottlenose and dusky – a particularly social species sometimes seen in the hundreds) and New Zealand fur seals. There's also plenty of birdlife, including albatrosses and blue penguins.

Your choices are boat, plane or helicopter. Aerial options are shorter and pricier, but allow you to see the whole whale, as opposed to just a tail, flipper or spout. During summer, book your tour a few weeks ahead, and allow some leeway for lousy weather.

Air Kaikoura WHALE WATCHING
(☑03 319 6579; www.airkaikoura.co.nz; Kaikoura Airport, 627 Kaikoura South Rd, Peketa; 30/40min flights $150/180) The local aero club offers professional and highly successful whale-watching tours plus scenic and charter flights. If you want to cross 'piloting a two-seater plane' off your bucketlist, it offers that too (20 minutes, $120).

Wings over Whales WHALE WATCHING
(☑03-319 6580; www.whales.co.nz; Kaikoura South Rd, Peketa; 30min flights adult/child $195/100; ⊙8am-5pm) Light-plane flights departing from Kaikōura Airport, 8km south of town on SH1. Whale-spotting success rate: 95%.

South Pacific Helicopters WHALE WATCHING
(☑03-319 5548; www.southpacificwhales.co.nz; 72 West End; per person $275-950) Offers a wide range of whale-watching and flightseeing trips by helicopter.

Kaikōura Helicopters WHALE WATCHING
(☑03-319 6609; www.worldofwhales.co.nz; Whaleway Station Rd) Reliable whale-spotting flights plus jaunts around the peninsula, Mt Fyffe and peaks beyond. Ask about flights taking in the area's spectacular post-earthquake landscapes from above.

Whale Watch Kaikoura WHALE WATCHING
(☑03-319 6767; www.whalewatch.co.nz; Whaleway Station Rd; tours adult/child $150/60) ✐ With knowledgeable guides and fascinating onboard animation, Kaikōura's biggest operator heads out on boat trips (with admirable frequency) in search of some of the big fellas. It'll refund 80% of your fare if no whales

are sighted (success rate: 95%). If this trip is a must for you, allow a few days' flexibility in case the weather turns to custard.

Albatross Encounter   BIRDWATCHING
(☑03-319 6777; www.albatrossencounter.co.nz; 96 Esplanade; adult/child $130/65; ☺tours 9am & 1pm year-round, plus 6am Nov-Apr) 🏊 Even if you don't consider yourself a bird-nerd, you'll love this boat trip providing close encounters with pelagic species such as shearwaters, shags, mollymawks and petrels. It's the various albatross species, however, that steal the show.

Seal Swim Kaikōura   WILDLIFE
(☑03-319 6182; www.sealswimkaikoura.co.nz; 58 West End; adult/child $120/80, viewing $60/40; ☺Nov-Apr) 🏊 Take a warmly wet-suited swim with Kaikōura's healthy population of playful seals – including very cute pups – on guided snorkelling tours (by boat).

Dolphin Encounter   WILDLIFE
(☑03-319 6777; www.encounterkaikoura.co.nz; 96 Esplanade; adult/child swim $180/165, observation $95/55; ☺tours 8.30am & 12.30pm year-round, plus 5.30am Nov-Apr) 🏊 Claiming NZ's highest success rate (over 90%) for locating dolphins, this operator runs DOC-permitted three-hour tours, which often encounter sizeable pods of sociable duskies. Note that while concerns over the impact of swimming tours on the bottlenose dolphins in the Bay of Islands have caused such tours to be banned, they are currently still allowed here.

Clarence River Rafting   RAFTING
(☑03-319 6993; www.clarenceriverrafting.co.nz; 1/3802 SH1, Clarence; half-day trips adult/child $140/80) Raft the rapids of the Clarence/ Waiau-Toa River and experience the spectacular uplift and changes to the landscape following the 2016 Kaikōura earthquake. Half-day trips incorporate 2½ hours on the water, while longer journeys include a three- to five-day adventure with wilderness camping. Based on SH1, 35km north of Kaikōura near the Clarence Bridge. Grade II; all gear provided.

Kaikoura Kayaks   KAYAKING
(☑03-319 7118; www.kaikourakayaks.nz; 19 Killarney St; 3hr tours adult/child $110/70; 🚐) Excellent, family-friendly, guided sea-kayak tours to view fur seals and explore the peninsula's coastline. Kayak fishing and other on-demand trips available, plus freedom kayak and paddleboard hire. Ask about visiting

Hope Springs, a sulphurous, bubbling section of the ocean that was discovered following the 2016 earthquake.

Seal Kayak Kaikoura   KAYAKING
(☑027 261 0124; www.sealkayakkaikoura.com; 18 Beach Rd; adult/child $95/69) Sightseeing, seal encounters, sunset tours and fishing trips using pedal kayaks, which provide the option of propelling the craft either with your arms or legs.

🛏 Sleeping

Albatross Backpacker Inn   HOSTEL $
(☑03-319 6090; www.albatross-kaikoura.co.nz; 1 Torquay St; dm/tw/d without bathroom from $32/79/84; P🐾🛜) 🏊 This arty backpackers resides in three sweet buildings, one a former post office. It's colourful and close to the beach but sheltered from the breeze. As well as a laid-back lounge with musical instruments for jamming, there are decks and verandas to spread out on.

Kaikoura Cottage Motels   MOTEL $$
(☑03-319 5599; www.kaikouracottagemotels.co .nz; 7 Old Beach Rd; units $150-180; ☺Sep-May; P🛜) This enclave of eight modern freestanding units looks mighty fine, surrounded by attractive native plantings. Oriented for mountain views, the spick-and-span self-contained units sleep four between an open-plan studio-style living room and one private bedroom. Lovely hosts seal the deal.

Anchor Inn   MOTEL $$
(☑03-319 5426; www.anchorinn.co.nz; 208 Esplanade; units from $175; P❄🛜) These sharp and spacious units are a pleasant 15-minute walk from town and about 10 seconds from the ocean. Choose between studios with either sea or garden views, or a one- or two-bedroom apartment, sleeping up to five people.

Bay Cottages   MOTEL $$
(☑03-319 7165; www.baycottages.co.nz; 29a South Bay Pde; cottages $150-170; P🛜) Here's a great-value option in South Bay, a few kilometres south of town, close to Kaikōura's new harbour. Five cottages sleeping up to four all feature a kitchen, lounge area and free Netflix. The surrounding area is private and quiet, and there's even a barbecue to grill your fish on.

Kaikoura Boutique Hotel   BOUTIQUE HOTEL $$$
(☑03-319 5748; www.kaikouraboutiquehotel.co.nz; 146 Esplanade; r $188-399; P🛜) Occupying a gorgeous heritage building halfway along the

Esplanade, this chic hotel has plush rooms in the main building and a brace of smaller rooms edging the back garden. Quirky art, excellent bathrooms, balconies with sea views and chandeliers like disco balls elevate the waterfront rooms out of the ordinary.

Lemon Tree Lodge   B&B $$$
(✍ 03-319 7464; www.lemontree.co.nz; 31 Adelphi Tce; r $320-380; ☻Nov-Mar; ☏) Enjoying superb ocean and mountain views, Lemon Tree Lodge combines four charming and stylish rooms in the main house with two quiet and secluded garden units. Our favourites are the Ocean View Suites with expansive windows and private balconies showcasing brilliant Pacific vistas. The well-travelled and friendly owners have plenty of great advice on how best to enjoy the region.

Nikau Lodge   B&B $$$
(✍ 03-319 6973; www.nikaulodge.com; 53 Deal St; d $220-280; ☻Oct-Mar; P☏) Expect high standards and grand-scale vistas at this beautiful B&B high on the hill. The five ensuite rooms are plush and comfy, with additional satisfaction arriving in the form of cafe-quality breakfasts accompanied by fresh local coffee. Good humour, home baking, free wi-fi, complimentary drinks, a hot tub and blooming gardens: you may want to move in.

✖ Eating

Beach House Cafe   CAFE $
(✍ 03-319 6035; 39 Beach Rd; mains $7-19; ☻7am-3.30pm; ☏) Beachy artwork fills the walls of this cosy cottage cafe but, despite the name, it's on the highway with no water in sight. Choose between tasty muffins and an excellent eggs Benedict for breakfast, and return at lunchtime for seafood chowder, souvlaki or burgers.

Kaikoura Seafood BBQ   SEAFOOD $
(✍ 027 376 3619; www.facebook.com/kkseafood bbq; Fyffe Quay; items $10-12; ☻9.30am-5pm Sun-Fri, 11am-3pm Sat, extended hours in summer) Conveniently located on the way to the Point Kean Seal Colony, this long-standing roadside barbecue is a great spot to sample local seafood, including crayfish (half from $45), chowder and whitebait fritters.

Cods & Crayfish   SEAFOOD $
(✍ 03-319 7899; www.codsncray.co.nz; 81 Beach Rd; mains $8-12; ☻8am-6pm; ☏) This combo fish shop and fast-food joint serves fish and chips, fish burgers and half crays grilled to order. Scoff them on the outdoor tables or at the nearby beach.

Hislops Wholefoods Cafe   CAFE $$
(✍ 03-319 6971; www.hislops-wholefoods.co.nz; 33 Beach Rd; breakfast $13-19, lunch $18-26; ☻8.30am-4pm; ☏✍) ✍ Organic ingredients shine at this long-established Kaikōura eatery. Come for breakfast on the shaded deck and enjoy blueberry hotcakes with blueberries, a chia bircher or coconut rice with harissa. Throughout the day, homestyle baking blurs the line between healthy and tasty, and the coffee is always good.

Pier Hotel   PUB FOOD $$
(✍ 03-319 5037; www.thepierhotel.co.nz; 1 Avoca St; lunch $15-36, dinner $24-36; ☻11am-late) Situated in a primo seaside spot, with panoramic views over the water to the Inland Kaikōura Range, this venerable pub (built in 1885) is a friendly place for a drink and respectable food, including crayfish and paua (abalone). You'll find beers here from Kaikōura's two craft breweries: Emporium Brewing and the Kaikōura Brewing Company.

Green Dolphin   EUROPEAN $$
(✍ 03-319 6666; www.greendolphin.co.nz; 12 Avoca St; mains $28-39; ☻5pm-late Tue-Sat) Under new ownership, this upmarket place continues to deliver French-style fare using top-quality local produce including crayfish, paua, beef, lamb and venison. There are also lovely homemade pasta dishes. Ask for a window table to enjoy the ocean and mountain views.

Zephyr   BISTRO $$$
(✍ 03-319 6999; www.zephyrrestaurant.co.nz; 40 West End; mains $34-37; ☻5.30pm-late Mon-Sat) Focusing on a concise and seasonal menu, Zephyr's modern dining room is a good place to enjoy seafood chowder, mushroom-crusted venison or local fish with a gourmet spin. The wine and beer list is equally focused and well curated.

❶ Information

Kaikōura i-SITE (✍ 03-319 5641; www.kaik oura.co.nz; West End; ☻9am-5pm, extended hours Dec-Mar) Helpful staff make tour, accommodation and transport bookings, and help with DOC-related matters.

❶ Getting There & Away

The 2016 earthquake resulted in 85 landslides on SH1 on either side of Kaikōura. Roadworks are still continuing, with lots of stop/go, one-way sections; expect delays.

BUS

InterCity (p294) buses stop outside the i-SITE, with two buses a day heading to/from Christchurch (from $22, three hours), Waipara (from $20, 1¾ hours), Blenheim (from $19, 1¾ hours) and Picton (from $25, 2½ hours).

TRAIN

KiwiRail's scenic Coastal Pacific (p92) service operates daily from October to April, heading to/from Picton (three hours), Blenheim (2½ hours) and Christchurch (3¼ hours); fares start from $59.

ⓘ Getting Around

Kaikoura Shuttles (☑ 03-319 6166; www.kaikourashuttles.co.nz) will run you around the local sights as well as to and from the airport. For local car hire, contact **Kaikoura Rentals** (☑ 03-319 3311; www.kaikourarentals.co.nz; 94 Churchill St).

Lewis Pass

The northernmost of the three main mountain passes connecting the West Coast to the east, 864m-high Lewis Pass is not as steep as the others (Arthur's and Haast), but the drive is arguably just as scenic. Vegetation comprises mainly beech (red and silver) and kowhai trees growing along river terraces. From Lewis Pass the highway wiggles east for 62km before reaching the turn-off to Hanmer Springs. Heading northeast to Kaikōura, the road travels through Waiau before reaching SH1.

⊙ Sights

Marble Hill   FOREST
(www.doc.govt.nz; SH7) Located within Lewis Pass Scenic Reserve, Marble Hill is home to one of NZ's most beautiful DOC camping grounds – a row of sites tucked into beech forest, overlooking a grassy meadow and encircled by snow-capped mountains.

This special place represents a landmark victory for NZ's conservation movement. Back in the 1970s, this significant forest was saved from the chop by a 341,159-signature petition known as the 'Maruia Declaration', which played a part in the Department of Conservation's establishment in 1987.

🏃 Activities

The area has some interesting **hikes**, passing through beech forest backed by snow-capped mountains, lakes and alpine tarns. Popular tracks include the **St James Walkway** (66km; four to five days) and those

through **Lake Sumner Forest Park**; see the DOC pamphlet *Lake Sumner & Lewis Pass* ($2). Subalpine conditions apply; make sure you sign the intentions books at the huts.

Maruia Springs   HOT SPRINGS
(☑ 03-523 8840; www.maruiahotsprings.co.nz; SH7; adult/child $40/18; ⊙ 8am-9pm) Maruia Springs is a small hot-spring resort on the banks of the Maruia River. The water temperature varies between 36°C and 42°C across a variety of pools, including outdoor rock pools, indoor baths, a sauna and a cold plunge pool. It's a magical setting during winter (June to September) but mind the sandflies in summer (December to March).

New owners have recently invested in the resort with renovations and improvements including new outdoor bathing pools and private spas. Accommodation is available in simple but cosy rooms (doubles from $249); guests have 24-hour access to the pools. There's also an overnight campground and a cafe with a sunny deck overlooking the river. It's 6km west of Lewis Pass.

ⓘ Getting There & Away

East West Coaches (☑ 03-789 6251; www.eastwestcoaches.co.nz) runs between Christchurch and Westport via the Lewis Pass daily except Saturday stopping at Maruia Springs and the St James Walkway.

Hanmer Springs

POP 840

Ringed by mountains, pretty Hanmer Springs has a slightly European feel, enhanced by the fact that many of the streets are named after English spa towns (Bath, Harrogate, Leamington). The town is the main thermal resort on the South Island, and it's a pleasantly low-key spot to indulge yourself, whether by soaking in hot pools, dining out, or being pampered in the spa complex. If that all sounds too soporific, fear not; there are plenty of family-friendly outdoor activities on offer, including a few to get the adrenaline pumping.

🏃 Activities

★**Hanmer Springs**
Thermal Pools   HOT SPRINGS
(☑ 03-315 0000; www.hanmersprings.co.nz; 42 Amuri Ave; adult/child $35/20, locker per 2hr $3; ⊙ 10am-9pm; 🛝) 🔄 Māori legend has it that these hot springs are the result of embers

from Mt Ngauruhoe on the North Island falling from the sky. Whatever their origin, visitors flock to Hanmer Springs year-round to soak in the warming waters. The main complex consists of a series of large pools of various temperatures.

There are also smaller, adult-only land-scaped rock pools, a freshwater 25m lap pool, private thermal pools, a cafe and an adjacent spa. Kids of all ages will love the water slides – including the biggest in NZ, Conical Hill – and the whirl-down-the-plughole-thrill of the Superbowl ($10).

Hanmer Horse Trekking   HORSE RIDING

(☑ 022 462 1435; www.hanmerhorsetrekking.com; 1/2hr $80/120, half/full day $160/350; 🚸) 🖉 Treks exploring the forest and mountain scenery around Hanmer. Riders of all levels of experience are catered for and longer ex-cursions venture into the rugged and remote St James Station area.

Hanmer Forest Park   HIKING, MOUNTAIN BIKING

(www.visithurunui.co.nz; 🚸) 🖉 Trampers and mountain bikers will find plenty of room to move within the 130 sq km expanse of forest abutting Hanmer Springs. The easy Wood-land Walk starts 1km up Jollies Pass Rd and goes through Douglas fir, poplar and red-wood stands before joining Majuba Walk, which leads to Conical Hill Lookout and then back towards town (1½ hours).

The Waterfall Track is an excellent half-day tramp starting at the end of McIntyre Rd. The i-SITE (p110) stocks a *Forest Park Walks* booklet and a mountain-biking map (both $3).

Hanmer Springs Spa   SPA

(☑ 03-315 0000, 0800 873 529; www.thespa hanmersprings.nz; 42 Amuri Ave; ⊙ 10am-9pm) If you're looking to be pampered, you've come to the right place. Hanmer Springs Spa offers every kind of treatment you would expect from an international-standard spa, includ-ing facials (from $110), hot-stone massages ($180) and full-body treatments ($320).

Mt Lyford Alpine Resort   SKIING

(☑ 03-366 1220, 027 471 0717; www.mtlyford.co.nz; day passes adult/child $83/40; ⊙ lifts 9am-4pm) Around 60km from both Hanmer Springs and Kaikōura, this is more of a 'resort' than most NZ ski fields, with accommodation and eating options. There's a good mix of runs and a terrain park.

A shuttle service runs from Mt Lyford village (a 45-minute drive from Hanmer

Hanmer Springs

Springs) during the season – enquire at Hanmer Springs Adventure Centre.

Hanmer Springs Ski Area   SKIING

(☏027 434 1806; www.skihanmer.co.nz; daily lift passes adult/child/family $60/30/130; 🚌) Only 17km from town via an unsealed road, this small complex has runs to suit all levels of ability. The Hanmer Springs Adventure Centre provides shuttles during the ski season (adult/child return $40/32) and also has gear for rent.

Hanmer Springs Adventure Centre   ADVENTURE SPORTS

(☏0800 368 7386, 03-315 7233; www.hanmer adventure.co.nz; 20 Conical Hill Rd; ⏰9am-5pm; 🚌) Offers quad biking (from $139), mountain-bike shuttles to the top of Jack's Pass ($125), clay-shooting ($59) and archery ($45). You can also book local tours and rent mountain bikes (from $25/60 per hour/day), fishing rods ($29 per day), camping equipment and ski/snowboard gear.

Hanmer Springs Attractions   ADVENTURE SPORTS

(☏03-315 7046, 0800 661 538; www.hanmer springsattractions.nz; 839 Hanmer Springs Rd; ⏰9am-5.30pm) Bungy off a 35m-high bridge ($169), jetboat the Waiau Gorge (one hour, adult/child $125/70), explore the Waiau River by raft (two hours, adult/child $169/99), get dirty on a quad bike (two hours, adult/child $169/99), or self-drive an off-road buggy (two hours, $249). The activities base is next to the bridge near the turn-off from SH7, but there's also a **booking office** (☏0800 661 538, 03-315 7346; www.hanmer springsattractions.nz; 12 Conical Hill Rd; ⏰9am-5pm) in town.

A free shuttle bus is available from your accommodation to the activities base.

🛏 Sleeping

Hanmer Springs has a wide range of accommodation options, from basic camping through to luxury B&Bs and swanky apartments. If you're planning on staying awhile, check out websites like www.alpineholiday homes.co.nz and www.hanmerholiday homes.co.nz for local rentals.

Kakapo Lodge   HOSTEL $

(☏03-315 7472; www.kakapolodge.co.nz; 14 Amuri Ave; dm $33, d with/without bathroom from $100/80; 🅿🛜) The YHA-affiliated Kakapo has a cheery owner, a roomy kitchen and lounge, chill-busting underfloor heating and a 1st-floor sundeck. Bunk-free dorms (some with bathrooms) and spotless double rooms are available.

Jack in the Green   HOSTEL $

(☏03-315 5111; www.jackinthegreen.co.nz; 3 Devon St; sites per person $20, dm $32, d with/without bathroom $92/76; 🅿🛜) This charming converted old home is a 10-minute walk from the town centre. Large rooms (no bunks), relaxing gardens and a cosy lounge area are the main drawcards. For extra privacy, book an en suite garden 'chalet'. Excellent mountain bikes can be rented ($35 per day).

Hanmer Springs Top 10   HOLIDAY PARK $

(☏0800 904 545, 03-315 7113; www.hanmer springstop10.co.nz; 5 Hanmer Springs Rd; sites $44-54, units with/without bathroom from $154/99; 🅿@🛜🚌) This family-friendly park is just a few minutes' walk from the town's eponymous pools. Kids will love the playground and jumping pillow. Take your pick from basic cabins (BYO everything) to attractive motel units with everything supplied. Extremely comfortable new two-bedroom apartments were opened in late 2019.

★ Woodbank Park Cottages   COTTAGE $$

(☏03-315 5075; www.woodbankcottages.co.nz; 381 Woodbank Rd; d $190-225; 🅿❄) Nestled among the trees, these two plush cottages are a six-minute drive from Hanmer but feel a million miles away. Decor is crisp and modern, with wrap-around wooden decks that come equipped with gas barbecues and rural views. Log-burning fireplaces and well-stocked kitchens seal the deal.

Drifters Inn   LODGE $$

(☏03-315 7554; www.driftersinn.co.nz; 2 Harrogate St; d from $120; 🅿🛜) Compact and spotless rooms combine with spacious shared facilities, including a modern and well-equipped kitchen and comfortable lounge, providing guests at Drifters Inn with the advantages of both a motel and a lodge. Save money by cooking up a storm and you'll have more holiday funds for Hanmer's attractions and activities. Book online for good discounts.

Chalets Motel   MOTEL $$

(☏03-315 7097; www.chaletsmotel.co.nz; 56 Jacks Pass Rd; d $170-210; 🅿🛜) Soak up the mountain views from these tidy, reasonably priced, free-standing wooden chalets, set on the slopes behind the town centre. All chalets have full kitchens; the larger spa unit is the pick of the bunch.

OFF THE BEATEN TRACK

MOLESWORTH STATION

Filling up 1807 mountainous sq km between Hanmer Springs and Blenheim, Molesworth Station is NZ's largest farm, with the country's largest cattle herd (up to 10,000). It's also an area of national ecological significance and the entire farm is now administered by DOC (Map p319; ☑03-572 9100; www.doc.govt.nz; Gee St, Renwick).

Visits are usually only possible when the Acheron Rd through the station is open from November to early April, weather permitting; check with DOC or at the Hanmer Springs i-SITE (p110). Note that the gates are only open from 7am to 7pm. Pick up DOC's *Molesworth Station* brochure from the i-SITE or download it from the website.

Highlights of a visit include wild and spectacular scenery, scree-covered mountains, expansive river valleys and windswept tussocky slopes.

Overnight camping (adult/child $6/3) is permitted in certain areas (no open fires allowed). There are also a couple of basic DOC huts (adult/child $5/2.50).

Molesworth Heritage Tours (☑027 201 4536, 03-315 7401; www.molesworth.co.nz; tours $235-770; ☺Oct-May) leads 4WD coach trips to the station from Hanmer Springs. Day tours include a picnic lunch, but there's also a five-hour 'no frills' option. From the Blenheim side, **Molesworth Tours** (☑03-572 8025; www.molesworthtours.co.nz) offers one- to four-day all-inclusive heritage and 4WD trips ($220 to $1487), as well as four-day fully supported (and catered) mountain-bike adventures (from $1460).

Cheltenham House　　　　　B&B **$$$**
(☑03-315 7545; www.cheltenham.co.nz; 13 Cheltenham St; r $255-295; P☎) This large 1930s house has room for both a billiard table and a grand piano. There are four art-filled suites in the main house and two in cosy garden cottages. Cooked gourmet breakfasts are delivered to the rooms and wine is served in the evening.

St James　　　　　APARTMENT **$$$**
(☑03-315 5225, 0508 785 2637; www.thestjames.co.nz; 20 Chisholm Cres; d $245-295, apt from $320; P❋☎) Luxuriate in a stylish modern apartment with all the mod cons, including an iPod dock and fully equipped kitchen. Sizes range from studios to two-bedroom apartments; most have mountain views.

Eating

Hanmer Springs Bakery　　　　　BAKERY **$**
(☑03-315 7714; 24 Conical Hill Rd; pies $5-6, rolls from $6; ☺6am-4pm) In peak season queues stretch out the door for this humble bakery's meat pies and filled rolls.

Coriander Leaf　　　　　INDIAN **$$**
(☑03-315 7616; www.corianderleaf.co.nz; Chisholm Cres; mains $16-22; ☺noon-2pm & 5-10pm Tue-Sun; ☑) Spice up your life at this brightly painted North Indian restaurant complete with *bhangra*-beats soundtrack. There are plenty of tasty lamb, chicken and seafood dishes to choose from, plus a fine vegetarian selection.

Takeaways are especially popular and we can recommend the vegetable samosas.

Powerhouse Cafe　　　　　CAFE **$$**
(☑03-315 5252; www.powerhousecafe.co.nz; 8 Jacks Pass Rd; mains $16-28; ☺7.30am-2pm; ☑) Delicious cakes and good-quality coffee are on the menu at this local favourite, tucked away off the main street. Power up with a huge High Country breakfast or try the Highland Fling – caramelised, whisky-infused porridge topped with banana. Lunch offerings are equally palatable.

No. 31　　　　　MODERN NZ **$$$**
(☑03-315 7031; www.restaurant-no31.nz; 31 Amuri Ave; mains $37-40; ☺5-11pm) Substantial servings of good-quality, albeit conservative, cuisine are on offer in this pretty wooden cottage. The upmarket ambience befits the prices, though you're also paying for the location, directly opposite the hot springs. Canterbury lamb and venison feature along with craft beer and wine from the nearby Waipara region. Book ahead on weekends.

Drinking & Nightlife

Monteith's Brewery Bar　　　　　PUB
(☑03-315 5133; www.mbbh.co.nz; 47 Amuri Ave; ☺9am-11pm) This large, slightly worn pub is the town's busiest watering hole. The kitchen serves decent pub-style meals all day (mains $22 to $35). Live musicians kick off from 4pm Sundays.

ℹ Information

Hanmer Springs i-SITE (☑ 03-315 0020, 0800 442 663; www.visithanmersprings.co.nz; 40 Amuri Ave; ⊙10am-5pm) Books transport, accommodation and activities.

ℹ Getting There & Away

The **main bus stop** is near the corner of Amuri Ave and Jacks Pass Rd.

Hanmer Connection (☑ 0800 242 663, 03-382 2952; www.hanmerconnection.co.nz; adult/child one way $30/20, return $50/30) Runs a daily bus to/from Christchurch via Waipara and Amberley, departing Christchurch at 9am and Hanmer Springs at 4.30pm.

Hanmer Tours & Shuttle (☑ 03-315 7418; www.hanmertours.co.nz) Runs daily buses to/from Culverden ($15, 30 minutes), Waikari ($15, 45 minutes), Waipara ($20, one hour), Amberley ($20, one hour), Christchurch city centre ($35, two hours) and Christchurch Airport ($45, two hours).

Waipara Valley

POP 5200

Conveniently stretched along SH1 60km north of Christchurch, this resolutely rural area makes for a tasty pit stop. The valley's warm dry summers followed by cool autumn nights have proved a winning formula for growing grapes, olives, hazelnuts and lavender. While Waipara accounts for less than 3% of NZ's vines, it nonetheless produces some of the country's finest cool-climate wines, including riesling, pinot noir and gewürztraminer.

Of the region's 30 or so wineries, around a dozen have cellar doors to visit, four with restaurants. To explore the valley's bounty fully, pick up a copy of the *North Canterbury Wine Region* map (www.northcanterburywines.co.nz). Otherwise, you'll spot several of the big players from the highway. The area's main towns are tiny Waipara and slightly larger Amberley, but you're likely to spend most of your time in the countryside between the two.

◉ Sights

★ Pegasus Bay   WINERY

(☑ 03-314 6869; www.pegasusbay.com; Stockgrove Rd; ⊙restaurant noon-4pm Thu-Mon, tastings 10am-5pm daily) It's fitting that Waipara Valley's premier winery should have the loveliest setting and one of Canterbury's best restaurants (mains $36 to $43). Verdant manicured gardens set the scene, but it's the contemporary NZ menu and luscious paired wines that steal the show.

Black Estate   WINERY

(☑ 03-314 6085; www.blackestate.co.nz; 614 Omihi Rd, SH1; ⊙10am-5pm, shorter hours Jun-Oct) 🍷 Perched on a hillside overlooking the valley, this striking black barn is home to some excellent drops – try the pinot noirs from the winery's three nearby vineyards, each of which have a distinctive terroir of their own. The attached light-filled restaurant offers stunning views and food that champions local producers (mains $32 to $38).

Brew Moon   BREWERY

(☑ 03-314 8036; www.brewmoon.co.nz; 12 Markham St, Amberley; ⊙3pm-late Wed-Fri, from noon Sat & Sun) The variety of craft beers available to taste at this wee brewery never wanes. Stop in to fill a rigger (flagon) to take away, or sup an ale alongside a tasty woodfired pizza in the cosy bar (pizzas $16 to $22). Our favourite brew is the Wolf of Washington American Pale Ale and there's always interesting seasonal beers on offer.

🛏 Sleeping & Eating

Old Glenmark Vicarage   B&B $$$

(☑ 03-314 6775; www.glenmarkvicarage.co.nz; 161 Church Rd, Waipara; d $230, barn d $250; 🅿🛜🏊) There are two divine options in this beautifully restored vicarage: cosy up with bed and breakfast in the main house, or lounge around in the character-filled, converted barn that sleeps up to six (perfect for families or groups). The lovely gardens and swimming pool are a blessed bonus.

Little Vintage Espresso   CAFE $

(20 Markham St, Amberley; breakfast $10-21; ⊙7am-4pm Mon-Fri, to 2pm Sat) This petite whitewashed cottage just off SH1 has the best coffee in town, with food to match. All-day breakfasts, gourmet sandwiches and delectable homemade cakes are all on offer.

Pukeko Junction   CAFE, DELI $$

(☑ 03-314 8834; www.pukekojunction.co.nz; 458 Ashworths Rd, SH1, Leithfield; mains $7.50-20; ⊙9am-4.30pm Tue-Sun; 🍴) A deservedly popular roadside stop, this bright, friendly cafe in Leithfield (south of Amberley) serves delicious bakery fare, like gourmet sausage rolls and tarts filled with goat's cheese, leek and walnut. The attached shop stocks an excellent selection of local wines.

ⓘ Getting There & Away

Hanmer Connection (📞 0800 242 663; www.hanmerconnection.co.nz) One daily bus stops in Waipara on request on the road between Hanmer Springs ($20, 50 minutes) and Christchurch ($20, 1¼ hours).

Hanmer Tours & Shuttle (📞 03-315 7418; www.hanmertours.co.nz) Runs a daily shuttle to/from Hanmer Springs ($20), Christchurch city centre ($15) and Christchurch Airport ($25).

InterCity (📞 03-365 1113; www.intercity.co.nz) Coaches head to/from Picton (from $34, five hours), Kaikōura (from $18, 1¾ hours) and Christchurch (from $15, one hour) at least daily.

CENTRAL CANTERBURY

While the dead-flat agricultural heartland of the Canterbury Plains blankets the majority of the region, there's plenty of interest for travellers in the west, where the Southern Alps soar to snowy peaks. Here you'll find numerous ski fields and some brilliant wilderness walks.

Unusually for NZ, the most scenic routes avoid the coast, with most places of interest accessed from one of two spectacular roads: the Great Alpine Highway (SH73), which wends from the Canterbury Plains deep into the mountains and over to the West Coast, and the Inland Scenic Route (SH72), which skirts the mountain foothills on its way south towards Tekapo.

Selwyn District

POP 56,400

Named after NZ's first Anglican bishop, this largely rural district has swallowed an English map book and regurgitated place names such as Lincoln, Darfield and Sheffield. Yet any illusions of Britain are quickly dispelled by the looming presence of the snow-capped Southern Alps, providing a rugged retort to 'England's mountains green'.

The highly scenic Great Alpine Hwy pierces the heart of the district on its journey between Christchurch and the West Coast. On the Canterbury Plains, it passes through the small settlement of Springfield, notable for a monument to local Rewi Alley (1897–1987), who became a great hero of the Chinese Communist Party.

Selwyn's numerous ski fields may not be the country's most glamorous, but they provide plenty of thrills for ski bunnies. **Porters** (📞 03-318 4731; www.skiporters.co.nz; daily lift passes adult/child weekend $99/69, midweek $79/49; ⊙ lifts 9am-4pm) is the main commercial field; club fields include **Mt Olympus** (📞 03-318 5840; www.mtolympus.co.nz; daily lift passes adult/child $75/35), **Cheeseman** (📞 03-344 3247, snow phone 03-318 8794; www.mtcheeseman.co.nz; daily lift passes adult/child $79/39; ⊙ lifts 9am-4.30pm, shorter hours midweek), **Broken River** (📞 03-318 8713; www.brokenriver.co.nz; daily lift passes adult/child $75/35; ⊙ lifts 9am-4pm), **Craigieburn Valley** (📞 03-318 8711; www.craigieburn.co.nz; daily lift passes adult/child $75/35) and **Temple Basin** (📞 03-377 7788; www.templebasin.co.nz; daily lift passes adult/child $69/35).

🏃 Activities

Rubicon Valley Horse Treks   HORSE RIDING (📞 03-318 8886; www.rubiconvalley.co.nz; 534 Rubicon Rd, Springfield; 👶) Operating from a sheep farm 6km from Springfield, Rubicon offers a variety of horse treks to suit both beginner and advanced riders, including hour-long farm rides ($55), two-hour river or valley rides ($98), two-hour sunset rides ($120) and six-hour mountain trail rides ($285).

🍴 Sleeping & Eating

Smylies Accommodation   HOSTEL $ (📞 03-318 4740; www.smylies.co.nz; 5653 West Coast Rd, Springfield; dm/s/d $38/60/90; 🅿🛜) 🍃 This well-seasoned, welcoming, YHA-associated hostel has a piano, manga comics galore, a DVD library and a wood-burning fire in the large communal kitchen. As well as traditional dorms, there are also self-contained motel units ($105) and a three-bedroom cottage ($280). Winter packages (June to September), including ski-equipment rental and ski-field transport, are available.

Famous Sheffield Pie Shop   BAKERY $ (📞 03-318 3876; www.sheffieldpieshop.co.nz; 51 Main West Rd, Sheffield; pies $5-7; ⊙ 6.30am-4pm Mon-Fri, from 7am Sat & Sun) Blink and you'll miss this stellar roadside bakery, a purveyor of more than 20 varieties of pies, from traditional beef to more experimental flavour combinations – think whisky and venison, or chicken, camembert and apricot. While you're here, snaffle a bag of the exemplary Afghan biscuits – such cornflakey, chocolatey goodness!

ⓘ Getting There & Away

Public transport is limited in Selwyn District, so it's best to have your own transport.

Arthur's Pass

POP 30

Having left the Canterbury Plains at Springfield, the Great Alpine Hwy heads over Porter's Pass through the mountainous folds of the Torlesse and Craigieburn Ranges and into Arthur's Pass.

Māori used this pass to cross the Southern Alps long before its 'discovery' by Arthur Dobson in 1864. The Westland gold rush created the need for a dependable crossing over the Alps from Christchurch, and the coach road was completed within a year. Later, the coal and timber trade demanded a railway, duly completed in 1923.

Today it's an amazing journey. Successive valleys display their own character, not least the spectacular braided Waimakariri River Valley, encountered as you enter the national park proper.

Arthur's Pass village is 4km from the actual pass. At 900m, it's NZ's highest-altitude settlement and a handy base for tramps, climbs and skiing. The weather, however, is a bit of a shocker. Come prepared for rain.

○ Sights

★ Arthur's Pass
National Park   NATIONAL PARK
(www.doc.govt.nz) Straddling the Southern Alps, known to Māori as Ka Tiritiri o Te Moana (Steep Peak of Glistening White), this vast alpine wilderness became the South Island's first national park in 1929. Of its 1144 sq km, two-thirds lies on the Canterbury side of the main divide; the rest is in Westland. It is a rugged, mountainous area, cut by deep valleys, and ranging in altitude from 245m at the Taramakau River to 2408m at Mt Murchison.

There are plenty of well-marked day tramps throughout the park, especially around Arthur's Pass village. Pick up a copy of DOC's *Discover Arthur's Pass* booklet to read about popular tramps, including: the Arthur's Pass Walkway, a reasonably easy track from the village to the Dobson Memorial at the summit of the pass (2½ hours return); the one-hour return walk to Devils Punchbowl falls; and the steep walk to beautiful views at Temple Basin (three hours return). More challenging, full-day options include the Bealey Spur track and the classic summit hike to Avalanche Peak.

The park's many multiday trails are mostly valley routes with saddle climbs in between, such as Goat Pass and Cass-Lagoon Saddles Tracks, both two-day options. These and the park's longer tracks require previous hiking experience as flooding can make the rivers dangerous and the weather is extremely changeable. Always seek advice from DOC before setting out.

Cave Stream Scenic Reserve   CAVE
(www.doc.govt.nz) Near Broken River Bridge, 2km northeast of Castle Hill, you'll find this 594m-long cave. As indicated by the information panels in the car park, the walk through the cave is an achievable adventure, but only with a foolproof torch and warm clothing, and definitely only if the water level is less than waist deep where indicated. Heed all notices, take necessary precautions and revel in the spookiness.

Failing that, just wander around the 15-minute loop track for a gander at the surrounds, including limestone formations that featured in the *Chronicles of Narnia* movie.

Castle Hill/Kura Tawhiti   LANDMARK
Scattered across lush paddocks around 33km from Springfield, these limestone formations reach up to 30m high, and look so other-worldly they were named 'treasure from a distant land' by early Māori. A car park (with toilets) provides easy access to a short walk into the strange rock garden (10 minutes), favoured by rock climbers and photographers.

🛏 Sleeping

Camping is possible near the basic Avalanche Creek Shelter (www.doc.govt.nz; SH73; adult/child $8/4; P), opposite the DOC, where there's running water, tables, a sink and toilets. You can also camp for free at Klondyke Corner (www.doc.govt.nz; SH73; adult/child $8/4) or Hawdon Shelter (www.doc.govt.nz; Mount White Rd, off SH37), 8km and 24km south of Arthur's Pass respectively, where facilities are limited to toilets and stream water for boiling. If you're not camping, there are plenty of accommodation options in Arthur's Pass village and surrounds.

Mountain House YHA   HOSTEL $
(☑ 03-318 9258; www.trampers.co.nz; 83 Main Rd; dm/s/d/tr/q $34/94/94/120/144; P 🖵) This well-kept hostel has cosy dorms and private rooms and the efficient and enthusiastic manager can provide extensive local hiking information. Note all rooms share bathroom facilities. The family room set-up ($238) sleeping up to seven people is a good option for groups.

Arthur's Pass Village B&B B&B $$

(☑ 021 394 776; www.arthurspass.org.nz; 72 School Tce; d $160-180; ℗ 🛜) This lovingly restored former railway cottage is now a cosy B&B, with two well-appointed guest rooms. Breakfast on free-range bacon and eggs, pancakes and freshly baked bread, while enjoying the company of the friendly owners. Delicious home-cooked dinners ($40) and afternoon snacks and nibbles ($10) are also available.

Arthur's Pass Motel & Lodge MOTEL $$

(☑ 03-3189099; www.arthurspass-accommodation. com; 107 Main Rd; d/apt $169/226; ℗ 🛜) Stylishly decorated options at this diverse complex include modern bedrooms sharing a fully equipped kitchen, lounge and dining area – a good way to meet other travellers – and an apartment with a separate bedroom and en suite bathroom. Note the property is not available to families with children. Check online for good discounts.

Arthur's Pass Alpine Motel MOTEL $$

(☑ 03-318 9233; www.apam.co.nz; 52 Main Rd; d $130; ℗ 🛜) On the southern approach to the village, this cabin-style motel complex combines the homey charms of yesteryear with the beauty of double-glazing and the advice of active, enthusiastic hosts.

Flock Hill Lodge MOTEL, HOSTEL $$

(☑ 03-318 8196; www.flockhill.co.nz; Great Alpine Hwy, Craigieburn Valley; dm/d $35/100, cottages $170-300; ℗ @ 🛜) Near Craigieburn Forest Park and Lake Pearson, this historic high-country sheep station offers a genuine taste of rural life in its Shearers' Quarters bunkhouse, set in a picturesque farmyard. Tidy cottage units enjoy a more manicured garden setting.

Wilderness Lodge LODGE $$$

(☑ 03-318 9246; www.wildernesslodge.co.nz; Cora Lynn Rd, Bealey; half board s $595-810, d $980-1300; ℗ 🛜) 🖉 For tranquillity and natural grandeur, this midsize alpine lodge tucked into beech forest just off the highway takes some beating. It's a class act, with a focus on immersive, nature-based experiences. Two daily guided activities (such as hiking and kayaking) are included in the tariff, along with gourmet breakfast and dinner.

✖ Eating

There are only two mediocre dining options in the village – stock up on self-catering supplies before you leave the plains.

Arthur's Pass Store & Cafe CAFE $

(85 Main Rd; breakfast & lunch $7-24; ☉ 8am-5pm; 🛜) If you want to stock up on supplies, this is your best chance, with odds-on for egg sandwiches, hot chips, decent coffee, basic groceries and petrol.

Wobbly Kea CAFE $$

(www.wobblykea.co.nz; 108 Main Rd; mains $25-27; ☉ 11am-7pm Mon-Thu, to 8pm Fri & Sat) Don your big-eatin' pants for brunch, lunch or dinner at the Wobbly Kea, which offers a short menu of simple but tasty home-cooked meals, such as meaty stew and curry. Pricey pizza ($33) is available to take away.

ⓘ Information

DOC Arthur's Pass Visitor Centre (☑ 03-318 9211; www.doc.govt.nz; Main Rd; ☉ 8.30am-4.30pm) Helpful staff can provide advice on suitable tramps and the all-important weather forecast. Detailed route guides and topographical maps are also available, as are locator beacons for hire. Before you leave, log your trip details on AdventureSmart (www.adventuresmart.org.nz) via the on-site computer.

ⓘ Getting There & Away

Fill your fuel tank before you leave Springfield (or Hokitika or Greymouth, if you're coming from the west). There's a pump at Arthur's Pass Store but it's expensive and only operates from 8am until 5pm.

Buses depart from various stops all a stone's throw from the store – check with the bus company for the latest information.

Atomic Shuttles (☑ 03-349 0697; www.atomictravel.co.nz) From Arthur's Pass buses head to/from Christchurch ($40, 2¼ hours), Springfield ($40, one hour), Lake Brunner ($30, 50 minutes) and Greymouth ($40, 1¼ hours).

East West Coaches (☑ 0800 142 622; www.eastwestcoaches.co.nz) Buses stopping at Arthur's Pass head to/from Christchurch ($45, 2¾ hours) and Greymouth ($35, 1¾ hours).

TranzAlpine (☑ 0800 872 467, 04-495 0775; www.greatjourneysofnz.co.nz/tranzalpine; fares from $89) One train daily in each direction stops in Arthur's Pass, heading to/from Springfield (1½ hours) and Christchurch (2½ hours), or Lake Brunner (one hour) and Greymouth (two hours).

Methven

POP 1700

Methven is busiest in winter (June to September), when it fills up with snow bunnies heading to nearby Mt Hutt. At other times tumbleweeds don't quite blow down the main street – much to the disappointment of the wannabe gunslingers arriving for the raucous October rodeo. Over summer (December to March) it's a low-key and affordable base for trampers and mountain bikers heading into the spectacular mountain foothills.

🏃 Activities

Most people come to Methven for the nearby ski slopes, but there are plenty of other activities nearby. Ask at the i-SITE about local walks (including the town heritage trail and Methven Walk/Cycleway) and longer tramps, horse riding, mountain biking, fishing, clay-shooting, archery, golfing, scenic helicopter flights, and jetboating through the nearby Rakaia Gorge.

Rakaia Gorge Walkway　　　WALKING
(www.doc.govt.nz; Rakaia Gorge Bridge, SH72) Following river terraces into the upper gorge, this well-graded tramp passes through forest and past the historic ferryman's cottage and coal mines, with plenty of pretty picnic spots. The highlight is the lookout at the end with epic alpine views. The walk is four hours return, but a shorter tramp to the lower lookout (one hour return) is also worthwhile.

Black Diamond Safaris　　　SKIING
(027 450 8283; www.blackdiamondsafaris.co.nz) Provides access to uncrowded club ski fields by 4WD. Prices start from $150 for transport, safety equipment and familiarisation, while $295 includes a lift pass, lunch and a guide.

Methven Heliski　　　SKIING
(03-302 8108; www.methvenheli.co.nz; Main St; 5-run day trips $1110) Epic guided, all-inclusive backcountry heliski trips, featuring five runs averaging drops of 750 to 1000 vertical metres.

Discovery Jet　　　BOATING
(0800 538 2628, 021 538 386; www.discoveryjet.co.nz; Rakaia Gorge Bridge, SH72; adult/child $99/75;) A speedy, exhilarating way to explore the Rakaia Gorge is via jetboat. Discovery Jet, based downstream of the bridge, offers a 45-minute blood-pumping ride with twists, turns and 360-degree spins, all with a backdrop of majestic mountain scenery. Shorter joyrides are also available.

Skydiving Kiwis　　　SKYDIVING
(0800 359 549; www.skydivingkiwis.com; Ashburton Airport, Seafield Rd) Offers tandem jumps from 6000ft ($249), 9000ft ($299) and 13,000ft ($360) departing Ashburton Airport.

Shuttles leave from central Christchurch if you don't have your own transport.

🛏 Sleeping

Methven is a hub for skiers headed to nearby Mt Hutt, and there is a wide range of accommodation available in town for all budgets. Book ahead during the ski season, especially for budget accommodation. Prices can rise significantly in winter (June to September); some places close in the summer months from December through February

Alpenhorn Chalet　　　HOSTEL $
(03-302 8779; www.alpenhorn.co.nz; 44 Allen St; dm $30, d $65-85;) This small, inviting home has a leafy conservatory housing an indoor spa pool, a log fire and complimentary espresso coffee. Bedrooms are spacious and brightly coloured, with lots of warm, natural wood; one double room has an en suite bathroom.

Mt Hutt Bunkhouse　　　HOSTEL $
(03-302 8894; www.mthuttbunkhouse.co.nz; 8 Lampard St; dm $32, d $72-80, cottage $280-350;) Enthusiastic on-site owners run this basic, well-equipped, bright and breezy hostel. There's a comfy lounge, and a large garden sporting a barbecue and a volleyball court. The cottage (sleeps up to 18) is economical for large groups.

Big Tree Lodge　　　HOSTEL $
(03-302 9575; www.bigtreelodge.co.nz; 25 South Belt; dm $30-40, d $75-90, apt $110-130;) Once a vicarage, this relaxed hostel has bunk-free dorms and wood-trimmed bathrooms. Tucked just behind is Little Tree Studio, a self-contained unit sleeping up to four people.

**Rakaia Gorge
Camping Ground**　　　CAMPGROUND $
(03-302 9353; 6686 Arundel-Rakaia Gorge Rd; sites per adult/child under 12yr $10/free) There are no powered sites here, only toilets, showers and a small kitchen shelter, but don't let that put you off. This is the best camping ground for miles, perched picturesquely above the ultra-blue Rakaia River, and a good base for exploring the area. Amenities closed May to September.

Redwood Lodge　　　HOSTEL, LODGE $$
(03-302 8964; www.redwoodlodge.co.nz; 3 Wayne Pl; s $65-75, d $115-129;) Expect a warm welcome and no dorms at this charming and peaceful family-friendly lodge. Most rooms are en suite, and bigger rooms can be reconfigured to accommodate

families. The large shared lounge is ideal for resting ski-weary limbs.

Whitestone Cottages   RENTAL HOUSE **$$$**
(⏵03-928 8050; www.whitestonecottages.co.nz; 3016 Methven Hwy; cottages $275; Ⓟ🛜) When you just want to spread out, cook a meal, do your laundry and have your own space, these four large free-standing cottages in leafy grounds are just the ticket. Each sleeps six in two en suite bedrooms. Rates are for two people; each extra person is $35.

🍴 Eating & Drinking

★ Dubliner   BISTRO **$$**
(⏵03-302 8259; www.dubliner.co.nz; 116 Main St; meals $19-34; ⏲5pm-late daily mid-Jun–Mar, Wed-Sat only Apr–mid-Jun) This atmospheric Irish bar and restaurant is housed in Methven's lovingly restored old post office. Great food includes pizza, Irish stew and other hearty fare suitable for washing down with a pint of beer. It's very popular and booking for dinner on Friday and Saturday nights is recommended.

Topp Country Cafe   CAFE **$$**
(⏵03-302 9393; 45 Forest Dr; mains $15-25; ⏲8am-3pm Mon-Fri, from 9am Sat & Sun) The Topp Twins are NZ entertainment legends and this cafe owned by Dame Lynda Topp and her wife Donna is a fine addition to Methven's dining scene. Check out the cosy rural vibe and ease into the day with a stonking cooked breakfast or come back for a burger for lunch. A mid-afternoon coffee and caramel slice is also recommended.

Aqua   JAPANESE **$$**
(⏵03-302 8335; 112 Main St; mains $9-23; ⏲11.30am-2pm & 5.30-9pm Thu-Sun) A ski-season stalwart with unpredictable hours at other times (ring ahead), this tiny restaurant sports kimono-clad waitresses and traditional Japanese cuisine, including *yakisoba* (fried noodles), ramen (noodle soup) and izakaya-style small plates to share, with ice-cold beer or warming sake. Booking ahead for dinner is recommended and note credit cards are not accepted.

Blue Pub   PUB
(⏵03-302 8046; www.thebluepub.co.nz; 2 Barkers Rd; ⏲11am-late; 🛜) Have a drink at the bar, crafted from a huge slab of native timber, or tuck into robust meals in the quieter cafe (mains $28 to $36). Afterwards, challenge the locals to a game of pool or listen to regular live music. Check the website for what's on.

MT HUTT

One of the highest ski areas in the southern hemisphere **Mt Hutt** (⏵0800 697 547; www.mthutt.co.nz; daily lift passes adult/child $119/59; ⏲9am-4pm) has one of the largest skiable areas of any of NZ's commercial fields (365 hectares). The ski field is only 26km from Methven but in wintry conditions the drive takes about 40 minutes; allow two hours from Christchurch. Road access is steep: be extremely cautious in lousy weather.

Methven Travel runs shuttle buses from Methven during the ski season ($25). Return bus transport from Christchurch ($60) is also available when the mountain is open for skiing. Check the website for departure details. Half of the terrain is suitable for intermediate skiers, with a quarter each for beginning and advanced skiers. The longest run stretches for 2km. Other attractions include chairlifts, heliskiing and wide-open faces that are good for learning to snowboard. The season usually runs from mid-June to mid-October.

☆ Entertainment

Cinema Paradiso   CINEMA
(⏵03-302 1975; www.cinemaparadiso.co.nz; 112 Main St; adult/child $17/12; ⏲Wed-Sun) Quirky 35-seat cinema with an art-house slant.

ℹ Information

Medical Centre (⏵03-302 8105; The Square, Main St; ⏲8.30am-5.30pm)

Methven i-SITE (⏵03-302 8955; www.methvenmthutt.co.nz; 160 Main St; ⏲8.30am-5.30pm Mon-Fri Jun-Sep, 9am-5pm Mon-Fri Oct-May, 11am-3pm Sat & Sun year round; 🛜) Ask staff here about local walks and other activities. Methven Travel are also based here for transport needs and there's a convenient guest services desk for Mt Hutt during winter.

ℹ Getting There & Away

Methven Travel (⏵03-302 8106, 0800 684 888; www.methventravel.co.nz; 160 Main St) Runs shuttles between Methven and Christchurch Airport (adult/child $47/30) three times a week from October to June, increasing to three times daily during the ski season. Also runs shuttles up to Mt Hutt ski field from June to September (adult return $25, kids free with paying adult). Also return transport from Christchurch to Mt Hutt ($60) in winter when the mountain is open for skiing.

Mt Somers

POP 2650

The small settlement of Mt Somers sits on the edge of the Southern Alps, beneath the mountain of the same name. The biggest drawcard to the area is the **Mt Somers track** (26km), a two-day tramp circling the mountain, linking the popular picnic spots of Sharplin Falls and Woolshed Creek. Trail highlights include volcanic formations, Māori rock drawings, deep river canyons and botanical diversity. The route is subject to sudden weather changes, so precautions should be taken.

There are two DOC huts on the track: Pinnacles Hut and Woolshed Creek Hut (adult/child $15/7.50). Hut tickets and information are available at Mt Somers General Store and Staveley Store.

🛏 Sleeping & Eating

Mt Somers Holiday Park   HOLIDAY PARK **$**
(🖉 03-303 9719; www.mountsomers.co.nz; 87 Hoods Rd; sites $20-32, cabins with/without bathroom $90/60; **P**) This small, friendly-vibe park offers pleasant sites in leafy grounds along with standard (bring your own linen) and en suite cabins. All guests have access to basic shared kitchen and lounge areas.

Staveley Store & Cafe   CAFE **$**
(🖉 03-303 0859; www.staveleystore.co.nz; 2 Burgess Rd, Staveley; mains $6-13; ⊙ 9am-4.30pm) Call into this cute little country store for the best coffee for miles around, as well as tasty lunch rolls, delectable cakes, gourmet ice cream and locally sourced groceries. Also sells hut tickets for the Mt Somers track.

Stronechrubie   BISTRO **$$**
(🖉 03-303 9814; www.stronechrubie.co.nz; cnr Hoods Rd & SH72; mains bistro $18-30, restaurant $39-41; ⊙ bistro 5.30pm-late Thu-Sat, restaurant 6.30pm-late Wed-Sat, Sun lunch by appointment; 🛜) This motel complex offers comfortable chalets overlooking bird-filled gardens (doubles $140 to $160), but it's the up-and-coming culinary hub that's the main draw here. Enjoy a more formal meal in the lauded, long-standing restaurant, or head to the flash bar and bistro for modern, tapas-style fare alongside lovely wines and craft beer. Reservations recommended.

ⓘ Information

Mt Somers General Store (🖉 03-303 9831; 61 Pattons Rd; ⊙ 7am-5.30pm Mon-Fri, 8am-5.30pm Sat, 9am-5pm Sun) Hut tickets for the Mt Somers track, plus information, petrol and basic groceries.

ⓘ Getting There & Away

There are no public buses to/from Mt Somers village, so you will need your own transport.

SOUTH CANTERBURY

After crossing the Rangitata River into South Canterbury, SH1 and the Inland Scenic Route (SH72) narrow to within 8km of each other at the quaint town of Geraldine. Here you can choose to take the busy coastal highway through the port city of Timaru, or continue inland on SH79 into Mackenzie Country, where NZ's tallest peaks rise above powder-blue lakes.

The Mackenzie Basin is a wild, tussock-strewn bowl at the foot of the Southern Alps, carved out by ancient glaciers. It takes its name from the legendary James 'Jock' McKenzie, who ran his stolen flocks in this then-uninhabited region in the 1840s.

Director Sir Peter Jackson made the most of this rugged and untamed landscape while filming the *Lord of the Rings,* choosing Mt Cook Village as the setting for Minas Tirith and a sheep station near Twizel as Gondor's Pelennor Fields.

Timaru

POP 29,000

Trucking on along the SH1 through Timaru, travellers could be forgiven for thinking that this small port city is merely a handy place for food and fuel halfway between Christchurch and Dunedin. Drop the anchors, people! Straying into the CBD reveals a remarkably intact Edwardian precinct boasting some good dining and interesting shopping, not to mention a clutch of cultural attractions and lovely parks, all of which sustain at least a day's stopover.

The town's name comes from the Māori name Te Maru, meaning 'place of shelter'. No permanent settlement existed here until 1839, when the Weller brothers set up a whaling station. The *Caroline,* a sailing ship that transported whale oil, gave the picturesque bay its name.

◉ Sights

★ Aigantighe Art Gallery GALLERY

(www.aigantighe.co.nz; 49 Wai-iti Rd; ⊙10am-4pm Tue-Fri, from noon Sat & Sun) **FREE** One of the South Island's largest public galleries, this 1908 mansion houses a notable collection of NZ and European art across various eras, alongside temporary exhibitions staged by the gallery's ardent supporters. The Gaelic name means 'at home' and is pronounced 'egg-and-tie'.

Sacred Heart Basilica CHURCH

(7 Craigie Ave, Parkside) Roman Catholic with a definite emphasis on the Roman, this beautiful neoclassical church (1911) impresses with multiple domes, Ionian columns and richly coloured stained glass. Its architect, Francis Petre, also designed the large basilicas in Christchurch (now in ruins) and Ōamaru. Inside, there's an art-nouveau feel to the plasterwork, which includes intertwined floral and sacred-heart motifs. There are no set opening hours; try the side door.

Caroline Bay Park PARK, BEACH

(Marine Pde) Fronting the town, this expansive park ranges over an Edwardian-style garden under the Bay Hill cliff, then across broad lawns to low sand dunes and the beach itself. It has something for everyone between the playground, skate park, soundshell, ice-cream kiosk, minigolf, splash park and myriad other attractions. Don't miss the **Trevor Griffiths Rose Garden** (Caroline Bay Park, Marine Pde), a triumphant collection of heritage varieties, and consider an evening picnic making the most of the late sun. If you're lucky enough to spot a seal or penguin on the beach, do keep your distance.

Te Ana Māori Rock Art Centre MUSEUM

(☑03-684 9141; www.teana.co.nz; 2 George St; adult/child $22/11, tours $130/52; ⊙10am-3pm) Passionate Ngāi Tahu guides bring this innovative multimedia exhibition about Māori rock paintings to life. You can also take a three-hour excursion (departing at 2pm, November to April) to see isolated rock art in situ; prior booking is essential.

Timaru Botanic Gardens GARDENS

(cnr King & Queen Sts; ⊙8am-dusk) Established in 1864, these gardens are a restful place to while away an hour or two, with a pond, lush lawns, shady trees, a playground and vibrant floral displays. With luck you'll arrive during rhododendron or rose bloom time. Enter from Queen St, south of the city centre.

South Canterbury Museum MUSEUM

(http://museum.timaru.govt.nz; Perth St; admission by donation; ⊙10am-4.30pm Tue-Fri, 1-4.30pm Sat & Sun) Historic and natural artefacts of the region are displayed here. Highlights include the Māori section, a full-scale model of a ship's cabin from 1859, and a replica of the aeroplane designed and flown by local pioneer aviator and inventor Richard Pearse. It's speculated that his mildly successful attempts at flight came before the Wright brothers' famous achievement in 1903.

✸ Festivals & Events

Timaru Festival of Roses CULTURAL

(www.festivalofroses.co.nz; ⊙Nov/Dec) Featuring a market day, concerts and family fun, this week-long celebration capitalises on Timaru's obsession with all things rosy. The festival is held annually for one week at the end of November or early December.

⊨ Sleeping

Timaru Top 10 Holiday Park HOLIDAY PARK $

(☑03-684 7690; www.timaruholidaypark.co.nz; 154a Selwyn St, Marwiel; sites $40-45, cabins & units $70-140; ℗◉◧) ✐ Tucked away in the suburbs, this excellent holiday park has clean, colourful amenities and a host of accommodation options throughout mature, leafy grounds. Helpful staff go out of their way to assist with local advice and bookings.

Grosvenor HOTEL $

(☑03-687 9190; www.thegrosvenor.co.nz; 26 Cains Tce; s/d from $95/125; ℗◉) In a heritage building right in the centre of town, this good-value budget hotel offers clean, no-frills rooms with comfy beds, fridge and TV. The quirky Mondrian-styled corridors give the place a hip vibe. Try and book ahead as it's popular.

Glendeer Lodge B&B $$$

(☑03-686 9274; www.glendeer.co.nz; 51 Scarborough Rd, Scarborough; d $210-260; ℗◉) ✐ Set on 5 acres 4km south of Timaru, this purpose-built lodge is a peaceful option away from busy SH1. Walk to the lighthouse, relax in the garden watching fallow deer nibbling the paddock, then retire to the plush, self-contained lodge offering three en suite rooms. The owners' fly-fishing guiding business lends a wilderness vibe.

CHRISTCHURCH & CANTERBURY TIMARU

Timaru

Timaru

✗ Eating & Drinking

Arthur Street Kitchen
CAFE $

(www.arthurskitchen.co.nz; 8 Arthur St; mains $11-21; ⊙7am-5pm Mon-Fri, 9am-3pm Sat; 🖉) Timaru's hippest coffee house follows the recipe for success: namely great coffee, contemporary cafe fare, good tunes and a mix of arty inside and sunny outside seating. Made with flair and care, the food offering includes grainy salads, refined sandwiches and pastry treats, plus an à la carte breakfast and lunch menu.

★ Oxford
MODERN NZ $$

(☎03-688 3297; www.theoxford.co.nz; 152 Stafford St; mains $31-34; ⊙10am-late Mon & Wed-Fri, 9.30am-late Sat & Sun) This sophisticated corner restaurant honours its 1925 building with stylish monochrome decor and a feature wall commemorating the day Timaru went bust. The menu offers high-class comfort food, starring local produce like venison, beef and salmon, while an alluring drinks list encourages you to pop in for pinot and cheese, or a glass of sticky wine alongside golden syrup pudding.

Street Food Kitchen   STREET FOOD **$$**
(📞 03-686 6036; www.streetfoodkitchen.co.nz; 2 George St; shared plates $14-17; ⏱11.30am-late Tue-Sun) Asian and Mediterranean flavours underpin the concise menu of shared plates at Street Food Kitchen. Highlights include the steamed bao buns with crispy pork belly and the pumpkin and Parmesan arancini. Good cocktails and Timaru's best selection of NZ craft beers also make it a fine spot for an end-of-the-day drink.

Speight's Ale House   PUB
(📞 03-686 6030; www.timarualehouse.co.nz; 2 George St; ⏱11.30am-late; 📶) The pub most likely to be registering a pulse of an evening, this enterprise – housed in an interesting 1870s stone warehouse – redeems its overly ostentatious branding with friendly staff and a sunny courtyard, including bean bags for slumping in.

ⓘ Information

Timaru Information Centre (📞 03-687 9997; www.southcanterbury.org.nz; 2 George St; ⏱10am-4pm Mon-Fri, to 3pm Sat & Sun; 📶) Across from the train station (trains in this area only carry freight, not passengers), the visitor centre shares its building with the Te Ana Māori Rock Art Centre (p117). There's free wi-fi throughout Timaru's CBD and Caroline Bay Park.

ⓘ Getting There & Away

AIR
Air New Zealand (📞 0800 737 000; www. airnewzealand.co.nz) Flies from Timaru's Richard Pearse Airport to/from Wellington at least once daily.

BUS
Atomic Shuttles (📞 03-349 0697; www.atomictravel.co.nz) Stops by the Timaru Information Centre twice daily, en route to Christchurch ($30, 2½ hours), Ōamaru ($25,1¼ hours) and Dunedin ($30, 2¾ hours).

Budget Buses & Shuttles (📞 03-615 5119; www.budgetshuttles.co.nz; ⏱Mon-Sat) Offers door-to-door shuttles to Christchurch ($55).

InterCity (📞 03-365 1113; www.intercity.co.nz) Stops outside the train station.

DESTINATION	FARES ($) FROM	DURATION (HR)
Christchurch	20	2½
Dunedin	34	3
Gore	51	6
Ōamaru	23	1

Inland & Mackenzie Country

Heading to Queenstown and the southern lakes from Christchurch means a turn off SH1 onto SH79, a scenic route towards the high country and the Aoraki/Mt Cook National Park's eastern foothills. The road passes through Geraldine and Fairlie before joining SH8, which heads over Burkes Pass to the sparkling blue Lake Tekapo.

The expansive high ground from which the scenic peaks of Aoraki/Mt Cook National Park escalate is known as Mackenzie Country, after the legendary James 'Jock' McKenzie, who ran his stolen flocks in this then-uninhabited region in the 1840s. When he was finally caught, other settlers realised the potential of the land and followed in his footsteps. The first people to traverse the Mackenzie were the Māori, trekking from Banks Peninsula to Otago hundreds of years ago.

Peel Forest

POP 180

Tucked away between the foothills of the Southern Alps and the Rangitata River, Peel Forest is a small but important remnant of indigenous podocarp (conifer) forest. Many of the totara, kahikatea and matai trees here are hundreds of years old and are home to an abundance of birdlife, including riflemen, kereru (wood pigeons), bellbirds, fantails and grey warblers. There's a small settlement, mostly to serve the visitors who come to tramp, ride and raft the beautiful surrounds.

A road from nearby Mt Peel sheep station leads to Mesopotamia, the run of English writer Samuel Butler in the 1860s. His experiences here partly inspired his famous satire *Erewhon* ('nowhere' backwards, almost).

⊙ Sights

St Stephen's Church   CHURCH
(1200 Peel Forest Rd) Sitting in a pretty glade right next to the general store, this gorgeous little Anglican church (1885) has a warm wooden interior and some interesting

stained glass. Look for St Francis of Assisi surrounded by NZ flora and fauna (get the kids to play spot the tuatara).

Activities

Big Tree Walk (30 minutes return) is a gentle stroll through the forest to a particularly fine example of a totara, which is 31m tall, has a circumference of 9m and is over 1000 years old. There are also trails to **Emily Falls** (1½ hours return), **Rata Falls** (two hours return) and **Acland Falls** (one hour return). Pick up the *Peel Forest Area* brochure from the Green Man at Peel Forest cafe or download it from the DOC website (www.doc.govt.nz).

★**Rangitata Rafts**　　　　　RAFTING
(☑0800 251 251; www.rafts.co.nz; Rangitata Gorge Rd; ☺Oct-May; ☝) Begin your adventure in the stupendously beautiful braided Rangitata River valley before heading on an exhilarating two-hour ride through the gorge's Grade V rapids ($219, minimum age 15). A gentler alternative route encounters only Grade II rapids ($179, minimum age six).

Peel Forest Horse Trekking　　HORSE RIDING
(☑03-696 3703; www.peelforesthorsetrekking. co.nz; 105 Dennistoun Rd; 1hr/2hr/half day/full day $65/120/220/320, multiday $800-1450; ☝) Ride through lush forest on short rides or multiday treks with experienced guides. Accommodation packages are available in conjunction with Peel Forest Lodge.

Hidden Valleys　　　　　　RAFTING
(☑03-696 3560; www.hiddenvalleys.co.nz; ☺Sep-May) They may be based in Peel Forest but this crew doesn't limit itself to rafting the Rangitata. Multiday expeditions head to the Waimakariri, Waiau, Landsborough, and Grey and Waiatoto Rivers, peaking with a five-day trip ($1750) down the Clarence near Kaikōura. Shorter, child-friendly trips on the Rangitata River are also available (adult $120 to $200, child $80 to $160).

Sleeping & Eating

★**Peel Forest DOC Campsite**　CAMPGROUND $
(☑03-696 3567; www.thegreenmanpeelforest.co. nz; sites per adult/child powered $23/11.50, unpowered $20/10, cabins $50-80) Near the Rangitata River, around 3km north of Green Man at Peel Forest store, this lovely camping ground is equipped with basic two- to four-berth cabins (bring your own sleeping bag), hot showers and a kitchen. Check in at the store. The campsite is only open from mid-September to April.

Peel Forest Lodge　　　　LODGE $$$
(☑03-696 3703; www.peelforestlodge.co.nz; 96 Brake Rd; d $400, additional adult/child $45/25; P☎) This delightful log cabin hidden in the forest has four rooms and sleeps eight people. It only takes one booking at a time, so you and your posse will have the place to yourself. The cabin is fully self-contained, but meals can be arranged, as can horse treks, rafting trips and other explorations of the beautiful surrounds.

Green Man at Peel Forest　　　CAFE $$
(☑03-696 3567; www.thegreenmanpeelforest.co.nz; 1202 Peel Forest Rd; mains lunch $6-19, dinner $21-30; ☺cafe 9.30am-4.30pm daily, bar 6pm-late Wed-Sat; ☎) Your one-stop shop for basic groceries, hut tickets, internet access and DOC campsite bookings. The attached cafe has good espresso coffee and does a roaring trade in toasties and burgers come lunchtime. There's occasionally live music in the evenings; check the website for dates. Make a night of it with decent craft beer.

❶ Getting There & Away

InterCity (p122) buses will get you as close as Geraldine, but you'll need your own transport or a lift to get to Peel Forest itself.

Geraldine

POP 2300

Consummately Canterbury in its dedication to English-style gardening, pretty Geraldine has a village vibe and an active arts scene. In spring (September to November), duck behind the war memorial on Talbot St to the River Garden Walk, where green-fingered locals have gone completely bonkers planting azaleas and rhododendrons. If you've still got energy to burn, try the well-marked trails in Talbot Forest on the town fringe.

◎ Sights & Activities

Geraldine Historical Museum　　MUSEUM
(☑03-693 7028; 5 Cox St; ☺10am-3pm Mon-Sat, from 12.30pm Sun) FREE Occupying the photogenic Town Board Office building (1885), this cute little museum tells the town's story with an eclectic mix of exhibits, including an extensive collection of photographs.

**Geraldine Vintage Car &
Machinery Museum**　　　　MUSEUM
(☑03-693 8756; 178 Talbot St; adult/child $15/ free; ☺9.30am-4pm Oct-May, 10am-4pm Sat & Sun Jun-Sep) Rev-heads will enjoy this lovingly

maintained vintage car collection, featuring a 1907 De Dion-Bouton and a gleaming 1926 Bentley. There's also a purpose-built Daimler used for the 1954 royal tour, plus some very nice Jags, 1970s muscle cars and all sorts of farm machinery.

Big Rock Canyons   ADVENTURE SPORTS
(☏0800 244 762; www.bigrockcanyons.co.nz; tours from $219; ⊗Oct-Apr) Offers slippy, slidey day-long adventures in the Kaumira Canyon near Geraldine, as well as in five other canyons with varying degrees of difficulty. Pickup is available in Geraldine or Christchurch.

🛏 Sleeping

Geraldine Top 10 Holiday Park   HOLIDAY PARK $
(☏03-693 8147; www.geraldinetop10.co.nz; 39 Hislop St; sites $39-46, d $60-142; P@🛜👶) 🏊 This top-notch holiday park is set amid well-established parkland right in the centre of town. Tidy accommodation ranges from budget cabins to plusher motel units, plus there's a TV room and playground.

Rawhiti Backpackers   HOSTEL $
(☏03-693 8252; www.rawhitibackpackers.co.nz; 27 Hewlings St; dm/s/tw/d $38/54/84/84; P🛜) On a hillside on the edge of town, this former maternity hospital is now a sunny and spacious hostel with well-maintained communal areas, bright rooms with colourful bed linen, a lemon tree and three cute cats. The guests' kitchen is spacious and modern, and the hosts have plenty of ideas for exploring the region.

★Vicarage   BOUTIQUE HOTEL $$$
(www.thevicaragegeraldine.co.nz; 69 Talbot St; r/ste $250/395; P🛜) Housed in a restored Anglican vicarage, this charming boutique hotel is a very relaxing place to stay. Named after former vicars of Geraldine, the seven rooms and suites are stylish and modern, with heritage design features blending with contemporary decor. In-room facilities include Nespresso coffee machines, and it's just metres to good eating at the associated Barker's Foodstore & Eatery.

🍴 Eating

Long overdue to be lauded 'Cheese & Pickle Capital of NZ', Geraldine is paradise for self-caterers. Numerous artisan producers line the Four Peaks Plaza; seek out a bag of Heartland potato chips, made just down the road. There's an excellent **farmers market** (Talbot St, St Mary's Church car park; ⊗9am-

12.30pm Sat Oct-Apr) 🏊, and, if you're not in the mood to DIY, there are also a few good cafes in town.

Talbot Forest Cheese   DELI $
(www.talbotforestcheese.co.nz; Four Peaks Plaza, Talbot St; cheeses $5-10; ⊗9am-5pm; 🏊) This little shop not only showcases the plethora of cheeses made on-site (including delicious Parmesan- and Gruyère-style ones), it doubles as a deli with all you need for a tasty picnic. Fans of funky cheeses should check out the Mt Talbot Blue.

Verde   CAFE $
(☏03-693 9616; 45 Talbot St; mains $9-18; ⊗9am-4pm; 🏊) Down the lane beside the old post office and set in beautiful gardens, this excellent cafe is one of Geraldine's best eateries. Drop in for coffee and cake, or linger over a lazy lunch of salads, soup, sandwiches and the like.

Barker's Foodstore & Eatery   DELI $$
(☏03-693 9727; www.barkersfoodstore.nz; 71 Talbot St; mains $15-25; ⊗8.30am-4.30pm; 🏊) Relocated in late 2019 to include an excellent cafe and boutique accommodation, Barker's is a long-standing producer of favourite fruity preserves, including raspberry jam, tamarillo chutney and cherry juice. It's the perfect spot to stock up on picnic essentials or enjoy excellent cafe fare. Try the lamb burger or a tasting platter ($25 to $45) with a selection of Barker's products.

Running Duck   BURGERS $$
(☏03-693 8320; www.therunningduck.co.nz; 1 Peel St; burgers $8-19; ⊗8am-4pm Mon, Wed & Thu, to 8pm Fri, 9am-4pm Sat & Sun; 👶) This hip burger joint is the perfect setting to feast on tasty gourmet burgers and crispy fries, topped with chef Al's special spicy sauce. There's a fridge full of NZ craft beers and an adjacent food truck open on summer evenings serving fish and chips.

☆ Entertainment

Geraldine Cinema   CINEMA
(☏03-693 8118; www.geraldinecinema.co.nz; 78 Talbot St; adult/child $12/8) Snuggle into an old sofa to watch a Hollywood favourite or an art-house surprise at this ageing dame, built in 1924. There's also occasional live music, usually with a folk, blues or country spin.

ℹ Information

Geraldine Visitor Information Centre (☏03-693 1101; www.southcanterbury.org.nz; 38 Waihi Tce; ⊗8am-5.30pm) Located inside the Kiwi Country visitor complex. Don't miss the world's biggest woollen jumper (sweater) hanging on the wall.

ℹ Getting There & Away

Budget Buses & Shuttles (☑ 03-615 5119; www.budgetshuttles.co.nz; ⊙ Mon-Sat) Offers a door-to-door shuttle to Christchurch ($65).

InterCity (☑ 03-365 1113; www.intercity.co.nz) Runs daily services to the following:

DESTINATION	FARES ($) FROM	DURATION (HR)
Christchurch	37	2¼
Cromwell	47	4¾
Lake Tekapo	25	1¼
Mt Cook Village	111	3
Queenstown	49	5¾

Fairlie

POP 720

Leafy Fairlie describes itself as 'the gateway to the Mackenzie', but in reality this wee, rural town feels a world away from tussocky Mackenzie Country over Burkes Pass, to the west. The bakery and picnic area make it a good lunchtime stop.

◉ Sights & Activities

The information centre can provide details on nearby **hiking and mountain-biking** tracks. The main ski resort, **Mt Dobson** (☑ 03-281 5509; www.mtdobson.co.nz; daily lift passes adult/child $88/43), lies in a 3km-wide treeless basin 26km northwest of Fairlie. There's also a club ski field 29km northwest at **Fox Peak** (☑ 03-685 8539, snow phone 03-688 0044; www.foxpeak.co.nz; daily lift passes adult/child $70/20) in the Two Thumb Range.

Fairlie Heritage Museum   MUSEUM
(www.fairlieheritagemuseum.co.nz; 49 Mt Cook Rd; adult/child $10/free; ⊙ 9.30am-5pm; 🚗) A somewhat dusty window on to rural NZ of old, this museum endears with its farm machinery, model aeroplanes, dodgy dioramas and eclectic ephemera. Highlights include the homespun gyrocopter, historic cottage and new automotive wing featuring tractors. The attached Swiss-owned cafe has superb cakes and delicious hot chocolate.

🛏 Sleeping & Eating

Musterer's   MOTEL $$
(☑ 03-685 8284; www.musterers.co.nz; 9 Gordon St; units $95-205; 🅿🛜) On the western edge

of Fairlie, these stylish self-contained cottages afford all mod cons with the bonus of a shared barbecue area and woolshed 'lounge' – complete with donkeys, goats and a pony to pet. Units are plush and spacious; the larger ones come complete with their own wood-fired hot tub ($45 extra) for a stargazing soak.

★**Fairlie Bakehouse**   BAKERY $
(☑ 03-685 6063; www.liebers.co.nz; 74 Main St; pies $5-8.50; ⊙ 7.30am-4.30pm Mon-Sat, to 4pm Sun; 🚗🛜) Famous for miles around and the top-ranking reason to stop in Fairlie, this superb bakery turns out exceptional pies, including the legendary salmon and bacon. The ultimate steak pie with cheese and mushroom is also a winner. On the sweet side, American doughnuts and raspberry cheesecake feature alongside Kiwi classics such as custard squares and cream buns. An essential stop.

ℹ Information

Fairlie Heartland Resource & Information Centre (☑ 03-685 8496; www.fairlienz.com; 67 Main St; ⊙ 10am-4pm Mon-Fri) Has maps and brochures, and can advise on nearby activities.

ℹ Getting There & Away

InterCity (☑ 03-365 1113; www.intercity.co.nz) runs daily services to the following:

DESTINATION	FARES ($) FROM	DURATION (HR)
Christchurch	41	3¼
Cromwell	43	4
Lake Tekapo	19	¾
Mt Cook Village	87	2½
Queenstown	47	5

Lake Tekapo

POP 370

Born of a hydropower scheme completed in 1953, today Tekapo is booming off the back of a tourism explosion, although it has long been a popular tour-bus stop on the route between Christchurch and Queenstown. Its popularity is well deserved: the town faces out across the turquoise lake to a backdrop of snow-capped mountains.

Such splendid Mackenzie Country and Southern Alps views are reason enough to linger, but there's infinitely more to see if you wait till dark. In 2012 the Aoraki Mackenzie area was declared an International Dark Sky Reserve, one of only 12 in the world, and Tekapo's Mt John – under light-pollution-free

AORAKI MACKENZIE INTERNATIONAL DARK SKY RESERVE

The stars really do seem brighter in Mackenzie Country. A unique combination of clear skies and next to no light pollution makes this region one of the best stargazing sites in the world – a fact that led to 4367 sq km of Aoraki/Mt Cook National Park and the Mackenzie Basin being declared the southern hemisphere's first International Dark Sky Reserve in 2012.

If you're up for some amateur stargazing, all you'll need are a cloud-free night and some warm clothes. For best results, time your visit to coincide with a new moon, when the skies will be at their darkest. For those who'd like a bit more guidance, join one of the nightly tours of the Mt John Observatory run by the Dark Sky Project. Ask at the information centre (p125) about other smaller local companies also offering stargazing.

skies – is the ultimate place to experience the region's glorious night sky.

Sights

Church of the Good Shepherd　　　CHURCH
(Pioneer Dr; ⊙9am-5pm) The picture window behind the altar of this pretty stone church (built in 1935) gives worshippers a distractingly divine view of the lake and mountains; needless to say, it's a firm favourite for weddings. Come early in the morning or late afternoon to avoid the peace-shattering crowds – this is the prime disembarkation point for tour buses. Nearby is a statue of a collie, a tribute to the sheepdogs that helped develop Mackenzie Country.

Activities

Lake Tekapo is a great base for outdoor activities enthusiasts. In winter (June to September), snow bunnies can go downhill skiing at Mt Dobson and **Roundhill** (☑021 680 694, snow phone 03-680 6977; www.roundhill. co.nz; daily lift passes adult/child $84/36), and cross-country skiing on the **Two Thumb Range**.

When the Mackenzie Basin was scoured out by glaciers, **Mt John** (1029m) remained as an island of tough bedrock in the centre of a vast river of ice. Nowadays, a road leads to the summit, or you can tramp via a circuit track (2½ hours return) for rewarding views. To extend it to an all-day tramp, continue on to **Alexandrina** and **McGregor Lakes**.

The free town map details this and other walks in the area, along with cycling tracks, including **Cowan's Hill** and those in **Lake Tekapo Regional Park**.

Dark Sky Project　　　STARGAZING
(☑0800 327 5759; www.darkskyproject.co.nz; SH8; ⊕) 🖉 A recognised International Dark Sky Reserve, the Mackenzie region is one of the world's best places for stargazing. Night-

ly tours head up to the University of Canterbury's observatory on Mt John (adult/child $175/99), where you'll get a guided tour of the sky from qualified astronomers. Other options include a multi-media presentation blending science and Māori astronomy at Dark Sky Project's new lakefront Rehua base, stargazing at the Church of the Good Shepherd, and viewing the night sky from Cowan's Observatory.

Dark Sky Project's spectacular lakefront base includes a good cafe and gift shop, and is also home to the Brashear Telescope, an 1894 telescope recently restored after being in storage at the University of Canterbury. It's hoped the telescope, crafted of brass, iron, steel and wood, will once again be used for surveying the Southern Hemisphere night sky in the future.

**Mackenzie Alpine
Horse Trekking**　　　HORSE RIDING
(☑0800 628 269; www.maht.co.nz; Godley Peaks Rd; 30min/1hr/2hr $50/90/140; ⊙Oct-May; ⊕) Located on the road to Mt John, this place runs various treks taking in the area's amazing scenery, catering for everyone from novice to experienced riders.

Tekapo Springs　　　SPA
(☑03-680 6550; www.tekaposprings.co.nz; 6 Lakeside Dr; adult/child pools $27/15, ice skating $19/14; ⊙10am-9pm; ⊕) There's nothing nicer on a chilly day than soaking in the thermal waters of these landscaped outdoor pools, with views over the lake to the snow-capped mountains beyond. Pools range in temperature from 28°C to 40°C, and include an artificial beach and aqua play area. There's also a steam room and sauna ($6 extra), along with a day spa. During the colder months (May to September) the attached ice-skating rink and snow-tubing slide are available, while in summer (December to March) there's the

DON'T MISS

LAKE PUKAKI LOOKOUT

The largest of the Mackenzie's three alpine lakes, Pukaki is a vast jewel of totally surreal colour. On its shore, just off SH8 between Twizel and Lake Tekapo, is a well-signed and perennially popular lookout affording picture-perfect views across the water all the way up to snow-capped Aoraki/Mt Cook and its surrounding peaks. Opened in 2019, the **Ngāi Tahu Lake Pukaki Centre** (SH8, Lake Pukaki; ⊘24hr) FREE presents the historical, geological and Māori cultural background of the lake and the region. Don't miss the superb lake and mountain views from the centre's windows.

Near the centre and the lookout, there's a retail outlet for **Mt Cook Alpine Salmon** (www.mtcookalpinesalmon. com; SH8, Lake Pukaki; ⊘8.30am-5.30pm Oct-Jun, 9am-5pm Jul-Sep), the highest salmon farm on the planet, which operates in a hydroelectric canal system some distance away. Pick up some sashimi (from $10) and snack with stellar views.

world's largest inflatable slide and slippery-slope tubing.

Air Safaris   SCENIC FLIGHTS
(☑03-680 6880; www.airsafaris.co.nz; SH8) Awe-inspiring views of Aoraki/Mt Cook National Park's peaks and glaciers are offered on the 'Grand Traverse' fixed-wing flight (adult/child $395/295); there are also various other flights available, including similar trips in a helicopter.

Sleeping

Lake Tekapo Motels &
Holiday Park   HOLIDAY PARK $
(☑03-680 6825; www.laketekapo-accommodation. co.nz; 2 Lakeside Dr; sites $50-60, dm $38, d $110-180; P☎🖥) With a prime position right on the lakefront, this sprawling complex has something for everyone. Backpackers get the cosy, log-cabin lodge, while others can enjoy cute Kiwi bachs, basic cabins, glamping tents or smart en suite units with particularly good views. Campervaners and campers are spoilt for choice, and share the sparkling amenities block.

YHA Lake Tekapo   HOSTEL $
(☑03-680 6857; www.yha.co.nz; 5 Motuariki Lane; dm $37-42, s/d from $125/140; ☎) New Zealand's newest YHA is also one of the country's best with colourful dorms and private rooms, excellent shared spaces including an upstairs lounge with lake and mountain views, and a modern and spacious kitchen. Downstairs, check out Our Dog Friday for burgers and craft beer.

Tailor Made Tekapo Backpackers   HOSTEL $
(☑03-680 6700; www.tekapohostelnz.com; 11 Aorangi Cres; dm $30-40, d $100-120, d without bathroom $80-100; ☎) Spread over three well-tended houses on a peaceful street five minutes' walk from town, this sociable hostel offers bright dorms (with no bunks) and cosy doubles. There's also a large garden complete with barbecue, hammock, chickens and bunnies, plus tennis and basketball courts next door for the energetic.

Chalet Boutique Motel   APARTMENT $$$
(☑03-680 6774; www.thechalet.co.nz; 14 Pioneer Dr; units from $235; P☎) The 'boutique motel' tag doesn't do justice to this collection of attractive accommodation options in three adjacent properties beside the lake. The wonderfully private 'Henkel hut' is a stylish option for lovebirds. Charming hosts will happily provide all the local information you need.

Eating & Drinking

Astro Café   CAFE $
(Mt John University Observatory; mains $8-18; ⊘9am-6pm Oct-Apr, 10am-5pm May-Sep, weather dependent; 🖥) This glass-walled pavilion atop Mt John has spectacular 360-degree views across the entire Mackenzie Basin – just maybe one of the planet's best locations for a cafe. Tuck into bagels with salmon or a stonking slice of bacon and egg pie. There is a charge of $8 per car to access Mt John, but it's worth it for the views.

Blue Lake Eatery & Bar   BISTRO $$
(☑03-680 6677; www.facebook.com/bluelaketekapo; SH8; mains $29, pizza $26, platters $26-59; ⊘3-9pm Mon & Tue, to 10pm Wed, Thu & Sun, to 11pm Fri & Sat) Craft beers from the Mackenzie Country's Burkes Brewing Co partner a seasonal menu including platters and pizza at this cosmopolitan spot in Lake Tekapo's commercial hub. Smaller plates could include porcini mushroom croquettes, and there's always interesting dishes with local South Island lamb and Mt Cook alpine salmon. Ask if any

Belgian-style beers from Ōamaru's tiny Craftwork Brewery are available.

Kohan   JAPANESE $$

(📞 03-680 6688; www.kohannz.com; SH8; dishes $6-20, bento $28-39; ⊙ 11am-2pm daily, plus 6-9pm Mon-Sat; 🐾) Despite its basic decor, this is one of Tekapo's best dining options, both for its distracting lake views and its authentic Japanese food, including fresh-off-the-boat sashimi. Leave room for the handmade green-tea ice cream.

Greedy Cow   CAFE $$

(📞 027 434 4445; www.greedycowtekapo.com; 16 Rapuwai Lane; mains $13-22; ⊙ 7.30am-4pm; 🐾📷) Classic breakfast dishes (until 2.30pm), a cabinet full of cakes, pies and sandwiches, good espresso and free wi-fi are all reasons to visit this petite cafe. Gourmet deli items – including freshly baked ciabatta – will tempt the self-catering crew.

ℹ Information

Kiwi Treasures & Information Centre (📞 03-680 6686; SH8; ⊙ 8am-5.30pm Mon-Fri, to 6pm Sat & Sun) This little gift shop doubles as the post office and info centre with local maps and advice, plus bookings for nearby activities and national bus services.

Tekapo Springs Sales & Information Centre (📞 03-680 6579; SH8; ⊙ 10am-6pm) The folks from Tekapo Springs dispense brochures and advice, as well as take bookings for their own complex down the road. See also www.tekapo-tourism.co.nz.

ℹ Getting There & Away

Cook Connection (📞 0800 266 526; www.cookconnect.co.nz) Has a shuttle service to Mt Cook Village ($42, 2¼ hours).

InterCity (📞 03-365 1113; www.intercity.co.nz) Runs daily services to the following:

DESTINATION	FARES ($) FROM	DURATION (HR)
Christchurch	41	3¾
Cromwell	41	2¾
Geraldine	24	1
Mt Cook Village	87	2½
Queenstown	40	4

Twizel

POP 1200

Pronounced 'twy-zel' but teased with 'Twizzel' and even 'Twizzelsticks' by outsiders, Twizel gets the last laugh. The town was

DON'T MISS

ALPS 2 OCEAN CYCLE TRAIL

One of the best Great Rides within the New Zealand Cycle Trail (www.nzcycletrail.com), the 'A2O' serves up epic vistas on its way from the foot of the Southern Alps all the way to the Pacific Ocean at Ōamaru.

New Zealand's highest mountain – Aoraki/Mt Cook – is just one of many stunning sights. Others include braided rivers, glacier-carved valleys, turquoise hydro-lakes, tussock-covered highlands and lush farmland. Off-the-bike activities include wine tasting, penguin spotting, glider flights and soaking in alfresco hot tubs. Country hospitality, including food and accommodation, along with shuttles and other services, make the whole trip easy to organise and enjoy.

The trail is divided into nine easy-to-intermediate sections across terrain varying from canal paths, quiet country roads, old railway lines and expertly cut cross-country track, to some rougher, hilly stuff for the eager. The whole journey takes around four to six days, but it can easily be sliced into short sections.

Twizel is an excellent base for day rides. Options include taking a shuttle to Lake Tekapo (p122) for a five- to six-hour, big-sky ride back to Twizel, or riding from Twizel out to Lake Ohau Lodge (p126) for lunch or dinner. Both rides serve up the sublime lake and mountain scenery for which the Mackenzie is famous.

The trail is well supported by tour companies offering bike hire, shuttles, luggage transfers and accommodation. These include Twizel-based **Cycle Journeys** (📞 0800 224 475, 03-435 0578; www.cyclejourneys.co.nz; 3 Benmore Pl; all-inclusive packages from $1389) and **Jollie Biker** (📞 03-435 0517, 027 223 1761; www.thejolliebiker.co.nz; 193 Glen Lyon Rd; bike hire per day from $50). The Alps 2 Ocean website (www.alps2ocean.com) has comprehensive details.

OFF THE BEATEN TRACK

RUATANIWHA CONSERVATION PARK

Stretched between Lake Pukaki and Lake Ohau, the 368-sq-km protected area of **Ruataniwha Conservation Park** (www.doc.govt.nz) includes the rugged Ben Ohau Range along with the Dobson, Hopkins, Huxley, Temple and Maitland Valleys. It offers plenty of hiking and mountain-biking opportunities, as detailed in DOC's *Ruataniwha Conservation Park* pamphlet (available online), with several easy day trails close to Twizel.

DOC huts and camping areas are scattered throughout the park, and a more comfortable stay is available at Lake Ohau Lodge (p126). Passing through these parts is the Alps 2 Ocean Cycle Trail (p125), a great way to survey the majestic surroundings.

built in 1968 to service construction of the nearby hydroelectric power station, and was due for obliteration in 1984 when the project was completed. But there was no way the locals were upping their twizzlesticks and relinquishing their relaxed, mountain country lifestyle.

Today the town is thriving with a modest boom in holiday-home subdivisions and recognition from travellers that – as everyday as it may be – Twizel is actually in the middle of everything and has almost everything one might need (within reason).

🏃 Activities

Twizel sits amid some spectacular country offering all sorts of adventure opportunities. **Lake Ruataniwha** is popular for rowing, boating and windsurfing. Nearby hiking and cycling trails are illustrated on the excellent town map, available from the information centre (p127), including a nice river ramble. Twizel is also the best hub for rides on the Alps 2 Ocean Cycle Trail (p125).

Fishing in local rivers, canals and lakes is big business; enquire at the information centre about local guides, and ask them about swimming in **Loch Cameron** while you're at it (but don't tell them we tipped you off!).

☞ Tours

OneRing Tours   TOURS
(🞄03-435 0073, 0800 213 868; www.lordofthe ringstour.com; cnr Ostler & Wairepo Sts; �➔) How

often do you get the opportunity to charge around like a mad thing wielding replica *LOTR* gear? Not often enough! A range of tours is available – head to the sheep station used for the location of the Battle of the Pelennor Fields (adult/child $89/59), or take a lunchtime visit to Laketown (adult/child $119/89), as seen in the *Hobbit* films.

There's also a breakfast tour (adult/child $109/89) or an adults-only twilight tour ($139); enjoy beer, wine and nibbles as the sun sets over Gondor.

Helicopter Line   SCENIC FLIGHTS
(🞄03-435 0370; www.helicopter.co.nz; Pukaki Airport, Harry Wigley Dr) Flights range from the hour-long Tasman Glacier Experience ($750) to the 20-minute Alpine Experience ($280), with several options in between. All but the shortest guarantee snow landings.

🛏 Sleeping

Twizel Holiday Park   HOLIDAY PARK $
(🞄03-435 0507; www.twizelholidaypark.co.nz; 122 Mackenzie Dr; sites from $44, cabins & units $85-180; P 🛜 ♿) Offers green, flower-filled grounds, with grassed sites and tidy communal facilities. Basic rooms are available in an old converted maternity hospital. The modern, self-contained cottages are particularly good value. Bike hire is also available.

Lake Ohau Lodge   LODGE $$
(🞄03-438 9885; www.ohau.co.nz; Lake Ohau Rd; s $114-225, d $123-246; P 🛜) Idyllically sited on the western shore of remote Lake Ohau, 42km west of Twizel, accommodation includes everything from budget rooms with shared facilities to upmarket rooms with decks and mountain views. The lodge is the buzzy wintertime hub of the **Ohau Ski Field** (🞄03-438 9885; www.ohau.co.nz; daily lift passes adult/child $100/40), which runs from June to September. In summer (December to February) it's a quieter retreat. Half-board packages are available (the nearest dining options are in Twizel).

Omahau Downs   LODGE, COTTAGE $$
(🞄03-435 0199; www.omahau.co.nz; SH8; d $165-170, cottages from $180; ⊘closed Jun-Aug; P 🛜) This farmstead, 2km north of Twizel, has three cosy, self-contained cottages (one sleeping up to 15), and a lodge with sparkling, modern rooms and a deck looking out at the Ben Ohau Range.

★Lakestone Lodge   LODGE $$$
(🞄03-971 1871; www.lakestonelodge.co.nz; 4589 Tekapo-Twizel Hwy, Lake Pukaki; r/ste $595/655;

P 🛜) 🛏 Daytime views from Lakestone Lodge's spectacular hilltop location include Lake Pukaki and alpine peaks, and there's a guests-only opportunity to survey the region's night sky after dark. Rooms are modern and exceedingly comfortable, and the lodge is well situated for day adventures on the nearby Alps 2 Ocean Cycle Trail. Breakfast is provided and dinners are also available ($90 per person).

Heartland Lodge
B&B, APARTMENT **$$$**

(📋 03-435 0008; www.heartland-lodge.co.nz; 19 North West Arch; d $310-370, apt $145; P 🛜) On the leafy outskirts of town, this elegant modern house offers spacious, en suite rooms and a comfortable, convivial communal space. Friendly hosts prepare a cooked breakfast using organic, local produce where possible. The adjacent 'retreat' apartment sleeps up to six and has its own kitchenette (breakfast is not provided).

✖️ Eating & Drinking

Shawty's
CAFE **$$**

(📋 03-435 3155; www.shawtys.co.nz; 4 Market Pl; mains $17-24; ☻7.30am-3.30pm) The town centre's best cafe serves up big breakfasts including waffles with bacon and maple syrup, and Middle Eastern-inspired shakshuka baked eggs. For lunch the global menu includes a great Korean chicken burger and Thai-style Massaman lamb curry. Local flavours and ingredients include beer-battered blue cod and a warm smoked salmon salad. Look forward to good beers and wine too.

Poppies Cafe
CAFE **$$**

(📋 03-435 0848; www.poppiescafe.com; 1 Benmore Pl; mains brunch $10-21, dinner $27-38; ☻9am-9pm; 🛜) A favourite with locals, this well-run cafe serves up classic brunch faves and good coffee in the mornings, while come evening you'll find tasty curries, fresh fish and pasta dishes on the menu. Craft beer encourages a wee sup and snack, if you're not going the whole hog. It's south of town just off SH8.

High Country Salmon
SEAFOOD **$$**

(📋 0800 400 385; www.highcountrysalmonfarm. co.nz; SH8; salmon per kg from $38; ☻8am-6pm) The glacial waters of this floating fish farm, 3km from Twizel, produce mighty delicious fish, available to buy as fresh whole fillets and smoked portions. Our pick is the hot-smoked salmon, flaked into hot pasta, perhaps with a dash of cream. There's also a small cafe selling sashimi and other salmon-inspired dishes. Try the delicious Hawaiian-style poke.

MoW Bar & Eatery
BAR

(📋 03-435 3257; www.facebook.com/Ministryof WorksBarandEatery; 2 Market Pl; ☻4.30-9pm Sun-Thu, 3-10pm Fri & Sat) A decent selection of NZ craft beers and ciders partners with good pizza ($20 to $26) and bar snacks at this convivial hybrid of bar and restaurant. Score an outdoor table on a warm summer's evening or cosy up inside on cooler nights. The industrial decor references NZ's Ministry of Works, the government agency responsible for Twizel's development in the 1960s.

🛍️ Shopping

Twizel Bookshop
BOOKS

(📋 027 464 5062; www.twizelbookshop.co.nz; 12b Market Pl; ☻9am-5pm Mon-Fri, shorter hours Sat & Sun) A sweet, well-curated bookshop offering both new and secondhand titles.

ℹ️ Information

Twizel Information Centre (📋 03-435 3124; www.twizel.info; Market Pl; ☻8.30am-5pm Mon-Fri, 10am-3pm Sat) Can advise on hiking and cycling paths in the area, as well as book accommodation. Also offers bike hire (one hour/three hours/full day $25/35/45).

ℹ️ Getting There & Away

Cook Connection (📋 0800 266 526; www. cookconnect.co.nz) Runs daily shuttle services to Mt Cook Village (one way/return $30/55, one hour).

InterCity (📋 03-365 1113; www.intercity.co.nz) Runs daily services to the following:

DESTINATION	FARES ($) FROM	DURATION
Christchurch	47	5¼hr
Cromwell	32	2hr
Lake Tekapo	19	50min
Mt Cook Village	78	1hr
Queenstown	39	3hr

Naked Bus (www.nakedbus.com) Services Christchurch and Queenstown/Wānaka.

Aoraki/Mt Cook National Park

POP 200

The spectacular 700-sq-km Aoraki/Mt Cook National Park is part of the Southwest New Zealand (Te Wāhipounamu) World Heritage

Aoraki/Mt Cook National Park

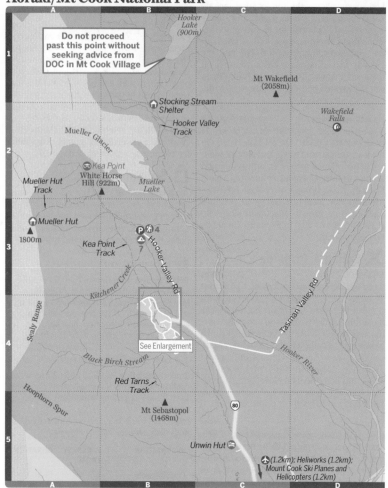

Do not proceed past this point without seeking advice from DOC in Mt Cook Village

Hooker Lake (900m)

Mt Wakefield (2058m)

Wakefield Falls

Stocking Stream Shelter

Hooker Valley Track

Mueller Glacier

Kea Point

White Horse Hill (922m)

Mueller Lake

Mueller Hut Track

Mueller Hut

1800m

Kea Point Track

Hooker Valley Rd

Sealy Range

Kitchener Creek

Tasman Valley Rd

See Enlargement

Black Birch Stream

Hooker River

Hoophorn Spur

Red Tarns Track

Mt Sebastopol (1468m)

80

Unwin Hut

(1.2km); Heliworks (1.2km); Mount Cook Ski Planes and Helicopters (1.2km)

Area, which extends from Westland's Cook River down to Fiordland. More than one-third of the park has a blanket of permanent snow and glacial ice; of the 23 NZ mountains over 3000m, 19 are in this park. The highest is mighty Aoraki/Mt Cook – at 3724m, the tallest peak in Australasia. Among the region's other great peaks are Sefton, Tasman, Silberhorn, Malte Brun, La Perouse, Hicks, De la Beche, Douglas and the Minarets.

Aoraki/Mt Cook is a wonderful sight, assuming there's no cloud in the way. Most visitors arrive on tour buses, stop at the Hermitage hotel for photos, and then zoom off back down SH80. Hang around to soak up this awesome peak and the surrounding landscape, and to try the excellent short walks in the area, including to the Tasman Glacier.

History

Known to Māori as Aoraki (Cloud Piercer), after an ancestral deity in Māori mythology, the mountain was given its English name in 1851, in honour of explorer Captain James Cook.

This region has always been the focus of climbing in NZ. On 2 March 1882 William Spotswood Green and two Swiss alpinists failed to reach the summit after an epic 62-hour ascent. Two years later a trio of local climbers – Tom Fyfe, George Graham and

Aoraki/Mt Cook National Park

◎ Top Sights
1 Aoraki/Mt Cook National Park
    Visitor Centre...................... E4

◎ Sights
2 Sir Edmund Hillary Alpine Centre...... E4

◐ Activities, Courses & Tours
3 Alpine Guides.............................E5
    Big Sky Stargazing......................(see 8)
    Glacier Explorers.........................(see 8)
    Glacier Kayaking........................(see 10)
4 Hooker Valley Track.......................... B3
    Kea Point Track .... (see 1)
    Sealy Tarns Track ....(see 4)
    Southern Alps Guiding ....(see 10)
    Tasman Valley 4WD Tours ....(see 8)

◎ Sleeping
5 Aoraki Court Motel...........................F5
6 Aoraki/Mt Cook Alpine Lodge.............E5
7 DOC White Horse Hill Campground.. B3
8 Hermitage E4
9 YHA Aoraki Mt Cook F5

◎ Eating
10 Old Mountaineers' Cafe..................... E4

◎ Drinking & Nightlife
11 Chamois Bar & Grill...........................F5

◐ Transport
12 Cook Connection........................ E4
    InterCity.......................................(see 12)

◉ Sights

★ **Aoraki/Mt Cook National Park Visitor Centre**   MUSEUM
(☑ 03-435 1186; www.doc.govt.nz; 1 Larch Grove; ⊙ 8.30am-5pm Oct-Apr, to 4.30pm May-Sep) **FREE** Arguably the best DOC visitor centre in NZ. It not only dispatches all necessary information and advice on hiking routes and weather conditions, it also houses excellent displays on the park's natural and human history. It's a fabulous place to commune with the wilderness, even on a rainy day. Most activities can be booked here.

Tasman Glacier   GLACIER
(www.doc.govt.nz) At 27km long and up to 4km wide, the Tasman is the largest of NZ's glaciers, but it's melting fast, losing hundreds of metres of length each year. It is also melting from the surface, shrinking around 150m in depth since it was first surveyed in 1891. Despite this considerable shrinkage, at its thickest point the ice is still estimated to be over 600m deep.

Jack Clarke – were spurred into action by the news that two well-known European alpinists were coming to attempt the peak, and set off to climb it before the visitors. On Christmas Day 1894 they ascended the Hooker Glacier and north ridge to stand on the summit.

In 1913 Australian climber Freda du Faur became the first woman to reach the summit. New Zealander Edmund Hillary first climbed the south ridge in 1948; Hillary went on to become one of the first two people to reach the summit of Mt Everest. Since then, most of the daunting face routes have been climbed.

In its lower section the melts have exposed rocks, stones and boulders, which form a solid unsightly mass on top of the ice.

Tasman Lake, at the foot of the glacier, started to form only in the early 1970s and now stretches to 7km. The ongoing effects of climate change are expected to extend it much further in the next decade. The lake is covered by a maze of huge icebergs, which are continuously being sheared off the glacier's terminal face. On 22 February 2011 the Christchurch earthquake caused a 1.3km-long, 300m-high, 30-million-tonne chunk of ice to break off, causing 3.5m waves to roll into the tourist boats on the lake at the time (no one was injured). You can kayak on Tasman Lake with Glacier Kayaking.

In the glacier's last major advance (17,000 years ago), the glacier crept south far enough to carve out Lake Pukaki. A later advance did not reach out to the valley sides, so there's a gap between the outer valley walls and the lateral moraines of this later advance. The unsealed Tasman Valley Rd, which branches off Mt Cook Rd 800m south of Mt Cook Village, travels through this gap. From the Blue Lakes shelter, 8km along the road, the **Tasman Glacier View Track** (30 minutes return) climbs interminable steps to an aptly rewarding viewpoint on the moraine wall, with a side trip to Blue Lakes on the way. Now only replenished by rainfall, the Blue Lakes have reduced in size and are now a muddy green colour.

Sir Edmund Hillary Alpine Centre MUSEUM
(www.hermitage.co.nz; Hermitage, Terrace Rd; adult/child $20/10; ⏰7.30am-9.30pm Oct-Mar, 8am-7pm Apr-Sep) This multimedia museum opened just three weeks before the 2008 death of the man regarded by many as the greatest New Zealander of all time, explorer and mountain climber Sir Edmund Hillary. The main attraction is a cinema and domed digital planetarium that screens films all day, including the *Mt Cook Magic* 3D movie and a fascinating 75-minute documentary about Sir Ed's conquest of Everest. The foyer houses memorabilia both from St Ed's various expeditions and from the 1884-built Hermitage (p132) hotel itself.

🏃 **Activities**

Hiking & Climbing

Various easy tramps from the village are outlined in the (multilingual) *Walking & Cycling Tracks* pamphlet available from the Aoraki/Mt Cook National Park Visitor Centre (p129) and online. On the trails, look

for the thar, a Himalayan goat; the chamois, smaller and of lighter build than the thar, and originally hailing from Europe; and red deer, also European. Summertime (December through March) brings into bloom the Mt Cook lily, a large mountain buttercup, and mountain daisies, gentians and edelweiss.

Longer tramps are only recommended for those with mountaineering experience, as tracks and conditions at higher altitudes can become dangerous. Highly changeable weather is typical: Aoraki/Mt Cook is only 44km from the coast and weather conditions rolling in from the Tasman Sea can mean sudden storms.

As for climbing, there's unlimited scope for the experienced, but those without experience must go with a guide. Regardless of your skills, take every precaution – more than 200 people have died in climbing accidents in the park. The bleak *In Memoriam* book in the visitor centre begins with the first death on Aoraki/Mt Cook in 1907; since then more than 80 climbers have died on the peak.

Check with the park rangers before attempting any climb and always heed their advice. If you're climbing, or even going on a longer tramp, fill out an intentions card before starting out so rangers can check on you if you're overdue coming back. Sign out again when you return. The visitor centre also hires locator beacons ($30/40 per three/seven days).

If you intend to stay at any of the park's huts, it's essential to register your intentions at the visitor centre and pay the hut fees. Walkers can use the public shelter in Mt Cook Village, which has running water, toilets and coin-operated showers. Note that this shelter cannot be used for overnight stays.

Hooker Valley Track HIKING
Perhaps the best of the area's day walks, this track (three hours return from the DOC White Horse Hill Campground; p132) heads up the Hooker Valley and crosses three swing bridges to the Stocking Stream and the terminus of the Hooker Glacier. After the second swing bridge, Aoraki/Mt Cook totally dominates the valley, and you may see icebergs floating in Hooker Lake.

Kea Point Track HIKING
The trail to Kea Point (two hours return from the visitor centre) is lined with native plants and ends with excellent views of Aoraki/Mt Cook, the Hooker Valley, and the ice faces of Mt Sefton and the Footstool. De-

spite the name, you're no more likely to see a kea (bird) here than anywhere else. If you do, don't feed it.

Sealy Tarns Track   HIKING
The walk to Sealy Tarns (three to four hours return) branches off the Kea Point Track (p130) and continues up the ridge to Mueller Hut (dorm $36), a comfortable 28-bunk hut with gas, cooking facilities and long-drop toilets.

Southern Alps Guiding   CLIMBING
(☑03-435 1890; www.mtcook.com; Old Mountaineers' Cafe, Bowen Dr) Offers mountaineering instruction and guiding, plus three- to four-hour helihiking trips on Tasman Glacier year-round ($599). From June to October heliskiers can head up the Tasman, Murchison and Mannering Glaciers for a series of 5km to 15km runs (four runs, from $1250; extra runs per person from $125).

Alpine Guides   CLIMBING
(☑03-435 1834; www.alpineguides.co.nz; 81 Bowen Dr; beginners climbing course from $2350) Offers guided climbs and mountaineering courses for all skill levels, along with ski-touring, including heli options. It also stocks outdoor clothing and mountaineering gear, and rents ice axes, crampons, day packs and sleeping bags.

Alpine Recreation   TRAMPING
(☑03-680 6736, 0800 006 096; www.alpinerecreation.com; guided tramps 2/4/6 days from $810/1750/2590) Based in Lake Tekapo, these folks organise high-altitude guided tramps, as well as mountaineering courses and ski touring. Also on offer are guided ascents of Aoraki/Mt Cook, Mt Tasman and other peaks.

Other Activities

Glacier Kayaking   KAYAKING
(☑03-435 1890; www.mtcook.com; Old Mountaineers' Cafe, Bowen Dr; per person $250; ☉Oct-Apr) Suitable for paddlers with just an ounce of experience, these guided kayaking trips head out on the terminal lake of the Tasman or Mueller Glaciers. With luck there will be icebergs to negotiate, but regardless there will be spectacular scenery, with a fascinating geology lesson thrown in. Trips last four to six hours, depending on conditions; book at the Old Mountaineers' Cafe (p132).

Big Sky Stargazing   STARGAZING
(☑03-435 1809, 0800 686 800; www.hermitage.co.nz; Hermitage, Terrace Rd; adult/child $80/45; ☀) New Zealand's southern sky is introduced with a 45-minute presentation in the Alpine Centre's digital planetarium. Afterwards participants venture outside to study the real deal with telescopes, binoculars and an astronomy guide.

👉 Tours

Mount Cook Ski Planes & Helicopters   SCENIC FLIGHTS
(☑03-430 8026; www.mtcookskiplanes.com; Mt Cook Airport) Get an aerial view of Mt Cook and surrounding glaciers via ski plane or helicopter with this outfit, based at Mt Cook Airport. Most flights include a snow or glacier landing; options include the 45-minute Grand Circle (adult/child $599/479) and the 35-minute Tasman Experience (adult/child $359/295).

Glacier Explorers   BOATING
(☑03-435 1641; www.glacierexplorers.com; Hermitage, Terrace Rd; adult/child $170/87; ☉Sep-May; ☀) Head out on the terminal lake of the Tasman Glacier for this small-boat tour, which gets up close and personal with old icebergs and crazy moraines. Includes a 30-minute walk. Book at the activities desk at the Hermitage (p132).

Helicopter Line   SCENIC FLIGHTS
(☑03-435 1801; www.helicopter.co.nz; Glentanner Park, Mt Cook Rd, Glentanner) Departing from Glentanner Park, the Helicopter Line offers 20-minute Alpine Vista flights ($270), an exhilarating 35-minute flight over the Ben Ohau Range ($415), and a 40-minute Mountains High flight over the Tasman Glacier and alongside Aoraki/Mt Cook ($480). All feature snow landings.

Heliworks   SCENIC FLIGHTS
(☑0800 666 668, 03-435 1460; www.queenstownhelicopters.nz; Mt Cook Airport; flights per person $380-605) Offers a range of scenic helicopter flights over some of NZ's most majestic scenery, all with a glacier landing. The 55-minute Aoraki/Mt Cook Ultimate flight ($605) circumnavigates the country's highest peak.

Tasman Valley 4WD Tours   TOURS
(☑0800 686 800; www.hermitage.co.nz/en/activities/tasman-valley-tour; adult/child $68/48; ☀) Offers two-hour 4WD tours to the Tasman Glacier and its terminal lake, with alpine flora and interesting commentary along the way. Book online or at the Hermitage (p132) activities desk.

🛏 Sleeping

YHA Aoraki Mt Cook   HOSTEL $

(📋 03-435 1820; www.yha.co.nz; 1 Bowen Dr; dm/d $41/145; P 🔊) 🏷 Handsomely decked out in pine, this excellent hostel has a free sauna, a drying room, log fires, a large kitchen and friendly, helpful staff. Rooms are clean and warm, although some are a tight squeeze (particularly the twin bunk rooms).

DOC White Horse Hill Campground   CAMPGROUND $

(📋 03-435 1186; www.doc.govt.nz; Hooker Valley Rd; sites per adult/child $15/7.50; P) Located 2km up the Hooker Valley from Mt Cook Village, this self-registration camping ground has a basic shelter with (cold water) sinks, tables and toilets, along with blissful views and close proximity to various walking tracks.

Glentanner Park Centre   HOLIDAY PARK $

(📋 03-435 1855; www.glentanner.co.nz; SH80, Glentanner; sites $22-25, dm $40, units $125-240; P @ 🔊) 🏷 On the northern shore of Lake Pukaki, 22km south of Mt Cook village, this is the nearest fully equipped camping ground to the national park. Features include cabins and motel units, a bunk room, a cafe and free-roaming rabbits.

★ Aoraki/Mt Cook Alpine Lodge   LODGE $$

(📋 03-435 1860; www.aorakialpinelodge.co.nz; Bowen Dr; d $185-260; P 🔊) This lovely family-run lodge has en suite rooms, including some suitable for families and two with kitchenettes; most have views. The huge lounge and kitchen area also has a superb mountain outlook, as does the barbecue area – a rather inspiring spot to sizzle your dinner.

Aoraki Court Motel   MOTEL $$$

(📋 03-435 1111; www.aorakicourt.co.nz; 26 Bowen Dr; d $325-455; P 🔊) While they wouldn't command these prices elsewhere, this clump of modern motel units offers classy decor, all the requisite mod cons and good views. Some units have spa baths, and there are bikes for hire.

Hermitage   HOTEL $$$

(📋 03-435 1809; www.hermitage.co.nz; Terrace Rd; r $184-429; P @ 🔊) Completely dominating Mt Cook Village, this famous hotel offers awesome views. While the corridors in some of the older wings can seem a little hospital-like, all of the rooms have been renovated to a reasonable standard (the cheapest do not have mountain views). In addition to the on-site shop and Alpine Centre, there are three dining options of reasonable standard.

🍴 Eating & Drinking

Old Mountaineers' Cafe   CAFE $$

(www.mtcook.com; Bowen Dr; mains breakfast $10-18, lunch $18-30, dinner $26-40; ⊙ 10am-9pm; 🔊) 🏷 Encouraging lingering with books, memorabilia and mountain views through picture windows, the village's best eatery also supports local and organic suppliers via an all-day menu offering salmon and bacon pies, cooked breakfasts, burgers and pizza.

Chamois Bar & Grill   PUB

(Bowen Dr; ⊙ 4pm-late; 🔊) This large bar offers basic pub meals, a pool table, a big-screen TV and the occasional live gig. The views are its best feature. Come at sunset and watch the mountains change colour.

ℹ Information

The Aoraki/Mt Cook National Park Visitor Centre (p129) is the best source of local information. The nearest ATM and supermarket are in Twizel.

ℹ Getting There & Away

Mt Cook Village's small airport only serves aerial sightseeing companies. Some of these may be willing to combine transport to the West Coast (ie Franz Josef) with a scenic flight, but flights are heavily dependent on weather.

If you're driving, fill up at Lake Tekapo or Twizel. There is a self-service pump at Mt Cook, but it's expensive.

Cook Connection (📋 0800 266 526; www.cookconnect.co.nz) runs shuttle services to Lake Tekapo ($42, 2¼ hours) and Twizel ($30, 45 minutes).

InterCity (📋 03-365 1113; www.intercity.co.nz) coaches stop at the Hermitage; however, they are operated as part of a 'tour' and can be pricey – you might be better off catching a shuttle back to Twizel and picking up an InterCity connection from there.

DESTINATION	FARES ($) FROM	DURATION (HR)
Christchurch	162	5¼
Lake Tekapo	78	2½
Queenstown	186	4

Dunedin & Otago

Best Places to Eat

➡ Riverstone Kitchen (p145)

➡ Fleur's Place (p145)

➡ Good Good (p154)

➡ Cucina (p144)

➡ Bracken (p154)

Best Places to Stay

➡ Pen-y-bryn Lodge (p143)

➡ Oliver's (p169)

➡ Oamaru Backpackers (p143)

➡ Terminus Hotel (p152)

➡ Hogwartz (p152)

Why Go?

Wine, wildlife, the weird and the wonderful – travellers who take the time to explore this quirky corner of the country are in for a treat.

Cruising down the coast from Christchurch you come to seaside Ōamaru, a town that has let its gracious Victorian buildings weave a steampunk fantasy of costume and creativity around its residents. The coastal road also sweeps past the sweet Moeraki Boulders and two of New Zealand's most acclaimed restaurants (both of which are sprinkled with eccentricity in keeping with the region) on the way to Dunedin. This city is full of hidden treasures, from the world-class street art down every alley to the stunning coastline providing sanctuary to royal albatross, fur seals and penguins.

Heading inland you soon find yourself on deserted roads stretching to mountains on the far horizon and dotted with isolated gold-rush villages. It's perfect cycling country, and there are plenty of chances to do just that, including the famous Otago Central Rail Trail. Nearby in Cromwell and Bannockburn, charming wineries are busy producing the best pinot noir in NZ.

When to Go

➡ February and March have sunny, settled weather (usually...), and the juicy appeal of fresh apricots, peaches and cherries.

➡ At Easter, hook yourself a 'Southern Man' at the biennial Middlemarch Singles Ball, or drown your sorrows at the Clyde Wine & Food Festival.

➡ Take to two wheels on the Otago Central Rail Trail during the quieter months of September and October.

➡ In November, watch the pros battle it out at the Highlands Motorsport Park, then ride graciously into the past on a penny-farthing bicycle at Ōamaru's Victorian Heritage Celebrations.

Dunedin & Otago Highlights

1 **Dunedin** (p146) Hunting for street-art Easter eggs down Dunedin's alleyways.

2 **Ōamaru** (p137) Going bonkers for steampunk in this town of vintage costumery and warehouses of offbeat art.

3 **Otago Peninsula** (p157) Peering at penguins, admiring albatross and staring at seals.

4 **Otago Central Rail Trail** (p162) Cycling through breathtaking vistas and frontier towns.

5 **Naseby** (p165) Relishing the wintry delights of curling, luging, skating and stargazing.

6 **Taieri Gorge Railway** (p150) Winding through gorges, along canyons and across viaducts on this snaking heritage railway.

7 **Cromwell** (p169) Taste-testing some of the planet's best pinot noir in the wineries scattered around the fruit bowl of the south.

ⓘ Getting There & Away

From Dunedin, **Air New Zealand** (☑ 0800 737 000; www.airnewzealand.co.nz) flies to Christchurch, Wellington and Auckland, **Jetstar** (☑ 0800 800 995; www.jetstar.com) flies to Auckland and **Virgin** (☑ 0800 670 000; www. virginaustralia.com) flies direct to Brisbane (Australia).

The only train services are heritage trips (p150) from Dunedin to Pukerangi or Waitati.

The main bus routes follow SH1 or SH8.

WAITAKI DISTRICT

The broad, braided Waitaki River provides a clear dividing line between Otago and Canterbury to the region's north. The Waitaki Valley is a direct but less-travelled route from the Southern Alps to the sea, featuring freaky limestone formations, Māori rock paintings and ancient fossils, spotlighted in the Waitaki Whitestone Geopark (p137). The area is also one of New Zealand's newest winemaking regions, and is a major component of the Alps 2 Ocean Cycle Trail (p125), which links Aoraki/Mt Cook National Park to the coast. The district's main town, Ōamaru, is a place of penguins, steampunk and glorious heritage architecture.

Ōmarama

POP 270

At the head of the Waitaki Valley, sleepy Ōmarama is surrounded by mountain ranges and fabulous landscapes. Busy times include the rodeo (28 December) and the sheepdog trials (March).

⊙ Sights & Activities

Clay Cliffs Paritea LANDMARK
(Henburn Rd; cars $5) About as 'hidden gem' as you can get in an area rife with nosy tourists, these eerie and kinda creepy pinnacles, ravines and ridges have been shaped by around two million years of erosion along the active Ostler fault. Short trails lead around and between the forms to make you feel like an ant crawling in a sandcastle. Be careful – some look like they could crumble at any moment.

★ Omarama Hot Tubs SPA
(☑ 03-438 9703; www.hottubsomarama.co.nz; 29 Omarama Ave, SH8; 1-/2-/3-/4-person tub $56/98/123/148, pod $85/160/210/240; ⊙ 11am-

late) ✒ If your legs are weary after mountain biking or hiking, or you just want to cosy up with your significant other, these private, wood-fired hot tubs could be just the ticket. Choose between a 90-minute soak in a tub (each has its own dressing room) or a two-hour session in a 'wellness pod', which includes a sauna.

These tubs are popular – book ahead online (last booking 8.30pm). Clothing is optional and the chemical-free glacier and snow-melt water is changed after each booking; the used water is recycled for irrigation. The concept is Japanese, but with the surrounding mountain ranges, the lakeside setting and a pristine night sky, you could well be on the South Island of NZ. Therapeutic massages (30/60/90 minutes $65/120/170) and other treatments are also available.

Glide Omarama GLIDING
(☑ 03-438 9555; www.glideomarama.com; Airport Rd, Omarama Airfield; ⊙ 8.30am-6.30pm) Ōmarama's unique westerlies and warm summer thermals allow for world-class gliding over the hills and spectacular Southern Alps. This outfit offers lessons and scenic flights ranging from 30 minutes ($386) to five hours ($1735).

Sleeping & Eating

Buscot Station FARMSTAY $

(☑ 027 222 1754; www.bbh.co.nz; 912 SH8; sites/dm/s/d from $10/25/40/60; ℗) For a completely different and uniquely Kiwi experience, grab a room in the home-style farmhouse attached to a huge sheep and cattle station, or a bed in the large dormitory out the back. The sunset views are terrific and there's plenty of acreage for quiet explorations. Look for it on SH8, 10km north of Ōmarama.

Omarama Top 10
Holiday Park HOLIDAY PARK $

(☑ 03-438 9875; www.omaramatop10.co.nz; 1 Omarama Ave, SH8; sites from $45, units with/without bathroom $150/80; ℗ 🖨 🏋) 🚲 Facilities are good at this holiday park, squeezed between the highway and a stream. Standard cabins are on the cosy side, but larger en-suite cabins and self-contained motel units are also available.

Wrinkly Rams CAFE $$

(☑ 03-438 9751; www.thewrinklyrams.co.nz; 24-30 Omarama Ave, SH8; mains $12-30; ⊙ 6.30am-4.30pm; 🖨) Restaurants attached to tourist attractions can be dodgy, but the meals here are perfectly fine (the coffee is hit and miss, though). Big glass windows and outside tables give a nice view of the mountains while you eat. If a group has booked, you can tag along to see a sheepdog or shearing show (adult/child $25/12.50).

❶ Information

Omarama Information Centre (☑ 021 195 5572; www.facebook.com/omaramainfo; 4 Omarama Ave; ⊙ 10am-4pm) This friendly centre can assist with accommodation and help you organise an Alps 2 Ocean Cycle Trail (p125) trip.

❶ Getting There & Away

The road from Ōmarama to Cromwell heads over the striking Lindis Pass.

Cycle Journeys (☑ 03-377 2060; www.cyclejourneys.co.nz; ⊙ Oct-Apr) Runs seasonal shuttles for cyclists on the Alps 2 Ocean Cycle Trail between Ōmarama and Ōamaru ($50), stopping at Kurow and Duntroon – call ahead to see if you can book a seat.

InterCity (☑ 03-471 7143; www.intercity.co.nz) Has two coaches a day heading to/from Christchurch (from $49, six hours), Twizel (from $19, 25 minutes), Cromwell (from $27, 1½ hours) and Queenstown (from $37, 2½ hours),

and one heading to/from Mt Cook Village ($78, 3½ hours).

Waitaki Valley

Wine, waterskiing and salmon-fishing are just some of the treats on offer along this little-travelled route. Coming from Ōmarama, the winding SH83 passes a series of glassy blue lakes. For a scenic detour along the north bank (with basic lakeside camping in summer for $10), leave the highway at Otematata and cross over Benmore Dam, then cross back over Aviemore Dam to rejoin the route.

A succession of sleepy little towns line the highway. One of the most appealing is tiny Kurow, the home town of World Cup–winning retired All Blacks captain Richie McCaw, with a handful of lovely cafes. At almost-as-cute **Duntroon**, a couple of heritage buildings, including an evocative blacksmiths shop, have been restored.

Although they've got a way to go to attain the global reputation of Central Otago, a few winemaking pioneers in Waitaki Valley are producing wine of which international experts are taking notice.

◎ Sights

◎ Kurow

Kurow Heritage &
Information Centre MUSEUM

(☑ 03-436 0950; www.kurow.org.nz; 57 Bledisloe St, Kurow; ⊙ 9am-5pm Mon-Fri, 10am-4pm Sat & Sun Oct-Mar, 9am-4pm Mon-Fri Apr-Sep) FREE Local hero Richie McCaw rates a mention at this very sweet community-run museum, filled with lovingly preserved curios. Staff are knowledgeable and friendly, and can give excellent advice on local activities and routes. It's celebrating 50 years in operation in 2020.

Vintner's Drop WINERY

(☑ 03-436 0545; www.ostlerwine.co.nz; 45 Bledisloe St, Kurow; tastings 3/5 wines $10/15; ⊙ noon-5pm Nov-Mar, to 3.30pm Mon-Fri Apr-Oct) Housed in Kurow's old post office, Vintner's Drop acts as a tasting room for Ostler Vineyards, along with other small local producers. Try the signature Caroline's pinot noir.

River T Estate WINERY

(☑ 021 190 8875; www.rivertestate.co.nz; SH83; lunch $13-16; ⊙ 9am-6pm Oct-Mar, from 11am Apr-Sep) Offering over 40 local wines by the glass, including River T's own well-regarded pinot gris and chardonnay, this new cellar door is gaining a reputation for its platters featuring local Waitaki Valley produce ($20 per person). Dine overlooking the vines – you're encouraged to stroll around and sample the grapes when they're in season.

◉ Duntroon & Around

Takiroa Māori
Rock Painting Site   ARCHAEOLOGICAL SITE
(SH83) FREE Hidden within the honeycomb cliffs lining the highway, this well-signposted site, 3km west of Duntroon, is of special significance to the Ngāi Tahu. It features mainly 19th-century drawings, including people riding horses and European sailing ships.

Elephant Rocks   LANDMARK
Sculpted by wind, rain and rivers, the huge limestone boulders of this bizarre landscape were used as Aslan's Camp in the NZ-filmed *Narnia* movies (2005–10). They're located on farmland about 5.5km south of the highway; follow the signs after crossing the Maerewhenua River. To climb them, contact Cycle Ventures (p143) in Ōamaru.

Vanished
World Centre   MUSEUM
(☑ 03-431 2024; www.vanishedworld.co.nz; 7 Campbell St, Duntroon; adult/child $10/free; ⊙ 10am-4.30pm; ⛟) Stop into this volunteer-run centre to dig out your own real limestone fossils (to keep!) or check out the frightening 25-million-year-old shark-toothed dolphin and giant penguin. There are lots of activities for kids, and you can pick up a copy of the Vanished World Trail map ($6.50) outlining 20 different interesting geological locations around the Waitaki Valley and North Otago coast.

🛏 Sleeping

Valley Views
Glamping   TENTED CAMP $$$
(☑ 021 192 8282; www.valleyviews.co.nz; 161 Domett Rd, Otiake; dome for 2 incl breakfast $280-350) 🍃 Camp in luxury in this scattering of spacious geodesic domes on a working cattle farm 13km from Kurow. Each has a private deck and a huge window overlooking the valley. Bathrooms are shared – including standard facilities in the lodge and four outdoor baths in the forest. Running on solar

> ## WAITAKI WHITESTONE GEOPARK
> ●
> Earth scientists and fossil fans should check out this geopark (www.white stonegeopark.nz), a collection of sites linking coastal geology and culture, from 60 million years ago to the present. It includes the Moeraki Boulders (p145), Clay Cliffs Paritea (p135), Takiroa, Maerewhenua, Elephant Rocks and more, and is currently shortlisted to become the first Unesco Global Geopark in Australasia (to be decided in early 2021). Download the free app to check it out.

power and good vibes, this is a great romantic getaway.

Three-course meals are available Wednesday to Sunday for $50 per person.

❶ Getting There & Away

Cycle Journeys runs seasonal shuttles for cyclists on the Alps 2 Ocean Cycle Trail between Ōamaru and Ōmarama ($50), stopping at Kurow ($35) and Duntroon ($25) – call ahead to see if you can book a seat on board. Otherwise you'll need your own car or bike along this route.

Ōamaru

POP 13,670
Ōamaru is offbeat small-town New Zealand at its very best. Rattling around inside its enormous and ramshackle Victorian warehouses are oddballs, antiquarians and bohemians of all stripes who make art, age fruity whisky and dress up at the drop of a top hat. Most visible are the steampunks, boldly celebrating the past and the future with an ethos of 'tomorrow as it used to be'. Plus there's the penguins. The nightly beach waddle of adorable blue penguins draws plenty of visitors to Ōamaru, but many find they are just as charmed by the creative community of humans. Put simply, Ōamaru is *cool*.

Away from the docks, the town's gracious whitestone buildings harbour an increasing array of restaurants and bars, and some excellent accommodation options are available. You may find find yourself lingering in this laid-back coastal town.

Ōamaru

History

Ōamaru used to be rich and ambitious. In its 1880s heyday, it was about the same size as Los Angeles was at the time. Refrigerated meat-shipping had its origins nearby and the town became wealthy enough to erect the imposing buildings that grace Thames St today.

These buildings are all the more striking as they were constructed from the milky local limestone (known as Ōamaru stone or whitestone), with their forms reflecting the fashion of the times; there's a particular emphasis on the neoclassical. Impressive examples include the 1883 Forrester Gallery (p142),

the 1882 North Otago Museum (p142), the 1873 **St Patrick's Basilica** (📞03-434 8543; www.cdd.org.nz/st-patrick-oamaru; 68 Reed St) and the 1907 Opera House (p144). Many heritage buildings along Thames St are lit with coloured lights at night.

However, after the building boom, the town overreached itself and spent the end of the 19th century teetering on the verge of bankruptcy. Economic decline in the 20th century meant that there wasn't the impetus to swing the wrecking ball here with the same reckless abandon that wiped out much of the built heritage of NZ's main centres. It's

Ōamaru

DUNEDIN & OTAGO ŌAMARU

only in recent decades that canny creative types have cottoned on to the uniqueness of Ōamaru's surviving Victorian streetscapes and have started to unlock this otherwise unremarkable town's potential for extreme kookiness.

⊙ Sights

★**Victorian Precinct**   AREA
Consisting of only a couple of blocks centred on Harbour and Tyne Sts, this atmospheric enclave has some of NZ's best-preserved Victorian commercial buildings. Descend on a dark and foggy night and it's downright Dickensian. It's also ground zero for all that is hip, cool and freaky in Ōamaru, and one of the best places to window shop on the entire South Island.

Wander around during the day and you'll discover antiquarian bookshops, antique stores, galleries, vintage clothing shops, artist studios and artisan bookbinders.

The precinct is at its liveliest on Sunday when the excellent **Ōamaru farmers market** is in full swing, the **steam train** (www.oamaru-steam.org.nz; adult/child/family return $10/4/24; ⊙11am-3pm Sun; 🚂) is running, and artisans are busy in their studios.

★**Blue Penguin Colony**   BIRD SANCTUARY
(📞03-433 1195; www.penguins.co.nz; 2 Waterfront Rd; adult/child evening visit from $40/25, day $25/15; ⊙10am-2hr after sunset) 🐧 Every

evening the tykes from the Ōamaru blue penguin colony surf in and wade ashore, heading to their nests in an old stone quarry near the waterfront. Stands are set up on either side of the waddle route. General admission will give you a good view of the action but the premium stand (adult/child $55/32), accessed by a boardwalk through the nesting area, will get you closer.

You'll see the most penguins (up to 250) in November and December. From March to August there may be only 10 to 50 birds. They arrive in groups called rafts just before dark (around 5.30pm in midwinter and 9.30pm midsummer), and it takes about an hour for them all to come ashore; nightly viewing times are posted at the i-SITE (p144). Use of cameras is prohibited and you're advised to dress warmly.

To understand the centre's conservation work and its success in increasing the penguin population, take the daytime behind-the-scenes tour, when you can (usually) peer into the underground world of nesting penguins in residence; packages that combine night viewing and the daytime tour are also available.

Do not under any circumstances wander around the rocks beside the sea here at night looking for penguins. It's damaging to their environment and spoils studies into the human effects on the birds.

UWE ARANAS/SHUTTERSTOCK ©

1. Dunedin Railway Station (p146)
Built between 1903 and 1906, Dunedin's railway station claims to be NZ's most-photographed building.

2. Moeraki Boulders (p145)
These large and spherical boulders lie along a stretch of Koekohe Beach in the Waitaki Whitestone Geopark.

3. Toitū Otago Settlers Museum (p146)
This excellent interactive museum traces the history of human settlement on the South Island.

4. Elephant Rocks (p137)
These huge limestone boulders were used as Aslan's Camp in the NZ-filmed *Narnia* movies.

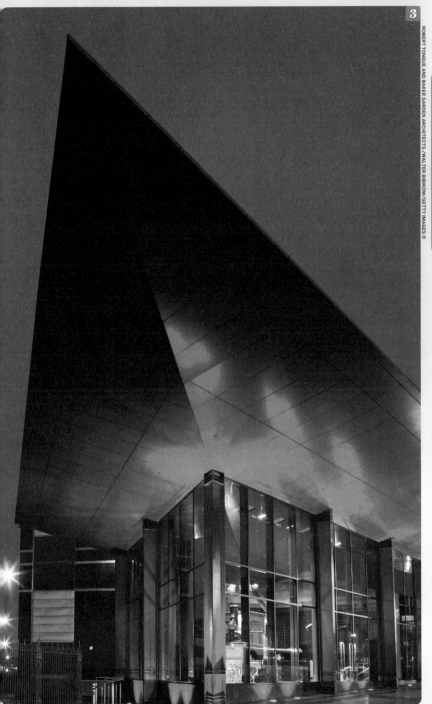

MĀORI NZ: DUNEDIN & OTAGO

The early Māori history of Otago echoes that of Canterbury (p92), with Ngāi Tahu the dominant tribe at the time the British arrived. One of the first parcels of land that Ngāi Tahu sold was called the Otago block, a 1618-sq-km parcel of land that changed hands in 1844 for £2400. The name Otago reflects the Ngāi Tahu pronunciation of Ōtākou, a small village on the far reaches of the Otago Peninsula, where there's still a *marae* (meeting place).

Dunedin's Otago Museum (p147) has the finest Māori exhibition on the South Island, including an ornately carved *waka taua* (war canoe) and a finely crafted *pounamu* (greenstone); there's wonderful exhibits at Toitū Otago Settlers Museum (p146) too. One of the most important collections of first settlement Māori artefacts in the country can be viewed at Ōamaru's North Otago Museum. Māori rock art can be seen in situ in the Waitaki Valley (p137), which was an important *ara tawhito* (travel route).

Steampunk HQ
GALLERY

(📞 027 778 6547; www.steampunkoamaru.co.nz; 1 Humber St; adult/child $10/2; ⏰10am-5pm) Discover an alternative past – or maybe a quirky version of the future – at this fascinating art project celebrating steampunk culture. Ancient machines wheeze and splutter, and the industrial detritus of the last century or so is repurposed and reimagined to creepy effect. Bring a $2 coin to fire up the sparking, space-age locomotive out the front.

The brainchild of artists Don Patterson, Jac Grenfell and Brian de Geest in 2011, at this whimsical workshop you can play the Metagalactic Pipe Organ of extraterrestrial sounds, and visit the Portal, an infinity light chamber. You are allowed to touch everything and photography is encouraged.

Grainstore Gallery
GALLERY

(📞 027 366 6201; 9 Harbour St; ⏰10.30am-2.30pm) Crammed with weird theatrical sculpture, papier-mâché masks and vintage curiosities, this former Victorian grain store houses an ever-changing cornucopia of creativity. Owner Donna Dementé shows her evocative portraits here, as well as the work of other local talents, and hosts occasional live music and other delightful distractions.

Whitestone City
MUSEUM

(📞 0508 978 663; www.whitestonecity.com; 12 Harbour St; adult/child $15/10; ⏰10am-6pm, to 4.30pm winter) Ōamaru's heyday is brought to life by costumed guides inside this 1882 grain store – and you too can don vintage costumes (adult/child $20/10) and get some shots of yourself dining at a Victorian table. Stroll through the replica Victorian streetscape, visit the schoolroom complete with slates, play old-fashioned games in the dimly lit saloon, and take a ride on the pièce de résistance – a penny-farthing carousel.

Art-house movies are shown in the theatre – check the website for details.

Yellow-Eyed Penguin Colony
BIRD SANCTUARY

(Bushy Beach Rd) FREE Larger and much rarer than their little blue cousins, yellow-eyed penguins waddle ashore at Bushy Beach in the late afternoon from a day of fishing. In order to protect these endangered birds, the beach is closed to people from 3pm onwards, but there are hides set up on the cliffs (you'll need binoculars for a decent view). The best time to see them is two hours before sunset.

Childhood Home of Janet Frame
HISTORIC BUILDING

(📞 03-434 1656; www.jfestrust.org.nz; 56 Eden St; $5; ⏰2-4pm Nov-Apr, or by appointment) Nobel Prize–nominated writer Janet Frame (1924–2004) grew up in this simple suburban home and drew on her time here to write her three acclaimed autobiographies, *To the Is-Land* (1982), *An Angel at My Table* (1984) and *The Envoy from Mirror City* (1984). Frame's typewriter is here, as is her writing desk.

Forrester Gallery
GALLERY

(📞 03-433 0853; www.culturewaitaki.org.nz/forrester-gallery; 9 Thames St; ⏰10.30am-4.30pm Mon-Fri, from 1pm Sat & Sun; ♿) FREE Housed in an elegant, temple-like former bank building, the Forrester Gallery was closed for renovations at the time of research but reopening in 2020. It stages excellent temporary exhibitions of local and NZ art, and the 2nd floor hosts interactive exhibitions especially designed for children.

North Otago Museum
MUSEUM

(📞 03-433 0852; www.culturewaitaki.org.nz; 58-60 Thames St; ⏰10am-4.30pm Mon-Fri, from 1pm Sat & Sun) FREE This weighty museum was renovated in early 2020. The new space houses Waitaki Taonga (the Willetts Collection), one of the most important collections of first settlement Māori artefacts in NZ, as well as exhibitions linked to the Waitaki Whitestone Geopark (p137) and European heritage, including the Victorian era.

Activities

Whitestone Cheese Factory   FOOD & DRINK
(📞03-434 0182; www.whitestonecheese.com; 3 Torridge St; adult/child $30/free, with wine $45; ⏰shop 9am-5pm Mon-Fri, 10am-4pm Sat & Sun) The home of award-winning artisanal cheeses, Whitestone is a local culinary institution. Tours run at 10am and 11.45am (45 to 60 minutes), and you get a goodie bag at the end. Pick up some cheesy souvenirs in its shop, or try the NZ 'Deep South' classic – the mighty cheese roll. They're a bargain here at three for $6. Book tours online.

Cycle Ventures   CYCLING
(📞03-434 5010; www.verticalventures.co.nz; 4 Wansbeck St; ⏰10am-5pm Mon-Fri, to 12.30pm Sat summer, 10am-5.30pm Thu & Fri, 10am-1pm Sat winter) Hire a mountain bike (from $45 per day), or join guided mountain-biking trips, including the Alps 2 Ocean Cycle Trail (seven days including transport, food and accommodation from $3095). You can also arrange rock-climbing day trips (from $150 per person).

Festivals & Events

Victorian Heritage Celebrations   CULTURAL
(www.vhc.co.nz; ⏰mid-Nov) Five days of costumed capers and historical hi jinks, culminating in a grand fete.

Steampunk Festival   ART
(www.steampunk.org.nz; ⏰late May-early Jun) Celebrating the Queen's Birthday holiday (Queen Victoria that is), Ōamaru dusts off her bonnet and kicks up her heels at a gala ball, monster teapot races and tea-duelling championships.

Sleeping

⭐**Oamaru Backpackers**   HOSTEL $
(📞021 190 0069; www.oamarubackpackers.co.nz; 47 Tees St; dm/s/d/tr from $32/52/90/95; 🅿🛜) A stone's throw from the Victorian quarter, this snug hostel has lovely, individually decorated rooms and a great dorm with privacy curtains and individual outlets. Best of all is the view of the harbour from the giant windows (with telescope) in the airy, light-filled lounge.

Old Bones Lodge   LODGE $
(📞03-434 8115; www.oldbones.co.nz; Beach Rd; r $100; 🅿🛜) Five kilometres south of Ōama-

ru on the coast road, this top-notch lodge has tidy rooms off a huge, sunny, central space. Great for groups. Listen to the surf crashing over the road while relaxing by the wood-burning fire, or book one of the hot tubs (from $90 for two people) and drift into ecstasy while gazing at the stars.

Oamaru Top 10
Holiday Park   HOLIDAY PARK $
(📞03-434 7666; www.oamarutop10.co.nz; 30 Chelmer St; sites $40, units with/without bathroom from $99/75; 🅿🛜) Grassy and well maintained, this Top 10 has trees out the back and is right next door to the lush public gardens. Standard cabins are basic, but the other units (with varying levels of self-contained comfort) are much nicer. There's a spa pool and a jumping pillow for kids.

Highfield Mews   MOTEL $$
(📞03-434 3437; www.highfieldmews.co.nz; 244 Thames St; units from $175; 🅿🛜) The units at this motel are basically smart apartments, with kitchens, desks, stereos and tiled bathrooms, most with spa baths.

⭐**Poshtel**   BOUTIQUE HOTEL $$$
(📞03-434 8888; www.poshtelnz.com; 126 Thames St; d from $259; 🅿🛜) Anyone for polo? Crammed with sporty vintage collectables in themed rooms (like the Steeplechase room or the Antarctic Explorer Suite), this plush new hotel is the perfect balance of quirk and luxury. Thick whitestone walls, deep carpets and comfy beds keep you snug and the odd steampunk firearm keeps you interested. Great location on the main street.

Check out the excellent on-site art gallery specialising in NZ and Pacific art.

⭐**Pen-y-bryn Lodge**   B&B $$$
(📞03-434 7939; www.penybryn.co.nz; 41 Towey St; r May-Sep $495-750, Oct-Apr $525-825; 🅿🛜) Well-travelled foodie owners have thoroughly revitalised this beautiful 1889 residence and continue to upgrade. There are two rooms in the main house but the three recently and luxuriously refurbished ones in the rear annexe are nicer. Complimentary predinner drinks and canapés are served in the antique-studded drawing room; arrange a four-course dinner in the fabulous dining room (from $135 per person).

Eating

Harbour St Bakery   BAKERY $
(📞021 0248 5351; 4 Harbour St; pies $5.50; ⏰8am-4pm Tue-Sat, to 2pm Sun & Mon) Artisan

sourdough bread and simply enormous pies, croissants and pastries – all baked to perfection using German, Dutch and Kiwi traditions. Try a Kiwi favourite: the custard square.

Steam
CAFE $

(www.facebook.com/steamoamaru; 7 Thames St; mains $10-13; ⏰7am-4pm Mon-Sat, 8am-3pm Sun; 🛜) This popular little cafe near the Victorian quarter roasts its own coffee in-house – it's a good spot to stock up on freshly ground beans for your own travels. Check the counter cabinet for the day's culinary choices, including freshly baked muffins, croissants and the like.

Fat Sally's
PUB FOOD $$

(📞03-434 8368; www.fatsallys.co.nz; 84 Thames St; mains $22-30; ⏰11.30am-late Tue-Sun) Fat Sally's is a cosy pub in a heritage building with sports on the telly and Speights on the taps. There's a nice open fire, and friendly staff will happily adapt the meat-heavy menu for vegos. Quiz night is Wednesday from 7pm. There's often live music on Saturday night.

★Cucina
ITALIAN $$$

(📞03-434 5696; www.cucinaoamaru.co.nz; 1 Tees St; mains $24-38; ⏰5pm-late Mon-Sat) Cucina is the most sophisticated kitchen in Ōamaru and serves up superb seasonal food in a heritage dining room painted black and filled with plants. Here you can try dishes like 55-day-aged rib-eye with smoked pommes Anna, broccolini and caramelised baby onion, or beetroot rigatoni with salt-baked beetroot, mint pesto and marinated feta. The chef's menu is $115/65 with/without wine.

🍷 Drinking & Nightlife

Scott's Brewing Co.
BREWERY

(📞03-434 2244; www.scottsbrewing.co.nz; 1 Wansbeck St; ⏰11am-9.30pm Mon-Thu, to 11pm Fri, 10am-11pm Sat, 10am-9.30pm Sun) Drop into this old waterfront warehouse to sample the output of Ōamaru's popular craft brewers. Slouch against the counter for a tasting or head out onto the sunny deck for a pint (including many gluten-free options) and an excellent pizza.

New Zealand Whisky Collection
DISTILLERY

(📞027 942 5739; www.thenzwhisky.com; Harbour St; per glass $18-25, 4-whisky flight $30; ⏰10.30am-4.30pm) This is actually a maturation house rather than a distillery, where the whiskies are uniquely aged in red-wine barrels, giving them spicy, cherry-plum, Christmas-cake flavours. There are six whiskies for you to taste and the selection changes regularly, or you can also try a hot toddy ($10).

☆ Entertainment

Oamaru

Opera House
THEATRE

(📞03-433 0770; www.oamaruoperahouse.co.nz; 94 Thames St; ⏰ticket office 10am-4pm Mon-Fri, to 1pm Sat) First opened in 1907 and now beautifully restored to its original glory, Ōamaru's opera house hosts a variety of shows, including music, dance, theatre and comedy. The main auditorium seats 500-plus patrons under the stunning 1900s cupola and chandelier, while the smaller **Inkbox** theatre is home to more intimate performances.

Penguin Club
LIVE MUSIC

(www.thepenguinclub.co.nz; Emulsion Lane, off Harbour St; cover charge varies) Tucked down an atmospheric alley off a 19th-century street, the Penguin's unusual location matches its acts: everything from touring Kiwi bands to punky/grungy/rocky/country locals. It's a members club (you can join at the door) and shows are intermittent (check ahead of your visit on www.facebook.com/the penguinclub).

ℹ Information

Ōamaru i-SITE (📞03-434 1656; www.waitaki nz.com; 1 Thames St; ⏰9am-5pm; 🛜) The friendly staff at this i-SITE can offer you mountains of information including details on local walking trips and wildlife, plus they'll give you daily penguin-viewing times. There's also an interesting 10-minute film on the history of the town.

ℹ Getting There & Away

Ōamaru sits on the main SH1 coastal route between Christchurch (3¼ hours) and Dunedin (1½ hours).

Most buses and shuttles depart from the **Lagonda Tearooms** (📞03-434 8716; www. facebook.com/lagondatearooms.oamaru; 191 Thames St; ⏰9am-4.30pm; 🛜). Note that both the tearooms and the i-SITE take bookings.

RIVERSTONE

This idiosyncratic complex, 14km north of Ōamaru, is the home of **Riverstone Kitchen** (☑ 03-431 3505; www.riverstonekitchen.co.nz; 1431 SH1, Waitaki Bridge; mains $25-36, feasting menu $70; ⊙ 9am-late Thu-Sat, to 5pm Sun & Mon), a sophisticated destination restaurant headed by award-winning chef Bevan Smith. Much of the produce comes from the extensive on-site kitchen gardens (go for a stroll, they're impressive), plus locally sourced venison, pork, salmon, beef and wine. It's a smashing brunch option, with excellent coffee and legendary truffled scrambled eggs. Save room for dessert, too.

Next door, behind a set of fake heritage shopfronts, **Riverstone Country** (☑ 03-431 3872; 1431 SH1, Waitaki Bridge; ⊙ 9am-5.30pm) is literally packed to the rafters with gifts, crafts, homewares, fake flowers, garden ornaments and Christmas decorations, like the cast-offs of an overstocked kingdom of cute. And what's that looming over the complex? A moated **castle** of course. It's all the brainchild of Bevan's mum Dot Smith, one of the owners of Riverstone and queen of the castle.

Atomic Shuttles (☑ 210 867 6001; www.atomictravel.co.nz) Buses once daily to/from Christchurch ($35, four hours), Timaru ($25, 1¼ hours), Moeraki Boulders ($20, 30 minutes) and Dunedin ($25, 1¼ hours).

Coast Line Tours (☑ 03-434 7744; www.coastline-tours.co.nz) Shuttles once daily to/from Dunedin (adult/child $40/25); pick-up at your accommodation. Detours to Moeraki and Dunedin Airport can be arranged.

InterCity (☑ 03-471 7143; www.intercity.co.nz) Three or four daily coaches to/from Christchurch (from $24, four hours), Timaru (from $16, one hour), the Moeraki turn-off (from $12, 28 minutes) and Dunedin (from $16, 1½ hours), and one to Te Anau (from $48, 6½ hours).

Moeraki

POP 60

The name Moeraki means 'a place to sleep by day', which should give you some clue as to the pace of life in this little fishing village. You might be surprised to learn that this was one of the first European settlements in New Zealand, with a whaling station established here in 1836. Since then, Moeraki has nurtured the creation of several national treasures, from Frances Hodgkins' paintings to author Keri Hulme's *The Bone People,* and Fleur Sullivan's cooking. Apart from Fleur's eponymous restaurant, the main reason travellers stop in town is the **Moeraki Boulders** (Te Kaihinaki; off SH1), beloved of photographers and children alike.

Riverside Haven Lodge & Holiday Park   CAMPGROUND $
(☑ 03-439 5830; www.riversidehaven.nz; 2328 Herbert Hampden Rd/SH1, Waianakarua; unpow-ered/powered sites from $29/32, d with/without bathroom from $110/90; ☎) ✿ Nestled in a loop of the Waianakarua River, 12km north of the Moeraki turn-off, this certified-organic riverside property offers both bucolic camping sites and colourful lodge rooms, some with en suites. Kids will love the playground and farm animals; parents will love the spa and peaceful vibe.

Moeraki Haven Motel   COTTAGE $$
(☑ 03-439 4859; www.moerakihavenmotel.co.nz; 28 Haven St; 1-/3-bed units from $150/165, studio from $125; P ☎) Commanding jaw-dropping views over the shoreline, these spic-and-span, self-contained units perched high above the ocean are a great choice for families or groups. The owners have a range of accommodation in the area.

★**Fleur's Place**   SEAFOOD $$$
(☑ 03-439 4480; www.fleursplace.com; Old Jetty, 169 Haven St; mains $22-45; ⊙ 10.30am-late Wed-Sun) There's a rumble-tumble look about it, but this tin-and-timber fishing hut houses one of the South Island's best – and most popular – seafood restaurants. The straightforward, scribble-covered decor mirrors the simple, clean handling of the food. Tuck into fresh shellfish, tender blue cod and other recently landed ocean bounty. There's a smokehouse on-site and you can try mutton bird here too. Book ahead.

❶ Getting There & Away

Moeraki is on SH1, a 30-minute drive from Ōamaru and one hour from Dunedin. Buses travelling between the two stop on SH1 by the Moeraki turn-off, if you ask in advance. From here it's about a 2km walk to both the centre of the village and to the boulders.

DUNEDIN

POP 130,700

Dunedin is full of hidden surprises. Firmly on the international street-art map since A-list Belgian aerosol artist ROA put up his beautiful tuatara at 7 Bath St in 2014, it now has artists from around the world vying for the best wall space in town. Many of them are drawn to the city's blossoming warehouse precinct, south of The Octagon, home to funky burger joints and vegan cafes. Dunedin also boasts a vibrant live-music scene, supported by the students of New Zealand's oldest university, and the wildlife-rich Otago Peninsula, which officially lies within the city limits.

And Dunedin has not forgotten its roots. The 'Edinburgh of the South' is immensely proud of its Scottish heritage, never missing an opportunity to break out the haggis and bagpipes on civic occasions. In fact, the very name Dunedin is derived from the Scottish Gaelic name for Edinburgh – Dùn Èideann – and the city even has its own tartan.

History

The first permanent European settlers, two shiploads of pious, hard-working Scots, arrived at Port Chalmers in 1848, including the nephew of Scotland's favourite son, Robbie Burns. A statue of the poet dominates The Octagon, the city's civic heart.

In the 1980s Dunedin spawned its own internationally influential indie music scene, with Flying Nun Records and the 'Dunedin sound'. And not to be left out of this creative profusion, Dunedin's literary heritage and culture was recognised in 2014 when the city became NZ's first Unesco City of Literature.

◉ Sights

◉ City Centre

★ **Toitū Otago Settlers Museum**   MUSEUM
(Map p148; ☑03-477 5052; www.toituosm.com; 31 Queens Gardens; ⊙10am-5pm; ♠) FREE Storytelling is the focus of this excellent interactive museum, which traces the history of human settlement on the South Island. Pass through the new albatross *waharoa* (entranceway) by master carver James York to enter the engrossing Māori section, followed by a large gallery where floor-to-ceiling portraits of Victorian-era settlers stare out from behind their whiskers and lace. Walk through a re-created passenger-ship cabin (you can try out a bunk) and check out the fascinating array of obsolete technology.

Dunedin Railway Station   HISTORIC BUILDING
(Map p148; 22 Anzac Ave; ⊙8am-5pm Mon-Fri, 8.30am-3pm Sat & Sun) Featuring mosaic-tile floors and glorious stained-glass windows, Dunedin's striking bluestone railway station (built between 1903 and 1906) claims to be NZ's most photographed building. Head upstairs for the **New Zealand Sports Hall of Fame** (Map p148; ☑03-477 7775; www.nzhalloffame.co.nz; Dunedin Railway Station, 22 Anzac Ave; adult/child $6/2; ⊙10am-4pm), a small museum devoted to the nation's obsession, and the **Art Station** (Map p148; ☑03-477 9465; www.otagoartsociety.co.nz; Dunedin Railway Station, 22 Anzac Ave; ⊙10am-4pm) FREE, the local Art Society's gallery and shop. The station is the departure point for several popular scenic rail journeys (p150).

Dunedin Public Art Gallery   GALLERY
(Map p148; ☑03-474 3240; www.dunedin.art.museum; 30 The Octagon; ⊙10am-5pm; ♠) FREE Gaze upon local and international art – including a small collection of Impressionists – at this expansive and airy gallery. Only a fraction of the collection is displayed at any given time, with most of the space given over to often-edgy temporary exhibitions with a focus on interactive art. A new playspace (open 10am to 4.30pm) encourages kids to get crafty and hands-on.

St Paul's Cathedral   CHURCH
(Map p148; www.stpauls.net.nz; Moray Pl; ⊙10am-4pm Oct-Apr, to 3pm May-Sep) Even in Presbyterian Dunedin, the 'established church' (aka the Church of England) gets the prime spot on The Octagon. A Romanesque portal leads into the Gothic interior of this beautiful Anglican cathedral, where soaring white Ōamaru-stone pillars spread into a vaulted ceiling. The main part of the church dates from 1919, although the sanctuary was left unfinished until 1971, hence the slightly jarring modern extension. The massive organ (3500 pipes) is said to be one of the finest in the southern hemisphere.

Dunedin Chinese Garden   GARDENS
(Map p148; ☑03-477 3248; www.dunedinchinesegarden.com; cnr Rattray & Cumberland Sts; adult/child $9.50/free; ⊙10am-5pm) Built to recognise the contribution of Dunedin's Chinese community, this walled garden was constructed in Shanghai before being dismantled and reassembled in its current location. The tranquil confines contain all of the elements of a classical Chinese garden, including ponds, pavilions, rockeries, stone bridges and a tea

UNESCO CITY OF LITERATURE

Dunedin was designated a Unesco City of Literature in 2014, in recognition of the profound creative energy of this small southern city. If you'd like to explore Dunedin's literary side during your stay, check out the City of Literature office's website (www.cityofliterature.co.nz) for information about readings, launches and other literary events, or take a **Literary Walking Tour** (☑ 027 444 4788; www.literarytours.nz; tours from $25).

Nowhere is Dunedin's bookishness more evident than in the city's bookstores, whose number seems at odds with Dunedin's relatively small population. As well as the usual chain stores and the excellent **University Book Shop** (Map p148; ☑ 03-477 6976; www.unibooks.co.nz; 378 Great King St, North Dunedin; ⊗ 8.30am-5.30pm Mon-Fri, 10am-4pm Sat & Sun), be sure to seek out some of the city's abundance of secondhand bookshops, which are all packed to the ceiling with intriguing volumes. Favourites include **Dead Souls** (Map p148; ☑ 021 0270 8540; www.deadsouls.co.nz; 393 Princes St; ⊗ 10am-6pm Mon-Sat), **Scribes** (Map p148; ☑ 03-477 6874; 546 Great King St; ⊗ 10am-5.30pm Mon-Fri, to 4.30pm Sat & Sun) and **Hard to Find Books** (Map p148; ☑ 03-471 8518; www.hardtofind.co.nz; 20 Dowling St; ⊗ 10am-6pm).

house. There's also a small display on the history of the local Chinese community.

Speight's Brewery
BREWERY

(Map p148; ☑ 03-477 7697; www.speights.co.nz; 200 Rattray St; adult/child $30/14; ⊗ tours noon, 2pm, 4pm Apr-Sep, plus 5pm, 6pm & 7pm Oct-Mar) Speight's has been churning out beer on this site since the late 19th century and is the oldest operating brewery in NZ. The 60-minute tour gives an insight into the history of the building, the company and the brewing process, and finishes up in the tasting room for a guided 30-minute, six-beer sampling session. On the street outside, a tap delivers the chemical-free spring water that feeds the brewery to passers-by. Donations go to local wetland rehabilitation. Tours can be combined with a meal at **Speight's Ale House** (Map p148; ☑ 03-471-9050; www.thealehouse.co.nz; 200 Rattray St; ⊗ 11.30am-2pm & 5-9pm).

⊙ North Dunedin

★ Olveston
HOUSE

(Map p148; ☑ 03-477 3320; www.olveston.co.nz; 42 Royal Tce, Roslyn; adult/child $23/13; ⊗ tours 9.30am, 10.45am, noon, 1.30pm, 2.45pm & 4pm) Although it's a youngster by European standards, this spectacular 1906 mansion provides a wonderful window into Dunedin's past. Entry is via fascinating one-hour guided tours; it pays to book ahead. There's also a pretty little garden to explore (entry free) with a beautifully preserved 1921 Fiat 510 on display.

Until 1966 Olveston was the family home of the wealthy Theomin family, notable patrons of the arts who were heavily involved with endowing the Public Art Gallery. This artistic bent is evident in Olveston's grand interiors, which include works by Charles Goldie and Frances Hodgkins (a family friend). A particular passion was Japanese art, and the home is liberally peppered with exquisite examples. The family was Jewish, and the grand dining table is set up as if for Shabbat dinner.

Otago Museum
MUSEUM

(Map p148; ☑ 03-474 7474; www.otagomuseum.nz; 419 Great King St, North Dunedin; ⊗ 10am-5pm) 🏷 FREE The centrepiece of this august institution is Southern Land, Southern People, showcasing Otago's cultural and physical past and present, from geology and dinosaurs to the modern day. The Tāngata Whenua Māori gallery houses an impressive *waka taua* (war canoe), wonderfully worn old carvings, and some lovely *pounamu* (greenstone) weapons, tools and jewellery. Other major galleries include Pacific Cultures, People of the World (including the requisite mummy), Nature, Maritime and the Animal Attic. The **Tūhura Otago Community Trust Science Centre** (adult/child $15/10) boasts 45 hands-on interactive science displays, a Tropical Forest butterfly enclosure and a 7.5m-high double helix slide. There's also a **planetarium** ($12/7), which screens films on its 360-degree dome.

Guided tours depart from the information desk at 11am, 1pm, 2pm and 3pm daily ($15 per person).

Dunedin Museum of Natural Mystery
MUSEUM

(Map p148; ☑ 021 032 9906; www.royaldunedinmuseum.com; 61 Royal Tce; adult/child $5/free; ⊗ noon-5pm Fri, from 10am Sat & Sun) This oddball collection of skulls, body bits, ethnographic art and beautiful bone sculptures

Central Dunedin

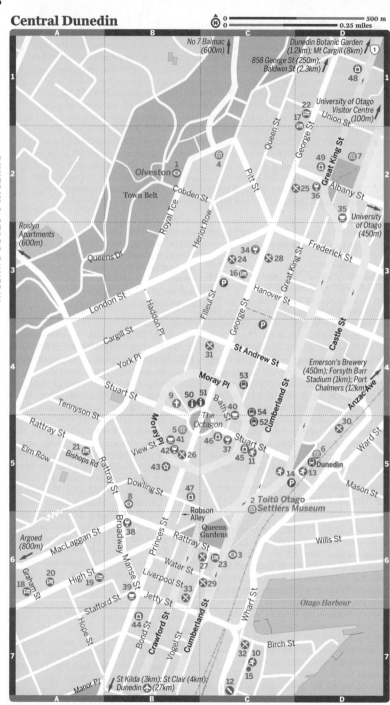

0   500 m
0   0.25 miles

No 7 Balmac
(600m)

Dunedin Botanic Garden
(1.2km); Mt Cargill (8km)

858 George St (250m);
Baldwin St (2.3km)

48

University of Otago
Visitor Centre
(100m)

22
17

49

7

Olveston   1

4

25   36

Town Belt

Cobden St

Royal Tce

Pitt St

35

University
of Otago
(450m)

Roslyn
Apartments
(600m)

Queens Dr

Heriot Row

Albany St

Frederick St

34
24   28

16

London St

Filleul St

Hanover St

Cargill St

Haddon Pl

George St

Great King St

Castle St

York Pl

31

St Andrew St

Emerson's Brewery
(450m); Forsyth Barr
Stadium (1km); Port
Chalmers (12km)

Moray Pl

53

9   51
50

40

54
52

Anzac Ave

Stuart St

Tennyson St

The
Octagon

46   37

30

Rattray St

5   41
42   26

45   11

6

Elm Row

21
Bishops Rd

43

14   13   Dunedin

Mason St

Dowling St

47

8

Robson
Alley

2 Toitū Otago
Settlers Museum

Argoed
(800m)

38

Queens
Gardens

Wills St

MacLaggan St

Broadway

Princes St

Manse St

Rattray St

Water St

3

27   23

20

High St

19

Liverpool St

39   33

Otago Harbour

18
Graham St

Stafford St

Jetty St

29

44

Bond St

Crawford St

Vogel St

Cumberland St

Wharf St

Birch St

Hope St

32   10

15

Manor Pl

St Kilda (3km); St Clair (4km);
Dunedin ✈ (27km)

12

Central Dunedin

DUNEDIN & OTAGO DUNEDIN

has been assembled by local mural artist and sculptor Bruce Mahalski. If you feel at home with a few skeletons in the closet, you can stay here too (double from $120).

Emerson's Brewery BREWERY
(Map p158; ☎ 03-477 1812; www.emersons.co.nz; 70 Anzac Ave; tours per person $28; ⊙ tours 10am, noon, 2pm, 4pm & 6pm Oct-Mar, 11am, 2pm & 6pm Apr-Sep, restaurant 10am-late, cellar door 10am-8pm) This impressive brick-and-glass structure is the flash home of Emerson's, the microbrewery founded by local-boy-made-good Richard Emerson in 1992. Forty-five-minute tours take you behind the scenes of the brewing process, ending with the all-important tasting. There's also a cellar door where you can fill a rigger with your favourite drop – or, if you'd like to linger longer, drop into the

lively, cavernous restaurant for hearty meals (mains $17 to $35).

Baldwin Street LANDMARK
(Map p158; North East Valley) This street proudly held the title of steepest street in the world until July 2019, when Ffordd Pen Llech in the Welsh town of Harlech was officially recognised as steeper by Guinness World Records. Dunedin went into shock and at the time of writing local surveyor Toby Stoff was mounting a challenge to the controversial decision. Stay tuned... However, not even the Welsh can deny that Baldwin St is pretty bloody steep, with a gradient of 1 in 2.86 (19 degrees).

To reach the street from the city centre, head 2km north up Great King St and stay in the right-hand lane to continue on when the left lane branches off towards Timaru. Baldwin St is signposted after 1km.

University of Otago HISTORIC BUILDING
(Map p158; www.otago.ac.nz; 362 Leith St) Founded in 1869, the University of Otago is NZ's oldest. Today the university is home to some 21,000 students, and is well worth a wander, with many magnificent bluestone buildings to admire. The historic heart – bounded by Leith, St David and Castle Sts – is the most photogenic part of the campus. Check the university website for a self-guided tour map. You can buy uni merch from the **visitor centre** (Map p158; www.otago.ac.nz; cnr Cumberland & David Sts; ⊙9am-4.30pm Mon-Fri, 10.30am-3pm Sat).

 Activities

Swimming, Surfing & Diving

St Clair and St Kilda are both popular swimming beaches (though you need to watch for rips at St Clair). Both have consistently good left-hand breaks, and you'll also find good surfing further south at Blackhead, and at Aramoana on Otago Harbour's North Shore.

Esplanade Surf School SURFING
(Map p158; ☑0800 484 141; www.espsurfschool. co.nz; 1 Esplanade, St Clair; 90min group lesson $60, private instruction $120) Operating from a van parked at St Clair Beach in summer whenever the surf is up (call at other times), this experienced crew provides board hire ($40 for two hours including wetsuit) and lessons to suit all levels.

St Clair Hot Salt Water Pool SWIMMING
(Map p158; www.dunedin.govt.nz; Esplanade, St Clair; adult/child $6.70/3; ⊙6am-7pm Mon-Fri, from 7am Sat & Sun Oct-Mar) This heated outdoor pool, averaging 28°C, sits on the western headland of St Clair Beach.

Dive Otago DIVING
(Map p148; ☑03-466 4370; www.diveotago.co.nz; 2 Wharf St; full-day guided dive from $150; ⊙8.30am-5.30pm Mon-Sat) Guided shore dives to see the likes of inquisitive blue cod and sea lions. You can also hire gear ($100) and tanks ($20).

Walking

Tunnel Beach Walkway WALKING
(Tunnel Beach Rd, Blackhead) This short but extremely steep pathway (20 minutes down, 40 back up) brings you to a dramatic stretch of coast where the wild Pacific has carved sea stacks, arches and unusual formations

out of the limestone. The tunnel is cut off at high tide so check tide times online or with the i-SITE (p156) before you set off. Strong currents make swimming here dangerous, but the views are spectacular.

Mt Cargill-Bethunes Gully Walkway WALKING
(Map p158; www.doc.govt.nz; Norwood St, Normanby) Yes, it's possible to drive up 676m Mt Cargill, but that's not the point. The track (four hours, 8.5km return) starts from Norwood St, which is accessed from North Rd. From Mt Cargill, a trail continues to the 10-million-year-old, lava-formed Organ Pipes and, after another half hour, to Mt Cargill Rd on the other side of the mountain.

Other Activities

★**Dunedin Railways** RAIL
(Map p148; ☑03-477 4449; www.dunedinrailways. co.nz; Dunedin Railway Station, 22 Anzac Ave; ⊙office 8am-5pm Mon-Fri, 8.30am-3pm Sat & Sun) Two scenic heritage train journeys set off from Dunedin's railway station (p146). The best is the **Taieri Gorge Railway**, with narrow tunnels, deep gorges, winding tracks, rugged canyons and viaduct crossings. The four-hour return trip aboard 1920s heritage coaches travels to Pukerangi (one way/return adult $72/115, child $19/29), 58km away, leaving at 9.30am and 3pm daily.

On Sundays Taieri Gorge trains carry on for another 20km from Pukerangi to Middlemarch (adult/child one way from Dunedin $81/21) – the start of the Otago Central Rail Trail (p162).

The **Seasider** heads north along the coast as far as Waitati (adult/child return $70/25, two hours) once or twice daily, depending on the season. Aim for a seat on the right-hand side of the train for better sea views.

Check the website for precise schedules.

Ocho FOOD & DRINK
(Map p148; ☑03-425 7819; www.ocho.co.nz; 10 Roberts St; adult/child $25/15; ⊙tours 11am & 2pm Mon-Sat) Dunedin chocaholics shed a tear when Cadbury World shut down its much-loved chocolate factory tours in 2018. But filling the gap is indie choccy maker Ocho, with single-origin chocolate sourced from PNG, the Solomons and further afield that is far less processed than its big competitor. Drop into the **Bay Road Peanut Butter** (Map p148; ☑022 679 6420; www.bayroad.nz; 8 Roberts St; ⊙7.30am-1.30pm Mon-Fri) roastery next door too.

🏃 Walking Tour
Street Art Stroll

START TOITŪ OTAGO SETTLERS MUSEUM
END SPEIGHT'S BREWERY
LENGTH 2KM; THREE HOURS

Wander through the excellent ❶ **Toitū Otago Settlers Museum** (p146) to emerge just outside street-art central. Cross Cumberland St and head a block west then left down Vogel St. You'll spot a number of pieces as you make your way to ❷ **Vogel St Kitchen** (p154), which sports UK artist Phlegm's stunning artwork of a fish swallowing an armada of *waka* and other boats. Swing up Jetty St and up to Bond St to see Polish artist Natalia Rak's ❸ **Love is in the Air** featuring portraits of herself and her husband, fellow street-artist Bezt, as children – she's stealing a kiss. Back on Jetty St, check out Italian Pixel Poncho's floral/robot ❹ **Riding Dreams**. Cross Princes St and duck around the corner to see the ❺ **collaboration piece** by Pixel Poncho and Phlegm. Each started at a diagonal corner of the wall and their unique styles intertwined as they met in the middle. Continue along Stafford for Chinese artist DALeast's portrayal of NZ's extinct ❻ **Haast eagle**, a creation of shining steel ribbons. Duck back up Manse St, past another Phlegm wall, ❼ **Song Pipe Organ**, then right down High St to Polish artist Bezt's enormous painting of a dying woman ❽ **The Hunter has Been Hunted**, featuring a fantail (*pīwakawaka*), a Māori symbol of death.

Head east down High St, north on Princes and right onto Rattray and through the car park on your left to see the stunning 3D chrome-style ❾ **bull** by Puerto Rico's Bik-Ismo. Head back west on Rattray to see Australian artist Fintan Magee's ❿ **Chasing the Thin White Cloud** featuring three local kids netting the famous symbol of Aotearoa. Round the corner of the ⓫ **Crown Hotel** (p155) to the Broadway-facing wall where Dunedin's Aroha Novak and Guy Howard Smith pay tribute to Chi Fooi, an early citizen whose four grandsons still run the pub. Have a drink here or cross the road to ⓬ **Speight's** (p147), where they brew with water from the natural spring below.

Escape

Dunedin Prison   LIVE CHALLENGE

(Map p148; ☑ 027 783 8811; www.escapedunedin.
com; 2 Castle St; 2-/3-person game $50/75) Dunedin Prison (which operated from 1896 until 2007) now hosts an escape room. Perfect for a rainy day.

Cycle World   CYCLING

(Map p148; ☑ 03-477 7473; www.cycleworld.co.nz; 67 Stuart St; per day from $50; ⊙ 8.30am-5.30pm Mon-Fri, 9.30am-3.30pm Sat, 10am-3pm Sun) Bike hire, repair and information.

🖝 Tours

★ Dunedin Street Art
Walking Tour   WALKING

(☑ 027 389 9060; adult/child $30/free; ⊙ 10.30am) She may be a self-described 'senior entrepreneur' but Victoria Gilliand, aka Street Kiwi, is a huge street-art fan girl (and practitioner: she's a yarn-bomber) who personally gets to know all the local and international artists contributing to Dunedin's world-class walls. Follow her down alleyways and through car parks on this two-hour tour to find out all the goss. Book ahead at the i-SITE (p156).

🎆 Festivals & Events

Dunedin
Fringe Festival   PERFORMING ARTS

(www.dunedinfringe.nz; ⊙ Mar) The world's southernmost fringe festival puts arty events in venues across town.

🛌 Sleeping

Rates in Dunedin skyrocket when big events are in town and at the start of the academic year (mid to late February). Also take into account the calf-burning climb if you choose a place uphill.

🛏 City Centre

★ Hogwartz   HOSTEL $

(Map p148; ☑ 03-474 1487; www.hogwartz.co.nz; 277 Rattray St; dm/s/d from $28/60/80, d with bathroom $95, studio $120; ⊙ Oct-Jun; 🅿 @ 🛜) The Catholic bishop's residence from 1872 to 1999, this beautiful building is now a fascinating warren of comfortable and sunny rooms, many with harbour views. Shared bathrooms include welcome touches like waterfall showers and underfloor heat-

ing. The old coach house and stables have swankier en suite rooms and apartments.

Chalet
Backpackers   HOSTEL $

(Map p148; ☑ 03-479 2075; www.chaletbackpackers.
co.nz; 296 High St; dm/s/d without bathrooom from $21/44/72; @ 🛜) At the top of the High St hill, this rambling old building offers sweeping views of the city from its sunny lounge and dining room; there's also a pool table, a piano and rumours of a ghost. Rooms are ageing but tidy.

315 Euro   MOTEL $$

(Map p148; ☑ 03-477 9929; www.eurodunedin.
co.nz; 315 George St; studio from $178, 1-bed apt from $210; 🅿 @ 🛜) This sleek complex is accessed by an unlikely looking alley off Dunedin's main retail strip. Choose from modern studios or larger one-bedroom apartments with full kitchens and laundries. Double glazing keeps George St's incessant buzz at bay.

Dunedin
Palms Motel   MOTEL $$

(Map p148; ☑ 03-477 8293; www.dunedinpalms
motel.co.nz; 185-195 High St; units with/without spa from $189/179; 🅿 🛜) Located a mercifully short stroll up from the city centre, the Palms has smartly renovated studios and one- and two-bedroom units arrayed around a central car park. All have kitchen facilities.

★ Terminus Hotel   APARTMENT $$$

(Map p148; ☑ 021 762 667; www.warehousepre
cinct.co.nz/terminus-apartments; 42 Queens Gardens; 1-/2-bedroom apt from $225/330; 🛜) This late-Victorian building always had great bones, with its high ceilings and arched windows, but owners Steve and Antonia have worked makeover magic turning the once dilapidated hotel into chic apartments. Some have balconies and loft spaces; all have beautiful exposed red-brick walls, a modern kitchen, a laundry and everything else you need for a comfy stay – even a popcorn machine.

Fletcher Lodge   B&B $$$

(Map p148; ☑ 03-474 5552; www.fletcherlodge.
co.nz; 276 High St; s/d incl breakfast from $310/355; 🅿 🛜) 🍃 Originally home to one of NZ's wealthiest industrialists, this gorgeous red-brick mansion is just minutes from the

city, but the secluded gardens feel wonderfully remote. Rooms are elegantly trimmed with antique furniture and ornate plaster ceilings and are snug on cold nights with underfloor bathroom heating.

North Dunedin

★ Kiwi's Nest
HOSTEL $

(Map p148; ☑03-471 9540; www.kiwisnest. co.nz; 597 George St, North Dunedin; dm $28, s with/without bathroom $80/55, d $100/80, apt $120; P @ ⚘) Kiwi's Nest is a wonderfully homey two-storey house with a range of tidy centrally heated rooms, some with en suite, fridge and kettle. Plus it's a flat walk to The Octagon – something few Dunedin hostels can boast.

858 George St
MOTEL $$$

(Map p158; ☑03-474 0047; www.858georgestreet motel.co.nz; 858 George St, North Dunedin; units $180-325; P ⚘) ✈ Recently refreshed with new furniture and a paint job, this top-quality motel complex has modern units ranging in size from studios to two bedrooms. Studios are fitted with a microwave, fridge, toaster and a kettle, while the larger units also have a stove top or a full oven.

Bluestone on George
APARTMENT $$$

(Map p148; ☑03-477 9201; www.bluestonedune din.co.nz; 571 George St, North Dunedin; apt from $225; P @ ⚘) If you're expecting an imposing old bluestone building, think again: this four-storey block couldn't be more contemporary. The elegant studio units are decked out in muted tones, with kitchenettes, laundry facilities and decks or tiny balconies – some with harbour views. There's also a small gym and a guest lounge.

St Clair

★ Majestic Mansions – Apartments at St Clair
APARTMENT $$

(Map p158; ☑03-456 5000; www.apartmentsatst clair.co.nz; 15 Bedford St, St Clair; 1-/2-bedroom apt from $179/250; P ⚘) One street back from St Clair Beach, this venerable art-deco apartment block has been thoroughly renovated and restyled by its new owners, sprucing it up with feature wallpaper and smart furnishings. Each has a kitchen and laundry facilities and some have sea views. Prices drop in low season.

Hotel St Clair
HOTEL $$$

(Map p158; ☑03-456 0555; www.hotelstclair.com; 24 Esplanade, St Clair; r $234-394; P ⚘) Soak up St Clair's surfy vibe from the balcony of your chic room in this contemporary medium-rise hotel. All but the cheapest rooms have ocean views, and the beach is only metres from the front door.

Other Suburbs

Dunedin Top 10 Holiday Park
HOLIDAY PARK $

(Map p158; www.aaronlodgetop10.co.nz; 162 Kaikorai Valley Rd, Kaikorai; sites from $28, d cabins from $78, motel r $142-169; P ⚘ ⚞) About 2.5km from the city centre, this spic-and-span park has great facilities and some fun extras like a trampoline, a petanque court, a spa and a heated pool. There's a range of accommodation packed in quite tight.

Argoed
B&B $$$

(Map p158; ☑03-474 1639; www.argoed.co.nz; 504 Queens Dr, Belleknowes; r from $175-250; P ⚘) Roses and rhododendrons encircle this gracious two-storey wooden villa, built in the 1880s. Each of the three charmingly old-fashioned bedrooms has its own bathroom, though only one is en suite. Guests can relax in the conservatory or tinkle the ivories of the grand piano in the lounge.

✕ Eating

Forage for cheap eats from around the world, from Khmer to Mexican, along George St, or hit the hip nosh spots in the converted warehouses along Vogel St. There's a cluster of relaxed bars and cafes in North East Valley, on the way to Baldwin St, while the beachy ambience of St Clair is great for a lazy brunch or sunset drinks.

✕ City Centre

★ Otago Farmers Market
MARKET $

(Map p148; www.otagofarmersmarket.org.nz; Dunedin Railway Station; ⊙8am-12.30pm Sat) This thriving market is all local, all edible (or drinkable) and mostly organic. Grab a freshly baked pastry and a flat white to sustain you while you browse, and stock up on fresh meat, seafood, veggies and cheese for your journey. Sorted.

JUST GIVE ME THE COFFEE & NO ONE WILL GET HURT

Dunedin has loads of excellent coffee bars in which you can refuel and re-charge. Try these:

Mazagran Espresso Bar (Map p148; 36 Moray Pl; ⊗8am-4.30pm Mon-Fri, to 2pm Sat)

Insomnia by Strictly Coffee (Map p148; ☑03-479 0017; www.strictlycoffee. co.nz; 23 Bath St; ⊗7.30am-4pm Mon-Fri)

Allpress (Map p148; ☑03-477 7162; www. allpressespresso.com; 12 Emily Siedeberg Pl; ⊗8am-4pm Mon-Fri)

Daily Coffee Co (Map p148; ☑021 054 0736; 366a Princes St; ⊗7.30am-2.30pm Mon-Sat; 🛜) 🍴

★ **Good Good** BURGERS $
(Map p148; www.goodgood.co.nz; 22 Vogel St; burgers $15; ⊗11.30am-2.30pm & 5-8pm) The crafty cooks here sizzle up famously good burgers from a kitchen in a retro caravan parked inside a cool warehouse space. There's tags on the walls, couches on the floor, electronica on the speakers and occasionally someone playing live. Nice place for a drink, too.

Kind Grocer VEGAN $
(Map p148; ☑021 217 4910; www.facebook.com/ kindgrocernz; 49 Vogel St; lunch $9-13; ⊗10am-5pm Tue-Fri, to 3pm Sat & Sun; 🛜☑) Fully vegan and fully delicious, you can dig into the likes of loaded jackfruit with nasturtium and delectable cakes such as raw salted caramel snickers cheesecake or gluten-free chocolate fudge. Then pick up some fresh veg and treats for your travels, including plant pastrami, vegan jerky or marshmallows.

Harry's Kitchen JAPANESE $
(Map p148; ☑03-477 0123; 358 George St; noodles $14; ⊗11am-8pm) Student favourite with authentic Japanese and Korean dishes at a great price. Get your ramen fix here.

Vogel St Kitchen CAFE $$
(Map p148; ☑03-477 3623; www.vogelstkitchen. co.nz; 76 Vogel St; sandwiches $16, pizzas $25; ⊗7.30am-3pm Mon-Fri, 8.30am-4pm Sat & Sun; 🛜) In the heart of Dunedin's warehouse precinct, Vogel St Kitchen offers smashing breakfasts and wood-fired pizzas in a cavernous two-storey red-brick building. It gets especially busy on weekends, when local residents make the most of large shared tables for long lazy brunches.

Etrusco at the Savoy ITALIAN $$
(Map p148; ☑03-477 3737; www.etrusco.co.nz; 8a Moray Pl; mains $18-27; ⊗5.30pm-late) This boisterous pizza-and-pasta joint resides in the elegant Edwardian dining room of the Savoy, with its moulded ceilings, stained-glass crests and green Ionian columns. It's a slightly strange fit but it works, with hearty food and chandeliers setting just the right tone for big birthday celebrations and students taking out-of-town parents to dinner.

Paasha TURKISH $$
(Map p148; ☑03-477 7181; www.paasha.co.nz; 31 St Andrew St; mains lunch $13-20, dinner $19-36; ⊗11.30am-3pm & 5-9pm Mon-Wed, from 11am Thu-Sun; 🍴) Authentic kebabs, dips and salads are on the menu at this long-running Dunedin favourite. It's a top place for takeaways, and most nights the spacious and warm interior is filled with groups drinking Efes beer and sharing heaving platters of tasty Turkish goodness.

★ **Bracken** MODERN NZ $$$
(Map p148; ☑03-477 9779; www.brackenrestaurant.co.nz; 95 Filleul St; menus from $55; ⊗11.30am-2pm & 5pm-late Tue-Sat) 🍴 Bracken's seasonal tasting menus offer a succession of pretty little plates bursting with flavour. While the dishes are intricate, nothing's overly gimmicky, and the setting, in an old wooden house, is classy without being too formal. Meals can be paired with wine (from $45) or whisky (from $35).

Plato MODERN NZ $$$
(Map p148; ☑03-477 4235; www.platocafe.co.nz; 2 Birch St; mains lunch $20-25, dinner $36; ⊗noon-2pm Wed-Sun, 6pm-late daily) The unpromising locale and kooky decor (including collections of toys and beer tankards) gives little indication of the seriously good food on offer at this relaxed eatery. Fresh fish and shellfish, including oysters in season, feature prominently. Try the house-brewed beer.

🍴 North Dunedin

Buster Greens CAFE $$
(Map p148; ☑03-470 1233; 466 George St, North Dunedin; mains $22-25; ⊗6.30am-3.30pm Mon-Fri, from 7.30am Sat, from 8.30am Sun; ☑) Bright and bustling cafe with top-notch brunches, healthy raw sweet treats and colourful salads. Great vegan selection. There's more

seating downstairs and blankets to ward off the chill at the tables outside.

St Clair

Starfish
CAFE $$

(Map p158; 03-455 5940; www.starfishcafe.co.nz; 7/240 Forbury Rd, St Clair; mains $15-24; 6.30am-late Tue-Sat, to 5pm Sun, to 4.30pm Mon) Part of the growing restaurant scene at St Clair Beach, Starfish is a popular all-day eatery offering decadent brunch dishes, good coffee and a great buzz. Pop in for a quick lunch on the balcony overlooking the beach, or drop by in the evening for a hearty dinner accompanied by a glass of wine or a wide selection of craft beer.

Esplanade
ITALIAN $$

(Map p158; 03-456 2544; www.esplanade.co; 2 Esplanade, St Clair; mains $21-26; 8am-late;) A prime position overlooking St Clair Beach is only the beginning at this relaxed Italian cafe-restaurant from the same team as No 7 Balmac. Drop in during the morning for an espresso and a panino, or come by in the evening for authentic thin-crust pizzas. At sunset the windows offer the perfect frame as lavender twilight descends over the beach.

Other Suburbs

No 7 Balmac
CAFE $$$

(Map p158; 03-464 0064; www.no7balmac.co.nz; 7 Balmacewen Rd, Maori Hill; mains brunch $14-26, dinner $35-40; 7am-late Mon-Fri, from 8am Sat, 8am-5pm Sun;) We wouldn't recommend walking to this sophisticated cafe at the top of Maori Hill, but luckily it's well worth the price of a cab. The fancy cafe fare stretches from smashing brunches to the likes of confit duck and applewood-grilled pork and fennel. Take a stroll through the organic garden where many of the greens are sourced.

Drinking & Nightlife

★ Dog with Two Tails
BAR

(Map p148; 03-477 4188; www.dogwithtwotails.co.nz; 25 Moray Pl; 11am-late Tue-Fri, from 10am Sat, 10am-4pm Sun) Nightly events here range from jazz jams and soulful singer-songwriters, to indie rock and literary readings with a peppering of quiz nights and open mics. Tuck into its signature crêpes ($6.50 to $12) in the red-painted room under a beautiful stained-glass entranceway.

★ Pequeno
COCKTAIL BAR

(Map p148; 03-477 7830; www.pequeno.co.nz; behind 12 Moray Pl; 5pm-late Mon-Fri, from 7pm Sat) Head down the alley opposite the Rialto Cinema, with the black-and-white *kākāpō* street-art piece by Phelgm, to discover this intimate and sophisticated lounge bar. Music is generally laid-back, with regular live acts. The leather couches, fireplace, tapas menu and excellent wine and cocktail list make this backstreet bar perfect for a chilled night out.

Inch Bar
BAR

(Map p158; 03-473 6496; 8 Bank St, North East Valley; 3pm-late) Make the short trek from town to this cosy bar for its selection of Kiwi craft beers and tasty nibbles, and the cute indoor/outdoor beer garden. Despite its diminutive dimensions, it hosts live music on Friday and Saturday nights, plus there's Vinyl Revival on Monday, open-mic music on Wednesday (free drink if you play) and open-mic comedy Thursday.

Carousel
COCKTAIL BAR

(Map p148; 03-477 4141; 141 Stuart St; 5pm-midnight Wed, to 2am Thu, to 3am Fri & Sat) Monochrome tartan wallpaper, a roof deck and great cocktails leave the classy

---

DUNEDIN'S LIVE-MUSIC SCENE

Don't miss the chance to check out Dunedin's live-music scene. Consult Under the Radar (www.undertheradar.co.nz/utr/gig_guide/otago) for upcoming gigs, or try your luck at one of these venues:

The Cook (Map p148; 03-777 3603; www.thecook.nz; 354 Great King St; 10am-late Sat, to 3.30pm Sun) Raucous rock driven by nearby uni students.

Dog with Two Tails Indie folk, singer-songwriters, and spoken word.

Pequeno Underground bar with stylish loungers tapping toes to jazz and fusion.

The Crown (Map p148; 03-477 0132; 179 Rattray St; 11am-2.30am Fri & Sat, to 11pm Mon-Thu) Anything from punk to funk with posters from Dunedin's dirty '90s on the walls.

Inch Bar Blues, country and local musos.

clientele looking pleased to be seen somewhere so deadly cool. It gets going around 10pm and DJs spin deep house until late. Find it upstairs.

Aika + Co BAR

(Map p148; 357 George St; ⊙7.30am-5pm Mon-Thu, to 7pm Fri, 9am-7pm Sat, 9am-3pm Sun) 'Dunedin's littlest bar' might only be 1.8m wide, but this bolthole on George St is still full of punters. There's sometimes even live musicians squeezed in here in summer. By day, it's a handy caffeine-refuelling spot.

☆ Entertainment

Forsyth Barr Stadium STADIUM

(Map p158; www.forsythbarrstadium.co.nz; 130 Anzac Ave) Constructed for the 2011 Rugby World Cup, this is the only major stadium in NZ with a fully covered roof, and it holds 30,000 spectators. It's the home ground of the Highlanders Super 15 rugby team (www.thehighlanders.co.nz) and the Otago rugby team (www.orfu.co.nz), and also plays regular host to the All Blacks, international sporting matches, concerts and shows.

Rialto Cinemas CINEMA

(Map p148; ☑03-474 2200; www.rialto.co.nz; 11 Moray Pl; adult/child $16/10) Screens blockbusters and art-house flicks. Tickets are cheaper ($9) on Tuesdays.

🛍 Shopping

Gallery De Novo ART

(Map p148; ☑03-474 9200; www.gallerydenovo.co.nz; 101 Stuart St; ⊙9.30am-5.30pm Mon-Fri, 10am-3pm Sat & Sun) This interesting, contemporary, fine-art gallery is worth a peek whether you're likely to invest in a substantial piece of Kiwi art or not.

Guild FASHION & ACCESSORIES

(Map p148; www.guilddunedin.co.nz; 145 Stuart St; ⊙10am-5pm Mon-Sat) This cooperative of Dunedin designers sells high-end fashion, jewellery and homewares made by its 12 members and special guests. You'll find bright and beautiful fabrics, artful clothing cuts and very wearable designs. Pop in for a chat with a local maker – it's always staffed by a member of the co-op.

ℹ Information

The **Dunedin i-SITE** (Map p148; ☑03-474 3300; www.isitedunedin.co.nz; 50 The Octagon; ⊙8.30am-5.30pm Mon-Fri, from 8.45am Sat & Sun) incorporates the **DOC Visitor Centre**

(Department of Conservation; Map p148; ☑03-474 3300; www.doc.govt.nz; 50 The Octagon; ⊙8.30am-5.30pm Mon-Fri), providing a one-stop shop for all of your information needs, including Great Walks and hut bookings.

Dunedin Hospital (☑03-474 0999; 201 Great King St)

Urgent Doctors (☑03-479 2900; www.dunedinurgentdoctors.co.nz; 18 Filleul St; ⊙8am-10pm) There's also a late-night pharmacy next door.

ℹ Getting There & Away

AIR

Air New Zealand (☑0800 737 000; www.airnewzealand.co.nz) flies to/from Auckland, Wellington and Christchurch.

Jetstar (☑0800 800 995; www.jetstar.com) flies to/from Auckland.

Virgin Australia (p135) flies to/from Brisbane, Australia.

BUS

Regional buses leave from Moray Pl, just around the corner from the Bus Hub.

Atomic Shuttles (Map p148; ☑210 867 6001; www.atomictravel.co.nz; 331 Moray Pl) Buses to/from Christchurch ($40, 5¾ hours), Timaru ($30, three hours) and Ōamaru ($25, 1¾ hours), once daily.

Catch-a-Bus (☑03-449 2150; www.trailjourneys.co.nz) Bike-friendly shuttles to/from key Rail Trail towns, including Middlemarch ($55, one hour), Ranfurly ($55, two hours), Alexandra ($60, 3¼ hours) and Clyde ($60, 3½ hours).

InterCity (Map p148; ☑03-471 7143; www.intercity.co.nz; 331 Moray Pl) Coaches run to/from Christchurch (from $29, 5½ hours), Ōamaru (from $23, 1½ hours), Cromwell (from $23, 3¼ hours) and Queenstown (from $24, 4¼ hours) around four times daily, and once daily to Gore (from $15, 2¾ hours) and Te Anau (from $19, 4½ hours). There's also a direct service once weekly to Invercargill (from $23, 3¼ hours).

ℹ Getting Around

TO/FROM THE AIRPORT

Dunedin Airport (DUD; ☑03-486 2879; www.dunedinairport.co.nz; 25 Miller Rd, Momona; 🛜) is 27km southwest of the city. There is no public transport to the airport. A standard taxi ride to/from the city costs around $100. For door-to-door shuttles, try **Kiwi Shuttles** (☑03-487 9790; www.kiwishuttles.co.nz; per 1/2/3/4 passengers $20/36/48/60) or **Super Shuttle** (☑0800 748 885; www.supershuttle.co.nz; per 1/2/3/4 passengers $20/30/40/50) – book in advance.

BUS

Dunedin's **Orbus** (☑ 0800 672 8736; www.orc. govt.nz/public-transport/dunedin-buses; adult $1.92-11.41) network extends across the city. It's particularly handy for getting to St Clair, St Kilda and Port Chalmers, and as far afield as Palmerston or the Otago Peninsula. Buses run regularly from the **Bus Hub** (Map p148; ☑ 0800 672 8736; www.orc.govt.nz/public-transport/dunedin-buses; Great King St) in the city Monday to Friday, with reduced services on weekends.

Individual tickets are available from the bus driver; for longer stays, invest in a GoCard – purchase from bus drivers, from the council offices in The Octagon, or from the University Book Shop (p147) – which offers reduced fares.

CAR

The big international car-hire companies all have offices in Dunedin; local outfits include **Hanson Rental Vehicles** (☑ 03-453 6576; www.hanson. net.nz; 313 Kaikorai Valley Rd; ⊙ 7.30am-5.30pm) and **Ezi Car Rental** (☑ 03-486 1245; www.ezicarrental.co.nz; Dunedin Airport; ⊙ 7.30am-2pm).

SCOOTER

Lime electric scooters (www.li.me; $1, plus per minute 38¢) have arrived in Dunedin. You're allowed to ride them on the footpath if you're considerate of pedestrians.

TAXI

There are several taxi companies in Dunedin. Options include:
Dunedin Taxis (☑ 03-477 7777; www.dunedin taxis.co.nz)
Southern Taxis (☑ 03-476 6300; www.south erntaxis.co.nz)
Green Cabs (☑ 0800 46 47 336; www.green cabs.co.nz).

AROUND DUNEDIN

Port Chalmers

POP 1365

Little Port Chalmers is only 13km from central Dunedin but it feels a world away. Somewhere between working class and bohemian, Port Chalmers is dominated by its huge container terminal, but the coastal landscapes surrounding it are beautiful and the town has long attracted Dunedin's arty types. The main drag, George St, is home to a handful of cafes, design stores and galleries, perfect for a half-day's worth of wandering, browsing and sipping away from the city crush.

Orokonui Ecosanctuary   WILDLIFE RESERVE
(Map p158; ☑ 03-482 1755; www.orokonui.nz; 600 Blueskin Rd; adult/child $20/10; ⊙ 9.30am-4.30pm) From the impressive visitor centre there are great views over this 307-hectare predator-free nature reserve, which encloses cloud forest on the mountainous ridge above Port Chalmers and stretches to the estuary on the opposite side. Its mission is to provide a mainland refuge for species usually exiled to offshore islands for their own protection. Visiting options include self-guided explorations, hour-long 'highlights' tours (adult/child $35/17.50; 11am and 1.30pm daily) and two-hour 'forest explorer' tours (adult/child $50/25; 11am daily).

Hare Hill   HORSE RIDING
(Map p158; ☑ 03-472 8496; www.horseriding-dunedin.co.nz; 207 Aramoana Rd, Deborah Bay; treks $110-220) Horse treks include thrilling beach rides and harbour views.

Carey's Bay Hotel   PUB FOOD **$$**
(Map p158; ☑ 03-472 8022; www.careysbayhotel. co.nz; 17 Macandrew Rd, Carey's Bay; mains $22-35; ⊙ 10am-late) Just around the corner from Port Chalmers you'll find this cosy historic pub, popular with locals for its hearty meals and unbeatable location – on sunny days grab a table out the front.

❶ Getting There & Away

On weekdays bus 14 (adult/child $6/3.60, 30 minutes, half-hourly) travels between Dunedin's Bus Hub and Port Chalmers between 6.30am and 9.30pm (11.30pm on Friday). On Saturday buses run hourly between 8.30am and 11.30pm, and between 9.30am and 5.30pm on Sunday. The Port to Port (p161) private ferry operates from Port Chalmers' Back Beach to Portobello on the Otago Peninsula up to three times daily.

Otago Peninsula

POP 5000

It's hard to believe that the Otago Peninsula – a picturesque haven of rolling hills, secluded bays, sandy beaches and clifftop vistas – is only half an hour's drive from downtown Dunedin. As well as interesting historical sites and wild walking trails, this small sliver of land is home to the South Island's most accessible diversity of wildlife, including albatross, penguins, fur seals and sea lions. The peninsula's only town is the petite Portobello and, despite a host of tours exploring the region, it maintains its quiet rural air.

Dunedin & the Otago Peninsula

⊙ Sights

★ **Nature's Wonders**
Naturally   WILDLIFE RESERVE
(Map p158; ☑03-478 1150; www.natureswonders.
co.nz; Taiaroa Head; adult/child Argo $99/45,
coach $45/22.50, boat $55/22.50; ⊙tours
10.15am-sunset) What makes the improbably
beautiful beaches of this coastal sheep farm
different from other important wildlife
habitats is that (apart from pest eradication
and the like) they're left completely alone.
Many of the multiple private beaches haven't suffered a human footprint in years.
The result is that yellow-eyed penguins can
often be spotted (through binoculars) at
any time of the day, and NZ fur seals laze
around rocky swimming holes, blissfully
unfazed by tour groups passing by.

Depending on the time of year, you might
also see whales and little penguin chicks.
The tour is conducted in 'go-anywhere' Argo
vehicles by enthusiastic guides, at least some

of whom double as true-blue Kiwi farmers.
A less bumpy coach option is also available,
and there's also the *Albatross Express* boat
tour, departing 3km south from Wellers
Rock Wharf (p161), devoted to spotting albatross and sea birds. Combo tours are available.

Royal Albatross Centre
& Fort Taiaroa   BIRD SANCTUARY
(Map p158; ☑03-478 0499; www.albatross.org.nz;
Taiaroa Head; adult/child albatross $52/15, fort
$26/10, combined $62/20; ⊙10.15am-sunset)
Taiaroa Head (Pukekura), at the peninsula's
northern tip, has the world's only mainland
royal albatross colony, along with a late
19th-century military fort. The only public
access to the area is by guided tour. There's
an hour-long albatross tour and a 30-minute
fort tour available, or the two can also be
combined. Otherwise you can just call into
the centre to look at the displays and have a
bite in the cafe.

Dunedin & the Otago Peninsula

◎ Top Sights

◎ Sights

✪ Activities, Courses & Tours

🛏 Sleeping

✕ Eating

◎ Drinking & Nightlife

✪ Entertainment

🛍 Shopping

Albatross are present on Taiaroa Head throughout the year, but the best time to see them is from December to March, when one parent is constantly guarding the young while the other delivers food throughout the day. Sightings are most common in the afternoon when the winds pick up; calm days don't see as many birds in flight.

Little penguins swim ashore at Pilots Beach (just below the car park) around dusk to head to their nests in the dunes. For their protection, the beach is closed to the public every evening one hour before sunset, but viewing is possible from a specially constructed wooden platform (adult/child $35/10). Depending on the time of year, 50 to 200 penguins might waddle past. Photos are allowed, but no flashes.

Fort Taiaroa was built in 1885 in response to a perceived threat of Russian invasion. Its **Armstrong Disappearing Gun** was designed to be loaded and aimed under-ground, then popped up like the world's slowest jack-in-the-box to be fired.

Larnach Castle   CASTLE
(Map p158; ☎ 03-476 1616; www.larnachcastle. co.nz; 145 Camp Rd; adult/child castle & grounds $34/12, grounds only $17/5; ⊗ 8am-7pm Oct-Apr, 9am-5pm May-Sep) 🏆 Standing proudly on

top of a hill overlooking the peninsula, this gorgeous Gothic Revival mansion was built in 1871 by Dunedin banker, merchant and Member of Parliament William Larnach. The castle fell into disrepair after Lanarch's death, until it was purchased by the Barker family in 1967, and a long period of restoration began. The four floors are now filled with intricate woodwork and exquisite antique furnishings, and the crenellated tower offers expansive views.

Penguin Place   BIRD SANCTUARY
(Map p158; ☑03-478 0286; www.penguinplace. co.nz; 45 Pakihau Rd, Harington Point; adult/child $55/16; ☉tours from 10.15am Oct-Mar, 3.45pm Apr-Sep) On private farmland, this reserve protects nesting sites of the rare yellow-eyed penguin (hoiho). The 90-minute tours cover 2km and focus on penguin conservation and close-up viewing from a system of hides. Bookings are recommended.

 Activities

A popular walking destination is beautiful **Sandfly Bay**, reached from Seal Point Rd (one hour return). You can also follow a track from the end of Sandymount Rd to the **Sandymount summit** and on to the impressive **Chasm and Lovers Leap** (one hour return). Note that this track is closed from September to mid-October for lambing. Download the helpful DOC *Dunedin Walks* brochure to plan your hike.

 Tours

Back to Nature Tours   BUS
(☑0800 286 000; www.backtonaturetours.co. nz) ◢ The full-day Royal Peninsula tour (adult/child $205/130) heads to points of interest around Dunedin before hitting the Otago Peninsula. Stops include Larnach Castle's (p159) gardens (castle entry is extra), Penguin Place and the Royal Albatross Centre (p158). There's also a half-day option that visits various beaches ($85/55) and another tackling the Lovers Leap walking track ($99/55). Will pick up from your accommodation.

Wild Earth Adventures   KAYAKING
(☑03-489 1951; www.wildearth.co.nz; per person $115) Offers guided tours in double sea kayaks, with wildlife often sighted en route. Tours take between three and five hours, with pick-ups from The Octagon in Dunedin.

Elm Wildlife Tours   WILDLIFE
(☑03-454 4121; www.elmwildlifetours.co.nz; tours from $103) ◢ Well-regarded, small-group, wildlife-focused tours, with options to add the Royal Albatross Centre (p158) or a Monarch Cruise. Pick-up and drop-off from Dunedin is included.

Monarch Wildlife Cruises & Tours   BOATING
(☑03-477 4276; www.wildlife.co.nz) ◢ One-hour boat trips departing from Wellers Rock Wharf (adult/child $57/22), as well as half-day ($95/35) and full-day ($257/125) tours cruising right along the harbour from Dunedin. You may spot sea lions, penguins, albatross and seals. The full-day option includes admission to the Royal Albatross Centre and Penguin Place.

 Sleeping & Eating

McFarmers Backpackers   HOSTEL $
(Map p158; ☑03-478 0389; mcfarmers@xtra.co.nz; 774 Portobello Rd, Broad Bay; s/d $35/70) On a working sheep farm with harbour views, the rustic timber lodge and self-contained cottage here are steeped in character and feel instantly like home. The Portobello bus goes past the gate.

★**Portobello Motel**   MOTEL $$
(Map p158; ☑03-478 0155; www.portobellomotels. com; 10 Harington Point Rd, Portobello; d units $180; ℙ🐾) These sunny, modern units are thoughtfully decorated and outfitted with all mod cons. The studio units are the pick of the bunch, each with small private decks overlooking the bay. Spacious one- and two-bedroom versions are the same price, but lack the views.

Larnach Castle   B&B $$$
(Map p158; ☑03-476 1616; www.larnachcastle. co.nz; 145 Camp Rd; d stable/lodge/estate $170/330/540; ℙ@🐾) ◢ Larnach Castle's pricey back-garden lodge has 12 unique, whimsically decorated rooms with views. Less frivolous are the atmospheric rooms in the 140-year-old stables (bathrooms are shared). A few hundred metres from the castle, Camp Estate has luxury suites worthy of a romantic splurge. Each option includes breakfast and castle entry; dinner in the castle is extra ($70).

Portobello Hotel & Bistro   PUB FOOD $$
(Map p158; ☑03-478 0759; www.portobellohotel andbistro.com; 2 Harington Point Rd, Portobello;

mains lunch $18-23, dinner $23-36; ⊙11.30am-9pm, to late Fri & Sat) Refreshing thirsty travellers since 1874, the Portobello pub is still a popular pit stop. Grab a table in the sun and tuck into the chef's special seafood chowder, a burger or a fillet of freshly caught blue cod. On Wednesday the kitchen closes after lunch.

1908 Cafe CAFE, BISTRO $$
(Map p158; ☑03-478 0801; www.1908cafe.co.nz; 7 Harington Point Rd, Portobello; mains lunch $12-28, dinner $14-34; ⊙noon-2pm & 5-8.30pm, closed Mon & Tue Apr-Oct) Salmon, venison and steak are joined by fresh fish and blackboard specials at this casual eatery. Cafe fare, such as soup and toasted sandwiches, is served at lunch. As the name suggests, the building originally opened as a tearoom in 1908, and many of the original features are still in place.

ⓘ Getting There & Away

Portobello is a scenic 20km drive from Dunedin along the harbour. A $64 million upgrade to the road was underway at the time of research, with a cycleway/walkway to Portobello along the stunning coastline expected to be completed in 2020.

On weekdays, buses make the journey from Dunedin's Bus Hub to Portobello Village from 7.30am to 10.30pm (adult/child $6/3.60, one hour, half-hourly), with four services continuing to Harington Point ($10.20/6.10) at the tip of the peninsula. On weekends the service reduces to hourly from 8.30am.

The **Port to Port** (☑020 4162 4250; www.porttoport.co.nz; adult/child $12/6) private ferry operates from Port Chalmers' Back Beach to Portobello up to three times daily. This 10-minute trip is an economical way to get out on the water with the possibility of seeing wildlife. The company also runs two-hour wildlife cruises (adult/child $90/46) from **Wellers Rock Wharf** (Map p158; Harrington Point Rd).

Once on the peninsula, it's tough to get around without your own transport. Most tours will pick you up from your Dunedin accommodation.

CENTRAL OTAGO

Central Otago is a remote region of far horizons, rolling hills and distant mountains that turn from green to gold in the relentless summer sun and are blanketed in snow in winter and spring. These lonely landscapes provide a backdrop to a succession of tiny, charming gold-rush towns where farmers mingle with Lycra-clad cyclists in lost-in-time pubs. As well as being one of the coun-

try's top wine regions, the area provides fantastic opportunities for those on two wheels, whether mountain biking along old gold-mining trails or traversing the district on the Otago Central Rail Trail (p162).

Middlemarch
POP 156

With the Rock and Pillar Range as an impressive backdrop, the small town of Middlemarch is the terminus of both the Taieri Gorge Railway and the Otago Central Rail Trail. It's famous in New Zealand for the **Middlemarch Singles Ball** (www.facebook.com/middlemarchsinglesdance; held over Easter in odd-numbered years), where southern men gather to entice city gals to the country life.

🏃 Activities

There are a number of reliable companies offering bike hire and logistical support to riders on the Otago Central Rail Trail. (p162) This includes shuttles, bag transfers and an accommodation booking service.

Trail Journeys CYCLING
(☑03-464 3213; www.trailjourneys.co.nz; 20 Swansea St; per day from $50, e-bikes from $100; ⊙8.30am-4.30pm Sep-May) Provides bike hire and logistical support to riders on the Otago Central Rail Trail. Also has a depot in Clyde (p168), at the other end of the trail.

Cycle Surgery CYCLING
(☑03-464 3630, 0800 292 534; www.cyclesurgery.co.nz; cnr Swansea & Aberafon Sts; per day from $45; ⊙depot 8.30am-5pm mid-Sep–mid-May) Bikes and logistics for Rail Trailers. At the time of writing the company was renovating the historic Dunstan Hotel on Clyde's main street (33 Sunderland St) to be its new depot at the other end of the trail. Until then you can organise for pick-up/drop off by shuttle in Clyde.

🛏 Sleeping & Eating

Otago Central Hotel B&B $$
(☑027 544 4800; www.otagocentralhotelhyde.com; SH87, Hyde; d with/without bathroom from $170/130; ⊙Oct-Apr) Most of the tidy rooms in this cool old hotel, 27km along the trail from Middlemarch, have private bathrooms, but not en suite.

There's a very sweet pop-up 'honesty cafe' on the veranda for passing Rail Trailers.

CYCLING IN OTAGO

OTAGO CENTRAL RAIL TRAIL

START CLYDE OR MIDDLEMARCH
END MIDDLEMARCH OR CLYDE
DURATION 3 TO 4 DAYS
DISTANCE 152KM
DIFFICULTY EASY

From the early 20th century through to the 1990s, the Central Otago rail line linked small, inland goldfield towns between Dunedin and Clyde. After the 150km stretch from Middlemarch to Clyde was permanently closed, the rails were ripped up and the trail resurfaced. The result is a year-round, mainly gravel cycling and walking trail. Culverts, beautiful old rail bridges, viaducts, dramatic rock cuttings and spooky tunnels remove most of the ups and downs, making this a very accessible trail popular with families, older folks and weekend cyclists.

With excellent trailside facilities (toilets, shelters and information), gob-smacking scenery and profound remoteness, the trail attracts over 80,000 users annually. March

is the busiest time, when there are so many city slickers on the track that you might have to wait 30 minutes at cafes en route for a panini. Consider September/October for a quieter ride.

The trail can be followed in either direction – Clyde (p168) to Middlemarch (p161) is the most popular. The whole thing takes three to four days to complete by bike (or a week on foot), but you can obviously choose to do as short or as long a stretch as suits your plans. There are also easy detours to towns such as Naseby (p165) and St Bathans (p164).

Due to the popularity of the trail, a whole raft of sleeping and eating options have sprung up in remote locales en route, like Alexandra (p166), Ophir (p166), Oturehua (p167), Ranfurly (p164) and Waipiata (p164).

However, some sections are less well served than others, particularly the 52km between Waipiata and Middlemarch. This, combined with the fact that much of the accommodation is closed in low season (June

Otago is the most popular destination for cycle touring in the whole of New Zealand. These three trails can easily be linked together to make one mega ride.

to August) and in high demand during peak season (November to April), means it's well worth getting one of the outfitters to book accommodation for you – they don't charge extra for this service. Any of the area's i-SITEs can also provide detailed information and bookings. See www.otagocentralrailtrail. co.nz and www.otagorailtrail.co.nz for track information, recommended timings, accommodation options and tour companies.

One-way bike hire, secure parking and transport back to the start is easily arranged with bike operators. They also offer shuttle transport to the trailheads at Clyde and Middlemarch from Queenstown and Dunedin.

The gorgeous heritage tourist trains operated by **Dunedin Railways** (p150) can be used as a transport connection between Middlemarch and Dunedin. The Taieri Gorge Railway travels between Dunedin and Pukerangi twice daily – Rail Trail operators can shuttle you between Pukerangi and the trailhead at Middlemarch, 20km away (around $30). On Sunday trains go all the way to Middlemarch.

ROXBURGH GORGE TRAIL

START ALEXANDRA
END ROXBURGH DAM
DURATION 4 TO 5 HOURS
DISTANCE 21KM CYCLE, 13KM BOAT RIDE
DIFFICULTY MODERATE

Opened to considerable fanfare in 2013, this well-constructed mountain-biking and walking track was intended to connect Alexandra to Roxburgh Dam. As access through some of the farmland in the middle section wasn't successfully negotiated, however, riding the 'full trail' requires prearranging a scenic 13km jet-boat ride (adult/child $110/65, October to May) via the local information centres or directly with **Clutha River Cruises** (p167).

An alternative is to make a return trip from each end: Alexandra–Doctors Point (20km return) or Roxburgh Dam–Shingle Creek (22km return).

It's requested that you purchase a $10 day tag to assist with the maintenance of the track, although this is not compulsory. They can be bought at i-SITEs, cycle shops and tour operators. For more information see www.centralotagonz.com/roxburgh-gorge-trail.

CLUTHA GOLD TRAIL

START ROXBURGH DAM
END LAWRENCE
DURATION 2 TO 4 DAYS
DISTANCE 73KM
DIFFICULTY EASY

From Roxburgh Dam you can continue on this far easier trail that follows the turquoise Clutha (Mata-au) River through Roxburgh to Beaumont and then on to Lawrence. The same voluntary maintenance fee tag system covers both tracks.

Look out for evidence of the area's gold-mining past during the 10km ride from the dam to the Roxburgh (p168) township. The following 20km stretch to Millers Flat is flanked by unusual rock formations and native kanuka (tea tree); stop for a cooling dip at Pinders Pond. From Millers Flat it's 25km to Beaumont, passing through farmland and beneath the Horseshoe Bend suspension bridge. The trail climbs from Beaumont to the highest point of the track and then heads through 434m Big Hill Tunnel on its way to Lawrence.

InterCity has direct buses from Lawrence to Dunedin (from $16, 1½ hours). Bikes are allowed as checked luggage if you pre-book and collapse them down (both wheels removed, the handlebars turned sideways and the chain covered).

BIKE HIRE & LOGISTICS

Bikes and equipment can be hired in **Dunedin** (p152), Middlemarch (p161), **Alexandra** (p167), Clyde (p168) and **Roxburgh** (p168). Bike-hire companies, especially those located on the relevant route, offer detailed information and logistical support to get you out on the trails.

WORTH A TRIP

ST BATHANS

A 17km detour north from SH85 heads into the foothills of the imposing Dunstan Mountains and on to diminutive St Bathans. This once thriving gold-mining town of 2000 people is now home to only half a dozen permanent residents living amid a cluster of cutesy 19th-century buildings. There's not much in town but the historic **Vulcan Hotel** (🕿 03-447 3629; mj.kavanagh@xtra.co.nz; Main St; r per person $70, dinner $28-35) – an atmospheric (and famously haunted) spot to drink, eat or stay.

The **Blue Lake** is an accidental attraction: a large hollow filled with blue water that has run off abandoned gold workings. Walk along the sculpted cliffs to the lookout for a better view of the alien landscape (one hour return).

Kissing Gate Cafe   CAFE $
(🕿 03-464 3224; 2 Swansea St; mains $7-15; ⏰ 7.30am-3.30pm; 🛜) Sit out under the fruit trees in the pretty garden of this lovely little wooden cottage and tuck into a cooked breakfast, a meat pie, a zingy salad or some home baking. Nana-chic at its best.

❶ Getting There & Away

Middlemarch is an hour's scenic drive from Dunedin.

Both of the main cycle companies offer shuttles to Dunedin, Pukerangi and the Rail Trail towns. In the warmer months, Trail Journey's **Catch-a-Bus** (🕿 03-449 2150; www.trailjourneys.co.nz; ⏰ Oct-Apr) has scheduled daily services to/from Dunedin ($55, one hour), Ranfurly ($25, one hour), Alexandra ($55, 2¼ hours) and Clyde ($55, 2½ hours).

The scenic **Taieri Gorge Railway** (🕿 03-477 4449; www.dunedinrailways.co.nz) runs between Dunedin and Pukerangi (adult/child $72/19), leaving Dunedin at 9.30am and 3pm daily. On Sunday trains run all the way to Middlemarch ($81/21).

Ranfurly & Waipiata

POP 663

After a series of fires in the 1930s, Ranfurly was rebuilt in the architectural style of the day, and a few attractive art-deco buildings still line its sleepy main drag.

Most travellers come through Ranfurly as part of a journey on the Otago Central Rail Trail (p162), which passes right through town. Much smaller Waipiata, 10km closer to Middlemarch along the Rail Trail, with a lovely pub and accommodation, is also a handy stop.

🏃 Activities

Real Dog Adventures   DOG SLEDDING
(🕿 03-444 9952; www.realdog.co.nz; 2 Bypass Rd, Ranfurly; sled dog team ride $150; ⏰ Apr-Oct) Six to eight Alaskan malamutes or Siberian huskies are harnessed to a snow sled when there's enough snow (otherwise a dog rig with bike-style wheels) and off you go for a 4km run through the forest. In summer (November to March) you can still do a kennel tour ($40). Book ahead.

🛏 Sleeping

Old Post Office Backpackers   HOSTEL $
(🕿 03-444 9588; www.oldpobackpackers.co.nz; 11 Pery St, Ranfurly; dm $35, s/d with shared bathroom $55/80; ⏰ closed Jun-Sep; 🅿🛜) Tidy rooms with bright paint and a cheery lounge-room fire make this backpackers a welcome sight for Rail Trailers. Discounts on laundry and loads of DVDs to borrow.

Behind the Bike Sheds   B&B $$
(🕿 022 352 3147; www.behindthebikesheds.co.nz; 32 Waipiata Domain Rd, Waipiata; per person with shared bathroom $70) 🚲 Two sweet handmade cabins (a double and a four-bed bunkhouse) in the garden comprise this lovely B&B on the Rail Trail. There's a composting loo and an outdoor bath for stargazing, heated by a gas-fired burner underneath – watch your toes! Breakfast includes homemade jams and jellies. It's across the trail from the Waipiata pub.

Hawkdun Lodge   MOTEL $$
(🕿 03-444 9750; www.hawkdunlodge.co.nz; 1 Bute St, Ranfurly; s/d from $125/150; 🛜) 🚲 This smart boutique motel is the best option in Ranfurly's town centre by far, with a spa pool and free laundry facilities. Even studio units are spacious, with kitchenettes, sitting areas and en suites. Travelling chefs can flex their skills in the smart guest kitchen and dining area. Breakfast costs $15.

Kokonga Lodge   B&B $$$
(🕿 03-444 9774; www.kokongalodge.co.nz; 33 Kokonga-Waipiata Rd; s/d $265/295; @🛜) Just off SH87 between Waipiata and Hyde, this

upmarket rural property offers six contemporary en suite rooms, newly refurbished in neutral tones. One was occupied by Sir Peter Jackson when he was filming *The Hobbit* in the area. It's right on the Rail Trail.

Eating & Drinking

Maniototo Cafe CAFE **$**
(📞03-444 9023; www.maniototocafe.co.nz; 1 Pery St, Ranfurly; mains $8; ⊙7am-4.30pm Mon-Fri, 8am-5pm Sat & Sun) Attached to the Four Square supermarket, this sunny cafe is a good lunch option, with a tempting array of sandwiches, sausage rolls and cakes, like spiced apricot, Brie and chicken pretzel rolls.

Waipiata
Country Hotel PUB
(📞03-444 9470; www.waipiatahotel.co.nz; 29 Main St, Waipiata; ⊙10am-late; 🛜) Around 10km from Ranfurly, this friendly country pub right on the Rail Trail is a great spot to quench your post-ride thirst. It also offers good pub meals – like slow-cooked beef and smokey cheese pies or grilled haloumi salad. It also has rooms available (doubles with/ without bathroom $150/140) and a comfortable lodge (doubles $160) down the road.

ℹ Information

Ranfurly i-SITE (📞03-262 7999; www.central otagonz.com; 3 Charlemont St, Ranfurly; ⊙9am-5pm; 🛜) Call into the Ranfurly i-SITE in the old train station. While you're there, check out the short film about the Rail Trail and interesting local history displays.

ℹ Getting There & Away

Both on the Rail Trail, Ranfurly sits on route SH85, 1¾ hours' drive from Dunedin, while Waipiata is 10km off SH85. In the warmer months, Trail Journey's **Catch-a-Bus** (📞03-449 2150; www.trailjourneys.co.nz; ⊙Oct-Apr) passes through Ranfurly and Waipiata on its way between Clyde ($55, two hours) and Dunedin ($55, two hours). Seasonal local shuttles can take you to Naseby and other locales; enquire at the i-SITE.

Naseby

POP 100

Cute as a button, surrounded by forest and dotted with 19th-century stone buildings and heritage shopfronts, Naseby (*naze*-bee) is the kind of small settlement where life moves slowly. That the town is pleasantly obsessed with the fairly insignificant world of New Zealand curling (a Winter Olympic sport resembling lawn bowls on ice) indicates the pace of life here. It's that lazy small-town vibe, along with summer swimming dams and good mountain-biking and walking trails through the surrounding forest, that makes Naseby a delightful stopover.

Activities

Maniototo Curling
International ICE SKATING
(📞03-444 9878; www.curling.co.nz; 1057 Channel Rd; adult/child per 90min $40/15; ⊙10am-5.30pm May-Oct, 9am-6pm Nov-Apr) All year round you can shimmy after curling stones at this indoor ice rink; tuition and grippy shoes included. Upstairs you can watch the games from the bar.

Naseby Ice Luge SNOW SPORTS
(📞03-444 9270; www.lugenz.com; 1057 Channel Rd; adult/child $35/25; ⊙10am-4pm Jun-Aug) In winter, hurtle 360m down a hillside on a wooden sled on the southern hemisphere's only ice luge. Weather dependent; call ahead, bookings recommended. There's also an outdoor ice rink to skate around.

Naseby Night Sky Tours OUTDOORS
(📞03-444-9908; https://nasebynightskytours. wixsite.com/home; 17 Leven St; per person $35) Astrophysicist Paul Bishop leads fascinating tours to see planets, star clusters and constellations with the aid of two telescopes, binoculars and Naseby's low-light-pollution skies.

🛏 Sleeping & Eating

Naseby Lodge APARTMENT **$$**
(📞03-444 8222; www.nasebylodge.co.nz; cnr Derwent & Oughter Sts; 1-/2-bedroom apt $170/260) These free-standing modern apartments are smart and spacious, with fully equipped kitchens and underfloor heating in the bathrooms. There's also a good restaurant, constructed of straw-bale walls sheathed in rustic corrugated iron, and a bike-repair workshop.

Old Doctor's Residence B&B **$$$**
(📞03-444 9775; www.olddoctorsresidence.co.nz; 58 Derwent St; r/ste $295/350; 🛜) 🌿 Old doctors take note: this is how to reside! Sitting behind a pretty garden, this gorgeous 1870s house offers two luxurious guest rooms and a lounge where wine and nibbles are served in the evening. The suite has both a sitting room and an en suite bathroom,

while the smaller room's bathroom is accessed from the corridor.

Black Forest Cafe CAFE **$**
(☑ 03-444 9820; 7 Derwent St; mains $8-19; ☺ 9am-3pm Wed-Mon; ☎) Inside this cute old building with a skylight, a sunny deck and an undulating wooden floor, you'll find hearty soups, cakes and toasties. Plus great coffee.

ℹ Information

Naseby Information Centre (☑ 03-444 9961; www.nasebyinfo.org.nz; Old Post Office, Derwent St; ☺ 11am-2pm Fri, Sun & Mon, to 4pm Sat, extended hours summer) Gold pans ($20) sold.

ℹ Getting There & Away

The Ranfurly–Naseby Rd leaves SH85, 4km north of Ranfurly. There's no public transport and cyclists should factor in a 12km detour from the Rail Trail. Many accommodation providers will collect you, or you can arrange seasonal shuttles with local operators – be sure to ask at the information centre or at Ranfurly i-SITE (p165).

From Naseby, you can wind your way on unsealed roads northeast through spectacular scenery to Danseys Pass and through to Duntroon in the Waitaki Valley.

Lauder, Omakau & Ophir

Separated by 8km of SH85, tiny Lauder (population 18) and larger Omakau (population 260) are good stops if you're a hungry cyclist in need of a feed and a bed. However, the area's real gem is Ophir (population 50), 2km from Omakau across the Manuherikia River.

Ophir was bypassed by the railway in 1904, leaving its main street trapped in time. The most photogenic of its heritage buildings is the 1886 **post office** (www.historic.org. nz; 53 Swindon St, Ophir; ☺ 9am-noon Mon-Fri). At the far end of town, the road heads over the heritage-listed 1870s **Dan O'Connell Bridge**, a bumpy but scenic crossing that loops back to SH85.

Ophir lays claim to the country's widest range of recorded temperatures: from -21.6°C to 35°C.

🛏 Sleeping & Eating

Blacks Hotel PUB **$$**
(☑ 03-447 3826; www.blackshotel.co.nz; 170 Swindon St, Ophir; r $155; ☺ 4pm-late Mon, from 11am Tue-Sat, from noon Sun; P ☎) Decorated like an OTT wedding in a Scots hunting lodge, this popular local watering hole is a great spot to enjoy a pint or a pub-style meal (mains $23 to $30). Sit under the wall of pink roses and be licked clean by the friendly resident dogs. Out the back is a row of basic, clean en suite rooms.

Chatto Creek Tavern HERITAGE HOTEL **$$**
(☑ 03-447 3710; www.chattocreektavern.co.nz; 1544 SH85, Chatto Creek; dm/s/d without bathroom $60/100/130; ☺ 10am-late; P ☎) Dating from 1886, this attractive stone hotel sits right beside the Rail Trail and highway, 10km southwest of Omakau. Pop in for hearty pub meals (mains $17 to $30), or rest your weary calf muscles in a dorm bed or a double room. Rates include breakfast. Informal camping is also possible.

Stationside Cafe CAFE **$**
(☑ 03-447 3580; Lauder-Matakanui Rd, Lauder; mains $9-18; ☺ 8am-4pm Oct-Apr) Country hospitality is on show at this great little trailside place with wonderfully charming hosts. Options include tasty breakfasts, healthy salads and soups, as well as a mouthwatering selection of just-baked scones, cakes and muffins.

Pitches Store RESTAURANT **$$$**
(☑ 03-447 3240; www.pitches-store.co.nz; 45 Swindon St, Ophir; lunch $19-28, dinner $26-40; ☺ 10am-8.30pm daily Nov-Apr, to 4pm Thu & Mon, to 8.30pm Fri-Sun May & Sep-Oct, closed Jun-Aug) Formerly a general store and butcher, this heritage building has been sensitively transformed into a humdinger of a cafe-restaurant. Exposed stone walls may speak of the past but the menu offers contemporary gourmet fare. There are also six elegant guest rooms ($296) here.

ℹ Getting There & Away

There's no public transport to these parts but many of the bike crews servicing the Otago Central Rail Trail provide shuttles, and many accommodation providers can pick you up from the trail if you enquire in advance.

Alexandra

POP 5510

Unless you've come especially for the Easter Bunny Hunt or the springtime Blossom Festival (www.blossom.co.nz) and NZ Merino

OTUREHUA

Well worth a stop on the Rail Trail, Oturehua boasts New Zealand's oldest continually operating store, the lost-in-time **Gilchrist Store** (☑ 03-444 5808; www.gilchriststore.co.nz; 3353 Ida Valley-Omakau Rd; ⊙ 7.30am-5pm Mon-Fri, 8am-4pm Sat & Sun), established in 1902, where floor-to-ceiling wooden shelves are still stocked with old boxes of soap powder, rolling tobacco and laxative tablets.

Also here is **Hayes Engineering Works** (☑ 03-444 5801; www.hayesengineering.co.nz; 39 Hayes Rd; adult/child $12/free; ⊙ 10am-5pm Sep-May), where you can wander about the workshop where inventor and engineer Ernest Hayes manufactured all manner of useful farm devices, including his famous fencing wire strainer (1924). Also visit the homestead (1920), fitted with mod cons from piped radio to electricity.

Stay overnight at **Marchburn Country Lodge** (☑ 021 253 1941; www.marchburn.co.nz; 16 Reef Rd; r $295; 🛜) to enjoy amazing views of the snow-covered peaks right from your bed through the big windows. A crackling fire, big leather lounges and a fine collection of vintage books make for a cosy evening.

Shearing Championships, the main reason to visit unassuming Alexandra is mountain biking. It's the biggest Otago Central Rail Trail (p162) settlement by far, offering more eating and sleeping options than the rest of the one-horse (or fewer) towns on the route. It's also the start of the Roxburgh Gorge Trail (p163).

Alex, as it's known to the locals, marks the southeastern corner of the acclaimed Central Otago wine region. Of the 25 wineries in the Alexandra Basin (www.alexandra basinwines.co.nz), only 10 are seasonally open for tastings. These are detailed on the *Central Otago Wine Map,* available from the i-SITE (p168).

⊙ Sights

Central Stories   MUSEUM
(☑ 03-448 6230; www.centralstories.com; 21 Centennial Ave; by donation; ⊙ 10am-4pm) Central Otago's history of gold mining, winemaking, fruit growing and sheep farming is covered in this excellent regional museum and gallery, which shares a building with the i-SITE.

🏃 Activities

As well as the obvious – the Otago Central Rail Trail and Roxburgh Gorge Trail – walkers and mountain bikers will love the old gold trails weaving through the hills; contact Altitude Bikes, or download the Trailforks app (www.trailforks.com).

Altitude Bikes   CYCLING
(☑ 021 456 918; www.altitudebikes.co.nz; 88 Centennial Ave; adult/child per day $50/35; ⊙ 8.30am-

5.30pm Mon-Fri, 9am-1pm Sat) Altitude Bikes hires bikes in conjunction with Henderson Cycles and organises logistics for riders on the Otago Central, Clutha Gold and Roxburgh Gorge Trails. Be sure to also get in touch for info on local mountain-biking trails.

Clutha
River Cruises   BOATING
(☑ 022 068 3302; www.cluthararivercruises.co.nz; boat ramp, Dunorling St; adult/child $95/55; ⊙ 2.30pm Oct-Apr) Explore the scenery and history of the region on a 2½-hour heritage cruise. The same company also runs the jetboat transfer for cyclists on the Roxburgh Gorge Trail (adult/child $110/65, October to May).

🛌 Sleeping & Eating
Asure
Avenue Motel   MOTEL $$
(☑ 03-448 6919; www.avenue-motel.co.nz; 117 Centennial Ave; units $145-170; 🅿🛜) The pick of the motels on the main drag, these clean, modern units have all the mod cons, and full kitchens, too. Studio, one- and two-bedroom apartments are available.

Courthouse
Cafe & Larder   CAFE $$
(☑ 03-448 7818; www.packingshedcompany.com; 8 Centennial Ave; mains $11-24; ⊙ 6.15am-4pm Mon-Fri, from 9am Sat) Bounteous botanical displays dispel any lingering austerity in this stone courthouse building, dating from 1878. The counter groans under the weight of an extraordinary array of baked goods (cakes, doughnuts, croissants and more),

ALEXANDRA TO MILTON ON SH8

Heading south from Alexandra, SH8 winds along rugged, rock-strewn hills above the Clutha River as it passes Central Otago's famous orchards. In season (roughly December to March) roadside fruit stalls sell just-picked stone fruit, cherries and berries. En route there's a scattering of small towns, many dating from gold-rush days.

Further south, the Clutha broadens into **Lake Roxburgh**, with a large hydroelectric power station at its terminus, before rushing past Roxburgh itself. Call into the friendly **i-SITE** (☑ 03-262 7999; www.centralotagonz.com; 120 Scotland St; ☺ 9am-5pm daily Oct-Apr, Mon-Fri May-Sep) for information on cycling and seasonal fruit picking (December to April) in the surrounding apple and stone-fruit orchards. You can hire bikes and get all the information you need for the Clutha Gold and Roxburgh Gorge Trails from **Highland Bike Hire** (☑ 03-446 8009; www.highlandbikehire.co.nz; 107 Scotland St; adult/child per day from $40/25; ☺ 9am-5.30pm Mon-Thu, to 7pm Fri, plus 10am-2pm Sat Sep-May).

Before you leave Roxburgh, drop into **Jimmy's Pies** (☑ 03-446 9012; www.jimmyspies.co.nz; 143 Scotland St; pies from $3.50; ☺ 7.30am-5pm Mon-Fri), renowned across the South Island since 1959. If you're at a loss as to which of the 20 different varieties of pies to choose, try the apricot chicken – you're in orchard country, after all.

Continuing south from Roxburgh, the road passes through **Lawrence** and the **Manuka Gorge Scenic Reserve**, a picturesque route through wooded hills and gullies. SH8 joins SH1 near Milton.

which compete with gourmet brunch and lunch options.

ℹ Getting There & Away

Alexandra lies on SH8, around 2½ hours' drive from Dunedin and 1¼ hours from Queenstown.
Catch-a-Bus (☑ 03-449 2150; www.trailjourneys.co.nz) Door-to-door shuttles to Clyde ($15, 10 minutes), Ranfurly ($55, one hour), Middlemarch ($55, two hours) and Dunedin ($60, 3¼ hours).

InterCity (☑ 03-442 4922; www.intercity.co.nz) coaches head to/from Dunedin (from $23, three hours), Roxburgh (from $14, 34 minutes), Clyde (from $10, nine minutes), Cromwell (from $11, 24 minutes) and Queenstown (from $15, 1½ hours).

Clyde

POP 1010

More charming than his buddy Alex, 8km down the road, Clyde looks more like a 19th-century gold-rush film set than a real town. Set on the banks of the emerald-green Clutha River, Clyde retains a friendly, small-town feel, even when holidaymakers arrive in numbers over summer. It's also the trailhead of the Otago Central Rail Trail (p162).

🏃 Activities

Pick up a copy of *Walk Around Historic Clyde* from the Alexandra i-SITE.

The **Alexandra–Clyde 150th Anniversary Walk** (12.8km, three hours one way) is a riverside walking and cycling trail that's fairly flat, with ample resting spots and shade. This makes a nicer riverside cycle than the official Rail Trail route between the towns. A new cycle trail from Clyde to Cromwell, through the Cromwell Gorge, is also in development, aiming to open in 2021.

Trail Journeys   CYCLING
(☑ 03-449 2150; www.trailjourneys.co.nz; 16 Springvale Rd; rental per day from $50, e-bikes from $100; ☺ 9am-5pm Mon-Fri May-Oct, from 8am daily Nov-Apr) 🚲 Right by the Otago Central Rail trailhead (1.7km from the town centre), Trail Journeys rents bikes and arranges cycling tours, baggage transfers and shuttles. It also has a depot in Middlemarch (p161).

🎉 Festivals & Events

Clyde Wine & Food Festival   WINE, FOOD
(www.promotedunstan.org.nz; adult/child $15/free; ☺ 10.30am-4.30pm Easter Sun) Held in the main street on Easter Sunday each year, this local festival showcasing the region's produce and wines brings folks from across the South Island.

🛏 Sleeping & Eating

Postmaster's House BOUTIQUE HOTEL **$$**
(☑ 03-449 2488; www.postofficecafeclyde.co.nz; 4
Blyth St; d with/without bathroom $140/105; P)
Antique furnishings are dotted around the
large and lovely rooms in this pretty 1865
stone cottage. Two of the three rooms share
a bathroom; the third has its own. Wi-fi is
available in the attached restaurant.

Dunstan House B&B **$$$**
(☑ 03-449 2295; www.dunstanhouse.co.nz; 29
Sunderland St; s/d without bathroom from
$110/130, d/ste with bathroom from $220/265; 🛜)
This restored late-Victorian balconied inn
has cosy lounge areas, a magnificent kauri
staircase and stylish rooms decorated with
William Morris wallpaper. The less expensive rooms share bathrooms but are just as
comfortable and atmospheric. Breakfast is
served in the lovely licensed cafe (open 7am
to 4pm), which specialises in gluten-free, vegan and keto dishes.

★ Oliver's B&B **$$$**
(☑ 03-449 2600; www.oliverscentralotago.co.nz;
Holloway Rd; d $255-465; P 🛜) 🍴 Oliver's fills
an 1860s merchant's house and stone sta-
bles with luxurious rooms decked out with
old maps, heritage furniture and claw-foot
baths. Most of the rooms open onto a seclud-
ed garden courtyard. The attached **restau-
rant** (☑ 03-449 2805; www.oliverscentralotago.
co.nz; 34 Sunderland St; mains lunch $21-26, din-
ner $34-43; ☺ restaurant noon-2pm & 6-8pm, bar
noon-late, shorter hours Jun-Aug), housed in a
gold-rush-era general store, incorporates a
bar, cafe-deli and bistro showcasing the best
local produce with dishes like braised hare
leg and apricot-frangipani pie.

**Paulina's Restaurant
& Bar** MULTICUISINE **$$**
(☑ 03-449 3236; www.paulinasrestaurant.co.nz;
6 Naylor St; lunch $22, dinner $30-36; ☺ noon-
2.30pm & 5.30pm-late) International dishes are
whipped up here, including in the traditional wood-fire oven, but Paulina particularly
showcases her South American heritage
with treats such as *gambas al ajillo* (garlic
prawns) and Peruvian-style blue cod on the
menu, and pisco sours behind the bar.

ℹ Getting There & Away

Catch-a-Bus (☑ 03-449 2150; www.trailjour
neys.co.nz; ☺ Oct-Apr) Door-to-door shuttles
to/from Alexandra ($15, 10 minutes), Ranfurly
($55, 1½ hours), Middlemarch ($55, 2½ hours)

and Dunedin ($60, 3½ hours) during the main
cycling season.
InterCity (☑ 03-471 7143; www.intercity.co.nz)
Coaches head to/from Dunedin (from $23,
three hours), Roxburgh (from $14, 44 minutes),
Alexandra (from $10, nine minutes), Cromwell
(from $10, 14 minutes) and Queenstown (from
$14, 1½ hours).

Cromwell

POP 4143

Cromwell has a charming lakeside historic precinct, a great weekly farmers market
and perhaps the South Island's most OTT
'big thing' – a selection of giant fruit by the
highway, representing the area's extensive
fruit-growing industry.

During the cherry season (mid-December
to February) local growers sell fruit on the
roadsides and put out 'PYO' ('pick your own')
signs. You can pick up seasonal work here
too – contact Seasonal Solutions Cooperative
(www.ssco.co.nz).

It's also at the very heart of the prestigious Central Otago wine region (www.cowa.
org.nz), known for its extraordinarily good
pinot noir and, to a lesser extent, riesling,
pinot gris and chardonnay. The Cromwell
Basin – which stretches from Bannockburn,
7km southwest of Cromwell, to north of
Lake Dunstan – accounts for over 70% of
Central Otago's total wine production. Pick
up the *Central Otago Wine Map* for details
of upwards of 50 local wineries.

⊙ Sights & Activities

Cromwell Heritage Precinct HISTORIC SITE
(www.cromwellheritageprecinct.co.nz; Melmore
Tce; ☺ 10am-4pm) **FREE** When the Clyde Dam
was completed in 1992 it flooded Cromwell's
historic town centre – 280 homes, six farms
and 17 orchards. Many historic buildings
were disassembled before the flooding and
have since been rebuilt in a pedestrianised
precinct beside Lake Dunstan. While some
have been set up as period museum pieces
(stables, newspaper presses and the like),
others house good cafes, galleries and some
interesting shops – look for the shop selling
a rainbow of hand-spun yarn.

In summer the area plays host to an excellent weekly farmers market (p171).

Bendigo Historic Reserve HISTORIC SITE
(www.doc.govt.nz; Bendigo) **FREE** Gold was
discovered in Bendigo in 1862; relics from
the rush can be seen at this historic reserve,

accessible off SH8, near the north of Lake Dunstan. Sights include mine shafts and tunnels, ruined buildings and water races. Reaching the site is part of the adventure – it's up an extremely steep dirt road, accessible by 2WD, but only just. Don't attempt this in wet weather or if your car's a bit dodgy. Signposted walking trails thread through the ruins and offer great views.

Highlands

Motorsport Park
ADVENTURE SPORTS
(☏ 03-445 4052; www.highlands.co.nz; cnr SH6 & Sandflat Rd; ⊙ 10am-4pm winter, to 5pm summer) Transformed from a paddock into a top-notch 4km racing circuit in just 18 months, this revheads' paradise hosted its first major event in 2013. The action isn't reserved just for the professionals, with various high-octane experiences on offer, along with an excellent museum.

Budding speed freaks can start out on the go-karts ($49 per 10 minutes) before taking a 200km/h ride in the Highlands Taxi ($129 for up to four people), completing a lap in a Ferrari 488 at 230km/h ($179), or having a go at the wheel of a V8 muscle car ($395).

If you'd prefer a less racy experience, the National Motorsport Museum (adult/child $25/10) showcases racing cars and displays about Kiwi legends such as Bruce McLaren, Possum Bourne, Emma Gilmour and Scott Dixon. There's minigolf (free with museum entry) and a good cafe.

Also check out the New Zealand Endurance Championship in November, a weekend-long motor-sports festival, and the Highlands Festival of Speed, classic motor racing in early April.

Tours

Goldfields Jet
ADVENTURE
(☏ 03-445 1038; www.goldfieldsjet.co.nz; SH6; adult/child 40min $125/65, 20min $89/59; ⊙ 9am-5pm) Zip through the Kawarau Gorge on a jetboat ride.

Central Otago
Motorcycle Hire
TOURS
(☏ 03-445 4487; www.comotorcyclehire.co.nz; 271 Bannockburn Rd; per day from $185) The sinuous and hilly roads of Central Otago are perfect for negotiating on two wheels. This crew hires out motorbikes and advises on improbably scenic routes. It also offers guided trail-bike tours (from $195 per person for two people) and extended road tours (from $575).

Goldfields Mining Tours
WALKING
(☏ 0800 111 038; www.goldfieldsmining.co.nz; SH6; adult/child $25/10; ⊙ 9am-5pm) Take a tour of the goldfields, including the Chinese Village, or wander around with a self-guided map. Either way, you'll be taught how to pan for gold – and you get to keep your finds. It's 8km from Cromwell.

Sleeping

Cromwell Backpackers
HOSTEL $
(☏ 03-445 1378, 028 406 4088; www.cromwellbackpackers.co.nz; 33 The Mall; dm per night/week from $35/170; P ✿) This small, popular and somewhat ramshackle hostel is right in the centre of town, with bunk beds packed quite tight. There's a no-shoes policy, instruments to play in the lounge, a decent coffee machine and a share-house vibe. It's the sort of place where long-stayers keep their toothbrushes in the bathroom.

There's one women-only dorm. This backpackers is a good place to hook up fruit-picking work June to September.

Firewood Creek House
B&B $$
(☏ 021 209 1705; www.firewoodcreekhouse.com; 10 Roberts Dr; d incl breakfast from $160; P ✿ ✹) A roomy retreat just outside the town centre. You can take in the mountains from the outdoor pool or spa in summer. Spotless rooms, fantastic cooked brekkie, private balconies, electric blankets and a beautiful garden make for a comfortable stay.

Burn Cottage Retreat
B&B, COTTAGE $$$
(☏ 027 208 8565; www.burncottageretreat.co.nz; 168 Burn Cottage Rd; cottage $235-265; P ✿) Set among walnut trees and gardens 3km north-west of Cromwell, this peaceful retreat has three luxurious, self-contained cottages with classy decor, spacious kitchens and modern bathrooms. Enjoy the gorgeous garden with a game of petanque.

Eating

For a small town, Cromwell's dining scene encompasses a wide range of international flavours, including Italian, Japanese, Mexican, Turkish, Indian and Thai.

Black Rabbit Kitchen & Bar
CAFE $
(☏ 03-445 1553; www.blackrabbit.nz; 430a Bannockburn Rd, Bannockburn; baked items $8-10; ⊙ 9am-2pm Tue & Wed, to 3pm Thu, to 8.30pm Fri, Sat & Sun) It's much cheaper to get a takeaway from this hip cafe in Bannockburn,

CELLAR-DOOR DINING

A fantastic way to sample some local wine is to dine at one of the local wineries.

As well as making the region's most prestigious pinot noir, **Mt Difficulty** (☑ 03-445 3445; www.mtdifficulty.co.nz; 73 Felton Rd, Bannockburn; mains $34-39, tastings from $5; ☺ tastings 10.30am-4.30pm, restaurant noon-4pm) is a lovely spot for a leisurely lunch looking down over the valley. There are large, wine-friendly platters to share, but save room for the decadent desserts. Book ahead.

The winery dates back to the early 1990s, when five growers collaborated to produce wine from the promising but unproven Central Otago region. Not only does it offer the chance to taste various wines at its welcoming cellar door, its spectacular perch overlooking the Cromwell Basin encourages a very long lunch. Sharp and modern, with scrumptious fare and alfresco dining on the terrace, it pays to book a table and sort out well in advance who's responsible for driving onward.

The stylish restaurant at **Carrick** (☑ 03-445 3480; www.carrick.co.nz; Cairnmuir Rd, Bannockburn; tastings from $15, mains $35; ☺ tastings 10am-5pm, restaurant 11am-4pm) opens out on to a terrace and lush lawns. The seasonal menu features excellent share platters and is a pleasurable complement to the wine range. The flagship drop is the intense, spicy pinot noir, as well as a rich, toasty chardonnay and citrusy aromatic varietals.

Round the back of a fruit-and-veg shed, the outdoor kitchen **Stoaker Room** (☑ 03-445 4841; www.thestoakerroom.co.nz; 180 SH8B, Cromwell; mains $20-25; ☺ 10am-10pm) will smoke your meal in an old French-oak pinot-noir wine barrel and serve it with a tasty Wild Earth wine. Sit in the outdoor space beside the orchard and after lunch taste some more wine from the two other cellar doors in the complex.

like a spinach and feta roll with homemade chutney ($8). But you can also sit down for an excellent meal – try the famous seafood chowder, or a gourmet pizza with venison, capsicum, blueberry, red onion, blue cheese and mozzarella ($30); pizzas are half price on Sunday night.

Amigos MEXICAN $$
(☑ 03-445 8263; www.amigosmexicangrill.co.nz; 50 The Mall; mains $29; ☺ 11am-9.30pm; ⏏) A local favourite with a creative menu of Mexican-inspired fare from rattlesnake wings to tacos with sweet potato, beetroot and mint puree. Don't miss the house-made chipotle and jalapeño sauces. If you find the place is packed, step across the mall to Bargarita, a great little cocktail bar run by Amigos' owners where you can order off the same menu.

🛍 Shopping

Cromwell Farmers Market MARKET
(www.cromwellheritageprecinct.co.nz; ☺ 9am-1pm Sun late-Oct–Easter) In summer the Cromwell Heritage Precinct plays host to an excellent farmers market, running every Sunday from Labour weekend (late October) to Easter.

❶ Getting There & Away

InterCity (☑ 03-471 7143; www.intercity.co.nz) Coaches to Queenstown (from $11, one hour, frequent), Fox Glacier (from $52, 6½ hours, one daily), Christchurch (from $54, 7½ hours, three daily), Alexandra (from $11, 24 minutes, four daily) and Dunedin (from $22, 3½ hours, four daily).

Ritchies (☑ 0800 405 066; www.ritchies.co.nz/queenstown) Scheduled shuttles to/from Wānaka ($20, 45 minutes), Queenstown Airport ($20, one hour) and Queenstown CBD ($20, 1¼ hours).

Fiordland & Southland

Best Places to Eat

➡ Niagara Falls (p182)

➡ Orepuki Beach Cafe (p187)

➡ Redcliff Cafe (p199)

➡ Church Hill (p192)

➡ Louie's (p184)

Best Places to Stay

➡ Te Anau Lodge (p198)

➡ Newhaven Holiday Park (p179)

➡ Southern Comfort Backpackers (p183)

➡ Slope Point Accommodation (p181)

➡ Manapouri Motels & Holiday Park (p194)

Why Go?

Brace yourself for sublime scenery on a breathtaking scale. Fiordland National Park's mountains, forests and mirror-smooth waters hold visitors in thrall. Framed by kilometre-high cliffs, Milford Sound was carved by epic battles between rock and ice over millennia. Leading here is the Milford Hwy, which reveals a magnificent alpine view at every bend. Shying away from attention is Doubtful Sound, the pristine 'place of silence' (which leaves many admiring visitors speechless, too).

From here, a chain of towns characterised by friendliness and fresh seafood is strung along the Southern Scenic Route. The road snakes through Southland to the Catlins, where meadows roll to golden bays and sawtooth cliffs are speckled with dozing seals.

Then there's the end of the line – Stewart Island/Rakiura, an isolated isle seemingly lost in time, and home to New Zealand's beloved icon, the kiwi.

When to Go

➡ Late October to late April is the Great Walks season for the Milford, Kepler and Routeburn Tracks – book in advance if you want to hike these popular routes.

➡ Visit from December to April for the best chance of settled weather in Fiordland's notoriously fickle climate (although chances are, you'll still see rain!).

➡ Stewart Island/Rakiura's changeable weather can bring four seasons in a day, at any time of year. Tackle the island's walks in summer (December to February), or come in winter for the stargazing.

Fiordland & Southland Highlights

1 Milford Sound (p201)
Being overwhelmed by your first glimpse of Mitre Peak rising from the fiord's inky waters.

2 Kepler Track (p175)
Feeling on top of the world traversing a sharp ridgeline among Fiordland peaks.

3 Stewart Island/Rakiura (p188) Savouring solitude on NZ's 'third island', a haven for bird life.

4 Doubtful Sound (p194)
Embracing silence when the boat engine snaps off on this remote cruise.

5 Nugget Point (p178)
Watching waves crash against stepping-stone islands extending into the ocean.

6 Slope Point (p181)
Trudging through a cow paddock to the sea-ravaged cliffs at the South Island's southernmost point.

7 Papatowai (p180)
Discovering forest waterfalls, acoustic sea caves and an organic mechanic.

HIKING IN SOUTHLAND

MILFORD TRACK

START GLADE WHARF
END SANDFLY POINT
DURATION 4 DAYS
DISTANCE 53.5KM
DIFFICULTY MODERATE

Dubbed 'the finest walk in the world' in 1908 by London's *Spectator,* the Milford remains an absolute stunner, complete with rainforest, deep glaciated valleys, a glorious alpine pass surrounded by towering peaks and powerful waterfalls, including the legendary Sutherland Falls, one of the loftiest in the world. All these account for its popularity: around 8000 hikers complete the track each summer.

During the Great Walks season (late October to April), you must book huts in advance ($140 per hut); camping is not permitted. Bookings open sometime between February and June and fill up extremely quickly – for the 2019/2020 season, the December/January peak sold out in six minutes. Keep an eye on www.doc.govt.nz/milfordtrack for the announcement of the booking opening date and be ready to move fast. If you miss out, it's worth checking back as there are sometimes cancellations.

During the season, you can only walk in one direction and you must stay at Clinton Hut the first night, despite it being only one hour from the start of the track. You must also complete the trip in the prescribed three nights and four days. This is perfectly acceptable if the weather is kind, but when the weather turns sour you'll still have to push on across the alpine Mackinnon Pass and may miss some rather spectacular views. It's all down to the luck of the draw.

The track starts at Glade Wharf, at the head of Lake Te Anau, accessible by a 1¼-hour boat trip from Te Anau Downs, itself 29km from Te Anau on the road to Milford Sound. It finishes at Sandfly Point, a 15-minute boat trip from Milford Sound village, from where you can return by road to Te Anau, around two hours away. You must book these connecting transfers in advance

and you'll be given options to do this online when you book your hut tickets.

DOC advises against tackling the Milford Track between early May and late October because of the significant risk of avalanches and floods, and the fact that bridges at risk of avalanche are removed. It's wet, very cold, and snow conceals trail markers. If

The deep-green deep south, a still-untamed outdoor treasure, is home to some of New Zealand's most famous tracks including four of its Great Walks.

you're a well-equipped hiking pro considering the Milford Track out of season, get DOC advice on weather conditions. During this low season, huts revert to the basic 'serviced' category ($15).

Tracknet (p200) offers transport from Queenstown and Te Anau to connect with boats at Te Anau Downs and Milford Sound. There are other options for transport to and from the track; **Fiordland i-SITE** (p199) and the **Fiordland National Park Visitor Centre** (p199) can advise on options to best suit you.

An alternative is to book a guided hike package through **Ultimate Hikes** (p198), which includes transfers and private en-suite rooms in comfortable lodges with all meals included.

HOLLYFORD TRACK

START LOWER HOLLYFORD RD
END MARTINS BAY
DURATION 4-5 DAYS (ONE WAY)
DISTANCE 56.8KM
DIFFICULTY ADVANCED

The four- to five-day (each way), 56km Hollyford Track is a backcountry hike requiring navigation and river-crossing skills. It passes through the lower Hollyford – the longest valley in Fiordland National Park – to remote Martins Bay. Expect splendid mountain and lake vistas, forest, extensive bird life and magical coast, as well as fewer crowds than the Great Walks in the region.

The majority of hikers start at Lower Hollyford Rd then turn tail at Martins Bay and retrace their steps back to the start; however, you can also connect by air to/from Martins Bay so you only have to walk one way. Advanced hikers can take the super challenging Pyke–Big Bay Route back from Martins Bay to create a round trip of around 10 days.

Hikers have the use of six DOC huts on the track; most are serviced huts ($15). Camping ($5) is permitted next to the huts, although sandflies will prevent this from being remotely enjoyable. Tickets should be obtained in advance.

Tracknet (p200) runs one daily shuttle to/from the Lower Hollyford Rd trailhead ($62 from Te Anau). **Trips & Tramps** (p197) offers return services from Te Anau – flying you into Martins Bay and picking you up from Lower Hollyford Rd after the hike ($410). Nine kilometres (two hours' walk) shy of the trailhead is **Gunn's Camp** (p202), a good bolthole before or after the feat, with car storage available.

For a less rugged experience in this wilderness, Ngāi Tahu–owned **Hollyford Track** (p198) leads three-day guided trips for small groups on the Hollyford, staying at luxurious private huts or lodges. A jetboat trip and a scenic flight to Milford Sound shorten the journey.

KEPLER TRACK

START/END LAKE TE ANAU CONTROL GATES
DURATION 3-4 DAYS
DISTANCE 60.1KM
DIFFICULTY MODERATE

Opened in 1988, the Kepler is one of NZ's best-planned tracks and now one of its most popular. This Great Walk takes the form of a moderately strenuous 60km loop beginning and ending at the Waiau River control gates at the southern end of Lake Te Anau. It features an all-day hike above the bushline, traversing the sharp edge of a ridge with incredible panoramas to either side, including the lake, the Jackson Peaks and the Kepler Mountains. Along the way it passes tussock lands, waterfalls, peaceful beech forest, lakeside beaches and cheeky kea.

The route is usually covered in four days, staying in all three huts ($130 per hut), although some people skip a hut or two. For example you can skip Moturau Hut and combine two mostly flat days and even cut 10km from this section by starting or leaving the track at the Rainbow Reach swing bridge. However, spending a night at Moturau Hut on the shore of Lake Manapōuri (maybe with a dip in the lake) is beautiful. The track can be walked in either direction, although the most popular (and safest in high winds) is Luxmore–Iris Burn–Moturau.

This is a heavily weather-dependent track at any time of year and the alpine sections require a good level of fitness. Parts of the track may be hazardous or impassible in winter.

You must book in advance during the Great Walk Season (late October to April). In the low season (highly inadvisable for all but the most experienced NZ hikers) the huts revert to the 'serviced' category ($15). There are campsites (in/out of season $40/5) at Brod Bay and Iris Burn.

Conveniently, the track begins under an hour's walk from the **Fiordland National Park Visitor Centre** (p199), via the lakeside track alongside the Manapōuri–Te Anau Rd (SH95). There's a car park and a shelter near the control gates. **Tracknet** (p200) and **Topline Tours** (p200) both run shuttles to and from both the control gates and Rainbow Reach trailheads. **Kepler Water Taxi** (p197) offers morning boat services across Lake Te Anau to Brod Bay, slicing 1½ hours off the first day's hike.

DUSKY TRACK
START LAKE HAUROKO
END WEST ARM
DURATION 8-10 DAYS
DISTANCE 84KM
DIFFICULTY ADVANCED

This challenging track begins (or ends) on the northern shores of dark, brooding Lake Hauroko, the deepest lake in NZ (462m). An epic journey, it only suits hikers at the top of their game: you'll wobble across 21 three-wire bridges, wade through rivers and trudge through knee-deep mud. Book a boat with Clifden-based **Lake Hauroko Tours** (☎03-225 5677, 0800 376 174; www.wjet.co.nz; track transport $99; ⏰ 8.30am Thu Nov–mid-Dec & Feb-Apr, Mon & Thu mid-Dec–Jan) to access the southern trailhead. **Trips & Tramps** (p197) offers transport ($55 per head) from Te Anau to Clifden Suspension Bridge, 12km north of Tuatapere, timed to meet boats near their launching point for the Dusky Track trailhead.

As there's only one or two boats per week accessing the southern trailhead, it's far better to embark on the walk from the south. The northern trailhead at Manapōuri is well served by four boats per day. This is useful, because the walk can take longer than expected – delays due to weather and conditions are common. Take extra food for

this reason. It's also a good idea to pack a tent – the standard DOC huts ($5, pit toilets, no cooking facilities) cannot be booked and are sometimes filled with multiday stayers or people visiting by helicopter.

HUMP RIDGE TRACK
START/END RARAKAU CAR PARK
DURATION 3-4 DAYS
DISTANCE 62KM
DIFFICULTY MODERATE

This track is rich in natural and cultural history, from coastal and alpine scenery to the relics of a historic timber town. The hiking days are long (up to nine hours on the first two days, ascending 890m on the first) and the terrain suits intermediate-level hikers. There's bird life aplenty, and the chance to see Hector's dolphins on the lonely windswept coast. En route the path crosses a number of towering historic wooden viaducts, including NZ's highest. At the time of writing the Hump Ridge Track was being upgraded to a Great Walk, with improvements to the coastal section and the construction of a third hut, expected to be launched in February 2020.

However, unlike the other Great Walks, the Hump Ridge Track will continue to be operated privately, with upmarket lodges featuring extras like chefs in the kitchen, shops selling food and well-stocked bars. There are options ranging from Freedom Walks ($245 per person sleeping in a dorm, including a hot breakfast) through to Guided Walks ($1695) that include three-course meals, motel-style rooms, a helicopter connection and pack transfer. Any walker can upgrade to a private room for $100 per night or take a hot shower ($20).

To hike the track you need to book through the **Hump Ridge Track Office** (p188). Transport connections to the trailhead (19km from Tuatapere) are available to/from Queenstown, Invercargill, Te Anau and Tuatapere. For hardy walkers, limited backcountry accommodation is available in winter ($50). Advance bookings are essential. Camping is not permitted.

RAKIURA TRACK
START/END OBAN, STEWART ISLAND/RAKIURA
DURATION 2-3 DAYS
DISTANCE 39KM
DIFFICULTY MODERATE

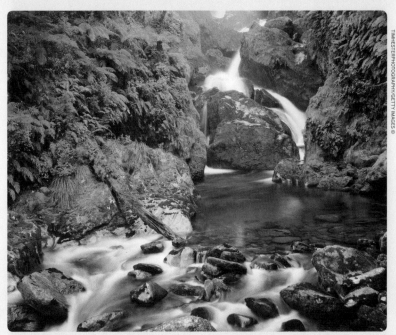

TIM HESTER PHOTOGRAPHY/GETTY IMAGES ©

Waterfall on Milford Track (p174)

One of NZ's Great Walks, the 32km, two-to-three-day Rakiura Track is a peaceful loop that sidles around beautiful beaches before climbing over a 250m-high forested ridge and traversing the sheltered shores of **Paterson Inlet/Whaka ā Te Wera**. It passes sites of historical interest, including Māori sites and sawmilling relics, and introduces many common sea and forest birds.

Rakiura Track is 32km long, but adding in the road sections at either end bumps it up to 39km, conveniently forming a circuit from Oban. It's a well-defined loop requiring a moderate level of fitness, suitable for hiking year-round. Being a Great Walk, it has been gravelled to eliminate much of the mud for which the island is infamous, though some boot-deep sections remain.

There are two Great Walk huts ($22 to $24; kids free) en route at Port William and North Arm, which need to be booked in advance via the DOC website (www.great walks.co.nz). They have toilets, water and a fireplace for heating, but no cooking facilities. Camping (adult/child $6/free) can be booked at the 'standard' campsites near (but not adjacent to) the huts, and also at Māori Beach.

NORTH WEST CIRCUIT TRACK

START/END OBAN, STEWART ISLAND/RAKIURA
DURATION 9-11 DAYS
DISTANCE 125KM
DIFFICULTY ADVANCED

The North West Circuit Track is Stewart Island/Rakiura's legendary hike, a demanding coastal epic around a remote coastline featuring isolated beaches, sand dunes, birds galore and miles of mud. It's 125km, and takes nine to 11 days, although there are several options for shortening it involving boats and planes.

There are well-spaced huts along the way, all of which are 'standard' ($5) except for two Great Walk Huts ($22 to $24), which must be booked in advance. A North West Circuit Pass ($35), available only at the **Rakiura National Park visitor centre** (p193), provides for a night in each of the 'standard' huts.

Locator beacons are advised and be sure to call into the visitor centre for up-to-date information and to purchase the essential topographical maps. You should also register your intentions with a friend (see www.adventuresmart.org.nz) as this is no easy walk in the park.

ⓘ Getting There & Away

Invercargill is the main transport hub, with flights to/from Wellington, Christchurch, Auckland and Stewart Island/Rakiura, and buses from as far afield as Queenstown and Dunedin. Te Anau has direct bus connections with Queenstown, Dunedin and Christchurch.

THE CATLINS

The Catlins' meandering roads thread together a medley of pretty-as-a-picture landscapes. Bypassed entirely by SH1, this southeasterly swathe of the South Island is a road-tripper's dream. Narrow winding roads weave past golden-sand bays, zip through bucolic meadows and trace boulder-studded coast, while gravelly detours expose you to startled sheep and even more startled farmers.

ⓘ Information

Get maps and local tips at the small Owaka Museum & Catlins Information Centre and the even smaller **Waikawa Museum & Information Centre** (☑ 03-246 8464; waikawamuseum@hyper. net.nz; 604 Niagara–Waikawa Rd; ☺ 10am-5pm). En route to the Catlins, you can also grab lots of info from the i-SITEs in Invercargill (p184) and **Balclutha** (☑ 03-418 0388; www.cluthanz. com; 4 Clyde St, Balclutha; ☺ 8.30am-5pm Mon-Fri year-round, 9.30am-3.30pm Sat & Sun Nov-Apr, 10am-2pm Sat & Sun May-Oct).

For further information, see www.catlins.org. nz, www.cluthanz.com and www.catlins-nz.com.

There are no banks in the Catlins but there's an ATM at the **Four Square** (☑ 03-415 8201; 3 Ovenden St; ☺ 7.30am-7pm) supermarket in Owaka. Most businesses accept credit cards but we recommend bringing some cash.

ⓘ Getting There & Away

There is no public transport in the Catlins area so you'll need your own vehicle or you can take a tour – try Catch-a-Bus South (p185) or Headfirst Travel (https://headfirsttravel.com).

Kaka Point

The township might be sedate but the views at Kaka Point, 23km east of Owaka, are among the most mesmerising in the Catlins. The primary draws of this small coastal community of holiday homes are Nugget Point, a remarkable rock-studded peninsular shoreline, and Roaring Bay, where (with good timing) you can spot yellow-eyed penguins (hoiho). A much more common sight are sea lions and fur seals, which you'll see basking on beaches and camouflaging themselves among the rocks.

★ **Nugget Point**   NATURAL FEATURE
(off Nugget Point Rd) Reach one of the South Island's most jaw-dropping coastal lookouts via the 900m Nugget Point (Tokatā) walkway. Wave-thrashed cliffs give way abruptly to sapphire waters dotted with toothy islets known as the Nuggets. The track to the lighthouse is dotted with poetic placards, and you can spot seals and sea lions lolling below. Look out for bird life, such as soaring tītī (muttonbird) and spoonbills huddling in the lee of the breeze.

Roaring Bay   VIEWPOINT
(Nugget Point Rd) Your best chance of spotting rare yellow-eyed penguins (hoiho) is from a hide at Roaring Bay, 8km south of Kaka Point's main drag. The hide is accessible throughout daylight hours but suggested viewing times are posted on a noticeboard at the car park. Penguin behaviour changes seasonally but times are usually before 7am or after 3pm or 4pm; ask locally or at your guesthouse.

Kaka Point Motels   MOTEL $$
(☑ 03-412 8602; www.catlins.co.nz; 24 Rata St; d units $145-165; ⓟ ⓪) Recently upgraded, these modern units all have beautiful views over the ocean. Some have kitchenettes, double-glazed windows and heat pumps to keep out the chill, and a couple have two bedrooms so you can spread out. Free use of surf and body boards.

Point Cafe & Bar   PUB
(☑ 03-412 8800; 58 Esplanade; ☺ restaurant noon-3pm & 5.30-7.30pm Jun-Aug, longer hours Sep-May, shop 11am-6pm, bar noon-late) A one-stop shop for souvenirs, takeaway fried everything or decent full-blown meals of blue cod or lamb shank (mains $19.50 to $29), the Point is best for a beer at a window seat facing the sea – try the locally brewed Catlins Yellow Eyed Pilsner. You can also hire bikes here for $50/40 per day per adult/child.

ⓘ Getting There & Away

Kaka Point is 20km south of Balclutha on the Southern Scenic Route. You'll need your own vehicle – there is no public transport in the Catlins area.

The Catlins

Owaka

Languid Owaka township may be tiny but it has a top-quality museum, a few eating options and a supermarket and petrol station (no vain boast in these parts).

It makes a good base for exploring the Catlins, but most people prefer to stay close to the beach. There's good options 4km southeast of Owaka town at **Pounawea**, a beautiful hamlet on the edge of the Catlins River Estuary and just across the inlet at **Surat Bay**, notable for the sea lions that lie around the beach between here and **Cannibal Bay**, an hour's beach-walk away.

★**Purakaunui Falls**   WATERFALL
(Purakaunui Falls Rd) If you only see one waterfall in the Catlins, make it this magnificent cascade down three tiers of jet-black rock. It's an easy 10-minute clamber to reach the falls from the small parking area. Purakaunui Falls are almost equidistant between Owaka and Papatowai (respectively 15km and 12km by road).

Owaka Museum &
Catlins Information Centre   MUSEUM
(☑ info centre 03-415 8371, museum 03-415 8323; www.owakamuseum.org.nz; 10 Campbell St; museum adult/child $6/free; ☉9.30am-4.30pm Mon-Fri, 10am-4pm Sat & Sun) Vaguely canoe-shaped in honour of the town name (Owaka means 'place of the canoe'), this modern museum is a pleasant surprise. Salty tales of shipwrecks are well explained in short video presentations, Māori and frontier stories grippingly displayed, and an interesting array of artefacts exhibited. It doubles as the main in-formation centre for the Catlins; ask about the 24km **Catlins River–Wisp Loop Track** (www.doc.govt.nz).

Teapotland   LANDMARK
(21 Main Rd) Get a selfie in this wacky collections of teapots and statuettes arranged in Graham Renwick's garden.

Catlins Horse Riding   HORSE RIDING
(☑ 027 629 2904; www.catlinshorseriding.co.nz; 41 Newhaven Rd, Owaka; 1/2/3hr rides from $70/110/150) Learners' treks and the full-gallop available, and trips are tailored to your level of experience. Full safety briefing (and glorious coastal views) included. Book ahead. Full-day treks also available (per person from $230).

★**Newhaven Holiday Park**   HOLIDAY PARK $
(☑ 03-415 8834; www.catlinsnewhavenholiday park.com; 324 Newhaven Rd, Surat Bay; unpowered/powered sites from $35/40, units from $85, with bathroom from $120; ☉ Aug-May; ☜) This exemplary holiday park is on an incredible beach at the entrance to Surat Bay, 5km from Owaka, where sea lion pups can be spotted in December and January. It has a choice of cabins and self-contained units and bags of camping space. The best site is steps from the sand. There's a merry village atmosphere throughout. Showers are $2.

Pounawea Grove Motel   MOTEL $$
(☑ 03-415 8339; www.pounaweagrove.co.nz; 5 Ocean Grove, Pounawea; d & tw $150; ☜) More sophisticated than the average motel, Pounawea Grove has a boutique feel thanks to its roomy units with sharp, modern bathrooms, kitchenettes and plush textiles.

Throw in a warm welcome and the bucolic estuary setting, and a relaxing stay is almost guaranteed.

★ **Mohua Park**   COTTAGE $$$
(☑ 03-415 8613; www.catlinsmohuapark.co.nz; 744 Catlins Valley Rd, Tawanui; cottages $250; 🛜)
🪺 Situated on the edge of a peaceful 14-hectare nature reserve (7km off the highway), these four spacious self-contained cottages offer peace, quiet and privacy with stunning views. Instead of TV, you'll watch birds flitting through the forest on your doorstep and sigh at views of rolling hills.

ℹ️ Getting There & Away
You'll need your own wheels to reach Owaka.

Papatowai
Nature shows off some of her best angles at Papatowai, which is perched at a meeting of forest, sea and the Tahakopa River. The leafy village has barely 40 inhabitants but swells with holidaymakers in summer, drawn by a languid vibe and glittering views of waterfalls and golden bays.

◉ Sights

Cathedral Caves   CAVE
(www.cathedralcaves.co.nz; 1069 Chaslands Hwy; adult/child $5/1; ⊙ Nov-May) Cutting back into cliffs right on the beach, the huge, arched Cathedral Caves were carved out of the limestone by 160 million years of waves. Named for their acoustic properties, they are only accessible for two hours at either side of low tide (tide timetables are posted on the website, at the highway turn-off and at visitor information centres) – and even then they can be closed at short notice if the conditions are deemed dangerous. Cash only.

★ **Lost Gypsy Gallery**   GALLERY
(☑ 021 122 8102; www.thelostgypsy.com; 2532 Papatowai Hwy; gallery $8; ⊙ 10am-5pm Thu-Tue Nov–Apr) Fashioned from remaindered bits and bobs, artist and 'organic mechanic' Blair Somerville's intricately crafted automata are wonderfully irreverent. The bamboozling collection inside a converted bus (free entry) is a teaser for the carnival of creations through the gate (kids under 13 years not allowed, sorry...). The buzz, bong and bright lights of the organ are bound to tickle your ribs. Food truck and wi-fi on-site.

🏃 Activities
Eight kilometres north of Papatowai a short walk through verdant forest takes you to **Matai & Horseshoe Falls** (Papatowai Hwy, Caberfeidh) (30 minutes return); from here you can also access the 2km **Matai Rail Trail** following a former rail line through deep cuttings and over high embankments.

Four kilometres west of town, an easy walk along moss-scented pathways and boardwalks takes you out onto the waters of pretty **Lake Wilkie** (Chaslands Hwy) (30 minutes return). If you're pressed for time but want a photo of this Ice Age mirror lake, it's a 10-minute return walk to a lookout point.

A further 7km west, at the Whistling Frog, is the turn-off to **McLean Falls** (off Rewcastle Rd, Chaslands), reached by a thrilling walk along fern-fringed trails. Allow 40 minutes to walk to the falls and back; the car park is 4km from the main highway along a rough road.

Papatowai Freedom Kayak Hire   KAYAKING
(☑ 021 024 12925; www.catlinskayakhirepapatowai. com; 2519 Papatowai Hwy, Papatowai; single/double 2hr rental $45/59, 4hr $55/69) With over 25km of paddle-able waterways, this river-filled region is a great place to kayak. Explore native forest filled with birdsong, fertile estuaries and farmland on a self-guided paddle. Safety briefing, route advice, maps and transport to the river included, no experience necessary.

🛏️ Sleeping & Eating

Hilltop   LODGE $
(☑ 03-415 8028; 77 Tahakopa Valley Rd, Papatowai; s/d $100/110) High on a hill 1.5km out of town, with native forest at the back door and surrounded by a sheep farm, these two ship-shape cottages command spectacular views of the Tahakopa Valley and coast. Rent by the room or the whole house ($340 for nine people); the en-suite double is the pick of a very nice bunch.

★ **Whistling Frog**   CAFE $$
(☑ 03-415 8338; www.whistlingfrogresort.com; 9 Rewcastle Rd, Chaslands; mains $17-42.50; ⊙ 8.30am-8pm Nov-Mar, 10am-6pm Apr, May & Oct, closed Jun-Sep; 🛜) Colourful and fun, the Frog is the best dining option in the Catlins, offering craft beer on tap and crowd-pleasing meals, often garnished with flowers from the garden. We're talking seafood chowder, wood-fired pizza, gourmet burgers, craft-beer-battered blue cod, and veggie feeds like risotto and big salads. Excellent coffee and breakfast spreads, too. Ribbit!

There's a holiday park here also with powered/unpowered sites from $55/45, cabins without bathrooms from $110 and motel units from $165.

❶ Getting There & Away

There is no public transport in the Catlins. Papatowai is a pleasant 36km drive east from Waikawa, or 25km west of Owaka.

Curio Bay

Chasing sun and surf, droves of holiday-makers descend on Curio Bay in summer. For beach lovers the focal point is Porpoise Bay, a reliably wave-lashed arc of sand and arguably the best swimming beach in the Catlins. Hector's dolphins come here to rear their young.

Nearby, other natural curiosities merit a visit: a Jurassic-age forest lies just south in Curio Bay while 15km west is the trailhead for a short walk to Slope Point, South Island's most southerly point.

Curio Bay is whisper-quiet in winter (June to August). Regardless of the season, it's handy to bring food provisions and a full tank of fuel along this sparse stretch of coast.

◉ Sights & Activities

★ **Slope Point**   LANDMARK
(Slope Point Rd, Haldane) South Island's true southerly point lies not in Bluff, as many mistakenly believe, but at the end of a 20-minute trudge through a cliff-side cow paddock. From the car park, walk towards the sea and veer left along the fencing; a humble signpost marks this spectacular spot where blackened rocks tumble into turquoise sea while waves smash and swirl below.

Curioscape   MUSEUM
(📞03-246 8897; www.curioscape.co.nz; 590 Waikawa Curio Bay Rd, Curio Bay; museum adult/child $15/2; ⊙10am-10pm Tue-Sun, to 7pm Mon Nov-Apr, shorter hours May-Oct) Incorporated in this new centre is a pleasant cafe (lunch mains $10 to $22, dinner $26 to $38), visitor centre and the **Gateway**, a modern museum with a multiscreen film experience describing the evolution of the area, and a touchwall to learn about the petrified forest, penguins and local history.

To the side of the centre is the start of the walk to the petrified forest, via a **penguin boardwalk** that takes you over nesting grounds for endangered yellow-eyed penguin (hoiho). They waddle ashore from the beach at dusk and you might see them through the peep flaps, but do the right thing and keep your distance (at least 50m).

Petrified Forest   NATURAL FEATURE
(Curio Bay) [FREE] Marvel at the rare phenomenon of fossilised forest, extending south of Curio Bay. Preserved by silica in the ashy floodwaters that submerged these Jurassic-era trees, craggy stumps and entire logs create a dramatic contrast with the frothing waves. The wood grain is still clearly visible. The petrified forest is revealed for around four hours either side of low tide.

Waipapā Lighthouse   LIGHTHOUSE
(Waipapā Lighthouse Rd, Otara) [FREE] Standing on a desolate but beautiful point surrounded by farmland, this 13.4m-high lighthouse was built after the SS *Tararua* disaster, an 1881 shipwreck that claimed 131 lives.

Catlins Surf   SURFING
(📞021 208 0501; www.catlins-surf.co.nz; 601 Curio Bay Rd; 2hr lesson $60, 3hr board & suit hire $50; ⊙Oct-Apr) Based at the **Curioscape Campground** (📞03-246 8897; www.curioscape.co.nz; 601 Curio Bay Rd; unpowered/powered sites for 2 from $35/40), this surf school offers lessons on Porpoise Bay, much to the amusement of any passing dolphins.

⊨ Sleeping & Eating

★ **Slope Point Accommodation** FARMSTAY $
(📞03-246 8420; www.slopepoint.co.nz; 164 Slope Point Rd, Slope Point; dm $27, d with/without bathroom $90/60, 3-bed cottage for 2 $100; 🛜) In the midst of a working farm 4km north of Slope Point, this family-run accommodation plunges you into the rhythms of rural life: calf-feeding time, scampering pets, and kids eager to introduce you to their favourite lamb. Double rooms and self-contained units are cosy and modern, or there's a whole cottage up the road with amazing views of the estuary.

Lazy Dolphin Lodge   HOSTEL $
(📞03-246 8579; www.lazydolphinlodge.co.nz; 529 Curio Bay Rd; dm/r without bathroom $40/90; @🛜) This perfect hybrid of seaside holiday home and hostel has light-filled bedrooms sporting cheerful linen. There are two kitchens and lounges, but you'll want to hang out upstairs on the deck overlooking Porpoise Bay. A path at the rear of the property leads directly to the beach.

FIORDLAND & SOUTHLAND CURIO BAY

★**Curio Bay**
Accommodation APARTMENT **$$**
(📞03-246 8797; www.curiobay.co.nz; 521a Curio Bay Rd; apt $190-260; 🛜) Three plush units are on offer here – one apartment attached to the hosts' house, and two similar units down the road. All are self-contained, decorated in rustic, beachy style, with big windows and sun-drenched decks right next to the beach. There's also an old-fashioned Kiwi bach, sleeping up to six people. No TV, but plenty of books and games to occupy you instead.

★**Niagara Falls** CAFE **$$**
(📞03-246 8577; www.niagarafallscafe.co.nz; 256 Niagara–Waikawa Rd, Niagara; mains $15-25; ⊙10am-3pm & 9pm-late daily Dec-Feb, 11am-4pm Thu-Mon Mar-May & Jul-Nov, closed Jun; 🛜📶) 🌿 Located in a former Victorian schoolhouse, this excellent 'old-school' cafe puts the emphasis on local produce – free-range eggs, veggies from the garden, house-smoked salmon and spring water (fill your bottle). Chef Laura Thompson moonlights as coach of the NZ Paralympic cycling team – her gold, silver and bronze medals for riding as tandem bicycle pilot at London and Rio are casually displayed in the corner.

ⓘ Getting There & Away

There is no public transport to Curio Bay. Curio and Porpoise Bays are 4km south of Waikawa.

ESSENTIAL FIORDLAND & SOUTHLAND
· ·
Eat Bluff oysters, a New Zealand gourmet obsession, followed by Stewart Island salmon, whitebait and blue cod.

Drink Hokonui Moonshine Whisky in Gore.

Read poems by Hone Tuwhare (1922–2008), who drew inspiration from the landscapes of the Catlins.

Listen to roaring surf in Te Waewae, the crackle of static on road trips (radio signal is patchy), and dead silence in Doubtful Sound.

Watch *The World's Fastest Indian* (director: Roger Donaldson, 2005), to understand Invercargill's devotion to the legacy of Burt Munro.

Go online www.fiordland.org.nz, https://southlandnz.com

CENTRAL SOUTHLAND

Sandwiched between world-famous Fiordland National Park and the scene-stealing Catlins, Central Southland is often forgotten about by travellers. But its peaceful farmland and savage coast form a memorable contrast, while its seam of small-town quirk is heaps of fun.

There's Gore, with a proud history of moonshine distilling; oyster-mad Bluff; and Tuatapere, famous for its challenging hiking trails. Invercargill, the closest thing to a city slicker in Central Southland, has a long-standing revhead culture and a slew of impressive museums dedicated to classic cars, fast bikes and big diggers.

Gore
POP 12,033

Gore struts to its own beat. The town declares itself New Zealand's 'home of country music', and 'brown trout capital of the world'. If that wasn't enough to boast about, it also had a proud history of illegal distilleries and creative collectors, all of which it celebrates through the **Gold Guitar Awards** (www.goldguitars.co.nz; ⊙May/Jun), the **Hokonui Moonshine Festival** (📞03-208 9907; www.moonshinefest.co.nz) and its excellent set of distinctive museums.

Hokonui Moonshine Museum MUSEUM
(📞03-203 9288; www.gorenz.com/visit/things-to-see-do/hokonui-moonshine-museum; 16 Hokonui Dr; adult/child $5/free; ⊙9am-4.30pm Mon-Fri, to 3pm Sat & Sun) In the early 20th century, Gore's enterprising Scottish immigrants responded to 50 years of prohibition by distilling their own moonshine. This museum shines a tongue-in-cheek light on some colourful characters and whisky-drenched escapades of the era. On display is fascinating homemade distilling apparatus hidden for decades in the back of local sheds.

Admission includes three tastes of the local tipple ranging from rough to polished – 'fast and furious', 'whisky wannabe' and 'dessert'; also available for purchase.

Located in the Hokonui Heritage Centre at the time of research, the museum will expand into its own building in late 2020, and launch an on-site distillery.

Eastern Southland Gallery GALLERY
(📞03-208 9907; www.facebook.com/easternsouthlandgallery; 14 Hokonui Dr; ⊙10am-4.30pm Mon-Fri, 1-4pm Sat & Sun) **FREE** Nicknamed the

'Goreggenheim', this gallery has a truly impressive treasury of contemporary New Zealand art, including a large Ralph Hotere collection and works by esteemed NZ artist Rita Angus. There's also a fascinating indigenous folk art collection from West Africa and Australia. It's worth breaking up a road trip in Gore purely to step inside this attractive brick building; allow an hour to sidle between hefty Congolese statues, Ivory Coast masks and temporary exhibitions of thought-provoking modern art.

Croydon Aviation
Heritage Centre   SCENIC FLIGHTS
(☑03-208 6046; www.croydonaviation.co.nz; 1558 Waimea Hwy, SH94; adult/child $12/free; ☺ 9.30am-4.30pm Mon-Fri Oct-Apr, 10am-4pm May-Sep) Aircraft from the 1930s and '40s are lovingly restored and showcased within Croydon Aviation's hangar, 16km northwest of Gore on SH94 (towards Queenstown). But that's just a taster of life in the air: you can also book a flight in a two-seater 1930s Tiger Moth biplane or other wee aircraft (from $150 for 15 minutes). A restored steam railway runs once a month on open days (adult/child $5/2.50). There's a stylish **cafe** (☑03-208 9662; www.misscocoa.co.nz; 1558 Waimea Hwy, SH94; mains $20; ☺7am-4pm Mon-Fri, 10am-4pm Sat & Sun) and gift store attached to the aviation centre.

❶ Information

Gore Visitor Centre (www.gorevisitorcentre.co.nz; 16 Hokonui Dr; ☺9am-5pm Mon-Fri, 3pm Sat & Sun) Sharing the premises is the **Gore Historical Museum** (☑03-203 9288; www.gorenz.com/visit/things-to-see-do/gore-museum; 16 Hokonui Dr; admission free; ☺9am-4.30pm Mon-Fri, to 3pm Sat & Sun), which celebrates the town's history.

❶ Getting There & Away

Gore is a 66km drive northeast of Invercargill. Most buses on the Te Anau–Dunedin, Invercargill–Queenstown and Invercargill–Dunedin routes stop in Gore, including **Intercity** (☑03-471 7143; www.intercity.co.nz), which runs to Invercargill (from $13, one hour), Dunedin (from $22, two hours), Te Anau (from $33, 1½ hours) and Queenstown (from $71, 9½ hours).

Invercargill

POP 51,700

Poor old Invercargill has lost much of its mojo lately with the closure of both its Anderson Park gallery and Southland Museum

due to earthquake risks and the transformation of its inner city into a construction site as a new mall is built.

Thank goodness for its trio of motoring attractions, which keep alive the legacy of Burt Munro. The local legend still holds the world land-speed record for an under-1000cc motorcycle, which he set in 1967 at the age of 68 riding a 47-year-old bike that he modified himself in Invercargill.

◉ Sights

★ **Transport World**   MUSEUM
(☑0800 151 252; www.transportworld.co.nz; 491 Tay St; adult/child $30/20; ☺10am-5pm; 🅿) A kingdom of shiny chrome lies beyond the doors of Transport World, touted as the largest private automotive museum on the planet. Across 15,000 sq metres of warehouse space you'll find classic cars, hulking tractors and vintage petrol pumps (even the bathrooms are on theme). Kids' play areas, a miniature movie theatre, displays of fashions of yesteryear and a great cafe round out Transport World as a crowd-pleaser, rather than just one for the petrolheads.

Revved up for more? Smaller museum **Classic Motorcycle Mecca** (☑0800 151 252; www.transportworld.co.nz; 25 Tay St; adult/child $25/15; ☺10am-5pm) holds a collection of bikes, while **Dig This** (☑0800 151 252; www.transportworld.co.nz; 84 Otepuni Ave; ☺9am-5pm; 🅿) puts you behind the controls of a bulldozer to dig ditches, stack tyres and smash cars. A 'Turbo Pass' (adult/child $48/28) grants access to both Transport World and Classic Motorcycle Mecca.

E Hayes & Sons   MUSEUM
(☑03-218 2059; www.ehayes.co.nz; 168 Dee St; ☺7.30am-5.30pm Mon-Fri, 9am-4pm Sat & Sun) **FREE** Hardware shops aren't usually a must-see, but this one holds a piece of motoring history. In among the aisles of bolts, barbecues and brooms in this classic art-deco building are more than 100 items of motoring memorabilia, including the actual motorbike on which the late Burt Munro broke the world speed record (as immortalised in the 2005 film *The World's Fastest Indian*, starring Sir Anthony Hopkins).

🛏 Sleeping

★ **Southern Comfort**
Backpackers   HOSTEL $
(☑03-218 3838; www.southerncomfortbackpackers.com; 30 Thomson St, Avenal; dm/d without bathroom from $32/75; @🛜) A mix of snug and swish, this large Victorian house has

(side margin) FIORDLAND & SOUTHLAND INVERCARGILL

a lounge with a fireplace, a fully equipped kitchen and peaceful gardens. Adding to the perks are the use of two free bikes, a laundry and a herb garden where you can pluck your own garnish. A restful package, just five minutes' walk from town.

Invercargill Top 10   HOLIDAY PARK **$**
(☑ 03-215 9032, 0800 486 873; www.invercargill top10.co.nz; 77 McIvor Rd, Waikiwi; campervan sites per person from $22, units $115, d without bathroom $85; 🤶) 🧭 Continually upgrading and adding facilities, this well-kept park has backpacker dorms, modern motels and plenty of lush grass to camp upon, along with well-tended communal kitchens, laundry facilities and lounges. It's 6.5km north of town. Consider the new shingled hobbit pod ($100) near the outdoor pizza oven.

Victoria Railway Hotel   HOTEL **$$**
(☑ 0800 777557, 03-218 1281; www.hotelinvercargill. com; cnr Leven & Esk Sts; r $155-185; 🅿🤶) This beautifully restored 1896 building is awash with nostalgia and is a little worn, but comfy, like a favourite armchair. With old portraits and an old-fashioned bar, the dining area feels like a snapshot of more genteel times, amplified by kind, personalised service.

Quest Apartments   APARTMENT **$$$**
(☑ 03-211 3966; www.questapartments.co.nz; 10 Dee St; studio $124-204; 🤶) The vibe is business more than pleasure, but serviced apartments from this accommodation chain have perfectly kitted-out studios and apartments (good cotton bedsheets, trim kitchens, modern bathrooms, in-room laundry, solid wifi) within easy walking distance of Dee St's food and drink scene. Good value.

🍴 Eating & Drinking

Seriously Good
Chocolate Company   CAFE **$**
(☑ 03-218 8060; www.seriouslygoodchocolate.nz; 147 Spey St; bakery items $6.90-8.40; ⊙8am-4pm Mon-Fri, 8.30am-1.30pm Sat) The fantastic smell hits you as soon as you walk in the door: house-made chocolates. This is a great place to pick up tasty Kiwi gifts, like chocolate-covered Allpress coffee beans, hokey pokey, and suspicious but delicious 'sheep poo'. If you don't have a sweet tooth, it also does great lunch and coffee.

★Batch   CAFE **$$**
(☑ 03-214 6357; 173 Spey St; mains $13.50-20; ⊙7am-4.30pm Mon-Fri, 8am-4pm Sat & Sun;

🤶🖉) Large shared tables, a relaxed beachy ambience, and top-notch coffee and smoothies give this cafe its reputation as Southland's best. Delicious counter food includes bagels, generously crammed rolls, cheese scones and great salads, along with full-blown brunches and cakes that are little works of art.

★Louie's   MODERN NZ **$$**
(☑ 03-214 2913; www.facebook.com/pg/Louies Restaurant; 142 Dee St; tapas $13-16, mains $32-35; ⊙5.30pm-late Tue-Sat) Part tapas and cocktail bar, part chic fusion eatery, Louie's is a great place to while away an evening snuggled into a sofa or a fireside nook. The seasonally changing menu veers from creative tapas (venison tacos, muttonbird, mussels with lime and chilli) to more substantial mains. Slow-cooked pork, locally sourced blue cod, magnificent steaks...you can't go wrong.

Elegance at 148 on Elles   FRENCH, BRITISH **$$$**
(☑ 03-216 1000; 148 Elles Rd, Georgetown; mains $37-40; ⊙6-11pm Mon-Sat; 🖉) Welcome to 1984, and we mean that in a completely affectionate way. Where else can you still get a shrimp cocktail? Elegance is the sort of old-fashioned, upmarket, regional restaurant where the menu is vaguely French, vaguely British, and the venison is perfectly cooked atop a bed of creamy mash. Vegos: ask for the special menu.

Tillermans Music Lounge   BAR, CLUB
(☑ 027 482 2677; www.facebook.com/tillermans; 16 Don St; ⊙10pm-3.30am Thu-Sat) The saviour of Southland's live-music scene, Tillerman's hosts everything from thrash to flash, with a battered old dance floor to show for it. Visit the fun downstairs Vinyl Bar, which is open from 8pm Friday and Saturday, to find out what's coming up. It's behind Devil Burger.

ℹ Information

Invercargill i-SITE (☑ 03-211 0895; www. southlandnz.com; Wachner Pl; ⊙8.30am-5pm Mon-Fri, to 4pm Sat & Sun) The i-SITE can help with general enquiries, including about Stewart Island/Rakiura and the Catlins.

ℹ Getting There & Away

AIR
Air New Zealand (www.airnewzealand.com) Flights link Invercargill Airport to Christchurch and Wellington daily and Auckland around four times weekly.

Invercargill

Invercargill

Sights
1 Classic Motorcycle Mecca B2
2 E Hayes & Sons B1

Sleeping
3 Quest Apartments B2
4 Southern Comfort
    Backpackers B1
5 Victoria Railway Hotel B2

Eating
6 Batch C2
7 Louie's B1
8 Seriously Good Chocolate Company ... C2

Drinking & Nightlife
9 Tillermans Music Lounge B2

Transport
10 InterCity B2
    Tracknet .... (see 10)

Stewart Island Flights (☑ 03-218 9129; www.
stewartislandflights.co.nz; Airport Ave; adult/
child return $220/135) Connects Invercargill
to Stewart Island/Rakiura three times a day
year-round.

BUS

Buses leave from Dee St outside the Invercargill
i-SITE (p184), where you can also book your
tickets.

Catch-a-Bus South (☑ 24hr 027 449 7994;
www.catchabussouth.com) Offers scheduled
shuttle services at least daily to Bluff ($25,
35 minutes), Queenstown ($60, three to 3¼
hours), Queenstown Airport ($65, three hours),
Gore ($30, 1½ hours) and Dunedin ($60, 3½
hours). Book ahead.

InterCity (☑ 03-471 7143; www.intercity.co.nz)
Direct coaches to and from Gore ($14, one

hour, two or three daily), Queenstown ($49, 3½
hours, daily) and Queenstown Airport (from
$49, 3½ hours, daily).

Tracknet (☑ 03-249 7777; https://tracknet.
net) Runs to Te Anau ($51) and Queenstown
($51) once daily.

Getting Around

Invercargill Airport (☑ 03-218 6920; www.
invercargillairport.co.nz; 106 Airport Ave) is
3km west of central Invercargill. The door-to-
door **Executive Car Service** (☑ 03-214 3434;
https://executivecarservice.co.nz) costs
around $20 from the city centre; more for resi-
dential pickup. By taxi it's around $20; try **Blue
Star Taxis** (☑ 03-217 7777; www.bluestar
taxis.co.nz).

Bluff

POP 1794

Mention Bluff to a New Zealander and the first thing they'll think of is oysters. Bluff is Invercargill's port, windswept and more than a little bleak, located at the end of a protruding strip of land, 27km south of the city. Bluff's bulging bivalves are among the South Island's most prized produce, guzzled with gusto between March and August, and feted with a festival in May.

Outside oyster season, the main reason folk come here is to catch the ferry to Stewart Island/Rakiura.

Bluff Maritime Museum   MUSEUM
(☑03-212 7534; 241 Foreshore Rd; adult/child $3/1; ⊙10am-4.30pm Mon-Fri year-round, plus 12.30-4.30pm Sat & Sun Oct-Apr; ⊕) Salty tales whisper from the portholes, driftwood and barnacle-clung planks displayed at Bluff's small museum by the container port. The best part is clambering aboard the *Monica* and posing at the control of this 1909 oystering boat, though steam and pump engines (which clank to action at the touch of a button) come a close second.

> ### BLUFF OYSTERS
>
> Bluff oysters are in huge demand from the minute they come into season (late March to late August). Top restaurants as far away as Auckland compete to be the first to add them to their menus. As oysters go, they're whoppers. Don't expect to be able to slurp one down in a dainty gulp – these beasts take some chewing. If you want to know what all the fuss is about, you can buy fresh or battered Bluff oysters when they're in season from Fowlers Oysters, on the left-hand side as you head into town.
>
> Up by the signpost for **Stirling Point** (off SH1) is **Oyster Cove** (☑03-212 8855; www.oystercove.co.nz; 8 Ward Pde; half-dozen oysters from $27, mains $25-32; ⊙11am-7.30pm Sep-Mar, to 4pm Apr-Aug; ☎), where you can guzzle oysters while admiring sea views through epic, wraparound windows. Or time your visit for the annual **Bluff Oyster & Food Festival** (www.bluffoysterfest. co.nz; ⊙May).

Jimi Rabbitz Gallery   ART STUDIO
(☑03-212 7611; https://helenback.com; 158 Gore St; ⊙11am-4pm Sat & Sun, or by appointment) With characters that are part cheeky, part creepy, award-winning sculptor Helen Back makes whimsical works that look like they've stepped from the pages of a dark fairy tale. Stop by her studio on Bluff's main street to take a peek.

Fowlers Oysters   SEAFOOD $$
(☑03-212 8792; www.facebook.com/fowlers oysters; 99 Ocean Beach Rd; half-dozen battered $12, dozen raw from $24; ⊙9am-7pm Mar-Aug) Whether you like your oysters battered or freshly shucked, stop at Fowlers during oyster season for the best bivalves on the South Island. It's on the left-hand side as you head into Bluff. Battered blue cod and hot dogs are available for those squeamish about slurping on molluscs. Hours vary, cash or NZ bank cards only.

❶ Getting There & Away

Catch-a-Bus South (☑03-479 9960; www. catchabussouth.com) Offers scheduled shuttle services to Invercargill ($25, 30 minutes, two daily), Gore ($47, two hours, two daily) and Dunedin ($85, four hours, two daily). With prior notice, daily buses reach Queenstown Airport ($90, 3½ hours) and Queenstown ($85, 3¾ hours).

Stewart Island Experience (☑03-212 7660; www.stewartislandexperience.co.nz) Runs a shuttle (adult/child $28/14) between Bluff and Invercargill connecting with its Stewart Island/Rakiura ferry. Transfers from Te Anau and Queenstown to Bluff are available from late November to April.

Riverton

POP 1430

Quiet and friendly little Riverton (in Māori, Aparima) is worth a detour for its dreamy bay views and gripping museum of local history. If near-Antarctic swimming takes your fancy, the long, broad sands of **Taramea Bay** are good for a dip; otherwise take a stroll along **Palmerston St**, studded with cafes and 19th-century buildings.

★ **Te Hikoi Southern Journey**   MUSEUM
(☑03-234 8260; www.tehikoi.co.nz; 172 Palmerston St; adult/child $9/free; ⊙10am-4pm Apr-Sep, to 5pm Oct-Mar) Oh, that all small-town museums could be this good! The riveting Riverton museum starts with a 16-minute film about Pākehā sealer Jack Price and his

Māori wife Hinewhitia who were stranded on the Solander Islands, far south of Fiordland. Legends behind the landscape are entertainingly told, as are anecdotes about characters including cabbage-tree rum distillers, heroic castaways and the first recorded Pākehā (white European) Māori, James Caddell.

Southland Surf School
SURFING

(📱 027 864 7230; www.facebook.com/www.surfing nz.co.nz; 1½hr group lessons incl gear from $50, private lessons from $120; ⏰ Nov-Apr) Despite the chill, Riverton is an excellent place to learn to surf, with a very reliable, gentle break at Riverton Rocks on Taramea Beach. Former NZ champion surfer Jess Terrill runs this surf school and rents gear ($50 per day for suit and surfboard or paddleboard). She also has studio accommodation (doubles with en suite and kitchenette $150) right opposite the beach.

★ Beach House
MODERN NZ $$

(📱 03-234 8274; www.rivertonbeachhouse.co.nz; 126 Rocks Hwy; mains lunch $18-32, dinner $34-44; ⏰10am-4pm Mon & Tue, until late Wed-Sun Nov-Mar, 10am-4pm Wed, until late Thu-Sun Apr-Oct; 🛜) Looking over Taramea Bay, Beach House is a stylish, comfortable cafe famous for seafood, especially its creamy chowder studded with juicy mussels and hunks of salmon. On a sunny day with a warm breeze wafting off Foveaux Strait you can admire the distant snow-capped peaks from the outside tables. The other 90% of the time, retire inside to admire them through the windows.

❶ Getting There & Away

Riverton is on SH99, on the Southern Scenic Route. **Riverton Freight** (📱 027 433 9678; $8.50) runs twice daily on weekdays to/from Invercargill.

Te Waewae & Colac Bays

Between Riverton and Tuatapere on SH99, a section of the Southern Scenic Route, long, moody bays set a steely glare towards Antarctica. If you're travelling from the east, driving this stretch of SH99 provides a first glimpse of the snow-capped Southern Alps descending into the sea, framing the western end of the bay.

Colac Bay has a small but dedicated following among hardy surfers, but most travellers simply stop for a brisk dip or a beach stroll before continuing the drive. Further west, **Monkey Island** (off SH99, Orepuki) is a former Māori whaling lookout accessible at low tide. And just beyond, what's this? A beacon of gastronomic hope, beaming out good vibes along a desolate stretch of highway? The chipper, award-winning **Orepuki Beach Cafe** (📱 03-234 5211; www.facebook. com/pg/orepukibeachcafe; cnr Dudley & Stafford Sts, SH99, Orepuki; mains $19-29; ⏰9am-5pm Sun-Thu, to 11pm Fri & Sat; 📱) 🌱 grows its own salad veg, bakes its own bread, grinds its own beef and rears its own lamb right there on the paddock between the cafe and the ocean. Pure seaside charm.

One kilometre further is **Orepuki Beach**, nicknamed 'Gemstone Beach' for the lovely stones that occasionally wash up here, including quartz, jasper and even sapphire. Seven kilometres further, pause at **McCracken's Rest** (SH99), a lovely lookout point with views of wind-lashed Te Waewae Bay (and, if you're lucky, Hector's dolphins and southern right whales).

Tuatapere
POP 558

Formerly a timber-milling town, sleepy Tuatapere is gently shaken awake by hikers who pass through before embarking on the Hump Ridge (p176) or Dusky (p176) Tracks. The town's early woodcutters were very efficient, so only a remnant of a once-large tract of native podocarp (conifer) forest remains.

Wairaurahiri Wilderness Jet
BOATING

(📱 0800 270 556; www.river-jet.co.nz; 17 Main St, Otautau; day tours incl lunch from $270) Offers jetboat rides on the Wairaurahiri River, packaged together with a guided forest walk (total six hours). Other options include a jetboat-helicopter combo or overnighting at the remote Waitutu Lodge.

Clifden Caves
CAVING

(www.doc.govt.nz; Clifden Gorge Rd) `FREE` Around 16km north of Tuatapere (1km north of Clifden), this 22-million-year-old natural limestone cave is a strange find in a sheep paddock. You can travel the 300m underground route marked by orange triangles (allow 1½ to two hours) to see stalactites, stalagmites and glow worms (titiwai). It requires some ladder-climbing, squeezing, crawling and a sidle along a narrow ledge.

FIORDLAND & SOUTHLAND TE WAEWAE & COLAC BAYS

Bring two torches (flashlights) per person in case one fails, tell someone your plans and don't take any unmarked corridors. It's signposted from the highway – download the DOC brochure for more information.

Last Light Lodge CAFE **$$**
(☑ 03-226 6667; www.lastlightlodge.com; 2 Clifden Hwy; mains $19-37; ⊘ 8.30am-late; 🛜) 🍴 This friendly cafe, surrounded by food gardens, bees and a chook run, stands out for its homemade cookies, pies and truffles, and smoothies thick enough to hold up a straw. There's a good all-day selection of food: fish and chips, panini, chicken curry and plenty more. The deck is a fine place to tackle a beer in fair weather.

It also has fairly ordinary rooms in a former forestry workers' bunkhouse (single/double $60/90), though its campsites (from $16), edged with edible plants, are lovely. Dorm beds in a yurt are $22, though they get hot in summer.

ℹ Information

Hump Ridge Track Office (☑ 03-226 6739, 0800 486 774; www.humpridgetrack.co.nz; 31 Orawia Rd; ⊘ 7.30am-5.30pm Nov-Apr) Assists with local information, accommodation, Hump Ridge hut passes and transport.

ℹ Getting There & Away

Buses must be booked through the Hump Ridge Track Office; with demand, services go to/from Queenstown ($95, 2½ to 3¾ hours), Te Anau ($50, 1¾ hours) and Invercargill ($60, 1½ hours), and also to the Rarakau car park at the trailhead ($45 return).

STEWART ISLAND/ RAKIURA

POP 380

Visitors to Stewart Island often imagine they've been transported to a primordial wilderness, dominated by birds and filled with ferny gullies that spill down to pristine beaches – the kind where a moa might step into view at any moment. Time travel aside, this is a great place to spot the moa's more compact cousin, the kiwi, in the wild. The island is a bird sanctuary of international repute, and even amateur spotters will be distracted by the glorious squawking, singing and flitting of feathery flocks.

It's also famous for its amazing walks, from 10-minute strolls to 10-day treks, including a Great Walk. Some people even get lucky and see the aurora australis (the Southern Lights). Stewart Island is the world's southernmost International Dark Sky Sanctuary (for an aurora forecast check www.aurora-service.net/aurora-forecast).

The main community of **Oban** is a welcoming town with everything you need for a comfortable stay. But don't get stuck here or you'll miss the best the island has to offer. Get out on the trails!

History

Stewart Island's Māori name is Rakiura (Glowing Skies). According to myth, New Zealand was hauled up from the ocean by Māui, who said, 'Let us go out of sight of land, far out in the open sea, and when we have quite lost sight of land, then let the anchor be dropped'. The North Island was the

---

SPOTTING A KIWI

Stewart Island/Rakiura is one of the few places on earth where you can spot a kiwi in the wild. As big as a barnyard chicken, with a population estimated to number around 13,000 birds, the Stewart Island/Rakiura brown kiwi (*Apteryx australis lawryi*, also known as the tokoeka) is larger in size, longer in the beak and thicker in the legs than its northern cousins.

The birds are most easily spotted in grassed areas where they are less camouflaged, and sometimes even on beaches where they mine sandhoppers under washed-up kelp. Use a red torch (or put red cellophane over your usual torch) to increase your chances. If you spot one, keep silent, and stay still and well away. The birds' poor eyesight and single-mindedness in searching for food will sometimes lead them to bump right into you.

Organised tours are your best bet for a sighting, as locals know where kiwi families have most recently been spotted. Given the island's fickle weather – with tours sometimes cancelled – allow a few nights here if you're desperate for an encounter. Otherwise, some people get lucky and spot the birds in and around Oban itself. Try the bushy fringes of Traill Park or the path to Bathing Beach after sundown.

fish that Māui caught, the South Island his canoe and Rakiura the anchor – Te Punga o te Waka o Māui. The sculpture of the giant chain at the start of the Rakiura Track, which (symbolically) runs beneath the Foveaux Strait to reemerge at Stirling Point (p186) in Bluff, is a reference to this story.

There is evidence that parts of Rakiura were occupied by moa (bird) hunters as early as the 13th century. The tītī (muttonbird) on adjacent islands were an important seasonal food source for the southern Māori.

The first European visitor was Captain Cook. Sailing around the eastern, southern and western coasts in 1770 he mistook it for the bottom end of the South Island and promptly named it South Cape. In 1809 the sealing vessel *Pegasus* circumnavigated Rakiura and named it after its first officer, William Stewart.

Flora & Fauna

With an absence of mustelids (ferrets, stoats and weasels) and large areas of intact forest, Stewart Island/Rakiura has one of the largest and most diverse bird populations of anywhere in NZ. Even in the streets of Oban the air resonates with birds such as tui, bellbirds and kaka, which share their island home with weka, kakariki, fernbirds, robins and Rakiura tokoeka/kiwi. There are also plenty of shore- and seabirds, including dotterels, shags, mollymawks (albatross), prions and petrels, as well as the tītī (muttonbirds), which are seen in large numbers during breeding season. Ask locals about the evening parade of penguins on cliffs near the wharf; and *please* – don't feed the birds. It's bad for them.

Exotic animals include two species of deer, the red and the Virginia (whitetail), introduced in the early 20th century, as were brushtail possums, which are now numerous throughout the island and destructive to the native bush. Stewart Island/Rakiura also has NZ fur seals, NZ sea lions and (rare) elephant seals dawdling on its beaches and rocky shores.

Beech, the tree that dominates much of NZ, is absent from Stewart Island/Rakiura. The predominant lowland bush is podocarp (conifer) forest, with exceptionally tall rimu, miro and totara forming the canopy. Because of mild winters, frequent rainfall and porous soil, most of the island is a lush forest, thick with vines and carpeted in deep green ferns and mosses.

WALKING RAKIURA

Rakiura National Park protects 85% of the island, making it a paradise for hikers and birdwatchers. There are plenty of trails to explore the wilderness, including short, easy tracks from Oban – pick up the *Stewart Island/Rakiura Short Walks* brochure ($2) from DOC's visitor centre (p193) or download it for free. Popular day-hike destinations include Māori Beach or nearby Port William (p177), **Ackers Point** or **Observation Rock** (Map p192).

For multiday hikers who have booked ahead there's the stunning Rakiura Track Great Walk (p177), the advanced 71.5km Southern Circuit Track and the epic North West Circuit (p177), one of New Zealand's most isolated backcountry hikes.

Longer hikes can also be shortened via water taxis (p193) or an air hop with Stewart Island Flights (p193). The latter offers the fulfilling day-long Coast to Coast cross-island hike with air and water transfers ($235).

⊙ Sights & Activities

★**Ulva Island**   WILDLIFE RESERVE
(Te Wharawhara) A tiny paradise covering only 269 hectares, Ulva Island / Te Wharawhara is a great place to see lots of native birds. Established as a bird sanctuary in 1922, it remains one of Stewart Island/Rakiura's wildest corners. The island was declared rat-free in 1997 and three years later was chosen as the site to release endangered South Island saddlebacks. Any water-taxi company will run you to the island (around $25 return) from Stewart Island's Golden Bay wharf, with scheduled services offered by **Ulva Island Ferry** (☑03-219 1013; return adult/child $20/10; ⊙departs 9am, 10am, noon, 2pm, 4pm, returns 12.15pm, 2.15pm, 4.15pm Sep-May, also returns 6pm Dec-Feb).

Rakiura Museum   MUSEUM
(Map p192; ☑03-219 1221; www.rakiuramuseum.co.nz; 9 Ayr St, Halfmoon Bay; adult/child $2/50c; ⊙10am-1.30pm Mon-Sat, noon-2pm Sun) Historic photographs are the stars of this small museum focused on local natural and human history, and featuring Māori artefacts, whaling gear and household items. Cash only.

Stewart Island/Rakiura (North)

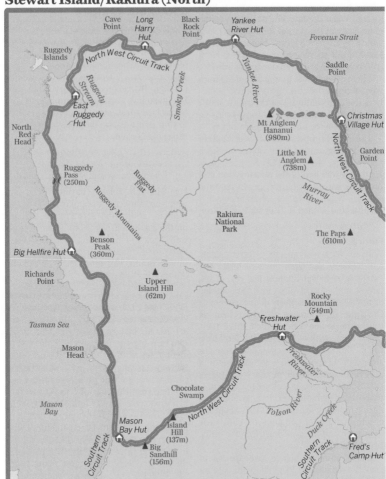

Big plans are in the works for a revamped, state-of-the-art Rakiura Museum to open on Main Rd, next to the DOC office, in mid-2020.

Rakiura Jade   ARTS & CRAFTS
(Map p192; ☏ 021 025 93958; www.rakiurajade.co.nz; 45 Elgin Tce; $180; ⏱10.30am-3pm Oct-Apr, reduced hours May, Aug & Sep) Step into Dave Goodin's atmospheric workshop suspended right over the water to learn the skills of carving *pounamu* (greenstone). Over 4½ hours Dave will guide you through selecting the right piece of stone, carving and polishing it, and even braiding the twine to hang it around your neck.

Tours

Beaks & Feathers   WALKING
(Map p192; ☏ 027 316 3077; www.beaksandfeathers.co.nz; 12 Main Rd, Oban; ⏱9am-5pm Oct-Jun) Small-group tours with Ange, a passionate local guide, including half-day tours of Ulva Island (from $220), kiwi spotting on the airstrip (from $100), as well as tours with a holistic healing slant, such as a mindful meditation walk (from $140) and a walk focused on medicinal and healing native plants (from $140).

Ruggedy Range

Wilderness Experience ECOTOUR

(Map p192; ☑ 027 478 4433, 03-219 1066; www.
ruggedyrange.com; 14 Main Rd, Oban) ✦ Highly customisable tours with a nature focus
offered on land and water (through co-owned **Aihe Eco Charters & Water Taxi**,
www.aihe.co.nz). Options include walking,
cruising, flying, bus touring, wildlife viewing (including kiwi), photography and combo packages featuring any of these, tailored
to your interests. See the websites for a wide
range of offerings.

Rakiura Charters & Water Taxi BOATING

(Map p192; ☑ 03-219 1487, 0800 725 487; www.rak
iuracharters.co.nz; 10 Main Rd, Oban; adult/child
from $130/90) Pelagic birding tours and
water-taxi services. A popular trip is to Port
William (adult/child $50/25), the first hut
on the Rakiura Track, from where you can
walk back to Oban along the track (12km,
three to five hours). Trips can be tailored
to suit timing and interests, such as wildlife-spotting and hiking.

Phil's Sea Kayak KAYAKING

(☑ 027 444 2323; www.seakayakstewartisland.nz;
2½-/4½-hour trips $90/145; ⊘ Oct–May) Stewart Island/Rakiura's only kayaking guide,
Phil runs trips on Paterson Inlet tailored for
all abilities, with sightings of wildlife along
the way.

Stewart Island Experience TOURS

(Map p192; ☑ 03-219 0056, 0800 000 511; www.
stewartislandexperience.co.nz; 12 Elgin Tce) ✦
This large operator runs 2½-hour Ulva Island Explorer cruises (adult/child $99/30),
including a 1¼-hour guided walk; and 1½-hour minibus tours of Oban and the surrounding bays ($49/30). There's also a Wild
Kiwi Encounter between September and
May ($199).

Ulva's Guided Walks WALKING

(☑ 027 688 1332; www.ulva.co.nz) ✦ Focused
firmly on birding and guided by expert
naturalists, these excellent half-day tours
(adult/child $145/70; transport included)
explore Ulva Island in small groups, developed by Ulva Goodwillie who is named after the island. Book at the **Stewart Island
Gift Shop** (Map p192; ☑ 03-219 1453; www.
facebook.com/StewartIslandGiftShop; 20 Main Rd,
Oban; ⊘ 10.30am-5pm Sep-Apr, by appointment
May-Aug). There are also kiwi-spotting tours
to Mamaku Point (from $130 per person including transport).

🛏 Sleeping

Finding accommodation can be difficult,
especially in the low season when many
places shut down – book ahead. The island has many holiday rentals, which
are often good value and offer the benefit of self-catering, which is especially
handy if you do a spot of fishing. (Note
that many impose a two-night minimum
stay or charge a surcharge for one night.)
For holiday listings, see www.stewartis
land.co.nz.

Oban

Jo & Andy's B&B   B&B $
(Map p192; ☎027 455 2191, 03-219 1230; jriksem@
gmail.com; 22 Main Rd, Oban; s $70, d & tw $100;
℗🖵) A great option for budget travellers,
this cosy blue home offers rooms with
shared-bathroom facilities. A big breakfast
of muesli, fruit and eggs prepares you for
the most active of days and free transfers
are available. Jo is splendid company and
there are hundreds of books if the weather packs up. Bookings essential; two-night
minimum stay.

Bunkers Backpackers   HOSTEL $
(Map p192; ☎027 738 1796; www.bunkersback
packers.co.nz; 14 Argyle St, Oban; dm/d $35/85;
⊙closed May-Sep; 🖵) A converted wooden
villa houses Stewart Island/Rakiura's smaller, but better, hostel option. It's somewhat
squeezed but offers the benefits of a cosy
lounge, a sunny garden, an inner-village location and a friendly, shoes-off vibe. Perks
include a barbecue area, hammock chairs
and board games.

Bay Motel   MOTEL $$
(Map p192; ☎03-219 1119; www.baymotel.co.nz;
9 Dundee St, Oban; units from $180, with spa from
$205; ℗🖵) This hillside motel offers spa-
cious, comfortable units with lots of light,
views over the harbour and a shared bal-
cony. Some rooms have spa baths, all have

kitchens, and two are wheelchair-accessible;
kids under 12 years are not allowed. Compli-
mentary pickup from the wharf or airport
with advance notice.

★**Observation Rock Lodge**   B&B $$$
(Map p192; ☎027 444 1802, 03-219 1444; www.
observationrocklodge.co.nz; 7 Leonard St, Oban; r
with/without bathroom $395/195; 🖵) Secluded
in bird-filled bush, and angled for sea, sunset and aurora views, are three stylish, luxurious rooms with private decks and a shared
lounge. Guided activities, a sauna, a hot tub
and Annett's gourmet dinners are included
in the deluxe package ($780) or by arrange-
ment as additions to the standard B&B rate.

✕ Eating & Drinking

★**Church Hill**   MODERN NZ $$$
(Map p192; ☎03-219 1123; www.churchhill.co.nz; 36
Kamahi Rd, Oban; mains $38-41; ⊙6pm-late daily
Sep-May) 🍴 Top-notch nosh is prepared at
this friendly restaurant, making use of home-
grown veggies, house-made pasta and Stew-

art Island/Rakiara seafood, such as mussels, crayfish and salmon. Dishes like paua ravioli, muttonbird and watercress dumplings and *hāngi*-baked kumara bring local flavours together in refined modern style. During summer the heritage villa's sunny deck provides hilltop views, in cooler months there's an open fire. Bookings advisable.

South Sea Hotel PUB
(☑ 03-219 1059; www.stewart-island.co.nz; 26 Elgin Tce, Oban; ☺ 7am-9pm; 🛜) Welcome to one of NZ's classic pubs, complete with stellar cod and chips, beer by the quart, a reliable restaurant (mains $16 to $33) and plenty of friendly banter in the public bar. Great at any time of day (or night), and the Sunday-night quiz offers an unforgettable slice of island life. Basic rooms (single/double from $75/95) are available, too.

🛈 Information

Rakiura National Park Visitor Centre (Map p192; ☑ 03-219 0009; www.doc.govt.nz; 15 Main Rd, Oban; ☺ 8am-5pm Dec-Mar, 8.30am-4.30pm Mon-Fri, 8am-4pm Sat & Sun Apr, May, Oct & Nov, 8.30am-4.30pm Mon-Fri, 10am-2pm Sat & Sun Jun-Sep) Stop in to obtain information on walking tracks, as well as hut bookings and passes, topographical maps, locator beacons, books and a few hiking essentials, such as insect repellent and wool socks. Information displays introduce Stewart Island/Rakiura's flora and fauna, while a video library provides entertainment and education (a good rainy-day Plan B).

Red Shed Oban Visitor Centre (Map p192; ☑ 03-219 0056, 0800 000 511; www.stewart islandexperience.co.nz; 12 Elgin Tce, Oban; ☺ 8am-6.30pm Oct-Apr, to 5pm May-Sep) Conveniently located next to the wharf, this Stewart Island Experience (p191) booking office can hook you up with nearly everything on and around the island, including guided tours, boat trips, bikes, scooters and hire cars.

Stewart Island/Rakiura has no banks. In the Four Square supermarket there's an ATM, which has a mind of its own; credit cards are accepted for most activities except water taxis.

🛈 Getting There & Away

AIR

Stewart Island Flights (☑ 03-218 9129; www.stewartislandflights.co.nz; Elgin Tce, Oban; adult/child one way $130/85, return $220/135; ☺ 7.30am-5pm Mon-Fri, 8.30am-4pm Sat & Sun, reduced hours Jun-Aug) Flies between the island and Invercargill at least three times daily, with good standby discounts. The price includes transfers between the island airport

and its office on the Oban waterfront. It also offers charter flights and tours.

BOAT

The passenger-only ferry **Stewart Island Experience** (Map p192; ☑ 03-219 0034, 0800 000 511; www.stewartislandexperience.co.nz; Main Wharf, Oban; adult/child one way $79/40, return $139/80) runs between Bluff and Oban up to four times daily (reduced to twice daily June to August). Book a few days ahead in summer (December to February). The crossing takes one hour and can be a rough ride. The company also runs a shuttle between Bluff and Invercargill (adult/child $28/14), with pickups and drop-offs in Invercargill at the i-SITE, inner-city hotels and Invercargill Airport.

Vehicles can be stored in a secure car park at Bluff for an additional cost (one/two/three/four/five days $21/31/41/52/62); there's also free unsecured parking opposite the wharf.

🛈 Getting Around

Roads on the island are limited to Oban and the bays surrounding it. Stewart Island Experience offers car and scooter hire from the Red Shed. E-bikes can be hired from the **Electric Bike Depot** (☑ 020 4023 8155; www.landsea.co.nz; 4 Main Rd; 1hr $35, half-/full day $55/84; ☺ 9-11am, 1-2pm & 4-5pm or by appointment).

Water taxis offer pickups and drop-offs for trips to Ulva Island and to remote parts of the main island – a handy service for hikers. Operators include Aihe Eco Charters & Water Taxi (p191), Ulva Island Ferry (p189) and Rakiura Charters & Water Taxi (p191).

FIORDLAND

If you picture New Zealand, it might just be Fiordland National Park that flashes into your mind's eye. Part of the Te Wāhipounamu (Southwest New Zealand) World Heritage Area, this formidable tract of mountains and forest spanning 26,000 sq km has deeply recessed sounds (technically fiords) that spider inland from the Tasman Sea.

Some of the South Island's most iconic destinations are here. Along the world-famous Milford Hwy, views of mountains and mirror lakes are only surpassed in beauty by the road's end point, Milford Sound. Here, granite giants cast their reflection in waters where dolphins and penguins frolic. Even more secluded is Doubtful Sound: the Māori-named 'place of silence' is teeming with wildlife; it's larger than Milford Sound, but much less visited.

Cruises enter the watery wilderness but walkers can delve deepest into Fiordland either on the multiday Milford, Kepler and Hollyford Tracks or shorter walks, easily reached from the highway.

Before embarking on a multiday hike, register your intentions with a friend – see AdventureSmart (www.adventuresmart.org. nz) for details.

Manapōuri

POP 228

Manapōuri, 20km south of Te Anau, is the jumping-off point for cruises to Doubtful Sound. Most visitors head straight to Pearl Harbour for the ferry to West Arm across Lake Manapōuri, known to early Māori as Roto Ua or 'Rainy Lake', and later as Moturau, the 'Many Island Lake'.

But little Manapōuri has a few tricks up its sleeve. The town can't compete with Te Anau's abundance of restaurants and motels but even the locals admit its mountain-backed lake views are more impressive. At 440m, Lake Manapōuri is the second-deepest lake in New Zealand. And with far fewer overnight visitors than Te Anau, you can enjoy the spectacular sunsets all to yourself.

🏃 Activities

Manapōuri is a staging point for the remote and challenging Dusky Track (p176).

By crossing the Waiau River at Pearl Harbour (p195) you can embark on day walks as detailed in DOC's *Fiordland Day Walks* brochure ($3 from the DOC office or download for free). A classic circuit with glimmering lake views (and occasional steep parts) is the Circle Track (3½ hours), or you can take the branch to Hope Arm (five to six hours return). Cross the Waiau River aboard a water taxi operated by Adventure Manapouri (📱021 925 577, 03-249 8070; www.adventurem-anapouri.co.nz; water taxi per person return $20; ⏱Oct-May), departing Pearl Harbour at 11am daily and returning at 3pm (also available on demand by arrangement).

Running between the northern entrance to Manapōuri township and Pearl Harbour, the 30-minute Frasers Beach walk offers picnic and swimming spots as well as fantastic views across the lake.

🛏 Sleeping & Eating

Possum Lodge   HOLIDAY PARK $
(📱03-249 6623; www.possumlodge.co.nz; 13 Murrell Ave; campervan sites $38-42, dm $25, units with/without bathroom $129/69; 🛜) Nestled into forest near the lake, Possum Lodge is old-fashioned in the best kind of way. There's basic cabins, time-worn motel units, enviably green campervan sites, laundry facilities and a fully equipped kitchen.

★ Manapouri Motels & Holiday Park   HOLIDAY PARK $
(📱03-249 6624; www.manapourimotels.co.nz; 86 Cathedral Dr; unpowered/powered sites from $20/ 50, s/d from $100/120, without bathroom from $75; 🛜) Ramshackle and eccentric, Manapouri Motels is not everyone's cup of tea, but if you like the sound of staying in a little wooden cabin that's part Swiss Alpine chalet, part hobbit house, you may find yourself at home. There's also a lovely green camping area, a fleet of Morris Minors and a games room full of old pinball machines.

The Church   PUB FOOD $$
(📱03-249 6001; www.facebook.com/pg/manap ouri.co.nz; 23 Waiau St; mains $10-30; ⏱4-8pm Tue, to 9pm Wed, noon-10pm Thu, to midnight Fri & Sat, to 9pm Sun; 🛜) No need to head up to Te Anau for a satisfying feed and a few beers, hurrah! Plates heavy with steaks, burgers and butter chicken are hauled to tables in the mezzanine of this converted church building, now a merry pub with exceptionally welcoming staff.

ℹ Getting There & Away

Topline Tours (p200) Offers year-round shuttles between Te Anau and Manapōuri (from $25). Shuttles must be booked in advance.

Tracknet (p200) One to two daily buses to/from Te Anau ($25, 20 minutes) from November to April, and on demand at other times of the year.

Doubtful Sound

Remote Doubtful Sound is humbling in size and beauty. Carved by glaciers, it's one of New Zealand's largest fiords – at least three times the length of more popular Milford. Boats gliding through this maze of forested valleys have good chances of encountering fur seals, bottlenose dolphins and Fiordland penguins. Aside from haunting birdsong, Doubtful Sound deserves its Māori name, Patea, the 'Place of Silence'.

Until relatively recently, Doubtful Sound was isolated from all but intrepid explorers. Even Captain Cook only observed it from off the coast in 1770, because he was 'doubtful' whether winds would be sufficient to blow the ship back to sea. Access improved when the road over Wilmot Pass opened in 1959 to facilitate construction of the underground West Arm power station, NZ's second-largest power generator.

Boat and coach transfers from Manapōuri to Deep Cove are easily organised through tour operators, but time-consuming enough to deter some travellers...ideal for those who want to enjoy the silence.

★ **Real Journeys**   CRUISE
(✆0800 656 501; www.realjourneys.co.nz) ✐ A family-run tourism trailblazer, Real Journeys is ecofriendly, and just plain friendly. One-day 'wilderness cruises' (adult/child from $265/80) include a 2¾-hour journey aboard a modern catamaran with a specialist nature guide. The overnight cruise, which runs from September to May, is aboard the *Fiordland Navigator*, which sleeps 72 in ensuite cabins (quad share $503, single/double from $785/1570).

Deep Cove Charters   CRUISE
(✆03-249 6828; https://doubtfulsoundcruise.nz; s $650, cabin tw/d $1450/1550; ⊙mid-Nov–mid-Mar) Overnight cruises onboard the *Seafinn* (maximum 12 passengers) run by home-grown crew who nimbly tailor the cruise to the day's weather and wildlife-spotting conditions. There are options to kayak and fish, but they had us at 'crayfish lunch and venison supper included'.

Doubtful Sound Kayak   KAYAKING
(✆0800 452 9257, 03-249 7777; www.fiordland adventure.co.nz; day tours $359; ⊙Oct-Apr) Runs day trips to Doubtful Sound, including four hours of paddling time, suitable for beginners or seasoned kayakers. Tours depart Te Anau at 6.30am.

Go Orange   CRUISE
(✆0800 505 504, 03-442 7340; www.goorange. co.nz) Real Journeys' low-cost sister operation runs kayak tours (from $259) and cruises in a 45-seater vessel (from $199) on Doubtful.

ⓘ **Getting There & Away**

Getting to Doubtful Sound is only possible by guided tour. This involves boarding a boat at **Pearl Harbour** (Waiau St, Manapōuri) for a one-

SOUTHERN SCENIC ROUTE

The Southern Scenic Route (www. southernscenicroute.co.nz) skirts lonesome beaches, forest-clad lakes and awe-inspiring lookout points, cutting a lazy arc from Queenstown to Te Anau, Manapōuri, Tuatapere, Riverton and Invercargill. From Invercargill it continues east and then north through the Catlins to Dunedin. Yes, there are more direct routes than this 610km meander, but these roads were custom-made for relaxed motoring with scenic stops sprinkled liberally along the way. See Lonely Planet's *New Zealand's Best Trips* or pick up the free *Southern Scenic Route* map to join all the dots.

hour trip to West Arm power station, followed by a 22km (40-minute) drive over Wilmot Pass to Deep Cove (permanent population: two), where you hop aboard a boat for your cruise or kayak on the sound. Tour operators will arrange all your transfers. Manapōuri is the closest place to base yourself, although Te Anau (20km) and Queenstown (170km) pickups are standard offerings (for an extra fee).

Te Anau

POP 1911

Picturesque Te Anau is the main gateway to Milford Sound and three Great Walks: the Milford, Kepler and Routeburn Tracks. Firmly focused on servicing travellers and holidaymakers, there's a sizeable accommodation scene, an array of places to eat, and the chance to stock up on dehydrated food and hiking gear. And while Te Anau doesn't party nearly as hard as effervescent Queenstown, there are a few places to sink a beer – which will taste all the better after a long day of hiking, kayaking or driving the unforgettable Milford Hwy.

Te Anau stretches along Lake Te Anau, New Zealand's second-largest lake, whose glacier-gouged fiords spider into secluded forest on its western shore. To the east are the pastoral areas of central Southland, while west across Lake Te Anau lie the rugged mountains of Fiordland. A day or two in town is more than enough before you'll be itching to get out into the wilderness.

Te Anau

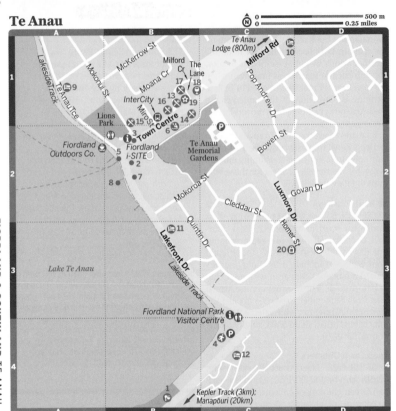

⊙ Sights

Te Anau Glowworm Caves CAVE
(☑0800 656 501; www.realjourneys.co.nz; adult/child $103/30) Stare up at constellations of glowworms on an underground boat ride. First described in Māori stories, this 200m-long cave system was lost in time until it was 'rediscovered' in 1948. Its sculpted rocks, waterfalls and whirlpools are impressive by themselves, but the bluish sparkle of glowworms, peculiar territorial larvae who lure prey with their come-hither lights, is the main draw. The caves can only be reached by a 2¼-hour guided tour with Real Journeys (p197), departing from its office on Lakefront Dr.

🏃 Activities

Lake2Lake CYCLING
(www.trailstrust.co.nz) A local-community initiative, this easy cycle trail along the Waiau River will eventually link Te Anau with Man-apōuri, starting from the DOC visitor centre (p199). At the time of research the section between Balloon Loop, 19km from Te Anau, and Supply Bay Rd, 4.7km from Manapōuri, was not yet complete (though a detour along the highway is possible for this section).

Bike Fiordland (☑03-280 0116, 0800 960 096; www.wildridesfiordland.co.nz; 68 Town Centre; bike hire 2/4hr $30/39, full day $50, ebikes 2/4hr $55/75; ⊙9am-6pm daily Nov-Apr, 10am-4pm Tue-Fri, to 3pm Sat May-Oct) offers regular shuttles to or from Balloon Loop ($78 including bike hire).

Day Hikes

Te Anau's **Lakeside Track** makes for a very pleasant stroll or cycle in either direction – north to the marina and around to the Upukerora River (about an hour return), or south past the Fiordland National Park Visitor Centre and **Punanga Manu o Te Anau** (Te Anau Bird Sanctuary; www.doc.govt.nz/teanaubirdsanctuary; Te Anau–Manapōuri Rd;

Te Anau

⊙dawn–dusk) **FREE** bird sanctuary to the Waiau River control gates and the start of the Kepler Track (50 minutes).

Day hikes in the national park are readily accessible from Te Anau. **Kepler Water Taxi** (⎇0800 004 191, 021 197 4555; www.fiordlandoutdoors.co.nz; one way $25; ⊙Oct–Apr) can scoot you over to **Brod Bay**, from where you can walk back along the Kepler and Lakeside Tracks to Te Anau (two to three hours).

Or take a cab or twice-daily Tracknet (p200) shuttle to **Rainbow Reach**, from where you can cross the swing bridge and walk 15km along the Kepler and Lakeside Tracks back to Te Anau.

During summer, **Trips & Tramps** (⎇0800 305 807, 03-249 7081; www.tripsandtramps.com) offers small-group, guided day hikes on the Milford, Kepler and Routeburn Tracks with the aid of helicopter and boat transfers. Real Journeys (p195) runs guided day hikes (adult/child $195/99, November to mid-April) along an 11km stretch of the Milford Track. Southern Lakes Helicopters (p198) offers a heli-hike ($270) on the Kepler flying into Luxmore Hut for the downhill walk to Brod Bay, with a boat pickup from there.

For self-guided adventures, pick up DOC's *Fiordland Day Walks* brochure ($3) from the Fiordland i-SITE (p199) or Fiordland National Park Visitor Centre (p199), or download it for free at www.doc.govt.nz.

Multiday Hikes

Te Anau is the gateway to three Great Walks – the Kepler (p175), Milford (p174) and **Routeburn** (www.doc.govt.nz; huts/camping $65/20, outside of Great Walks season $15/5) – and the less visited but equally worthy Hol-

lyford (p175). The Kepler trailhead is walking distance from Te Anau, the other walks are accessed from the Milford Hwy. Detailed information can be found in Lonely Planet's *Hiking & Tramping New Zealand* guide, and from the helpful folk at the Fiordland National Park Visitor Centre (p199). If you need gear, you can hire everything from **Bev's Tramping Gear Hire** (⎇03-249 7389, 027 249 7389; www.bevs-hire.co.nz; 16 Homer St; ⊙9am–noon & 6-7pm Mon-Fri Oct–Apr, or by arrangement). The Great Walks special ($160) includes warm clothing, a quality sleeping bag, a pack, cooking gear and other bits and pieces.

🢂 Tours

★**Real Journeys** TOURS
(⎇0800 656 501; www.realjourneys.co.nz; 85 Lakefront Dr; ⊙7am-8.30pm Mar-Oct, 6.45am-9.30pm Nov-Apr) 🗸 You can count on sharp service and well-organised tours from this major player, which offers cruises on Doubtful and Milford Sounds on its big menu of tours, walks and outdoor activities – always with sensitivity to local wildlife.

To see the highlights, take the Fiordland Inside and Out tour (adult/child including lunch $211/99), combining a cruise on Milford with a tour of the glowworm caves (p196) and a guided walk at Lake Gunn.

Fiordland Jet ADVENTURE SPORTS
(⎇0800 253 826; www.fjet.nz; 84 Lakefront Dr; adult/child $159/79) Thrilling two-hour jet-boating trips on the Upper Waiau River (in *Lord of the Rings*, the River Anduin), zipping between mountain-backed beech

forest, with commentary on the area's natural (and fictional) highlights.

Hollyford Track
HIKING

(☑ 03-442 3000; www.hollyfordtrack.com; adult/child from $2050/1625; ☉ late Oct-Apr) 🏃 Brimming with insight into Māori history and Fiordland wildlife, this Ngāi Tahu–owned operator leads small-group (less than 16 people) three-day guided trips on the Hollyford staying at private huts or lodges. The journey is shortened with a jetboat trip down the river and Lake McKerrow on day two, and ends with a scenic flight to Milford Sound.

A two-day helicopter and jetboating experience with short walks (7km) around Martins Bay is also available ($1890).

Ultimate Hikes
HIKING

(☑ 03-450 1940, 0800 659 255; www.ultimate hikes.co.nz; 5-day hikes incl food dm/s/d $2295/3330/5590; ☉ Nov–mid-Apr) 🏃 Booking yourself onto a guided hike of the Milford Track with Queenstown-based Ultimate Hikes puts route planning and logistics in the capable hands of an experienced operator. The guides' expert knowledge of fauna and flora enhances the journey, and walkers will overnight in lodges with hot showers and proper food.

Southern Lakes Helicopters
SCENIC FLIGHTS

(☑ 03-249 7167; www.southernlakeshelicopters.co. nz; Lakefront Dr) Offering flights over Te Anau for 30 minutes ($240), half-day heli-hike options to Luxmore Hut on the Kepler Track ($270), and longer trips with landings over Doubtful, Dusky and Milford Sounds (from $685), this operator's three decades of experience in Fiordland will reassure nervous flyers.

🛌 Sleeping

★ Te Anau Lakefront Backpackers
HOSTEL $

(☑ 03-249 7713, 0800 200 074; www.teanauback packers.co.nz; 48-50 Lakefront Dr; tent sites $25, dm $37, d with/without bathroom from $135/88; 🅿🛜) Tidy dorm and private rooms with a lakefront location hoist this backpackers to the top spot among Te Anau's budget beds. There's a range of options, including garden cabins ($120) and glamping tented dorms in summer ($32). Ask for a room with a view. The place has a cosy, lived-in feel, plus two lounges, two kitchens and a barbecue area.

Te Anau Lakeview Kiwi Holiday Park & Motels
HOLIDAY PARK $

(☑ 03-249 7457, 0800 483 262; www.teanauhol idaypark.co.nz; 77 Manapōuri–Te Anau Hwy; unpowered/powered sites $25/26, dm/s/d without bathroom from $36/59/80, d units from $379; 🅿@🛜) This 9-hectare grassy lakeside holiday park has plenty of space to pitch your tent or park your van. It also has a wide range of accommodation from basic dorms through to tidy cabins and the rather swanky Marakura two-bedroom motel units with enviable lake and mountain views. Friendly staff will hook you up with local activities and transport.

Getaway Te Anau
HOLIDAY PARK $$

(☑ 0800 249 746, 03-249 7462; www.getawayte anau.co.nz; 128 Te Anau Tce; 2-person powered sites from $68, cabins without bathroom from $119, units with bathroom $199-700; @🛜🎿) Accommodation at this holiday park covers all budgets: motel units have slate-grey decor and compact kitchens, while private tent sites and cabins share modern kitchen facilities and bathrooms. A playground, bike hire, a games room and a sauna provide distractions for kids and parents alike, but the best feature is the private lake-facing hot tubs, perfect for soaking away your hiking pains.

Keiko's Cottages
B&B $$

(☑ 03-249 9248; www.keikos.co.nz; 228 Milford Rd; d $145-190; ☉ closed Jun-Aug; 🛜) Surrounded by Japanese-style flower gardens, complete with babbling water features and a fish pond, Keiko's self-contained cottages are private, comfortable and decorated with feminine flair. The welcome is ebullient and breakfast ($25 per person) poses a difficult choice: Kiwi-style or a full Japanese banquet? The spa and sauna are worthy extras.

★ Te Anau Lodge
B&B $$$

(☑ 03-249 7477; www.teanaulodge.com; 52 Howden St; s $225-325, d $250-350, tr $300-375, all incl breakfast; 🛜) In a sea of functional but fusty motels, Te Anau's former Sisters of Mercy Convent distinguishes itself with unique history. The place oozes comfort and historic character from the elaborate confession box in reception to the complimentary fireside wine and ample continental breakfast. For a real treat, book into the heritage train carriage in the garden, complete with claw-foot bath.

Eating

★ **Bao Now** FOOD TRUCK **$**
(www.facebook.com/baonowbyhabitfoods; cnr Wong Way & Milford Cres; baos $13; ⊘9am-7.30pm Mar-Oct, to 9pm Nov-Apr) Fantastic food truck delivering Kiwi-Asian fusion baos, rice burgers and salads to hungry travellers and locals alike. Try the Bambi Bao, with wild Fiordland venison, or the Vega, with crispy tofu, shiitake and chilli mayo. Good luck getting your mouth around one of these bulging baos – grab extra napkins. Cash only.

Next door another truck, Fumi, makes sushi fresh to order.

Sandfly Cafe CAFE **$**
(☑03-249 9529; 9 The Lane; mains $11.50-21; ⊘7am-4.30pm; 🛜) As popular with locals as travellers, Sandfly serves the town's best espresso alongside breakfasts, light meals of pasta or club sandwiches, and an impressive rack of sweet treats from caramel slices to berry friands. Sun yourself on the lawn, or try to get maximum mileage out of the free 15 minutes of wi-fi.

Ristorante Paradiso ITALIAN **$$**
(Pizzeria da Toni; ☑03-249 4305; www.paradiso pizzeria.co.nz; 1 Milford Cres; mains $23-35; ⊘11am-10pm; 🚗) Simple wood-fired pizzas and homemade pastas are the stars of the show at this surprisingly authentic Italian restaurant, which scoops gelato from its streetside trolley and flies its *fiocchi* in from Italy. Vespa decorations and the odd splash of Italian art don't quite transport you to Rome but the marinara sauce comes close.

★ **Redcliff Cafe** MODERN NZ **$$$**
(☑03-249 7431; www.theredcliff.co.nz; 12 Mokonui St; mains $32-40; ⊘restaurant 11am-2pm & 5-9.30pm, bar 11am-late Sep-May) Housed in a replica settler's cottage, candlelit and cosy Redcliff offers well-executed, locally sourced food amid nostalgic decor (including old photos and antique sewing machines). Hearty meals include succulent slow-roasted pork belly with pear chutney or NZ prime beef with chimichurri. But Redcliff is just as good for a drink in the antique bar or on the sunny outdoor terrace.

Kepler's SOUTH AMERICAN **$$$**
(☑03-249 7909; 90 Town Centre; mains $29-45; ⊘5-9.30pm) Mountains of crayfish, mouthwatering ceviche and perfectly seared steaks are whisked to tables at this efficient but friendly family-run place. South American

flair permeates the menu (quinoa salads, empanadas, Argentine *carménère*); but for Kiwi flare try the lamb – roasted whole over coals in the centre of the restaurant – with a generous pour of merlot.

🍷 Drinking & Entertainment

Ranch Bar & Grill PUB
(☑03-249 8801; www.theranchbar.co.nz; 111 Town Centre; ⊘8am-late) An open fire and chalet-style eaves heighten the appeal of this popular local pub, most loved for its hefty Sunday roast dinners ($17.50), Thursday jam nights and sports matches on big screens. Show up for big pancake breakfasts (until 11.30am) or generous schnitzels and mostly meaty mains like surf 'n' turf and BBQ pork ribs ($28 to $45).

Fiordland Cinema CINEMA
(☑03 249 8844; www.fiordlandcinema.co.nz; 7 The Lane; adult/child $16/10; 🛜) In between regular showings of the excellent *Ata Whenua/Fiordland on Film* (adult/child $12/6), essentially a 32-minute advertisement for Fiordland scenery, Fiordland Cinema serves as the local movie house.

The **Black Dog Bar** (☑03-249 9089; www. blackdogbar.co.nz; 7 The Lane; ⊘10am-late Oct-Apr, 2.30pm-late May-Sep; 🛜), next to the cinema, is the town's most sophisticated watering hole.

ℹ Information

Fiordland i-SITE (☑03-249 8900; www. fiordland.org.nz; 19 Town Centre; ⊘9am-5pm May-Sep, 8.30am-7pm Oct-Apr) The official information centre, offering activity, accommodation and transport bookings.

Fiordland Medical Practice (☑03-249 7007; 25 Luxmore Dr; ⊘8.15am-5pm Mon-Fri, 9am-noon Sat, 10-10.30am & 5-5.30pm Sun) If you need medical help after hours, the centre's number will give the details of an on-call GP.

Fiordland National Park Visitor Centre (DOC; ☑03-249 7924; www.doc.govt.nz; cnr Lakefront Dr & Te Anau–Manapōuri Rd; ⊘8am-5pm daily Nov-Apr, 8.30am-4.30pm Mon-Fri, to 4pm Sat & Sun May-Oct) Can assist with Great Walks bookings, general hut tickets and information, with the bonus of a natural-history display and a shop stocking hiking supplies and essential topographical maps for backcountry trips.

ℹ Getting There & Away

InterCity (☑03-442 4922; www.intercity. co.nz; Miro St) Services to Milford Sound (from $33, three hours, two to three daily) and Queenstown (from $33, 2¼ hours, four daily), and daily 8am buses to Gore (from $33,

1¾ hours), Dunedin (from $26, 4¾ hours) and Christchurch (from $42, 11¼ hours). Buses depart from a stop on Miro St outside Kiwi Country, at the Town Centre end.

Topline Tours (☑ 03-249 8059; www.topline tours.co.nz; 32 Caswell Rd) Offers year-round shuttles between Te Anau and Manapōuri (from $25), and transfers from Te Anau to the Kepler Track trailheads at the control gates (from $5) and Rainbow Reach (from $10). Shuttles must be booked in advance.

Tracknet (☑ 0800 483 262; www.tracknet. net) From November to April Te Anau–based Tracknet has at least three daily scheduled buses to/from Te Anau Downs ($29, 30 minutes), the Divide ($43, 1¼ hours) and Milford Sound ($55, 2¼ hours), two buses to/from Manapōuri ($25, 20 minutes), one to Invercargill ($51) and four daily to Queenstown ($49, 2¾ hours). In winter, services are by demand. Buses depart from near the Te Anau Lakeview Kiwi Holiday Park (p198).

Milford Hwy

Expert travellers know it's all about the journey, and that's certainly true of the 119km road stretching north of Te Anau – though in this case the destination is not bad either. The Milford Hwy offers the most easily accessible experience of Fiordland in all its diversity, taking in expanses of beautiful beech forest, gentle river valleys, mirror-like lakes, exquisite alpine scenery and ending at arguably New Zealand's most breathtaking vista, Milford Sound.

The journey should take 2½ hours each way, but expect to spend time dawdling along walking trails and maxing out your camera's memory card. Most travellers embark on the Milford Hwy as a day trip from Te Anau, with a cruise on Milford Sound to break up the return journey. But the prospect of longer hikes or camping beneath jagged mountains might entice you to stay.

◉ Sights & Activities

Leaving Te Anau north along the Milford Hwy (SH94), the road meanders through rolling farmland atop the lateral moraine of the glacier that once gouged out Lake Te Anau. At the 29km mark it passes **Te Anau Downs**, where boats for the Milford Track depart. From here, an easy 45-minute return walk leads through forest to **Lake Mistletoe** (Te Anau Downs), a small glacier-formed lake.

The road then heads into the **Eglinton Valley**, at first pocketed with sheepy pasture, then reaching deeper wilderness immersion as it crosses the boundary into Fiordland National Park: knobby peaks, thick beech forest, lupin-lined riverbanks and grassy meadows.

Just past the **Mackay Creek Campsite** (at 51km) are the **Eglinton Flats**, a wide-open space exposing truly epic views of Pyramid Peak (2295m) and Ngatimamoe Peak (2164m). The most popular roadside stop is **Mirror Lakes** (SH94; at 58km). A short boardwalk (five minutes' walk) overlooks glassy waters, their surface interrupted by occasional mallards. If you're lucky enough to stop by on a calm, clear day, the lakes perfectly reflect the mountains across the valley.

At the 77km mark, after an enchanting stretch of forest-framed road, is **Cascade Creek** and **Lake Gunn**. This area was known to Māori as O Tapara, and a stopover for parties heading to Anita Bay in search of *pounamu* (greenstone). The bewitching **Lake Gunn Nature Walk** (SH94; 45 minutes return) loops through tall red beech forest. Moss-clung logs and a chorus of birdsong create a fairy-tale atmosphere, and side tracks lead to quiet lakeside beaches.

At 84km you pass across the **Divide**, the lowest east–west pass in the Southern Alps; from here the highway narrows and weaves. This is a trailhead for the Routeburn and Greenstone and Caples Tracks; those with less time can embark on a marvellous three-hour return walk along the start of the Routeburn, climbing up through beech forest to the alpine tussockland of **Key Summit**. On a good day the views of the Humboldt and Darran Mountains are sure to knock your socks off, and there's a nature walk around the boggy summit through stands of twisted beech.

From the Divide, the road falls into the beech forest of the Hollyford Valley – stop at **Pop's View** (SH94) for a great outlook...if you can get a parking space. The road climbs through a cascade-tastic valley to the **Homer Tunnel**, 101km from Te Anau and framed by a high-walled, ice-carved amphitheatre. Begun as a relief project in the 1930s and completed in 1953, the tunnel is one way (traffic lights direct vehicle flow – patience required). Kea (alpine parrots) hang around the tunnel entrance looking for food from tourists, but don't feed them as it's bad for their health. Dark, rough-hewn and dripping with water, the 1270m-long tunnel delivers you to the head of the spectacular **Cleddau Valley**. Any spare 'wows' might pop out about now.

About 10km before Milford Sound, the wheelchair- and pram-friendly **Chasm Walk** (SH94; 20 minutes return) affords staggering views over the churning Cleddau River. Pebbles caught in its frenetic currents have hollowed boulders into shapes reminiscent of a Salvador Dalí scene. An espresso van parks here November to April. Along the final 9km to Milford Sound, watch for glimpses of **Mt Tutoko** (2723m), Fiordland's highest peak, above the beech forest.

🛏 Sleeping

There are eight basic first-come, first-served DOC campsites (per adult/child $15/7.50) along the highway; the closest to Milford Sound is Cascade Creek, 43km away. Be warned they are popular with sandflies. There's no freedom camping on the Milford Hwy, the closest is at Lumsden, 78km east of Te Anau.

If you prefer four walls to canvas or camper vans, find more robust accommodation at Te Anau Downs at **Fiordland National Park Lodge** (📋 03-249 7811; www.fiordlandnational parklodge.com; 2681 Milford Hwy, Te Anau Downs; d/ste from $175/290; 🛜) or the attached Lone Moose Backpackers (dorms/doubles from $35/110); **Knob's Flat** (📋 03-249 9122; www. knobsflat.co.nz; 6178 SH94; unpowered sites per adult/child $20/10, d $150-180); or reserve a frontier-feel cabin at Gunn's Camp (p202). Otherwise, you're better off returning to the abundant accommodation choices in Te Anau, 119km south.

ℹ Getting There & Away

Check when you book bus tickets whether the operator is purely A-to-B or incorporates scenic lookouts.

➡ InterCity (p199) runs three daily bus services to Milford Sound from Te Anau (from $33, three hours) and Queenstown (from $66, six hours).

➡ Tracknet (p200) is handy for hikers. From November to April Te Anau–based Tracknet has at least three daily scheduled buses between Te Anau and Te Anau Downs ($29, 30 minutes), the Divide ($43, 1¼ hours) and Milford Sound ($55, 2¼ hours). Two of these connect all the way to Queenstown (from Milford Sound $95, five hours). One service runs to the Hollyford Rd end (from Te Anau/Queenstown $62/95) for the Hollyford Track. In winter (June to August), services are by demand.

Milford Sound

POP 200

The pot of gold at the end of Milford Hwy (SH94) is sublime Milford Sound (Piopiotahi). Rising above the fiord's indigo water is Mitre Peak (Rahotu), the deserved focal point of millions of photographs. Tapering to a cloud-piercing summit, the 1692m-high mountain appears sculpted by a divine hand.

In truth, it's the action of glaciers that carved these razor-edge cliffs. Scoured into the bare rock are pathways from tree avalanches, where entangled roots dragged whole forests down into darkly glittering water. When rain comes (and that's often), dozens of temporary waterfalls curtain the cliffs. Stirling and Lady Bowen Falls gush on in fine weather, with rainbows bouncing from their mists when sunlight strikes just right.

Milford Sound receives an estimated one million annual visitors which is an almighty challenge to keep its beauty pristine. But out on the water, all human activity – cruise ships, divers, kayakers – seems dwarfed into insignificance.

ℹ **MILFORD MOTORING**

The Milford Hwy is notorious throughout New Zealand for terrible driving. The majority of drivers along its 119km length are sightseers. Be on the lookout for cars decelerating suddenly, drifting across the centre line or parking dangerously. Fill up with fuel before you set out, allow plenty of time for your journey and leave adequate space between cars to avoid annoyance at fellow drivers (or worse).

In an effort to keep traffic under control, a parking fee of $10 per hour has been introduced in the main car park at Milford Sound. If you're heading up the highway on a day trip, consider taking a coach. These services stop for photos in key spots, and some have glass ceilings, through which you'll see a lot more scenery than if your eyes are glued to that winding road.

OFF THE BEATEN TRACK

HUMBOLDT FALLS & GUNN'S CAMP

Three kilometres north of the Divide, look out for a northeasterly detour off SH94. Follow the unsealed road (leading to the Hollyford Track) for 8km to reach **Gunn's Camp**. Blow dust off antique agricultural implements in the **museum** (Hollyford Rd; adult/child $2/free; ⊙ hours vary). A further 9km northeast is the trailhead for the Hollyford Track, where you will find the track to **Humboldt Falls** (off Hollyford Rd; 30 mins return). It's an easy 1.2km hike through rainforest to a viewing platform where you can spy this distant 275m-high cascade.

◉ Sights & Activities

Milford Underwater Observatory   AQUARIUM

(www.southerndiscoveries.co.nz; Harrison Cove; ⊙ 8am-5pm) Run by Southern Discoveries, this small observatory is NZ's only floating underwater observatory, with displays on the unique natural environment of the fiord. The centre offers a chance to view corals, tube anemones and bottom-dwelling sea perch from 10m below the waterline. It's only accessible on a cruise by any of the operators – some include a visit (such as Southern Discoveries' Scenic Cruise, from $90/55 per adult/child), others offer it as an add-on; check when you book.

Rosco's Milford Kayaks   KAYAKING

(☑ 03-249 8500, 0800 476 726; www.roscos milfordkayaks.com; 72 Town Centre, Te Anau; trips $115-225) Offers guided tandem-kayak trips such as the 'Morning Glory' ($225), a challenging paddle the full length of the fiord to Dale Point, and the 'Stirling Sunriser' ($219), which ventures beneath the 151m-high Stirling Falls for a 'glacial facial'. Beginners can take it easy on a two-hour paddle on the sound ($115) assisted by water taxi transfers.

Descend Scubadiving   DIVING

(☑ 027 337 2363; www.descend.co.nz; dives incl gear from $345) Black coral, more than 150 species of fish, the possibility of dolphins... Milford Sound is as beautiful underwater as it is above. Descend's six-hour trips offer a sampler of both realms: cruising on Milford Sound in a 10m boat and one or two dives along the way. There are excursions for experienced divers and novices. Transport, equipment, hot drinks and snacks included.

High rainfall at Milford Sound ensures a near-permanent layer of fresh water floats on the sea water. This blocks the light and tricks species that are usually only found at depths of up to 100m into shallow waters. You can expect to see black and red coral at just 8m, along with deepwater sea dragons.

☞ Tours

Fiordland's most accessible experience is a cruise on Milford Sound, usually lasting 90 minutes or more. Numerous companies have booking desks in the flash cruise terminal, a 10-minute walk from the main car park, but it's always wiser to book ahead.

Each cruise company claims to be quieter, smaller, bigger, cheaper or in some way preferable to the rest. What really makes a difference is timing. Buses coming all the way from Queenstown aim for sailings between around noon and 2pm, so if you avoid that time of day there will be fewer people on the boat, fewer boats on the water and fewer buses on the road. Cruises outside this window are also around 30% cheaper.

Most companies offer coach transfers from Te Anau for an additional cost. Day trips from Queenstown are common, but they make for a very long 13-hour day, about eight hours of which is spent sitting on a bus. Air transfers are also available.

★ Real Journeys   BOATING

(☑ 0800 656 501, 03-249 7416; www.realjourneys. co.nz; adult/child from $81/30) 🏊 Milford's biggest and most venerable operator runs a popular 1¾-hour scenic cruise. More specialised is the 2¼-hour nature cruise (adult/child from $89/30), which homes in on wildlife with commentary from a nature guide. Overnight cruises (from $363) are also available, from which you can take nature tours in small boats en route.

Southern Discoveries   BOATING

(☑ 0800 264 536, 03-441 1137; www.southerndis coveries.co.nz; adult/child from $55/30) A major operator with a range of Milford Sound trips, from standard scenic tours on large boats (1½ hours) to wildlife-focused cruises on smaller, 75-passenger vessels (2¼ hours;

adult/child from $99/30), always with engaging commentary and complimentary hot drinks. Add-ons include kayaking or visits to the Underwater Observatory. There's a booking office in **Te Anau** (☑0800 264 536; www.southerndiscoveries.co.nz; 80 Lakefront Dr; ⊙9am-6pm).

Cruise Milford   BOATING
(☑0800 645 367; www.cruisemilfordnz.com; adult/child from $99/18; ⊙10.45am, 12.45pm & 2.45pm) Offering a more personal touch than some of the big-boat tours, Cruise Milford's smaller vessels head out at least three times a day on 1¾-hour cruises, divulging great info from tectonics to wildlife. It never books more than half the seats so there's plenty of room.

Go Orange   BOATING
(☑0800 505 504, 03-442 7340; www.goorange. co.nz; adult/child from $57/25; ⊙9am, 12.30pm & 3pm) These low-cost two-hour cruises along the full length of Milford Sound have a cafe and a bar on board serving own-brewed beer. There's also kayaking trips (from $159, four to five hours on the water). You can book at Milford Sound or **Te Anau** (☑03-442 7340, 0800 505 504; www.goorange. co.nz; 21 Town Centre; ⊙8am-8pm Nov-Mar, 9am-4pm Apr-Oct), with transfers available for an extra fee.

Mitre Peak Cruises   BOATING
(☑0800 744 633, 03-249 8110; www.mitrepeak. com; adult/child from $95/30) Two-hour cruises in smallish boats (maximum capacity 75), allowing closer views of waterfalls and wildlife than larger vessels. The 4.30pm cruise is the last of the day, and a good choice because many larger boats are heading back at this time.

Milford Helicopters   SCENIC FLIGHTS
(☑03-249 8384; www.milfordhelicopters.com; Milford Airport; scenic flights from $265; ⊙8.30am-5.30pm Nov-Apr, 10am-4pm May-Oct) Swing past Mitre Peak, follow the Milford Track from above or land on a glacier on a scenic flight. Also offers air transfers to Te Anau and Queenstown ($800).

🛏 Sleeping

Milford Sound Lodge   LODGE $$$
(☑03-249 8071; www.milfordlodge.com; SH94; powered campervan sites per person $35, chalets $615-849; ☞) Alongside the Cleddau River, 1.5km from the Milford hub (there's a free shuttle), this modern lodge is the only accommodation at the sound. It offers luxurious self-contained chalets with a lovely riverside setting. The forest-clad campervan area (no tents please) suits smaller budgets. There's a chic restaurant (mains $28 to $41) here, open to nonguests. Book far in advance for November to April.

ℹ Information

Although it's run by Southern Discoveries, the **Discover Milford Sound Information Centre** (☑03-249 7931; www.southerndiscoveries.co.nz; SH94; ⊙8am-4pm Nov-Apr, from 9am May-Oct) near Milford's main car park sells tickets for most of the operators. There's a cafe attached.

ℹ Getting There & Away

BUS
➡ InterCity (p199) runs two to three daily buses to Milford Sound from Te Anau (from $33, three hours) and Queenstown (from $66, six hours); you can also include a cruise (from $115/125 from Te Anau/Queenstown).

➡ Tracknet (p200) has three daily scheduled buses to/from the Divide ($42), Te Anau Downs ($54) and Te Anau ($55), and two to Queenstown ($95) from November to April. In winter (June to August) services are by demand.

CAR & MOTORCYCLE
A parking fee of $10 per hour ($20 overnight) applies in the main car park. There's also a free car park on Deepwater Basin Rd about 1.5km before the cruise terminal (a free shuttle runs from here to the terminal every 15 to 20 minutes).

If you decide to drive, fill up with petrol in Te Anau before setting off. There are no petrol stations on the road to Milford Sound, and you'll want to avoid the high prices at Milford's self-serve petrol pump – the next closest, near Gunn's Camp (p202), is also costly and only accepts cash. Snow chains must be carried on ice- and avalanche-risk days from May to November (there will be signs on the road), and can be hired from petrol stations in Te Anau.

Queenstown & Wānaka

Best Places to Eat

➜ Amisfield Bistro & Cellar Door (p232)

➜ Aosta (p233)

➜ Akarua Wines & Kitchen by Artisan (p232)

➜ Fergbaker (p222)

➜ Yonder (p222)

Best Places to Stay

➜ Camp Glenorchy (p229)

➜ Adventure Queenstown (p220)

➜ Wanaka Haven (p240)

➜ Criffel Peak View (p239)

➜ Millbrook Resort (p232)

Why Go?

Few people come to Queenstown to wind down. The self-styled 'adventure capital of the world' is a place where visitors come to throw their inhibitions out the window...and throw themselves out of planes and off mountain tops and bridges.

The region has a cinematic backdrop of mountains and lakes and a smattering of valley towns just as enticing as Queenstown itself. Wānaka may resemble Queenstown – a lakeside setting, a fringe of mountains, a lengthy menu of adventures – but it runs at a less frenetic pace. Glenorchy is even more sedate, and yet it's the final stop for many on their way into arguably the finest alpine hiking terrain in New Zealand.

History makes its home in gold-rush Arrowtown, where the main-street facades still hint at past glory. Settle in for dinner and a drink after the crowds disperse – the following day there'll be plenty more opportunities to dive back into Queenstown's action-packed whirlwind.

When to Go

➜ The fine and settled summer weather from January to March is the perfect backdrop to Queenstown's active menu of adventure sports and outdoor exploration.

➜ Gold returns to Arrowtown in autumn (March to May) with a vivid display of colour in the turning of the leaves.

➜ In late June the Queenstown Winter Festival celebrates the coming of the ski season. From June to August, the slopes of the four ski fields surrounding Queenstown and Wānaka are flush with skiers and snowboarders.

➜ The winter play season ends with a flourish in August with Queenstown's Winter Pride and the Remarkables Ice & Mixed Festival.

Queenstown & Wānaka Highlights

1 Queenstown (p210)
Taking the literal leap into any number of once-in-a-lifetime activities in this paradise for thrill seekers.

2 Wānaka (p234) Scaling a waterfall via ferrata before dining at one of the lakeside town's bevy of interesting restaurants and cafes.

3 Arrowtown (p230) Spending a day in a lower gear strolling this historic gold-rush town before discovering some very chic restaurants and bars.

4 Routeburn Track (p206) Hiking high into the mountains on arguably the greatest of NZ's Great Walks.

5 Blue Pools Walk (p243) Taking a short stroll to a luminous bloom of river colour just outside Makarora.

6 Glenorchy (p228) Discovering that Paradise really is just around the corner at one of NZ's most enticing hiking bases.

HIKING AROUND QUEENSTOWN & WĀNAKA

ROUTEBURN TRACK

START ROUTEBURN SHELTER
END THE DIVIDE
DURATION 2-4 DAYS
DISTANCE 32KM
DIFFICULTY MODERATE

Some hikers say the Routeburn Track is the greatest Great Walk of all. It's a high-level mountain route with fantastic views all the way – expansive panoramas of other ranges, and near-at-hand views of mirror-like tarns, waterfalls, fairy glades lined with plush moss, and gnarled trees with long, straggly, lichen beards.

The track can be started from either end. From the Routeburn Flats end, you'll walk along the top of **Routeburn Gorge** and then ascend past the impressive **Routeburn Falls**. Arriving at alpine **Lake Harris** is an awe-inspiring mountain moment, as is the moment you rise onto **Harris Saddle** with its vast view. From here, if you have any energy left, you can make a steep 1½- to two-hour

detour up **Conical Hill**. On a clear day you can see waves breaking at Martins Bay, far away on the west coast, but it's not worth the climb on a cloudy or windy day. Shortly before you reach the Divide, a highly recommended one-hour detour heads up to the **Key Summit**, where there are views of the Hollyford Valley and the Eglinton and Greenstone Valleys.

During the Great Walks season (late October through April) you'll need to book ahead, which should be done online at www.doc.govt.nz. You'll then need to call into the DOC visitor centre in either **Queenstown** (p226) or **Te Anau** (p199) to collect actual tickets, either the day before or on the day of departure. Outside of the season, bookings aren't required, but you'll still need to visit one of the DOC centres to purchase your hut and campsite tickets. There are four basic huts along the track: Routeburn Flats, Routeburn Falls, Lake Mackenzie and Lake Howden. Both the Routeburn Flats and Lake Mackenzie huts have campsites near-

At the quiet end of Lake Wakatipu some of New Zealand's finest mountain country awaits, but you barely need to leave Wānaka for a memorable hike.

by. The other option is to take a guided walk, staying at private lodges along the way, operated by **Ultimate Hikes** (p213).

The Routeburn Track remains open in winter, though traversing the alpine section after the snow falls is not recommended for casual hikers, as winter mountaineering skills are required. There are 32 avalanche paths across the section between Routeburn Falls and Lake Howden, and the avalanche risk continues through to spring. Always check conditions with DOC.

There are car parks at both ends of the track, but they're unattended, so don't leave any valuables in your vehicle. Track shuttles are plentiful, and many people arrange to get dropped at the Divide to start their walk after a Milford Sound tour or, alternatively, time the end of their walk to catch one of the Milford Sound buses. This needs to be arranged in advance as there's no mobile phone reception on the track.

GREENSTONE CAPLES TRACKS

START/END GREENSTONE CAR PARK
DURATION 4 DAYS
DISTANCE 61KM
DIFFICULTY MODERATE

From the shores of Lake Wakatipu, this scenic route circuits through the Caples and Greenstone Valleys, crossing the subalpine McKellar Saddle, where it almost intersects with the Routeburn Track.

The name of the Greenstone Valley hints at its ancient use as a route for Māori to access the Dart Valley to collect highly prized *pounamu* (greenstone/jade), though no Māori archaeological sites have been found in the Greenstone and Caples Valleys themselves. Europeans would later traverse the valleys in search of grazing sites, with farming commencing in the Caples in 1880. The Greenstone and Pass Burn were utilised as stock routes.

The Greenstone Valley is wide and open with tussock flats and beech forest. The Caples is narrower and more heavily forested, interspersed with grassy clearings. Many hikers consider the Caples, with its park-like appearance, to be the more beautiful of the two.

The two tracks link at McKellar Saddle and again near Greenstone car park, where the road links to Glenorchy and on to Queenstown. Hikers can choose to walk just one track in one direction (joining the end of the Routeburn Track down to the Divide), or traverse both as a there-and-back journey of four days. Routeburn hikers planning to continue on the Greenstone can easily walk from Lake Mackenzie Hut to McKellar Hut, which takes around five to seven hours.

REES-DART TRACK

START MUDDY CREEK CAR PARK
END CHINAMANS FLAT
DURATION 4 DAYS
DISTANCE 63KM
DIFFICULTY DEMANDING

The Rees-Dart Track connects two splendid schist-lined valleys shaped by glaciation. The relatively small **Dart Glacier** was once part of an enormous system that terminated at Kingston, 135km away at the southern end of Lake Wakatipu.

As this hike winds up one valley and back down the other, it takes in a variety of scenery, such as meadows of flowering herbs and mighty bluffs and moraine walls.

Pinched between the Routeburn Track and Cascade Saddle, the Rees-Dart has become a popular hike, but it is longer and definitely more challenging than either the Routeburn or Greenstone Caples, and has several stream crossings, which can be hazardous in heavy rain or snowmelt.

The most common approach to the hike is to head up the Rees Valley and return down the Dart; this is the easiest direction in which to climb **Rees Saddle**. Plan an extra night at Dart Hut if you want to include a day trip to Dart Glacier or even on to Cascade Saddle.

CASCADE SADDLE

START/END RASPBERRY CREEK
CAR PARK
DURATION 3 DAYS
DISTANCE 30KM
DIFFICULTY DEMANDING

Cascade Saddle is one of the most beautiful and dramatic of all the passes that hikers can reach in New Zealand. Pinched between the West Matukituki and Dart Valleys, it's a very steep and demanding climb. On a fine day, the rewards are as numerous as the mountains you can see from atop the alpine pass, including an eyeball-to-eyeball view of Tititea/Mt Aspiring.

Cascade Saddle can also be reached from Dart Hut on the Rees-Dart Track, providing an enticing opportunity for a four-day hike, crossing the pass from the West Matukituki Valley and exiting along the Dart Valley. The recommended approach is from the West Matukituki.

The West Matukituki is hiking royalty in the South Island, and it's worth building in a couple of extra days to explore upstream to Liverpool Hut, and take a detour out to **Rob Roy Glacier**. You could easily while away a decent week based at Aspiring Hut, branching out on day walks and soaking up the spectacular mountain scenes.

Be warned: Cascade Saddle is a difficult climb, partially smothered in super-slippery snow grass, and hikers have fallen to their deaths here. It should not be attempted by inexperienced hikers, or in adverse conditions. If you have any doubts, seek advice from the warden in Aspiring Hut (staffed only in summer), who will have current weather forecasts on hand, or from the **DOC Visitor Centre** (p241) in Wānaka.

ROB ROY TRACK

START/END RASPBERRY CREEK
CAR PARK
DURATION 3–4 HOURS
DISTANCE 10KM
DIFFICULTY EASY TO MODERATE

It's not uncommon to hear this short hike, into a side pocket of the Matukituki Valley, described as the finest day walk in the South Island, and it's not difficult to understand why. Few tracks provide such large-scale mountain scenery in such a short time

Lake Harris, Routeburn Track (p206)

frame, with the walk beginning along the Matukituki Valley before climbing 400m through beech forest into a high and dramatic enclosure of mountains, providing a spectacular view of the **Rob Roy Glacier**.

The mix of beech forest and the clear blue water of Rob Roy Stream creates a bit of a fantasy land, before it all peels back to reveal the sort of mountain scene you might normally expect to find only after days of wilderness hiking.

Pay careful heed to the avalanche advisories if you're hiking in winter or spring, as the track beyond the lower lookout is susceptible to avalanches from the sheer-sided walls of the valley.

GILLESPIE PASS CIRCUIT

START/END MAKARORA
DURATION 3 DAYS
DISTANCE 58KM
DIFFICULTY MODERATE TO DEMANDING

Located in the northern reaches of Mt Aspiring National Park, this popular hike offers outstanding mountain scenery – some

ONFOKUS/GETTY IMAGES ©

Rob Roy Track

would say it rivals both the Matukituki and Glenorchy area hikes.

There is plenty to see and enjoy along this route, including valleys filled with silver beech (tawhai), and alpine tussock fields alive with grasshoppers, black butterflies, buttercups and mountain daisies. The bird life you might encounter includes the fantail, tomtit and rifleman, as well as the mōhua (yellowhead) and the parakeet known as the kākāriki.

The hike, which should only be undertaken by experienced parties, is best approached from the Young Valley to the Wilkin Valley, the easiest way to cross Gillespie Pass. This also makes for a thrilling finish if you choose, as many do, to eschew the final four to five hours' walking in favour of a jetboat ride (and thus avoiding a river crossing).

It is recommended that you carry a tent, as huts are often overcrowded in summer.

ROY'S PEAK

START/END WĀNAKA–MT ASPIRING RD
DURATION 5–6 HOURS
DISTANCE 16KM
DIFFICULTY MODERATE

If you've seen any one photo of Lake Wānaka (other than of *that* tree), it's likely to have been taken from the Roy's Peak Track, which provides a particularly photogenic vantage point. In the kindest of descriptions, the climb to Roy's Peak is a grind, ascending 1220m from near the lakeshore to the antenna-tipped summit, but oh, those views... It truly is a spectacular vista.

Those very views have made this an extremely popular track, though many hikers aspire only to reach the ridge, about three-quarters of the way up, from where the famous 'selfie with Lake Wānaka' moment bombards Instagram. If you'd prefer to escape the narcissists and experience a little more solitude, there are plenty of alternative viewpoints in the vicinity (p235).

ℹ Getting There & Away

Domestic flights head to Queenstown from Auckland, Wellington and Christchurch. There are also direct international flights from Australia (Melbourne, Sydney, the Gold Coast and Brisbane). Queenstown is the main bus hub for the region, with services radiating out to the West Coast (via Wānaka and Haast Pass), Christchurch, Dunedin (via Central Otago) and Invercargill.

QUEENSTOWN

POP 15,800

Queenstown is as much a verb as a noun, a place of doing that likes to spruik itself as the 'adventure capital of the world'. It's famously the birthplace of bungy jumping, and the list of adventures you can throw yourself into here is encyclopedic – from alpine heliskiing to ziplining. It's rare that a visitor leaves without having tried something that ups their heart rate, but to pigeonhole Queenstown as just a playground is to overlook its cosmopolitan dining and arts scene, its fine vineyards, and the diverse range of bars that can make evenings as fun-filled as the days.

Leap, lunge or luge here, but also find time to simply sit at the lakeside and watch the ever-dynamic play of light on the Remarkables and Lake Wakatipu, creating one of the most beautiful and dramatic natural scenes in NZ.

Expect big crowds, especially in summer and winter, but also big experiences.

History

The Queenstown region was deserted when the first British people arrived in the mid-1850s, although there is evidence of previous Māori settlement. Sheep farmers came first, but after two shearers discovered gold on the banks of the Shotover River in 1862, a deluge of prospectors followed.

Within a year the settlement was a mining town with streets, permanent buildings and a population of several thousand. It was declared 'fit for a queen' by the NZ government; hence Queenstown was born. Lake Wakatipu was the principal means of transport, and at the height of the boom there were four paddle steamers and 30 other craft plying the waters.

By 1900 the gold had petered out and the population was a mere 190. It wasn't until the 1950s that Queenstown became a popular holiday destination.

◎ Sights

★ Lake Wakatipu   LAKE

(Map p214) Shaped like a cartoon lightning bolt, Lake Wakatipu is NZ's third-largest lake. It reaches a depth of 372m, meaning the lake bed actually sits below sea level. Five rivers flow into it but only one (the Kawarau) flows out, making it prone to sometimes dramatic floods. The lake can be experienced at any number of speeds: the classic TSS Earnslaw (p220) steamboat trip, a spin with KJet (p216), below decks in the Time Tripper (p212), or a shark's-eye view with Hydro Attack (p216).

If the water looks clean, that's because it is. Scientists have rated it as 99.9% pure – you're better off dipping your glass in the lake than buying bottled water. It's also very cold. That beach by Marine Pde may look tempting on a scorching day, but trust us – you won't want to splash about for long in water that hovers around 11.5°C year-round. Because cold water increases the risk of drowning, local by-laws require the wearing of life jackets in all boats under 6m, including kayaks, on the lake (and all of the district's lakes).

Māori tradition sees the lake's shape as the burnt outline of the evil giant Matau sleeping with his knees drawn up. Local lad Matakauri set fire to the bed of bracken on which the giant slept in order to rescue his beloved Manata, a chief's daughter who was kidnapped by the giant. The fat from Matau's body created a fire so intense that it burnt a hole deep into the ground.

Queenstown Gardens   PARK

(Map p214; Park St) Set on its own tongue of land framing Queenstown Bay, this pretty park is the perfect city escape right within the city. Laid out in 1876, it features an 18-'hole' frisbee golf course (Map p214; www.queenstowndiscgolf.co.nz; Queenstown Gardens) FREE, a skate park, lawn-bowls club, tennis courts, Queenstown Ice Arena (Map p214; ☏03-441 8000; www.queenstownicearena.co.nz; 29 Park St; entry incl skate hire $19; ⊙ hours vary), mature exotic trees (including large sequoias and some fab monkey puzzles by the rotunda) and a rose garden.

Near the tip of the gardens there's a memorial to Captain Robert Scott (1868–1912), leader of the doomed South Pole expedition, which includes an engraving of his moving final message.

Queenstown Region

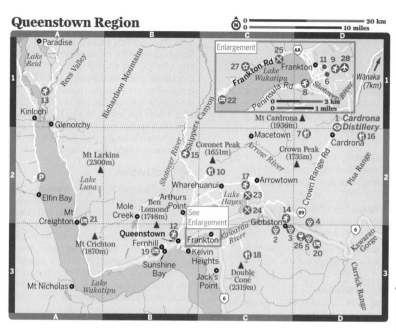

St Peter's on Church St CHURCH
(Map p218; ☎03-442 8391; www.stpeters.co.nz; 2 Church St) This pretty Anglican church, built in 1932 from local greywacke stone, has colour-ful stained glass and an impressive gilded and painted organ. Take a look at the eagle-shaped cedar lectern, carved and donated in 1874 by John Ah Tong, a Chinese immigrant.

ESSENTIAL QUEENSTOWN & WĀNAKA

Eat at a winery by Lake Hayes or in the Gibbston Valley.

Drink vodka or gin from the Cardrona Distillery (p242).

Read Robert Scott's final message, displayed on his memorial in Queenstown Gardens (p210).

Listen to *Out of the Woods* (2014) by Taylor Swift and re-enact the video, which was partly shot around Lake Wakatipu.

Watch *Top of the Lake*, the Jane Campion–directed TV series set around Glenorchy.

Go online www.queenstownnz.co.nz, www.lakewanaka.co.nz

Skyline Gondola
CABLE CAR

(Map p214; ☑03-441 0101; www.skyline.co.nz; Brecon St; adult/child return $44/26; ☺9am-9pm) Hop aboard for fantastic views as the gondola squeezes through pine forest to its grandstand location 400m above Queenstown. At the top there's the inevitable cafe, restaurant, souvenir shop and observation deck, as well as the Queenstown Bike Park (p215), Skyline Luge (p217), Ledge Bungy (p215), Ledge Swing (p215), GForce Paragliding (p217) and Ziptrek Ecotours (p216). At night there are stargazing tours (including gondola, adult/child $99/54).

Walking trails include the **Skyline Loop track** through the Douglas firs (30 minutes return). The energetic (or frugal) can forgo the gondola and hike to the top on the **Tiki Trail** (Map p214), while the popular Ben Lomond Track (p213) climbs on another 940m.

Kiwi Birdlife Park
BIRD SANCTUARY

(Map p214; ☑03-442 8059; www.kiwibird.co.nz; Brecon St; adult/child $55/25; ☺9am-5pm) 🖋 These 2 hectares are home to 10,000 native plants, geckos, skinks, tuatara (an endemic reptile) and scores of birds, including kiwi, kea (alpine parrots), kārearea (NZ falcons), kākāriki (parakeets) and the endangered whio (blue ducks). Stroll around the aviaries, watch the conservation show and tiptoe quietly into the darkened kiwi houses. Kiwi feedings take place five times a day.

Time Tripper
VIEWPOINT

(Map p218; ☑03-409 0000; www.timetripper.co.nz; Main Town Pier; adult/child $25/12; ☺9am-5pm) Located in the old underwater observatory beneath the main pier, this 30-minute experience promises a journey back in time, explaining Lake Wakatipu's geology and mythology by way of a 30-minute animation, after which the screen lifts so that you can peer through the windows at the lake life. Large brown trout abound, and look out for freshwater eels and scaup ducks.

🏃 Activities

Head to Shotover St to get a handle on the baffling array of activities on offer in Queenstown. This street, particularly the two blocks between Stanley and Brecon Sts, is wall-to-wall with adventure-tour operators selling their products, interspersed with travel agencies and 'information centres' hawking the very same products. Adding to the confusion is the fact that some stores change their name from summer to winter, while some tour operators list street addresses that are primarily their pick-up points rather than distinct shopfronts for the business.

Several operators are based at The Station, a large hub on the corner of Shotover St and Camp St; various tours and shuttle buses depart from here.

If you're planning on tackling several activities, various combination tickets are available, including those offered by **Queenstown Combos** (Map p218; ☑03-442 7318; www.combos.co.nz; The Station, cnr Shotover St & Camp St).

Skiing & Snowboarding

Queenstown has two excellent ski fields: **The Remarkables** (Map p211; ☑03-441 1456; www.theremarkables.co.nz; Remarkables Ski Field Access Rd; daily lift pass adult/child $129/69) and **Coronet Peak** (Map p211; ☑03-441 1516; www.coronetpeak.co.nz; Coronet Peak Rd; daily lift pass adult/child $129/69), both of which can be booked from the **Queenstown Snow Centre** (Map p218; ☑03-442 4615; www.nzski.co.nz; 9 Duke St). You can hire gear here too, and the NZSki Snowline Express Ski Bus (p227) leaves from out the front. Coronet Peak is the only field to offer night skiing (staying open until 9pm on Wednesdays, Fridays and Saturdays at the peak of the season), which is an experience not to be missed if you strike a starry night. If you fancy a change of scenery, there's also Cardrona Alpine Resort (p242) and Treble Cone (p235) near Wānaka.

The ski season generally lasts from around June to early October. In winter, shops throughout Queenstown are full of ski gear for purchase and hire; Outside Sports (p215) and **Small Planet Outdoors** (Map p218; 03-442 5397; www.smallplanetsports.com; 15-17 Shotover St; 8am-8pm) are reliable options.

Heliskiing is an option for serious, cashed-up skiers; try Over the Top (p218), **Harris Mountains Heli-Ski** (Map p218; 03-442 6722; www.heliski.co.nz; 19 Shotover St; from $995; Jul-Sep), **Southern Lakes Heliski** (Map p218; 03-442 6222; www.southernlakesheliski.com; Torpedo 7, 20 Athol St; from $975) or **Alpine Heliski** (Map p218; 03-441 2300; www.alpineheliski.com; Info & Snow, 37 Shotover St; from $975; Jul-Sep).

Hiking

DOC publishes a dedicated *Wakatipu Walks* brochure, as well as the *Head of Lake Wakatipu* brochure, which covers trails closer to Glenorchy. Between them, they outline more than 60 day walks in the area. They can be picked up from the DOC Visitor Centre (p226) or downloaded from its website.

★ **Ben Lomond Track**   HIKING
(Map p214; www.doc.govt.nz) The popular, six-to eight-hour (return) track to Ben Lomond (1748m) culminates in probably the best accessible view in the area. From the top gondola station, the track climbs almost 1000m, and past Ben Lomond Saddle it gets pretty steep and rocky, but the views are incredible, stretching over Lake Wakatipu and as far as Tititea/Mt Aspiring.

Snow and ice can make it even more difficult, so in winter, check at the DOC Visitor Centre (p226) before setting out.

★ **Queenstown Hill/**
Te Tapunui Time Walk   HIKING
(Map p214) Ascend 500m to the summit of Queenstown Hill/Te Tapunui for a 360-degree view over the lake and along the Remarkables. The walk takes around three hours return. Access is from Belfast Tce.

Ultimate Hikes   HIKING
(Map p218; 03-450 1940; www.ultimatehikes.co.nz; The Station, Duke St; Nov-Apr) ✿ If you like your adventure with a little comfort, Ultimate Hikes offers three-day guided hikes on the Routeburn (from $1375) and Milford (from $2130) Tracks, staying in its own well-appointed private lodges. It also runs day walks on both tracks (from $179) and a couple of combinations of tracks. Prices include transfers from Queenstown, meals and accommodation.

In winter the office is rebranded as Snowbiz and rents skis and snowboards.

Guided Walks
New Zealand   HIKING
(Map p211; 03-442 3000; www.nzwalks.com; unit 29, 159 Gorge Rd) Guided walks ranging from half-day nature walks near Queenstown (adult/child $119/79) to a day on the Routeburn Track ($199/140) and the full three-day Hollyford Track (from $2050/1625). It also offers snowshoeing in winter.

QUEENSTOWN WITH CHILDREN

While Queenstown is brimming with activities, some of them have age restrictions that may exclude the youngest in your group. Nevertheless, you shouldn't have any trouble keeping the littlies busy.

All-age attractions include the Kiwi Birdlife Park (p212) and lake cruises on the TSS Earnslaw (p220). There's a good beachside playground (Map p214) off Marine Pde, near the entrance to the Queenstown Gardens (p210). Also in the gardens, Queenstown Ice Arena (p210) is great for a rainy day, and a round of frisbee golf (p210) will easily fill in a couple of hours. The Skyline Gondola (p212) offers a slow-moving activity with a dizzying view. Even small children can ride the luge (p217) with an adult, but need to be at least 110cm in height to go it alone.

Family Adventures (p217) runs gentle rafting trips suitable for three-year-olds. Under-fives can ride on the Shotover Jet (p216) for free, provided they're over 1m in height, and six-year-olds can tackle the ziplines with Ziptrek Ecotours (p216). Children as young as eight can tackle the Kawarau Zipride (p215), though eight- and nine-year-olds must ride tandem with an adult.

For more ideas and information, including details of local babysitters, visit the i-SITE (p227) or www.kidzgo.co.nz.

Queenstown

0   500 m
0   0.25 miles

Queenstown Hill Recreation Reserve

Belfast Tce

Edinburgh Dr

Villa del Lago (250m)

Frankton Rd

6A

Walking Track to Frankton

Frankton Arm

Suburb St

Panorama Tce

Dublin St

The Terrace

Suburb St

Kent St

York St

Hallenstein St

Adelaide St

Melbourne St

Sydney St

Frankton Rd

Hobart St

Ballarat St

Stanley St

Coronation Dr

Park St

Park St

Anderson Heights

Guided Walks New Zealand (650m)

Gorge Rd

Weaver St

Turner St

Robins Rd

See Central Queenstown Map (p218)

Shotover St

Brecon St

Hamilton Rd

Lake St

TSS Earnslaw Route

Queenstown Bay

Lake Esp

St Omer Park

Brunswick St

Lomond Ave

Thompson St

Hidden (2.2km)

Fernhill (1km)

Lake Wakatipu

Cycling

Since the opening of the Queenstown Bike Park in 2011, the town has become entrenched as an international destination for mountain bikers. Coronet Peak (p212) also opens from December to March, with cross-country and downhill trails (day pass adult/child $55/35) and a shuttle from Queenstown ($25 return).

One of NZ's 22 Great Rides, the **Queenstown Trail** (www.queenstowntrail.co.nz) links various scenic cycling routes that radiate out like spokes to Arrowtown, Gibbston, Jack's Point, Lake Hayes and along the shores of Lake Wakatipu – 130km of off-road trails in total. The trail is suitable for cyclists of all levels. Bike-hire places such as **Charge-About** (Map p211; ☑03-442 6376; www.chargeabout.co.nz; Hilton Hotel, 79 Peninsula Rd, Kelvin Heights; e-bike half/full day from $79/119; ☉10am-5pm) and Arrowtown Bike Hire (p232) typically offer packages that include shuttle-bus pick-ups from Gibbston – ride one way, sip a few wines and get a designated driver for the return trip.

Your best bets for hiring serious wheels in central Queenstown are **Vertigo Bikes** (Map p218; ☑03-442 8378; www.vertigobikes.co.nz; 4 Brecon St; rental half/full day from $39/59; ☉8am-7pm Oct-May) and **Outside Sports** (Map p218; ☑03-441 0074; www.outsidesports.co.nz; 9 Shotover St; ☉8am-9pm).

Queenstown Bike Park MOUNTAIN BIKING
(Map p214; ☑03-441 0101; www.skyline.co.nz; Skyline Gondola; day pass incl gondola adult/child $110/75; ☉9am-7pm mid-Sep–mid-May) More than 30 different trails – from easy (green) to extreme (double black) – radiate out from the top of the Skyline Gondola. Once you've descended the 400m of vertical, simply jump on the gondola and do it all over again. The best trail for novice riders is the 6km-long **Hammy's Track**, which is studded with lake views and picnic spots.

Bungy & Swings

AJ Hackett Bungy BUNGY JUMPING
(Map p218; ☑03-450 1300; www.bungy.co.nz; The Station, cnr Camp St & Shotover St) The bungy originator now offers jumps from three sites in the Queenstown area, with giant swings available at two of them. It all started at the historic 1880 **Kawarau Bridge** (Map p211; ☑03-450 1300; www.bungy.co.nz; Gibbston Hwy; adult/child $205/155), 23km from Queenstown, which became the world's first commercial bungy site in 1988. The 43m river leap is the only bungy site in the region to offer tandem jumps.

The Kawarau Bridge site also features the **Kawarau Zipride** (Map p211; ☑03-450 1300; www.bungy.co.nz; Gibbston Hwy; adult/child $50/40, 3-/5-ride pack $105/150), a flying fox zooming above the riverbank that reaches speeds of 60km/h. Multiride packs can be split between groups, making it a far cheaper alternative to the bungy.

The closest options to Queenstown are the **Ledge Bungy** (Map p214; ☑0800 286 4958; www.bungy.co.nz; Skyline Gondola; adult/child $205/155) and **Ledge Swing** (Map p214; www.bungy.co.nz; Skyline Gondola; adult/child $165/115), set just beneath the top station of the Skyline Gondola. The drop is 47m, but it's 400m above town. From July to September you can even leap into the dark.

Queenstown

FIXING THE KNOTS

After days of adventure and activity, your body might well be craving a break in the pace. Here's our pick of the best ways to slow down and recharge in Queenstown.

➡ **Onsen Hot Pools** (☎03-442 5707; www.onsen.co.nz; 160 Arthurs Point Rd, Arthurs Point; 1/2/3/4 people from $88/126/175/212; ☺9am-11pm) has private Japanese-style hot tubs with mountain views. Book ahead and one will be warmed up for you.

➡ Make the short trek to Millbrook Resort near Arrowtown, where the **Spa at Millbrook** (Map p211; ☎03-441 7017; www.millbrook.co.nz/spa; treatments from $79) is regularly rated as one of NZ's best spas.

➡ Catch a water taxi across the lake to **Eforea Spa at Hilton** (Map p211; ☎03-450 9416; www.queenstownhilton.com; 79 Peninsula Rd, Kelvin Heights; treatments from $85; ☺9am-8pm).

Last but most airy is the **Nevis Bungy** (☎03-450 1300; www.bungy.co.nz; bungy $275), the highest leap in New Zealand. From Queenstown, 4WD buses will transport you onto private farmland where you can jump from a specially constructed pod, 134m above the Nevis River. The **Nevis Swing** (☎03-450 1300; www.bungy.co.nz; adult/child $225/175, tandem $440) starts 160m above the river and cuts a 300m arc across the canyon on a rope longer than a rugby field – yes, it's the world's biggest swing.

If you're keen to try more than one AJ Hackett experience, enquire about the range of combo tickets.

Shotover Canyon

Swing & Fox   ADVENTURE SPORTS
(Map p218; ☎03-442 9186; www.canyonswing.co.nz; 34 Shotover St; swing $249, fox $169, swing & fox combo $299) 🏃 Pick from any number of jump styles – backwards, in a chair, upside down – and then leap from a 109m cliff above the **Shotover River**, with 60m of free fall and a wild swing across the canyon at 150km/h. The Canyon Fox zipline can have you whizzing across the Shotover Canyon, more than 180m above the river. The price includes transfer from the Queenstown booking office, and if you liked the swing the first time, you can go again for $45.

Ziptrek Ecotours   ADVENTURE SPORTS
(Map p214; ☎03-441 2102; www.ziptrek.co.nz; Skyline Gondola; 🐾) 🏃 Incorporating a series of flying foxes, this thrill-ride takes you whirring through the forest canopy, from treetop platform to treetop platform, high above Queenstown. Choose from the two-hour, four-line Moa (adult/child $145/99); the gnarlier and faster three-hour, six-line Kea ($195/149); and the one-hour, two-line Keruru ($99), which evens with a 21m controlled drop.

Jetboating

Skippers Canyon Jet   BOATING
(Map p211; ☎03-442 9434; www.skipperscanyonjet.co.nz; Skippers Rd; adult/child $159/85) 🏃 A 30-minute jetboat blast through the remote and hard-to-access Skippers Canyon, among the narrowest gorges on the **Shotover River**. Trips pick up from The Station in Queenstown, taking around three hours in total. It also offers a scenic bus tour of the canyon (adult/child $155/95), which can be combined with the jetboat ($195/115).

Shotover Jet   BOATING
(☎03-442 8570; www.shotoverjet.com; 3 Arthurs Point Rd, Arthurs Point; adult/child $159/89) 🏃 Half-hour jetboat trips through the narrow Shotover Canyon, with lots of thrilling 360-degree spins and reaching speeds of 90km/h.

KJet   BOATING
(Map p218; ☎03-409 0000; www.kjet.co.nz; Main Town Pier; adult/child/family $135/69/307; ☺9am-5pm) Skim, skid and spin around Lake Wakatipu and the Kawarau and Lower Shotover Rivers on these one-hour trips, leaving every hour on the hour.

Hydro Attack   BOATING
(Map p218; ☎0508 493 762; www.hydroattack.co.nz; Lapsley Butson Wharf; 25min ride $154; ☺9am-6pm Nov-Mar, 10am-4.30pm Apr-Oct) That shark you see buzzing about Lake Wakatipu is the Hydro Attack – jump inside, strap yourself in and take a ride. This 'Seabreacher X' watercraft can travel at 80km/h on the water, dive 2m underneath and then launch itself nearly 6m into the air. It's mesmerising to watch, let alone travel inside.

Riverboarding & Rafting

Serious Fun Riverboarding   ADVENTURE SPORTS
(Map p218; ☎03-442 5262; www.riverboarding.co.nz; Info & Track, 37 Shotover St; from $225) Steer buoyant sledges or bodyboards on the rapids and whirlpools of the Kawarau River.

The gentlest option is bodyboard drifting ($255, January and February only), followed by sledging ($235, November to March) and full-on riversurfing ($235, September to May).

Family Adventures   RAFTING
(Map p218; ☑ 03-442 8836; www.familyadventures.co.nz; 39 Shotover St; adult/child $189/120; ☺ Oct-Apr; 🏠) These gentle (Grades I to II) and good-humoured rafting trips on the Shotover River are much loved by families as they're suitable for even three-year-olds. Trips depart from Browns Ski Shop and include a 45-minute scenic drive to the Skippers Canyon launch site, which *Lord of the Rings* nuts will recognise as the Ford of Bruinen.

Go Orange Rafting   RAFTING
(Map p218; ☑ 03-442 7340; www.goorange.co.nz; 35 Shotover St; rafting/helirafting from $189/299; ☺ 7.30am-7pm) 🛶 Rafts year-round on the churning Shotover River (Grades III to V) and calmer Kawarau River (Grades II to III). The Kawarau trips include a thrilling 30-minute jetboat ride from town to the launch site, then two hours on the water. Accessing the Shotover site involves a scenic coach trip along Skippers Canyon, but in snow a helicopter is required.

Paragliding, Parasailing & Skydiving
GForce Paragliding   PARAGLIDING
(Map p214; ☑ 03-441 8581; www.nzgforce.com; Skyline Gondola; flight $239) Tandem paragliding from the top of the gondola (early departures are $20 cheaper).

Queenstown Paraflights   PARASAILING
(Map p218; ☑ 03-441 2242; www.paraflights.co.nz; Main Town Pier; solo/tandem/triple per person $199/129/99) Take a solo, tandem or triple paraflight, zipping along 180m above the lake, pulled behind a boat.

NZone   SKYDIVING
(Map p218; ☑ 03-442 5867; www.nzoneskydive.co.nz; 35 Shotover St; from $299) Jump out of a perfectly good airplane from 9000, 12,000 or 15,000ft...in tandem with someone who actually knows what they're doing.

Other Activities
If you've heard it can be done, it's likely that it can be done in Queenstown. To save us writing an activities encyclopedia, check in at the i-SITE (p227) if you're interested in the likes of golf, minigolf, sailing or diving.

Climbing Queenstown   CLIMBING
(Map p211; ☑ 027 477 9393; www.climbingqueenstown.com; Basecamp Adventures Climbing Centre, 3/15 Red Oaks Dr, Frankton; half-/full day $179/299) Rock-climbing, mountaineering and guided hiking and snowshoeing trips in the Remarkables. Trips depart from Outside Sports (p215).

Canyoning Queenstown   CLIMBING
(Map p218; ☑ 03-441 3003; www.canyonexplorers.nz; 39 Camp St; ☺ Oct-Apr) Jump, slide, zip line and abseil your way through Queenstown Canyon (half day $219), 10 minutes' drive from town, or the remote Routeburn Canyon (full day $319) out past Glenorchy. It also operates via ferrata trips on Queenstown Hill ($189), climbing cliffs that overlook Queenstown using metal rungs and safety cables.

Skyline Luge   ADVENTURE SPORTS
(Map p214; ☑ 03-441 0101; www.skyline.co.nz; Skyline Gondola; 2/3/5 rides incl gondola adult $61/63/67, child $43/45/49; ☺ 10am-8pm) 🛷 Ride the gondola to the top, then hop on a three-wheeled cart to ride 800m of track. Your first run must be on the easy Blue Track then you're allowed to advance to the Red Track, with its banked corners and tunnel. Children must be over 110cm in height to ride the Blue Track and over 135cm for the Red.

☞ Tours
Winery Tours
Most winery tours include cellar-door stops in the Lake Hayes, Gibbston, Bannockburn and Cromwell Basin subregions.

New Zealand Wine Tours   WINE
(☑ 0800 666 778; www.nzwinetours.co.nz; from $235) Small-group (maximum seven people) or private winery tours, including lunch – platter, degustation or à la carte, depending on the tour.

Appellation Wine Tours   WINE
(☑ 03-442 0246; www.appellationcentral.co.nz; from $169) Take a tipple at wineries in Gibbston, Bannockburn and Cromwell, including cheese platters (on half-day tours) or a platter or degustation lunch. It also offers general sightseeing tours and combinations of the two.

Hop on Hop off Wine Tours   WINE
(☑ 0800 6937 2273; www.hoponhopoffwinetours.com; half-/full day $60/80) Jump on outside

QUEENSTOWN & WĀNAKA QUEENSTOWN

Central Queenstown

The Station for a 17-stop loop around Lake Hayes and Gibbston wineries, breweries and notable sites such as the Shotover Jet, Arrowtown and the original AJ Hackett bungy site.

Scenic Flights

Air Milford   SCENIC FLIGHTS
(Map p211; ☑ 03-442 2351; www.airmilford.co.nz; 3 Tex Smith Lane, Frankton) Options include a Milford Sound & Big Five Glaciers flyover (adult/child $420/260), a fly-cruise-fly combo (from $565/340), and longer flights to Doubtful Sound (summer only) and Aoraki/Mt Cook.

Glenorchy Air   SCENIC FLIGHTS
(Map p211; ☑ 03-442 2207; www.glenorchyair.co.nz; Queenstown Airport, Frankton) Scenic trips include a Milford Sound fly-cruise-fly option (adult/child $535/360), an Aoraki/Mt Cook glacier flight with a landing ($685/415), and various kayaking and hiking combos.

Over The Top   SCENIC FLIGHTS
(Map p211; ☑ 03-442 2233; www.flynz.co.nz; 10 Tex Smith Lane, Frankton) Offers a range of helicopter flights, from a picnic on a peak near town (per person $995) to an Ultimate Milford flight with four landings (from $7950). From July to October it offers heliskiing.

Milford Sound Tours

Day trips from Queenstown to Milford Sound via Te Anau take 12 to 13 hours, including a cruise on the sound. Bus-cruise-flight options are also available, as is pick-up from the Routeburn Track (p206) trailhead at the Divide. It's a long day in the saddle, so you might consider visiting Milford from Te Anau. Another way to speed things up are plane or helicopter sightseeing flights to Milford.

BBQ Bus by Altitude Tours   TOURS
(☑ 03-441 4788; www.bbqbus.co.nz; adult/child $250/125) Small-group bus tours to Milford Sound (maximum 19 people), including a

Central Queenstown

barbecue lunch followed by a cruise. Te Anau drop-offs and pick-ups are $40 cheaper.

Real Journeys TOURS
(Map p218; ☎0800 656 501; www.realjourneys.co.nz; Steamer Wharf) 🏊 Runs a host of trips, including day and overnight tours to Milford (from $210) and Doubtful (from $285) Sounds.

Other Tours
Off Road Adventure Centre DRIVING
(Map p218; ☎03-442 7858; www.offroad.co.nz; 61a Shotover St) Exciting off-road trips by quad

bike (from $219), dirt bike (from $309) or buggy (two-seater $368), with exclusive access to a 4500-hectare property along the Kawarau River and Nevis Range. Also on offer are 4WD sightseeing tours (from $189) to Glenorchy or Skippers Canyon.

Private Discovery Tours DRIVING
(☎03-442 2299; www.privatediscoverytours.co.nz) Offers a range of small-group 4WD tours, including the half-day High Country Discovery (adult/child $195/98) offering exclusive access to Mt Earnslaw Station, a sheep farm in a remote valley past Glenorchy, complete

with Middle-earth movie locations. The station is also included on the full-day Paradise Discovery ($395/205), which visits the Dart River, Paradise, Diamond Lake and further Hobbit-infested sites.

Nomad Safaris
DRIVING

(Map p218; ☑ 03-442 6699; www.nomadsafaris. co.nz; 37 Shotover St; adult/child from $195/95) Runs 4WD tours into hard-to-get-to backcountry destinations such as Skippers Canyon and Macetown, as well as a trip through Middle-earth locations around Glenorchy and the Wakatipu Basin. You can also quadbike through a sheep station on Queenstown Hill ($275).

TSS Earnslaw
CRUISE

(Map p218; ☑ 03-249 6000; www.realjourneys.co. nz; Steamer Wharf) The stately, steam-powered TSS *Earnslaw* was built in the same year as the *Titanic* (1912) but has fared somewhat better. The ship was once the lake's major means of transport, though now its ever-present cloud of black soot (it burns a tonne of coal an hour) seems a little incongruous in such a pristine setting.

🎉 Festivals & Events

Queenstown
Winter Festival
CARNIVAL

(www.winterfestival.co.nz; ☺ Jun) Four days of wacky ski and snowboard activities, live music, comedy, fireworks, a community carnival, parade, ball and plenty of frigid frivolity in late June.

Winter Pride
LGBT

(www.winterpride.co.nz; ☺ Aug/Sep) The South Island's biggest and best gay-and-lesbian event, held over 10 party-packed days in late August/early September.

🛏 Sleeping

🛏 Central Queenstown

Flaming Kiwi Backpackers
HOSTEL $

(Map p214; ☑ 03-442 5494; www.flamingkiwi.co. nz; 39 Robins Rd; dm/r without bathroom from $35/90; ℗ 🛜) Close to the town centre but still quietly removed, this friendly hostel offers tidy dorms with a locker for every bed, three kitchens, unlimited wi-fi and a bottle of sunblock at reception. The lounge is like being back at home, and there are free bikes, frisbees and international phone calls to 21 countries.

Haka Lodge
HOSTEL $

(Map p218; ☑ 03-442 4970; www.hakalodges. com; 6 Henry St; dm/apt from $33/216, r with/ without bathroom $103/94; ℗ ❄ 🛜) Part of a small Kiwi chain of higher-brow hostels, the warren-like Haka has cosy dorms with solid bunks that include large lockable storage chests, privacy curtains, personal lights and electrical sockets. There's a one-bedroom apartment attached, with its own kitchen, spacious lounge, laundry facilities and private deck where you can watch paragliders swirl down from the gondola.

Butterfli Lodge
HOSTEL $

(Map p214; ☑ 03-442 6367; www.butterfli.co.nz; 62 Thompson St; dm/r from $35/95; ℗ 🛜) This little hostel sits on a quiet hillside west of the town centre. There are no bunks but no en suites either. The views from the deck are like a sightseeing tour in themselves.

★ Adventure Queenstown
HOSTEL $$

(Map p218; ☑ 03-409 0862; www.aqhostel.co.nz; 36 Camp St; dm $38-44, r $140; ❄ 🛜) Run by experienced travellers (as the photos displayed throughout testify), this central hostel has spotless dorms, a modern kitchen and balconies that are like a window onto the city. The private room has an en suite, as do some of the dorms. There are activities every night, from an in-house quiz to a Saturday pub crawl.

Adventure Q2 Hostel
HOSTEL $$

(Map p218; ☑ 03-927 4625; www.adventureq2. co.nz; 5 Athol St; dm $37-39, r $135; 🛜) Opened in 2016, this sister hostel to Adventure Queenstown is pretty much its twin (complete with the nightly activities etc), but with sturdier bunks, disabled-access bathrooms and an elevator.

Creeksyde Queenstown
Holiday Park & Motels
HOLIDAY PARK $$

(Map p214; ☑ 03-442 9447; www.camp.co.nz; 54 Robins Rd; sites $65, r with/without bathroom $139/95, apt $159-329; ℗ 🛜) 🌿 In a pretty garden setting, this extremely well-kept holiday park has accommodation ranging from powered sites to fully self-contained two-bedroom apartments. There are quirky sculptures throughout and an ablutions block disguised as a medieval oast house (hop kiln). In 2018 it became the first holiday park in the world to be environmentally certified by EarthCheck.

Queenstown Motel Apartments
MOTEL $$

(Map p214; ☑ 03-442 6095; www.qma.co.nz; 62 Frankton Rd; unit from $170; ℗ 🛜) This well-run, sunlit spot is like two distinct properties in one – smallish but comfortable newer units at the front and cheaper 1970s-style units (with renovated bathrooms) lined along the back. It has good views across the lake to Cecil and Walter Peaks. No children under 18.

YHA Queenstown Lakefront HOSTEL $$
(Map p214; ☑ 03-442 8413; www.yha.co.nz; 88-90 Lake Esplanade; dm/s/tw/d without bathroom from $34/90/110/115, r with bathroom $150-160; P ☎) ✎ This large lakefront hostel, fully renovated in 2017, has basic but neat-as-a-pin bunkrooms and an industrial-sized kitchen with window benches to absorb the view. The TV room is filled with beanbags and there are even a couple of massage chairs in the lounge. Lakeview rooms get a shared balcony (and some traffic noise).

Nomads HOSTEL $$
(Map p218; ☑ 03-441 3922; www.nomadsworld. com; 5-11 Church St; dm/r from $32/154; ☎) With a prime location in the heart of Queenstown's nightlife, this massive hostel has facilities galore, including its own mini-cinema, private en-suite rooms, a large lounge with a pool table, a free sauna and an on-site travel agency. Dorms range from three to 12 beds, and some have en suites, too.

Bumbles HOSTEL $$
(Map p214; ☑ 03-442 6298; www.bumblesback packers.co.nz; cnr Lake Esplanade & Brunswick St; site/dm/tw/d from $40/33/135/145; P @ ☎) Enjoying a prime lakeside location, this popular wee hive has a supremely laid-back vibe. All of the rooms share bathrooms, and even the dorms get lake views. The beanbag-filled lounge has a colourful mural on one side and a more colourful vista of the Remarkables out the other. There's limited space for tents out the back.

Queenstown Park BOUTIQUE HOTEL $$$
(Map p214; ☑ 03-441 8441; www.queenstownpark hotel.co.nz; 21 Robins Rd; r from $405; P ❄ ☎) ✎ White curtains billow over beds decked out in luxurious linen at this very chic 19-room hotel. The 'Remarkables' rooms overlook a park, to the namesake mountain range (there aren't any lake views), while the 'Gondola' rooms are smaller but have courtyards or balconies. All have kitchenettes, and there's free wine and nibbles during 'canapé hour' (6pm to 7pm).

The Dairy BOUTIQUE HOTEL $$$
(Map p218; ☑ 03-442 5164; www.thedairy.co.nz; cnr Brecon & Isle Sts; r/ste from $337/480; P ❄ ☎) Its dining room was once a corner store, but the Dairy is now a luxury B&B with 13 rooms packed with classy touches such as designer bed linen, silk cushions and luxurious mohair rugs. Rates include cooked breakfasts and complimentary NZ bubbly on arrival.

Lomond Lodge MOTEL $$$
(Map p218; ☑ 03-442 8235; www.lomondlodge. com; 33 Man St; r from $255; P ☎) This lodge on the fringe of the town centre has smartly designed rooms with indulgent bathrooms and USB sockets, and a landscaped, sunny terrace and barbecue area out back. It's worth splurging on one of the upstairs Lake View rooms, which come with lookout-worthy balconies.

🛌 Surrounds

Queenstown Top 10 HOLIDAY PARK $$
(☑ 03-442 9306; www.qtowntop10.co.nz; 70 Arthurs Point Rd, Arthurs Point; sites from $60, r with bathroom $121, units with/without bathroom from $155/95; P ☎ ⛷) ✎ High above the Shotover River, this relatively small and extremely neat park with better-than-the-norm motel units is 10 minutes' drive from the hustle and bustle of Queenstown. There's bike storage, a ski drying room and a complimentary shuttle bus into town. Fall out of your campervan straight onto the famous Shotover Jet.

Villa del Lago APARTMENT $$$
(Map p211; ☑ 03-442 5727; www.villadellago.co.nz; 249 Frankton Rd, Queenstown East; apt from $333; P ☎) Clinging to the slopes between the highway and the lake, these spacious one- to three-bedroom apartments have lake-facing terraces, incredible views and all the mod cons, including full kitchens, laundries and gas fires. The water taxi can stop at the private jetty, or you can walk along the lake to Queenstown in 25 minutes.

Hidden B&B $$$
(Map p211; ☑ 03-442 6636; www.hiddenlodge queenstown.co.nz; 28 Evergreen Pl, Sunshine Bay; r from $595-695; P @ ☎) The well-named Hidden is literally the last place west in Queenstown. Tucked away in Sunshine Bay, it has enormous rooms, unfettered lake and mountain views, complimentary beer and wine, and an outdoor hot tub.

Platinum Villas RENTAL HOUSE $$$
(Map p214; ☑ 03-746 7700; www.platinumqueens town.co.nz; 96 Fernhill Rd, Fernhill; house from $485; P ☎) Nab one of these 36 identical, luxurious, three-bedroom townhouses and make yourself at home. Each has a large open-plan living area with a big stone

ℹ QUEENSTOWN ON A BUDGET

Queenstown is a notoriously expensive destination, especially if you're planning on undertaking the thrill-seeking adventures it's famous for. However, not everything costs a small fortune.

➡ Play frisbee golf (p210) for free in Queenstown Gardens.

➡ Shun the gondola and hike to a view on Queenstown Hill (p213) or the Tiki Trail (p212); for a free and full day out to Queenstown's finest view, continue along the Ben Lomond Track (p213).

➡ Fuel up at Fergbaker, Taco Medic, Empanada Kitchen or Caribe Latin Kitchen.

➡ Skip an organised lake tour and ride the ferry (p228) across to Kelvin Heights.

fireplace, bespoke furniture, laundry facilities and most have a garage. 'Lakeview' villas get the better outlook, but 'Alpine' villas get the melodic burble of the creek below.

Groups aged under 25 not accepted.

🍴 Eating

🍴 Central Queenstown

⭐**Fergbaker** BAKERY $
(Map p218; 03-441 1206; 40 Shotover St; items $3-7.50; ⏱6.30am-4.30am) The sweeter sister of Fergburger bakes all manner of tempting treats – and though most things look tasty with 3am beer goggles on, it withstands the daylight test admirably. Goodies include inventive pies (such as venison and portobello mushroom) and breads, filled rolls and a sugary wealth of sweet treats. If you're after gelato, call into **Mrs Ferg** next door.

Caribe Latin Kitchen LATIN AMERICAN $
(Map p218; 03-442 6658; www.caribelatin kitchen.com; 36 The Mall; mains $8-16; ⏱10.30am-11pm; 🍴) One of the Mall's more characterful and colourful restaurants, Caribe is a small nook dishing out quality tacos, quesadillas and burritos stuffed fuller than a piñata. The tiled decor plays to a Day of the Dead theme, and the few tables are brighter than a Mexican sun. Excellent value.

Empanada Kitchen EMPANADAS $
(Map p218; 021 0279 2109; www.theempanada kitchen.com; 60 Beach St; empanadas $5.50; ⏱10am-5.30pm) Yes, this little hole-in-the-wall kiosk is built into a public toilet, but that's far from a statement about its food. The empanadas are absolutely delicious, with flavours that change daily and include savoury and sweet options.

Taco Medic TACOS $
(Map p218; 03-442 8174; www.tacomedic.co.nz; 3 Searle Lane; tacos $8; ⏱11am-10pm) Taco Medic began life as a food truck, but has put on the handbrake to become a stylishly simple bolthole eatery. Cosy up to the bar and choose from eight tacos made with local free-farmed meats and a changing fish-of-the-day taco.

Erik's Fish & Chips FISH & CHIPS $
(Map p218; 03-441 3474; www.eriksfishand chips.co.nz; 13 Earl St; fish $6.50-12; ⏱noon-9pm) A pair of food trucks squeezed into a lane between buildings – order your hoki, monkfish or blue cod from one, and eat inside the other. Ever fancied a deep-fried kiwifruit to finish your meal? You've come to the right place.

Patagonia SWEETS $
(Map p218; 03-409 2465; www.patagoniachoc olates.co.nz; 2 Rees St; ice cream $6-9, breakfast $9-14; ⏱9am-9pm; 🛜) Its popularity is its only detraction, but fight your way in and you'll find 24 superb ice-cream flavours, a host of chocolate and the truly Patagonian touch of churros and *dulce de leche* ice cream.

⭐**Yonder** CAFE $$
(Map p218; 03-409 0994; www.yonderqt.co.nz; 14 Church St; mains $12-24; ⏱8am-late; 🛜) With a menu inspired by 'the things we've loved around our travels', this cafe brings to the table a cosmopolitan assortment of dishes: bacon butties, kimchi bowls, salmon poké bowls. There are power points and USB ports by many of the indoor tables, but when the sun's out you'll want to be on the outdoor patio.

Bespoke Kitchen CAFE $$
(Map p218; 03-409 0552; www.bespokekitchen. co.nz; 9 Isle St; mains $20-25; ⏱8am-5pm; 🛜🍴) Occupying a light-filled corner site near the gondola, Bespoke delivers everything you'd expect of a smart Kiwi cafe. It has a mouth-watering selection of counter food, beautifully presented cooked options, outside seating in sight of the mountains and, of course, great coffee. Vegans will find plenty of choice, too.

Blue Kanu FUSION **$$**

(Map p218; ☑03-442 6060; www.bluekanu.co.nz; 16 Church St; mains $29-36; ⏱4pm-late) Disproving the rule that all tiki houses are inherently tacky, Blue Kanu serves up a food style it calls 'Polynasian' – Fijian *kokoda* (raw fish with coconut and lime) in one hand, XO pork dumplings in the other. It's relaxed and personable, and although the marriage of the Polynesian decor and chopsticks sounds impossible to pull off, it works.

Vudu Cafe & Larder CAFE **$$**

(Map p218; ☑03-4418370; www.vudu.co.nz; 16 Rees St; mains $9-25; ⏱7.30am-6pm) At this ever-popular cafe, excellent home-style baking combines with great coffee and the sort of breakfasts that make bacon and eggs seem very passé – try the French-toast pudding. Admire the huge photo of a far less populated Queenstown from an inside table, or head outside to graze by the lake. Service can be slow, but that's the weight of numbers.

The Taj INDIAN **$$**

(Map p218; ☑03-442 5270; www.thetajqueenstown.co.nz; 75 Beach St; mains $27-36; ⏱noon-10pm) For a tiny place (only seven tables) this upmarket Indian restaurant sure has a long menu. Try the *maacher jhol*, a delicious Bengali-style fish curry served with pickled vegetables.

Eichardt's Bar TAPAS **$$**

(Map p218; ☑03-441 0450; www.eichardtsdining.com; Marine Pde; breakfast $16-20, tapas $8-13; ⏱7.30am-late) Elegant without being stuffy, the small bar attached to Eichardt's Private Hotel is a wonderful refuge from the buzz of the streets. The breakfast menu is full of interesting options (smashed edamame, chorizo hash). From lunchtime, the focus shifts to tapas, and though the selection isn't particularly Spanish (steamed buns or grilled brushcetta, for example), it is particularly delicious.

Fergburger BURGERS **$$**

(Map p218; ☑03-441 1232; www.fergburger.com; 42 Shotover St; burgers $13-20; ⏱8am-5am) Who knew a burger joint could ever be a destination restaurant? Such are the queues at Fergburger that it often looks like an All Blacks scrum out the front. The burgers are as tasty and satisfying as ever, but the wait can be horrendous and the menu has more choices than the place has seats.

Devil Burger BURGERS **$$**

(Map p218; ☑03-442 4666; www.devilburger.com; 5/11 Church St; burgers $11-20; ⏱10am-midnight Sun-Wed, to 3am Thu-Sat; ✐🏫) If gluttony is a sin, this Devil is doing its job, with 18 burgers coming in sizes regular and large. Wraps include the hangover-busting 'Walk of Shame', which is basically a rolled-up full cooked breakfast. It gives Fergburger a run for its bun, even if purely for the lack of queues.

Winnie's PIZZA **$$**

(Map p218; ☑03-442 8635; www.winnies.co.nz; 1st fl, 7-9 The Mall; mains $18-37; ⏱noon-late; 🗢🏫) It's a Tardis-like journey leaving the mall and finding Winnie's – part pizza joint and part bar, looking a little like a '50s diner with a drinking habit. Pizzas come in various accents – Moroccan, Mexican, Chinese – along with burgers, nachos, chicken wings and salads. On balmy nights the roof opens up and the party continues into the wee smalls.

Halo Forbidden Bite CAFE **$$**

(Map p218; ☑03-441 1411; www.haloforbiddenbite.co.nz; 1 Earl St; brunch $18-25, dinner $25-29; ⏱6am-9pm; 🗢) Pitching itself as both heavenly and devilish, Halo is a stylish, sunny place that effortlessly blurs the line between breakfast, lunch and dinner. The breakfast burrito will set you up for a day's adventuring. There's almost as much seating outside as in.

Tatsumi JAPANESE **$$$**

(Map p218; ☑03-442 5888; www.tatsumi.co.nz; 9 Beach St; dishes $15-35, lunch/dinner set menu from $50/75; ⏱4pm-late) Since losing its original business in the Christchurch earthquakes, Tatsumi has brought its blend of traditional and modern Japanese 'tapas' to central Queenstown. The service is exemplary and the food consistently excellent, including gorgeous sashimi platters, delicate squid-ink-tempura calamari and crispy *kara-age* chicken. Set menus of signature dishes, and indulgent dégustation dining, are also offered.

Rātā INTERNATIONAL **$$$**

(Map p218; ☑03-442 9393; www.ratadining.co.nz; 43 Ballarat St; mains $42-48, 2-/3-course lunch $38/45; ⏱noon-late) After gaining Michelin stars for restaurants in London, New York and LA, chef-owner Josh Emett now wields his exceptional but surprisingly unflashy cooking back home in this upmarket yet informal back-lane eatery. Native bush, edging the windows and in a large-scale photographic mural, sets the scene for a short menu showcasing the best seasonal NZ produce.

Botswana Butchery INTERNATIONAL **$$$**

(Map p218; ☑03-442 6994; www.botswanabutchery.co.nz; 17 Marine Pde; lunch mains $23-34, dinner $40-48; ⊗noon-11pm) This swish lakefront restaurant is one of the flag-bearers of Queenstown high-end dining. Despite that, it doesn't come across as sniffy, especially at lunch when prices drop and a casual air pervades. The menu bounces from a decadent French onion soup to curries and game meats. Evenings are predominantly but not exclusively meaty – a 1.4kg cut of Cardrona lamb, anyone?

✖ Frankton & Kelvin Heights

Boat Shed
CAFE $$

(Map p211; ☑03-441 4146; www.boatshedqueens town.com; Frankton Marina, 847 Frankton Rd, Frankton; mains $17-26; ⊗8am-5pm; 🐾) Occupying a historic NZ Railways shipping office right by the lake, this great little cafe serves excellent, artfully arranged breakfasts and the likes of beef cheeks and *cioppino* (seafood stew) for lunch. It's the perfect pit stop if you're cycling or walking the lakeside trail. Service can be slow at busy times.

Wakatipu Grill
EUROPEAN $$$

(Map p211; ☑03-450 9402; www.queenstownhilton. com; Hilton Queenstown, Peninsula Rd, Kelvin Heights; mains $30-49; ⊗6-10.30am & 4-10pm) The Hilton sprawls along the lakeside by the Kawarau River outlet, and part of the fun of visiting its signature restaurant is the ferry ride. As the name implies, there's always a decent selection of steak on the menu, but much more besides, including locally sourced fish and lamb.

🍷 Drinking & Entertainment

Pick up a copy of *Source* (www.sourcemaga zine.co.nz), a free monthly publication with articles and details of goings-on around the Southern Lakes.

Perky's
BAR

(Map p218; ☑021 664 043; www.facebook.com/ perkysqueenstown; Lapsley Butson Wharf; ⊗noon-11pm) That hint of wobbliness you feel isn't the alcohol (yet), it's the fact that you're drinking on an old tour boat that's now permanently moored at the lakeshore. If you're feeling peckish, you're welcome to bring your own food aboard.

Atlas Beer Cafe
CRAFT BEER

(Map p218; ☑03-442 5995; www.atlasbeercafe. com; Steamer Wharf; ⊗10am-late) There are usually 23 craft beers on tap at this pint-sized lakefront bar, headlined by brews from Dunedin's Emerson's Brewery and

Queenstown's Altitude; pick four to sample on a tasting paddle. It also serves excellent cooked breakfasts ($17 to $22), and simple substantial fare such as steaks and burgers.

Smiths Craft Beer House
CRAFT BEER

(Map p218; ☑03-409 2337; www.smithscraftbeer. co.nz; 1st floor, 53 Shotover St; ⊗noon-late; 🐾) It's back to basics in everything but the taps, with bare concrete floors and industrial tables and chairs, but 36 creative NZ craft beers to sample. The folks behind the bar will chat brews as long as you'll listen, and there's a menu (mains $17 to $20) of burgers and po'boys (Louisiana-style sandwiches) to mop up the suds.

Zephyr
BAR

(Map p218; ☑03-409 0852; www.facebook.com/ zephyrqt; 1 Searle Lane; ⊗7pm-4am) Queenstown's hippest rock bar is located – as all such places should be – in a dark, grungy, concrete-floored space off a back lane. There's a popular pool table and live bands on Wednesday nights. Beer comes only in bottles, and there's a permanently raucous soundtrack.

1789
BAR

(Map p218; ☑03-450 0045; www.sofitel-queens town.com; entry on Brecon St; ⊗4pm-late) Tucked into a corner of the Sofitel, this velvet-smooth jazz lounge is named for the French Revolution, with a bloody colour scheme to suit. There are around 350 wines by the bottle and 50 by the glass, and live jazz sessions on Friday and Saturday evenings.

Bunker
COCKTAIL BAR

(Map p218; ☑03-441 8030; www.thebunker.co.nz; 14 Cow Lane; ⊗4pm-4am) Bunkered upstairs rather than down, this chi-chi little bar clearly fancies itself as the kind of place Sean Connery's James Bond might frequent, if the decor is anything to go by. Best of all is the outside terrace, with couches, a fire in winter and a projector screening classic movies onto the wall of a neighbouring building.

World Bar
BAR

(Map p218; ☑03-450 0008; www.theworldbar. co.nz; 12 Church St; ⊗11.30am-late) Queenstown's legendary party hub before it was destroyed by fire in 2013, the World is once again spinning. Decor swings between degrees of eclectic, from the mounted moose head with halo, to the cocktails that come in teapots. The food's good, there are regular DJs and the outdoor area is prime real estate on balmy afternoons and evenings.

EXPLORING THE GIBBSTON VALLEY

Queenstown's adrenaline junkies might be happiest dangling off a giant rubber band, but as they're plunging towards the Kawarau River, they might not realise they're in the heart of Gibbston, one of Central Otago's main wine subregions, accounting for around 20% of plantings.

Strung along Gibbston Hwy (SH6) is an interesting and beautiful selection of vineyards. Almost opposite the Kawarau Bridge, a precipitous 2km gravel road leads to **Chard Farm** (Map p211; ☑ 03-442 8452; www.chardfarm.co.nz; 205 Chard Rd; ☉10am-5pm) **FREE**, the most picturesque of the wineries. A further 1km along SH6 is **Gibbston Valley** (Map p211; ☑ 03-442 6910; www.gibbstonvalley.com; 1820 Gibbston Hwy; ☉10am-5pm), the area's oldest commercial winery. As well as tastings ($5 to $15), it has a restaurant, cheesery, tours of the winery ($35) and NZ's largest wine cave ($20), as well as bike hire. It also operates its own bus from Queenstown ($35 return) – you could always take the bus and then hire a bike to get between cellar doors.

Another 3km along SH6, **Peregrine** (Map p211; ☑ 03-442 4000; www.peregrinewines. co.nz; 2127 Gibbston Hwy/SH6; ☉11am-5pm) **FREE** has an impressive, award-winning cellar door – a bunker-like building with a roof reminiscent of a falcon's wing in flight. As well as tastings, you can take a stroll through the adjoining barrel room.

The **Gibbston River Trail**, part of the Queenstown Trail, is a walking and cycling track that follows the Kawarau River for 11km from the Kawarau Bridge, passing all of the wineries. From Peregrine, walkers (but not cyclists) can swing onto the **Peregrine Loop** (one hour, 2.7km), which crosses over old mining works on 11 timber and two steel bridges, one of which passes through the branches of a willow tree.

While you're in the area, be sure to call into the rustic **Gibbston Tavern** (Map p211; ☑ 03-409 0508; www.gibbstontavern.co.nz; 8 Coalpit Rd; ☉11am-8pm), just off the highway past Peregrine. It stocks Gibbston wines, fires up good pizzas and has the cellar door for **Rockburn** (Map p211; ☑ 03-445 0555; www.rockburn.co.nz; 8 Coalpit Rd; tastings $10, free if you buy two bottles; ☉noon-4pm) in the front yard, producers of one of the region's most acclaimed pinot noirs.

If you're keen to explore the valley's wineries without needing to contemplate a drive afterwards, consider staying among the vines at **Kinross** (Map p211; ☑ 03-746 7269; www. kinrosscottages.co.nz; 2300 Gibbston Hwy; r from $266; 🅿🛜), where the heritage-looking cottages are a front for modern, luxurious studio rooms. It has its own cellar door, representing six Central Otago vineyards (tastings $15, free with purchases over $50), plus a bistro and bike-hire outlet.

Ask at the Queenstown i-SITE (p227) for maps and information about touring the area.

Vinyl Underground CLUB
(Map p218; www.facebook.com/Vinylundergroundqt; 12b Church St; ☉10pm-4am Tue-Sat) Enter the underworld, or at least the space under the World Bar, to find the heartbeat of Queenstown's late-night life. It's a proper, sweaty, industrial-style bunker club – the bar alone must weigh several tonnes.

Bardeaux WINE BAR
(Map p218; ☑ 03-442 8284; www.goodgroup.co. nz; Eureka Arcade, off The Mall; ☉4pm-4am) This small, cavelike wine bar is all class. Under a low ceiling are plush leather armchairs and a fireplace made from Central Otago schist. Whisky is king here, but the wine list is extraordinary, especially if you're keen to drop $4500 on a bottle once in your life. It's surprisingly relaxed for a place with such lofty tastes.

Pub on Wharf PUB
(Map p218; ☑ 03-441 2155; www.pubonwharf.co.nz; 88 Beach St; ☉10am-late) Schmick interior design combines with handsome woodwork at this popular pub, with fake sheep heads to remind you that you're still in NZ. Mac's beers on tap, scrummy nibbles and a decent wine list make this a great place to settle in for the evening. There's live music every night and comedy occasionally.

Little Blackwood COCKTAIL BAR
(Map p218; ☑ 03-441 8066; www.littleblackwood. com; Steamer Wharf; ☉2pm-2am) Slink into the darkened interior of this slick bar for a sneaky afternoon cocktail, or perch yourself on the waterfront terrace for views over the lake.

The Winery
WINE BAR

(Map p218; ☑ 03-409 2226; www.thewinery.co.nz; 14 Beach St; ⏰ 10.30am-late) Ignore the uninspiring location and settle in for a journey around NZ wine. Load up cash on a smart card and then help yourself to tasting pours or glasses of more than 80 NZ wines dispensed through an automated gas-closure system. There's also a whisky corner, and cheese and salami platters are available. Wines are arranged by varietals along the walls.

Sherwood
LIVE MUSIC

(Map p211; ☑ 03-450 1090; www.sherwoodqueens town.nz; 554 Frankton Rd) The faux-Tudor motel architecture might have you expecting lutes and folk ballads, but the Sherwood is Queenstown's go-to spot for visiting musos. Many of NZ's bigger names have performed here; check the website for coming gigs. The food's great, too.

🛍 Shopping

Vesta
ARTS & CRAFTS

(Map p218; ☑ 03-442 5687; www.vestadesign. co.nz; 19 Marine Pde; ⏰ 9am-5pm Mon-Sat) Arguably Queenstown's most interesting store, inside inarguably the town's oldest building; Vesta sells a collection of prints, jewellery and homeware as fascinating as the original wallpaper and warped-by-time floorboards of the 1864 wooden cottage.

Artbay Gallery
ART

(Map p218; ☑ 03-442 9090; www.artbay.co.nz; 13 Marine Pde; ⏰ 10am-5pm) Occupying an attractive 1863-built Freemason's Hall on the lakefront, Artbay is always an interesting place to peruse, even if you don't have $10,000 to drop on a painting. It showcases the work

---

MĀORI NZ: QUEENSTOWN & WĀNAKA

Like in other parts of the South Island, this region was first settled by moa hunters before being ruled by Waitaha, Ngāti Māmoe and then Ngāi Tahu. Lake Wakatipu is shrouded in legend, and sites to its north were highly valued sources of *pounamu* (greenstone/jade).

The Ngāi Tahu *iwi* (tribe) owns Shotover Jet (p216), Guided Walks New Zealand (p213) and Dart River Adventures (p228), the last of which offers a cultural component with its jetboat excursions.

---

of contemporary NZ artists, most of whom have a connection to the region.

Romer Gallery
PHOTOGRAPHY

(Map p218; ☑ 021 171 1771; www.romer-gallery. com; 15 Earl St; ⏰ 11am-5.30pm) Call in to ogle large-format, perspex-finished NZ landscapes from Queenstown-based photographer Stephan Romer. You may want to leave your credit card in the hotel safe, though; images are up to $12,500 a pop.

Ivan Clarke Gallery
ART

(Map p218; ☑ 03-442 5232; www.ivanclarkeartist. com; 39 Camp St; ⏰ 10am-6pm) Be prepared for industrial-strength levels of whimsy in this gallery devoted to the work of pooch-loving local artist, Ivan Clarke. Hanging alongside his large-scale landscapes is his *Lonely Dog* series (dogs skiing, dogs playing guitar, dogs riding motorbikes etc), which have also been published as part of an illustrated novel. There are even dog-shaped suits of armour.

Walk in Wardrobe
CLOTHING

(Map p218; ☑ 03-409 0190; www.thewalkinward robe.co.nz; Beech Tree Arcade, 34 Shotover St; ⏰ 10am-6pm Tue & Wed, to 8.30pm Thu-Mon) Benefitting from travellers lightening their suitcases before jetting out, this 'preloved fashion boutique' is a great place to hunt for bargain designer duds. Womenswear fills most of the racks.

Creative Queenstown Arts 'n Crafts Market
MARKET

(Map p218; www.queenstownmarket.com; Earnslaw Park; ⏰ 9.30am-3.30pm Sat) Gifts and souvenirs crafted from around the South Island; on the lakefront beside Steamer Wharf.

Remarkable Sweet Shop
FOOD

(Map p218; ☑ 03-409 2630; www.rss.co.nz; 39 Beach St; ⏰ 9am-11pm) Stock up on local and imported confectionery (fudge, chocolate truffles, boiled lollies – you name it!) at this Wonka-esque pantry. There's another branch in Arrowtown (☑ 03-442 1374; 27 Buckingham St; ⏰ 8.30am-6pm).

ℹ Information

Queenstown has free wi-fi in four town-centre locations: the Village Green, Earnslaw Park, Beach St and the Mall.

DOC Whakatipu-wai-Māori/Queenstown Visitor Centre (Map p218; ☑ 03-442 7935; www.doc.govt.nz; 50 Stanley St; ⏰ 8.30am-4.30pm) Head here for advice about hiking tracks, as well as maps, backcountry hut passes, locator beacons, weather alerts and to check in for your Routeburn Track booking.

Queenstown i-SITE (Map p218; 03-442 4100; www.queenstownsite.com; cnr Shotover & Camp Sts; 8.30am-8pm) Friendly and informative despite being perpetually frantic, the saintly staff here can help with bookings and information on the Southern Lakes region and further afield.

Getting There & Away

AIR

Air New Zealand (0800 737 000; www.air newzealand.co.nz) flies directly to Queenstown from Auckland, Wellington and Christchurch, as well as Melbourne, Sydney and Brisbane.

Jetstar (0800 800 995; www.jetstar.com) also flies the Auckland and Wellington routes, along with Melbourne, Sydney and the Gold Coast.

Qantas (www.qantas.com) and **Virgin Australia** (www.virginaustralia.com) fly directly from Australia (Melbourne, Sydney and Brisbane).

BUS

Most buses and shuttles stop on Athol St or Camp St; check when you book.

InterCity (03-442 4922; www.intercity. co.nz) The main operator; destinations include Wānaka (from $24, 1¾ hours, two daily), Franz Josef ($73, 8½ hours, daily), Dunedin (from $27, 4¼ hours, two daily), Invercargill ($51, three hours, daily) and Christchurch (from $62, 8¾ to 11¾ hours, two daily).

Ritchies (03-441 4471; www.ritchies.co.nz;) Operates the Expresslink shuttle to/from Wānaka four times daily ($30, 1¾ hours), with three stopping in Cromwell ($20, one hour). For Arrowtown services, see Orbus (p228).

Catch-a-Bus South (03-214 4014; www. catchabussouth.co.nz) Door-to-door daily bus from Invercargill ($60, 3¼ hours) and Bluff ($75, 3¾ hours), heading via Gore ($61, 2½ hours) three times a week.

HIKERS' & SKIERS' TRANSPORT

All of the following services are seasonal, heading either to the snowfields during the ski season or to the tracks in the warmer months.

Buckley Track Transport (03-442 8215; www.buckleytracktransport.nz) Has scheduled shuttles between Queenstown and the Routeburn trailheads – Routeburn Shelter ($50), The Divide ($85), into one and out of the other ($125) – Te Anau ($50), Te Anau Downs for the Milford Track ($75) and the Greenstone trailhead ($60).

EasyHike (021 445 341; www.easyhike. co.nz) Offers a car-relocation service for the Milford ($299), Routeburn ($299) and Kepler ($99) Tracks, dropping you at the start and shifting your car to the end. It can also kit you out entirely for the hike, offering a range of packages up to a 'Premium' service that includes booking your hut tickets, track transport, food and all the gear you'll need.

Info & Track (Map p218; 03-442 9708; www. infotrack.co.nz; 37 Shotover St; 7.30am-9pm) During the Great Walks season, this agency provides scheduled transfers to Glenorchy ($25), the Routeburn Shelter ($47), The Divide ($84) and the Rees, Dart and Greenstone trailheads (all $60). In winter it morphs into **Info & Snow** and heads to the Coronet Peak ($35), Remarkables ($35), Cardrona ($55) and Treble Cone ($60) ski fields instead.

Ski Bus (Map p218; 0800 697 547; www. nzski.com) During the ski season shuttles depart from outside the Snow Centre on Duke St every 20 minutes from 8am until 11.30am (noon for Coronet Peak), heading to both Coronet Peak and the Remarkables (return $25). Buses return as they fill up, from 1.30pm onwards. They also depart on the hour from 3pm to 6pm for night skiing at Coronet Peak, returning on the half-hour (last bus 9pm). From December to March it also runs a summer bus service to Coronet.

Trackhopper (021 187 7732; www.trackhop per.co.nz) Offers a handy car-relocation service for the Routeburn (from $285), Milford ($260), Greenstone Caples ($180) and Rees-Dart ($180) Tracks, driving you to one end of the track and leaving your car for you at the other.

Tracknet (03-249 7777; www.tracknet.net) This Te Anau–based outfit offers Queenstown connections to the Routeburn, Kepler, Hollyford and Milford Tracks throughout the Great Walks season. Its Invercargill bus service can connect with transport to the Rakiura Track on Stewart Island. It continues to operate on a restricted timetable in winter.

Getting Around

TO/FROM THE AIRPORT

Queenstown Airport (ZQN; Map p211; 03-450 9031; www.queenstownairport.co.nz; Sir Henry Wrigley Dr, Frankton) is 7km east of the town centre.

Blue Bubble Taxis (0800 228 294; www. queenstown.bluebubbletaxi.co.nz) and **Green Cabs** (0800 464 7336; www.greencabs. co.nz) charge around $45 to $50 for trips between the airport and town.

Orbus (p228) buses run every 15 minutes on route 1 between Queenstown and the airport ($10).

Super Shuttle (0800 748 885; www. supershuttle.co.nz) runs a door-to-door service (shared shuttle from $15).

BOAT

Queenstown Ferries (Map p218; ☑ 03-441 1124; www.queenstownferries.co.nz; Steamer Wharf; single/return $9/15; ☺ departs Queenstown 7.45am-9.45pm Sun-Thu, to 10.45pm Fri & Sat) zip across the lake from the town centre to the Hilton Hotel on the Kelvin Peninsula (and four stops in between). Pay the driver on the boat either in cash or electronically.

PUBLIC TRANSPORT

Orbus (☑ 0800 672 8778; www.orc.govt.nz/orbusqt; cash/GoCard trip $5/2) has four main routes, reaching Sunshine Bay, Fernhill, Arthurs Point, Frankton, Lake Hayes and Arrowtown. Cash fares are a standard $5 per trip, regardless of distance ($10 for the airport). If you're staying in Queenstown for a while, consider buying a GoCard ($5, minimum top-up $10), which drops the fare to $2. Pick up a route map and timetable from the i-SITE (p227); buses leave from directly outside, on Camp St.

AROUND QUEENSTOWN

Glenorchy

POP 363

Perhaps best known as the gateway to the Routeburn Track (p206), Glenorchy sits on a rare shelf of flat land at the head of Lake Wakatipu. The small town is a great option if you want to be beside the lake and the mountains but prefer to stay once removed from the bustle and bluster of Queenstown. The hiking around Glenorchy is sensational, and the town is also a base for horse treks, jetboat rides, helicopter flights and skydives. It's Queenstown on sedatives.

There's often a sense of déjà vu when you arrive in Glenorchy, with areas around the town featuring heavily in the *Lord of the Rings* trilogy, as well as being the setting for Jane Campion's *Top of the Lake* BBC series.

The town centre sits slightly back from the lake, so be sure to wander down to the picturesque wharf.

🏃 Activities

Shuttles from Queenstown to the Routeburn (p206), Rees-Dart (p207) and Greenstone Caples Tracks (p207) pass through Glenorchy; you can be picked up here along the way. Other activities on offer include farm tours, fly-fishing and guided photography tours; enquire at the Queenstown i-SITE (p227) or the Glenorchy Information Centre & Store.

Hiking

DOC's *Head of Lake Wakatipu* and *Wakatipu Walks* brochures detail more than 60 day walks in the area. Both brochures can be downloaded from the DOC website (www.doc.govt.nz). Two of the best short tracks are the **Routeburn Flats** (four hours return), which follows the first section of the Routeburn Track (p206), and **Lake Sylvan** (1½ hours return).

Another good wander, especially if you like birds, is the **Glenorchy Walkway**, which starts in the town centre and loops around Glenorchy lagoon, switching to boardwalks for the swampy bits. It's split into the Southern Circuit (30 minutes) and the Northern Circuit (one hour) and there are plenty of seats along the way, well positioned for views over the water to the Humboldt Mountains.

Before setting out on any longer hikes, call into DOC's Queenstown Visitor Centre (p226) for the latest track conditions and to purchase detailed maps. Another good resource is Lonely Planet's *Hiking & Tramping in New Zealand*.

For track snacks or meals, stock up on groceries in Queenstown, though you'll also find a small selection of trail-perfect fodder at **Mrs Woolly's General Store** (☑ 03-409 0051; www.theheadwaters.co.nz; 64 Oban St; ☺ 8am-7pm). Track transport is at a premium during the Great Walks season (late October to April), so try to book in advance.

Other Activities

Heli Glenorchy   SCENIC FLIGHTS
(☑ 03-442 9971; www.heliglenorchy.co.nz; 35 Mull St) It takes the best part of a day to drive from Glenorchy to Milford Sound, but it's only 15 minutes by helicopter. Options include a three-hour Milford Sound heli-cruise-heli package ($1025) and a wilderness drop-off so that you can walk the last few kilometres of the Milford Track before being whisked back over the mountains ($1725 for two people).

Dart River Adventures   ADVENTURE
(☑ 03-442 9992; www.dartriver.co.nz; 45 Mull St, Glenorchy; adult/child from $279/169) The only jetboat operator on the Dart River, with trips including a 30-minute walk through the rainforest. It also offers horse riding, guided wilderness walks, kayaking and jetboat rides combined with a river descent in an inflatable three-seater 'funyak' (adult/child from $399/305). Prices include Queenstown pick-ups, which depart an hour before each trip.

High Country Horses
HORSE RIDING

(Map p211; ☑03-442 9915; www.highcountryhorses.
nz; 243 Priory Rd) Offers more equine options than the Auckland Cup, from the easy
90-minute 'Isengard *Lord of the Rings*' trek
(with/without Queenstown transfer $195/175)
to an overnight 'Around the Mountain' trek
($850 including Queenstown transfer).

🛏 Sleeping

Little Paradise Lodge
LODGE $$

(Map p211; ☑03-442 6196; www.littleparadise.co.
nz; Glenorchy–Queenstown Rd, Mt Creighton; s/d
without bathroom from $110/160, r with bathroom
$195; ℗) This isolated and peaceful lodge,
almost midway between Queenstown and
Glenorchy, is a whimsical gem. From the
toilet-cistern aquariums to the huge garden
with 3000 roses, monkey puzzle trees and
the Swiss owner's own sculptural work, you
won't have seen a place like it.

Glenorchy Motel
MOTEL $$

(☑03-442 6993; www.glenorchymotels.co.nz; 87
Oban St; unit $180; ℗❄🛜) Given the full nip
and tuck by new owners in 2017, the seven
units here have some design savvy: an outdoor hot tub has been added, and there's a
wood sauna out the back if you need to thaw
some limbs after a day on the trails.

★ Camp Glenorchy
HOLIDAY PARK $$$

(☑03-409 0401; www.campglenorchy.co.nz; 42
Oban St; dm/site/cabin from $68/75/315; ℗🛜) 🌱
As much a statement about sustainability as
it is a fabulous place to stay, this main street
'eco retreat' offers luxurious designer-rus-
tic cottages showcasing recycled materials,
odourless composting toilets, and digital
controls that allow you to adjust the ambient
temperature and see how much electricity
you're drawing from or adding to the grid.
There's a big communal kitchen, too.

Glenorchy Lake House
B&B $$$

(☑03-442 4900; www.glenorchylakehouse.co.nz;
13 Mull St; r/house $340/565; 🛜) 🌱 The suit-
ably-named Lake House (it's the closest
place in town to the lake) is a boutique
B&B attached to the excellent Trading Post
store and cafe. The two guest bedrooms are
decked out with Egyptian cotton sheets and
TVs and there's an outdoor spa in which to
soak away the rigours of a day's hiking.

🍴 Eating

Glenorchy Cafe
CAFE $$

(GYC; ☑03-442 9978; www.facebook.com/glen
orchycafe; 25 Mull St; mains $12-20; ⊗10am-

4.30pm Sun-Fri, to 1.30am Sat) Grab a sunny
table out the back of this cute little cottage
and tuck into cooked breakfasts, sandwich-
es and soup. Head inside on Saturday night
to partake in pizza and beer underneath the
oddball light fixtures.

Queenie's Dumplings
DUMPLINGS $$

(☑03-442 6070; www.queeniesdumplings.wixsite.
com/queeniesdumplings; 19 Mull St; mains $14-19;
⊗11am-4pm) Where else would you expect to
find an authentic little dumpling joint than
far-flung, rural Glenorchy? Choose from
seven types of dumplings, or a handful of
noodle soups.

ℹ Information

Glenorchy Information Centre & Store (☑03-
409 2049; www.glenorchyinfocentre.co.nz;
42-50 Mull St; ⊗8.30am-9pm) Attached to the
Glenorchy Hotel, this little shop is a good source
of weather and track information. Fishing rods
and mountain bikes can be hired, and it sells
hiking supplies, including gas canisters and a
good selection of maps. It also has a bottle shop,
bless it.

ℹ Getting There & Away

Glenorchy is a scenic 45-minute (46km) drive
northwest from Queenstown, winding around
bluffs and coves with sweeping views over the
lake and its frame of mountains. There are no
bus services, but there are hikers' shuttles
(p227) during the Great Walks season (late
October to April).

QUEENSTOWN & WĀNAKA GLENORCHY

KINLOCH
....

Just 3km from Glenorchy, but 26km by road **Kinloch Lodge** (☑03-442 4900; www.kin lochlodge.co.nz; 862 Kinloch Rd; dm $45, r with/without bathroom from $195/120, cabin $435; 🛜) is the perfect escape if getting away from it all to Glenorchy isn't getting away from it all enough. This wonderfully remote 1868 lodge has small heritage rooms with shared bathrooms, while rooms in the YHA-associated hostel next door are comfy and colourful. The open-air hot tub has cracking views.

By way of complete contrast, it's also rents two 'EcoScapes' cabins. Built using passive design, they feature ultra-modern furnishings, en-suite bathrooms and feel almost like a city apartment plonked into the wilderness. The view from the bed across the lake is better than TV, but if you really must watch something else, the electronic blinds whirr down to become a screen for a data projector with Apple TV and Netflix.

The lodge also has mountain bikes and fishing rods for hire, offers guided kayaking (one/two hours $60/110) and provides transfers to the Routeburn ($27) and Greenstone Caples ($22) trailheads.

It's worth driving here just to gaze across the lake from the terrace of its restaurant (mains $27 to $37). It's open year-round for drinks and simple meals (the venison stew is a great winter warmer), although you'll need to pre-order dinner in the off-season.

Arrowtown

POP 2450

Beloved by day-trippers from Queenstown, exceedingly quaint Arrowtown sprang up in the 1860s following the discovery of gold in the Arrow River. Today its pretty, tree-lined avenues retain more than 60 of their original gold-rush buildings, and history is so ingrained here that even the golf course wraps around the ruined cottages and relics of the town's gold-mining heyday. But don't be fooled by the rustic facades; Arrowtown has a thriving contemporary scene, with chic modern dining, a cool cinema and a couple of drinking dens to rival the finest in Queenstown.

The pace in Arrowtown is very different to that of Queenstown, just 20km away. Strolling Buckingham St, with its gold-era facades, is the major activity here; when you need something more, there are gentle bike rides along the valleys, or an expanding network of walks along the Arrow River and Bush Creek.

◉ Sights

Arrowtown Chinese Settlement
HISTORIC SITE

(Buckingham St; ⊙24hr) **FREE** Strung along the creek, near the site of Arrowtown's first gold find, is NZ's best example of an early Chinese settlement. Interpretive signs explain the lives of Chinese miners during and after the gold rush (the last resident died in 1932), while restored huts and the only re-

maining Chinese store in the southern goldfields make the story more tangible. Subjected to significant racism, the Chinese often had little choice but to rework old tailings rather than seek new claims.

Lakes District Museum & Gallery
MUSEUM

(☑03-442 1824; www.museumqueenstown.com; 49 Buckingham St; adult/child $10/3; ⊙8.30am-5pm) Exhibits cover the gold-rush era and the early days of Chinese settlement around Arrowtown. Kids are kept engaged by the likes of an 'Odd One Out' game that they can play as you wander the exhibits. You can also hire pans ($3) to try your luck panning for gold on the Arrow River; you're more likely to find some traces if you head away from the town centre. There's a good gift shop, too.

Arrowtown Gaol
HISTORIC BUILDING

(Cardigan St) **FREE** With gold rushes came lawlessness. Arrowtown's prisoners were originally manacled to logs, but in 1876 this schist jail, now surrounded by homes, was constructed. The building was used as a jail as recently as 1987 when two men were held here for drunkenness. The jail is kept locked, but you can grab the key ($10 deposit) from the Lakes District Museum.

St Patrick's Catholic Church
CHURCH

(www.stjosephsqueenstown.co.nz; 7 Hertford St) Apart from its impressive Star of David–shaped rose window, this 1874 stone Gothic Revival church, built from local schist rock, wouldn't be worth noting if it weren't for its connection to Australasia's only Catholic

Arrowtown

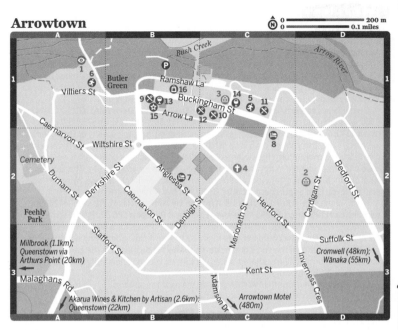

Arrowtown

◎ Sights

⊕ Activities, Courses & Tours

⊜ Sleeping

⊗ Eating

⊝ Drinking & Nightlife

⊛ Entertainment

⊜ Shopping

ⓘ Information

saint. Acclaimed educator St Mary of the Cross, aka Mary MacKillop (1842–1909), founded a convent in the tiny 1870s miners cottage next door. There are interesting displays about the saint in the church and in the restored cottage. The church and cottage are usually unlocked – go to the back door of the cottage.

🏃 Activities

The information centre stocks a *Cycling & Walking Trail* brochure ($1) outlining some excellent tracks in the area. One particularly good cycling route is the **Arrow River Bridges Ride** (12km) from Arrowtown to the Kawarau Bridge, which traverses various purpose-built suspension bridges and a tunnel cut under the highway. If you have more time and energy, you can connect onto the Gibbston River Trail at the Kawarau Bridge to cycle past a string of cellar doors. Local walks include hour-long strolls along Bush Creek and the Arrow River, and the enjoyable, well-marked **Sawpit Gully Trail** (two-to-three-hour loop).

LAKE HAYES

Around 14,000 years ago, little Lake Hayes was joined to the Frankton Arm of Lake Wakatipu. Now it sits in quiet isolation, its often-mirror-perfect reflections of the surrounding hills and mountains leading some to claim it as the most photographed lake in New Zealand. It's a great place for an easy stroll, with the 8km, bike-friendly **Lake Hayes Walkway** looping right around it. Allow two to three hours to walk it.

On the lake's eastern flank is **Amisfield Bistro & Cellar Door** (Map p211; ☑03-442 0556; www.amisfield.co.nz; 10 Arrowtown–Lake Hayes Rd; 3-/5-course lunch $75/95, 7-course dinner $140; ☺cellar door 10am-6pm, restaurant noon-8pm), a match for any of the wineries in nearby Gibbston, though it's the stylish bistro that's the real showstopper. It's an exercise in trust: simply inform the waiters of any dietary restrictions or aversions you might have and strap yourself in for whatever the chefs choose for you that day. The focus is on local produce, including foraged ingredients, presented in whimsical ways. Wine tastings are free if you dine or purchase a bottle, or $10 for five wines otherwise.

North of the lake, **Akarua Wines & Kitchen by Artisan** (Map p211; ☑03-442 1090; www.akaruaandartisan.co.nz; 265 Arrowtown–Lake Hayes Rd; mains $25-32; ☺9am-5pm) features a restaurant inside a cottage originally built as offices for a flour mill, and a cellar door in a shipping container (tastings $10, or free if dining or buying a bottle). The most enticing option if the sun's out, however, will be the beanbags in the garden. Lunch comes in the form of hearty shared plates or platters; we wholeheartedly endorse the confit duck ($58 for two).

Lake Hayes is 4km south of Arrowtown, on the road to Frankton.

Arrowtown Bike Hire CYCLING

(☑03-441 1144; www.arrowtownbikehire.co.nz; 59 Buckingham St; half-/full-day hire $42/55, e-bikes $85/120; ☺8.30am-5.30pm daily Sep-Apr, Tue-Sat May-Aug) Hires out bikes and provides great advice about local trails. If you fancy tackling the 16km Arrow River Bridges ride through to the Gibbston wineries, a pick-up service (from $10 per person, minimum $50) is offered. Multiday hires are also available, and bikes can be delivered to your Arrowtown accommodation.

Better by Bike CYCLING

(☑03-442 0339; www.betterbybike.co.nz; Dudley's Cottage, 4 Buckingham St; half-/full-day hire $45/55) Offers straightforward bike hire (including e-bikes) along with packages including hire and return transport from Queenstown, Gibbston or Lake Hayes (adult/child $95/55, minimum two people). It operates on a bookings-only basis through winter, so call ahead to secure your wheels.

Arrowtown Time Walks WALKING

(☑021 782 278; www.arrowtowntimewalks.com; adult/child $20/12) Guided walks (1½ hours) depart from the Lakes District Museum on demand, tracing a path through Arrowtown's golden past, pointing out places of interest along the way and delving into goldrush history. Book through the website, or in person at the museum (p230).

🛏 Sleeping

Arrowtown Motel MOTEL $$

(☑03-442 1833; www.arrowtownmotel.co.nz; 48 Adamson Dr; units $164-229; 🅿🛜🌳) This child of the 1980s is better on the inside than the outside, with spacious units with colourful feature walls, soft furnishings and interesting art. It's on a suburban road, facing onto a reserve, so peace and quiet is all but assured.

Shades of Arrowtown MOTEL $$

(☑03-442 1613; www.shadesofarrowtown.co.nz; 9 Merioneth St; units from $155; 🅿🛜) Tall shady trees and a garden setting give these bungalow-type cottages a relaxed air. Some have full kitchens and spa baths. The two-bedroom, self-contained cottage is good value if you're travelling with the whole clan.

⭐**Millbrook Resort** RESORT $$$

(☑03-441 7000; www.millbrook.co.nz; 1124 Malaghans Rd; r from $355; 🅿🛜🏊) 🌿 Further from Arrowtown in aesthetics than kilometres, this massive manicured resort is a town unto itself. Rooms range from studios to luxury homes overlooking the fairways of the resort's golf course, which has been rated among the top 10 courses in NZ. At the end of the day, take your pick from five restaurants, or relax at the spa (p216).

Arrowtown Lodge B&B $$$

(☑03-442 1101; www.arrowtownlodge.co.nz; 7 Anglesea St; r/cottage from $232/395; 🅿🛜) From the outside, the guest rooms look like her-

MACETOWN

Macetown, 15km north of Arrowtown, is a gold-rush ghost town, built in the 1860s but abandoned by the 1930s. Many of its buildings have been restored, creating an isolated and evocative destination. It's reached along a rugged, flood-prone road (the original miners' wagon track) that crosses the Arrow River more than 25 times.

Don't even think about taking your hire car here. A much more sensible option is the 4WD tour offered by Nomad Safaris (p220), which also includes gold panning in the Arrow River. Or you can hike from Arrowtown (15km each way, three to four hours one way), but it's particularly tricky in winter and spring; check with the information centre (p234) about conditions before heading out. An alternative route (four to five hours each way) climbs over Big Hill, avoiding many of the river crossings. This track climbs above 1000m, however, so shouldn't be attempted if the weather forecast isn't looking good.

The road to Macetown can also be tackled on a mountain bike (two to three hours each way), but it's not for beginners. You'll need a good bike and there are some steep drop-offs, and almost no mobile-phone coverage if you do get into trouble.

itage cottages, but inside they're cosy and modern, with en-suite bathrooms. There are three rooms, including a large cottage with its own outdoor living space and spa. Continental breakfast is provided, and Buckingham St is a two-minute walk away.

✖ Eating

Slow Cuts   GRILL $$
(☑ 03-442 0066; www.slowcuts.co.nz; 46-50 Buckingham St; mains $12-38; ☺ noon-9pm; 🛜 🚼) From the *amigas* at La Rumbla comes Slow Cuts, dishing up fast food in slow motion. There are rotisserie chickens, burgers, ribs, smashed fries, a delicious smoked beef sandwich, craft beers and a good wine list.

Provisions   CAFE $$
(☑ 03-442 0714; www.provisionsofarrowtown.co.nz; 65 Buckingham St; mains $15-24; ☺ 8am-5pm; 🛜 🥗 🚼) In a strip of old miners' cottages, this cute cafe serves up inventive creations – the likes of black rice ginger porridge, vegan Bombay bowls and dukkah poached eggs. Everything is baked on-site, including bread, bagels and the deservedly famous sticky buns.

La Rumbla   TAPAS $$
(☑ 03-442 0509; www.larumbla.co.nz; 54 Buckingham St; tapas $17-34; ☺ 4pm-late Tue-Sun) Tucked behind the post office, this little gem does a brilliant job of bringing the bold flavours and late-dining habits of Spain to sleepy little Arrowtown. Local produce is showcased in tasty bites on an ever-changing menu, and the cocktail list goes long and strong in the evening.

★ Aosta   ITALIAN $$$
(☑ 03-442 0131; www.aosta.nz; 18 Buckingham St; mains $26-42; ☺ 5pm-late Mon-Thu, noon-3pm

& 5pm-late Fri-Sun) Everything at this elegant restaurant is designed to be shared, from the *cicchetti* (Venetian-style bar snacks) to the pasta and substantial *secondi* (mains). Highlights include crayfish dumplings, wild thar *polpette* (meatballs), goats' cheese tortellini and inventive salads. We're also fond of the big, bubbly light fixtures over the bar and the white flying saucers illuminating the tables.

Kobe Cuisine   JAPANESE $$$
(Map p211; ☑ 03-441 7070; www.millbrook.co.nz; Millbrook Resort, 1124 Malaghans Rd; dishes $24-42; ☺ 5.30-9pm daily Jul-Apr, Tue-Sat May & Jun) An open kitchen occupies an entire wall of this relaxed Japanese restaurant in the heart of Millbrook Resort. Alongside the greatest hits of Japanese cuisine (sashimi, sushi, gyoza, ramen, teppanyaki... all deftly executed) are some more unusual choices, such as sushi tacos and (our favourite) Cardrona merino *kohitsuji* – perfectly barbecued lamb ribs served with black-garlic custard. Charming service, too.

🍷 Drinking & Entertainment

★ Blue Door   BAR
(☑ 03-442 0415; www.facebook.com/TheBlueDoor Bar; 18 Buckingham St; ☺ 4.30pm-12.30am; 🛜) The only indications that you've arrived are the unmarked blue doors – push them open and it's like stepping into a prohibition-era speakeasy. The low-lit little bar has a formidable wine list and enough rustic ambience to keep you mellow for the evening. Low ceilings, an open fire and abundant candles create an intimate setting.

Fork & Tap   PUB
(☑ 03-442 1860; www.theforkandtap.co.nz; 51 Buckingham St; ☺ 11am-11pm; 🚼) Built as a bank in

QUEENSTOWN & WĀNAKA ARROWTOWN

1870, Fork and Tap's currency is now craft beer, with up to 19 suds on tap. Add in good food, including shared meat and cheese platters, and a large, sunny, kid-friendly back garden, and you have the pick of Arrowtown's pubs. Grab a tasting paddle of four 150mL beers of your choice ($16). There's Irish music every Wednesday night, and live music in the garden on summer Sunday evenings.

Dorothy Browns   CINEMA
(☑ 03-442 1964; www.dorothybrowns.com; 18 Buckingham St; adult/child $18.50/15) This is what a cinema should be like: wide, ultra-comfortable seating with fine local wine, cheese boards and olives available to accompany the mostly art-house films on offer. Most screenings in the main theatre have an intermission – the perfect opportunity to tuck into a tub of gourmet ice cream. The cinema doubles as a neat little bookstore.

ⓘ Information

Arrowtown Visitor Information Centre (☑ 03-442 1824; www.arrowtown.com; 49 Buckingham St; ⊙ 8.30am-5pm) Shares premises with the Lakes District Museum & Gallery. Sells maps and a selection of NZ books.

ⓘ Getting There & Away

Orbus (p228) buses (line 2) run hourly from 6am to 10pm between Arrowtown and Arthurs Point (49 minutes), via Frankton (25 minutes) and Queenstown (36 minutes). The terminus is on Ranshaw Lane, directly behind the Lakes District Museum.

WĀNAKA

POP 6480

So long described as Queenstown's smaller and more demure sibling, Wānaka now feels grown up enough to have moved out of home and asserted its own identity.

What it does share with Queenstown is the fact that they're both lake and mountain towns bristling with outdoors and adventure opportunities. Wānaka's list of adventure options is impressive by almost any measure, except against the Queenstown ruler. The breadth and selection of adventures here might not be as comprehensive, but the lakefront is more natural and less developed – complete with a day-at-the-beach feel on sunny days – and the town centre has a more soulful atmosphere.

Despite constant growth – in both size and costs – Wānaka retains a fairly laidback, small-town atmosphere. Days are invariably active here, but evenings are an invitation into a wave of new eateries and some truly quirky bars.

◉ Sights

Rippon   WINERY
(☑ 03-443 8084; www.rippon.co.nz; 246 Mt Aspiring Rd; ⊙ 11am-5pm) It's worth raising a glass to the view alone at Rippon since the Tuscan-styled cellar door has surely the finest winery view in NZ. In a bid to contain numbers, the popular free tastings must now be booked in advance online. Tasting sessions are limited to 12 people and commence promptly on the hour, sampling four to six wines over 30 to 45 minutes.

Wānaka Station Park   PARK
(Homestead Cl; 🅟) Wānaka Station Park is a piece of Wānaka that existed before Wānaka did. This remnant of the sheep station that once covered the entire south side of the lake is a beautiful, secluded space with a playground and plenty of mature trees. These include giant sequoias, three immense Douglas firs, Himalayan cedars, a large walnut tree, an enormous rhododendron hedge and the station's surviving orchard, with pears and apples that are free for picking.

The park extends to the lake's edge, where you'll find one of the true stars of the Instagram age: **That Wānaka Tree**. Sprouted from a fence post but now almost as famous as the town itself, this water-bound willow provides a classically photogenic prop to the mountains and Ruby Island behind. If you are here for the Instagram moment, come at dawn, when reflections are typically at their best.

If you think it's a bit strange that there's now a constant stream of tourists queuing to get a shot of this particular tree, you're not alone. Arguably the scrum of would-be influencers is more of a spectacle than the tree itself.

Puzzling World   AMUSEMENT PARK
(☑ 03-443 7489; www.puzzlingworld.co.nz; 188 Wānaka–Luggate Hwy; adult/child $23/16, maze or illusions only $18/14; ⊙ 8.30am-5.30pm; 🅟) A 3D Great Maze and lots of fascinating brain-bending visual illusions serve to keep people of all ages bemused, bothered and bewildered at this entertaining little attraction. Even the cafe tables come equipped with puzzles. It's 2km from town, en route to Cromwell.

National Transport & Toy Museum   MUSEUM
(☑ 03-443 8765; www.nttmuseumwanaka.co.nz; 891 Wānaka–Luggate Hwy; adult/child $19/5;

⊙8.30am-5pm; 🖼) Mixing Smurfs with Studebakers and skidoos (and an authentic MiG jet fighter flown by the Polish Air Force), this completely eclectic and absorbing collection of more than 60,000 items fills four huge hangars (one mostly filled with vintage fire engines). Suitably, it's as jumbled as a toy box, making it all a bit of a treasure hunt, but it's a nostalgic journey even if you're only young enough to remember as far back as the Sylvanian Families.

Warbirds & Wheels   MUSEUM
(📞03-443 7010; www.warbirdsandwheels.com; 11 Lloyd Dunn Ave, Wānaka Airport; adult/child $20/5; ⊙8am-4pm) Dedicated to NZ combat pilots, the aircraft they flew and the sacrifices they made, this museum features a replica of a Hawker Hurricane, a de Havilland FB5 Vampire and twin rows of gleaming classic cars – pride of place goes to the 1934 Duesenberg Model J, described as the finest car ever made in the USA. There's a retro diner attached.

🏃 Activities

Wānaka might not have bridges to leap off, but you could still bottle the adrenaline here. For powder monkeys it's the gateway to the Treble Cone, Cardrona (p242) and Snow Farm (p242) ski areas, and it's the last stop before Mt Aspiring National Park for those in hiking boots.

Skiing

Like Queenstown, the ski season lasts from roughly June to September. From Wānaka the Cardrona (p242) and Treble Cone ski fields are roughly equidistant (about 24km). At the time of writing, Cardrona was seeking Commerce Commission approval to purchase Treble Cone; watch this space.

During the season, Treble Cone offers free shuttles from outside its **office** (📞03-443 1406; 24 Dungarvon St; ⊙7am-6pm Jun-Oct, 8.30am-5pm Mon-Fri Nov-May), departing at 8am and 8.45am and returning from the mountain at 4pm and 4.30pm; book your spot online. There are also free shuttles from the base of the mountain to the ski field, departing every 20 to 30 minutes.

Cardrona's Wānaka base of operations is **Cardrona Corner** (📞03-443 4512; www.cardrona.com; 20 Helwick St; ⊙7am-7pm Jun-Oct, 9am-5pm Nov-May). You can book your ski packages, purchase outdoorsy clothing and hire gear here, and mountain shuttles depart nearby (adult/child $35/30 return). In summer, its focus shifts to mountain biking.

Treble Cone   SKIING
(📞03-443 7443; www.treblecone.com; Treble Cone Access Rd; daily lift pass adult/child $149/75) 🅿
The highest and largest of the region's ski areas, spectacular Treble Cone delivers powder with panoramas. Its steep slopes are suitable for intermediate to advanced skiers, with a beginners' area that includes free lift access. There's around 700m of vertical, as well as numerous half-pipes.

Hiking

For walks close to town, including various lakeside wanders, download DOC's *Wānaka Outdoor Pursuits* brochure or pick it up from the visitor centre ($3.50). For something low-level, the **Glendhu Bay Track** bobbles along the southern shore of Lake Wānaka, passing That Wānaka Tree and Rippon before rolling into Glendhu Bay after three to four hours. It's also a good track for a gentle mountain-bike ride.

Roy's Peak (p209) is Wānaka's hike *du jour* for the Instagram mob, though you can get lofty views with far less effort atop **Mt Iron** (527m, 1½ hours return) – although it's a rather grandiose name for what's really just a hill. Other excellent (many would say far superior) alternatives to Roy's Peak include **Diamond Lake** (circuit: 45 minutes; Lake Wānaka lookout: two hours return) and **Isthmus Peak** (1385m, five to seven hours return); both reward your efforts with views of an additional lake.

Two highly scenic Mt Aspiring National Park tracks start from Raspberry Creek at the end of Mt Aspiring Rd, 50km from Wānaka: the excellent half-day Rob Roy Track (p208) and the challenging, multiday Cascade Saddle (p208). The road to Raspberry Creek is unsealed for 30km and involves eight creek fords. It's usually fine in a 2WD, except in very wet conditions; check at the visitor centre, which can also provide you with contacts and/or bookings for the three main shuttle operators ($40 to $50 per person).

Cycling

Hundreds of kilometres of tracks in the region are open to mountain bikers; see **Bike Wanaka** (www.bikewanaka.org.nz) for interactive maps. DOC's *Wānaka Outdoor Pursuits* brochure also describes a range of rides, including the popular **Deans Bank Track** (12km).

One particularly scenic route is the **Newcastle Track** (12km), which follows the raging blue waters of the Clutha River from Albert Town to the Red Bridge on Kane Rd.

You can make it a 30km loop by joining the **Upper Clutha River Track** at Luggate.

The **Glendhu Bay Track** provides easy riding along the shore of Lake Wānaka. **Sticky Forest** is a local favourite, with around 30km of purpose-built trails through pine forest on the edge of town, complete with jumps, drops and berms.

Bike hire is easy to find in town – try **Outside Sports** (☑03-443 7966; www.outside sports.co.nz; 17/23 Dunmore St; half/full day from $35/55; ☺bike hire 9am-6pm) for a quality dual-suspension, downhill mountain bike or e-bike. **Good Rotations** (☑03-443 4349; www.goodrotations.co; 34 Anderson Rd; half/full day from $59/89; ☺10am-5pm Tue-Fri, extended summer) specialises in e-bikes.

Wanaka Bike Tours   CYCLING
(☑03-443 6363; www.wanakabiketours.co.nz; from $199) Offers bike rentals (from $65 per day), bike and shuttle packages for self-guided one-way spins (adult/child from $85/55), Clutha River jetboat/bike combos ($199/112), guided e-bike tours (from $299) and helibiking (from $650).

Climbing, Canyoning & Mountaineering

Excellent rock climbing can be found at Hospital Flat, around 20km from Wānaka towards Mt Aspiring National Park, and the adjoining Diamond Lake Conservation Area.

★ **Wild Wire**   CLIMBING
(☑0800 9453 9473; www.wildwire.co.nz; 1 Umbers St) The Italian world of *via ferrata* – climbing using the likes of iron rungs, plank bridges and cables – arrives in Wānaka, scaling the cliffs beside (and sometimes across) Twin Falls. Make the half-day climb partway up the falls (from $199), or go the whole hog on 'Lord of the Rungs' ($599), the world's highest waterfall *via ferrata*, with a helicopter flight back down.

Wanaka Rock Climbing   CLIMBING
(☑022 015 4458; www.wanakarock.co.nz; 99 Ardmore St; ☺8.30am-12.30pm, by apt winter) ✐ This long-standing and highly respected operator offers introductory rock-climbing courses (half/full day $203/293), a half-day abseiling intro on 40m-high rock walls ($203) and guided climbs around the region.

Basecamp Adventures   CLIMBING
(☑03-443 1110; www.basecampadventures.co.nz; 50 Cardrona Valley Rd; day pass adult/child $20/17; ☺noon-7pm Mon-Fri, 10am-5pm Sat & Sun) At this indoor climbing centre at the town's edge, even fearless three-year-olds can have

a go on the Clip 'n Climb automatic belay system (from $11, booking recommended). It also offers outdoor climbs, including intro sessions (half-/full day $189/299), family adventures (from $299) and more advanced ascents. Plus there's snowshoeing (half-/full day $189/299), guided alpine hikes and mountaineering, too.

Deep Canyon   ADVENTURE SPORTS
(☑03-443 7922; www.deepcanyon.co.nz; Log Cabin, 100 Ardmore St; from $290; ☺Oct-Apr) Climb, walk, leap, zip-line and abseil your way through narrow, wild gorges on a canyoning expedition. There are 10 options on offer, rated either 'Get Into It' (easy), 'Step It Up' (intermediate) or 'Go Big' (advanced).

Adventure Consultants   ADVENTURE SPORTS
(☑03-443 8711; www.adventureconsultants.com; 20 Brownston St) This highly respected mountain guiding outfit (it's been leading climbs on Everest for decades) offers treks to Brewster Glacier (two days, from $890) and Gillespie Pass (four days, from $1450). It runs mountaineering and ice-climbing courses, too.

Other Activities

Paddle Wanaka   KAYAKING
(☑0800 926 925; www.paddlewanaka.co.nz; lakefront, Ardmore St; ☺9am-6pm Oct-Apr, 10am-4pm May & Jul-Sep) Offers kayaks (one/two hours $20/30) and stand-up paddle boards (SUP, $20 per hour) for hire, and guided paddle-powered tours of the lake (half/full day $179/349) and the rapids of the Clutha River (half day $199). It also offers jetboat pickups if you'd prefer a one-way lake paddle. For something unique, how about a heli-SUP trip to a remote mountain lake?

Wanaka River Journeys   ADVENTURE SPORTS
(☑03-443 4416; www.wanakariverjourneys.co.nz; adult/child $249/149) ✐ Combination walk (50 minutes) and jetboat ride in the gorgeous Matukituki Valley. Also offers packrafting and heli-jetboating.

Skydive Wanaka   SKYDIVING
(☑03-443 7207; www.skydivewanaka.com; 14 Mustang Lane, Wānaka Airport) Grab some airtime, jumping from 9000ft ($299), 12,000ft ($369), or going the whole banana with a 15,000ft leap ($469) and 60 seconds of free fall.

☞ Tours
Scenic Flights

Classic Flights   SCENIC FLIGHTS
(☑03-443 4043; www.classicflights.co.nz; 6 Spitfire Lane, Wānaka Airport; from $299) Sightseeing flights in a vintage Tiger Moth biplane.

Wānaka

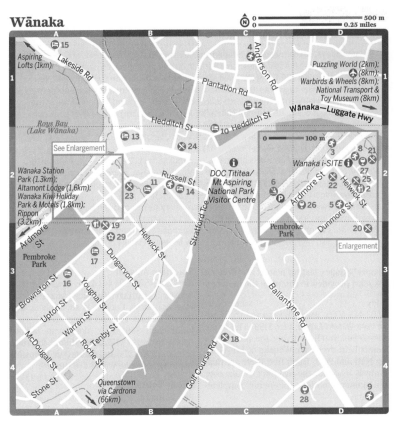

N 0 _____ 500 m
0 _____ 0.25 miles

Wānaka

🟠 Activities, Courses & Tours
1 Adventure Consultants	B2
2 Cardrona Corner	D2
3 Deep Canyon	D2
4 Good Rotations	C1
5 Outside Sports	D2
6 Paddle Wanaka	C2
7 Treble Cone office	A3
8 Wanaka Rock Climbing	D2
9 Wild Wire	D4

🟢 Sleeping
10 Archway	C2
11 Asure Brookvale Motel	B2
12 Criffel Peak View	C1
13 Lakeside	B2
14 Mountain View Backpackers	B2
15 Wanaka Bakpaka	A1
16 Wanaka View Motel	A3
17 YHA Wanaka Purple Cow	A3

🟠 Eating
18 Bistro Gentil	C4
19 Charlie Brown	B3
20 Federal Diner	D3
21 Francesca's Italian Kitchen	D2
22 Kai Whaka Pai	D2
23 Kika	B2
24 Red Star	B2
Relishescafé	(see 8)
25 Ritual	D2

🔵 Drinking & Nightlife
26 Gin & Raspberry	D2
27 Lalaland	D2
28 Rhyme x Reason	D4

🟠 Entertainment
29 Paradiso	B3

MT ASPIRING NATIONAL PARK

Verdant valleys, alpine meadows, braided glacial rivers, craggy mountains and more than 100 glaciers make Mt Aspiring National Park an outdoor enthusiast's paradise. Protected as a national park in 1964, and later included in the Te Wāhipounamu (Southwest New Zealand) World Heritage Area, the park now blankets 3555 sq km along the Southern Alps, from the Haast River in the north to its border with Fiordland National Park in the south. Lording it over all is colossal Tititea/Mt Aspiring (3033m), the highest peak outside the Aoraki/Mt Cook area.

While the southern end of the national park near Glenorchy includes famed hikes such as the Routeburn (p206), Rees-Dart (p207) and Greenstone Caples Tracks (p207), there are plenty of blissful short walks and more demanding multiday hikes in the **Matukituki Valley**, close to Wānaka. These include the dramatic Rob Roy Track (p208) and challenging Cascade Saddle (p208); see DOC's *Matukituki Valley Tracks* brochure, which can be downloaded from its website (www.doc.govt.nz).

Many of these tracks are prone to snow and avalanche risk and can be treacherous. It is extremely important to consult with the DOC staff at the Tititea/Mt Aspiring National Park Visitors Centre (p241) in Wānaka and to purchase hut tickets before heading off. You should also register your intentions on www.adventuresmart.org.nz.

'Biggles' goggles, leather helmet and flowing silk scarf provided to complete the moment.

U-Fly SCENIC FLIGHTS
(03-443 4005; www.u-flywanaka.co.nz; 8 Spitfire Lane, Wānaka Airport; from $199) The name doesn't lie...you'll be flying the plane on a scenic flight over Lake Wānaka or Mt Aspiring National Park. Don't fret; there are dual controls ready for the real pilot to take over at a moment's notice – they're not completely insane.

Alpine Helicopters SCENIC FLIGHTS
(03-443 4000; www.alpineheli.co.nz; 10 Lloyd Dunn Ave, Wānaka Airport) Options range from a 20-minute flight over Wānaka with a hilltop landing ($295), to the half-day Fiordland Heli Traverse ($2865), which includes multiple landings, checking crayfish pots on the fiords and scoffing the bounty during a remote alpine picnic.

Aspiring Helicopters SCENIC FLIGHTS
(03-443 7152; www.aspiringhelicopters.co.nz; Cattle Flat Station, 2211 Mt Aspiring Rd) Offers a range of flight options, from a 20-minute buzz over Lake Wānaka ($225) to a three-hour flight to Milford Sound ($1460), choppering along the sound's length and making four landings.

Wanaka Helicopters SCENIC FLIGHTS
(03-443 1085; www.wanakahelicopters.co.nz; 6 Lloyd Dunn Ave, Wānaka Airport) Options range from a 25-minute 'Wanaka Experience' ($250, one landing) to a three-hour trip to Aoraki/Mt Cook ($1595, two landings).

Southern Alps Air SCENIC FLIGHTS
(0800 345 666, 03-443 4385; www.southernalpsair.co.nz; 12 Lloyd Dunn Ave, Wānaka Airport) Flights over Aoraki/Mt Cook in a small plane, taking in Tasman, Fox and Franz Josef Glaciers (adult/child $505/340), along with Milford Sound flyovers ($475/320), Milford fly-cruise combos ($560/375) and whirls over Tititea/Mt Aspiring and Lake Wānaka ($310/225).

Other Tours

Eco Wanaka OUTDOORS
(03-443 2869; www.ecowanaka.co.nz) Trips include a full-day walk to the Rob Roy Glacier (adult/child $315/215), a four-hour cruise and walk on Mou Waho Island to find a lake within a lake ($245/165), and a full-day cruise-4WD combo ($494/295). Also offers helihikes.

Ridgeline Adventures DRIVING
(0800 234 000; www.ridgelinenz.com) Choose from a range of 4WD explorations ranging from a 'safari' through a high-country farm (adult/child $249/130) to a 4WD/jetboat/helicopter combo ($939/584).

Funny French Cars DRIVING
(027 386 6932; www.funnyfrenchcars.co.nz) Ride in a classic Citroën around local wineries and/or craft breweries ($199), or tour scenic highlights of Wānaka ($159).

Festivals & Events

TUKI MUSIC
(www.tukifestival.nz; tickets from $140; Feb) One-day music festival featuring big-name

Kiwi artists, held in even-numbered years in Glendhu Bay.

Warbirds Over Wanaka AIR SHOW
(☑03-443 8619; www.warbirdsoverwanaka.com; Wānaka Airport; 1-/3-day pass from $60/189) Held every second Easter (in even-numbered years), this incredibly popular international airshow attracts upwards of 50,000 people.

🛏 Sleeping

🛏 Central Wānaka

Wanaka Bakpaka HOSTEL $
(☑03-443 7837; www.wanakabakpaka.co.nz; 117 Lakeside Rd; dm $32-33, r with/without bathroom from $94/66; P@🛜) The only lakeside hostel in town delivers million-dollar views at backpacker prices. Amenities are top-shelf and it's worth paying a bit extra for the en-suite double with the gorgeous views, though you can also just lap it all up from the wide lounge windows. There are bikes for hire and the hot-water bottles come free.

Altamont Lodge LODGE $
(☑03-443 8864; www.altamontlodge.co.nz; 121 Mt Aspiring Rd; s/d $89/109; 🛜) At the quiet end of town, Altamont is like a hostel for grown-ups. There are no dorms but the 12 tidy little rooms share spotless bathrooms and a spacious, well-equipped kitchen. Pine-lined walls give it a ski-lodge ambience, while the spa pool and roaring fire in the lounge with its views of Roy's Peak will warm you up post-slopes.

Mountain View Backpackers HOSTEL $
(☑03-443 9010; www.mtnview.co.nz; 7 Russell St; dm/r without bathroom from $34/84; P🛜) Set beneath Monument Lookout, the Mountain View is effectively a hostel within a house, complete with a back lawn and clothesline. Rooms are simple but warm and comfortable, and there's a drying room for ski gear.

★Criffel Peak View B&B $$
(☑03-443 5511; www.criffelpeakview.co.nz; 98 Hedditch St; r from $180; P🛜) Situated in a quiet cul-de-sac, this excellent B&B has three rooms sharing a large lounge with a log fire and a sunny wisteria-draped deck. The charming hostesses live in a separate house behind, which also has a self-contained two-bedroom apartment attached.

YHA Wanaka Purple Cow HOSTEL $$
(☑03-443 1880; www.yha.co.nz; 94 Brownston St; dm $39-48, r with/without bathroom from

$160/115; P🛜) 🌱 This Wānaka stalwart is older than many of its guests, and it has mellowed comfortably with age. It has a mix of dorms and private rooms, but best of all are the large lounge, with commanding lake and mountain views, and the quiet reading room. The giant topo map in the lounge is great for planning hikes.

**Wanaka Kiwi
Holiday Park & Motels** HOLIDAY PARK $$
(☑03-443 7766; www.wanakakiwiholidaypark.nz; 263 Studholme Rd North; sites $45-61, units with/without bathroom from $149/84; P✳🛜🐾) This charming and relaxing campground has grassy terraced sites for tents and campervans, lots of trees and pretty views. Facilities include a barbecue area with heaters, a spa pool and a sauna. Older-style motel units have been renovated, and the newest budget cabins are warm and cosy. There's a courtesy van for runs into (but not back from) town.

Wanaka View Motel MOTEL $$
(☑03-443 7480; www.wanakaviewmotel.co.nz; 122 Brownston St; units from $195; P🛜) The refurbished Wanaka View has five apartments with spa baths and full kitchens squeezed tightly into a standard section. The largest has three bedrooms and most have lake views. There's also a comfortable studio unit tucked around the back, which is cheaper but doesn't have a kitchen or view.

Archway MOTEL $$
(☑03-443 7698; www.archwaymotels.co.nz; 64 Hedditch St; unit from $165; P🛜) A short uphill walk from the town centre, this older-style motel has spacious units and pine-clad 'chalets' with kitchenettes. The cedar hot tubs with mountain views are an appealing perk.

Asure Brookvale Motel MOTEL $$
(☑03-443 8333; www.brookvale.co.nz; 35 Brownston St; unit from $166; P🛜🏊) The patios at this old-fashioned concrete-block motel open onto a grassy lawn edged by a gently flowing creek. It also has a barbecue, hot tub and plunge pool.

Lakeside APARTMENT $$$
(☑03-443 0188; www.lakesidewanaka.co.nz; 9 Lakeside Rd; apt from $349; P🛜🏊) Luxuriate in a modern apartment in a prime position overlooking the lake, right by the town centre. All 23 apartments have three bedrooms, but can be rented with only one or two bedrooms open. The swimming pool is a relative rarity in these parts, and if you hire ski gear

through the website it can be delivered to your door.

🛏 Surrounds

★ Wanaka Haven
B&B $$$

(📞 03-443 4995; www.wanakahaven.co.nz; 42 Halliday Rd; r from $425; 🅿🛜🏊) Luxurious B&Bs seem to be constantly sprouting in the Wānaka countryside. This one has the advantage of gorgeous views over manicured lawns to the mountains, and a heated outdoor swimming pool. There's also a large guest lounge where you can help yourself to tea and coffee from the machine.

Alpine View Lodge
B&B $$$

(📞 03-443 7111; www.alpineviewlodge.co.nz; 23 Studholme Rd Sth; r/cottage from $245/360; 🅿🛜) In a peaceful rural setting on the edge of town, this excellent lodge has three B&B rooms, one of which has its own private deck with mountain views. Little extras include homemade shortbread in the rooms and a hot tub. Alternatively, you can opt for one of the fully self-contained one-, two- or three-bedroom cottages.

Lime Tree Lodge
B&B $$$

(📞 03-443 7305; www.limetreelodge.co.nz; 672 Ballantyne Rd; r $395-495; 🅿🛜🏊) 🅿 Quietly removed from town, this intimate lodge has four luxury rooms and two suites. Outside there's a pool, spa, pétanque court and croquet lawn, while the lodge is centred on an inviting living area with open kitchen where the in-house chef prepares meals. The owners – former sheep farmers – host canapés and aperitifs every evening.

Wanaka

Alpine Lodge
B&B $$$

(📞 03-443 5355; www.wanakaalpinelodge.co.nz; 4 Monteith Rd, Albert Town; r $269-299; 🅿🛜) Guests in the four spacious, modern bedrooms are pampered with home baking and a cedar hot tub. It's 4km from town, tucked in behind Mt Iron, but there are bikes onsite for guests.

🍴 Eating

Red Star
BURGERS $

(📞 03-443 9322; www.redstarburgers.co.nz; 26 Ardmore St; burgers $12-16; ⊙ 11.30am-9pm) The burger menu is exhaustive and inventive – beef, chicken, venison, fish and vegie burgers on crunchy toasted buns. Grab a seat on the terrace and sip on a craft beer with your craft burger.

Charlie Brown
CRÊPES $

(www.charliebrowncrepes.co.nz; 77-79 Brownston St; crêpes $6-17; ⊙ 8am-9.30pm) Both the retro green 1975 caravan and its owners hail from France, so you can be sure that the sweet crêpes and savoury galettes whisked up within are *très français*, even if the name isn't. Seasonal specials are chalked up on a board, or you can opt for something from the permanent menu of perennial favourites.

Kai Whaka Pai
CAFE $$

(📞 03-443 7795; 121 Ardmore St; mains $14-25; ⊙ 7am-11pm; 🅿) As Wānaka as *that* tree, this local institution is where the town seems to congregate on a sunny evening for a liquid sundowner over excellent pizza. Locally brewed craft beers are on tap and there are Central Otago wines as well. There are plenty of vegetarian options, including some suitable for vegans.

Federal Diner
CAFE $$

(📞 03-443 5152; www.federaldiner.co.nz; Pembroke Lane; brunch $14-22, dinner $15-30; ⊙ 7am-3pm Sun & Mon, to 9.30pm Tue-Sat; 🛜🅿🚼) When it's this hidden away and still this popular, you know to expect good things. This cosmopolitan cafe delivers robust breakfasts, excellent coffee, legendary scones, croissants and salads. In the evenings the menu shifts to substantial dishes such as pork belly and slow-roasted lamb shoulder. There are vegan options, too.

Relishescafé
CAFE $$

(📞 03-443 9018; www.relishescafe.co.nz; 99 Ardmore St; brunch $17-24, dinner $32-36; ⊙ 7am-10pm) A cafe by day with good breakfast and lunch options, this place transforms into a sophisticated restaurant with a fine wine list at night. Central Otago wines take centre stage.

Francesca's Italian Kitchen
ITALIAN $$

(📞 03-443 5599; www.fransitalian.co.nz; 93 Ardmore St; mains $23-29; ⊙ noon-3pm & 5pm-late) Pretty much the matriarch of Wānaka eateries, perennially busy Francesca's has the big flavours and easy conviviality of an authentic Italian family *trattoria*. Even simple things such as pizza, pasta and polenta chips are exceptional.

Ritual
CAFE $$

(☑ 03-443 6662; 18 Helwick St; mains $12-21; ☺ 9am-5pm) A classic 21st-century Kiwi cafe, Ritual is smart but not too trendy, and filled to the gills with delicious food. The counter positively groans under the weight of tasty salads, slices and scones.

Kika
TAPAS $$$

(☑ 03-443 6536; www.kika.nz; 2 Dunmore St; plates $14-48; ☺ 5.30pm-late) One of Otago's best restaurants, Kika's menu is underpinned by modern Italian cuisine, served tapas-style in a casual dining space and enlivened by some Asian flavours. Unsure what to choose? Let the chefs decide with the 'Just Feed Me' menu.

Bistro Gentil
FRENCH $$$

(☑ 03-443 2299; www.bistrogentil.co.nz; 76a Golf Course Rd; mains $36-40; ☺ 6pm-late Tue-Sat) Far removed from the madding crowd, Gentil ticks plenty of boxes for a memorable night out. Expect a short, focused menu of delicious modern French cuisine, featuring the likes of confit duck and venison shortloin. On a balmy night, request an outside table. By day, the space transforms into the tasting room for Maude Wines (tastings $10).

🍺 Drinking & Nightlife

Rhyme x Reason
BREWERY

(☑ 03-265 1101; www.rhymeandreason.beer; 17 Gordon Rd; tasting paddles $18-22; ☺ noon-10.30pm) Beer-loving locals head to this inconspicuous tin shed – situated in a light-industrial strip on the edge of town – to escape the tourists down at the lakefront and to sip on quality crafts brewed by one of their own, Jess Wolfgang. Her regular range (including an award-winning *kölsch*) is joined on tap by seasonal and guest brews. Bring your own food.

Lalaland
COCKTAIL BAR

(☑ 03-443 4911; www.facebook.com/Lalaland wanaka; L1, 99 Ardmore St; ☺ 5pm-2.30am) Long before the Ryan Gosling and Emma Stone flick, there was already this Lalaland in Wānaka. Sink into a comfy chair at the little, low-lit palace/bordello, where bar staff concoct elixirs to suit every mood. The lake view might be better at other upstairs Ardmore St bars, but can they top this playlist or cocktail list? Enter via the rear stairs.

☆ Entertainment

Paradiso
CINEMA

(☑ 03-443 1505; www.paradiso.net.nz; 72 Brownston St; adult/child $15/9.50) Sprawl on a comfy couch, or recline in a dentist's chair or an old Morris Minor at this Wānaka institution, screening the best Hollywood and art-house flicks. At intermission head to the lobby for freshly baked cookies (simply follow your nose), though the homemade ice cream is just as enticing.

Ruby's
CINEMA

(☑ 03-443 6901; www.rubyscinema.co.nz; 50 Cardrona Valley Rd; adult/child $19/13) How very Wānaka that an art-house cinema should adjoin an indoor climbing wall. Channelling a lush New York or Shanghai vibe, Ruby's has a whiff of cinema's glory days. Watch a movie from a reclining leather chair with a warming blanket over your knees, or just chill in the red-velvet lounge with local craft beers and wine or classic cocktails.

Ruby's is in the Basecamp Wānaka (p236) building on the outskirts of town.

ℹ Information

DOC Tititea/Mt Aspiring National Park Visitor Centre (☑ 03-443 7660; www.doc.govt. nz; 1 Ballantyne Rd; ☺ 8am-5pm daily Dec-Apr, 8.30am-5pm Mon-Sat May-Nov) In an A-framed building on the edge of the town centre, this DOC office takes hut bookings and offers advice on tracks and conditions. Be sure to call in before undertaking any wilderness hikes.

Wanaka i-SITE (☑ 03-443 1233; www.lake wanaka.co.nz; 103 Ardmore St; ☺ 8am-7pm Nov-Mar, 9am-5.30pm Apr-Oct) This lakefront information office is ever helpful, but always busy.

Wanaka Lakes Health (☑ 03-443 0710; www. wanakamedical.co.nz; 23 Cardrona Valley Rd; ☺ 8am-6pm Mon-Fri, 9am-noon & 3-6pm Sat & Sun) The place to go if you need to patch up any adventure mishaps.

ℹ Getting There & Away

Buses depart from outside the Log Cabin on the lakefront.

➡ InterCity (p227) Destinations include Queenstown (from $24, 1¾ hours, two daily), Cromwell (from $24, 40 minutes, two daily), Lake Hāwea ($28, nine minutes, daily), Makarora ($28, 1½ hours, daily) and Franz Josef ($55, daily).

➡ Ritchies (p227) Operates the Expresslink shuttle to/from Queenstown four times daily ($30, 1¾ hours), with three stopping in Cromwell ($20, 40 minutes).

QUEENSTOWN & WĀNAKA WĀNAKA

ⓘ Getting Around

Adventure Car Rentals (☏ 03-443 6050; www.adventurerentals.co.nz; 51 Brownston St) Hires cars and 4WDs (the latter is the best option if you're heading to Mt Aspiring National Park).

Yello! (☏ 03-443 5555; www.yello.co.nz) Operates taxis and scheduled winter shuttles to the Snow Farm near Cardrona ($35 return).

AROUND WĀNAKA

Cardrona

Gouged between the Crown and Criffel Ranges, the cute settlement of Cardrona reached its zenith in the 1870s at the height of the gold rush, when its population numbered more than 1000. Today it's effectively a ski field balanced atop a pub, albeit perhaps the most recognisable and evocative pub in New Zealand.

Cardrona wakes with a jolt for the ski season, but even if you're not here for powder, it's well worth a visit. Drink in the views and the beer, take a horse ride through the open tussock country, be slightly bemused at the bra fence and understand that a distillery rightly belongs here since the landscape is so reminiscent of the Scottish Highlands.

◉ Sights & Activities

★**Cardrona Distillery**   DISTILLERY
(Map p211; ☏ 03-443 1393; www.cardronadistillery.com; 2125 Cardrona Valley Rd; tours $25; ⊙ 9.30am-5pm) Enter past the fence of bras (Bra-vo!) and you'll find the beautiful cellar door of this fledgling single-malt distillery inside a building made of local schist. Have a complimentary sip of the liqueurs, gin and unusual single-malt vodka, or take the 75-minute distillery tour, which leaves on the hour from 10am to 3pm. Its first whisky won't be completely ready until 2025, but it released a three-year-old teaser in 2018 and plans to follow up with a six-year-old in 2021.

Cardrona Alpine Resort   SKIING
(Map p211; ☏ 03-443 9284; www.cardrona.com; Cardrona Skifield Rd; daily lift passes adult/child $120/62; ⊙ 8.30am-4pm) Well organised and professional, this 345-hectare ski field offers runs to suit all abilities (25% beginners, 25% intermediate, 30% advanced, 20% expert) at elevations ranging from 1670m to 1860m. Cardrona has several high-capacity chairlifts (including a gondola cable car), beginners' tows and extreme snowboard terrain.

Buses run from Wānaka ($35) and Queenstown ($55) during ski season, and you can shuttle up from the base ($10 return) if you don't want to drive to the top; cheaper deals are available with lift passes.

In summer, the mountain bikers take over. The **Cardrona Peak to Pub**, from the ski fields to the Cardrona Hotel, is a classic NZ ride with 1270m of descent – the resort runs shuttles back up the mountain.

Snow Farm   SKIING
(Map p211; ☏ 03-443 7542; www.snowfarmnz.com; Snow Farm Access Rd; ski day pass adult/child $45/25, snowshoe day pass $20/10; ♿) In winter this is home to fantastic cross-country skiing and snowshoeing, with 55km of groomed ski trails and 24km of snowshoe trails. Lessons and ski hire are available.

The Cardrona   HORSE RIDING
(Map p211; ☏ 03-443 1228; www.thecardrona.co.nz; 2125 Cardrona Valley Rd) Guided horse rides through the Cardrona Valley, including a 'High Country Pub' ride (from $159) that'll have you tying up at the Cardrona Hotel hitching rail for a beer. Also runs quad-bike tours and 4WD buggy rides.

Backcountry Saddle Expeditions   HORSE RIDING
(Map p211; ☏ 03-443 8151; www.backcountrysaddles.co.nz; 2130 Cardrona Valley Rd; adult/child $100/80) Two-hour horse treks across Mt Cardrona Station on Appaloosa horses.

🛌 Sleeping

Waiorau Homestead   B&B $$$
(Map p211; ☏ 03-443 2225; www.waiorauhomestead.co.nz; 2127 Cardrona Valley Rd; r $280; 🅿🛜❄) Tucked away in a private bucolic nook near the distillery, this lovely stone house, fringed by an old stand of conifers, has deep verandas and three luxurious guest bedrooms, each with their own bathroom. Rates include a full cooked breakfast.

🍷 Drinking & Nightlife

Cardrona Hotel   PUB
(☏ 03-443 8153; www.cardronahotel.co.nz; 2312 Cardrona Valley Rd; ⊙ 9am-11pm; 🛜) The wood-panelled facade looks like a film set, but it's the real deal – NZ's most photographed pub is a gold-rush relic from 1863.

The sense of history is palpable and things get busy in the après-ski thawing hours. Meals are delicious (bao buns, burgers, beef stew; mains $24 to $36), and there are 14 lovingly restored rooms (from $150) if you don't want to leave.

❶ Getting There & Away

There are no scheduled bus services to Cardrona, but the Cardrona Alpine Resort runs buses from Wānaka ($35) and Queenstown ($55) during the ski season, and from Queenstown during the mountain biking season. Winter ski shuttles are also offered by Yello! (p242) in Wānaka, and Info & Snow (p227) in Queenstown.

The 45km drive from Queenstown to Cardrona along the Crown Range Rd is one of the South Island's most scenic drives. Topping out at 1076m, it's the highest sealed road in NZ. There are some great places to stop and ogle the view, particularly at the Queenstown end of the road. However, the road is narrow and winding, and needs to be tackled with care in poor weather. In winter it's sometimes closed after heavy snows, and you'll often need snow chains for your tyres.

Makarora

POP 40

Just 20km from Haast Pass, where the West Coast begins its wild ways, remote Makarora is very much a last frontier – and it certainly feels like it. Traffic to and from the West Coast rolls through, but then Makarora settles back to silence.

🏃 Activities

Haast Pass Lookout Track (one hour return, 3.5km) offers great views from above the bush line. If you really want the upstairs view, the Mt Shrimpton Track climbs high onto the McKerrow Range (five hours return to the bush line, 6km); the track begins just a few hundred metres north of the Wonderland Makarora Lodge (✆03-443 8372; www.makarora.co.nz; 5944 Haast Pass-Makarora Rd/SH6; ⊙7am-8pm; 🐾).

Longer hikes including the Gillespie Pass Circuit (p208) go deep into the valleys that radiate through the mountains around Makarora, but shouldn't be undertaken lightly. Changeable alpine and river conditions mean you must be well prepared; call into the DOC Tititea/Mt Aspiring National Park Visitor Centre (p241) in Wānaka to check conditions and routes before undertaking any wilderness hikes.

WORTH A TRIP

LAKE HĀWEA

People looking to escape the bright lights of Queenstown typically gravitate to Wānaka; those looking to escape the slightly less bright lights of Wānaka come to Lake Hāwea.

This small town, 15km north of Wānaka, is strung along the southern shore of its 141-sq-km namesake. Separated from Lake Wānaka by a narrow strip of land called the Neck, the blue-grey Lake Hāwea (with an average water temperature of just 9°C) is 35km long and 410m deep. It's particularly popular with fisherfolk looking to do battle with its trout and landlocked salmon. The lake was raised 20m in 1958 when it was dammed to facilitate the power stations downriver. There's little here, but that's the town's appeal.

★Blue Pools Walk   WALKING
(Haast Pass–Makarora Rd) Far and away the most popular walk in the Makarora area is the 750m (30-minute return) track to the point where the Makarora and Blue Rivers converge. The water is so clear you can see the trout seemingly suspended in it. The trailhead is around 8km north of the Wonderland Makarora Lodge.

If you want to stride out a bit further, you can continue along the track to the mouth of the Young River (three to four hours return).

Siberia Experience   ADVENTURE
(✆03-443 4385; www.siberiaexperience.co.nz; Wonderland Makarora Lodge, 5944 Haast Pass–Makarora Rd; adult/child $415/340) 🐾 This thrill-seeking extravaganza combines a 25-minute scenic flight, a three-hour hike through a remote valley and a half-hour jetboat trip down the Wilkin and Makarora Rivers in Tititea/Mt Aspiring National Park.

❶ Getting There & Away

InterCity (p227) has a daily coach to/from Queenstown ($33, 3¾ hours), Cromwell ($28, 2½ hours), Wānaka ($28, 1½ hours), Lake Hāwea ($28, 1¼ hours) and Franz Josef (from $46, 4¾ hours).

QUEENSTOWN & WĀNAKA MAKARORA

The South Island's Birds

New Zealand may lack for mammals, but that's conversely created a unique population of birds – a number of species are flightless, having had no need to take to the air to avoid predators. Check out the excellent Digital Encyclopedia of New Zealand Birds (www.nzbirdsonline.org.nz), the Department of Conservation website (www.doc.govt.nz/nature/native-animals/birds).

1. Kiwi
The national icon with an onomatopoeic name (OK only for the male, which cries 'kiwi!'; females make a sound more like someone with a sore throat). There are five different species, but the small population is endangered by habitat loss and predators.

2. Tui/Tūī
Common throughout town and country, up close the 'parson bird' is metallic bluey-green with white throat tufts. Sometimes tuneful, and sometimes cacophonous, it is always an aerobatic flapper.

3. Fantail/Pīwakawaka
This restless little charmer will entrance you up close, but in truth it cares not a jot about you, merely the insects they displace.

4. Pukeko/Pūkeko
Often seen pecking about in paddocks or crossing the road in front of high-speed traffic. Territorial, highly social and easily recognised, it looks like a smooth blue chicken with a red forehead.

5. Kererū
If you can hear heavy wingbeats overhead, it'll be the kererū, often spotted on powerlines and tree branches. This handsome native pigeon won Bird of the Year in 2019.

6. Silvereye/Tauhou
One of NZ's most prevalent birds, though originally a migrant from Australia, it's easily recognised by a green and grey plumage and silver-white eyes; listen for its sing-song call.

7. Bellbird/Korimako
More like a laser gun than a church bell, this enchanting songbird sounds big but is a small, olive-green slip of a thing, with a curved bill for eating nectar.

8. Grey Warbler/Riroriro
New Zealand's most widely distributed endemic bird species is also one of its smallest. It tends to hide in dense vegetation; you're more likely to hear one warbling its lungs out, than see one.

9. Woodhen/Weka
Often mistaken for a kiwi by visitors to NZ, this large flightless bird (similar in size to a chicken) has a keen nose for lunch crumbs and will often appear at well-frequented picnic spots.

10. Rifleman/Tititi Pounamu
New Zealand's smallest bird, this hyperactive forest-dweller produces a characteristic 'wing-flicking' while moving through the canopy and foraging up and down tree trunks.

11. Kea
Resident only in the mountainous region of South Island, this alpine parrot likes to play. Kea appear innately curious, but this is simply a pretence to peck destructively at your possessions.

12. Paradise Shelduck
This colourful, conspicuous and honking waterfowl could be mistaken for a small goose as it hangs out in wild wetlands, river flats, sports fields and other open grassed areas.

13. New Zealand Robin/Toutouwai
Inhabiting forest and scrub, the distinct North Island and South Island robins stand leggy and erect, sing loud and long, and will often approach very closely.

14. Tomtit/Miromiro
Widespread inhabitants of forest and shrubland, the tomtit songbird is often reclusive but easily identified when it appears: mostly black with a white bar at the base of its feathers.

15. New Zealand Falcon/Kārearea
The NZ falcon is a magpie-sized bird of prey found in both forest and open habitats such as tussocklands and roughly grazed hill country.

16. Kaka/Kākā
This screechy parrot flaps boldly across the sky and settles in a wide variety of native forest including podocarp and beech forest, and in Wellington city near Zealandia.

17. Morepork/Ruru
You'll probably hear this small, brown nocturnal owl rather than see it (listen for the 'more-pork' call; peculiar screeches), although it may eyeball you from a low branch in both native and exotic forests.

18. Blue Duck/Whio
Mostly confined to clear, fast-flowing rivers in the mountains, this darling little bird issues a shrill 'whio' whistle above the noise of turbulent waters.

19. New Zealand Parakeets/Kākāriki
Red- or yellow-crowned parakeets are rarely found on the mainland except for escapees from Zealandia near Wellington. Seen on Tiritiri Matangi and Ulva Islands.

13

16

17

18

19

The West Coast

Best Places to Eat

➡ Hokitika Sandwich
Company (p265)

➡ Matheson Cafe (p256)

➡ Stations Inn (p265)

➡ SnakeBite Brewery (p260)

➡ Monsoon (p260)

Best Places to
Stay

➡ Theatre Royal Hotel (p267)

➡ Omau Settlers Lodge
(p277)

➡ Code Time Lodge (p261)

➡ Bazil's Hostel & Surf
School (p277)

➡ Ross Beach Top 10 (p262)

Why Go?

Nowhere is solitude sweeter than on the West Coast (in Māori, Te Tai o Poutini). A few marvels pull big crowds – like Franz Josef and Fox Glaciers, and the magnificent Pancake Rocks – but you'll need jetboats, helicopter rides and hiking trails to explore its inner realms. Hemmed in by the Southern Alps and the savage Tasman Sea, the West Coast forms almost 9% of the land area of New Zealand (NZ) but contains less than 1% of its population.

Nineteenth-century European settlers in this region faced great hardships as fortunes built on gold, coal and timber wavered. A chain of ghost towns and forlorn pioneer cemeteries was left in their wake, and only the hardiest remained. Present-day Coasters exhibit the same grit, softened with ironic humour and unquestioning hospitality. Time spent in these indomitable communities will have you spinning yarns of the wild West Coast long into the future.

When to Go

➡ December through February is peak season, so book accommodation a couple of months ahead during this period.

➡ The shoulder months of October/November and March/April are increasingly busy, particularly around Punakaiki, Hokitika and the Glaciers.

➡ The West Coast gets serious rainfall – in places, up to 5m annually.

➡ May to September has fewer crowds and cheaper accommodation; though mild (for the South Island), it's reliably rainy.

➡ All year round, backcountry hikers should check conditions with local DOC (Department of Conservation) office staff. Rivers are treacherous and snow hangs around longer than you think.

The West Coast Highlights

❶ The Great Coast Road (p274) Admiring salt-sprayed beaches, dramatic sea cliffs and the unusual Pancake Rocks along an unforgettable 100km drive.

❷ Franz Josef Glacier (p256) Pondering the glacier's swift retreat from a distance or taking a guided helihike on the glistening ice.

❸ Ōkārito (p260) Kayaking through rainforest channels and watching the sun set over the pounding surf before joining a kiwi-spotting walk.

❹ Reefton (p280) Delving into the gold-mining past of the coast's quaintest town, and taking a tipple at its excellent distillery.

❺ Hokitika (p262) Hunting out authentic local *pounamu* (greenstone/jade) in working studios.

❻ Ōpārara Basin (p279) Craning your neck at limestone formations girded by dense forest.

HIKING & BIKING ON THE WEST COAST

PAPAROA TRACK

START SMOKE-HO CAR PARK, BLACKBALL
END PORORARI RIVER TRACK CAR PARK, PUNAKAIKI
DURATION/DISTANCE 3 DAYS/55KM
DIFFICULTY MODERATE

Opened in December 2019 as NZ's 10th official Great Walk, this track traverses alpine terrain, limestone karst and rainforest within the dense wilderness of Paparoa National Park. It starts by following the old Croesus mining track, passing relics of the mining glory days, and climbs to 1000m above sea level before exiting through a lush river valley lined with nikau palms and spectacular limestone formations. Hikers can walk it in either direction, but mountain bikers are restricted to riding from Blackball to Punakaiki.

Being a Great Walk, it's well marked and signposted, with huts equipped with bunks, toilets, heating, gas stoves and drinkable water (no showers though); book in advance and bring all your own food, bedding and utensils. However, it's steep in parts and can be muddy, so you'll need to be reasonably fit and well equipped.

For mountain bikers it's a two-day, Grade 4 ride – meaning that it's suited to experienced, hardy riders who are confident with traversing the various swing and suspension bridges along the way. Just before the Punakaiki end the track splits, with mountain bikers exiting via a slightly longer route (to Waikori car park) than the hikers.

Alternatives to the main route include exiting via the western end of the **Croesus Track** to Barrytown, or via the **Pike29 Memorial Track**. At the time of writing this track was still being finalised, but it's planned as an official memorial to the 29 men who died in the Pike River mining disaster in 2010. It connects near the middle of the Paparoa Track and terminates on the access road to the mine.

Take a walk on the wild side, literally. The West Coast is one of the most dynamic hiking and mountain biking regions in New Zealand, with an emerging network of tracks.

OLD GHOST ROAD

START LYELL CAMPSITE
END MOKIHINUI RD, SEDDONVILLE
DURATION/DISTANCE 5 DAYS/85KM
DIFFICULTY MODERATE

One of the gnarliest of NZ's mountain biking and hiking trails, the **Old Ghost Road** (☑ 0800 244 678; www.oldghostroad.org.nz) follows a historic miners' track that was started in the 1870s but never finished, as the gold rush petered out. Following a painstaking, volunteer-led build, the gruelling track now traverses native forests, tussock tops, river flats and valleys.

The southern trailhead is at Lyell, 50 minutes' drive (62km) east of Westport along the scenic Buller Gorge (SH6). The DOC campsite and day walks here have long been popular, with visitors drawn in by readily accessible historic sites, including a graveyard secreted in the bush. The northern trailhead is at Seddonville, 45 minutes' drive (50km) north of Westport off SH67, from where the track sidles along the steep-sided Mokihinui River. Joining the two ends is an alpine section, with entrancing views from sunrise to sunset.

The track is dual use, but favours walkers (allow five days). For advanced mountain bikers who can handle narrow trails and plenty of jolts, it is pretty much the Holy Grail, completed in two to four days, preferably from Lyell to Seddonville. The four huts along the way need to be booked in advance on the Old Ghost Road website, which also details a range of other ways to experience the track other than an end-to-end ride or hike. Day trips from either end are a rewarding, flexible way in, particularly from the Seddonville end, via the inimitable **Rough & Tumble Lodge** (p277).

Being a long and remote track through wild terrain, conditions can change quickly, so check the trail website for its status.

COPLAND TRACK

START/END KARANGARUA RIVER BRIDGE
DURATION/DISTANCE 2 DAYS/36KM
DIFFICULTY MODERATE

This hike up the Copland Valley to Welcome Flat Hut is a popular overnight return trip for visitors to the Glacier Region. It offers a window into Westland Tai Poutini National Park's spectacular forest, river and mountain scenery, while natural hot pools at Welcome Flat are an added attraction for foot-weary adventurers.

The forests of the Copland Valley have a healthy canopy of southern rata, and their bright red blooms make for a spectacular sight during the summer flowering season. The forest gives way at higher altitudes to the upper montane vegetation of tree daisies and *Dracophyllums*, which in turn give way to the truly alpine habitats of tussock grasslands and native herbs.

Regular possum control has been undertaken since the mid-1980s and as a result the forest damage is significantly less than in the neighbouring Karangarua Valley, which has extensive canopy dieback. The only real drawback of this hike is that you must eventually turn around and backtrack to SH6.

Note, there's a river and about a dozen streams to cross (keep your boots on), hence the track is closed in heavy rain; check in with the National Park Visitor Centre before setting out. Book the hut online and be aware that there are no cooking facilities; you'll need to carry all of your equipment with you.

ℹ Getting There & Away

Most travellers arrive by road from elsewhere in NZ. Buses head here from major South Island destinations, including Nelson, Christchurch and Queenstown. The TranzAlpine (p268) train between Christchurch and Greymouth is the most scenic mode of transport. There are flights between Hokitika and Christchurch, and between Westport and Wellington.

WESTLAND

Long, thin Westland is one of New Zealand's most sparsely populated districts, stretching from Mt Aspiring National Park in the south to the Taramakau River, north of Hokitika. Its sweeping beaches are lined with swamp forests, twisted rata trees aflutter with birdlife, and squabbling colonies of seals and penguins.

Amid this tapestry of farmland and rainforest, the most famous features are Fox and Franz Josef Glaciers. Though in retreat, these frosty monoliths hook thousands of admirers, many of whom stick around for pulse-thudding pursuits like mountain biking the West Coast Wilderness Trail, hiking the Copland Track, soaring above national parks by helicopter, or tiptoeing through the bush on kiwi-spotting walks.

There's culture, too, if you like it quaint and low-key: gold-rush sights in Ross and greenstone-carving classes in Hokitika provide a respite on days when you want to hang up your hiking boots.

Haast & Around

POP 240

A small settlement near the yawning mouth of the Haast River, Haast acts as a springboard to forests, sand dunes, craggy coast and tree-knotted lakes. Only in 1965 was Haast linked to the rest of the West Coast Hwy and the remote feeling endures. It's a handy stop for filling the tank and tummy if you're travelling between Central Otago and the West Coast glaciers. Note: check your fuel gauge as Haast has the last petrol station before Fox Glacier (120km north) and Makarora (78km southeast).

◉ Sights & Activities

Haast's main selling point is its frontier location, but plenty of hikes hereabouts are easy, hour-long affairs. Explore with the help of the free *Haast Visitor Map* or DOC's brochure *Walks and Activities in the Haast Area* ($2 from the visitor centre (p254), or downloadable online). Some are easily accessible from the highway heading to Fox Glacier, so build in extra travelling time for your journey north.

Knights Point   VIEWPOINT
(Haast Hwy) Admire expansive views of boulder-studded sea from this roadside lookout. A granite column commemorates the opening of this section of coastal highway in 1965. It's an easy pull-over off the highway, 25km northeast of Haast Junction.

HAAST PASS HIGHWAY

The 145km road careening between the West Coast and Central Otago is a spectacular drive. It takes roughly two hours from Haast to Wānaka, but allow more time to drive this Southern Alpine saddle if you want to stop at lookouts and waterfall trails.

Heading inland from Haast, the highway (SH6) snakes alongside the Haast River, crossing the boundary into Mt Aspiring National Park. The further you go, the narrower the river valley becomes, until the road clambers around sheer-sided valley walls streaked with waterfalls and scarred by rock slips. Princely sums are involved in keeping this highway clear, and even so it sets plenty of traps for unwary drivers. Stop at signposted lookouts and short walkways to admire the scenery, such as small, graceful **Fantail Falls** (10 minutes return) and aptly named **Thunder Creek Falls** (one hour return). These are detailed in DOC's booklet *Walks along the Haast Highway* ($2), but sufficient detail is provided at the trailheads. The highway tops out at the 563m mark, shortly after which you will reach food and fuel at Makarora. Hello Otago!

Early Māori travelled this route in their quest for *pounamu* (greenstone/jade), naming it Tioripātea, meaning 'Clear Path'. Northern chief Te Puoho led troops across the pass in 1836 to raid southern tribes. German geologist Julius von Haast led a party of Europeans across in 1863 – hence the name of the pass, river and town – but evidence suggests that Scottish prospector Charles Cameron may have pipped Haast to the post. It was clearly no mean feat: the terrain is such that the Haast Pass Hwy wasn't opened until 1965.

THE ROAD TO JACKSON BAY/OKAHU

Most travellers drive northeast from Haast Junction towards Fox and Franz Josef Glaciers, but the road less travelled makes an interesting detour. Steering southwest for 45km from Haast you'll find the pocket-sized outpost of Jackson Bay/Okahu, towered over by the Southern Alps. There's no through road: this fishing hamlet is truly the end of the line. Farms here stand testament to some of the hardiest souls who ever attempted settlement in New Zealand. Migrants arrived in 1875 under a doomed settlement scheme, their farming and timber-milling aspirations shattered by never-ending rain and the lack of a wharf, not built until 1938. Until the 1950s, the only way to reach Haast overland was via bush tracks from Hokitika and Wānaka. Supplies came by an infrequent coastal shipping service.

Unless you're in the market for whitebait, present-day Jackson Bay has few attractions other than some lovely walking tracks spread along the road leading to it.

Near Okuru, 10km west of Haast, is the **Hapuka Estuary Walk** (20 minutes), a winding boardwalk that loops through a sleepy wildlife sanctuary with good interpretation panels en route.

The road continues west to Arawhata Bridge, where a turn-off leads to the **Lake Ellery Track**, 3.5km south along unsealed Jackson River Rd. A one-hour round trip takes you through mossy beech forest to a lookout over peaceful **Lake Ellery**. There's not much besides a picnic bench when you arrive, but you'll likely have it to yourself.

From the end of Jackson Bay Rd the 40-minute return **Wharekai-Te Kou Walk** leads through bird-filled bush to Ocean Beach, a tiny boulder-strewn bay where penguins are known to nest. The muddy three- to four-hour **Smoothwater Track**, following an old pioneers' track, also begins nearby.

Lake Moeraki　　　　LAKE
(Haast Hwy) Alongside the highway, 32km northeast of Haast Junction, and within the bounds of the World Heritage wilderness, Lake Moeraki is an undeveloped and tranquil spot to contemplate the forested, mountainous surroundings. There's no trail all the way around, but there are lake beaches where you can park and ponder.

Wayne's Waiatoto River Safari　　CRUISE
(☑03-750 0780; www.riversafaris.co.nz; 1975 Haast-Jackson Bay Rd, Hannahs Clearing; adult/child $199/139; ⊙ trips 10am, 1pm & 4pm Nov-Mar, 11am Apr-Oct) 🏊 These two-hour river cruises offer an exhilarating taste of World Heritage wilderness. Knowledgeable operators point out bird life and features of the landscape as the jetboat buzzes past areas otherwise only accessible by helicopter. Birds chatter, ducks race alongside the boat, and there's the occasional white-knuckle rapid on this generally gentle-paced journey. The base is 20km southwest of Haast Junction.

Ship Creek Tauparikākā　　WALKING
(www.doc.govt.nz; Haast Hwy) Two contrasting walks begin at Ship Creek, 15km north of Haast, each with interesting interpretive panels. Stroll sand dunes, stunted forest and driftwood-strewn beaches on the **Dune Lake** Walk (30 minutes return), before embarking on the enchanting **Kahikatea Swamp Forest Walk** (20 minutes return), along boardwalks that hover above glistening marshland (the bird-watching is superb).

🛏 Sleeping & Eating

Haast River Motels & Holiday Park　　HOLIDAY PARK $$
(☑03-750 0020; www.haastrivermotels.co.nz; 52 Haast Pass Hwy, Haast Junction; sites/units from $44/139; 🅿@🛜🏄) A large red hangar serves as the communal facilities for campervan and tenting guests, while a horseshoe of two-storey buildings contains a variety of roomy and well-furnished motel units. On-site facilities include a laundry, a games room, a playground, and a book- and DVD-filled lounge surveyed by mounted deer heads.

Wilderness Lodge Lake Moeraki　　LODGE $$$
(☑03-750 0881; www.wildernesslodge.co.nz; Haast Hwy; s/d incl breakfast & dinner from $595/980; 🅿🛜) 🏊 Positioned in a verdant setting on the edge of the Moeraki River near Lake Moeraki, 30km north of Haast Junction, this is one of NZ's best nature lodges. It offers comfortable rooms and three-course dinners, but the real delights are the free guided outdoor activities such as kayak trips and coastal walks.

Hard Antler
PUB FOOD **$$**

(☑ 03-750 0034; www.facebook.com/HardAntler
BarHaast; Marks Rd; mains $15-32; ⊙ 11am-late)
Antlers and a fishing and shooting wall of
fame establish the hunting-lodge vibe of
Haast's best boozer. Mainly meaty main
courses (venison nachos, burgers, toasties
and tasty grilled blue cod) are served all day.

❶ Information

With outdoor water features, a hiker-friendly
toilet block and a brimming museum, the **DOC
Awarua/Haast Visitor Centre** (☑ 03-750
0809; www.doc.govt.nz; cnr Haast Pass Hwy
& Haast-Jackson Bay Rd, Haast Junction;
⊙ 9am-6pm Nov-Mar, to 4.30pm Apr-Oct) is
more than the average info centre. Displays
cover local Māori history, whitebaiting and Te
Wāhipounamu World Heritage Area. It also sells
insect repellent (essential).

General regional information and visitor ser-
vices listings can be found on www.haastnz.com.

❶ Getting There & Away

Intercity (☑ 03-365 1113; www.intercity.
co.nz) buses stop on Marks Rd on their daily
runs between Queenstown ($43, 5¼ hours)
and Franz Josef ($29, 3¼ hours) via Cromwell,
($33, four hours), Wānaka ($30, 3¼ hours) and
Fox Glacier ($28, 2¾ hours).

Fox Glacier
POP 306

Descending from the brooding Southern
Alps, Fox Glacier (in Māori, Te Moeka o
Tuawe) seems to flow steadily, ominously
towards the township below. But in this
fragile landscape it's the glacier that's at risk:
despite slight advances in the early years of
the millennia, this 13km glacier (named for
former New Zealand PM Sir William Fox)
has been steadily retreating over the past
century. And, sadly, enormous landslides in
2019 have permanently closed the roads and
tracks leading towards its terminus. Now,
unless you fork out for a pricey helicopter
trip, you'll have content yourself with admir-
ing it from a considerable distance.

Compared with the glacier, the epony-
mous township isn't nearly so dramatic; its
cafes, motels and tour operators occupy a
very short strip of SH6. However, there are
some interesting sights and walks to pursue
in the surrounding farmland.

◉ Sights

Lake Matheson
LAKE

(Lake Matheson Rd) On a good day, the famous
'mirror lake' reflects extraordinary views of

WESTLAND TAI POUTINI NATIONAL PARK

With colossal mountains, forests, glaciers and surf-pounded beaches, Westland Tai Pou-
tini National Park (www.doc.govt.nz) clobbers visitors with its mind-bending proportions.
Reaching from the coast to the razor peaks of the Southern Alps, the park's supreme
attractions are twin glaciers Fox and Franz Josef, served by townships 23km apart. The
official National Park Visitor Centre (p260) is in Franz Josef.

Diverse and often unique habitats are huddled into the national park's 1280 sq km.
Endangered bird species include kākāriki (parakeets), kākā and kea (parrots) and rowi
(Ōkārito kiwi). Also scampering through these forests are introduced ungulates such as
red deer, chamois and Himalayan tahr.

Out of more than 60 glaciers in the park, only Fox and Franz Josef are easy to view.
The glaciers are as fragile as they are amazing to behold. Rising temperatures have beat-
en the glaciers into retreat, reducing opportunities to view them on foot and clanging a
death knell for their long-term future if climate change continues unchecked. The gla-
ciers are the most majestic handiwork of the West Coast's ample precipitation. Snowfall
in the glaciers' broad accumulation zones fuses into clear ice at 20m depth, and then
creeps down the steep valleys. Nowhere else at this latitude do glaciers descend so close
to the ocean. During the last ice age (around 15,000 to 20,000 years ago) Westland's
twin glaciers reached the sea. In the ensuing thaw they may have crawled back even fur-
ther than their current positions, but around the 14th century a mini ice age caused them
to advance to their greatest modern-era extent around 1750, and the terminal moraines
from this time are still visible. The only way to get onto the ice safely is with a guided tour.
Both glacier terminal faces are roped off to prevent people being caught in icefalls and
river surges, which can flood the valleys in a matter of minutes. Obey warning signs and
stay out of roped-off areas.

distant Aoraki/Mt Cook and Mt Tasman in its forest-shaded waters. The best time to visit is early morning or when the sun is low in the late afternoon, although the presence of an excellent cafe (p256) means that any time is a good time. It's extraordinary to think that this lake was carved out by the now distant Fox Glacier before it started its long retreat.

The shady, moss-lined 2.6km **Lake Matheson Track** circumnavigates the lake; allow 90 minutes walking at a slow pace. At the far end of the circuit you may, weather permitting, get the money shot, but failing that you can buy a postcard at the excellent gift store by the car park.

Branching off from the eastern side of the main track is the 8km-return **Lake Gault Track**, which gradually climbs 200m through virgin podocarp forest to another mirror lake. Allow three to five hours and expect to get wet and muddy feet.

Peak Viewpoint   VIEWPOINT
(Gillespies Beach Rd) It's a very long way from the actual glacier, but this parking area provides a surprisingly good view over fields to Fox Glacier (weather permitting). There's not much here except a picnic table and a marker pointing out the various peaks. However, it's a good alternative to the two-hour (6km return) **Fox Glacier South Side Walk** along the slip-damaged old Glacier View Rd to a viewpoint that, while considerably closer, still won't give you a view of the terminus.

Gillespies Beach   BEACH
(www.doc.govt.nz; Gillespies Beach Rd) Follow Cook Flat Rd for its full 21km (the final 12km is narrow, winding and unsealed) to this remote beach, a ruggedly beautiful, wind-blasted length of slate-grey sand and shingle near an old mining settlement. Interesting walks from here include a 30-minute, partly sheltered circuit to a rusting gold dredge from 1932, and a 3½-hour return walk to **Galway Beach**, a seal hang-out; don't disturb them.

Five-hundred metres shy of the beach, signposted from the road, is a well-kept miners' **cemetery**, reached by a five-minute walk. There's a basic, eight-site **DOC campground** by the beach.

Activities

Short helicopter flights (10 to 20 minutes) offer a spectacular vantage point over Fox Glacier with a snow landing up top. On a longer flight (30 to 50 minutes) you can also enjoy sky-high sightseeing over Franz Josef

Glacier and Aoraki/Mt Cook. Children are admitted, though age restrictions vary; expect to pay around 70% of the adult price. Shop around: most operators are situated on the main road in Fox Glacier village.

Fox Glacier Guiding   ADVENTURE SPORTS
(03-751 0825; www.foxguides.co.nz; 44 Main Rd) The only way to get on the actual glacier, this friendly crew offers small-group helihikes. A five-minute helicopter ride whooshes you onto the ice for a three-hour hike (adult/child $499/475), or a more demanding seven-hour hike (adult $750). Scrambling through ice caves, peering into crevasses and sipping glacial meltwater is included with the animated commentary. Age restrictions vary by trip.

Helicopter Line   SCENIC FLIGHTS
(03-751 0767; www.helicopter.co.nz; cnr Main & Cook Flat Rds; 20-40min flights $280-490) Whisking travellers to giddy heights since 1986, this well-established operator has a big menu of scenic flights. It also operates from Franz Josef, where it offers a three-hour helihike option ($485) in conjunction with Franz Josef Glacier Guides (p258).

HeliServicesNZ   SCENIC FLIGHTS
(03-751 0866; www.scenic-flights.co.nz; 44 Main Rd; flights from $280; ⊙7am-9pm Nov-Mar, 8am-6pm Apr-Oct) Locally run operator zipping sightseers up and down the glaciers, always with a snow landing. A two-glacier flight ($325) is over all too quickly, but longer flights also soar around Aoraki/Mt Cook and Mt Tasman. It also has an office in Franz Josef.

Mountain Helicopters   SCENIC FLIGHTS
(03-751 0045; www.mountainhelicopters.co.nz; 43 Main Rd; flights from $129) Offers flights over Fox and Franz Josef Glaciers, ranging from a 10-minute taster to a 40-minute all-rounder with a snow landing and views of Aoraki/Mt Cook. It also has an office at Franz Josef.

Sleeping & Eating

Fox Glacier Top 10   HOLIDAY PARK $$
(03-751 0821; www.fghp.co.nz; Kerr Rd; sites $55-58, r with/without bathroom from $165/85; P♠⊛) Inspiring mountain views and ample amenities lift this reliable holiday park above its competition. Trim cabins, basic lodge rooms, and grassy tent and hard campervan sites make use of a quality communal kitchen and dining room. The upmarket self-contained units offer extra comfort and

style. A playground and tandem bikes pile on the family-fun factor.

★ Matheson Cafe   CAFE $$

(📞03-751 0878; www.lakematheson.com; Lake Matheson Rd; breakfast & lunch $13-22, dinner $25-39; ⊗8am-late Nov-Mar, to 3pm Apr-Oct; 🐟) At the start of the Lake Matheson Track, this cafe does everything right: sharp architecture that maximises mountain views, strong coffee, craft beers and upmarket fare. Bratwurst breakfasts are a good prelude to rambling round the lake, while beef ramen and merino lamb burgers are a delicious way to refuel afterwards. Check out the ReflectioNZ gift shop next door.

❶ Information

The main national park visitor centre and i-SITE is in Franz Josef (p260). Pick up a copy of DOC's excellent *Glacier Region Walks* booklet ($2), which provides maps and illuminating background reading. You can also find info online at www.glaciercountry.co.nz.

Fox Glacier Clinic (📞03-751 0836; www.wcdhb.health.nz; 3 Main Rd) is open from 9am-4pm Monday to Friday.

❶ Getting There & Away

InterCity (p254) services trundle through Fox Glacier daily, heading south to Queenstown ($69, eight hours) via Haast ($28, 2¾ hours), and north to Greymouth ($47, 4¾ hours) via Franz Josef ($28, 40 minutes) and Hokitika ($40, 3¼ hours). Buses stop outside the Fox Glacier Guiding building.

Glacier Shuttles & Charters (p260) runs scheduled shuttles to Fox Glacier village and Lake Matheson from Franz Josef ($30 return, three to four daily).

If you're heading south along the coast, be aware that Fox is your last chance for fuel before Haast, 120km away.

Franz Josef/Waiau

POP 444

Franz Josef Glacier's cloak of ice once flowed from the mountains to the sea. Following millennia of gradual retreat, the glacier is now 19km inland. In the last 10 years alone the glacier has receded by nearly a kilometre, and the dismal forecast of a rainier, warmer future is sure to bring further shrinkage.

Swarms of small aircraft from tourist-focused Franz Josef / Waiau village, 5km north, lift visitors to views of sparkling ice and toothy mountains. Some land on the

glacier to lead groups to blue-tinged caves and crevasses. A glacier experience is the crowning moment for thousands of annual visitors, but walking trails, hot pools and adventure sports provide a reason to linger.

Geologist Julius von Haast led the first European expedition here in 1865, and named the glacier after the Austrian emperor. Its Māori name is much more evocative: Kā Roimata o Hine Hukatere (Tears of the Avalanche Maiden).

◎ Sights & Activities

The **Franz Josef Glacier/Kā Roimata o Hine Hukatere Walk** (1½ hours return) starts from the glacier car park, 5km from the village. It heads through native bush and then along the broad, stony glacier valley to the best permissible view of the terminal face, an elusive 750m away. A series of information panels are positioned at the previous extents of the glacier at different dates in history, comparing the global temperatures, world population and atmospheric carbon dioxide concentration then to now – a sobering reminder of the effects of climate change.

Branching off from the beginning of the main walk is the steep, 20-minute return track to the top of **Sentinel Rock**. The lookout reveals either impressive views of the glacier valley, flanked by Mt Roon (2233m) and Bismarck Peak (2545m), or a mysterious panorama obscured by mist and cloud.

Other walks include the **Douglas Walk** (one hour return), off the Glacier Access Rd, which passes moraine piled up by the glacier's advance in 1750, and **Peters Pool**, a small kettle lake reflecting mountain views. The **Terrace Track** (15 minutes return) is an easy amble over bushy terraces behind the village, illuminated by glowworms at night. Two good rainforest walks, **Callery Gorge Walk** and **Tatare Tunnels** (both around 1½ hours return), start from Cowan St – bring a torch for the latter and boots that can deal with ankle-deep water.

Much more challenging walks, such as the five-hour **Roberts Point Track** and eight-hour **Alex Knob Track**, are suited to experienced hikers only. Get advice from DOC before setting out as they can be treacherous; people have died at Roberts Point. All of the main walks in the area are detailed in DOC's *Glacier Region Walks* booklet.

West Coast Wildlife Centre   NATURE CENTRE
(📞03-752 0600; www.wildkiwi.co.nz; cnr Cron & Cowan Sts; adult/child $39/20, incl backstage

pass $59/35; ☺8am-5.30pm) 🖉 The purpose of this feel-good attraction is breeding two of the world's rarest kiwi – the rowi and the Haast tokoeka. As well as a chance to hang out with kiwi in their darkened ferny enclosure, there are tuatara (native reptiles) and conservation, glacier and heritage displays. The backstage pass into the incubating and rearing area is a rare opportunity to learn how a species can be brought back from the brink of extinction.

Glacier Hot Pools   HOT SPRINGS
(🗐03-752 0099; www.glacierhotpools.co.nz; 63 Cron St; adult/child $29/25; ☺11am-9pm) Cleverly set into a pretty rainforest on the edge of town, this stylish and well-maintained outdoor hot-pool complex is perfect après-hike or on a rainy day. These aren't thermal springs but they do make use of glacial melt water and the three main pools are heated to 36°, 38° and 40°C. Private pools and massages are also available.

Skydive Franz Josef & Fox Glacier SKYDIVING
(🗐03-752 0714; www.skydivefranz.co.nz; Main Rd; 20,000/16,500/13,000/9000ft jump $649/429/339/289) This company claims to offer NZ's highest jump (20,000ft, 85+ seconds freefall) and, with the glaciers and Aoraki/Mt Cook in your sights, it's certainly one of the most scenic.

Air Safaris   SCENIC FLIGHTS
(🗐03-752 0716; www.airsafaris.co.nz; Main Rd) Franz's only fixed-wing flyer offers 50-minute 'grand traverse' ($395) flights that expose breathtaking views of the glaciers, Aoraki/Mt Cook, and far-flung valleys, lakes and waterways en route. Alternatively, take a 30-minute Twin Glacier flight ($305). Either way, charge your camera.

Glacier Helicopters   SCENIC FLIGHTS
(🗐03-752 0755; www.glacierhelicopters.co.nz; Main Rd; 20-40min flights $280-490) This reliable operator has been running scenic flights since 1970. Shorter flights take you to one of the glaciers, while the 40-minute option reaches both, as well as soaring to spectacular views of Aoraki/Mt Cook. There's a brief snow landing on each trip.

Glacier Country Helicopters   SCENIC FLIGHTS
(🗐03-752 0203; www.glaciercountryhelicopters.co.nz; 10 Main Rd; flights from $280) This family-owned and operated company offers the choice of scenic flights surveying one, two or three glaciers, including a snow landing.

ESSENTIAL WEST COAST

Eat spicy sausage from Blackball Salami Co (p272).

Drink Little Biddy gin from Reefton Distillery (p280).

Read *The Bone People* (1984), Ōkārito-based Keri Hulme's Booker Prize-winning novel, set on the West Coast.

Listen to Mel Parsons, a folksy alt-country singer-songwriter hailing from Cape Foulwind near Westport.

Watch the BBC adaptation of Eleanor Catton's 2013 Man Booker Prize–winning novel, *The Luminaries*, set in Hokitika.

Go green in Paparoa National Park.

Go online at www.westcoast.co.nz.

Franz Josef

Clay Target Shooting   OUTDOORS
(🗐027 772 6590; www.franzjosefclayshooting.co.nz; 20/30 targets $110/130; ☺by arrangement) Lock your sights onto clay discs hurtling through the air, before obliterating them... sound like fun? This operator offers exhilarating two-hour shoot-'em-ups. Sessions include transfers to and from the range, on a farm 6km south of Franz Josef township. Book ahead, by phone or through the i-SITE. It's perfect for rainy days: shooters stay undercover in a purpose-built hut.

👉 Tours

★**Glacier Country Kayaks**   KAYAKING
(🗐03-752 0230; www.glacierkayaks.com; 64 Cron St; 3hr kayak adult/child $120/70) 🖉 Enjoy a change of pace on a guided kayak trip on Lake Mapourika (10km north of Franz). The 'kayak classic' is three hours of birdspotting and mountain views. Alternatively, take the summer-only 'sunset classic' ($130/80) or a four-hour 'kayak & walk' (adult/child $145/85). It also offers SUP tours, rainforest walks, lake cruises, fishing charters and various combos.

Glacier Valley Eco Tours   ECOTOUR
(🗐0800 925 586; www.glaciervalley.co.nz; 20 Main Rd; adult/child $80/40) 🖉 These conservation-focused walking tours unlock the geological and wildlife secrets of Glacier Country. Three- to four-hour tours explore either Franz Josef, Fox Glacier, Ōkārito or Lake Matheson, with the Franz Josef tour getting closer to the terminal face than is otherwise

Franz Josef Glacier & Village

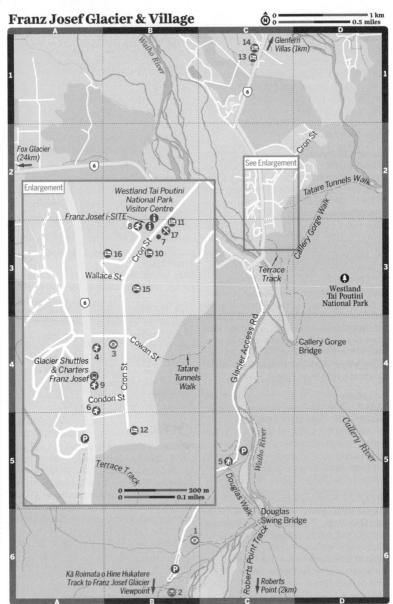

permitted. Full-day tours immerse you in local flora and fauna over seven hours of hiking (adult/child $180/90).

Franz Josef Glacier Guides ADVENTURE
(📞03-752 0763; www.franzjosefglacier.com; 63 Cron St) Take a helicopter ride to the ice and then experience two hours on the glacier exploring dazzling blue ice caves ($485). The daring can seize an ice pick for a four-hour ice climb ($609) or even camp on the glacier overnight ($999). Three-hour guided valley walks are also available (adult/child $82/67).

Franz Josef Glacier & Village

⊨ Sleeping

Rainforest Retreat
HOLIDAY PARK $

(☑ 03-752 0220; www.rainforest.nz; 46 Cron St; sites $48, dm/r/units from $37/100/195; P 🕏 🖼️) Options abound in these forested grounds: dorm rooms that sleep between four and six (four-bed 'flashpacker' en-suite rooms are worth the higher rate), en-suite doubles and luxurious free-standing cottages set among the trees, with underfloor heating, rain showers and private decks. Campervan sites are nestled in native bush. There's also a gigantic hot tub and an excellent on-site pub/restaurant, Monsoon (p260).

58 on Cron
MOTEL $$

(☑ 03-752 0627; www.58oncron.co.nz; 58 Cron St; units from $170; P 🕏) Guests staying in these 16 comfortable motel units, from petite studios to two-bedroom apartments, enjoy sweet service and a barbecue area. Bonus: you won't forget the motel's address.

Franz Josef Glacier YHA
HOSTEL $$

(☑ 03-752 0754; www.yha.co.nz; 2-4 Cron St; dm $33, s/d without bathroom $115/125, r with bathroom $145; P 🕏) 🖋️ Functional and friendly, the YHA has warm, spacious communal areas, family rooms, a large free sauna, and a booking desk for transport and activities. It can accommodate 115 people, but you'll still need to book ahead.

Franz Josef Top 10
HOLIDAY PARK $$

(☑ 03-752 0735; www.franzjoseftop10.co.nz; 2902 Franz Josef Hwy; sites $55, units with/without bathroom from $150/99; P @ 🕏 🖼️) 🖋️ Tents and motorhomes are afforded free-draining grassy sites away from the road at this spacious holiday park, 1.5km north of the township. Travellers who prefer four walls can choose cabins (sharing the well-maintained bathroom and kitchen areas) or trim self-contained units. A playground, games room and TV lounge provide distractions during rainy days.

Holly Homestead
B&B $$$

(☑ 03-752 0299; www.hollyhomestead.co.nz; 2900 Franz Josef Hwy; r $295-395; 🕏) This two-storey wisteria-draped B&B stays true to its 1926 beginnings with an old-fashioned welcome and freshly baked bread for breakfast. Choose between three characterful en-suite rooms or a suite, all of which share a classy lounge and a deck that's perfect for a sundowner. It's positioned on the highway, 1.5km to the north of the village.

Glenfern Villas
APARTMENT $$$

(☑ 03-752 0054; www.glenfern.co.nz; Franz Josef Hwy; villas $279-315; P 🕏) 🖋️ Forming something of a tiny, elite village 3km north of town, Glernfern's one- and two-bedroom houses are equipped with every comfort from quality beds to plump couches, gleaming kitchenettes and private decks where you can listen to birdsong. Book well ahead.

Te Waonui Forest Retreat
HOTEL $$$

(☑ 03-752 0555; www.tewaonui.co.nz; 3 Wallace St; s/d $679/809; ⊙ Sep-Apr; P 🕏) 🖋️ Luxurious Te Waonui is filled with design flourishes that evoke the land: twinkly lights suggest glowworms, coal-black walls nod to the mining past, and local stone provides an earthy backdrop. Beyond the gorgeous, greenery-facing rooms, the prime draw is the five-course degustation dinner (included in some packages). Top-notch green credentials include building materials that are either recycled or sustainably sourced.

THE WEST COAST FRANZ JOSEF/WAIAU

Aspen Court MOTEL $$$

(☑ 03-752 0210; www.aspencourtfranzjosef.co.nz; 76 Cron St; units $280-335; ⓟ 🛜) It couldn't be accused of being reasonably priced, but this motel near the visitor centre offers a brace of smart brick units grouped around a central car park. All have kitchens and some have spa baths. There's a communal barbecue, too.

✗ Eating

★ SnakeBite Brewery ASIAN $$

(☑ 03-752 0234; www.snakebite.co.nz; 28 Main Rd; mains $16-29; ⊙ 7.30am-10.30pm) SnakeBite's flavour-packed meals awaken taste buds after their long slumber through the West Coast's lamb-and-whitebait menus. Indonesian, Malaysian, Thai, Chinese and Japanese dishes all feature, along with burgers and pies. Try the mussel fritters with wasabi mayo and, the speciality, the beef-cheek rendang. Between courses, glug craft beers on tap or a 'snakebite' (cider with beer).

★ Monsoon PUB FOOD $$

(☑ 03-752 0101; www.monsoonbar.co.nz; 46 Cron St; mains $16-39; ⊙ 4.30pm-late) Sip drinks in the sunshine or within the cosy, chalet-style bar of the Rainforest Retreat (p259), which usually buzzes with a sociable crowd of travellers. Bar snacks, burgers, curries, roasts, steaks and posh pizzas ensure you needn't move from your comfy spot by the fire.

King Tiger ASIAN $$

(☑ 03-752 0060; www.kingtiger.co.nz; 70 Cron St; mains $21-30; ⊙ 11.30am-9.30pm; 🛜 ☑ ♿) Voyaging from India to China via Thailand, this atmospheric restaurant matches piquant dishes with Asian-inspired cocktails, red-and-black decor, Chinese lanterns, Buddha statues and a big gilded birdcage shaped like a maharaja's palace. There's a long menu but we're particularly partial to the lamb *saagwala* (spinach curry).

ℹ Information

Franz Josef Clinic (☑ 03-752 0700; www.wcdhb.health.nz; 97 Cron St; ⊙ 8.30am-5pm Mon-Fri) South Westland's main medical centre. After hours, calls connect to a local nurse.

Franz Josef i-SITE (☑ 0800 354 748; www.glaciercountry.co.nz; 63 Cron St; ⊙ 8.30am-5pm) Helpful local centre offering advice and booking service for activities, accommodation and transport in the local area and beyond.

Westland Tai Poutini National Park Visitor Centre (☑ 03-752 0360; www.doc.govt.nz; 69 Cron St; ⊙ 8.30am-5pm) Insightful exhibits, weather information, maps, locator beacons, and all-important track updates and weather forecasts.

ℹ Getting There & Away

➔ InterCity (p254) buses stop outside the Four Square supermarket on Main St. Daily services head south to Queenstown ($73, 8½ hours) via Fox Glacier ($28, 40 minutes) and Haast ($29, three hours), and north to Greymouth ($44, four hours) via Hokitika ($38, 2½ hours). Book online, or at the i-SITE or YHA.

➔ **Glacier Shuttles & Charters** (☑ 027 205 5922; www.glaciershuttlescharters.co.nz; 20 Main Rd) runs scheduled shuttles to the glacier car park ($12.50 return, five to six daily), Fox Glacier village and Lake Matheson ($30 return, three to four daily), Lake Mapourika ($15 return, two daily) and Ōkārito ($30 return, two daily).

Ōkārito

POP 30

The seaside hamlet of Ōkārito has a magnificent setting, with a pounding surf beach at its doorstep, the snow-capped Southern Alps as a backdrop, forest-clad hills on one flank and an expansive lagoon on the other.

Barely 10km from SH6, Ōkārito Lagoon is the largest unmodified wetland in NZ. More than 76 bird species preen and glide among its waterways, including the kōtuku (white heron). Hiding out in the forest are rowi kiwi, the rarest species of NZ's iconic land-bird – for a great chance of seeing one in the wild, hook up with the South Island's only licensed kiwi-tour operator, based in the village.

Ōkārito has no shops, limited visitor facilities and patchy phone reception, so stock up and book before you arrive. It's hard to believe that during the height of the gold rush, 4000 people lived here.

🏃 Activities & Tours

From a car park on the Strand you can begin the easy **Wetland Walk** (20 minutes), which leads into the 10km-long **Three Mile Pack Track** (3½ hours; the coastal return route is tide dependent, so check in with the locals for tide times). Otherwise, branch off on the **Ōkārito Trig Walk** (1½ hours return), where a jolly good puff to the top is rewarded with spectacular Southern Alps and Ōkārito Lagoon views (weather contingent).

★ Okarito Kiwi Tours BIRDWATCHING
(📞03-753 4330; www.okaritokiwitours.co.nz; 53 The Strand; 3-5hr tour $75) 🐾 Spotting the rare kiwi in Ōkārito's tangle of native forest isn't easy, but bird-whisperer Ian has a 98% success rate for his small-group evening tours. Patience, tiptoeing and fine weather are essential. If you have your heart set on a kiwi encounter, book ahead and be within reach of Ōkārito for a couple of nights, in case of poor weather.

Okarito Kayaks KAYAKING
(📞0800 652 748; www.okarito.co.nz; 1 The Strand; 2hr/3hr tour $110/130, half-/full-day rental $70/80; ⏱hours vary) This hands-on operator hires out kayaks for paddles across Ōkārito's shallow lagoon in the company of strutting waterfowl and beneath a breathtaking mountainscape. Honest advice is offered on weather, tides and paddling routes. Personalised guided kayaking trips are ideal for getting to know the landscape. It also serves homemade ice cream and cake, and surprisingly good coffee.

Okarito Boat Eco Tours BIRDWATCHING
(📞03-753 4223; www.okaritoboattours.co.nz; 31 Wharf St; ⏱late Oct–May) Runs bird-spotting lagoon tours, the most fruitful of which is the 80-minute 'early bird' (adult/child $85/40, 7.30am). The popular two-hour 'eco tour' offers deeper insights into this remarkable natural area ($95/45, 9am and 11.30am), or there's a 90-minute afternoon 'wetlands tour' ($75/35, 2.30pm) if you aren't a morning person. Book at least 24 hours in advance.

🛏 Sleeping

★ Code Time Lodge APARTMENT **$$$**
(📞021 037 2031; www.codetimelodge.co.nz; 8 Albert St; units $230; 🛜) Driftwood decorations and soft colour schemes impart a dreamy air to the Code Time Lodge, whose two roomy, self-contained apartments (kitchen included) are kept toasty by log-burning stoves. Essentials are provided for a do-it-yourself breakfast (eggs, bread, homemade jams).

ⓘ Getting There & Away

Ōkārito is 10km northwest off SH6 between Franz Josef and Whataroa. There are no buses but Glacier Shuttles & Charters (p260) runs scheduled shuttles to and from Franz Josef ($30 return, two daily).

Whataroa

POP 288

Although it's not much to look at, Whataroa (www.whataroa.org) is a gateway to rare natural wonders. Strung out along the SH6, 30km northwest of Franz Josef, this nondescript village is the departure point for tours of NZ's only nesting site for the kōtuku (white heron). With wings as delicately pretty as a bridal veil, these rare birds hold a special significance for Māori, who treasure their feathers and use 'kōtuku' as a compliment describing seldom-seen guests.

White Heron Sanctuary Tours BIRDWATCHING
(📞03-753 4120; www.whiteherontours.co.nz; 64 Main Rd; adult/child $150/75; ⏱tours 9am, 11am, 1pm & 3pm Oct-Feb) 🐾 The sight of scores of rare kōtuku nesting, nuzzling and soaring over the water is sheer delight, whether you're a bird-watcher or along for the ride. The 2½-hour tour involves a gentle jetboat ride to Waitangiroto Nature Reserve and a short boardwalk to the viewing hide, where you're also likely to see royal spoonbills and little shags. Book ahead.

Alpine Fault Tours OUTDOORS
(📞03-753 4236; www.alpinefaulttours.co.nz; 70 Main Rd; adult/child $60/25; ⏱tours 1pm, or by arrangement) Stand astride two tectonic plates, marvelling at Mother Nature's might, on a two-hour fault-line tour. The experience is geared towards casual tourists as much as geology buffs: small groups take a 20-minute 4WD bus to an area 10km from Whataroa where the Australian and Zealandia plates meet. Engaging commentary discuses the forces that created the Southern Alps. Book ahead.

Glacier Country Scenic Flights SCENIC FLIGHTS
(📞0800 423 463; www.glacieradventures.co.nz; off Whataroa Hwy; 20-50min flights $235-535) Offers a range of scenic flights and helihikes, lifting off from near the Whataroa River bridge. These guys give you more mountain-gawping for your buck than many of the operators flying from the glacier townships, with optional snow landings.

ⓘ Getting There & Away

This stretch of SH6 is serviced once daily by InterCity (p254) buses heading to/from Fox Glacier ($28, 1¼ hours), Franz Josef ($28, 44 minutes), Ross ($28, 1½ hours), Hokitika ($30, two hours) and Greymouth ($38, 3½ hours).

THE WEST COAST'S GREAT RIDE

One of the 22 Great Rides that together form the Ngā Haerenga NZ Cycle Trail, the easy (Grade 2) 133km **West Coast Wilderness Trail** (www.westcoastwildernesstrail.co.nz) stretches from Ross to Greymouth via Hokitika and Kumara, following gold-rush tracks, reservoirs, old tramways and railway lines. The trail reveals dense rainforest, glacial rivers, lakes and wetlands, and views to the Southern Alps and wild Tasman Sea.

The trail can be ridden in either direction and is gently graded most of the way. Although the full shebang takes a good four days by bike, it can easily be sliced up into sections of various lengths, catering to every ability and area of interest. Novice riders can tackle the relatively flat *Ross Railway* section between Ross and Hokitika (33km, three to five hours). Another goodie is the 49km *Majestic Forests & Lake Ride* from the Kawhaka Intake to Hokitika via Lake Kaniere, which takes in major highlights over seven hours, or a 45km ride following Kumara's gold trails (four hours).

Bike hire, transport and advice are available from the major setting-off points. In Hokitika, contact **Cycle Journeys** (☑021 263 3299; www.cyclejourneys.co.nz; 23 Hamilton St; bike hire per day from $55, shuttles $20-55) or Hokitika Cycles & Sports World (p264), and in Greymouth, Trail Transport (p271).

Ross

POP 297

When folks sensed gold in these hills in the 1860s, the township of Ross was hurriedly established. From 1865 to 1914 it was the most productive alluvial goldfield in NZ, reaching giddy heights of fame in 1909 with the discovery of the 'Honourable Roddy' gold nugget, weighing in at nearly 3kg (check out the replica in the Goldfields Heritage Centre). At its peak it was home to 3000 people, 10 times the current population.

It's the start or finish point of the West Coast Wilderness Trail, but its gold-rush history also makes Ross an interesting diversion on drives between the glacier towns and Hokitika. A cluster of gold-rush-era buildings on St James St are open to the public, free of charge, including **St Patrick's Catholic Church** from 1866, an 1885 **cottage** and a 1915 **gaol**. A **Chinese-style garden** and picnic area by the lake acknowledges the contribution of Chinese miners.

The **Ross Water Race Walkway** (one hour return) starts near the mildly interesting **Goldfields Heritage Centre** (☑03-755 4077; 4 Aylmer St; $2; ☺10am-3pm), passing old gold diggings, caves, tunnels and a cemetery. Hire a gold pan ($10) from the centre and head to Jones Creek to look for Roddy's great, great grandnuggets. Gold is still found here; there are three active mines in the area.

★**Ross Beach Top 10**   HOLIDAY PARK $
(☑03-429 8277; www.rossbeachtop10.co.nz; 145 Ross Beach Rd; sites $45-55, dm $35, pods with/

without bathroom from $110/101; ⓅⓈⓀ) ✈
Perched on a ruggedly beautiful stretch of windswept beach, 2km northwest of Ross, this holiday park has plenty of space for tents and motorhomes, as well as a neat amenities block with a kitchen and laundry. We adore the converted shipping containers, upcycled into chic, self-contained 'pods'.

Historic Empire Hotel   PUB
(☑03-755 4005; 19 Aylmer St; ☺10am-late)
Nostalgia wafts from every brightly painted beam of the Empire. Since 1866, West Coasters have huddled inside the pub, amid yellowing photographs and dusty antiques, to spin yarns and swap gossip about whitebaiting locations. Breathe in the authenticity, along with a whiff of woodsmoke, over a pint and a bowl of chowder.

❶ Getting There & Away

One daily InterCity (p254) bus heads to/from Fox Glacier ($34, 2¼ hours), Franz Josef ($30, 1¾ hours), Whataroa ($28, 1½ hours), Hokitika ($28, 25 minutes) and Greymouth ($28, two hours).

Hokitika & Around

POP 2970

Hokitika is the archetypal West Coast town, positioned between a surf-battered beach and the snow-capped Southern Alps. Of the coast's three major towns (the others being Greymouth and Westport), Hokitika is by far the most appealing. There are some good places to eat, and a thriving community of local artisans selling their wares in shops scattered around the compact town centre. The town's artsy credentials have been buoyed further by its starring role in Eleanor Catton's 2013 book *The Luminaries*. There are just enough grand buildings from Hokitika's golden days dotted about to capture the imagination of fans of the Man Booker–winning novel, set during the 1860s gold rush.

Radiant sunsets and a glowworm dell add extra sparkle to this coastal idyll, though many visitors prefer to work up a sweat on the West Coast Wilderness Trail and the scenic tracks at lakes Kaniere and Māhinapua.

◉ Sights

Hokitika Gorge   GORGE
(www.doc.govt.nz; Whitcombe Valley Rd) Water this turquoise doesn't come easily. Half a million years of glacial movement sculpted Hokitika's ravine; the rock 'flour' ground over millennia intensifies the water's hue. The gorge is a scenic 32km drive south of Hokitika, well signposted from Stafford St (past the dairy factory). From the car park it's a 150m walk to a viewing platform, then a further 300m to a swing bridge and 200m to a point where you can access the river.

En route, you will pass a poignant monument in Kōwhitirangi, the site of one of NZ's deadliest mass murders (immortalised in the 1982 classic film *Bad Blood*). Visitors can peer towards the farmstead site through a shaft bored through the stone.

Lake Māhinapua   LAKE
(www.doc.govt.nz; Shanghai Rd, Ruatapu) Serene Lake Māhinapua lies 10km southwest of Hokitika, screened from SH6 by its surrounding forest. The scenic reserve, gazetted in 1907, has a picnic area and DOC campsite that bask in mountain views, and the shallow water is warm enough for a paddle. There are several short walks (an hour return or less) signposted along the shore.

The starting point of the **Mahinapua Walkway** is on SH6, 8km south of Hokitika. It's an easy four- to five-hour return walk (6km each way) following an old logging tramway to Woodstock Rimu Rd, with a short spur track connecting to the lake.

Lake Kaniere   LAKE
(www.doc.govt.nz; Lake Kaniere Rd) Lying at the heart of a 7000-hectare scenic reserve, 18km southeast of Hokitika, beautiful Lake

Kaniere is 8km long, 2km wide, up to 195m deep, and freezing cold (as you'll discover if you swim). You can camp or picnic at **Hans Bay**, peer at **Dorothy Falls** (4km south of the campground), or undertake one of numerous walks, ranging from the 15-minute **Canoe Cove Walk** to the seven-hour return gut-buster up **Mt Tuhua**.

The historic **Kaniere Water Race Walkway** (3½ hours one-way) forms part of the West Coast Wilderness Trail.

Note: the road from Hans Bay to Dorothy Falls is narrow and unsealed, and hence not suitable for motorhomes.

Glowworm Dell   NATURAL FEATURE
(Kumara Junction Hwy) At nightfall, bring a torch (or grope your way) into this grotto on the northern edge of town, signposted off SH6. The dell is an easy opportunity to glimpse legions of glowworms (aka fungus gnat larvae), which emit an other-worldly blue light. An information panel at the entrance will further illuminate your way.

Sunset Point   VIEWPOINT
(Gibson Quay) A visit to Sunset Point is a quintessential Hokitika experience: watch the day's light fade away, observe whitebaiters casting nets, munch fish and chips, or stroll around the quayside shipwreck memorial.

Hokitika Museum   MUSEUM
(📞03-755 6898; www.hokitikamuseum.co.nz; 17 Hamilton St; ⊙10am-5pm Nov-Mar, to 2pm Apr-Oct) **FREE** Housed in the gorgeous, recently strengthened Carnegie Building (1908), this museum has displays on greenstone, gold mining, history and whitebait fishing.

National Kiwi Centre   NATURE CENTRE
(📞03-755 5251; www.thenationalkiwicentre.co.nz; 64 Tancred St; adult/child $26/15; ⊙9am-5pm; 🐾) Tiptoe through the darkened kiwi house to watch the birds rummage for tasty insects, or stare a tuatara – a reptile unchanged for 150 million years – in its beady eyes. There's also a pond where you can catch-and-return crayfish and a large tank full of giant eels, the oldest of which is thought to be over 120 years old.

Time your visit for eel feeding time (10am, noon and 3pm) when you can hold out scraps of meat for these slithery critters to grab from a pair of tongs (or your bare hands, if you dare).

Hokitika

🏃 Activities

Hokitika is a great base for walking and cycling. Be sure to download DOC's *Walks in the Hokitika Area*, and visit **Hokitika Cycles & Sports World** (📞03-755 8662; www.hokitikasportsworld.co.nz; 33 Tancred St; bike rental per day $55; ⊙9am-5pm Mon-Sat Oct-Mar, 9am-5pm Mon-Fri, to 1pm Sat Apr-Sep) for bike rental, repairs and valuable advice on tracks, including the West Coast Wilderness Trail (p262).

Bonz 'N' Stonz   ARTS & CRAFTS

(📞03-755 6504; www.bonz-n-stonz.co.nz; 16 Hamilton St; carving per hour $35) Design, carve and polish your own *pounamu* (greenstone/jade, $190), bone ($100) or paua-shell ($100) masterpiece, with tutelage from Steve Gwaliasi. Bookings recommended, and 'laughter therapy' included in the price. There's also a good range of Steve's accomplished carvings to purchase.

West Coast
Treetop Walk   OUTDOORS

(📞03-755 5052; www.treetopsnz.com; 1128 Woodstock-Rimu Rd, Ruatapu; adult/child $32/16; ⊙9am-3.15pm) Visitors strolling along this wobbly but wheelchair-friendly steel walkway, 450m long and 20m off the ground, can enjoy an unusual perspective on the canopy of native trees (allow 45 minutes). The highlight is the 47m-high tower, from which views extend to the Southern Alps and the Tasman Sea. It's 17km south of Hokitika, near the southern shore of Lake Māhinapua

Festivals & Events

Driftwood & Sand
ART
(www.driftwoodandsand.co.nz; Hokitika Beach; ☷Jan) Free spirits and budding artists transform flotsam and jetsam into sculptures on Hokitika Beach during the five-day, volunteer-led Driftwood & Sand festival. Participants range from beginners to pros, and accordingly their creations span the full spectrum from enigmatic to delightfully daft.

Wildfoods
Festival
FOOD & DRINK
(www.wildfoods.co.nz; Cass Sq; entry $35; ☷Mar) Give your taste buds the equivalent of a defibrillator shock at this one-day festival of daredevil eating held in early March. Fish eyes, pigs' ears, lamb testicles and huhu grubs usually grace the wild menu. Don't worry though, there are lots of other food stands to expunge the lingering taste of blood casserole.

Sleeping

Shining Star
HOLIDAY PARK $$
(☏03-755 8921; www.accommodationwestcoast. co.nz; 16 Richards Dr; sites/units from $30/140; P☏♨) This attractive and versatile beachfront spot has everything from camping to log-lined cabins facing the sea. Kids will love the menagerie, including pigs and alpacas straight from Dr Doolittle's appointment book. Parents might prefer the spa or sauna.

Drifting Sands
B&B $$
(☏021 0266 5154; www.driftingsands.nz; 197 Revell St; r from $133; ☏) Natural tones and textures, upcycled furniture and hip vibes make this boutique beachside guesthouse a winner on style and location. Heightening the feel-good factor, there's a lounge warmed by a log burner and fresh bread every morning, plus bikes to borrow. Bathrooms are shared.

Birdsong
HOSTEL $$
(☏03-755 7179; www.birdsong.co.nz; 124 Kumara Junction Hwy, Seaview; dm $37, s/d without bathroom $83/98, r with bathroom $134; P☏)

Sigh at sea views from the shared lounge and kitchen of this adorable YHA-affiliated hostel, 2.5km northeast of the town centre. Rooms are themed around native bird life. Our only gripe is that bathrooms could be bigger (and with better privacy than saloon-style doors).

Teichelmann's B&B
B&B $$$
(☏03-755 8232; www.teichelmanns.nz; 20 Hamilton St; s/d/cottages $200/280/300; ☏) Once home to surgeon, mountaineer and professional beard-cultivator Ebenezer Teichelmann, this B&B holds on to its venerable history but adds first-rate hospitality and complimentary port. Its six rooms each have an airy, restorative ambience, replete with great beds, quality cotton sheets and private bathrooms; the best enjoy fern-filled garden views. For added privacy, request self-contained Teichy's Garden Cottage.

Stopforths
MOTEL $$$
(☏03-755 7625; www.stopforths.co.nz; 30 Hall St; units $180-340; P☏) Several steps up from your average motel, friendly well-run Stopforths offers spacious, modern units with kitchenettes and king-sized beds, ranging from studios to two-bedroom apartments. Some have spa baths and desks.

Eating

★Hokitika
Sandwich Company
SANDWICHES $
(☏03-429 2019; www.facebook.com/TheHokitika SandwichCompany; 83a Revell St; half/full sandwiches $9/18; ☷10am-2pm Tue-Sat) To say this hip place is serious about sandwiches is a huge understatement. Everything is made to order and served on chunky slices of freshly baked bread, generously loaded with the best locally sourced goodies: free-range meat, organic vegetables, South Island cheeses and its own in-house condiments. Grab a seat on one of the communal tables and tuck in. Smoothies are also on the menu.

★Stations Inn
BISTRO $$
(☏03-755 5499; www.stationsinnhokitika.co.nz; 11 Blue Spur Rd; mains $29-39; ☷6-10pm Tue-Sat) Attached to an out-of-the-way but upmarket motel-style complex 4km southeast of the town centre, this restaurant delivers the best bistro-style fare in Hokitika. Expect hearty serves of pork, lamb, salmon, vegetarian

THE WEST COAST HOKITIKA & AROUND

pasta and a delicious Middle Eastern–style chicken on couscous.

Stella Cafe & Cheesery   CAFE $$
(☑ 03-755 5432; www.facebook.com/StellaCafe Hokitika; 84 Revell St; mains $10-24; ☺ 8am-4pm; ☏) Kids will love peering through the glass at the beehive in this large deli-style cafe, while their parents occupy themselves in the separate cheese room. Breakfasts of tasty omelettes and strong coffee are followed with burgers and pasta at lunch, along with a good range of counter food.

🛍 Shopping

Hokitika has a buzzing arts and crafts scene centred on carving and polishing *pounamu* (greenstone/jade) into ornaments and jewellery. Be aware that some galleries sell jade imported from Europe and Asia, so ask before you buy. Along for the ride are woodworkers, textile weavers and glass-blowers, all represented at classy boutiques in the centre of town.

★ Waewae Pounamu   ARTS & CRAFTS
(☑ 03-755 8304; www.waewaepounamu.co.nz; 39 Weld St; ☺ 8.30am-6.30pm Nov-Mar, 8.30am-5pm Mon-Fri, 10am-4pm Sat & Sun Apr-Oct) Linked to Ngāti Waewae, a local *hapū* (subtribe) of the broader Ngāi Tahu tribe, this stronghold of *pounamu* carving displays traditional and contemporary designs in its main-road gallery-boutique. Watch the carvers at work before deciding on a piece to purchase.

Wilderness Gallery   ARTS & CRAFTS
(☑ 03-755 7575; www.wildernessgallery.co.nz; 29 Tancred St; ☺ 10.30am-1.30pm Tue-Sun, extended summer) Juergen Schacke's large-scale nature photography takes centre stage at this gallery/gift shop, which also sells an excellent range of NZ-made craft: woodwork, pottery and carved *pounamu*, in particular.

Hokitika Glass Studio   ARTS & CRAFTS
(☑ 03-755 7775; www.hokitikaglass.co.nz; 9 Weld St; ☺ 8.30am-4.30pm Mon-Fri, 10am-3pm Sat & Sun) Call in on weekdays to watch the blowers at work at the furnace producing glistening glass birds, multicoloured bowls and stemware. And yes, these fragile objects are secured in oodles of protective wrapping.

Tectonic Jade   ARTS & CRAFTS
(☑ 03-755 6644; www.tectonicjade.com; 67 Revell St; ☺ 9am-5pm Oct-Apr) If you like your greenstone art and jewellery with a side-

order of spirituality, the lustrous *pounamu* carved by local artist Rex Scott will leave you entranced.

Sweet Alice's Fudge Kitchen   FOOD
(☑ 027 858 0802; 27 Tancred St; ☺ 11.30am-4.30pm Wed-Mon) Treat yourself to a slice of Alice's handmade fudge, real fruit ice cream or a bag of boiled lollies – or maybe all three. A slice of fudge costs around $7.

ℹ Information

Hokitika i-SITE (☑ 03-755 6166; www.hokitikainfo.co.nz; 36 Weld St; ☺ 9am-5pm) Information and bookings, including buses and DOC passes. It also rents locator beacons.

Westland Medical Centre (☑ 03-755 8180; www.westlandmedical.co.nz; 54a Sewell St; ☺ 8am-4.45pm Mon-Fri) Call ahead for appointments, or use the after-hours phone service (24 hours). For urgent cases on weekends, use the walk-in service at 10am and 5pm.

ℹ Getting There & Away

AIR
Hokitika Airport (HKK; ☑ 03-756 8050; www.hokitikaairport.co.nz; Airport Dr) is on the town's eastern fringe and has the usual collection of rental-car counters. **Air New Zealand** (www.airnewzealand.com) has two flights most days to/from Christchurch.

BUS
InterCity (p254) has a daily service between Greymouth ($28, 55 minutes) and Fox Glacier ($40, 3¼ hours) via Ross ($28, 25 minutes), Whataroa ($30, two hours) and Franz Josef ($38, 2½ hours). All buses stop outside both the National Kiwi Centre and the i-SITE.

ℹ Getting Around

Hokitika Taxis (☑ 03-755 5075; www.facebook.com/hokitikataxis) Expect to pay $10 to $15 for a cab to/from the airport.

Kumara
POP 309

Once upon a time, folks piled into Kumara's two theatres, waltzing until dawn and roaring with delight at travelling circus acts that passed through this gold-rush town. But with the glittering 1880s long faded into memory, only a scattering of well-preserved historic buildings remains, spread along the road to Arthur's Pass. Thanks to local enthusiasm for Kumara's boom time, display pan-

THE POWER OF POUNAMU

Pounamu (greenstone, NZ jade) was the most treasured natural resource in traditional Māori society, valued for its strength, durability and beauty. With no metal tools or weapons it was one of the hardest materials available, and it could be honed to a fine edge. It is believed that the stone can absorb spiritual energy from the people handling it and can accumulate *mana* (prestige) over time. For this reason, always ask permission before touching anyone's personal *pounamu*.

Only found on the South Island (in Māori, Te Waipounamu, meaning Waters of Greenstone), the ownership of all naturally occurring *pounamu* resides with the Ngāi Tahu *iwi* (tribe). It is, however, legal to rummage around beaches and rivers for stones, limited to what an individual can carry on their person. The exception is Westland's Arahura River, which is owned in its entirety by Ngāi Tahu.

The West Coast has a thriving community of artists sourcing the stone and carving it into sculptures and jewellery, particularly in Hokitika and Greymouth. It's considered luckier to buy greenstone for others, rather than yourself, and a few recurring shapes carry distinctive meanings.

Koru Unfurling spiral reminiscent of a fern shoot, signifying creation and growth.

Toki A wedge shape harking to traditional Māori tools; a symbol of strength.

Pikorua Contemporary 'twist' design symbolising bonds between people.

Hei matau Stylised fish hook with various meanings: health, safe travel and prosperity.

For authentic products by Māori artisans, try Garth Wilson Jade (p270) or Waewae Pounamu (p266), a studio linked to the Ngāti Waewae subtribe of Poutini Ngāi Tahu.

Ngāi Tahu also own and operate Franz Josef Glacier Guides (p258) and Glacier Hot Pools (p257).

els around town tell stories of feisty figures from yesteryear.

In recent times Kumara's main claim to fame is as the starting point of the multisport **Coast to Coast race** (www.coasttocoast.co.nz). Held each February, the strong, the brave and the totally knackered run, cycle and kayak a total of 243km all the way from Kumara Beach across the mountains to Christchurch, with top competitors dusting it off in around 11 hours. Kumara's also a stop on the West Coast Wilderness Trail (p262) and a good base for day cycles.

Don't expect big-ticket attractions, but Kumara has a couple of ramble-worthy sights where you can stretch your legs. There's a **glowworm dell** in the bush behind the Theatre Royal's miners' cottages. Some 800m south of town, off the highway, you'll find a **historic swimming pool** from the 1930s; at 46m by 30m it was once New Zealand's largest, though little but overgrown walls remain today.

Keep an eye out for the **Kumara Chinese Miner Memorial Reserve**, an attractive new garden that was in the process of being laid out alongside the main road when we last visited.

★ **Theatre Royal Hotel**   PUB $$
(☑ 03-736 9277; www.theatreroyalhotel.co.nz; 81 Seddon St; r/cottages from $144/200; P ☜) Themed around colourful figures from Kumara's past, rooms at this beautifully restored 1876 pub are reason enough to stay in town. We especially loved the feminine flourishes of Barbara Weldon's room, honouring a former lady of the night. Motel-style miners' cottages (sleeping up to four) are new but have vintage finishes such as clawfoot tubs.

The opulence continues with two suites in the picturesque Bank of New Zealand building across the road. The Theatre Royal's downstairs bar is a good spot for a hearty meal and a yarn with the locals; with a bit of encouragement, one of them might thump out a tune on the piano.

❶ Getting There & Away

East West Coaches (p278) stop outside the Theatre Royal Hotel daily, en route between Westport ($40, 1¾ hours) and Christchurch ($55, 3¼ hours) via Punakaiki ($25, 1¼ hours), Greymouth ($20, 10 minutes) and Arthur's Pass ($50, 1¼ hours).

GREY DISTRICT

The smallest of the three districts that make up the West Coast, Grey struggles to shrug off the lacklustre promise of its name. Its largest town, Greymouth, is big on services but light on attractions, although it is the northern trailhead of the West Coast Wilderness Trail (p262). Inland, Lake Brunner is a soothing spot for fishing or bird-watching, and remote Blackball is firmly in hikers' and mountain bikers' sights as a gateway to new Great Walk, the Paparoa Track (p250).

Even by NZ's standards, the Grey District is a standout for friendliness; its down-to-earth folk might be reason enough to dawdle here before you travel on.

Greymouth

POP 9660

Greymouth (in Māori, Māwhera) is the largest town on the West Coast and what passes for the Big Smoke in these parts. For locals it's an administrative and shopping pit stop; for travellers it's a noteworthy portal to hiking and biking trails, and the somewhat anticlimactic terminus of one of the world's most scenic rail journeys.

Arriving on a dreary day, it's no mystery why Greymouth, crouched at the mouth of the Grey River, is sometimes the butt of jokes. But with gold-mining history, a scattering of *pounamu* (greenstone/jade) studios, and worthy walks in its surrounds, it pays to look beyond the grey.

◉ Sights

Left Bank Art Gallery GALLERY

(🖉03-768 0038; www.bankarts.com; 1 Tainui St; ⊙10am-4pm Tue-Fri, 11am-2pm Sat) **FREE** A wide community of West Coast artists is represented in this former bank, which displays contemporary NZ prints, paintings, photographs, jewellery and ceramics; much of it is for sale.

Monteith's Brewing Co BREWERY

(🖉03-768 4149; www.thebrewery.co.nz; 60 Herbert St; tour $28; ⊙11am-9pm) The original Monteith's brewhouse is the HQ for this nationally famous beer brand: glossy and a wee bit corporate, but it delivers a high-quality experience. Book ahead for a guided tour (45 minutes, including generous samples) or DIY in the industrial-chic tasting room and bar, complete with a roaring fire, outdoor seating and a kitchen serving pizza, burgers and steaks.

Shantytown MUSEUM

(🖉03-762 6634; www.shantytown.co.nz; Rutherglen Rd, Paroa; adult/child $34/17; ⊙8.30am-5pm; 👶) Good fun for kids and young-at-heart travellers, Shantytown is a recreated 1860s gold-mining town, 10km south of Greymouth. Peer inside a church, a tavern, a hospital and a Chinese encampment, all painstakingly crafted to evoke the spirit of the era. Take cheesy souvenir pics in period costume and try gold-panning ($7), but the highlight is a steam train ride into the bush (five to seven daily, last departure 4pm).

🏃 Activities

TranzAlpine RAIL

(🖉04-4950775; www.greatjourneysofnz.co.nz; one-way adult/child from $119/83) The *TranzAlpine* is one of the world's great train journeys. It traverses the Southern Alps between Christchurch and Greymouth, through Arthur's Pass National Park, from the Pacific Ocean to the Tasman Sea. Dramatic landscapes span its 223km length, from the flat, alluvial Canterbury Plains, through alpine gorges, an 8.5km tunnel, beech-forested valleys and a lake fringed with cabbage trees.

Floodwall Walk WALKING

(Mawhera Quay) Once subject to serious flooding, Greymouth hasn't experienced a deluge since the building of this floodwall, masterminded after a flood in 1988. Take a 10-minute riverside stroll along Mawhera Quay, the start of the West Coast Wilderness Trail (p262), or stretch your legs by pressing on for the full 50-minute route.

The walk takes in the fishing boat harbour, Blaketown Beach and the breakwater at the mouth of the Grey River – a great place to experience the power of the ocean and savour a West Coast sunset. On Mawhera Quay, look out for the memorial to those lost in coal-mining incidents, including the 29 men killed at Pike River Mine in 2010.

🛏 Sleeping

Global Village HOSTEL **$**

(🖉03-768 7272; www.globalvillagebackpackers.co.nz; 42 Cowper St; dm/r without bathroom from $32/78; P @ 🛰) This colourful hostel has African, Asian and Pacific art on its walls, and a passionate traveller vibe at its core. Borrow a kayak to explore the adjacent wetlands or a bike to pedal around town. Relaxation comes easily with a spa, a sauna, a barbecue and a firepit.

Greymouth

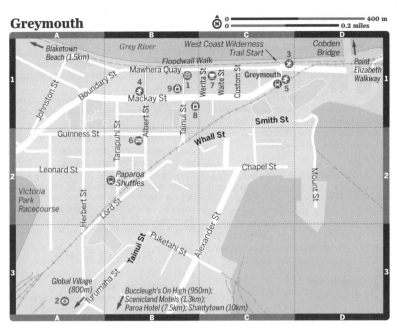

Greymouth

1 Left Bank Art Gallery B1
2 Monteith's Brewing Co A3

Activities, Courses & Tours
3 Floodwall Walk.......................................C1
4 Trail Transport..B1
5 TranzAlpine...C1

Sleeping
6 Duke B2

Drinking & Nightlife
7 DP1 Cafe C1

Shopping
8 Nimmo Gallery & Store B1
9 Shades of Jade.......................................B1

Information
Greymouth i-SITE ....(see 5)

Duke HOSTEL **$**
(☑03-768 9988; www.duke.co.nz; 27 Guinness St; dm $26, s/d without bathroom from $50/61, r with bathroom $85; ☎) The former Duke of Edinburgh Hotel dates to at least the 1870s, although we strongly suspect it wasn't painted purple and green then. New owners have been busily renovating the rooms, which circle a central light well upstairs. The best have sharp contemporary decor and en-suite bathrooms. Downstairs there's a huge kitchen and a guest lounge with a roaring fire.

Scenicland Motels MOTEL **$$**
(☑03-768 5100; www.sceniclandmotel.co.nz; 108-110 High St; units from $125; P※☎) The decor is simple-bordering-on-spartan but the units at this friendly motel are comfortable and well-kept. Opt for a studio with a kitchenette or a one- or two-bedroom unit with a full kitchen. Town's only a 20-minute walk away (or you can hire a bike if you'd prefer) and there's a very convenient supermarket next door.

Paroa Hotel MOTEL **$$**
(☑03-762 6860; www.paroa.co.nz; 508 Main South Rd, Paroa; units from $180; P☎) A family affair since 1954, the venerable Paroa has benefitted from a slick makeover. The sizeable motel-style units have kitchenettes and great beds, and share a garden. The warm service continues inside the noteworthy bar and restaurant. It's opposite the Shantytown turn-off, 8km south of Greymouth town centre.

✖ Eating & Drinking

Buccleugh's On High   BISTRO $$

(📞 03-768 5154; www.rechotel.co.nz; 68 High St; mains $25-37; 🕐 5.30-9pm) Out the back of the public bar of the Recreation Hotel, this bistro is Greymouth's best dining option – which isn't saying much. The menu offers what you'd expect from an upmarket pub (lamb shanks, steak, venison, roast/fish/pasta of the day), although the prices are a little higher than they should be.

DP1 Cafe   CAFE

(www.facebook.com/dp1cafe; 104 Mawhera Quay; 🕐 8am-5pm; 🛜) A stalwart of the Greymouth cafe scene, this quayside java joint is awash with local artwork. Hip clientele and friendly staff make it an excellent place to mingle while sipping the best espresso in town. The food is fairly standard but there are some options for vegetarians and vegans.

🛍 Shopping

Garth Wilson Jade   ARTS & CRAFTS

(📞 03-762 6226; www.garthwilsonjade.co.nz; 63 Rutherglen Rd, Paroa; 🕐 9am-5pm Mon-Fri or by appointment) *Whakapapa* (genealogy) links to two West Coast *hapū* (subtribes) give Garth the right to collect *pounamu* all along the coast, which he then carves in his home studio near Shantytown. Call in to watch him at work and to buy a truly authentic piece; he also takes commissions. Garth's an avid mountain biker,too; ask about local tracks.

Nimmo Gallery & Store   ARTS & CRAFTS

(📞 03-768 6499; www.nimmophoto.co.nz; 102 Mackay St; 🕐 9am-5pm Mon-Fri, 10am-2pm Sat & Sun) Ostensibly the gallery of local landscape photographer Stewart Nimmo, this stylish space overflows with cracking souvenirs (with more handicrafts and clothing sold in the courtyard out back). Honeyed beauty

products, postcards, *pounamu*, pottery, woodwork: it's got it all.

Shades of Jade   JEWELLERY

(📞 03-768 0794; www.shadesofjade.co.nz; 22 Tainui St; 🕐 9am-5pm Mon-Fri, 10am-2pm Sat & Sun) Browse *pounamu* jewellery – mainly in Māori-style designs but also crosses – all created from genuine West Coast greenstone.

ℹ Information

Grey Base Hospital (📞 03-769 7400; www.wcdhb.health.nz; 71 Water Walk Rd)

Greymouth i-SITE (📞 03-768 7080; www.westcoasttravel.co.nz; 164 Mackay St; 🕐 9am-5pm; 🛜) The helpful crew at the train station can assist with all manner of advice and bookings, including for DOC huts and transport connections. It also offers luggage storage.

ℹ Getting There & Away

BUS

All buses stop outside the train station.
➔ InterCity (p254) has daily buses north to Westport ($21, 2¼ hours) and Nelson ($48, six hours), and south to Hokitika ($28, 55 minutes), Franz Josef ($44, four hours) and Fox Glacier ($47, 4¾ hours).
➔ East West Coaches (p278) stop daily en route between Westport ($25, 1¼ hours) and Christchurch ($60, 3½ hours) via Punakaiki ($20, 45 minutes), Kumara ($20, 10 minutes) and Arthur's Pass ($40, 1½ hours).
➔ **Atomic Travel** (📞 021 0867 6001; www.atomictravel.co.nz) runs daily shuttle buses to/from Christchurch ($55, 3¾ hours) via Moana ($40, 25 minutes), Arthur's Pass ($40, 1½ hours) and Springfield ($50, 2½ hours).
➔ **Paparoa Shuttles** (📞 021 286 2233; www.paparoashuttles.co.nz; cnr Tarapuhi St & Sheilds Ln) offers timetabled transfers to Blackball ($20, 30 minutes, three daily), Paparoa Track's Smoke-ho trailhead ($30, 1½ hours, daily), Barrytown ($40, 40 minutes,

---

WHITEBAIT FEVER

If you visit the West Coast between September and mid-November, you're sure to catch a whiff of whitebait fever. The West Coast is gripped by an annual craze for tiny, transparent fish, and netting buckets of whitebait is an all-consuming, highly competitive passion.

In season you'll see whitebait sold from back doors and served in cafes and restaurants. They mostly surface in a pattie, made best with just an egg, and accompanied by a wedge of lemon or perhaps mint sauce. We've seen them topping pizzas and salads, too.

Whitebait are the young of native fish, including inanga, kokopu, smelt and eels. Conservationists say they shouldn't be eaten at all, with some species threatened or in decline. DOC applies stiff penalties for anyone breaching their rules on whitebaiting season and the size of nets, and they urge locals to keep their catch small.

two daily) and Punakaiki ($50, one hour, two daily); bikes cost $10 extra. **Trail Transport** (☑ 03-768 4060; www.trailtransport.co.nz; 53 Mackay St; bike hire per day from $50, shuttle transport $28-65) covers the same route, but on demand.

TRAIN

The TranzAlpine (p268) train takes a highly scenic route to/from Christchurch (from $119, 4½ hours) daily, via Moana (from $79, one hour), Arthur's Pass (from $139, 2¼ hours) and Springfield (from $119, 3½ hours).

❶ Getting Around

Greymouth Taxis (☑ 03-768 7078) A taxi to Shantytown will cost you around $35 (one-way).

Lake Brunner

Expect your pulse to slow almost as soon as you arrive at Lake Brunner. Named for England-born explorer Thomas Brunner (not the German footballer), this 40 sq km expanse of sapphire water lies 35km southeast of Greymouth. The lake is large but its main settlement **Moana** (population 270), on the northern shore, is minuscule. Nonetheless it brims with accommodation options to suit the families and trout-fishing enthusiasts drawn to this sedate spot.

Brunner is a scenic place to idle away a day or two strolling lakeside tracks, fishing or bird-watching. Book ahead in summer (and note that it's whisper-quiet in winter).

Brunner is a tranquil spot for bush walks, bird-spotting and water sports, including boating and fishing. Indeed, the local boast is that the lake and Arnold River are 'where the trout die of old age', which suggests that this is a good spot to dangle a line. Greymouth i-SITE can hook you up with a guide.

Lake Brunner Country Motel HOLIDAY PARK $$
(☑ 03-738 0144; www.lakebrunnermotel.co.nz; 2014 Arnold Valley Rd; sites $20-45, units with/without bathroom from $148/77; ❐@🔊) Birdsong, flower beds and 2.4 hectares of greenery... feeling relaxed yet? At this motel and campground, 2km from Lake Brunner, choose from powered and unpowered tent sites, and simple cabins, all of which share bathrooms and kitchen facilities. More plush are the self-contained cottages, complete with floral trimmings and nice bathrooms.

Stationhouse Cafe CAFE $$
(☑ 03-738 0158; www.lakebrunner.net; 40 Koe St, Moana; mains $17-23; ⊙ 10.30am-8.30pm Mon-Sat, 9am-10pm Sun) It's one of the only shows in town, but luckily the Stationhouse (built 1901) is a winner. The cafe serves fruit smoothies, good coffee, excellent eggs Benedict, savoury muffins and indulgent baked goods, along with a sizeable menu of main courses. In good weather, grab a spot on the deck for views of the water and Mt Alexander.

❶ Getting There & Away

Atomic Travel shuttle buses stop in Moana daily, en route between Greymouth ($40, 25 minutes) and Christchurch ($55, 3¼ hours) via Arthur's Pass ($40, one hour) and Springfield ($50, 2¼ hours).

The TranzAlpine (p268) train pulls into Moana train station daily on its journey from Christchurch (from $119, 3½ hours) to Greymouth (from $79, one hour) and back, via Arthur's Pass (from $139, 1½ hours) and Springfield (from $119, 2½ hours).

Blackball

POP 291

Ramshackle Blackball is a shadow of its mining glory days, but this spirited town offers more than meets the eye. Around 23km upriver of Greymouth, Blackball was established in 1866 to service gold diggers, before coal mining kicked off in 1890. The town is often trumpeted as the birthplace of the NZ Labour movement, after a successful miners' strike in 1908 led to the formation of a national Federation of Labour. It's been something of a low-key pilgrimage site for Labour supporters and politicians ever since.

When its coal mine closed in 1964, Blackball had a population of 1580 people. With most mining families forced out, the town was kept alive by the arrival of a small community of hippies, attracted by the cheap housing and lush natural setting.

The Paparoa Track (p250) – newly inscribed as a Great Walk – is a 55km hiking and mountain-biking trail through Paparoa National Park that starts at the Smoke-ho car park, 6km north of town.

At the time of research Blackball was gearing up for the opening of the Paparoa Track and the influx of hikers and mountain bikers expected to follow, but accommodation remained limited. Blackball Salami Co (p272) was in the process of installing modern shipping-container sized en-suite units in a field out the back. Formerly the Blackball Hilton offers simple, shared-bathroom pub rooms.

Formerly the
Blackball Hilton   HISTORIC BUILDING
(☑03-732 4705; www.blackballhilton.co.nz; 26 Hart St; ⊘midday-late, from 2.30pm Mon & Tue outside summer) Blackball's major talking point is this century-old pub, once known as the Dominion. When it was renamed in the 1990s, a certain global hotel chain got antsy – hence the addition of 'formerly' to its name. These days it's something of a shrine to the Labour movement, proudly bedecked in old trade-union banners, posters and portraits of significant politicians. Call in for a beer or pub meal and take some time to peruse the walls.

Blackball Museum of Working
Class History (Mahi Tūpuna)   MUSEUM
(☑03-732 4010; www.blackballmuseum.org.nz; 26 Hart St; ⊘24hr) FREE Consisting of outdoor displays and a couple of shipping containers, this appropriately humble 'museum' tells the fascinating story of how Blackball came to be so important to the story of workers' rights in NZ. Look out for the Workers' Memorial Wheel dedicated to people killed in their workplaces since 1990, with a special focus on the 29 men who died at nearby Pike River Mine in 2010.

Blackball Salami Company Ltd   FOOD
(☑03-732 4111; www.blackballsalami.co.nz; 11 Hilton St; ⊘8am-4pm Mon-Fri, 9am-2pm Sat) Take time to sample Blackball's namesake salami, beloved up and down the West Coast. The garlic and peppercorn varieties have a kick, the venison version is rich and distinctive, but we like the fattier 'Italian-style' cut. Also available from this humble shop are bacon, black pudding, cheeses and sausages.

❶ Getting There & Away

There's no bus service, but Paparoa Shuttles (p270) runs two or three timetabled transfers per day to Blackball from Greymouth ($20, 30 minutes), Barrytown ($50, 1¼ hours) and Punakaiki ($60, 1½ hours), which continue on to the Paparoa Track trailhead (add $10); bikes cost $10 extra.

Trail Transport (p271) offers on-demand shuttles to the trailhead from Greymouth (per person $60, minimum $140) and Punakaiki (per person $70, minimum $200); prices include bikes.

Runanga, Rapahoe & Barrytown
POP 1480

The southernmost stretch of the Great Coast Road, between Greymouth and Punakaiki, carves a path between rocky bays and the steep, bushy Paparoa Ranges. First you'll pass through tiny Runanga before hitting the coast at blink-and-you'll-miss-it Rapahoe, with its friendly local pub. Aside from some excellent walks, there's not much to do except to pull up along the coast and take in the expansive views.

Craggy islets strike dramatic poses off each headland as you head towards sleepy, sparsely populated Barrytown, where the mountains take a half step back from the sea allowing for a thin stretch of farmland. Barrytown is the western trailhead of the **Croesus Track**, an old mining trail that connects to the Paparoa Track (p250).

🏃 Activities

Coal Creek Track   WALKING
(www.doc.govt.nz; Ballance St, Runanga) This 30-minute (each way) walk through mixed beech-podocarp forest leads to a broad waterfall tumbling into a swimmable basin.

Point Elizabeth
Walkway   WALKING
(www.doc.govt.nz; North Beach Rd, Cobden) Starting in Cobden, 6km north of Greymouth, this enjoyable coastal track (three hours return) skirts around a richly forested headland in the shadow of the Rapahoe Range to an impressive ocean lookout, before continuing on to the northern trailhead at Rapahoe. If you want a shorter walk, it's 45 minutes to the ocean lookout (one-way).

Barrytown
Knifemaking   ARTS & CRAFTS
(☑03-731 1053; www.barrytownknifemaking.com; 2662 Coast Rd, Barrytown; classes $170) Fashion your own knife on a day-long course under the expert tutelage of Steve and Robyn. You'll hand-forge the steel blade and craft its handle from native rimu timber. Bonuses include axe-throwing, a big swing, and a stream of entertainingly bad jokes from Steve. Courses begin with an enthusiastic greeting from the dog and include a sandwich lunch. Bookings essential.

🛏️ Sleeping

Breakers   B&B $$$

(📞03-762 7743; www.breakers.co.nz; 1367 Coast Rd, Nine Mile Creek; r $285-405; 🅿️🛜) 🏄 Crafted to tug at the heart strings of surfers, every room at Breakers has a view and easy access to the shore. Tucked into a hillside nook 3km north of Rapahoe, all four units are tasteful and modern, with decks for sighing over the sunset. Knowledgeable hosts are on hand for surf tips.

ℹ️ Getting There & Away

➡ InterCity (p254) services ply this leg of the Great Coast Road once a day on their way between Greymouth ($10, 30 minutes) and Nelson ($45, 5¼ hours), via Punakaiki ($10, 20 minutes), Westport ($17, two hours) and Murchison ($29, 3½ hours).

➡ East West Coaches (p278) stop daily en route between Westport ($20, 40 minutes) and Christchurch ($70, 4¼ hours), via Greymouth ($20, 20 minutes).

➡ Paparoa Shuttles (p270) offers two daily time-tabled transfers to Barrytown from Punakaiki ($30, 20 minutes), Greymouth ($40, 40 minutes), Blackball ($50, 1½ hours) and the Paparoa Track's Smoke-ho trailhead ($70, two hours).

BULLER REGION

Forest and coast unite in dramatic form in the Buller Region. This northwesterly expanse of the South Island is a promised land for hikers. Riverside trails wend their way through primeval forest, accessing geological marvels like the Ōpārara Arch and Punakaiki's Pancake Rocks.

Gold was found in the Buller River in the mid-19th century, and coal mining scorched the landscape soon after. Mining history is carefully conserved in main towns Westport and Reefton, though agriculture and tourism are the Buller Region's prime moneymakers today. Mining history makes a pleasant diversion if you need a breather from muddy trails, white-water rafting and kayaking tannin-stained waterways.

Punakaiki & Paparoa National Park

Located midway between Westport and Greymouth is Punakaiki, a small settlement on the edge of rugged 430-sq-km Paparoa National Park. Most visitors come for a quick squiz at the Pancake Rocks, layers of limestone that resemble stacked crepes. But these are just one feature of the impressive, boulder-sprinkled shoreline. Pebble beaches (keep an eye out for greenstone/jade) are kissed by spectacular sunsets, and there are some riveting walking and mountain-biking trails into the national park, most notably the Paparoa Track, which became an official Great Walk in December 2019.

Paparoa National Park is blessed with high cliffs and empty beaches, a dramatic mountain range, crazy limestone river valleys, diverse flora and a profusion of bird life, including weka (native woodhens) and the Westland petrel, a rare sea bird that nests only here.

👁️ Sights & Activities

The Paparoa National Park Visitor Centre (p274) has free maps detailing hikes in the area, including the Paparoa Track (p250). Note that many of Paparoa's inland walks are susceptible to river flooding, so it is vital that you obtain updates from the centre before you depart, and always heed warning signs and roped-off trails.

Shorter walks include the wonderful **Truman Track** (1.4km, 30 minutes return), which leads through native bush to an isolated beach. It's well signposted from the highway, 1.5km north of the township.

For a taste of the Great Walk, take the **Punakaiki–Pororari Loop** (11km, three hours), which follows the **Pororari River Track** (a section of the Paparoa Track) along a spectacular Jurassic-looking limestone gorge lined with nikau palms. It then joins the **Inland Pack Track**, pops over a hill and heads back down the bouldery Punakaiki River; the last section is along the highway.

⭐**Pancake Rocks**   NATURAL FEATURE

(www.doc.govt.nz; SH6) Punakaiki's claim to fame is Dolomite Point, where a layering-weathering process called stylobedding has carved the limestone into what looks like piles of thick pancakes. Aim for high tide (tide timetables are posted at the visitor centre) when, if the swell and wind are cooperating, the sea surges into caverns and booms menacingly through blowholes. See it on a wild day and be reminded that nature really is the boss.

Allow 20 minutes for the straightforward walk, which loops from the highway out to the rocks and blowholes (or 40 minutes if

THE WEST COAST PUNAKAIKI & PAPAROA NATIONAL PARK

DON'T MISS

THE GREAT COAST ROAD

One hundred kilometres of salty vistas line the road between Westport and Greymouth. One of New Zealand's most beautiful drives, the Great Coast Road meanders past foaming surf and shingle beaches on one side, and forbidding, overhanging cliffs on the other. The best-known stop along this inspiring stretch of SH6 is Punakaiki's geologically fascinating Pancake Rocks (p273). But there are numerous wind-whipped lookouts where you can pull over to gaze at waves smashing against haggard turrets of stone. Fill up in Westport or Greymouth if you're low on petrol or cash.

you want to take photos). Parts of the trail are suitable for wheelchairs.

Punakaiki Horse Treks   HORSE RIDING
(☑03-731 1839; www.pancake-rocks.co.nz; 4224 SH6; 2½hr ride $200; ☺mid-Oct–early May) Trek through the beautiful Punakaiki Valley right onto the beach on these guided tours, suitable for all experience levels. Private rides start at $250 (minimum two people).

🛏 Sleeping

Te Nikau Retreat   HOSTEL $
(☑03-731 1111; www.tenikauretreat.co.nz; 19 Hartmount Pl; dm $32, s/d without bathroom from $50/85, r with bathroom $110, cottages $65-220; ⓟ☎) 🌿 Checking in to Te Nikau feels instantly restorative. Kindly staff establish a relaxing tone, and there are charming wooden cottages tucked into the rainforest, a short walk from the beach. Our favourite is tiny Stargazer: it's little more than a double bed in a low hut, but glass roof panels allow you to count constellations on clear nights.

Punakaiki Beach Hostel   HOSTEL $
(☑03-731 1852; www.punakaikibeachhostel.co.nz; 4 Webb St; sites/dm/d without bathroom $22/34/89; ☎) The ambience is laid-back but Punakaiki Beach is efficiently run. This spick-and-span hostel has all the amenities a traveller could need, from laundry and a shared kitchen to staff who smile because they mean it. Comfy dorm rooms aside, the en-suite house truck is the most novel stay, but cutesy Sunset Cottage is also worth a splurge (both $150).

Punakaiki Beachfront Motels   MOTEL $$
(☑03-731 1008; www.punakaikibeachfrontmotels. co.nz; Mabel St; units from $180; ☎) Six basic motel units are sandwiched between cliff and sea, with private access to a wind-blown pebble beach. Larger groups (up to nine) can rent a two-storey, four-bedroom house, or a two-bedroom 'kiwi bach' (old-fashioned holiday home). The setting feels pleasingly remote, but it's only 900m north of the visitor centre.

Hydrangea Cottages   COTTAGE $$$
(☑03-731 1839; www.pancake-rocks.co.nz; 4224 SH6; cottages $145-485; ⓟ☎) On a hillside overlooking the Tasman Sea, this set of stand-alone and mostly self-contained cottages is built from salvaged timber and stone. At the top of the price range is a chic self-contained cottage that sleeps up to 12 people; at the other end, the rustic Stables Hut is aimed at budget travellers. Occasional quirks like outdoor bathtubs add to the charm.

ⓘ Information

Paparoa National Park Visitor Centre (☑03-731 1895; www.doc.govt.nz; 4294 SH6; ☺9am-5pm) Across the road from the Pancake Rocks walkway, the visitor centre has information on the national park – including track conditions and tide times – and sells hut tickets.

Punakaiki Promotions (www.punakaiki.co.nz) Online directory of accommodation, activities and tide times.

ⓘ Getting There & Away

➡ InterCity (p254) services stop here for 45 minutes (long enough to admire the Pancake Rocks) en route between Greymouth ($11, 40 minutes) and Nelson ($44, 4¼ hours), via Barrytown ($10, 20 minutes), Westport ($16, 49 minutes) and Murchison ($28, 2¼ hours).

➡ East West Coaches (p278) stop daily en route between Westport ($20, 30 minutes) and Christchurch ($70, 4½ hours), via Greymouth ($20, 45 minutes) and Arthur's Pass ($40, 2½ hours).

➡ Paparoa Shuttles (p270) offers two daily timetabled transfers to Punakaiki from Barrytown ($30, 20 minutes), Greymouth ($50, one hour), Blackball ($60, 1½ hours) and the Paparoa Track's Smoke-ho trailhead ($80, 2¼ hours); bikes cost $10 extra.

➡ Trail Transport (p271) offers on-demand shuttles from Greymouth (per person $70, minimum $180) and the Smoke-ho trailhead (per person $70, minimum $200); prices include bikes.

Charleston & Around

POP 342

Heading north from Punakaiki the Great Coast Road continues to enthral, passing a series of dramatic bays and headlands; stop at one of the designated viewpoints to admire them safely. Just before it leaves the coast to cut across country to Westport, the highway passes through Charleston, an 1860s gold-rush boom town that once boasted 80 hotels, three breweries and thousands of thirsty gold-diggers staking claims along the Nile River. There's not much left now except a motel, a camping ground, a clutch of local houses, and a whole lot of tall tales.

Mitchells Gully Goldmine   MINE

(☑03-789 6257; www.mitchellsgullygoldmine.co. nz; SH6; adult/child $10/free; ☺9am-4pm) For a true taste of the region's gold-mining past, swing into this former mine, 3km north of Charleston. You'll get a friendly primer on the 1860s mining days and then be left to explore mining tunnels and railway tracks on a short bush walk, goggling at Charleston's last remaining waterwheel and stamping battery along the way. If you're staying in the area, reserve a spot on a night-time glowworm tour (adult/child $25/5).

Underworld Adventures   CAVING

(☑03-788 8168; www.caverafting.com; SH6) Glow with the flow on black-water rafting trips deep into the glowworm-filled **Nile River Caves** (adult/child $190/150, four hours). This friendly operator also runs cave excursions without rafting (adult/child $125/90). Short on time? Take the rainforest train ride (adult/child $25/20), a 1½-hour return journey departing two or three times daily. The Adventure Caving trip ($375, five hours) includes a 40m abseil into Te Tahi cave system, with rock squeezes, waterfalls, fossils and trippy cave formations.

Kids aged 10 and over can raft, while the cave tours suit anyone who can walk on slippery surfaces for a couple of hours.

Beaconstone Eco Lodge   LODGE $

(☑027 448 9007; www.beaconstoneecolodge.com; 115 Birds Ferry Rd; s/d without bathroom from $70/100; ☎) 🖉 Set in 42 serene hectares, 10km north of Charleston, this solar-powered, energy-efficient lodge is both eco- and guest-friendly. Fashioned from sustainably sourced native timber and featuring comfy beds and a laid-back communal area, the lodge's style is Americana cool meets West Coast charm. Bush walks start at the doorstep.

ⓘ Getting There & Away

➧ InterCity (p254) buses stop here en route between Greymouth ($19, two hours) and Nelson ($35, 3½ hours), via Punakaiki ($16, 30 minutes), Westport ($12, nine minutes) and Murchison ($19, two hours).

➧ East West Coaches (p278) stop daily en route between Westport ($10, 10 minutes) and Christchurch ($70, 4¾ hours), via Punakaiki ($20, 20 minutes), Greymouth ($25, 50 minutes) and Arthur's Pass ($50, 2¾ hours).

Westport & Around

POP 4040

The 'capital' of Buller District, Westport's fortunes have historically waxed and waned with the coal mining industry, but fishing, dairy farming and, increasingly, tourism are rapidly taking its place. Chief among the town's natural attractions are the long, sandy beaches on either side of the Buller River – Carters Beach and North Beach – and the craggy, seal- and seabird-populated headland of Cape Foulwind.

It would be a stretch to accuse Westport of being exciting, but it does have respectable visitor services and makes a good base for exploring the fascinating coast north to Denniston, Charming Creek, Karamea and Kahurangi National Park. It's also an increasingly popular surfing destination, with good breaks south of Cape Foulwind at Tauranga Bay and Nine Mile Beach.

⊙ Sights

The most interesting sights are beyond Westport's urban limits, particularly heading north on SH67, which passes **Granity**, **Ngakawau** (home to the well-named Charming Creek) and **Hector**, where there's a monument to Hector's dolphins, NZ's smallest, although you'll be lucky to see them unless your timing is impeccable. It's also worth taking a look at **Seddonville**, a small bush town on the Mokihinui River that's the northern trailhead for the thrilling Old Ghost Road (p251).

Coaltown Museum   MUSEUM

(☑03-789 6658; www.coaltown.co.nz; 123 Palmerston St; adult/child $10/2; ☺9am-4.30pm) Westport's 'black gold' is paid homage at this remarkably interesting museum, adjoining the i-SITE. A replica mine, well-scripted

Westport

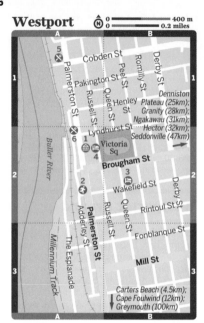

Denniston
Plateau (25km);
Granity (28km);
Ngakawau (31km);
Hector (32km);
Seddonville (47km)

Carters Beach (4.5km);
Cape Foulwind (12km);
Greymouth (100km)

Westport

display panels and an excellent selection of photographs and pioneer ephemera allow for an informative trip into the coal-blackened past. Best of all are the Denniston displays, including a whopping brake drum and panels explaining the daily tribulations of miners.

Denniston Plateau   HISTORIC SITE
(www.doc.govt.nz; Denniston Rd) FREE Six hundred metres above sea level, Denniston was once NZ's largest coal town, with 1500 residents in 1911. By 1981 there were eight. Its

claim to fame was the fantastically steep Denniston Incline, which hurtled laden wagons down a 45-degree hillside. Display panels bring the plateau's history to life and trails provide sweeping views and a direct route into the past. The turn-off to Denniston is 16km east of Westport at Waimangaroa; Denniston is a further eight winding kilometres inland.

🏃 Activities

There are some good walking and cycling trails in and around town. The **Millennium Track** (1km, 15 minutes) starts near the Buller Bridge and heads through bush alongside the river to the town centre. This is the first part of the **Kawatiri River Trail**, which continues, partly on road and then via boardwalks, up to North Beach and the mountain-biking trails through **Kawatiri Beach Reserve**.

Cape Foulwind Walkway   WALKING
(www.doc.govt.nz; Lighthouse Rd, Omau) Screaming gulls and crashing waves are the soundtrack to hikes around Cape Foulwind (one hour each way), as wind-battered a walk as its name promises. The trail traverses the coastal cliffs between Omau and Tauranga Bay, passing a **lighthouse**, mounted **astrolabe** (navigational instrument) and, near the southern end, a **seal colony**.

The seal colony is only a 15-minute walk along the cliffs from the southern trailhead at **Tauranga Bay**, a popular surfing beach. Depending on the season, up to 200 fur seals loll on the rocks below the track; binoculars are set up at the designated viewpoint to help you spot them. Nearby, another set of binoculars is trained on craggy **Wall Island**, an important nesting site for sea birds.

Abel Tasman was the first European to sight the Cape, in 1642, naming it Clyppygen Hoeck (Rocky Point). However, his name was supplanted by James Cook in 1770, who clearly found the Cape less than pleasing. From Westport, it's 12km to the parking area for the northern trailhead or 16km to the southern trailhead; both are well signposted.

Charming Creek Walkway   WALKING
(www.doc.govt.nz; Tyler Rd, Ngakawau) Starting from either Ngakawau (30km north of Westport), or near Seddonville, a few kilometres further on, this is one of the best day walks on the coast, taking around three hours each way (9.5km). It's also open to bikes.

Following an old coal line through the Ngakawau Gorge, the walkway passes tunnels, a suspension bridge, a waterfall, rusty relics galore, and lots of interesting plants and geological formations.

Habitat Sports CYCLING
(☑03-788 8002; www.habitatsports.co.nz; 234 Palmerston St; bike rental from $35; ⊙9am-5pm Mon-Fri, 9am-1pm Sat) As well as bike rental, repairs, maps and plentiful advice, this Westport sports shop offers transport to various track trailheads including Denniston ($35), Ngakawau ($40), Seddonville ($45), Lyell ($50) and Kōhaihai ($90); prices include bikes and are per person, with a minimum of two. It also offers a car relocation service ($200).

🛏 Sleeping

🛏 Westport

★**Bazil's Hostel & Surf School** HOSTEL $
(☑03-789 6410; www.bazils.com; 54 Russell St; dm $32, r with/without bathroom $110/78; ℙ﹖) Mural-painted Bazil's has well-maintained dorm and private rooms (some with kitchenettes, en-suite bathrooms and mezzanine bedrooms) in a sociable setting. It's managed by worldly types who offer surfing lessons (free if you stay for five nights), stand-up paddleboarding (SUP) trips, and social activities aplenty.

Archer House B&B $$$
(☑03-789 8778; www.archerhouse.co.nz; 75 Queen St; r $245; ﹖) This beautiful house, built in 1890 and formerly the home of a goldfields trader, has original features galore. There are three individually decorated rooms with private bathrooms, and three tastefully attired lounges in which to swirl a glass of complimentary wine while admiring the stained glass, tiled fireplaces and flourishing garden. A generous continental breakfast rounds out the experience.

🛏 Surrounds

Old Slaughterhouse HOSTEL $
(☑027 529 7640; www.oldslaughterhouse.co.nz; SH67, Hector; sites/dm/r without bathroom $22/40/95; ⊙Oct-Jun; ℙ﹖) 🌿 Perched on a hillside 32km northeast of Westport, this lodge offers epic views over the Tasman Sea. Powered largely by a waterwheel, the central lodge has a roomy lounge, shared kitchen,

reading nooks and a deck; wi fi is limited. A steep, 10-minute walk from the car park bolsters its off-the-grid charm.

Carters Beach Top 10 HOLIDAY PARK $
(☑03-789 8002; www.top10westport.co.nz; 57 Marine Pde, Carters Beach; sites from $40, units with/without bathroom from $119/71; ℙ﹖🐾) Right on Carters Beach, 5km from Westport, this tidy complex has pleasant sites as well as comfortable cabins and motel units. It's a good option for tourers seeking a peaceful stop-off with a swim (or on foul-weather days, a games room and playground to distract the kids).

★**Omau Settlers Lodge** MOTEL $$
(☑03-789 5200; www.omausettlerslodge.co.nz; 2 Omau Rd, Cape Foulwind; units $175-195; ℙ﹖) Relaxation is the mantra at this faultless motel near Cape Foulwind. Beds are plump, bathrooms are glossy and fragrant, plus there's a hot tub surrounded by bush. Chatty hosts Karen and Lee offer superb service, and lay out a satisfying free continental breakfast. Ask nicely and you might get a lift to the end of Cape Foulwind Walkway.

Rough & Tumble Lodge LODGE $$$
(☑03-782 1337; www.roughandtumble.co.nz; Mokihinui Rd, Seddonville; r $240; ﹖) 🌿 With invigorating views of river and bush, this luxe lodge sits in splendid isolation at the northern end of the Old Ghost Road. Its five split-level quad rooms have silver-birch banisters, posh bathrooms and verdant views. An onsite cafe provides meals and brews in the warmer months. Bonus: profits are poured back into the maintenance of the walking track.

🍴 Eating

PortSide Bistro & Bar BISTRO $$
(☑03-789 7133; www.portsidebistro.co.nz; 13 Cobden St; brunch $17-28, dinner $25-37; ⊙11am-late Tue-Fri, 9am-late Sat, 9am-3pm Sun; ﹖) Way up at the northern end of the main Palmerston St strip, this smart bistro serves cooked breakfasts on the weekends, along with the usual pubby bistro classics at lunch and dinner (burgers, steaks, market fish, pasta etc). Otherwise, just drop in for a beer on the deck.

PR's Cafe CAFE $$
(☑03-789 7779; www.facebook.com/PrsCafe; 124 Palmerston St; mains $7-23; ⊙7am-4.30pm Mon-Fri, to 3pm Sat & Sun, closed Mon winter; ﹖) Westport's most popular cafe has a cabinet full

of sandwiches and pastries, and a counter groaning under the weight of cakes and cookies. An all-day menu delivers the likes of salmon omelettes, fish and chips, pies, quiches and burgers.

Star Tavern   PUB FOOD $$
(📞 03-789 6923; www.facebook.com/TheStarTaven; 6 Lighthouse Rd, Cape Foulwind; meals $8-33; ⊗4-8.30pm Mon-Fri, noon-8.30pm Sat & Sun) Refuel after tackling the Cape Foulwind Walkway at this convivial rural pub. Options include lamb shanks, fish and chips, sizeable steaks doused with garlic butter, burgers and, that West Coast speciality, whitebait fritters.

ℹ Information

Buller Hospital (📞 03-788 9030; www.wcdhb. health.nz; Cobden St; ⊗24hr)
Westport i-SITE (📞 03-789 6658; www. coaltown.co.nz; 123 Palmerston St; ⊗9am-4.30pm; 🛜) Information on local tracks, tours, accommodation and transport. Self-help terminal for DOC information, hut and track bookings, and fishing licences.

ℹ Getting There & Away

AIR

Westport Airport is near the mouth of the Buller River, on the opposite side from town; a **taxi** (📞 03-789 6900; www.facebook.com/west portshuttles) costs around $25. **Sounds Air** (📞 03-520 3080; www.soundsair.com; adult/ child from $199/179) has one to six flights daily to/from Wellington (50 minutes).

BUS

➡ InterCity (p254) buses stop outside the i-SITE daily en route between Nelson ($36, 3½ hours) and Greymouth ($21, 2¼ hours) via Murchison ($19, 1½ hours), Charleston ($12, nine minutes) and Punakaiki ($16, 49 minutes).

➡ **East West Coaches** (📞 0800 142 622; www.eastwestcoaches.co.nz) has services to/ from Reefton ($25, 50 minutes, most days), Punakaiki ($20, 30 minutes, daily), Greymouth ($25, 1¼ hours, daily), Kumara ($40, 1¾ hours, daily) and Christchurch ($70, 3½ hours, two most days).

➡ Karamea Express (p280) heads to/from Karamea ($35, two hours) on weekdays year-round, and on Saturdays from October to April.

➡ From November to April, the Heaphy Bus (p280) stops here once or twice a week en route between Nelson ($65, 3½ hours) and the Heaphy Track trailhead at Kōhaihai ($60, 2½ hours), via Lyell ($50, 1¼ hours), Seddonville ($40, 40 minutes) and Karamea ($55, 2¼ hours).

From November to March, Golden Bay Coachlines (p294) has a daily service to Kōhaihai ($55, 1¾ hours) via Granity ($15, 20 minutes), Seddonville ($35, 40 minutes) and Karamea ($50, 1½ hours).

Track transport is also offered by Habitat Sports (p277) and **Trek Express** (📞 03-540 2042; www.trekexpress.co.nz).

Karamea & Around

POP 375

Friendly hiking-hub Karamea is colourful, pint-sized and perched by the enticing wilderness of Kahurangi National Park (p309). As the beginning (or end) point of the Heaphy and Wangapeka Tracks, it's common to see hikers gearing up for adventure (or shuffling wearily to the pub). You can delve into the national park on much shorter walks, in particular around the 35-million-year-old Ōpārara Basin, where rainforest hides limestone caverns and natural rock arches.

Never swim at Karamea's beaches, where currents are wild and waves smash the shore. If you must dip a toe in some water, ask at the information centre about freshwater swimming holes.

Karamea is 98 scenic (and petrol-station-free) kilometres north from Westport along SH67 (fill your tank before you set out). You'll find the main cluster of businesses at Market Cross, just across the bridge at the approach to the village.

◉ Sights & Activities

The outdoor wonderland of nikau palms, moss-clad forests and dramatic coastline is the prime reason to visit Karamea. The West Coast road continues (unsealed) for 14km north to **Kōhaihai**, the western trailhead (and most commonly, the finish point) of the Heaphy Track (p288), where there's a standard DOC campsite (adult/child $8/4).

The Karamea Information & Resource Centre (p279) distributes the free *Karamea Visitor Guide & Map*, which details walks such as the 800m **Karamea Estuary Walk**, a very pleasant stroll bordering the estuary and Karamea River; **Big Rimu** (45 minutes return to a whopping tree); and the **South Terrace Zig Zag** (one hour return), which accesses lookouts over peaceful farmland. At sunset, take a walk along **Karamea Beach**, which can be reached via Flagstaff Rd, north of town. Longer walks around Karamea include the **Fenian Track and Fenian Caves**

THE WEST COAST KARAMEA & AROUND

Loop Track (5km, three hours return, bring a torch) leading to three open-access caves. The Wangapeka Track (p288) is a four-to-six-day backcountry trip suitable for highly experienced hikers only.

Scotts Beach BEACH
It's almost an hour's walk each way from Kōhaihai along the beginning of the Heaphy Track and over the hill to Scotts Beach – a wild, empty shoreline shrouded in mist, awash in foamy waves, strewn with driftwood and backed by a nikau-palm-punctuated forest. Wander in wonder, but don't even think about dipping a toe in – there are dangerous currents at work. There's a DOC Great Walks campsite here; bookings required (adult/child $14/free).

About 30 minutes into the trail, you can detour to a lookout over the beach if you don't want to walk the whole distance.

★ Ōpārara Basin HIKING
Lying within Kahurangi National Park, the Ōpārara Basin is a hidden valley concealing limestone arches and caves within a thick forest of massive, moss-covered trees. The valley's signature sight is the 200m-long, 37m-high **Ōpārara Arch**, spanning the picturesque Ōpārara River, tannin-stained a fetching shade of caramel, which wends along the easy walkway (45 minutes return).

The main car park is the trailhead for walks of various lengths, and there are excellent information panels here, too. At the cave mouth of the Ōpārara Arch walk, some hikers continue uphill for lofty views but it's steep and treacherous (especially after rain), so we advise against it.

The smaller but no less impressive **Moria Gate Arch** (43m long, 19m high) is reached via a gorgeous forest loop walk (1½ hours), which also passes the **Mirror Tarn** (itself 15 minutes from the car park). The trail connects to the **Ōpārara Valley Track**, a rewarding five-hour (one-way) route through ancient forest, along the river, popping out at the Fenian Track car park.

Just a 10-minute walk from the second Ōpārara Basin car park are the **Crazy Paving and Box Canyon Caves**. Take your torch to enter a world of weird subterranean shapes and rare, leggy spiders.

Beyond this point are the superb **Honeycomb Hill Caves and Arch**, accessible only by guided tours ($150) run by the Karamea Information & Resource Centre; enquire about other guided tours of the area.

To drive to the basin from Karamea, travel 10km along the main road north and turn off at McCallum's Mill Rd, where signposts will direct you a further 14km up and over into the valley along a road that is winding, gravel, rough in places and sometimes steep. Don't attempt it with a campervan.

Karamea Outdoor Adventures OUTDOORS
(☑03-782 6181; www.karameaadventures.co.nz; Bridge St, Market Cross; kayaking/tubing/mountain-biking/horse-riding tour from $50/65/35/105) Guided and go-it-alone kayaking, tubing and riverbug trips, plus mountain-bike hire, horse treks, caving and a host of other ways to make your pulse race.

🛏 Sleeping & Eating

Last Resort LODGE $
(☑03-782 6617; www.lastresortkaramea.co.nz; 71 Waverley St; dm $37, r with/without bathroom $107/74, cottages $155; 🛜) Enclosed by greenery, this rambling resort suits most budgets, with dorms, a choice of private rooms with and without bathrooms, and self-contained two-bedroom cottages. Bonus points for laundry facilities, a comfy communal lounge with tea-making facilities, and showers for passing hikers ($5). The attached cafe/restaurant is one of the few options for a feed in Karamea.

Vinnie's CAFE $$
(☑027 781 1583; Bridge St, Market Cross; mains $8-22; ⊗9am-3pm) Operating from a hole-in-the-wall counter attached to a barn-like hall, Vinnie's dishes up strong coffee and simple fare such as cooked breakfasts, soup, toasties, omelettes and meat pies.

Karamea Village Hotel PUB FOOD $$
(☑03-782 6800; www.karameahotel.co.nz; 141 Waverley St; meals $25-34; ⊗noon-10pm Oct-Mar, 3-10pm Mon-Thu & noon-10pm Sat & Sun Apr-Sep) Within this 1876-built pub lie simple pleasures and warm hospitality: a game of pool, a pint of ale, and a choice of roast dinners, nachos and beer-battered whitebait, to a soundtrack of local gossip and dinging pokie machines. There are motel-style rooms out the back.

❶ Information

Karamea Information & Resource Centre
(☑03-782 6652; www.karameainfo.co.nz; 106 Bridge St, Market Cross; ⊗9am-4pm Mon-Fri, to 1pm Sat & Sun) This excellent, community-owned centre has the local low-down, internet

access, maps and DOC hut tickets. It also doubles as the petrol station. Enquire about guided tours to the Honeycomb Hill Caves and Arch ($150).

🛈 Getting There & Away

AIR

Golden Bay Air (📞 03-525 8725; www.golden bayair.co.nz; flights $99-209) has scheduled flights between Karamea and Takaka.

Adventure Flights Golden Bay (📞 03-525 6167; www.adventureflightsgoldenbay.co.nz) flies charters to/from the other Heaphy trailhead ($200), Takaka ($200), Motueka ($240) and Nelson ($285).

Helicopter Charter Karamea (📞 03-782 6111; www.helicharterkaramea.com; 78 Aerodrome Rd) offers charter flights to all of the main track trailheads.

BUS

Karamea Express (📞 03-782 6757; www.karameaexpress.co.nz) heads to/from Westport ($35, two hours) on weekdays year-round, and on Saturdays from October to April. It also offers a daily shuttle between Karamea and the Kōhaihai trailhead ($20); bookings essential. Wangapeka Track transport is also available.

From November to March, Golden Bay Coachlines (p294) has a daily service to Kōhaihai ($20, 15 minutes), Seddonville ($30, 50 minutes), Granity ($40, 70 minutes) and Westport ($50, 1½ hours).

From November to April, the **Heaphy Bus** (📞 03-540 2042; www.theheaphybus.co.nz) stops here once or twice a week en route between Nelson ($115, 5¾ hours) and Kōhaihai ($20, 15 minutes), via Lyell ($100, 3½ hours), Westport ($55, 2¼ hours) and Seddonville ($55, 1½ hours).

Reefton

POP 1030

In picturesque Reefton, the town's golden days are never far from mind, with nostalgia permeating every well-preserved goldrush-era building. Early adoption of hydro-electric power generation (1888) and street lighting (1923) gave Reefton its tag line 'the town of light', but these days it's the great outdoors that shines brightest.

Located on the Inangahua River, at the conjunction of the highways linking Westport and Greymouth to the Lewis Pass, the town is an increasingly appealing base for mountain biking, hiking and rafting. A hip distillery has recently been added to the antique stores, galleries and cafes lining Reefton's unrelentingly quaint main street.

◉ Sights & Activities

Pick up the *Walks and Tracks of Reefton* leaflet detailing the **Golden Fleece Walk** (15 minutes), **Bottled Lightning Powerhouse Walk** (30-minute loop) and other easy strolls. Note, a local charitable trust is working to re-establish the historic hydro-electric power station, with a new turbine in the historic shell and a visitor centre; it should be up and running by 2021.

Surrounding Reefton is the 206,000-hectare **Victoria Forest Park** (NZ's largest forest park), which hides historic sites, such as the old goldfields around Blacks Point. Starting at Blacks Point, the enjoyable **Murray Creek Track** is a four-hour return trip. Various walks, from 90 minutes to three hours, begin in or around the ghost town of Waiuta, 23km south of Reefton. Longer hikes in the Forest Park include the two- to three-day **Kirwans** or two-day **Big River Track**.

Many of these tracks can also be tackled on a mountain bike. Pick up the free *Reefton Mountain Biking* leaflet ($1 from the i-SITE) for an outline of 15 local tracks.

★ Reefton Distilling Co.   DISTILLERY

(📞 03-732 7083; www.reeftondistillingco.com; 10 Smith St; tour & tasting $35; ⊙10am-4pm Thu-Tue, from noon Wed) Every gold-rush town needs a still, and Reefton's got a goodie in the form of this operation that makes use of foraged botanicals and spring water sourced from the surrounding mountains. Book an hour-long tour or call in for a free tasting of its signature firewater, including the excellent Little Biddy gin, Wild Rain vodka, and Tayberry and Blueberry liqueurs. You'll have to wait a few years for the whisky.

Bearded Mining Company   HISTORIC BUILDING

(46 Broadway; admission by donation; ⊙9am-2pm) Looking like a ZZ Top tribute band, the straight-talkin', bearded fellas at this recreated high-street mining hut rollick your socks off with tales tall and true about the good ol' mining days. If you're lucky, you'll be served a cuppa from the billy along with local tips.

🛏 Sleeping & Eating

Reef Cottage B&B   B&B $$

(📞 03-732 8440; www.reefcottage.co.nz; 51-55 Broadway; s/d from $131/150; 🅿🤶) Enjoy total immersion into old-world Reefton at this converted 1887 solicitor's office. Compact rooms are furnished in period style, with modern touches like swish bathrooms and a well-equipped guest kitchen. In our favourite room, a vault has been converted into the bathroom. There's extra elbow room in the communal lounge and garden, too. Breakfast is in its cafe, next door.

Lantern Court Motels MOTEL $$
(☑ 03-732 8574; www.lanterncourtmotel.co.nz; 63 Broadway; units $130-220; ℙ🐾) Occupying a heritage building (formerly a draper's shop), this friendly establishment has self-catering options for everyone from singles to family groups. Next door, its newer motel block offers all mod cons with a nod to Victorian architecture.

Future Dough Co. CAFE $
(☑ 03-732 8497; www.thefuturedoughco.co.nz; 31 Broadway; mains $5-20; ⊙6.30am-4pm) Also known as the Broadway Tearooms, this wooden-floored bakery cafe gets by far the most daytime traffic in Reefton, whether for a freshly baked loaf, iced slices and shortbread to take away, or a bigger sit-down feed of sausage breakfasts, eggs Benedict, toasties and pies. On a sunny day, the outdoor tables are perfect for people-watching.

ℹ Information

Reefton i-SITE (☑ 03-732 8391; www.reefton.co.nz; 67-69 Broadway; ⊙9.30am-5pm Mon-Sat, 10am-2pm Sun Oct-Mar, 9.30am-4.30pm Mon-Sat Apr-Sep) This i-SITE has helpful staff, free maps, and you can visit a compact recreation of a mine inside (gold coin entry) and spark NZ's oldest winding engine into action ($2). Enquire about the mooted new Oceana gold-mining museum.

ℹ Getting There & Away

East West Coaches (p278) stops in Reefton every day except Saturday on the run between Westport ($25, 50 minutes) and Christchurch ($60, four hours) via Waipara ($54, three hours).

Murchison

POP 492

In Murchison, tumbling river rapids add freshness to the air and forested hills beckon bushwalkers. This humble township, 125km southwest of Nelson and 95km east of Westport, lies on the 'Four Rivers Plain'. The mightiest waterway is the Buller (in Māori, Kawatiri, meaning 'deep and swift'), where class II-IV rapids have made it hugely popu-

---

OFF THE BEATEN TRACK

GOLDEN GHOSTS

Remote **Waiuta** (www.waiuta.org.nz; Waiuta Rd) is one of the West Coast's most famous ghost towns. Spread over a plateau, this once-burgeoning gold town was swiftly abandoned after the mineshaft collapsed in 1951. Waiuta grew quickly after a gold discovery in 1905 but these days the forest-shrouded settlement is reduced to bits of rusting machinery, an overgrown swimming pool, stranded brick chimneys, fenced-off mine shafts and the odd intact building, including the old hospital (now a lodge).

From the signposted turn-off on SH7, 23km south of Reefton, it's another 17km to Waiuta, the last half of which is unsealed, winding and narrow in places but easy enough in a 2WD (keep your headlights on). Ask at Reefton's i-SITE for information and maps or consult the DOC website.

---

lar with experienced rafters, as well as those testing the waters for the first time (some jetboat operators have trips to suit kids... and risk-averse grown-ups).

Unless you have a passion for small-town history and antiques, Murchison itself won't excite you. But a day spent rafting or hiking here is a satisfying way to break up journeys between Nelson and the West Coast.

◉ Sights & Activities

Ask at the Murchison Information Centre (p282) about local walks, such as the **Skyline Walk**, a 90-minute hike through fern-filled beech and podocarp forest, and the **Johnson Creek Track**, a two-hour circuit through pine forest to the 'big slip', formed during the 1929 earthquake. Staff can also hook you up with mountain-bike hire and trout-fishing guides.

Murchison Museum & Information Service MUSEUM
(☑ 03-523 9392; www.visitmurchison.nz; 60 Fairfax St; ⊙10am-3pm) FREE This small volunteer-run museum showcases all sorts of local memorabilia (coins, minerals, telephones, sewing machines, toasters etc), the most interesting of which relate to the 1929 and 1968 earthquakes. In winter it covers as the information centre.

THE WEST COAST MURCHISON

★ **Wild Rivers Rafting** RAFTING
(☑03-789 8953; www.wildriversrafting.co.nz; departs Iron Bridge, SH6; 2hr rafting adult/child $160/85; ☺trips 10am & 2pm) Head out white-water rafting with Bruce and Marty on the particularly exciting Earthquake Rapids section of the beautiful Buller River (good luck with the 'gunslinger' and 'pop-up toaster'!). Kids aged 10 and up can join rafting tours, but check ahead – when the river's high, the minimum age is 13.

Ultimate Descents RAFTING
(☑03-523 9899; www.rivers.co.nz; 38 Waller St; ☎) This Murchison-based outfit offers white-water rafting and kayaking trips on the Buller, including the classic grade II-IV gorge trip ($160), and gentler family excursions (adult/child $130/100) suitable for kids aged five or more. You can usually count on departures at 9.30am and 1.30pm between September and April, but you'll need to book ahead in winter. Helirafting trips by arrangement ($500).

Buller Canyon Jet ADVENTURE SPORTS
(☑03-523 9883; www.bullercanyonjet.co.nz; 32 Waller St; adult/child $125/75; ☺Sep-May) Launching from the whopping 110m Buller Gorge Swingbridge, this is one of NZ's most scenic and best-value jetboat trips – 40 minutes of ripping through the beautiful Buller with a good-humoured captain. Its safety record is unblemished.

Natural Flames Experience TOURS
(☑027 698 7244; www.naturalflames.co.nz; 34 Waller St; adult/child $105/65) This informative half-day 4WD and bushwalking tour through verdant valleys and beech forest arrives at a hot spot where natural gas seeping out of the ground has been burning since 1922. Boil a billy on the flames and cook pancakes before returning to civilisation.

🛏 Sleeping

Lazy Cow HOSTEL $
(☑03-523 9451; www.lazycow.co.nz; 37 Waller St; dm $32-35, r with/without bathroom $110/90; ☎) It's easy to be a lazy cow here, with all the comforts of home in a stress-free, small-scale package. Dorms and private rooms all have electric blankets, and guests can order a pizza from the adjoining Cow Shed restaurant and scoff it in the backyard or cosy lounge.

Murchison Lodge B&B $$$
(☑03-523 9196; www.murchisonlodge.co.nz; 15 Grey St; d $240-280; ☎) This quality B&B surrounded by extensive gardens and paddocks is a short walk from the Buller River. Attractive timber features and charming hosts add to the comfortable feel. A hearty breakfast, home baking and plenty of local information are complimentary.

🍴 Eating

Cow Shed PIZZA $$
(☑03-523 9523; www.lazycow.co.nz; 37 Waller St; mains $18-24; ☺5-9pm Mon-Sat) Attached to the Lazy Cow hostel, the cute Cow Shed is a popular option for its crisp, generously topped pizzas served in intimate surrounds. Gluten-free options available.

🛍 Shopping

Dust & Rust ANTIQUES
(☑03-523 9300; www.dustandrust.nz; 35 Fairfax St; ☺10am-5pm daily Dec-Feb, Thu-Mon Sep-Nov & Mar-May) Rummage through an ever-changing array of vintage cars, foreign number-plates, hubcaps, 1970s kitchenware and vintage clothing at this impressive archive of curios housed in the historic Commercial Stables building. They're all originals – dust and rust comes included in the price.

ℹ Information

Murchison Information & Booking Centre
(☑03-523 9350; www.murchison.info; 47 Waller St; ☺9am-6pm Dec-Mar, 10am-4pm Mon-Fri Apr & Sep-Nov) Helpful tourist centre that assists with activity and hotel bookings, and offers bags of local info.

ℹ Getting There & Away

InterCity (p254) buses stop at Beechwoods Cafe on Waller St daily en route between Nelson ($23, 1¾ hours) and Greymouth ($31, four hours) via Westport ($19, 1½ hours), Charleston ($19, two hours) and Punakaiki ($28, 2¼ hours).

Nelson & Marlborough

Best Places to Eat

➡ Scotch Wine Bar (p322)

➡ Harry's Hawker House
(p292)

➡ Rock Ferry (p321)

➡ Urban (p293)

➡ Mills Bay Mussels (p313)

Best Places to Stay

➡ Adrift in Golden Bay
(p306)

➡ Kaiteri Motels &
Apartments (p299)

➡ Tombstone Backpackers
(p316)

➡ Eden's Edge Lodge (p300)

➡ Tasman Bay Backpackers
(p290)

Why Go?

For sauvignon blanc lovers the world over, the name Marlborough denotes crisp, herbaceous wine that seems to capture the very essence of summer sunshine and green spaces. The minute you set foot in this sun-soaked and verdant region, you'll see exactly how apposite an impression that is.

Consisting of the fertile Tasman and Marlborough districts, with the chilled-out city of Nelson squeezed in between, the 'Top of the South' has renowned coastal holiday spots – particularly Golden Bay, Tasman Bay and the curlicued emerald inlets of the Marlborough Sounds. There are also three national parks (Nelson Lakes, Abel Tasman and Kahurangi) and three of the country's most famous multiday hikes (the Abel Tasman Coast, Heaphy and Queen Charlotte tracks), two of which number among New Zealand's official list of Great Walks.

If you're arriving by ferry from often-blustery Wellington, it's an impressive introduction to what South Islanders refer to as 'the Mainland'.

When to Go

➡ The forecast is good: this area soaks up some of New Zealand's sunniest weather, with January and February being the warmest months.

➡ June and July are the coldest months, averaging highs of 12°C. However, the Top of the South sees some wonderful winter weather, with frosty mornings often giving way to clear skies and T-shirt temperatures.

➡ From around Christmas until the end of January, the whole region teems with Kiwi holidaymakers, so plan ahead during this time and be prepared to jostle for position with bucket-and-spade-wielding families.

Nelson & Marlborough Highlights

1 Abel Tasman National Park (p301) Kayaking or hiking to blissful golden-sand beaches.

2 Marlborough Wine Region (p320) Diving into a sea of sauvignon blanc in NZ's most famous wine region.

3 Queen Charlotte Track (p288) Hiking or biking through the myriad inlets of the Marlborough Sounds.

4 Great Taste Trail (p286) Pausing regularly for food, drink, art and beach breaks along this popular cycle trail.

5 Omaka Aviation Heritage Centre (p317) Immersing yourself in life-sized tableaux showcasing original WWI and WWII aircraft.

6 Farewell Spit (p308) Touring through a dunescape with gannets and godwits for company.

7 Heaphy Track (p288) Reaching the wild West Coast on foot, crossing through Kahurangi National Park.

❶ Getting There & Away

Picton is the South Island's main interisland ferry port, with multiple daily sailings to and from Wellington. Meanwhile Nelson has the busiest domestic airport, followed by Blenheim and Picton. Buses link the region to Canterbury and the West Coast. From October to April, KiwiRail's *Coastal Pacific* train takes the scenic journey between Picton and Christchurch.

NELSON

POP 46,400

Dishing up a winning combination of beautiful surroundings, sophisticated art and culinary scenes, and lashings of sunshine, Nelson has been hailed as one of New Zealand's most liveable cities. In summer it fills up with local and international visitors, there to take advantage of its proximity to both the Marlborough Sounds and the diverse natural attractions of the Tasman District.

Known to Māori as Whakatū, it was renamed Nelson after the hero of the Battle of Trafalgar by the canny New Zealand Company in 1841, in a bid to entice British colonists to its dubiously acquired settlement. In 1858 it was declared a city when it was still little more than a muddy village by dint of having acquired for itself a bishop and the promise of a cathedral. It still feels more like a big provincial town than a proper city, but that's part of Nelson's appeal.

◉ Sights

Tahunanui Beach   BEACH

(🏖) Nelson's primo playground takes the form of a long sandy beach (with lifeguards in summer) backed by dunes and a large grassy park with a playground, an espresso cart, a hydroslide, go-karts, a roller-skating rink and a model railway.

Christ Church Cathedral   CATHEDRAL

(Map p291; ☑ 03-548 1008; www.nelsoncathedral.org; Pikimai; ⊗9am-6pm) FREE The enduring symbol of Nelson, Christ Church lords it over the city from the top of Pikimai/Church Hill. It's an unusual mix of Gothic and art-deco style, with its nave constructed in Takaka marble in 1932 and the sanctuary and tower completed in ferroconcrete in 1972.

Nelson Provincial Museum   MUSEUM

(Map p291; ☑03-548 9588; www.nelsonmuseum.co.nz; 270 Trafalgar St; adult/child $5/3; ⊗10am-5pm) This modern museum is filled with a jumble of cultural heritage and natural history exhibits with a strong regional focus, including an almost Easter Island–esque stone statue, beautiful greenstone *hei-tiki* (stylised human figures) pendants, *patu* (warriors' clubs) and even the gown worn by Nobel Prize–winning scientist and Nelson College alumni Ernest Lord Rutherford at his christening. The top floor is given over to regular touring exhibitions (for which admission fees vary), and also features a roof garden.

Suter Art Gallery   GALLERY

(Map p291; ☑03-548 4699; www.thesuter.org.nz; 208 Bridge St; ⊗9.30am-4.30pm) FREE Redeveloped in 2016 with a series of contemporary, light-filled exhibition spaces, Nelson's public art gallery presents changing exhibitions from a collection that includes Kiwi big hitters such as Gordon Walters, Ralph Hotere and Don Binney. The complex incorporates an art-house cinema, an excellent gift shop and a riverside cafe.

HIKING & BIKING IN NELSON & MARLBOROUGH

GREAT TASTE TRAIL

ACTIVITY CYCLING
START NELSON
FINISH KAITERITERI
DURATION ONE OF TWO DAYS
DISTANCE 77KM
DIFFCULTY EASY

In a stroke of genius inspired by great weather and easy topography, the Tasman District has developed one of New Zealand's most popular cycle trails. Why is it so popular? Because no other route is so frequently punctuated by stops for food, wine, craft beer and art, as it passes through a range of landscapes from bucolic countryside to estuary boardwalk.

While the **Great Taste Trail** (www.heartof biking.org.nz) can be ridden in full in a few days, stopping at accommodation en route, it is more commonly ridden as day trips of various lengths. The most popular and diversion-filled section stretches from Nelson to Kaiteriteri (77km, six to nine hours), via Stoke, Richmond, Moturoa/Rabbit Island, Māpua, Motueka and Riwaka. To get from **Moturoa/Rabbit Island** (p296) to Māpua requires a trip on the Māpua Ferry; check the schedule before setting out.

The full Great Taste Trail circuit is still being completed but will eventually include a 1325m section of former rail tunnel (you'll need a light). The route doubles back from Kaiteriteri to Riwaka (6km, 30 minutes to one hour) and heads inland to Woodstock (31km, two to three hours). From here, the main circuit will head south to Kohatu, through the Spooners Tunnel and then northeast through Wakefield, Brightwater and Richmond. Until that's completed, an alternative, shorter route heads on road directly from Woodstock to Wakefield (29km, 1½ to three hours) and then back to Nelson (32km, two to 3½ hours).

Kiwi Journeys (Map p291; ☎03-548 0093; www.kiwijourneys.co.nz; 37-39 Halifax St; day tours

Welcome to the sunny side! This end of the South Island has more sunshine hours than any other part, which means long, sun-baked days perfect for getting outdoors.

from $99; ⊙9am-5pm) – which operates the bike-friendly Māpua Ferry and has depots in Nelson, Māpua Wharf and Kaiteriteri – is one of several excellent companies offering bike hire, drop-offs and cycle tours along this and other trails. Others include **Nelson Cycle Hire & Tours** (☑03-539 4193; www.nelson cyclehire.co.nz; Nelson Airport; day tours from $99), **Gentle Cycling Company** (☑03-929 5652; www. gentlecycling.co.nz; 411 Nayland Rd, Stoke; day tours from $75; ⊙Sep-Apr) and **Wheelie Fantastic** (☑03-543 2245; www.wheeliefantastic.co.nz; 151 Aranui Rd, Māpua; bike hire per day from $55).

ABEL TASMAN COAST TRACK

ACTIVITY HIKING
START MĀRAHAU
END WAINUI CAR PARK
DURATION 5 DAYS
DISTANCE 60KM
DIFFICULTY EASY

Think of this as a beach holiday on foot. Arguably the most beautiful of the Great Walks, the Abel Tasman Coast Track is a seductive combination of reliably pleasant weather, sparkling seas, golden sand, quintessential NZ coastal forest and hidden surprises with intriguing names such as Cleopatra's Pool. Another attraction is the terrain, for this is not a typical, rugged New Zealand track. It is better serviced than any other track in the country: well cut, well graded and well marked. It's difficult to get lost and can be hiked in a pair of running shoes. Leaving the boots behind is a bonus, as you'll probably get your feet wet – indeed, you'll probably want to get your feet wet.

This is a track with long stretches of beach walking and crazy tides to work around. The tidal ranges in the park are among the greatest in the country – up to a staggering 6m. At Awaroa Bay you have no choice but to plan on crossing at low tide. Daylight tide times are published on the DOC website (www.doc.govt.nz), and also displayed at DOC's **Whakatū/Nelson Visitor Centre** (p294)

and regional i-SITEs. It's important to consult these at the time of planning your trip, as the times of the tides will affect the huts or campsites that you use and the direction in which you walk the track.

The track is so well trodden that a topographical map isn't essential for navigation. The maps in DOC's trip information sheet and the *Abel Tasman Coast Track Guide* provide sufficient detail, and you can readily buy more illuminating maps at local visitor centres.

The path finishes at a car park near Wainui Bay, though most people extend their hike beyond Wainui by returning to Tōtaranui via the Gibbs Hill Track to pick up the water taxis back to Mārahau or Kaiteriteri. You could always just stop at Tōtaranui the first time you walk through, but by continuing north you will discover the most dramatic viewpoint (Separation Point), the least-crowded hut (Whariwharangi) and some of the best beaches (Anapai and Mutton Cove) in the park.

The entire hike takes only three to five days, although with water-taxi transport you can convert it into an almost endless array of options, particularly if you combine it with a kayak leg. Note, however, that kayaks aren't available from within the park and have to be brought in and out from Mārahau/Kaiteriteri each day. If you plan to combine a hike with kayaking, you should arrange the logistics with a kayak hire company before you book huts or campsites to ensure everything aligns.

Such is the pulling power of this track that it now attracts more than 37,000 hikers and kayakers each year who stay at least one night in the park. By way of comparison, the next most popular Great Walk is the Routeburn Track, which draws around 17,000. Don't expect to just turn up and hike; you'll need to plan and book your Great Walks huts and campsites online, well in advance, especially if you're planning to hike between Christmas and the end of January.

HEAPHY TRACK

ACTIVITY HIKING (ALL YEAR) OR
MOUNTAIN BIKING (MAY TO NOVEMBER)
START BROWN HUT
END KŌHAIHAI
DURATION 5 DAYS
DISTANCE 78.5KM
DIFFICULTY MODERATE

The Heaphy Track is one of the most popular hikes in the country. A Great Walk in every sense, it traverses diverse terrain – dense native forest, the mysterious Gouland Downs, secluded river valleys, and beaches dusted in salt spray and fringed by nikau palms.

Although quite long, the Heaphy is well cut and benched, making it easier than any other extended hike found in Kahurangi National Park. That said, you may still find it arduous, particularly in unfavourable weather.

Walking from east to west, most of the climbing is done on the first day and the scenic beach walk is saved for the end; a fitting and invigorating grand finale.

The track is open to mountain bikers between May and November. Factoring in distance, remoteness and the possibility of bad weather, this epic journey is only suited to well-equipped cyclists with advanced riding skills. A good port of call for more information is the **Quiet Revolution Cycle Shop** (p305) in Takaka.

A strong hiker could walk the Heaphy in three days, but most people take four or five days. For a detailed track description, see DOC's *Heaphy Track* brochure.

The seven designated Great Walk huts ($34) have bunks and kitchen areas, heating, toilets (composting or pit) and washbasins with cold water. Most but not all have gas rings; a couple have lighting. There are also nine Great Walk campsites ($14), plus the beachside **Kōhaihai Campsite** (www.doc. govt.nz; Karamea-Kohaihai Rd; site per adult/child $8/4) at the West Coast trailhead. Like all of the Great Walks, you'll need to book huts and campsites in advance.

WANGAPEKA TRACK

ACTIVITY HIKING
START ROLLING RIVER CAR PARK
END WANGAPEKA RD CAR PARK
DURATION 5 DAYS
DISTANCE 59KM
DIFFICULTY MODERATE TO DIFFICULT

The more challenging Wangapeka Track is not as well known as the Heaphy, but some advanced hikers consider it the more enjoyable Kahurangi National Park hike due to its rugged scenery and isolation. It traverses two saddles over 1000m and passes through beech forest in the Wangapeka, Karamea, Taipo and Little Wanganui River valleys.

There's a chain of DOC huts along the track; purchase your backcountry hut passes in advance and check with DOC before setting out.

QUEEN CHARLOTTE TRACK

ACTIVITY HIKING (ALL YEAR) OR
MOUNTAIN BIKING (MARCH TO NOVEMBER
ONLY)
START MERETOTO/SHIP COVE
END ANAKIWA
DURATION 4 DAYS
DISTANCE 71KM
DIFFICULTY MODERATE

The hugely popular, meandering Queen Charlotte Track (www.qctrack.co.nz) offers gorgeous coastal scenery on its way from historic Meretoto/Ship Cove to Anakiwa, passing through a mixture of privately owned land and DOC reserves. The coastal forest is lush, and from the ridges there are regular views into both Queen Charlotte and Kenepuru Sounds.

Queen Charlotte is a well-defined track, suitable for people of most fitness levels. It can be completed in three to five days, and can be walked in either direction, though Meretoto/Ship Cove is the usual (and recommended) starting point. This is mainly because it's easier to arrange a boat from Picton to Meretoto/Ship Cove than the reverse. It can also be walked in sections by hopping aboard numerous boat services. A good two-day hike is from Meretoto/Ship Cove to Punga Cove (27km), while recommended day walks include the sections from Mistletoe Bay to Anakiwa (12.5km), or Meretoto/Ship Cove to Furneaux Lodge (15km).

You can also turn the hike into a multisport outing by combining sections of hiking with kayaking or mountain biking. In 2013 the track was opened to cyclists, though they're forbidden from riding the section between Meretoto/Ship Cove and Kenepuru Saddle from 1 December to the end of February.

There are six DOC camping grounds along the route, while other accommodation ranges from old-fashioned homestays to luxury waterfront lodges. This is one of the enduring draws of the track – the chance to spend the day hiking, then to enjoy a hot shower and a cold beer at the end of it. Boat operators will also happily transport your pack along the track for you. At first it seems decadent...then it just seems welcome.

The district council, DOC and private landowners manage the track as a partnership. The private landowners are members of the Queen Charlotte Track Land Cooperative. They require each track user to purchase and display a pass for the private-land sections between Kenepuru Saddle and Bottle Bay (a one-day pass costs $12, while $25 covers you for up to five consecutive days). Passes can be purchased from various accommodation providers and boat operators near the track, from the Picton and Blenheim i-SITEs, and from the ticket machine at the Anakiwa trailhead.

NYDIA TRACK

ACTIVITY HIKING OR MOUNTAIN BIKING
START KAIUMA BAY
END DUNCAN BAY
DURATION 2 DAYS
DISTANCE 27KM
DIFFICULTY EASY

This track can be tackled as a very long day walk (9½ hours not counting breaks, or five hours on a mountain bike), but most people prefer the two-day option, staying in beautiful Nydia Bay along the way.

Hidden in the inner reaches of Pelorus Sound, the track crosses the Kaiuma Saddle (387m) before descending to Nydia Bay, the site of a long-gone sawmilling settlement. In the early 1900s, steam-powered haulers would drag logs from the saddles down to the bay where there was a large mill and a 300m wharf. Accommodation options here now include a DOC campsite and unhosted 50-bed lodge, and the excellent privately owned **On the Track Lodge** (p310).

The track then continues over the Nydia Saddle (347m) and through a patch of broadleafed coastal forest to Duncan Bay; allow around four to 4½ hours for the 15km walk.

Although rather remote, each trailhead is accessible by both water and road; there's no road to Nydia Bay.

LAKE ANGELUS TRACK

ACTIVITY HIKING
START/END MT ROBERT CAR PARK
DURATION 2 DAYS
DISTANCE 32.2KM
DIFFICULTY MODERATE TO DIFFICULT

Despite its relatively short length, this hike rates as one of the best in the country, showcasing all that's good about Nelson Lakes National Park. In fine weather, the walk along Robert Ridge is spectacular – seldom do hikes afford such an extended stretch across such open tops. The views will blow your socks off, as they will again as you descend into the extraordinary Lake Angelus basin (1650m) and Angelus Hut, which is a good base for short forays to the ridge above the lake and to Mt Angelus. A two-night stay at Angelus Hut is highly desirable, but be aware that bookings are required from December to April and it often books out.

Angelus Hut is an alpine hut and weather conditions can change rapidly. Snow, frost and freezing winds can occur even in midsummer, so hikers should be experienced and well equipped before attempting this route. Don't underestimate it: two people died here in 2019. Talk to the staff at the DOC Nelson Lakes Visitor Centre before setting out; locator beacons are recommended.

ST ARNAUD RANGE TRACK

ACTIVITY HIKING
START/END ST ARNAUD
DURATION 5 HOURS RETURN
DISTANCE 11KM
DIFFICULTY MODERATE

This popular up-and-down day walk provides one of the best viewpoints of Nelson Lakes National Park and beyond, surveyed from the top of the St Arnaud Range. It's around a 1000m ascent (and subsequent descent) from lake to ridge, but achy legs will be soothed by the splendour of beech forest – red, silver and mountain – that gradually changes with altitude.

Equally diverting is the chatter of native birds, the population of which is bolstered by the work of the Rotoiti Nature Recovery Project, through which this track passes.

Above the bushline (1400m) the views are worthy of a sit-down, but don't be content with gawping at the lake and Mt Robert from Parachute Rocks, as many hikers are. Fuel up with some scroggin (trail mix) and conquer the final 30-minute climb through alpine tussock to the ridge (1650m). You won't be disappointed.

Queen's Gardens
GARDENS

(Map p291; Bridge St) Immerse yourself in botanical history in this ornamental garden, founded in 1887 to commemorate the 50th jubilee of Queen Victoria's coronation. It's set around a horseshoe-shaped pond, with a bridge leading to a walled Chinese-style garden.

Botanical Reserve
PARK

(Milton St) Walking tracks through this 12-hectare reserve ascend Botanical Hill, where a spire proclaims the Centre of New Zealand. The actual centre is 55km southwest of here, but the views are great regardless. NZ's first-ever rugby match was played at the foot of the hill on 14 May 1870.

Founders Heritage Park
MUSEUM

(☑03-548 2649; www.founderspark.co.nz; 87 Atawhai Dr; adult/child/family $7/5/15; ☉10am-4.30pm) A collection of heritage buildings has been relocated to this site, 2km northeast of the city centre, creating a Victorian-era village complete with a church, pub, windmill and model railway (rides adult/child $6/4). Quaint shops now stock artisan products, while larger sheds display stagecoaches and vintage buses. Wet your whistle with a visit to McCashin's Hop Garden.

McCashin's Brewery
BREWERY

(☑03-547 5357; www.mkb.co.nz; 660 Main Rd, Stoke; tour incl tastings $25; ☉7am-4.30pm Mon-Wed, to 9.30pm Thu-Sat, 9am-4.30pm Sun) McCashin's was a forerunner of the craft brewing craze in NZ, which started way back in the 1980s. Visit the historic Rochdale Cider building in Stoke (8km southwest of central Nelson) for a tasting, bistro meal or tour.

🏃 Activities & Tours

There's plenty of walking and cycling to be enjoyed in and around the town, for which the i-SITE (p294) has maps. Nelson has two of the New Zealand Cycle Trail's 22 Great Rides: the Coppermine Trail (www.heartofbiking.org.nz), an awesome but challenging one-day ride ranging over the hills to the south of the city; and the Great Taste Trail (p286), which offers a blissfully flat meander through beautiful countryside dotted with wine, food and art stops.

Cable Bay Kayaks
KAYAKING

(☑027 223 6594; www.cablebaykayaks.co.nz; Cable Bay Rd, Pepin Island; half-/full-day guided trips $90/160) Twenty minutes' drive from Nelson city, this team offers richly rewarding guided sea-kayaking trips exploring the cave-indented coast around Pepin Island, where you'll likely meet local marine life (snorkelling gear on board helps).

Moana SUP
WATER SPORTS

(☑027 285 0772; www.moananzsup.co.nz; Bizley Walk, Tahunanui Beach; lessons from $70) Learn stand-up paddle boarding with the crew at Moana, or hire a board or kayak if you're already enlightened.

Nelson Tours & Travel
TOURS

(☑027 237 5007; www.nelsontoursandtravel.co.nz) CJ and crew run various small-group, flexible tours honing in on Nelson's wine, craft beer, art and scenic highlights. The five-hour 'Best of Both Worlds' tour ($160) includes beer, wine and lunch at the heritage Moutere Inn. Day tours of Marlborough wineries also available ($295).

🎆 Festivals & Events

For current info on Nelson's active events program, visit www.itson.co.nz.

Nelson Jazz Festival
MUSIC

(www.nelsonjazzclub.co.nz; ☉Jan) More scoo-be-doo-bop events over four days in January than you can shake a leg at. Features local and national acts.

Nelson Arts Festival
PERFORMING ARTS

(www.nelsonartsfestival.co.nz; ☉Oct) Held over two weeks in October; events include a street carnival, exhibitions, cabaret, writer talks, theatre and music.

🛏 Sleeping

★ Tasman Bay Backpackers
HOSTEL $

(☑03-548 7950; www.tasmanbaybackpackers.co.nz; 10 Weka St; dm $28-30, r with/without bathroom $88/76; @🛜) This well-designed, friendly hostel has airy communal spaces with a 100% Kiwi music soundtrack, colourful rooms, a sunny outdoor deck and a well-used hammock. Good freebies: wi-fi, decent bikes, breakfast during winter, and chocolate pudding and ice cream year-round.

Prince Albert
HOSTEL $

(Map p291; ☑03-548 8477; www.theprincealbert.co.nz; 113 Nile St; dm/s/d from $26/55/85; 🅿🛜) A five-minute walk from the city centre, this lively, well-run backpackers has roomy ensuite dorms surrounding a sunny courtyard. Private rooms are upstairs in the historic pub where guests can meet the locals and refuel with a good-value meal. A simple free breakfast is provided.

Central Nelson

Central Nelson

MĀORI NZ: NELSON & MARLBOROUGH

In Māori mythology the South Island was the canoe from which the demigod Māui fished up the North Island. Hence the top of the South Island is known as *Te Tau Ihu o te Waka a Māui* – the prow of Māui's canoe.

The Wairau Bar, near Blenheim, is the oldest known settlement site in the country, with finds radiocarbon-dated to the 13th century, some of which originated in East Polynesia. You'll find objects from this site, alongside other *taonga* (treasures), in the Nelson Provincial Museum (p285) and the Marlborough Museum (p318).

Control over the area has shifted between various *iwi* (tribes) over the centuries, most recently during the chaos of the early-19th-century Musket Wars, when it was invaded by displaced North Island tribes. Nowadays the tribal areas overlap substantially, and there's a confusing array of *iwi* with links to the region.

Significant *wāhi tapu* (sacred places) that can be visited include the Riuwaka Resurgence (p300) and Te Waikoropupū Springs (p304). At both sites, you're asked to refrain from eating and to keep out of the water.

Bug Backpackers
HOSTEL $

(☑03-539 4227; www.thebug.co.nz; 226 Vanguard St; dm $27-30, r with/without bathroom $82/69; @ 🛜) About 15 minutes' walk from town, the VW-themed Bug occupies a boldly painted converted villa, a modern building next door to it, and a self-contained unit sleeping up to four. Start the day with free breakfast, then return later for a backyard barbecue.

Cedar Grove Motor Lodge
MOTEL $$

(Map p291; ☑03-545 1133; www.cedargrove.co.nz; 59 Trafalgar St; unit from $160; P🛜) Set behind a large tree just across the bridge from the town centre, this modern motel offers studio, one-bedroom and two-bedroom units, each with cooking facilities and either patios or balconies.

Beaches
MOTEL $$

(☑03-548 6008; www.beachesnelson.nz; 71 Tahunanui Dr, Tahunanui; unit $159-219; P🛜) These 16 well-equipped units are closer to the highway than the beach but still handy for all of Tahunanui's watery attractions. All have patios or balconies, and free wi-fi.

Palazzo
MOTEL $$$

(Map p291; ☑03-545 8171; www.palazzomotorlodge.co.nz; 159 Rutherford St; unit $155-420; P✳🛜) This modern, Italian-tinged motor lodge offers stylish and comfortable studio, one-, two- and three-bedroom apartments within a block from the city centre. All have enviable kitchens with decent cooking equipment, classy glassware and a dishwasher.

Century Park Motor Lodge
MOTEL $$$

(Map p291; ☑03-546 6197; www.centuryparkmotorlodge.com; 197 Rutherford St; unit $169-285;

P✳🛜) Portraits of golden-era Hollywood stars add a sprinkle of glamour to these highly polished apartment-style studios and suites (including the super-duper two-bedroom 'presidential spa suite'). All have a patio or balcony catching the sunshine, along with pod coffee machines in the well-equipped kitchens. Continental breakfast is available, and pretty floral fringes take the edge off the car park.

🍴 Eating

Nelson has a lively cafe scene and a varied array of restaurants. Self-caterers can stock up on locally grown produce at the Nelson Market (p294) on Saturdays and the **Nelson Farmers' Market** (Map p291; ☑022 010 2776; www.nelsonfarmersmarket.org.nz; Kirby Lane, Bridge St; ☺8.30am-1.30pm Wed) on Wednesdays.

Swedish Bakery & Cafe
BAKERY $

(Map p291; ☑03-546 8685; www.facebook.com/TheSwedishBakeryandCafe; 54 Bridge St; mains $5.80-9; ☺8am-3pm Tue-Fri, to 1.30pm Sat) Nelson's resident Scandinavian baker serves up delicious breads, pastries, cakes and small chocolate treats in this bijou bakery cafe. The freshly filled baguettes and croissants are excellent, too. Take your goodies away or pray that one of three small tables is free.

★ Harry's Hawker House
ASIAN $$

(Map p291; ☑03-539 0905; www.hawkerhouse.co.nz; 296 Trafalgar St; dishes $8-28; ☺3pm-late Tue-Thu, from noon Fri-Sun) Step into a dimly lit room imbued with the glamour of old Shanghai and order a Singapore-style cocktail before delving into a menu filled with delectable dishes inspired by the street food of China and Southeast Asia, such as beef-cheek rendang roti rolls, pot stickers and curries. Don't miss the chicken laksa dumplings; the master broth they're served in is extraordinarily good.

★Urban
STREET FOOD $$

(Map p291; ☑03-546 7861; www.urbaneatery.co.nz; 278 Hardy St; dishes $18-27; ⊙4pm-late Mon, 11am-late Tue-Sat) Slurp oysters from the shell, or revitalise with sashimi and ceviche, then sate your cravings with street-food dishes such as *kung pao* Sichuan fried chicken or smoked venison tostadas. Black butchers' tiles, edgy artwork, craft beers and a fine wine list all bolster this metropolitan experience.

DeVille
CAFE $$

(Map p291; ☑03-545 6911; www.devillecafe.co.nz; 22 New St; meals $15-22; ⊙8am-4pm Mon-Sat, 9am-3pm Sun; 🐾🎵) Most of DeVille's tables lie in its sweet walled courtyard, a hidden boho oasis in the inner city and the perfect place for a meal or morning tea. The food's good and local – from fresh baking to a chorizo burrito brunch and proper burgers, washed down with regional wines and beers. It's open late for live music in summer.

Indian Café
INDIAN $$

(Map p291; ☑03-548 4089; www.theindiancafe.com; 94 Collingwood St; mains $14-20; ⊙noon-2pm Mon-Fri, 5pm-late daily; 🎵) This saffron-coloured Edwardian bungalow houses a convivial Indian restaurant serving impressive interpretations of standards such as tandoori chicken, rogan josh and beef Madras. Share the mixed platter to start, then mop up your mains with one of 10 different breads.

Falafel Gourmet
MIDDLE EASTERN $$

(Map p291; ☑03-545 6220; 195 Hardy St; mains $12-18; ⊙10am-4pm Mon-Sat; 🎵) This humble joint dishes out healthy pitta pockets, platters and the best kebabs for miles around. Choose between chicken, lamb or tasty falafels.

Hopgood's & Co
BISTRO $$$

(Map p291; ☑03-545 7191; www.hopgoods.co.nz; 284 Trafalgar St; mains $40-42; ⊙5.30pm-late Mon-Sat) Hopgood's relaxed approach to service and gastro-pub feel seem a little at odds with the hefty prices, although the bis-

tro menu (two/three courses $49/59, served Monday to Wednesday) lessens the pain somewhat. The food is deftly prepared but unfussy (roast duck, merino lamb), allowing quality local ingredients to shine. The five-course tasting menu ($95) affords the full Hopgood's experience.

Cod & Lobster
SEAFOOD $$$

(Map p291; ☑03-546 4300; www.codandlobster.com; 300 Trafalgar St; mains $36-38; ⊙11am-11pm Tue-Sun; 🐾) Stellar cocktails and a vast array of gin make the corner bar an essential destination, but this heritage space also serves up excellent food. A concise selection of steak, lamb and vegetarian dishes is available, but it's the briny-fresh catch of the day you're really here for. At lunchtime there's a good-value set menu (two/three courses $35/45).

Drinking & Entertainment

Free House
CRAFT BEER

(Map p291; ☑03-548 9391; www.freehouse.co.nz; 95 Collingwood St; ⊙3-10.30pm Mon-Thu, to midnight Fri, noon-midnight Sat, noon-10.30pm Sun) Tastefully converted from its original, more reverent purpose, this former church is now home to an excellent, oft-changing selection of NZ craft beers. Munch on bar snacks on the outside deck, and visit on a Friday or Saturday afternoon to browse the vinyl at the excellent Family Jewels Records pop-up store.

IN PURSUIT OF HOPPINESS
• •

Nelson and the neighbouring Tasman region lay claim to the title of craft-brewing capital of New Zealand. World-class hops have been grown here since the 1840s. Pick up a copy of the *Nelson Craft Beer Trail* map (available from the i-SITE (p294) and other outlets, and online at www.craftbrewingcapital.co.nz) and wind your way between brewers and pubs. Top picks for a tipple include Free House and Mc-Cashin's Hop Garden (p290) in Nelson, McCashin's Brewery (p290) in Stoke, Hop Federation (p300) in Riwaka, and the Townshend Brewery at Motueka's T.O.A.D Hall (p297).

Sprig & Fern CRAFT BEER
(Map p291; ☑03-548 1154; www.sprigandfern.
co.nz; 280 Hardy St; ⊙11am-midnight; 🛜) This
outpost of a Richmond brewery offers 18
brews on tap, including three limited releas-
es. No pokies and no TV; just decent beer, NZ
wines, pizza, $10 lunch specials, occasional
live music and a pleasant outdoor area. Look
for a second Sprig at 143 Milton St.

Theatre Royal THEATRE
(Mapp291;☑03-5483840;www.theatreroyalnelson.
co.nz; 78 Rutherford St; ⊙box office 10am-4pm
Mon-Fri) Built in 1878, this charmingly
restored heritage theatre hosts a full roster
of local and touring drama, dance and musical productions. Check the website for the
current programme or visit the box office.

🛍 Shopping

Nelson Market MARKET
(Map p291; ☑03-546 6454; www.nelsonmarket.
co.nz; Montgomery Sq; ⊙8am-1pm Sat) This big,
busy weekly market has fresh produce, food
stalls, fashion, local arts, crafts and buskers.

Jens Hansen JEWELLERY
(Map p291; ☑03-548 0640; www.jenshansen.com;
320 Trafalgar Sq; ⊙9am-5pm Mon-Fri, to 2pm Sat
year-round, 10am-1pm Sun Nov-Easter) Catapulted to fame after designing the One Ring for
the *Lord of the Rings* movies, this contemporary jeweller now does a brisk trade in
Elvish-inscribed engagement rings for those
unfazed by the prospect of their fiancé or fi-
ancée vanishing or turning into an evil mega-
alomaniac. There are plenty of other elegant
designs available for those with quibbles
about such things.

🛈 Information

MEDICAL SERVICES

Medical & Injury Centre (☑03-546 8881; 98
Waimea Rd; ⊙8am-10pm) Duty doctors working late at a clinic attached to Nelson Hospital.
Nelson Hospital (☑03-546 1800; www.
nmdhb.govt.nz; Tipahi St)

TOURIST INFORMATION

DOC Whakatū/Nelson Visitor Centre (Map
p291; ☑03-546 9339; www.doc.govt.nz; 77
Trafalgar St; ⊙8.30am-5pm) The main DOC
Visitor Centre for the Top of the South, includ-
ing the Kahurangi and Abel Tasman National
Parks. Call in for up-to-date information on
tracks including the Heaphy, Abel Tasman
Coast and Queen Charlotte.
Nelson i-SITE (Map p291; ☑03-548 2304; www.
nelsontasman.nz; 77 Trafalgar St; ⊙8.30am-

5pm Oct-Easter, 10am-4pm Easter-Sep) A slick,
information-packed tourist office, sharing space
with the DOC Visitor Centre. Pick up a copy of the
Nelson Tasman Visitor Guide.

🛈 Getting There & Away

AIR

Nelson Airport is 5km southwest of town, near
Tahunanui Beach. A taxi between the airport
and the town centre will cost around $30, while
Super Shuttle (☑0800 748 885; www.super-
shuttle.co.nz) offers a door-to-door service for
around $18.

Scheduled flights include:

Air New Zealand (☑0800 737 000; www.
airnewzealand.co.nz) To/from Auckland, Wellington and Christchurch;
Golden Bay Air (p305) To/from Takaka;
Originair (☑0800 380 380; www.originair.
co.nz) To/from Palmerston North and New Plymouth and Napier;
Sounds Air (☑03-520 3080; www.soundsair.
com) To/from Wellington and the Kāpiti Coast.

BUS

Regional buses depart from outside the centrally located **Nelson SBL Travel Centre** (Map p291;
☑03-548 1539; www.nelsoncoachlines.co.nz;
27 Bridge St; ⊙7am-5.15pm Mon-Fri).
ScenicNZ Abel Tasman (☑03-548 0285;
www.scenicnzabeltasman.co.nz) operates one
or two buses a day to Motueka ($14, one hour),
Kaiteriteri ($21, 1½ hours) and Mārahau ($21,
1¾ hours).
Golden Bay Coachlines (☑03-525 8352;
www.goldenbaycoachlines.co.nz) has a daily
service to Motueka ($14, 45 minutes) and
Takaka ($39, two hours) year-round, with a
second bus from November to March that continues on to Collingwood ($54, 2½ hours) and
the Heaphy Track trailhead ($65, three hours),
or to Pōhara ($49, 2¼ hours) and Tōtaranui
($59, three hours).
InterCity (☑03-365 1113; www.intercity.co.nz)
heads to destinations including Havelock ($15,
1¼ hours), Picton ($23, 2¼ hours), Blenheim
($23, 1¾ hours), Westport ($36, 3½ hours) and
Greymouth ($48, six hours).

🛈 Getting Around

NBus (☑03-548 3290; www.nbus.co.nz)
Nelson Suburban Bus Lines (SBL) operates
services between Nelson and Richmond ($4)
via Tahunanui ($3) and Stoke ($3.50). Buses
run from roughly 7am to 7pm; pay the driver in
cash or buy a 10-trip ticket. On weekends, the
Late Late Bus (flat fare $4) departs from the
Westpac Bank on Trafalgar St at 10pm, 11pm,
1am, 2am and 3.15am.

TASMAN DISTRICT

Named after Dutch explorer Abel Tasman, who landed here in 1642, the Tasman District stretches north to Farewell Spit at the very tip of the South Island and south to the Nelson Lakes. With the twin delights of Tasman Bay (Te Tai-o-Aorere) and Golden Bay (Mohua) along with three highly scenic national parks (Kahurangi, Abel Tasman and Nelson Lakes), it's easy to see why it's such a popular travel destination for international and domestic travellers alike. It's also one of New Zealand's sunniest spots.

Nelson Lakes National Park

Nelson Lakes National Park surrounds two lakes – Rotoiti ('small lake') and Rotoroa ('long lake') – fringed by sweet-smelling beech forest with a backdrop of greywacke mountains. Located at the northern end of the Southern Alps, and with a dramatic glacier-carved landscape, it's an awe-inspiring place to get up on high.

Part of the park, east of Lake Rotoiti, is classed as a 'mainland island' where a conservation scheme aims to eradicate introduced pests (rats, possums and stoats), and regenerate native flora and fauna. It offers excellent hiking, including short walks, lake scenery and one or two sandflies... The park is flush with bird life, and famous for brown-trout fishing. The human hub of the Nelson Lakes region is the small, low-key village of **St Arnaud**.

🏃 Activities

Many spectacular walks allow you to appreciate this rugged landscape, but before you tackle them, stop by the DOC Nelson Lakes Visitor Centre (p295) for maps, track and weather updates, and to pay your hut or camping fees.

There are two fantastic day hikes to be had: the St Arnaud Range Track (p289) and the five-hour **Mt Robert Circuit Track**, which starts at Mt Robert car park – a short, rough drive away from St Arnaud – and circumnavigates the mountain. The optional side trip along Robert Ridge offers staggering views into the heart of the national park. Only attempt these hikes in fine weather. At other times they are pointless (no views) and potentially dangerous.

There are also plenty of shorter (and flatter) walks from Lake Rotoiti's Kerr Bay and the road end at Lake Rotoroa. These and the longer day hikes are described in DOC's *Walks in Nelson Lakes National Park* pamphlet ($2). The fit and well equipped can embark upon longer hikes such as the Lake Angelus Track (p289).

🛏 Sleeping

Travers-Sabine Lodge HOSTEL $
(☑ 03-521 1887; www.nelsonlakes.co.nz; Main Rd, St Arnaud; dm/r without bathroom $35/79; 🅿 🖥) This hostel is a great base for outdoor adventure – it's a short walk to Lake Rotoiti, inexpensive, clean and comfortable. It also has particularly cheerful technicolor linen in the dorms, doubles and family room. The owners are experienced adventurers themselves, so advice comes as standard.

Alpine Lodge LODGE $$
(☑ 03-521 1869; www.alpinelodge.co.nz; Main Rd, St Arnaud; r from $180; 🅿 🖥) Family owned and a consistent performer, this large Swiss chalet–style complex offers a range of accommodation, the pick of which are the split-level studios with mezzanine bedrooms and spa baths. If nothing else, go for the inviting in-house restaurant – a snug affair sporting an open fire, mountain views, good food (mains $20 to $35) and local beer.

ℹ Information

DOC Nelson Lakes Visitor Centre (☑ 03-521 1806; www.doc.govt.nz; View Rd; ⊙ 9am-4pm) Proffers park-wide information (weather, track status, activities) and hut passes, plus displays on park ecology and history.

ℹ Getting There & Away

There's no public transport to this national park. If you don't have a car, your best bet is to book an on-demand hikers' shuttle with the likes of **Nelson Lakes Shuttles** (☑ 03-547 6896; www.nelsonlakesshuttles.co.nz) or **Trek Express** (☑ 03-540 2042; www.trekexpress.co.nz).

ℹ Getting Around

Lake Rotoiti Water Taxis (☑ 021 702 278; www.rotoitiwatertaxis.co.nz; Kerr Bay; up to 3/4 passengers $110/140) Runs to/from Kerr Bay (St Arnaud) to West Bay, Coldwater or Lakehead at the southern end of Rotoiti. It also hires out kayaks (per hour/day $15/75) and canoes ($25/100).

Ruby Coast & Moutere Hills

It's possible to blast between Nelson and Motueka in 40 minutes via SH6 and SH60 but, if you've got the time, there are plenty of interesting diversions to slow you down. This is the heart of Nelson's wine region; pick up the *Nelson Wine Guide* pamphlet (www.winenelson.co.nz), which lists details for 21 wineries.

A short detour leads along the Ruby Coast to little **Māpua** with its surprisingly hip wharf precinct consisting of cafes, artsy shops, a brewery, wine bar and coffee roastery. Alternatively, take the inland Moutere Hwy, which traverses gently rolling countryside dotted with farms, orchards and lifestyle blocks. It's a scenic and fruitful drive, particularly in high summer when roadside stalls are laden with fresh produce. The main settlement along the way is **Upper Moutere**, a sleepy hamlet that was first settled by German immigrants.

The whole area can be explored by bicycle on the Great Taste Trail (p286).

◉ Sights

The Nelson and Motueka i-SITEs stock a range of pamphlets – including *Great Taste Trail, Nelson Wine Guide, Nelson Art Guide, Nelson's Creative Pathways* and *Moutere Artisans map* (www.moutereartisans.co.nz) – outlining an eclectic set of stops in the area.

★ Motuoroa/Rabbit Island   ISLAND
(◷ dawn-dusk) With a Māori name that translates as 'Long Island', this low-lying expanse forms an 8km-long barrier to the ocean with a gorgeous sandy beach spread along its entire length. A pine plantation forest provides shade for the cyclists on the Great Taste Trail (p286), which passes through. You're likely to see weka, inquisitive flightless birds similar to kiwi but with much shorter beaks, here. Rabbit Island is the largest of a brace of islands at the mouth of the Waimea River with similarly prosaic names such as Best, Rough, Bird and Bell. A signposted turn-off from SH60 leads onto Redwood Rd, which passes by bridge onto Rough Island and then Rabbit Island. The bridge closes at sunset and overnight stays are not allowed. The island can also be reached by the Māpua Ferry ($12 return, 10 minutes), run by Kiwi Journeys (p286), but in winter this only operates on weekends.

Höglund Art Glass   GALLERY
(☑ 03-544 6500; www.hoglundartglass.com; 52 Lansdowne Rd, Appleby; ◷ 10am-5pm) The Höglunds have had their art glass exhibited internationally and even featured on a jointly issued Swedish and New Zealand postage stamp. Call into their shop to admire the colourful collection and then pop into the next room, which has displays on the process and windows facing onto the furnace and workshop. If you don't fancy weighing down your luggage with a signature vase, the jewellery and penguins make memorable souvenirs.

Neudorf Vineyards   WINERY
(☑ 03-543 2643; www.neudorf.co.nz; 138 Neudorf Rd, Upper Moutere; ◷ 11am-5pm Oct-Apr, hours vary May-Sep) ✿ Sitting pretty in Upper Moutere, with views across the grapes to the mountains of Kahurangi National Park, bijou Neudorf produces gorgeous wines including seductive pinot noir and some of NZ's finest chardonnay. A $5 donation to the local rescue helicopter service is requested for tastings. Cheese platters can be purchased, but you're welcome to bring your own picnic to enjoy in the grounds.

Seifried   WINERY
(☑ 03-544 5599; www.seifried.co.nz; 184 Redwood Rd, Appleby; ◷ 10am-4pm) Situated at the SH60 Motuoroa/Rabbit Island turn-off, Seifried is one of the region's biggest wineries. Try its chardonnay and delicious Sweet Agnes riesling.

✕ Eating & Drinking

Smokehouse   FISH & CHIPS $
(☑ 0800 540 2280; www.smokehouse.co.nz; Māpua Wharf, Māpua; fish & chips $9.40-13; ◷ 11am-7pm) Visit this Māpua institution to order fish and chips and eat them on the wharf while the gulls eye off your crispy bits. Get some wood-smoked fish and pâté to go.

Jester House   CAFE $$
(☑ 03-526 6742; www.jesterhouse.co.nz; 320 Aporo Rd, Tasman; mains $13-22; ◷ 9am-4.30pm, closed Aug; 🛜) Long-standing Jester House is reason alone to take this coastal detour, as much for its tame eels (friendly critters that like to be hand fed) as for the peaceful sculpture gardens that encourage you to linger over lunch. A short, simple menu includes a few twists (venison goulash; twice-cooked, three-cheese souffle). It's roughly 8km from both Māpua and Motueka.

Moutere Inn PUB

(✆03-543 2759; www.moutereinn.co.nz; 1406 Moutere Hwy, Upper Moutere; ⊗noon-9pm) One of NZ's oldest pubs, the Moutere Inn (built 1850) is a welcoming establishment serving meals (homemade burgers, fish and chips, curries) and craft beer, including its own Moutere Brewing Co range. Sit in the sunshine or settle inside on music nights, which have a folksy bent.

❶ Getting There & Away

Buses on the Nelson–Motueka route head along SH60 but there are no buses to the Ruby Coast or Moutere Hills. Biking the Great Taste Trail (p286) is a good way of exploring.

Motueka

POP 7600

Motueka (pronounced maw-tu-*eh*-ka) is a bustling agricultural hub and the closest decent-sized town to the Abel Tasman and Kahurangi National Parks. It has a good selection of accommodation and cafes, a large supermarket and roadside fruit stalls; stock up here if you're heading north. If you're cycling the Great Taste Trail (p286), it's a great place to break up the trip.

While you might not realise it from the main street, Motueka is just a stone's throw from the sea. Walk or cycle along the muddy estuary, with its saltwater baths and exposed shipwreck, then continue on foot along the **Motueka Sandspit**, an important habitat for birds such as oystercatchers, terns, shags and godwits. The last of these are known to migrate between here and Alaska's Yukon Delta – a distance of 11,500km – in less than a week, flying nonstop.

◉ Sights & Activities

Motueka District Museum MUSEUM

(Map p298; ✆03-528 7660; www.motuekadistrict museum.org.nz; 140 High St; ⊗10am-3pm Sun-Fri Dec-Mar, Tue-Fri & Sun Apr-Nov) 【FREE】 Housed in an attractive 1913-built school building, this museum has a tiny but interesting collection of regional artefacts.

Skydive Abel Tasman ADVENTURE SPORTS

(✆03-528 4091; www.skydive.co.nz; Motueka Aerodrome, 16 College St; jumps 9000/13,000/16,500ft $279/329/419) Move over, Taupō: we've jumped both and think Motueka takes the cake. Presumably so do the many sports jumpers who favour this drop zone, some of

whom you may see rocketing in. Spectators can spread out on the front lawn.

⌂ Sleeping

Motueka Top 10 Holiday Park HOLIDAY PARK $

(Map p298; ✆03-528 7189; www.motuekatop10. co.nz; 10 Fearon St; sites from $50, unit with/without bathroom from $120/66; ◎⧆⊕) Close to town and the Great Taste Trail, this place is packed with grassy, green charm – check out those lofty kahikatea trees! Shipshape communal amenities include a swimming pool, a spa and a jumping pillow. There are several accommodation options, from tent sites to smart cabins and a three-bedroom apartment. Staff can hire bikes, dispense advice and book local activities.

Equestrian Lodge Motel MOTEL $$

(Map p298; ✆03-528 9369; www.equestrianlodge. co.nz; 2 Avalon Ct; unit $150-225; ⏘◎⧆) No horses, no lodge, but no matter. This excellent motel complex is close to town and features expansive lawns, rose gardens, and a heated pool and spa alongside a series of continually refreshed units. Cheerful owners will hook you up with local activities.

✕ Eating & Drinking

Motueka Sunday Market MARKET $

(Map p298; ✆03-540 2709; https://motuekasun daymarket.co.nz; Decks Reserve car park, Wallace St; ⊗8am-1pm Sun) On Sunday mornings the car park behind the i-SITE fills up with trestle tables laden with produce, jewellery, clothing, secondhand books, art and crafts. Food trucks and coffee carts provide sustenance, while buskers provide entertainment.

T.O.A.D Hall CAFE $$

(Map p298; ✆03-528 6456; www.toadhallmotueka. co.nz; 502 High St; breakfast $17-22, lunch $9-28, dinner $25-31; ⊗8am-5pm Sun-Thu, to 10pm Fri & Sat; ⏘⊕) This fantastic cafe serves excellent breakfasts and lunches such as salmon hashcakes, lamb burgers, pies and some good vegan options, then stays open late on weekends for bistro-style meals and, in summer, live music. Also on offer are smoothies, juices, baked goods and selected groceries. Beer and cider are brewed on-site by Townshend Brewery and served in an adjacent taproom.

Smoking Barrel BARBECUE $$

(Map p298; ✆03-528 0693; www.facebook.com/ thesmokingbarrelnz; 105 High St; breakfast $16-22, lunch $9-24, dinner $24-40; ⊗8am-10pm Wed-Sun) An old Austin truck serves as the

Motueka

N 0 —————— 400 m
   0 —————— 0.2 miles

specialties, such as the venison yellow curry and the delicious *phad prik khing pla* (crispy fish red curry). Your next choice is 'mild', 'hot' or 'Thai hot'. Be warned: regular hot is pretty darned hot! There are lots of vegetarian options, too.

Precinct Dining Co   CAFE **$$**
(Map p298; ☑03-528 5332; www.precinctdining.com; 108 High St; breakfast & lunch $16-24, dinner $26-34; ⊙9am-late Tue-Sat) This relaxed cafe-bistro is a versatile slice of cosmopolitan cool. Kick off with eggs Benedict for brunch, before returning at dinner for fish and chips, a chicken burger or a rustic mushroom risotto with toasted hazelnuts. Good coffee and a savvy drinks list seal the deal.

Sprig & Fern   CRAFT BEER
(Map p298; ☑03-528 4684; www.sprigandfern.co.nz; Wallace St; ⊙2pm-late; 🛜🌐) A member of the local Sprig & Fern Brewery family, this back-lane tavern is the pick of Motueka's drinking holes. Small and pleasant, with two courtyards, it offers 20 hand-pulled brews, simple food (pizza, fish and chips, and an awesome burger; meals $16 to $25) and occasional live music.

ℹ Information

Motueka i-SITE (Map p298; ☑03-528 6543; www.nelsontasman.nz/visit-abel-tasman; 20 Wallace St; ⊙9am-6pm Nov-Mar, to 4pm Apr-Oct) An endlessly busy info centre with helpful staff handling bookings and providing local expertise. DOC information, bookings and passes are also available. There's even an e-bike charging station.

coffee station inside this hip, greenery-filled barbecue joint, where lamb and pork shoulders are grilled for 12 hours and served with flatbread or in Cubano sandwiches. On top of that there are burgers, steaks, bagels, chicken chimichangas and a crazy selection of doughnuts (bacon French toast flavour, anyone?).

Chokdee   THAI **$$**
(Map p298; ☑03-528 0318; www.chokdee.co.nz; 109 High St; mains $21-30; ⊙5pm-late Mon, 11am-2pm & 5pm-late Tue-Sun; ☑) There's a huge menu to peruse at this highly fragrant restaurant, so cut straight to the house

❶ Getting There & Away

ScenicNZ Abel Tasman (p294) runs daily buses to/from Nelson ($14, one hour), Kaiteriteri ($11, 20 minutes) and Mārahau ($11, 40 minutes). It adds a second bus from November to March.

Golden Bay Coachlines (p294) has a daily service to Nelson ($14, 45 minutes) and Takaka ($28, 1¼ hours) year-round, with a second bus from November to March that continues on to Collingwood ($41, 1¾ hours) and the Heaphy Track trailhead ($52, 2¼ hours), or to Pōhara ($38, 1½ hours) and Tōtaranui ($50, 2¼ hours).

Buses depart from outside the i-SITE.

Kaiteriteri

POP 789

Thanks to its gorgeous golden-sand beach, this seaside hamlet, 13km from Motueka, is the most popular resort town in the area. During the summer holidays there can be more towels than sand, but off-season it's a sleepy place. Kaiteriteri is also a major departure point for Abel Tasman National Park boats, although Mārahau is the main base.

Its other claim to fame is as a cycling destination. It's one of the main hopping-off points of the Great Taste Trail (p286), which passes through a corner of the wonderful **Kaiteriteri Mountain Bike Park** (✆03-527 8010; www.bikekaiteriteri.co.nz; Martin Farm Rd) **FREE** on its way into town. This free-to-access, 180-hectare parcel of DOC land has mountain-bike trails to suit all levels of ability. Call into **Kiwi Journeys** (✆03-548 0093; www.kiwijourneys.co.nz; 3 Kaiteriteri-Sandy Bay Rd), opposite the beach, for bike rental and advice.

★ **Kaiteri Motels & Apartments** MOTEL **$$**
(✆03-527 8063; www.kaiterimotelsandapartments. co.nz; 8 Kotare Pl, Little Kaiteriteri Beach; unit from $190; P ☎) Just 200m from Little Kaiteriteri Beach (around the corner from the main beach) is this congregation of comfortable, stylishly furnished, roomy units with full kitchens and laundry facilities. Guests can also make use of a ferny barbecue area and spa pool.

Bellbird Lodge B&B **$$$**
(✆03-527 8555; www.bellbirdlodge.co.nz; 160 Kaiteriteri-Sandy Bay Rd; s/d $350/375; ⊗Oct-Apr; P ❋ ☎) This upmarket B&B, 1.5km up the hill from Kaiteriteri Beach, offers two ensuite rooms, bush and sea views, extensive gardens, spectacular breakfasts (featuring homemade muesli and fruit compote), and gracious hosts.

❶ Getting There & Away

ScenicNZ Abel Tasman (p294) runs daily buses to/from Nelson ($21, 1½ hours), Motueka ($11, 20 minutes) and Mārahau ($8, 20 minutes); two daily in summer.

Mārahau

POP 120

Just up the coast from Kaiteriteri and 18km north of Motueka, Mārahau (properly pronounced '*Mah*-rah-ho') is the main gateway to Abel Tasman National Park. It's less of a town, more of a procession of holiday homes and tourist businesses lining a big beach.

🏃 Activities

Abel Tasman Horse Trekking HORSE RIDING
(✆03-527 8232; www.abeltasmanhorsetrekking. co.nz; Ocean View Chalets, 305 Sandy Bay–Mārahau Rd; 2hr ride $115) Head here for the chance to belt along the beach on horseback; training is available for newbie riders. Younger ones (under 12) can be led around a paddock on a pony for 30 minutes ($40) after helping to brush and saddle up their mount.

🛏 Sleeping

Adventure Inn HOSTEL **$**
(✆0800 713 000; www.adventureinn.co.nz; 269 Sandy Bay–Mārahau Rd; dm $35; P ❋ ☎) With a 20-seat cinema, two pool tables, takeaways served from an old bus, and air-conditioned dorms with personal lights and charging ports, this isn't your run-of-the-mill hostel. Plus there's a barbecue and a firepit – perfect for swapping Coast Track tips over a few beers.

The Barn HOSTEL **$**
(✆03-527 8043; www.barn.co.nz; 14 Harvey Rd; sites per person from $22, dm/tw/d without bathroom $30/89/99; P ☎) Part backpackers, part campground, The Barn offers comfortable dorms, private microcabins and a grassy camping field, along with alfresco kitchens and barbecue areas. The barn itself is the hub – the communal kitchen and lounge area are good for socialising, as is the central deck, which has a fireplace. Activity bookings and secure parking are available.

Ocean View Chalets CHALET **$$**
(✆03-527 8232; www.accommodationabeltasman. co.nz; 305 Sandy Bay–Mārahau Rd; unit from $145; P ☎) 🦮 On a leafy hillside affording plenty of privacy, these cheerful, cypress-lined chalets

NELSON & MARLBOROUGH MĀRAHAU

RIWAKA

Just over the river from Motueka, Riwaka is a small settlement at the heart of fertile plains planted with orchards, vineyards and hops. If you're peckish while you're careering along SH60, there is a couple of roadside cafes and, in season, a stall selling cherries.

It's well worth taking a 6km detour to the end of Riwaka Valley Rd where a 10-minute walk through native bush leads to the peaceful **Riuwaka Resurgence** (Te Puna o Riuwaka in Māori, meaning 'The Spring of Riuwaka'). In this pocket of Kahurangi National Park, the Riuwaka River emerges from the base of Takaka Hill in a crystalline pool set within a ferny glade. This *wāhi tapu* (sacred place) was once used by the local Te Ātiawa and Ngāti Rārua people for cleansing and healing rituals. If you're wondering about the different spellings, Riwaka is a historic misspelling of the Māori name Riuwaka. It's been officially corrected for the name of the river but not the town.

Hop Federation (☑03-528 0486; www.hopfederation.co.nz; 483 Main Rd; ⊙11am-6pm) Pop in for tastings and fill a flagon to go at this teeny-weeny but terrific craft brewery. Pick of the ales is the Red IPA.

Eden's Edge Lodge (☑03-528 4242; www.edensedge.co.nz; 137 Lodder Lane; d/tw/tr $120/120/150; ⓟ⊚) Surrounded by farmland, this friendly lodge's facilities include attractive, comfy, en-suite rooms and relaxed communal areas. A do-it-yourself breakfast is included – with organic eggs from the owners' hens – and there are fresh herbs aplenty in the garden for cooking up in the spotless kitchen. An arcade machine in the lounge is loaded with every game imaginable.

Resurgence (☑03-528 4664; www.resurgence.co.nz; 574 Riwaka Valley Rd; s/d from $725/745; ⓟ⊚⊠) Choose a luxurious en-suite room or a self-contained 'bush suite' chalet at this magical green retreat. At peak times, rates include breakfast as well as aperitifs and a four-course dinner. At other times B&B-only rates are available.

Ginger Dynamite (☑021 168 8736; www.gingerdynamite.co.nz; 488 Main Rd; mains $6-8; ⊙8am-2.30pm) Operating out of a pair of brightly painted shipping containers, one of them set up to resemble a 1970s Kiwi bach (holiday house), this quirky coffee cart serves tasty meat pies, seafood chowder and scones to passing cyclists and motorists.

are 300m from the Coast Track with views out to Motuareroiti/Fisherman Island. All except the cheapest studios are self-contained; buffet breakfast and packed lunches are available.

Abel Tasman Lodge   MOTEL $$$
(☑03-527 8250; www.abeltasmanlodge.co.nz; 295 Sandy Bay–Mārahau Rd; unit from $200; ⓟ❋⊚) ⌖ Evoke halcyon days in this renovated arc of studios and self-contained apartments with hip styling and cathedral ceilings, opening onto landscaped gardens. There's also a communal kitchen, barbecues and a spa pool. Tui and bellbirds squawk and warble in the bushy surrounds, and some of the interior decor is styled after local bird life.

✕ Eating

Fat Tui   BURGERS $
(☑03-527 8420; cnr Sandy Bay–Mārahau & Mārahau Valley Rds; mains $12-17; ⊙noon-8pm Nov-May) Everyone's heard about this bird, based in a caravan that isn't going anywhere. Thank goodness. It serves superlative burgers, such as the Cowpat (beef), the Ewe Beaut (Morrocan lamb) and Roots, Shoots & Leaves (vegie). Fish and chips, and coffee, too.

Hooked   CAFE $$
(☑03-527 8576; www.hookedonmarahau.co.nz; 229 Sandy Bay–Mārahau Rd; breakfast $17-20, mains $24-29; ⊙8am-10pm Dec-Mar, 8-11am & 4-8pm Mon, Tue, Thu & Fri, 8am-8pm Sat & Sun Oct, Nov & Apr; ☞) ⌖ The art-bedecked interior of this popular place opens on to an outdoor terrace with distracting views. Seafood is showcased on the menu, including *kokoda/ika mata* (Pasifika-style raw fish in lemon and coconut milk), fish and chips, grilled salmon, banana-leaf snapper and seafood spaghetti, alongside local lamb, burgers and salad bowls. Pop in for happy hour drinks from 4pm to 6pm.

Park Cafe   CAFE $$
(☑03-527 8270; www.parkcafe.co.nz; 350 Sandy Bay–Mārahau Rd; pizza $18-24; ⊙8am-late Wed-Sun Nov-May; ☞) At the Coast Track trailhead, this breezy cafe is perfect for fuelling up or

replenishing reserves. High-calorie options include the big breakfast, burgers and cakes, but there are also seafood and salad options, plus wood-fired pizza Wednesday through Saturday evenings. Enjoy in the room with a view or the sunny courtyard garden. Check online for occasional live music listings.

ⓘ Getting There & Away

ScenicNZ Abel Tasman (p294) runs daily buses to/from Nelson ($21, 1¾ hours), Motueka ($11, 40 minutes) and Kaiteriteri ($8, 20 minutes); two daily in summer.

Abel Tasman National Park

Coastal Abel Tasman National Park blankets the northern end of a range of marble and limestone hills that extends from Kahurangi National Park. There are various tracks in the park, although the Coast Track (p287) is what everyone is here for – it's New Zealand's most popular Great Walk.

The main reason for the track's popularity is that it traverses some of New Zealand's (and arguably the world's) finest golden-sand beaches. Only a few can be reached by road, but non–Great Walkers can access others by kayak, water taxi or one of the scheduled boat transfers.

🏃 Activities

Those wanting a quieter alternative to the Coast Track (p287) might like to consider the **Inland Track**, a tougher and much less frequented path taking three days. It explores the forested interior and hence doesn't compete with the coast in terms of scenery. It can be combined with the Coast Track to form a five- to six-day loop.

If you can only spare a couple of days, a deservedly popular option is the loop around the northern end of the park, hiking the Coast Track from Tōtaranui, passing Anapai and Mutton Cove, overnighting at Whariwharangi Hut, then returning to Tōtaranui via the **Gibbs Hill Track**. This will give you a slice of the park's best features (beaches, seals, coastal scenery) and will be far less crowded than any other segment.

Perhaps the best short non-coastal walk is the **Wainui Falls Track**, an easy 25-minute, 2km-each-way path through beautiful native bush. The track leads alongside a boulder-strewn river and across two suspension bridges to the waterfall, which crashes violently into a green-tinged pool. The car park is well signposted from Abel Tasman Drive, 11km east of Pōhara.

👉 Tours

Tour companies usually offer free Motueka pick-up/drop-off, with Nelson pick-up available at extra cost.

★**Abel Tasman Canyons** ADVENTURE (☑03-528 9800; www.abeltasmancanyons.co.nz; full-day trip $289; ⊗Oct-Apr) Few Abel Tasman visitors see the Torrent River, but here's your chance to journey down its staggeringly beautiful granite-lined canyon, via a fun-filled combination of swimming, sliding, abseiling, ziplining and big leaps into jewel-like pools. Other trips explore

THE PEOPLE'S BEACH

When an 800m arc of Awaroa Bay in Abel Tasman National Park was offered for sale by a private owner in late 2015, there was concern that overseas buyers could secure the sheltered slice of paradise. But following chats over a few beers on Christmas Day 2015, up stepped two proud South Islanders to rally the public of NZ and instigate the biggest crowd-funding campaign the country has ever seen.

Against the threat of offshore purchasers winning the tender for the 7 hectares of coastal perfection, Duane Major and Adam Gard'ner – both regular summertime visitors to the bays and coves of Abel Tasman National Park – launched a campaign on the NZ crowdfunding website, Givealittle, to secure the beach for all New Zealanders.

By the time the deadline was reached in February 2016, 29,239 private donors had raised $2,259,923, and, along with significant corporate donations and $350,000 from the NZ government, the winning tender of more than $2.8 million was reached.

Less than five months later, Awaroa Bay was officially incorporated into Abel Tasman National Park. With its now-protected status, there are ongoing efforts to restore the beach's sand-dune ecosystem, and native plant species are being replanted to improve the habitat for coastal birds, including oystercatchers, dotterel and godwits.

PADDLING THE ABEL TASMAN

The Abel Tasman Coast Track has long been hiking territory, but its coastal beauty makes it an equally seductive spot for sea kayaking, which can easily be combined with walking and camping.

A variety of professional outfits are able to float you out on the water, and the possibilities and permutations for guided or freedom trips are vast. You can kayak from half a day up to three days, staying in DOC huts or campsites (book in advance online before entering the park), or in any of the other park accommodation. You can kayak one day, camp overnight then walk back, or walk further into the park and catch a water taxi back.

Most operators offer similar trips at similar prices, focusing on the safer southern half of the park (as far as Onetahuti Beach). Mārahau is the main base, but trips also depart from Kaiteriteri. There are numerous day-trip options, including guided trips often departing from Mārahau and taking in bird-filled Motuareronui/Adele Island (around $200). There are also various multiday guided trips, with three days a common option, costing anything from $285 to $900 depending on accommodation and other inclusions.

Freedom rentals (double-kayak and equipment hire) are around $85/130 per person for one/two days; all depart from Mārahau with the exception of Golden Bay Kayaks (p307), which is based at Tata Beach in Golden Bay. Instruction is given to everyone, and most tour companies have a minimum age of either eight or 14 depending on the trip. None allow solo hires. Camping gear is usually provided on overnight trips; if you're disappearing into the park for a few days, most operators provide free car parking.

November to Easter is the busiest time, with December to February the absolute peak. You can, however, paddle all year round, with winter offering its own rewards; the weather is surprisingly amenable, the seals are more playful, and there's more bird life and less haze. Here are the key players in this competitive market (shop around):

Abel Tasman Kayaks (☑ 03-527 8022; www.abeltasmankayaks.co.nz; 273 Sandy Bay–Mārahau Rd, Mārahau; guided tours from $120, full-day rental $45) 🍃

Kahu Kayaks (☑ 03-527 8300; www.kahukayaks.co.nz; 325 Sandy Bay-Mārahau Rd, Mārahau; guided tour from $100, full-day rental $85)

Kaiteriteri Kayaks (☑ 03-527 8383; www.seakayak.co.nz; 3 Kaiteriteri-Sandy Bay Rd, Kaiteriteri; ⊙ half-day tour adult/child from $90/65, 1/2/3/4hr rental $30/45/55/60)

Mārahau Sea Kayaks (☑ 03-527 8176; www.msk.co.nz; 229 Sandy Bay-Mārahau Rd, Mārahau; tours from $130, full-day rental from $85) 🍃

R&R Kayaks (☑ 03-527 8197; www.rrkayaks.co.nz; 279 Sandy Bay-Mārahau Rd, Mārahau; tours from $150, full-day rental $85)

Wilsons (p302)

Kahurangi National Park and Mt Richmond Forest Park, and combo adventures including kayaking or skydiving are also available.

Wilsons OUTDOORS
(Map p298; ☑ 03-528 2027; www.abeltasman.co.nz; 409 High St, Motueka; walks, cruises $38-89, tours $79-185) This long-standing, family-owned operator offers an impressive array of cruises, walking, kayaking and combo tours. Overnight stays are available at Wilsons' lodges in pretty Awaroa and Torrent Bay for guided-tour guests. Offers an Explorer Pass for unlimited boat travel on three days over a seven-day period (adult/child $158/79).

🛏 Sleeping

Along the Abel Tasman Coast Track are four Great Walk huts ($75) with bunks, heating, flush toilets and limited lighting, but no cooking facilities. There are also 18 designated Great Walk campsites ($30). All Great Walks huts and campsites must be booked in advance online year-round (www.doc.govt.nz). Penalty fees apply to those who do not have a valid booking, and you may be required to leave the park if caught.

Tōtaranui Campground CAMPGROUND $
(☑ 03-528 8083; www.doc.govt.nz; adult/child $15/7.50) Not to be confused with the adjacent Tōtaranui Great Walk Campsite, this extremely popular facility has a whopping

Abel Tasman National Park

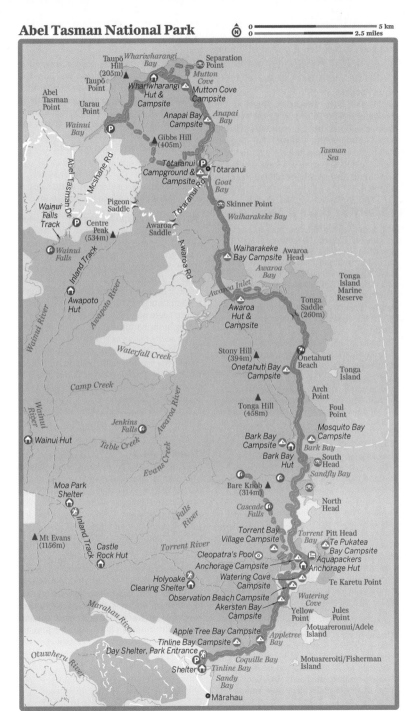

capacity (850 campers) and a splendid setting next to the beach backed by some of the best bush in the park. A staffed DOC office has interpretive displays, flush toilets, cold showers and a public phone.

Aqua Packers HOSTEL $$$
(☑ 027 430 7400; www.aquapackers.co.nz; Anchorage; dm/r $110/265; ☉ Oct-Easter) This specially converted, permanently moored 13m catamaran provides unusual but buoyant backpacker accommodation for 22. Facilities are basic but decent; prices include a barbecue dinner and simple breakfast. Bookings essential.

❶ Getting There & Away

Daily buses head to Mārahau, the park's southern gateway. Between November and March, Golden Bay Coachlines (p294) also has a daily bus to Tōtaranui and the Wainui car park from Nelson ($59, three hours), Motueka ($50, 2¼ hours), Takaka ($24, one hour) and Pōhara ($20, 50 minutes).

Heaphy Track Help (p309) offers car relocation ($250) from one trailhead to the other, in either direction.

Scheduled boat services depart from both Kaiteriteri and Mārahau. Most operators provide shuttles from Motueka.

Abel Tasman AquaTaxi (☑ 03-527 8083; www.aquataxi.co.nz; 275 Sandy Bay-Mārahau Rd, Mārahau) Up to four boats daily between Mārahau and Tōtaranui ($51, 1¾ hours) via Anchorage ($40, 45 minutes), Bark Bay ($44, one hour), Onetahuti ($46, 1¼ hours) and Awaroa ($49, 1½ hours).

Abel Tasman Sea Shuttle (☑ 03-527 8688; www.abeltasmanseashuttles.co.nz; 2 Kaiteriteri-Sandy Bay Road, Kaiteriteri) Two to four boats daily between Kaiteriteri and Tōtaranui ($48, 1½ hours) via Apple Tree Bay ($20, 25 minutes), Anchorage ($34, 50 minutes), Medlands Beach ($38, one hour), Tonga Quarry ($40, 1¼ hours) and Awaroa ($45, 1½ hours).

Marahau Water Taxis (☑ 03-527 8176; www.marahauwatertaxis.co.nz; 229 Sandy Bay-Mārahau Rd, Mārahau) Two to four boats a day between Mārahau and Tōtaranui ($49, two hours) via Anchorage ($37, 45 minutes), Bark Bay ($42, one hour), Onetahuti ($44, 1¼ hours) and Awaroa ($47, 1½ hours).

Wilsons (p302) One to four boats daily between Kaiteriteri and Tōtaranui ($51, two hours) via Apple Tree Bay ($35, 20 minutes), Anchorage ($40, 45 minutes), Torrent Bay ($40, 45 minutes), Medlands ($42, one hour), Tonga Quarry ($46, 1½ hours) and Awaroa ($49, 1¾ hours).

Takaka & Around
POP 1240

Boasting New Zealand's highest concentration of yoga pants, dreadlocks and bare feet in the high street, Takaka is a lovable little town and the last 'big' centre before the road west ends at Farewell Spit. You'll find most things you need here, and a few things you don't, but we all have an unworn tie-dyed tank top in our wardrobe, don't we?

◉ Sights

Many of Takaka's sights are a little out of town, but they can all be reached by bike.

★ **Te Waikoropupū Springs** SPRING
(www.doc.govt.nz; Pupu Springs Rd) Around 14,000L of water per second bubble up from underground vents here, making it the largest freshwater spring in the southern hemisphere. It's also among the clearest in the world. The colourful little lake is reached via a 45-minute forest loop from the car park, where there are Māori carvings and illuminating information panels. Māori consider this a *wāhi tapu* (sacred place), and hence the waters are off limits to all but the local tribe who use them for healing and other ceremonies. Tradition has it that a *taniwha* (a kind of dinosaur-like spiritual guardian) regularly visits here.

From Takaka, head 4km northwest on SH60 and follow the signs inland for 3km from Waitapu Bridge.

Rawhiti Cave CAVE
(www.doc.govt.nz) The ultimate in geological eye-candy around these parts are the phyto-karst features of Rawhiti Cave, a 15-minute drive from Takaka (reached via Motupipi, turning right into Glenview Rd, then left into Packard Rd and following the signs; the last 800m passes through farmland). The rugged two-hour-return walk is steep in places and can be dangerous in the wet.

Anatoki Salmon HATCHERY
(☑ 03-525 7251; www.anatokisalmon.co.nz; 230 McCallum Rd; ☉ 10am-4.30pm; 🖶) Here's your chance to catch a salmon and have it smoked for lunch or prepared as super-fresh sashimi. Rods and instructions are provided, but the fish pretty well catch themselves anyway. Other attractions beyond fishing include hand-feeding tame eels, a petting zoo for the kids and minigolf. There's no entrance fee, but expect to pay around $40 to $55 for your

salmon. Salmon snacks and platters (from $21) are available at the Salmon Cafe.

 Activities

Pupu Hydro Walkway   HIKING

(www.doc.govt.nz; Pupu Valley Rd) Part of Kahurangi National Park, this enjoyable two-hour circuit follows an old water race through beech forest, past engineering and gold-mining relics to the restored (and operational) Pupu Hydro Powerhouse, built in 1929. It's 9km from Takaka at the end of the unsealed but well-maintained Pupu Valley Rd; just follow the signs at the Te Waikoropupū Springs junction and be prepared to cross a couple of fords.

Golden Bay Air   SCENIC FLIGHTS

(☑03-525 8725; www.goldenbayair.co.nz; Takaka Aerodrome, 290 Takaka–Collingwood Hwy; scenic flights per person $50-290) As well as their scheduled flights, this crew offers scenic and charter flights around Golden Bay and its surrounds.

Adventure Flights Golden Bay   SCENIC FLIGHTS

(☑03-525 6167; www.adventureflightsgoldenbay. co.nz; Takaka Aerodrome, 290 Takaka-Collingwood Hwy; scenic flights per person $40-320) Offers scenic and charter flights over the national parks, Farewell Spit and the West Coast.

Quiet Revolution Cycle Shop   CYCLING

(☑03-525 9555; 11 Commercial St; bike hire per day from $25; ⊙9am-4.30pm Tue-Fri, to 12.30pm Sat) You'll get personal service at this most proper of bike shops. It offers town-, mountain- and e-bike hire, plus top-notch servicing and sales, local ride maps and a car relocation service for the Heaphy Track in winter, too.

🛏 Sleeping

Some of the area's best accommodation is out of the town centre, with a couple of great options by the beach at Tukurua, 18km to the north.

Golden Bay Holiday Park   HOLIDAY PARK $

(☑03-525 9742; www.goldenbayholidaypark.co.nz; 99 Tukurua Rd, Tukurua; site/cabin/house from $50/105/195; [P][@][🖥]) With a quiet beach right out front, this gem of a park has acres of grass, graceful shade trees and hedgerows, atoning for older communal facilities. There are tidy, family-friendly cabins for budget travellers, and luxury beach houses sleeping up to four.

Kiwiana Backpackers   HOSTEL $

(☑03-525 7676; www.kiwianabackpackers.co.nz; 73 Motupipi St; sites/dm/s/d $20/30/55/70; [🖥]) Beyond the welcoming garden and rainbow picket fence is a cute cottage where rooms are named after classic Kiwiana (the jandal, Buzzy Bee...). The garage has been converted into a convivial lounge, with wood-fired stove, table tennis, pool table, music, books and games; free bikes for guest use.

Golden Bay Motel   MOTEL $$

(☑03-525 9428; www.goldenbaymotel.co.nz; 132 Commercial St; unit from $145; [P][🖥][♿]) At the

---

TAKAKA HILL

Takaka Hill (791m) butts in between Tasman Bay and Golden Bay, and between the Abel Tasman and Kahurangi National Parks. It looks fairly bushy but closer inspection reveals a remarkable marble landscape formed by millions of years of erosion. Its smooth beauty is revealed on the one-hour drive over the hill road (SH60), a steep, winding route punctuated by spectacular lookout points and a smattering of other interesting stops.

Just before the summit is the turn-off to **Canaan Downs Scenic Reserve**, reached at the end of a rough 11km gravel road. This area stars in both *The Lord of the Rings* and *The Hobbit* movies, but **Harwoods Hole** is the most famous feature here. It's one of the largest *tomo* (caves) in the country at 357m deep and 70m wide, with a 176m vertical drop – although you can't really see much from ground level. It's a 30-minute walk from the car park. Allow us to state the obvious: the cave is off limits to all but the most experienced cavers.

It is possible, however, to take a guided tour of the **Ngarua Caves** (☑03-528 8093; www. ngaruacaves.co.nz; 1242 SH60; adult/child $20/8; ⊙45min tours hourly 10am-4pm Oct-Apr, phone ahead other months), situated on private land just below the summit of Takaka Hill. The myriad subterranean delights on display here include stalagmites, stalactites and moa bones.

Mountain bikers with intermediate-level skills can venture along a couple of loop tracks, or head all the way down to Takaka via the titillating **Rameka Track**. Also close to the top, the **Takaka Hill Walkway** is a 2½-hour loop through marble karst rock formations, native forest and farmland. For more walks, see DOC's *Walks in Golden Bay* brochure.

time of research, new owners were in the process of renovating this old motel, which has units in various configurations. Some of the decor's still a bit dated, but units have kitchens and there's a big garden at the rear with a kids' play set.

⭐ **Adrift in Golden Bay** COTTAGE $$$

(☑03-525 8353; www.adrift.co.nz; 53 Tukurua Rd, Tukurua; villa $399-488; ⊙Sep-May; 🅿🛜) 🄿 Adrift on a bed of beachside bliss is what you'll be in one of these five cottages dotted within gardens, right on the beach. Tuck into your breakfast hamper, then self-cater in the fully equipped kitchen, dine on the sunny deck, or soak in the spa bath. A minimum two-night stay usually applies. A stylish studio is also available.

🍴 Eating & Drinking

Wholemeal Cafe CAFE $

(☑03-525 9426; www.wholemealcafe.co.nz; 60 Commercial St; mains $9-22; ⊙7.30am-3pm Sun-Thu, to 7.30pm Fri & Sat; 🛜🄿♿) Within the cavernous, brightly painted interior of this old theatre is a cabinet groaning under the weight of tempting savoury and sweet options. They bake their own bread, which makes its way into cooked breakfasts and sandwiches. Lunch and dinner options include soup, curry and spanakopita; vegetarians and vegans are well catered for.

Curry Leaf FAST FOOD $

(☑03-525 8481; www.thecurryleaf.co.nz; 5a Commercial St; mains $10-19; ⊙11.30am-9pm; 🄿) Trust Takaka to have a kooky takeaway joint in a shipping container, painted with a giant squid mural. The menu isn't run-of-the-mill either. Sure, they do burgers, but there are also naan wraps, and various other Indian and Thai dishes. The fish green curry is excellent; enjoy it at one of the tables out the front or take it away.

Choco Loco SWEETS $

(☑027 363 6622; www.chocoloco.co.nz; 47b Commercial St; items $2.50-4.50; ⊙9am-3pm Mon-Fri, 10am-1pm Sat) Sweet-toothed travellers should start their days with a chocolate-and-almond croissant at this cute little shop, where all the chocolate truffles, brownies and cakes are handcrafted on-site. Order a coffee, tea or hot chocolate and choose a dainty receptacle for it from the 'cup library'.

Roots Bar PUB FOOD $$

(☑03-525 9592; www.rootsbar.co.nz; 1 Commercial St; mains $19-32; ⊙11am-late; 🛜) 🄿 Aside from being Takaka's best bar, this hip joint also turns out its most interesting food. Wild game meat finds its way into venison burgers, goat meatballs and Jamaican goat curries, served alongside lamb shanks, steaks and a large selection of burgers. There's a range of good local craft beers, too. Check online for details of regular gigs and DJ sets.

Dangerous Kitchen CAFE $$

(☑03-525 8686; www.thedangerouskitchen.co.nz; 46a Commercial St; ⊙9am-9pm Mon-Sat, closed Aug; 🄿♿) 🄿 This cafe serves good-value fare such as falafel salads, pizza, burritos, pasta and baked goods, as well as juices and local wines and craft beer. It's mellow and musical, with a sunny courtyard out the back and people-watching out the front. Check out the quirky mural near the entrance, and ask about occasional live music.

Mussel Inn PUB

(☑03-525 9241; www.musselinn.co.nz; 1259 Takaka–Collingwood Hwy, Ōnekakā; ⊙11am-late) You will find one of NZ's most beloved brewery-taverns halfway between Takaka and Collingwood. The Mussel Inn is rustic NZ at its most genuine, complete with creaking timbers, a rambling beer garden with a brazier, regular music and other events, and hearty, homemade food (snacks $6 to $19, dinner $30). Try the signature Captain Cooker, a brown beer brewed naturally with mānuka.

🛍 Shopping

Shopping in Takaka is a highlight if you enjoy homespun art and craft. Galleries along the main street are worthy of attention.

Dancing Sands Distillery DRINKS

(☑03-525 9899; www.dancingsands.com; 46a Commercial St; ⊙10am-4pm Mon-Sat Nov-Easter, Mon-Fri Easter-Oct) 🄿 Here's a surprise – an award-winning distillery tucked down a laneway off Takaka's main street. Its gin and vodka is crafted from water from the same aquifer that feeds the pristine waters of the nearby Te Waikoropupū Springs, and variations include NZ's first barrel-aged gin, and gin flavoured with wasabi, chocolate or saffron. Free tastings will help you choose.

ℹ Information

Golden Bay Visitor Centre (☑03-525 9136; www.goldenbaynz.co.nz; 8 Willow St; ⊙9am-5.30pm Oct-Easter, 9.30am-2.30pm Mon-Sat Easter-Sep) A friendly little centre with all the necessary information, including a free tourist map, bookings and DOC passes.

ℹ️ Getting There & Away

Golden Bay Air (p305) flies to/from Wellington, Nelson and Karamea.

Golden Bay Coachlines (p294) has a daily service from Nelson ($39, two hours) and Motueka ($28, 1¼ hours) year-round, with a second bus from November to March that continues on to Collingwood ($15, 25 minutes) and the Heaphy Track trailhead ($35, one hour), or to Pōhara ($12, 10 minutes) and Tōtaranui ($24, one hour).

Pōhara

POP 571

About 8km northeast of Takaka is pint-sized Pōhara, a beachy village with a population that quadruples over summer. It has more flash holiday homes than other parts of Golden Bay, but an agreeable air persists nonetheless, aided by decent food and lodging, and a beach that at low tide is as big as Heathrow's runway.

Pōhara lies close to the northern gateway of Abel Tasman National Park. The largely unsealed road into the park passes **Tarakohe Harbour** (Pōhara's working port), followed by **Ligar Bay** and beautiful **Tata Beach**. It's worth climbing to the Abel Tasman lookout as you pass by.

◉ Sights & Activities

Grove Scenic Reserve VIEWPOINT

(www.doc.govt.nz; Rocklands Rd, Clifton) Between Pōhara and Takaka (signposted down Clifton Rd), you will find this crazy limestone maze punctuated by gnarled old rata trees and tall pencil-thin nikau palms. The walkway takes around 10 minutes and passes an impressive lookout.

Golden Bay Kayaks KAYAKING

(📞 03-525 9095; www.goldenbaykayaks.co.nz; 29 Cornwall Pl, Tata Beach; half-day guided tours $100, half/full day rental $60/80; 🚣) Based at Tata Beach, this long-standing operator runs guided trips (including family-friendly options) and rents kayaks for hour-long to multiday paddles in Abel Tasman National Park, as well as stand-up paddle boards and sit-on-tops.

🛏️ Sleeping & Eating

The Sandcastle COTTAGE $$

(📞 03-525 9087; www.goldenbayaccommodation. co.nz; 32 Haile Lane; cottages $120-150; P🖥️) There's more than a hint of hippy to this complex of six colourful, self-contained cottages set in a peaceful garden with views to the ocean. Don't expect anything flash but there is a pizza oven, a tinkling water feature, and massage and yoga on offer.

Sans Souci Inn LODGE $$

(📞 03-525 8663; www.sanssouciinn.co.nz; 11 Richmond Rd; s/d $110/130, units from $170; ⊙mid-Sep–Jun; P🖥️) *Sans souci* means 'no worries' in French, and this will be your mantra too after staying in one of the seven Mediterranean-flavoured, mud-brick rooms. Guests share a plant-filled, mosaic bathroom with composting toilets, and an airy lounge and kitchen that open onto a semitropical courtyard. Dinner in the restaurant is highly recommended (bookings essential; summer only); breakfast by request.

Pohara Beach Top 10 HOLIDAY PARK $$

(📞 03-525 9500; www.poharabeach.com; 809 Abel Tasman Dr; sites $51-57, unit with/without bathroom $121/85; @🖥️) Lining grassy parkland between the dunes and the main road, this place is in prime position for some beach time. Some sites are right by the beach and there are some beaut cabins, but be warned – this is a favourite spot for NZ holidaymakers so it goes a bit mental in high summer. There's a general store and takeaway on-site.

Ratanui LODGE $$$

(📞 03-525 7998; www.ratanuilodge.com; 818 Abel Tasman Dr; r $425-455; ⊙closed Aug; 🖥️🏊) A romantic wisteria- and grapevine-draped haven close to the beach, this boutique lodge is styled with Victorian panache. It features myriad sensual stimulants such as perfumed rose gardens, a swimming pool, a spa, cocktails and a candelabra-lit restaurant showcasing local produce (open to the public; bookings required). Free bikes, too.

ℹ️ Getting There & Away

Between November and March, Golden Bay Coachlines (p294) has a daily bus to/from Tōtaranui ($20, 50 minutes), Takaka ($12, 10 minutes), Motueka ($38, 1½ hours) and Nelson ($49, 2¼ hours).

Collingwood & Around

POP 244

Far-flung Collingwood is the northernmost town in Golden Bay, and has a real end-of-the-line vibe. It's busy in summer, though for most people it's simply a launch pad for the Heaphy Track (p288) or Farewell Spit (p308).

OFF THE BEATEN TRACK

CAPE FAREWELL & FAREWELL SPIT

Bleak, exposed and positively sci-fi, **Farewell Spit** is a wetland of international importance and a renowned bird sanctuary. At low tide a large sandy intertidal zone is exposed on the Golden Bay side – the summer home of thousands of migratory waders, notably the godwit, Caspian tern and Australasian gannet. Unfortunately, the shallow waters are also notorious for mass strandings of pilot whales – in one incident in February 2017, over 400 beached themselves simultaneously; despite the best efforts of an army of volunteers, most of them died.

Walkers can explore the first 4km of the spit via a network of tracks (see DOC's *Farewell Spit & Puponga Farm Park* brochure; $2 or download from www.doc.govt.nz). Beyond that point, access is limited to trips with the brilliant Farewell Spit Tours (p308), scheduled according to tides.

The spit's 35km beach features colossal, crescent-shaped dunes, from where panoramic views extend across Golden Bay and a vast low-tide salt marsh. At the foot of the spit is a hilltop visitor-centre-cum-cafe – a convenient spot to write a postcard over a coffee, especially on an inclement day.

Wharariki Beach This remote, dramatically beautiful beach is a magnificent introduction to the West Coast, with a seal colony at its eastern end and otherworldly rock formations scattered about including, just offshore, the extraordinary Archway Islands. As inviting as the water may seem, don't even think about swimming: strong undertows make it incredibly dangerous. From the turn-off at Puponga it's 6km along an unsealed road, then a 1km walk from the car park over farmland (part of the DOC-administered Puponga Farm Park).

Cape Farewell Horse Treks (☑ 03-524 8031; www.horsetreksnz.com; 36 McGowan St, Puponga; treks from $100) Befitting a frontier, this is the place to saddle up. Treks in this wind-blown country range from 1½ hours along Puponga Beach to five hours, continuing over Old Man's Range to Wharariki Beach.

Like Takaka, it's got its fair share of hippies. Like Nelson, it's named after a British military hero: the admiral who was Nelson's second in charge at the Battle of Trafalgar.

⊙ Sights & Activities

Collingwood Museum MUSEUM
(☑ 03-524 8131; 2 Tasman St; ⊙ 9am-6pm) FREE
This tiny unstaffed museum fills a corridor of the former council office with a quirky collection of saddlery, moa bones, shells, sewing machines and old typewriters. Next door, the **Aorere Centre** has historic photographs of the town by pioneer photographer Fred Tyree.

★ **Farewell Spit Tours** ECOTOUR
(☑ 03-524 8257; www.farewellspit.com; 6 Tasman St; tours $135-170) 🌿 Operating for more than 70 years and employing expert, knowledgeable guides, this company runs memorable tours of Farewell Spit ranging from two to 6½ hours. Tours take in the lighthouse and plenty of birdwatching. Expect ripping yarns aplenty.

🛏 Sleeping & Eating

The Innlet HOSTEL $
(☑ 03-524 8040; www.theinnlet.co.nz; 839 Collingwood-Puponga Rd, Pakawau; dm $40 s/d with bathroom from $75/95, without $70/90; ⊙ Oct-May; 🛜) This leafy charmer is 10km from Collingwood on the way to Farewell Spit. The main house has attractive backpacker rooms, and self-contained options including a cottage sleeping six. Enjoy the garden and explore the local area on a bike, in a kayak or on foot.

Station House Motel MOTEL $$
(☑ 03-524 8464; www.accommodationcollingwood. co.nz; 7 Elizabeth St; r/unit from $120/135; 🛜) It seems like false modesty to call this charming accommodation a motel. Rather than a row of cookie-cutter units, there are two small cottages in the back garden and two rooms in an attractive century-old wooden villa. All four are self-contained with en-suite bathrooms and kitchenettes, and there's a guest barbecue, too.

Zatori Retreat LODGE $$$
(☑ 03-524 8692; www.zatori.co.nz; 2321 Takaka-Collingwood Hwy; s/tw/d without bathroom $55/

60/140, r with bathroom $229-399; ⓟ 🛜) 🥾 This former maternity hospital has been transformed into a stylish, relaxing retreat. Chic suites surround a spacious lounge area enlivened with colourful artworks from Asia, and offering brilliant views over the water. A separate wing houses rooms with shared bathrooms for budget travellers. The restaurant and bar are also open to nonguests.

MAD Café CAFE $$
(📞 03-524 8660; www.facebook.com/madcafegold enbay; 7 Tasman St; mains $16-28; ⊙ 8am-8pm Wed-Sun, daily summer; 🅿 ♿) 🥾 With oddball art on the walls and a barista that looks like he's been beamed in from Woodstock, this is the ultimate Golden Bay hippy cafe. The name stands for Make A Difference; don't be surprised if you stumble into an art class or other community event. The menu is succinct but tasty: breakfasts, laksa, slow-cooked venison, burgers and pan-fried fish.

❶ Getting There & Away

From November to March, Golden Bay Coachlines (p294) has a daily bus to/from the Heaphy Track trailhead ($25, 40 minutes), Takaka ($15, 25 minutes), Motueka ($41, 1¾ hours) and Nelson ($54, 2½ hours).

Kahurangi National Park

Kahurangi – 'blue skies' in one of several translations – is the second largest of New Zealand's national parks, and also one of its most diverse. Its most eye-catching features are geological, ranging from windswept beaches and sea cliffs to earthquake-shattered slopes and moraine-dammed lakes, and the smooth, strange karst forms of the interior tableland.

Around 85% of the 5173 sq km park is forested, and more than 50% of NZ's plant species can be found here, including more than 80% of its alpine plant species. Among the park's 60 bird species are great spotted kiwi, kea, kākā, takahē and whio (blue duck). There are creepy cave weta, weird beetles and a large, leggy spider, but there's also a majestic and ancient snail known as Powelliphanta – something of a flag bearer for the park's animal kingdom. If you like a field trip filled with the new and strange, Kahurangi National Park will certainly satisfy.

🏃 Activities

The Heaphy Track (p288) and Wangapeka Track (p288) are just part of a 650km network of trails that includes excellent full-day and overnight hikes such as those in the **Cobb Valley** and **Mt Arthur/Tablelands**. See www.doc.govt.nz for detailed information on all Kahurangi tracks.

❶ Getting There & Away

The two road ends of the Heaphy Track are an almost unfathomable distance apart: 449km to be precise. **Heaphy Track Help** (📞 027 446 0128; www.heaphytrackhelp.co.nz) offers car relocation ($375) from one trailhead to the other, in either direction.

From November to March, Golden Bay Coachlines (p294) has a daily service to the Brown Hut (northeastern) trailhead from Collingwood ($25, 40 minutes), Takaka ($35, one hour), Motueka ($52, 2¼ hours) and Nelson ($65, three hours); and to the Kōhaihai (southwestern) trailhead from Westport ($55, 1¾ hours), Granity ($45, 1½ hours) and Karamea ($20, 15 minutes).

Karamea Express (📞 03-782 6757; www.karameaexpress.co.nz) operates a daily shuttle between Karamea and the Kōhaihai trailhead ($20); booking ahead is essential. Wangapeka Track transport is also available.

From November to April, **Heaphy Bus** (📞 03-540 2042; www.theheaphybus.co.nz) offers a scheduled round-trip shuttle service from Nelson to each trailhead ($170); on-demand track transport is also available.

Adventure Flights Golden Bay (p305) will fly you to Karamea and the Brown Hut trailhead from Takaka, Motueka or Nelson. Per person prices range from $85 (Takaka–Brown Hut) to $285 (Nelson–Karamea); two people minimum.

Another option is to charter a flight to any of the Heaphy or Wangapeka trailheads with Helicopter Charter Karamea (p280).

MARLBOROUGH DISTRICT

Picton is a major gateway to the South Island and the main launching point for Marlborough Sounds exploration. A cork's pop south of Picton is Blenheim and its world-famous wineries. Highlights of this region include negotiating the famed Queen Charlotte Track, either on foot or by mountain bike, and discovering the many hidden bays and coves of the Marlborough Sounds by boat. At the end of a busy day, relaxing over a glass of local sauvignon blanc and a bowl of greenshell mussels is highly recommended.

History

Abel Tasman sheltered on the east coast of D'Urville Island in 1642, more than 100 years before James Cook blew through in 1770. It was Cook who named Queen Charlotte Sound (in Māori it's Tōtaranui); his reports made the area the best-known sheltered anchorage in the southern hemisphere. In 1827 French navigator Jules Dumont d'Urville discovered the narrow strait now known as French Pass. His officers named the island just to the north in his honour. In the same year a whaling station was established at Te Awaiti in Tory Channel, which brought about the first permanent European settlement in the district.

Marlborough Sounds

The Marlborough Sounds are a maze of peaks, bays, beaches and watery reaches, formed when the sea flooded deep river valleys after the last ice age. They are very convoluted: **Pelorus Sound**, for example, is 42km long but has 379km of shoreline.

The main gateways are Havelock, at the base of Pelorus Sound (Te Hoiere), and Picton, at the apex of **Queen Charlotte Sound**. The wiggly 35km route along **Queen Charlotte Drive** between the two is a great Sounds snapshot but, if you have a spare day, you're best to head out on the water. Better still, put aside four days to tackle the wonderful Queen Charlotte Track (p288).

There are loads of other hiking, kayaking, boating and biking opportunities, and there's diving as well – notably the wreck of the *Mikhail Lermontov,* a Russian cruise ship that sank in Port Gore in 1986.

◎ Sights & Activities

Motuara Island   WILDLIFE RESERVE
(www.doc.govt.nz) ✔ This DOC-managed, predator-free island reserve at the entrance to Queen Charlotte Sound is chock-full of rare NZ birds including the Ōkārito brown kiwi (rowi), wood pigeon (kererū), saddleback (tīeke) and king shag. You can get here by water taxi and on tours from Picton.

Lochmara   BAY
(☑ 03-573 4554; www.lochmara.co.nz; Lochmara Bay; day trips from $40) ✔ As well as offering lodge accommodation, this tourist complex can be visited on a variety of short cruises from Picton. Activities include kayaking; stand-up paddle boarding; bushwalks; a

sculpture walk; hand-feeding stingrays, eels and endangered kākāriki parakeets; and checking out Lochmara's underwater observatory (adult/child $20/10). Lunch and dinner options are also available.

Sea Kayak Adventures   KAYAKING, BIKING
(☑ 03-574 2765; www.nzseakayaking.com; cnr Queen Charlotte Dr & Anakiwa Rd; half-/full-day guided paddles $99/135) Guided kayaking and bike/hike options around Queen Charlotte, Kenepuru and Pelorus Sounds. It also offers kayak and mountain-bike rental (half-/full day $40/60).

🛏 Sleeping

Some Sounds sleeping options are accessible only by boat and are deliciously isolated, but the most popular are those on (or just off) the Queen Charlotte Track. Some places close over winter; call ahead to check. There are over 30 DOC camping grounds throughout the Sounds (many accessible only by boat), providing water and toilet facilities but not much else.

Smiths Farm Holiday Park   HOLIDAY PARK $
(☑ 03-574 2806; www.smithsfarm.co.nz; 1419 Queen Charlotte Dr, Linkwater; sites per person $20-22, units with/without bathroom from $120/65; 🅿🛜♿) ✔ Located on the aptly named Linkwater flat between Queen Charlotte and Pelorus, friendly Smiths makes a handy base camp for the track and beyond. Well-kept cabins and motel units face out onto the bushy hillside, while livestock nibble around the lush camping lawns. Short walks extend to a waterfall and magical glowworm dell.

On the Track Lodge   LODGE $$
(☑ 03-579 8411; www.onthetracklodge.nz; Nydia Bay; chalet s/d without bathroom $110/150, train s/d with bathroom $130/190, yurt $300; �;Nov-Apr) ✔ Providing an alternative to the DOC accommodation on the Nydia Track, this tranquil, ecofocused lodge offers breakfasts ($15), packed lunches ($20), evening meals (mains $25) and a hot tub. Accommodation options include a yurt, a 1930s railway carriage and cosy wooden chalets. There's no road access but the Pelorus Mail Boat stops in Nydia Bay twice a week.

Hopewell Lodge   LODGE $$
(☑ 03-573 4341; www.hopewell.co.nz; 7204 Kenepuru Rd, Double Bay; r with/without bathroom $165/125, cottage $265; ☐Sep-May; 🛜) Beloved of travellers, remote Hopewell sits waterside surrounded by native bush. Savour the long,

Marlborough Sounds

winding drive to get there, or take a water taxi from Te Mahia ($50 return). Stay a couple of days so you can chill out or enjoy the roll-call of activities: mountain biking, kayaking, sailing, fishing, eating pizza, soaking in the outdoor hot tub and more.

Anakiwa 401　　　　　　　GUESTHOUSE $$
(☏03-574 1388; www.anakiwa401.co.nz; 401 Anakiwa Rd, Anakiwa; s/tw without bathroom $85/110, r/apt with bathroom $140/160; ☺Aug-May; ⊚) At the southern end of the track, this former schoolhouse is a soothing spot to rest and reflect. There are two rooms (one en suite) and a beachy self-contained unit. Jocular owners will have you jumping off the jetty for joy and enjoying espresso and ice cream from their green caravan (open afternoons). Free bikes and kayaks.

Mistletoe Bay　　　　　　HOLIDAY PARK $$
(☏03-573 4048; www.mistletoebay.co.nz; Onahau Bay; sites per person $18, unit $140-190; ☺closed

Jul; ⊚) ✎ Surrounded by bushy hills, Mistletoe Bay offers attractive camping with no-frills facilities. There are also modern en-suite cabins and two self-contained

WORTH A TRIP

PELORUS BRIDGE SCENIC RESERVE

A pocket of deep, green forest tucked between paddocks and plantation forests, 18km west of Havelock, this scenic reserve contains one of the last stands of river-flat forest in Marlborough. It survived only because a town planned in 1865 didn't get off the ground by 1912, by which time obliterative logging made this little remnant look precious. Visitors can explore its many tracks, admire the historic bridge, take a dip in the limpid Pelorus River (alluring enough to star in Peter Jackson's *The Hobbit*), and partake in some home baking at the cafe. The fortunate few can stay overnight in DOC's small but perfectly formed **Pelorus Bridge (Kahikatea Flat) Campground** (☑03-571 6019; www.doc.govt.nz; SH6; sites per person $20-23), with its snazzy facilities building. Come sundown, keep an eye out for long-tailed bats – the reserve is home to one of the last remaining populations in Marlborough.

two-bedroom cottages (unusually, linen is an extra $7.50 per person). Environmental sustainability abounds, as does the opportunity to jump off the jetty, kayak in the bay, or hike the Queen Charlotte Track. There's a shop/cafe on-site.

Te Mahia Bay Resort   RESORT $$$

(☑03-573 4089; www.temahia.co.nz; 63 Te Mahia Rd; d $170-268; ☎) This lovely low-key resort is close to the Queen Charlotte Track in a picturesque bay on Kenepuru Sound. It has a range of delightful self-catering rooms-with-a-view, the pick of which are the good-value heritage units. The on-site shop has pizza, cakes, coffee and wine, plus personal chef and massage services are available.

Bay of Many Coves   RESORT $$$

(☑03-579 9771; www.bayofmanycoves.co.nz; Arthurs Bay; apt from $1345; ☎▨) Not accessible by road, these stylish, secluded apartments feature all mod cons and private balconies overlooking Queen Charlotte Sound. As well as upmarket cuisine, there are various indulgences such as massage, a spa and a hot tub. Kayaking and bush walks are also on the cards, as are adventures in the Sounds organised by the charming, hands-on owners and staff.

Mahana Lodge   LODGE $$$

(☑03-579 8373; www.mahanalodge.co.nz; Camp Bay, Endeavour Inlet; r $225-275; ⊙ Oct-Apr) ✒ This beautiful property features a pretty waterside lawn and purpose-built lodge with four en-suite doubles and a separate studio. Ecofriendly initiatives include bush regeneration, pest trapping and an organic vegetable garden. In fact, feel-good factors abound: free kayaks, home baking and a blooming conservatory where prearranged evening meals are served (three courses $75).

ℹ Getting There & Around

Sounds travel is invariably quicker by boat (for example, Punga Cove from Picton by car takes two hours, but just 45 minutes by boat). Fortunately, an armada of vessels offers scheduled cruises and on-demand boat services, with the bulk operating out of Picton for Queen Charlotte Sound, and some from Havelock for Kenepuru and Pelorus Sounds.

Options include **Arrow Water Taxis** (☑03-573 8229; www.arrowwatertaxis.co.nz; Town Wharf, Picton; fares from $30), **Kenepuru Water Taxi** (☑03-573 4344; www.kenepuru.co.nz; Havelock Marina), **Pelorus Sound Water Taxi** (☑027 444 2852; www.pelorussoundwatertaxis.co.nz; Pier C, Havelock Marina) and **Picton Water Taxis** (☑027 227 0284, 03-573 7853; www.pictonwatertaxis.co.nz; Town Wharf, Picton).

What roads there are along the ridges are narrow and occasionally unsealed; allow plenty of driving time and keep your wits about you.

Havelock

POP 486

Havelock (not to be confused with Havelock North in Hawkes Bay) sits at the head of Pelorus Sound and is the main hub for the western half of the Marlborough Sounds. It's the self-proclaimed 'Greenshell Mussel Capital of the World' and hence a great place to try this particular New Zealand delicacy. Aside from some well-preserved heritage buildings, there's not a lot to the town itself – but it's a good base from which to explore Pelorus and Kenepuru Sounds.

Māori knew Havelock as Motuweka (there's another town named Motueka in Tasman) and there were three major *pā* (fortified villages) in the area. The British followed the trend set with Nelson, Collingwood and Picton, and renamed it after one of their military heroes: Sir Henry Havelock, who had recently died during an uprising in India.

◎ Sights

Cullen Point Lookout   VIEWPOINT
Cullen Point curves around to the northeast of Havelock, sheltering the marina from the rest of Pelorus Sound. A 10-minute walk loops up and around the headland overlooking the village, the surrounding valleys and the Sound. Another track provides a hour-long loop along the coast. Both start from a car park 3km from Havelock along Queen Charlotte Dr.

Havelock Museum   MUSEUM
(www.havelockmuseum.nz; 74 Main Rd; ◎10am-4pm) **FREE** Inhabiting an old Methodist church, this cute, locally focused museum presents old colonial tales in a contemporary, easily digestible style.

🏃 Activities & Tours

Pelorus Mail Boat   CRUISE
(☑03-574 1088; www.themailboat.co.nz; Pier B, Havelock Marina; adult/child $132/free; ◎departs 10am daily Nov-Apr, Mon, Wed & Fri May-Oct) This popular full-day cruise heads through the far reaches of Pelorus Sound on a genuine postal delivery run, taking different routes on different days. Bookings essential; BYO lunch.

Pelorus Eco Adventures   KAYAKING
(☑021 133 3705; www.kayak-newzealand.com; Bluemoon Lodge, 48 Main Rd; adult/child $185/155) Float in an inflatable kayak on scenic Pelorus River, star of the barrel scene in *The Hobbit*. Wend your way down exhilarating rapids, through crystal-clear pools and past native forest and waterfalls. No experience required; tours last around four hours.

🛏 Sleeping

Bluemoon Lodge   HOSTEL $
(☑021 133 3705; www.bluemoonhavelock.co.nz; 48 Main Rd; dm/apt $37/132, r with/without bathroom from $102/84; P🐾🛜) 🐾 This pleasant and relaxed backpackers has homely rooms in the main house, a self-contained apartment with a spa bath, and bunk-filled cabins in the yard. Notable features include a sunny barbecue deck, inflatable kayak trips on the Pelorus River, and **Nydia Track** (www.doc.govt.nz) transport.

Havelock Garden Motel   MOTEL $$
(☑03-574 2387; www.gardenmotels.com; 71 Main Rd; units $130-160; P🛜) Set in a large gar-

den with old trees and blooms galore, these 1960s units have been tastefully revamped to offer home comforts. Local activities are happily booked for you.

🍴 Eating

★Mills Bay Mussels   SEAFOOD $
(☑03-574 2575; www.millsbaymussels.co.nz; 23a Inglis St; mains $6.50-17; ◎11am-3pm Thu, Sat & Sun, to 8pm Fri) How would you like your greenshell mussels? Steamed with white wine and garlic? Grilled in garlic butter? Beer-battered? Crumbed? In a chowder, fritter or Dutch-style croquette? If you can't decide, try a tasting platter ($30 for two). It's a simple set-up, right by the marina, with a shared table inside and more outside.

Slip Inn   CAFE $$
(☑03-574 2345; www.slipinn.co.nz; Havelock Marina; mains $21-28; ◎8am-4pm Mon-Wed, to 7.30pm Thu-Sun) With a deck jutting over the water, this brasserie-style cafe serves plenty of seafood: fish and chips, steamed greenshell mussels, and a particularly delicious *oka* – a Samoan dish of raw fish and mussels cured in a lime, coconut cream and green-chilli broth – served with lots of crusty ciabatta. Burgers, pizza, steaks, lamb and chicken Parmigiana are also offered.

ℹ Information

Havelock i-SITE (☑03-574 2161; www.marlboroughnz.com; 61 Main Rd; ◎9am-4pm Nov-Apr)

ℹ Getting There & Away

InterCity (p294) has a daily coach to/from Nelson ($15, 1¼ hours), Blenheim ($12, 25 minutes) and Picton ($14, one hour). Buses depart from near the i-SITE.

During the summer school holidays (Christmas through January) the **Link Bus** (☑027 314 8569; www.thelinkbus.co.nz) operates three to four timetabled shuttles per day (except Wednesday) between Havelock and Picton ($35, 1¼ hours) via Anakiwa.

Havelock is also linked to Picton by the 42km **Link Pathway** walking and cycling trail.

Picton

POP 2745

Half asleep in winter, but hyperactive in summer (with up to eight fully laden ferry arrivals per day), boaty Picton clusters around a deep and beautiful gulch at the head of Queen Charlotte Sound. It's a major

Picton

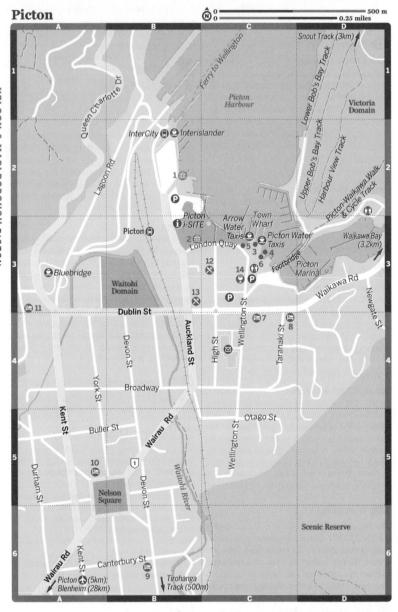

0   500 m
0   0.25 miles

Snout Track (3km)

Ferry to Wellington

Picton Harbour

Victoria Domain

Queen Charlotte Dr

Lagoon Rd

Lower Bob's Bay Track

Upper Bob's Bay Track

Harbour View Track

InterCity   Interislander

1

Picton i-SITE

Picton

Picton-Waikawa Walk- & Cycle Track

Waikawa Bay (3.2km)

Arrow Water Taxis

Town Wharf

Picton Water Taxis

2   London Quay

Bluebridge

Waitohi Domain

12

5
3   4
6

14

Footbridge

Picton Marina

Waikawa Rd

Newgate St

13

P

Dublin St

11

Devon St

York St

Broadway

High St

Wellington St

Taranaki St

7

8

Auckland St

Otago St

Wellington St

Kent St

Buller St

Wairau Rd

Waitohi River

Devon St

Durham St

10

Nelson Square

Scenic Reserve

Wairau Rd

Kent St

Canterbury St

9

Picton (5km);
Blenheim (28km)

Tirohanga
Track (500m)

---

entry point for the South Island, and the best base for tackling the Marlborough Sounds and Queen Charlotte Track. Over the last few years this little town has really bloomed, and offers visitors plenty of reasons to linger even after the obvious attractions are knocked off the list.

Originally called Waitohi, the British renamed it after (surprise, surprise) a military hero, Sir Thomas Picton, who died at the Battle of Waterloo. The local Te Ātiawa people joined their kin a little further up the coast at **Waipawa**, which still has the area's

Picton

main *marae* (community meeting place) along with a small beach and large marina.

◉ Sights

Edwin Fox Maritime Museum MUSEUM
(☏03-573 6868; www.edwinfoxsociety.com; Dunbar Wharf; adult/child $15/5; ◷9am-3pm) Built near Calcutta and launched in 1853, the *Edwin Fox* is purportedly the world's ninth-oldest surviving ship. During its chequered career it carried troops to the Crimean War, booze to India and immigrants to NZ. Most notably, it's the last remaining ship to have transported convicts to Australia. Displays relate this fascinating story but the real thrill is walking around the ship itself, moored in a dry dock next door.

Heritage & Whaling Museum MUSEUM
(☏03-573 8283; www.pictonmuseum-newzealand.com; 9 London Quay; adult/child $5/1; ◷10am-4pm) There's something quite appealing about this style of regional museum: it cheerfully leaps between displays on the local hospital and jail, Māori family portraits, whaling paraphernalia and a collection of old irons. It's well worth a look.

🏃 Activities & Tours

The town has some very pleasant walks. A free i-SITE map details many of these, including an easy 1km track to **Bob's Bay**. The Snout Track (three hours return) continues along the ridge offering superb water views. Climbing a hill behind the town, the **Tirohanga Track** is a two-hour leg-stretching loop offering the best view in the house. The **Link Pathway** (www.linkpathway.nz) is a 42km walking and cycling track connecting Picton to Havelock, with a spur heading to the Queen Charlotte Track trailhead at Anakiwa. When fully completed in 2020 it will all be off-road.

★**Wilderness Guides** OUTDOORS
(☏03-573 5432; www.wildernessguidesnz.com; Town Wharf; guided day trips from $130, kayak/bike hire per day $60) Guided kayaking, hiking and mountain-biking trips are offered by this popular crew, including combinations of all three over multiple days.

Marlborough Sounds Adventure Company OUTDOORS
(☏03-573 6078; www.marlboroughsounds.co.nz; Town Wharf; half-/full-day tour $105/140, kayak hire per half/full day $40/60, bike hire per 1/2/3 days $60/110/150) Bike-hike-kayak trips, with options to suit every inclination and interest. Trip durations range from half a day to five days, and the popular 'Paddle & Walk' option combines two days of kayaking with two days of hiking.

Cougar Line CRUISE
(☏03-573 7925; www.cougarline.co.nz; Town Wharf; adult/child from $95/48) Queen Charlotte Track transport, plus various half- and full-day cruise/walk trips, including the rather special (and flexible) ecocruise to Motuara Island (p310).

Beachcomber Cruises CRUISE
(☏03-573 6175; www.beachcombercruises.co.nz; Town Wharf; cruises from $87, track round trips $105) Various cruise adventures, including the classic 'Magic Mail Run', plus walking, biking and resort lunch options and round-trip track transport.

E-Ko Tours WILDLIFE
(☏03-573 8040; www.e-ko.nz; 1 Wellington St; adult/child from $75/34) Offers a variety of wildlife-focused tours including trips to Motuara Island (p310).

Escape to Marlborough BUS
(☏03-573 5573; www.escapetomarlborough.co.nz; day ticket $75; ◷8am-6pm) Hop-on/hop-off bus services linking Picton and Blenheim, and then stopping at 13 key attractions including vineyards and breweries. Bespoke

wine tours are also offered. Check the website for the service timetables.

🛏 Sleeping

★ Tombstone Backpackers   HOSTEL $

(☑03-573 7116; www.tombstonebp.co.nz; 16 Gravesend Pl; dm $30-40, r with/without bathroom $95/88, apt $120; P@🛜) Rest in peace in a smart dorm, double room or self-contained apartment at this hillside hostel, opposite the cemetery. Perks include a spa pool overlooking the harbour, free breakfast, a sunny reading room, table tennis, free internet, free bikes and two big fluffy cats.

Jugglers Rest   HOSTEL $

(☑03-573 5570; www.jugglersrest.com; 8 Canterbury St; dm/s/d/cabin without bathroom $35/75/80/90; ⊙Oct-May; 🛜) 🏊 A jocular host keeps all her balls in the air at this well-run, ecofriendly, bunk-free backpackers. It's peacefully located a 10-minute walk from town, or even less on one of its free bikes. The attractive gardens are a good place to socialise with fellow travellers, especially during the occasional circus-skills shows.

Sequoia Lodge Backpackers   HOSTEL $

(☑0800 222 257; www.sequoialodge.co.nz; 3a Nelson Sq; van site $23, dm $28-32, r with/without bathroom from $86/76; P🛜) This well-managed backpackers in a colourful Victorian house offers bikes, barbecues, a hot tub, free wi-fi and nightly chocolate pudding. A complimentary breakfast is served from May to October. In the special Netflix room, you can fire up your on-demand content of choice. Family rooms sleep up to five people.

Bay Vista Waterfront Motel   MOTEL $$

(☑03-573 6733; www.bayvistapicton.co.nz; 303 Waikawa Rd, Waikawa; unit from $145; 🛜) This smart motel enjoys an enviable position on the Waikawa foreshore, with views down Queen Charlotte Sound. All units have their own patio and share a large lawn. It's 4km from Picton (courtesy transfer available).

Whatamonga Homestay   B&B $$

(☑03-573 7192; www.whsl.co.nz; 425 Port Underwood Rd, Whatamango Bay; r with/without bathroom $195/180; P🛜) Follow Waikawa Rd, which becomes Port Underwood Rd, for 8km and you'll bump into this classy waterside option – two units with king-sized beds, kitchenettes and balconies with magical views. Two other rooms under the main house share a bathroom. Keen fisherfolk can borrow a dinghy and a rod and try their luck. Minimum two-night stay.

Gables B&B   B&B $$

(☑03-573 6772; www.thegables.co.nz; 20 Waikawa Rd; d $185-208, units $235; 🛜) This historic B&B (once home to Picton's mayor) has three individually styled rooms in the main house and two homely self-contained units out the back. The lovely hosts provide excellent local advice.

Harbour View Motel   MOTEL $$

(☑03-573 6259; www.harbourviewpicton.co.nz; 30 Waikawa Rd; unit from $153; P🛜) Its elevated position means this motel commands good views of Picton's mast-filled marina from the timber decks of its smart, self-contained studios and two-bedroom apartments. Luggage storage is offered for guests walking the Queen Charlotte Track.

🍴 Eating & Drinking

Picton Village Bakkerij   BAKERY $

(☑03-573 7082; www.facebook.com/PictonVillage Bakery; 46 Auckland St; items $3-8.50; ⊙6am-4pm Mon-Sat; 🅿) Dutch owners bake trays of European and Kiwi goodies here, including interesting breads, filled rolls, cakes, tarts and savoury pies. It's an excellent place to stock up for a packed lunch.

Gusto   CAFE $$

(☑03-573 7171; 33 High St; mains $8-22; ⊙7am-2.30pm Sun-Fri) With only a handful of tables and a bench by the window, this friendly joint does beaut cooked breakfasts including a warming porridge in winter. Lunch options include homemade savoury pies, local mussels, curry and pasta.

Seumus' Irish Bar   IRISH PUB

(☑03-573 5050; www.seumusirishbar.co.nz; 25 Wellington St; ⊙3-11pm Wed & Thu, noon-1am Fri & Sat, noon-10pm Sun; 🛜) Modelled on a bar in Northern Ireland, Seumus' is a cosy nest of dark wood and leather booths. Of course there's Guinness on tap and regular live music, and it also serves hearty fare such as fish and chips, bangers and mash, burgers, hot pots and Sunday roasts.

ℹ Information

Picton i-SITE (☑03-520 3113; www.marlbor oughnz.com; Auckland St; ⊙8.30am-6pm Dec-Feb, 9am-4pm Mar-Nov; 🛜) All vital tourist guff including maps, Queen Charlotte Track information, lockers and transport bookings.

Picton Library (67 High St; ⊙8am-5pm Mon-Fri, 10am-4pm Sat, 1-4pm Sun; 🛜) This flash modern library offers free wi-fi.

ℹ️ Getting There & Away

The main transport hub (with car-rental depots) is at the Interislander ferry terminal, which also has a cafe and internet facilities. Most buses also depart from here or at the nearby i-SITE.

AIR

Sounds Air (📞 03-520 3080, 0800 505 005; www.soundsair.co.nz; 10 London Quay; ⏱️7.30am-5.30pm Mon-Thu & Sat, to 7pm Fri, 9am-7pm Sun) flies between Picton and Wellington; a shuttle bus to/from the airstrip at Koromiko is available ($10).

BOAT

There are two operators crossing Cook Strait between Picton and Wellington, and although all ferries leave from more or less the same place, each has its own terminal. Crossings take around 3½ hours.

Bluebridge (📞 04-471 6188; www.bluebridge. co.nz; Lagoon Rd; adult/child/motorbike/car/ campervan from $50/26/54/120/150; 📶) has four sailings in each direction daily.

Interislander (📞 04-498 3302; www.great-journeysofnz.co.nz; Auckland St; adult/ child/motorbike/car/campervan from $56/26/43/111/132) has five sailings in each direction daily.

Picton is also the hub for water taxis and cruises along Queen Charlotte Sound (p312).

BUS

InterCity (📞 03-365 1113; www.intercity. co.nz; outside Interislander Ferry Terminal, Auckland St) has two coaches a day to/from Christchurch (from $37, six hours) via Blenheim (from $10, 30 minutes) and Kaikōura (from $25, 2½ hours); and one or two daily to Nelson ($23, 2¼ hours) via Blenheim and Havelock ($14, one hour).

Escape to Marlborough (p315) has three morning departures to Blenheim ($19), with two returning in the afternoon as part of its hop-on/ hop-off bus service.

There's also a bus to/from Blenheim ($4, 30 minutes), operated by Ritchies, which runs twice a day on Tuesdays and Thursdays only.

During the summer school holidays (Christmas through January) the Link Bus (p313) operates three or four shuttles per day (except Wednesday) between Picton and Havelock ($35, 1¼ hours) via Anakiwa ($20, 45 minutes).

TRAIN

KiwiRail's scenic **Coastal Pacific** (📞 04-495 0775; www.greatjourneysofnz.co.nz) service operates daily from October to April, heading to/from Christchurch (from $99, 6¼ hours) via Blenheim (from $39, 26 minutes) and Kaikōura (from $59, three hours).

Blenheim & Around

POP 31,600

Set on the fertile Wairau Plains, a large flat expanse wedged between the Richmond Ranges and the Wither Hills, Blenheim is very much an agricultural hub. While there's not a lot to get excited about in the town itself, wine lovers will find plenty of thrills in the surrounding countryside. This is the heart of the Marlborough Wine Region, the most famous and most productive of the country's viticultural areas. Blenheim is a good base from which to explore it, with a couple of interesting museums and an increasingly lively food scene.

◎ Sights

★ **Omaka Aviation
Heritage Centre**   MUSEUM

(Map p319; 📞 03-579 1305; www.omaka.org.nz; 79 Aerodrome Rd, Omaka; adult/child WWI $25/12, WWII $20/10, both $39/16; ⏱️10am-5pm) When Sir Peter Jackson has a passion for something, there are no half measures. That's abundantly clear in the 'Knights of the Sky' exhibition, which features the movie director's personal collection of WWI aircraft and memorabilia, brought to life in a series of life-sized dioramas that depict dramatic wartime scenes such as the death of the Red Baron. The other half of the centre, WWII-themed 'Dangerous Skies', is the work of local aviation enthusiasts.

The latter may not be as slick as Sir Peter's section – the backgrounds are hand painted and there are fewer of the hyper-realistic mannequins produced by the Oscar-winning Weta Workshop – but all of these aircraft have been restored and are airworthy, and it includes an eight-minute immersive 'Stalingrad Experience'.

Book ahead to take a flight in a US military biplane (10/20 minutes, $250/380 for up to two people) or a Soviet WWII fighter (20/30 minutes $2300/2599).

Omaka Classic Cars   MUSEUM

(Map p319; 📞 03-577 9419; www.omakaclassiccars. co.nz; Aerodrome Rd, Omaka; adult/child $15/free; ⏱️noon-4pm daily Oct-May, Fri-Sun Jun-Sep) Opposite the Aviation Heritage Centre is this collection of more than 100 restored cars dating from the 1950s to the '80s.

Pollard Park   PARK

(Map p319; Parker St) Ten minutes' walk from town, this 25-hectare park has beautiful

NELSON & MARLBOROUGH BLENHEIM & AROUND

blooming and scented gardens, a playground, tennis courts and a nine-hole golf course. It's pretty as a picture when lit up on summer evenings. Five minutes away, on the way to town, is the extensive **Taylor River Floodway Reserve**, a lovely place for a stroll.

Marlborough Museum
MUSEUM

(Map p319; ☑03-578 1712; www.marlborough museum.org.nz; 26 Arthur Baker Pl; adult/child $10/5; ☻10am-4pm) The history of NZ's wine industry is celebrated here, along with fascinating displays devoted to finds from Wairau Bar, the site of the country's earliest known settlement. Look out for the *karetao*, a traditional wooden puppet covered in *moko* (tattoos) and designed to perform a *haka* (ceremonial dance). The museum is situated within the **Bradshaw Heritage Park**, a collection of transported Victorian buildings that includes a miniature railway and a farm-machinery museum.

 Activities & Tours

Wither Hills Farm Park
WALKING

(Map p319; Rifle Range Pl, Witherlea) In a town as flat as a pancake, this hilly 11-sq-km working sheep and cattle farm provides welcome relief, offering over 60km of walking and mountain-biking trails with grand views across the Wairau Valley and out to Cloudy Bay. Pick up a map from the i-SITE (p322) or check the information panels at the many entrances.

Driftwood Eco-Tours
ECOTOUR

(☑03-577 7651; www.driftwoodecotours.co.nz; tours from $180) ✏ Tour through private farmland to the ecologically and historically significant Wairau Lagoon, 10 minutes' drive from Blenheim. Alternatively book one of the specialist-led themed day or multiday tours to learn about the flora and fauna.

Sleeping

Watson's Way Lodge
HOSTEL $

(Map p319; ☑027 800 4664; www.watsonsway lodge.co.nz; 56 High St, Renwick; sites from $15, dm $30, r with/without bathroom $99/88; ☻Oct-Jul; ☏) This traveller-focused lodge has spick-and-span rooms in a sweetly converted bungalow with a full kitchen and a comfy lounge with a pool table. There are also spacious leafy gardens dotted with fruit trees and hammocks, bikes for hire and local information aplenty.

St Leonards
COTTAGE $$

(Map p319; ☑03-577 8328; www.stleonards.co.nz; 18 St Leonards Rd, Springlands; cottage from $170; ☐☏☒) Tucked into the grounds of an 1886 homestead, these five stylish and rustic cottages offer privacy and a reason to stay put. Each is unique in its layout and perspective on the gardens and vines. Our pick is the capacious and cosy Woolshed, exuding agricultural chic. Resident sheep, chickens and deer await your attention.

Olde Mill House
B&B $$

(Map p319; ☑03-572 8458; www.oldemillhouse. co.nz; 9 Wilson St, Renwick; d $180-190; ☐☏) On an elevated section in otherwise flat Renwick, this charming old house is a treat. Home-grown fruit and homemade jams and pickles are offered as part of the continental breakfast. Free bikes, an outdoor spa pool and pretty gardens make this a tip-top choice in the heart of the wine country.

Montana Lodge Motel
MOTEL $$

(Map p319; ☑03-578 9259; www.montanalodge motel.co.nz; 71 Main St; units $135-160; ☐☏☒) One of the cheaper motels in a pricey town, this angular, 1970s-looking complex offers clean and comfortable units with kitchenettes, and a cute kidney-shaped pool.

Marlborough Vintners Hotel
HOTEL $$$

(Map p319; ☑03-572 5094; www.mvh.co.nz; 190 Rapaura Rd, Rapaura; r from $315; ☐☒☏) ✏ The 16 architecturally designed suites here make the most of valley views and are decked out with modern bathrooms and abstract art. The stylish reception building has a bar and restaurant opening out onto a cherry orchard and organic vegetable garden.

 Eating

Ritual
CAFE $

(Map p319; ☑03-578 6939; www.ritualcoffee.co.nz; 10 Maxwell Rd; mains $9-20; ☻7am-4pm Mon-Sat) A shopfront for a local fair-trade and organic coffee roaster, this cool little cafe is all leadlights and lampshades. Cooked breakfasts include the usual eggy options alongside more unusual dishes such as huevos rancheros (eggs served with a tortilla and a spicy tomato sauce). There's a good selection of quick-and-easy counter food, along with great coffee, naturally.

The Burleigh
PIES $

(Map p319; ☑03-579 2531; www.facebook.com/ theburleighnz; 72 New Renwick Rd, Burleigh; pies

Marlborough Wine Region

Marlborough Wine Region

MARLBOROUGH WINERIES

Marlborough is NZ's vinous colossus, producing around three-quarters of the country's wine. At last count, there were 244 sq km of vines planted – which is even more extraordinary when you consider that the modern industry only really kicked off in 1973 when the Yukich family expanded their West Auckland operations to here.

Sunny days and cool nights create the perfect conditions for cool-climate grapes: world-famous sauvignon blanc, top-notch pinot noir, and notable chardonnay, riesling, gewürztraminer, pinot gris and bubbly. Drifting between tasting rooms and dining among the vines is a quintessential South Island experience. The big annual event is the one-day **Marlborough Wine & Food Festival** (☎03-577 9299; www.wine-marlborough-festival.co.nz; tickets $63), held at Brancott Estate in mid-February.

A Taste of the Tastings

The *Marlborough Wine Trail* map – available from Blenheim i-SITE and online at www.wine-marlborough.co.nz – lists 35 wineries that are open to the public. Our picks provide a range of high-quality cellar-door experiences. Some wineries charge a small fee for tasting, normally refunded if you purchase a bottle.

Yealands Estate (☎03-575 7618; www.yealands.co.nz; cnr Seaview & Reserve Rds, Seddon; ⊙10am-4.30pm) Zero-carbon winemaking on a grand scale at this space-age winery out by itself near Seddon, 30km southeast of Blenheim. A 7km self-drive vineyard tour includes spectacular views over Cook Strait. If you're lucky, you'll see Yealands' compact babydoll sheep grazing between the vines. They're handy for keeping the grass down, but not tall enough to reach the grapes.

Wither Hills (Map p319; ☎03-520 8284; www.witherhills.co.nz; 211 New Renwick Rd, Burleigh; tastings $5, free with purchase; ⊙10am-4.30pm) Pull up a beanbag on the Hockneyesque lawns of this impressive complex and enjoy a three-wine flight ($10), or head into the cellar for a more traditional tasting session. It also offers a Wine Blending Experience ($60 for four people). The restaurant is excellent, too.

Brancott Estate (Map p319; ☎03-520 6975; www.brancottestate.com; 180 Brancott Rd, Fairhall; tastings $5-15, free with purchase; ⊙10am-4.30pm) Under its previous name, Montana Wines, this was the trailblazer of the wine region. Now it has Marlborough's most impressive cellar door and restaurant complex, poised atop a hillock overlooking the vines. It offers an hour-long **Vineyard Bike Tour** ($35, 10.30am) and, from December to March, a **Falcon Encounter** (adult/child $30/10, 11am) featuring the kārearea (NZ falcon); bookings essential.

Spy Valley Wines (Map p319; ☎03-572 6207; www.spyvalleywine.co.nz; 37 Lake Timara Rd West, Waihopai Valley; tastings $5-10, free with purchase; ⊙10.30am-4.30pm daily Nov-Apr, Mon-Fri May-Oct) Stylish, edgy architecture features at this espionage-themed winery with drops in the top echelons. Memorable merchandise.

Clos Henri Vineyard (☎03-572 7293; www.clos-henri.com; 639 State Hwy 63, Waihopai Valley; ⊙10am-4pm Mon-Sat Oct-Apr) French winemaking meets Marlborough terroir with *très bon* results. The cellar door is housed in a beautifully restored wooden church.

Bladen (Map p319; ☎03-572 9417; www.bladen.co.nz; 83 Conders Bend Rd, Renwick; ⊙11am-4.30pm Nov-Apr) Bijou family winery that's big on charm.

Framingham (Map p319; ☎03-572 8884; www.framingham.co.nz; 19 Conders Bend Rd, Renwick; tastings $5, free with purchase; ⊙10.30am-4.30pm) Consistent, quality wines including exceptional riesling and stellar dessert wines. Check out the '90s song lyrics on the pavers of the cloister.

Forrest (Map p319; ☎03-572 9084; www.forrest.co.nz; 19 Blicks Rd, Renwick; tastings free-$10; ⊙10am-4.30pm) Doctor-owners produce and prescribe a range of fine vinous medicines, including some mood-altering riesling.

Huia (Map p319; [☎]03-572 8326; www.huiavineyards.com; 22 Boyces Rd, Rapaura; [⊙]10.30am-4.30pm Nov-Mar) Sustainable, small-scale family winemaking and a personable cellar-door experience. Delectable dry-style gewürztraminer.

Allan Scott Family Winemakers (Map p319; [☎]03-572 9054; www.allanscott.com; 229 Jacksons Rd, Rapaura; tastings $3, free with purchase or lunch; [⊙]9am-4.30pm) Highlights of this esteemed range include a lovely gewürztraminer and a *méthode traditionnelle* sparkling wine. The attached Twelve Trees restaurant is good, too.

Cloudy Bay (Map p319; [☎]03-520 9147; www.cloudybay.co.nz; 230 Jacksons Rd, Rapaura; tastings $10-25; [⊙]10am-4pm) The most famous, most upmarket and most expensive tasting experience; private tastings and tours are also offered. Jack's Raw Bar shucks and serves oysters and clams from December to mid-April.

Saint Clair Estate (Map p319; [☎]03-570 5280; www.saintclair.co.nz; 13 Selmes Rd, Rapaura; tastings $5-10, free with meal or purchase; [⊙]9am-5pm Nov-Apr, 11am-4pm May-Oct) Prepare to be blown away by the Pioneer Block and Reserve range sauvignon blanc and pinot noir at Marlborough's most awarded winery. There's a good restaurant on-site, too.

Wining & Dining

Rock Ferry (Map p319; [☎]03-579 6430; www.rockferry.co.nz; 80 Hammerichs Rd; mains $28-30, tastings $5, free with purchase or meal; [⊙]cafe 11.30am-3pm, cellar door 10am-4.30pm) Although it calls itself a cafe, that doesn't really cover the sophisticated but concise modern NZ menu on offer here (for example, monkfish, steak and a delicious crusted baked salmon served on pearl barley). A very pleasant environment, inside and out.

Wairau River (Map p319; [☎]03-572 9800; www.wairauriverwines.com; 11 Rapaura Rd, Rapaura; mains $27-30, tastings $5, free with purchase or meal; [⊙]noon-3pm; [☎]) This modish, mud-brick cellar door and bistro has a wide veranda and beautiful gardens with plenty of shade. The adventurous cuisine-straddling menu may include the likes of *togarashi* (Japanese spice mix) prawns with miso mayo, Marlborough mussel chowder, braised beef cheeks with sambal (Malaysian chilli paste), hot-smoked salmon salad or tandoori chicken burger.

Arbour (Map p319; [☎]03-572 7989; www.arbour.co.nz; 36 Godfrey Rd, Renwick; set menu $89-109; [⊙]5.30-11pm Tue-Sat Aug-Jun) Located in the thick of Renwick wine country, Marlborough's most lauded restaurant focuses on local produce fashioned into top-notch contemporary dishes. Settle in for a multiple-course degustation, either with or without suggested matches from the mesmerising wine list.

Wine Tours

Wine tours are generally conducted in a minibus, last between four and seven hours, take in four to seven wineries and range in price from $95 to $130 (with a few grand tours costing up to around $250 for the day, including a winery lunch).

Bubbly Grape Wine Tours ([☎]027 672 2195; www.bubblygrape.co.nz; tours $100-195) Three different tours including a gourmet lunch option.

Highlight Wine Tours ([☎]03-577 9046; www.highlightwinetours.co.nz; tours $90-130) Tours visit a chocolate factory, too. Custom tours available.

Hop 'n Grape ([☎]021 157 4094; www.hopngrapetours.co.nz; half/full day $115/150) Winemaker-led, small-group wine tours with an optional side serving of beer.

Sounds Connection ([☎]03-573 8843; www.soundsconnection.co.nz; tours from $95) Some tour options combine tastings with a Marlborough Sounds cruise.

Bike 2 Wine (Map p319; [☎]03-572 8458; www.bike2wine.co.nz; 9 Wilson St, Renwick; standard/tandem per day $30/60, pick-ups within 15km $10; [⊙]10am-5.30pm) An alternative to the usual minibus tours, this operator offers self-guided, fully equipped and supported two-wheeled tours. There are more than 20 wineries in a 5km radius of its Renwick base, and it offers a pick-up service from Blenheim and its surrounds for $10 return.

$6-9; ⊙ 7.30am-3pm Tue-Fri, to 1.30pm Sat) The humble pie rises to stratospheric heights at this fabulous bakery-deli on Blenheim's rural fringes; try the pork-belly or steak and blue cheese, or perhaps both. Freshly filled baguettes, local sausage, French cheeses and great coffee also make tempting appearances. Avoid the lunchtime rush.

★ **Scotch Wine Bar**   TAPAS $$
(Map p319; ☑ 03-579 1176; www.scotchbar.co.nz; 24-26 Maxwell Rd; dishes $7-28, tasting menu $45; ⊙ 4pm-late Mon-Fri) A versatile and sociable spot in central Blenheim, Scotch offers local wines, craft beer on tap and delicious sharing plates in a range of sizes. The southern fried chicken with chilli mayo is a crispy and filling crowd-pleaser but, if you're feeling adventurous, we'd recommend the raw hangar steak with juniper, pine needles and sorrel.

Gramado's   BRAZILIAN $$$
(Map p319; ☑ 03-579 1192; www.gramadosrestau rant.com; 74 Main St; mains $37-40; ⊙ 4pm-late Tue-Sat; 🔊 ☑) Injecting a little Latin passion into the Blenheim dining scene, Gramado's is a fun place to tuck into unashamedly hearty meals such as lamb *assado*, feijoada (smoky pork and bean stew) and Brazilian-spiced fish. Kick things off with a caipirinha, of course.

🍷 Drinking & Entertainment

Moa Brewing Company   CRAFT BEER
(Map p319; ☑ 03-572 5146; www.moabeer.com; 258 Jacksons Rd, Rapaura; tastings $10; ⊙ 11am-6pm) Take a break from wine-tasting at Moa's laid-back beer-tasting room amid Rapaura's vineyards. Food trucks often rock up Thursday to Sunday, and there's always a few seasonal brews on tap. Travelling beer geeks should try Moa's excellent sour beers; the $28 beer flight is the equivalent of 2½ pints.

Dodson Street   CRAFT BEER
(Map p319; ☑ 03-577 8348; www.dodsonstreet. co.nz; 1 Dodson St; ⊙ 11am-11pm) This pub and garden has a beer-hall ambience and suitably Teutonic menu featuring pork knuckle, bratwurst and schnitzel (its pizza and burgers are also good). The stars of the show, however, are the 24 taps pouring quality, ever-changing craft beer from around Marlborough and the rest of NZ.

ASB Theatre Marlborough   THEATRE
(Map p319; ☑ 03-520 8558; www.asbtheatre.com; 2 Hutcheson St) Opened in 2016, this large, modern theatre presents a wide programme of concerts and performances. Check the website to see what's on.

🛍 Shopping

Makana Confections   CHOCOLATE
(Map p319; ☑ 03-570 5370; www.makana.co.nz; cnr Rapaura & O'Dwyers Rds, Rapaura; ⊙ 9am-5.30pm) Large windows face the factory, allowing you to watch the chocolates being made while you're engulfed in the most mouth-watering fragrances and tempted with free samples. Resistance is futile.

ℹ Information

Blenheim i-SITE (Map p319; ☑ 03-577 8080; www.marlboroughnz.com; Train Station, 8 Sinclair St; ⊙ 9am-4pm Mon-Fri, 10am-3pm Sat & Sun) Information on Marlborough and beyond, including wine-trail maps.

Wairau Hospital (☑ 03-520 9999; www. nmdhb.govt.nz; Hospital Rd, Witherlea)

ℹ Getting There & Away

AIR

Marlborough Airport (Map p319; ☑ 03-572 8651; www.marlboroughairport.co.nz; 1 Tancred Cres, Woodbourne) is 6km west of town.
Blenheim Shuttles (☑ 03-577 5277; www. blenheimshuttles.co.nz) provides door-to-door services between the airport and the town centre, as does **Marlborough Taxis** (☑ 03-577 5511); expect to pay around $20.
➜ Air New Zealand (p294) has direct flights to/from Wellington and Auckland.
➜ Sounds Air (p317) flies to Wellington, Kāpiti Coast and Christchurch.

BUS

InterCity (p294) buses depart from the Blenheim i-SITE. Destinations include Picton (from $10, 30 minutes), Havelock ($12, 25 minutes), Nelson ($23, 1¾ hours), Kaikōura (from $19, 1¾ hours) and Christchurch (from $37, 5½ hours).

There's also a bus to/from Picton ($4, 30 minutes), operated by Ritchies, which runs twice a day on Tuesdays and Thursdays only.

TRAIN

KiwiRail's scenic Coastal Pacific (p317) service operates daily from October to April, heading to/from Picton (from $39, 26 minutes), Kaikōura (from $59, 2½ hours) and Christchurch (from $99, 5¾ hours).

ℹ Getting Around

The **Blenheim Bus** (☑ 03-578 5467; www.ritch ies.co.nz/blenheim; adult/child $2/1), operated by Ritchies, runs on two loops around central Blenheim.

Understand the South Island

History

Western historians continue to unravel New Zealand's early history, with much of what they have discovered confirming traditional Māori narratives passed on through the generations. In less than 1000 years NZ has hosted two new peoples: the Polynesian Māori and European New Zealanders (or Pākehā). New Zealand shares some of its history with the rest of Polynesia, and with other European colonial nations. This cultural intermingling has created the unique Kiwi spirit you'll experience today.

Māori Settlement

Abel Tasman named NZ 'Stateland', assuming it was connected to Staten Island near Argentina. It was subsequently named after the province of Zeeland in Tasman's native Holland.

The first settlers of NZ were the Polynesian forebears of today's Māori. Archaeologists and anthropologists continue to search for the details, but the most widely accepted evidence suggests they arrived in the 13th century. The DNA of Polynesian rat bones found in NZ, dated to centuries earlier, has been written off as unreliable (and certainly not conclusive evidence of earlier settlement). Most historians now agree on 1280 as the Māori's likeliest arrival date. Scientists have sequenced the DNA of settlers buried at the Wairau Bar archaeological site on the South Island, and confirmed the settlers as originating from east Polynesia (though work is ongoing to pinpoint their origins more precisely). The genetic diversity of the buried settlers suggests a fairly large-scale settlement – a finding consistent with Māori narratives about numerous vessels reaching the islands.

Prime sites for first settlement were warm coastal gardens for the food plants brought from Polynesia (kumara or sweet potato, gourd, yam and taro); sources of workable stone for knives and adzes; and areas with abundant big game. New Zealand has no native land mammals apart from a few species of bat, but 'big game' is no exaggeration: the islands were home to a dozen species of moa (a large flightless bird) – the largest of which weighed up to 240kg, about twice the size of an ostrich – preyed upon by *Harpagornis moorei,* a whopping 15kg eagle that is now extinct. Other species of flightless birds and large sea mammals, such as fur seals, were easy game for hunters from small Pacific Islands. The first settlers spread far and fast, from the top of the North Island to the bottom of the

TIMELINE	AD 1280	1500–1642	1642
	Based on evidence from archaeological digs, the most likely arrival date of east Polynesians in NZ, now known as Māori.	The 'classic period' of Māori culture, when weapon-making and artistic techniques were refined. Many remain cultural hallmarks to this day.	First European contact: Abel Tasman arrives on an expedition from the Dutch East Indies (Indonesia) but leaves in a hurry after a sea skirmish with Māori.

One of NZ's most persistent legends is that Māori found mainland NZ already occupied by a more peaceful and racially distinct Melanesian people, known as the Moriori, whom they exterminated. This myth has been regularly debunked by scholars since the 1920s, but somehow persists.

To complicate matters, there were real 'Moriori', and Māori did treat them badly. The real Moriori were the people of the Chatham Islands, a windswept group about 900km east of the mainland. They were, however, fully Polynesian, and descended from Māori – 'Moriori' was their version of the same word. Mainland Māori arrived in the Chathams in 1835, as a spin-off of the Musket Wars, killing some Moriori and enslaving the rest, but they did not exterminate them.

South Island within the first 100 years. High-protein diets are likely to have boosted population growth.

By about 1400, however, with big-game supply dwindling, Māori economics turned from big game to small game – forest birds and rats – and from hunting to farming and fishing. A good living could still be made, but it required detailed local knowledge, steady effort and complex communal organisation, hence the rise of the Māori tribes. Competition for resources increased, conflict did likewise, and this led to the building of increasingly sophisticated *pā* (fortified villages), complete with wells and food-storage pits. Vestiges of *pā* earthworks can still be seen around the country (on the hilltops of Auckland, for example).

Around 1500 is considered the dawn of the 'classic period', when Māori developed a social structure and aesthetic that was truly distinct, rather than an offshoot of the parent Polynesian culture. Māori had no metals and no written language (and no alcoholic drinks or drugs). Traditional Māori culture from these times endures, including performance art like *kapa haka* (cultural dance) and unmistakable visual art, notably woodcarving, weaponry and *pounamu* (greenstone) carving.

Spiritual life was similarly distinctive. Below Ranginui (sky father) and Papatūānuku (earth mother) were various gods of land, forest and sea, joined by deified ancestors over time. The mischievous demigod Māui was particularly important. In legend, he vanquished the sun and fished up the North Island before meeting his death between the thighs of the goddess Hine-nui-te-pō in an attempt to bring immortality to humankind.

The Ministry for Culture & Heritage's history website (www.nzhistory.net.nz) is an excellent source of information on NZ's history.

Enter Europe

The first authenticated contact between Māori and European explorers took place in 1642. Seafarer Abel Tasman had just claimed Van Diemen's

1769	1772	1790s	1818–45
European contact recommences with visits by James Cook and Jean de Surville. Despite violence, both manage to communicate with Māori. This time NZ's link with the outside world proves permanent.	Marion du Fresne's French expedition arrives; it stays for some weeks at the Bay of Islands. Relations with Māori start well, but a breach of Māori *tapu* (sacred law) leads to violence.	Whaling ships and sealing gangs arrive in the country. Relations are established with Māori, with Europeans depending on the contact for essentials, such as food, water and protection.	Intertribal Māori 'Musket Wars' take place: tribes acquire muskets and win bloody victories against tribes without them. The wars taper off in the 30s, with a shift to economic rivalry.

Land (Tasmania) for the Dutch when rough winds steered his ships east, where he sighted New Zealand. Tasman's two ships were searching for southern land and anything valuable it might contain. Tasman was instructed to pretend to any natives he might meet 'that you are by no means eager for precious metals, so as to leave them ignorant of the value of the same'.

JAMES COOK'S ENDEAVOURS

Countless obelisks, faded plaques and graffiti-covered statues remember the renowned navigator James Cook (1728–79). It's impossible to travel the Pacific without encountering the captain's image and his controversial legacy in the lands he opened to the West.

Cook came from an extremely pinched and provincial background. The son of a day labourer in rural Yorkshire, he was born in a mud cottage, had little schooling and seemed destined for farm work. Instead, Cook went to sea as a teenager, worked his way up from coal-ship servant to naval officer, and attracted notice for his exceptional charts of Canada. But Cook remained a little-known second lieutenant until, in 1768, the Royal Navy chose him to command a daring voyage to the South Seas.

In a converted coal ship called *Endeavour*, Cook sailed to Tahiti and then became the first European to land in NZ and on the east coast of Australia. While he was there, Cook sailed and mapped NZ's coastline in full – with impressive accuracy. The ship almost sank after striking the Great Barrier Reef, and 40% of the crew died from disease and accidents, but somehow the *Endeavour* arrived home in 1771. On a return voyage (1772–75), Cook became the first navigator to pierce the Antarctic Circle and circled the globe near its southernmost latitude, demolishing the ancient myth that a vast, populous and fertile continent surrounded the South Pole.

Cook's travels made an enormous contribution to world thought. During his voyages, Cook and his crew took astronomical measurements. Botanists accompanied him on his voyages, diligently recording and studying the flora they encountered. Cook was also remarkable for completing a round-the-world voyage without any of his crew dying of scurvy – adding 'nutrition' to his impressive roster of specialist subjects.

But these achievements exist beneath a long shadow. Cook's travels spurred colonisation of the Pacific, and within a few decades of his death, missionaries, whalers, traders and settlers began transforming (and often devastating) island cultures. As a result, many indigenous people now revile Cook as an imperialist villain who introduced disease, dispossession and other ills to the region (hence the frequent vandalising of Cook monuments). However, as islanders revive traditional crafts and practices, from tattooing to *tapa* (traditional barkcloth), they have turned to the art and writing of Cook and his men as a resource for cultural renewal. Significant geographical features in NZ bear his name, including Aoraki/Mt Cook, Cook Strait and Cook River, along with countless streets and hotels.

For good and ill, a Yorkshire farm boy remains one of the single most significant figures in shaping the modern Pacific.

1837	1840	1844	1858
European settlers introduce possums from Australia to NZ, creating a possum population boom that comes to threaten native flora and bird life.	Starting at Waitangi in the Bay of Islands on 6 February, around 500 chiefs countrywide sign the Treaty of Waitangi to 'settle' sovereignty once and for all. NZ becomes a nominal British colony.	Young Ngāpuhi chief Hōne Heke challenges British sovereignty, first by cutting down the British flag at Kororāreka (now Russell), then by sacking the town itself. The ensuing Northland war continues until 1846.	The Waikato chief Te Wherowhero is installed as the first Māori king.

When Tasman's ships anchored in Wharewharangi Bay, local Māori came out in their canoes to make the traditional challenge: friends or foes? The Dutch blew their trumpets, unwittingly challenging back. When a boat was lowered to take a party between the two ships, it was attacked and four crewmen were killed. Having not even set foot on the land, Tasman sailed away and didn't return; nor did any other European for 127 years. But the Dutch did leave a name: initially 'Statenland', later changed to 'Nova Zeelandia' by cartographers.

Contact between Māori and Europeans was renewed in 1769, when English and French explorers arrived, under James Cook and Jean de Surville – Cook narrowly pipped the latter to the post, naming Doubtless Bay before the French party dropped anchor there. The first French exploration ended sourly, with mistrust between the ailing French seamen and Māori, one of whom they took prisoner (he died at sea). Bloody skirmishes took place during a second French expedition, led by Marc-Joseph Marion du Fresne, when cultural misunderstandings led to violent reprisals; later expeditions were more fruitful. Meanwhile Cook made two more visits between 1773 and 1777. Exploration continued, motivated by science, profit and political rivalry.

Unofficial visits, by whaling ships in the north and seal-hunting gangs in the south, began in the 1790s (though Māori living in New Zealand's interior remained largely unaffected). The first Christian missionaries established themselves in the Bay of Islands in 1814, followed by dozens of others – Anglican, Methodist and Catholic. Europe brought such things as pigs and potatoes, which benefited Māori and were even used as currency. Trade in flax and timber generated small European–Māori settlements by the 1820s. Surprisingly, the most numerous category of 'European' visitor was probably American. New England whaling ships favoured the Bay of Islands for rest and recreation. Their favourite haunt, the little town of Kororāreka (now Russell), was known as 'Gomorrah, the scourge of the Pacific'. As a result, New England visitors today may well have distant relatives among the locals.

One or two dozen bloody clashes dot the history of Māori–European contact before 1840, but given the number of visits, interracial conflict was modest. Europeans needed Māori protection, food and labour, and Māori came to need European articles, especially muskets. Whaling stations and mission stations were linked to local Māori groups by intermarriage, which helped keep the peace. Most warfare was between Māori: the terrible intertribal 'Musket Wars' of 1818–36. Because Northland had the majority of early contact with Europe, its Ngāpuhi tribe acquired muskets first. Under their great general Hongi Hika, Ngāpuhi then raided south, winning bloody victories against tribes without muskets. Once they acquired muskets, these tribes then saw off Ngāpuhi, but

One of the first European women to settle in NZ was Charlotte Badger, a convict mutineer/pirate who escaped to the Bay of Islands with her daughter in 1806, integrating into local society, learning Māori fluently and, later in life, Tongan, too.

HISTORY ENTER EUROPE

'I believe we were all glad to leave New Zealand. It is not a pleasant place. Amongst the natives there is absent that charming simplicity...and the greater part of the English are the very refuse of society.'

Charles Darwin, writing about his 1835 visit to Kororāreka (Russell).

1860–69	1861	1863–64	1867
The Taranaki wars are incited by the controversial swindling of Māori land by the government at Waitara, and continue with outrage over the confiscation of more land as a result.	Gold discovered in Otago by Gabriel Read, an Australian prospector. As a result, the population of Otago climbs from less than 13,000 to over 30,000 in six months.	Waikato Land War. Up to 5000 Māori resist an invasion mounted by 20,000 imperial, colonial and 'friendly' Māori troops. Despite surprising successes, Māori are defeated and much land is confiscated.	All Māori men (rather than individual landowners) are granted the right to vote.

'Kaore e mau te rongo – ake, ake!' (Peace never shall be made – never, never!) War chief Rewi Maniapoto in response to government troops at the battle of Orakau, 1864.

also raided further south in their turn. The domino effect continued to the far south of the South Island in 1836. The missionaries claimed that the Musket Wars then tapered off through their influence, but the restoration of the balance of power through the equal distribution of muskets was probably more important.

The Māori population for 1769 has been estimated at between 85,000 and 110,000. The Musket Wars killed perhaps 20,000, and new diseases (including typhoid, tuberculosis and venereal disease) did considerable damage, too. Fortunately NZ had the natural quarantine of distance: infected Europeans often recovered or died during the long voyage, and smallpox, for example, which devastated indigenous North Americans, never arrived. By 1840 Māori had been reduced to about 70,000, a decline of at least 20%. Māori bent under the weight of European contact, but they certainly did not break.

Growing Pains

Māori tribes valued the profit and prestige brought by the Pākehā and wanted both, along with protection from foreign powers. Accepting nominal British authority was the way to get them. James Busby was appointed New Zealand's first British Resident in 1833, though his powers were largely symbolic. Busby selected the country's first official flag and established the Declaration of the Independence of New Zealand. But he was too ineffectual to curb rampant colonisation.

By 1840 the British government was overcoming its reluctance to undertake potentially expensive intervention in NZ. The British were eager to secure their commercial interests, and they also believed, wrongly but sincerely, that Māori could not handle the increasing scale of unofficial European contact. In 1840 the two peoples struck a deal, symbolised by the treaty first signed at Waitangi on 6 February that year. The Treaty of Waitangi now has a standing not dissimilar to that of the Constitution in the US, but is even more contested. The original problem was a discrepancy between British and Māori understandings of it. The English version promised Māori full equality as British subjects in return for complete rights of government. The Māori version also promised that Māori would retain their chieftainship, which implied local rights of government. The problem was not great at first, because the Māori version applied outside the small European settlements. But as those settlements grew, conflict brewed.

In 1840 there were only about 2000 Europeans in NZ, with the shanty town of Kororāreka the capital and biggest settlement. By 1850 six new settlements had been formed, with 22,000 settlers between them. About half of these had arrived under the auspices of the New Zealand Company and its associates. The company was the brainchild of Edward

Situated on NZ's North Island, the Waitangi Treaty Grounds, where the Treaty of Waitangi was first signed in 1840, is now a tourist attraction for Kiwis and non-Kiwis alike. Each year on 6 February, Waitangi hosts treaty commemorations and protests.

1868–72	1886–87	1893	1901
East Coast war. Te Kooti, having led an escape from his prison on the Chatham Islands, leads a holy guerrilla war in the Urewera region. He finally retreats to establish the Ringatū Church.	Tuwharetoa tribe gifts the mountains of Ruapehu, Ngauruhoe and Tongariro to the government to establish NZ's first national park.	NZ becomes the first country in the world to grant the vote to women, following a campaign led by Kate Sheppard, who petitioned the government for years.	New Zealand politely declines the invitation to join the new Commonwealth of Australia, but thanks for asking.

Gibbon Wakefield, who also influenced the settlement of South Australia. Wakefield hoped to short-circuit the barbarous frontier phase of settlement with 'instant civilisation', but his success was limited. From the 1850s his settlers, who included a high proportion of upper-middle-class gentlefolk, were swamped by succeeding waves of immigrants, who continued to wash in until the 1880s. These people were part of the great British and Irish diaspora that also populated Australia and much of North America, but the NZ mix was distinctive. Lowland Scots settlers were more prominent in NZ than elsewhere, for example, with the possible exception of parts of Canada. New Zealand's Irish, even the Catholics, tended to come from the north of Ireland. New Zealand's English tended to come from the counties close to London. Small groups of Germans, Scandinavians and Chinese made their way in, though the last faced increasing racial prejudice from the 1880s, when the Pākehā population reached half a million.

Much of the mass immigration from the 1850s to the 1870s was assisted by the provincial and central governments, which also mounted large-scale public-works schemes, especially in the 1870s under Premier Julius Vogel. In 1876 Vogel abolished the provinces on the grounds that they were hampering his development efforts. The last imperial governor with substantial power was the talented but machiavellian George Grey, who ended his second governorship in 1868. Thereafter, the governors (governors-general from 1917) were largely just nominal heads of state; the head of government, the premier or prime minister, had more power. The central government, originally weaker than the provincial governments, the imperial governor and the Māori tribes, eventually exceeded the power of all three.

The Māori tribes did not go down without a fight. Indeed, their resistance was one of the most formidable ever mounted against European expansion. The first clash took place in 1843 in the Wairau Valley, now a wine-growing district. A posse of settlers set out to enforce the myth of British control, but encountered the reality of Māori control. Twenty-two

Revered NZ Prime Minister (1893–1906) Richard 'King Dick' Seddon popularised the country's self-proclaimed nickname 'Godzone' with his famous final telegraph: 'Just leaving for God's own country'.

HISTORY GROWING PAINS

THE NEW ZEALAND WARS

Starting in Northland and moving throughout the North Island, the New Zealand Wars had many complex causes, but *whenua* (land) was the one common factor. In these conflicts, also referred to as the Land Wars or Māori Wars, Māori fought both for and against the NZ government, on whose side stood the Imperial British Army, Australians and NZ's own Armed Constabulary. Land confiscations imposed on the Māori as punishment for involvement in these wars are still the source of conflict today, with the government struggling to finance compensation for what are now acknowledged to have been illegal seizures.

1908	1914–18	1931	1935–49
NZ physicist Ernest Rutherford is awarded the Nobel Prize in chemistry for 'splitting the atom', investigating the disintegration of elements and the chemistry of radioactive substances.	NZ's contribution to WWI is staggering: for a country of just over one million people, about 100,000 NZ men serve overseas. Some 60,000 become casualties, mostly on the Western Front in France.	A massive earthquake in Napier and Hastings kills at least 256 people.	First Labour government in power, under Michael Savage. This government creates NZ's pioneering version of the welfare state, and also takes some independent initiatives in foreign policy.

settlers were killed, including Wakefield's brother, Arthur, along with about six Māori. In 1845 more serious fighting broke out in the Bay of Islands, when Hōne Heke sacked a British settlement. Heke and his ally Kawiti baffled three British punitive expeditions, using a modern variant of the traditional *pā* fortification. Vestiges of these innovative earthworks can still be seen at Ruapekapeka (south of Kawakawa). Governor Grey claimed victory in the north, but few were convinced at the time. Grey had more success in the south, where he arrested the formidable Ngāti Toa chief Te Rauparaha, who until then wielded great influence on both sides of Cook Strait. Pākehā were able to swamp the few Māori living on the South Island, but the fighting of the 1840s confirmed that the North Island at that time comprised a European fringe around an independent Māori heartland.

In the 1850s settler population and aspirations grew, and fighting broke out again in 1860. The wars burned on sporadically until 1872 over much of the North Island. In the early years the King Movement, seeking to establish a monarchy that would allow Māori to assume a more equal footing with the European settlers, was the backbone of resistance. In later years some remarkable prophet-generals, notably Titokowaru and Te Kooti, took over. Most wars were small-scale, but the Waikato Land War of 1863–64 was not. This conflict, fought at the same time as the American Civil War, involved armoured steamships, ultra-modern heavy artillery, and 10 proud British regular regiments. Despite the odds, Māori forces won several battles, such as that at Gate Pā, near Tauranga, in 1864. But in the end they were ground down by European numbers and resources. Māori political, though not cultural, independence ebbed away in the last decades of the 19th century. It finally expired when police invaded the last Māori sanctuary, the Urewera Mountains, in 1916.

From Golden Rush to Welfare State

From the 1850s to the 1880s, despite conflict with Māori, the Pākehā economy boomed. A gold rush on the South Island made Dunedin NZ's biggest town, and a young, mostly male population chased their fortunes along the West Coast. Fretting over the imbalance in this frontier society, the British government tried to entice women to settle in NZ. Huge amounts of wool were exported, and there were unwise levels of overseas borrowing for development of railways and roads. By 1886 the population reached a tipping point: the population of non-Māori people were mostly born in NZ. Many still considered Britain their distant home, but a new identity was taking shape.

Depression hit in 1879, when wool prices slipped and gold production thinned out. Unemployment pushed some of the working population to Australia, and many of those who stayed suffered miserable working

Wellington-born Nancy Wake (code-named 'The White Mouse') led a guerrilla attack in France against the Nazis with a 7000-strong army. Her honours included being the Gestapo's most wanted person and a highly decorated Allied servicewoman. Her story has been told via books, a film and a TV miniseries.

New Zealand's staunch anti-nuclear stance earned it the nickname 'The Mouse That Roared'.

1936	1939–45	1953	1973
NZ aviatrix Jean Batten becomes the first aviator to fly solo directly from Britain to NZ.	NZ troops back Britain and the Allied war effort during WWII; from 1942 as many as 45,000 American soldiers camp in NZ to guard against Japanese attack.	New Zealander Edmund Hillary, with Tenzing Norgay, 'knocks the bastard off'; the pair become the first men to reach the summit of Mt Everest.	Fledgling Kiwi prog-rockers Split Enz enter a TV talent quest...finishing second to last.

conditions. There was still cause for optimism: NZ successfully exported frozen meat in 1882, raising hopes of a new backbone for the economy. Forests were enthusiastically cleared to make way for farmland.

In 1890 the Liberals, NZ's first organised political party, came to power. They stayed there until 1912, helped by a recovering economy. For decades, social-reform movements such as the Woman's Christian Temperance Union (WCTU) had lobbied for women's freedom, and NZ became the first country in the world to give women the vote in 1893. (Another major WCTU push, for countrywide prohibition, didn't take off.) Old-age pensions were introduced in 1898, but these social leaps forward didn't bring universal good news. Pensions only applied to those falling within a very particular definition of 'good character', and the pension reforms deliberately excluded the population of Chinese settlers who had arrived to labour in the goldfields. Meanwhile, the Liberals were obtaining more and more Māori land for settlement. By now, the non-Māori population outnumbered the Māori by 17 to one.

Nation Building

New Zealand had backed Britain in the Boer War (1899–1902) and WWI (1914–18), with dramatic losses in WWI. However, the bravery of Anzac (Australian and New Zealand Army Corps) forces in the failed Gallipoli campaign endures as a nation-building moment for NZ. In the 1930s NZ's experience of the Great Depression was as grim as any. The derelict farmhouses still seen in rural areas often date from this era. In 1935 a second reforming government took office, campaigning on a platform of social justice: the First Labour government, led by Australian-born Michael Joseph Savage. In WWII NZ formally declared war on Germany: 140,000 or so New Zealanders fought in Europe and the Middle East, while at home women took on increasing roles in the labour force.

By the 1930s giant ships were regularly carrying frozen meat, cheese and butter, as well as wool, on regular voyages from NZ to Britain. As the NZ economy adapted to the feeding of London, cultural links were also enhanced. New Zealand children studied British history and literature, not their own. New Zealand's leading scientists and writers, such as Ernest Rutherford and Katherine Mansfield, gravitated to Britain. Average living standards in NZ were normally better than in Britain, as were the welfare and lower-level education systems. New Zealanders had access to British markets and culture, and they contributed their share to the latter as equals. The list of 'British' writers, academics, scientists, military leaders, publishers and the like who were actually New Zealanders is long.

New Zealand prided itself on its affluence, equality and social harmony. But it was also conformist, even puritanical. The 1953 Marlon Brando movie, *The Wild One,* was banned until 1977. Full Sunday trading was not

Maurice Shadbolt's *Season of the Jew* (1987) is a semi-fictionalised story of bloody campaigns led by warrior Te Kooti against the British in Poverty Bay in the 1860s. Te Kooti and his followers compared themselves to the Israelites cast out of Egypt. Only available from secondhand booksellers. For more about the NZ Wars, visit www.newzealandwars.co.nz.

Former NZ prime minister Julius Vogel (1835–99) wrote a science-fiction novel *Anno Domini 2000* (1889) in which he imagines a utopian society led by women. Very prescient, considering NZ was the first country to give women the vote... Available on Kindle.

1974	1981	1985	1992
Pacific Island migrants who have outstayed visas (dubbed 'over-stayers') are subjected to Dawn Raids (crackdowns by immigration police). These raids continue until the early 1980s.	Springbok rugby tour divides the nation. Many New Zealanders show a strong anti-apartheid stance by protesting the games. Other Kiwis feel that sport and politics should not mix, and support the tour.	*Rainbow Warrior* sunk in Auckland Harbour by French agents to prevent the Greenpeace protest ship from making its intended voyage to Moruroa, where the French government is conducting nuclear tests.	Government begins reparations for land confiscated in the NZ Wars, and confirms Māori fishing rights in the 'Sealord deal'. Major settlements of historical confiscation follow.

allowed until 1989. Licensed restaurants hardly existed in 1960, nor did supermarkets or TV. Notoriously, from 1917 to 1967 pubs were obliged to shut at 6pm (which, ironically, paved the way for a culture of fast, heavy drinking before closing time). Yet puritanism was never the whole story. Opposition to Sunday trading stemmed not so much from belief in the sanctity of the sabbath, but from the belief that workers should have weekends, too. Six o'clock closing was a standing joke in rural areas. There was always something of a Kiwi counterculture, even before imported countercultures took root from the 1960s onward.

In 1973 'Mother England' ran off and joined the budding EU. New Zealand was beginning to develop alternative markets to Britain, and alternative exports to wool, meat and dairy products. Wide-bodied jet aircraft were allowing the world and NZ to visit each other on an increasing scale. Women were beginning to penetrate first the upper reaches of the workforce and then the political sphere. Gay people came out of the closet, despite vigorous efforts by moral conservatives to push them back in. University-educated youths were becoming more numerous and more assertive.

In 2015 there was a public referendum to decide between five proposed designs for a new national flag, and the winner was a black-and blue-backed silver fern. During a second referendum in 2016, Kiwis decided that, on reflection, they preferred the original flag – if it ain't broke...!

The Modern Age

From the 1930s, Māori experienced both a population explosion and massive urbanisation. Life expectancy was lengthening, the birth rate was high, and Māori people were moving to cities for occupations formerly filled by Pākehā servicemen. Almost 80% were urban dwellers by the mid-1980s, a staggering reversal of the status quo that brought cultural displacement but simultaneously triggered a movement to strengthen pride in Māori identity. Immigration was broadening, too, first encouraging Pacific Islanders in, for their labour, and then (East) Asians for their capital.

Then, in 1984, NZ's next great reforming government was elected – the fourth Labour government, led by David Lange, though in fact by Roger Douglas, the Minister of Finance. This government adopted a more market-led economic policy (dubbed 'Rogernomics'), delighting the right, and an anti-nuclear foreign policy, delighting the left. New Zealand's numerous economic controls were dismantled with breakneck speed. Revelling in their new freedom, NZ investors engaged in a frenzy of speculation, and suffered even more than the rest of the world from the economic crash of 1987.

Scottish settler influence is still apparent in NZ, particularly in the south of the South Island. Dunedin is called the Edinburgh of the south.

In 1985 French spies sank the Greenpeace anti-nuclear protest ship *Rainbow Warrior* in Auckland Harbour, killing one crewman. The lukewarm American condemnation of the French act brought middle NZ in behind the anti-nuclear policy, which became associated with national independence.

2004	2010	2011	2013
Māori TV begins broadcasting – for the first time a channel committed to NZ content and the revitalisation of Māori language and culture hits the small screen.	A cave-in at Pike River coalmine on the South Island's West Coast kills 29 miners.	A severe earthquake strikes Christchurch, killing 185 people and badly damaging the central business district.	New Zealand becomes one of just 15 countries in the world to legally recognise same-sex marriage.

Māori *poupou* wood carvings

From the 1990s, a change to a points-based immigration policy has woven an increasingly multicultural tapestry in NZ. Numbers of migrating Brits fell, while new arrivals from Pacific Islands, Asia, North Africa, the Middle East and other European countries increased, particularly to NZ's cities.

In 2017 NZ voted in a new face to show the world. Helmed by Jacinda Ardern, a coalition government was formed by Labour and NZ First, with support from the Green Party. New Zealand's third woman prime minister has faced challenges satisfying the various elements of her governing coalition while trying to tackle a national housing crisis and effect bigger investment in education and health. Ardern's response to the 2019 Christchurch mosque attacks was widely admired for her compassion and leadership. It's no wonder that her ascendancy has been touted as the dawn of a new period of major reform.

2013	2017	2017	2019
Auckland teenager Ella Yelich-O'Connor, aka Lorde, hits No 1 on the US music charts with her mesmeric tune 'Royals'.	Whanganui River is granted the same legal rights as a human being, a global first.	Jacinda Ardern becomes NZ's youngest PM for 150 years, heralding a new direction for NZ politics.	Terrorist shootings at two mosques in Christchurch kill 51 worshippers and shock the nation.

Environment

New Zealand's landforms have a diversity that you would expect to find across an entire continent: snow-dusted mountains, drowned glacial valleys, rainforests, dunelands and an otherworldly volcanic plateau. Straddling the boundary of two great colliding slabs of the earth's crust – the Pacific plate and the Indo-Australian plate – NZ is a plaything for nature's powerful forces.

The Land

New Zealand is a young country – its present shape is less than 10,000 years old. Having broken away from the supercontinent of Gondwanaland (which included Africa, Australia, Antarctica and South America) some 85 million years ago, it endured continual uplift and erosion, buckling and tearing, and the slow fall and rise of the sea as ice ages came and went.

Evidence of NZ's tumultuous past is everywhere. The South Island's mountainous spine – the 650km-long ranges of the Southern Alps – grew from the clash between plates at a rate of 20km over three million years; in geological terms, that's a sprint. Despite NZ's highest peak, Aoraki/Mt Cook, losing 10m from its summit overnight in a 1991 landslide (and a couple of dozen more metres to erosion), the Alps are overall believed to be some of the fastest-growing mountains in the world.

Earthquakes

Earthquakes are common in NZ, but most only rattle the glassware. A few have wrecked major towns. On the South Island, in September 2010, Christchurch was rocked by a magnitude 7.1 earthquake. Less than six months later, in February 2011, a magnitude 6.3 quake destroyed much of the city's historic heart and claimed 185 lives, making it the country's second-deadliest natural disaster and from which Christchurch is still recovering. Then in November 2016 an earthquake measuring 7.8 on the Richter scale struck Kaikōura – further up the coast – resulting in two deaths and widespread damage to local infrastructure. Roads and rail have since been rebuilt but the landscape stills wears the evidence.

Flora & Fauna

New Zealand's long isolation has allowed it to become a veritable warehouse of unique and varied plants. Separation of NZ's landmass occurred before mammals appeared on the scene, leaving birds and insects to evolve in spectacular ways. As one of the last places on earth to be colonised by humans, NZ was for millennia a safe laboratory for risky evolutionary strategies. But the arrival of Māori, and later Europeans, brought new threats and sometimes extinction.

The now-extinct flightless moa, the largest of which grew to 3.5m tall and weighed over 200kg, browsed open grasslands much as cattle do today (skeletons can be seen at the Canterbury Museum and Otago Museum), while the smaller kiwi still ekes out a nocturnal living rummaging among forest leaf litter for insects and worms. One of the country's most

> **NEW ZEALAND'S ANCIENT LIZARD**
> ....
> The largest native reptile in NZ is the tuatara, a crested lizard that can grow up to 50cm long. Thought to be unchanged for more than 220 million years, these endearing creatures can live for up to a century. Meet them at Hokitika's National Kiwi Centre (p263), and other zoos and sanctuaries around NZ.

ferocious-looking insects, the mouse-sized giant weta, meanwhile, has taken on a scavenging role that is elsewhere filled by rodents.

Many endemic creatures, including moa and the huia, an exquisite songbird, were driven to extinction, and the vast forests were cleared for their timber and to make way for agriculture. Destruction of habitat and the introduction of exotic animals and plants have taken a terrible environmental toll and New Zealanders are now fighting a rearguard battle to save what remains.

A specific plan and task force, Predator Free 2050, was established to coordinate environmental projects with specific short-term, as well as the obvious long-term, goals.

Birds & Bats

Pause in any NZ forest and listen: this country is aflutter with melodious feathered creatures. The country's first Polynesian settlers found little in the way of land mammals – just two species of bat – and most of NZ's present mammals are introduced species. New Zealand's birds generally aren't flashy, but they have an understated beauty that reveals itself in more delicate details: the lacy plumage of a rare white heron (kōtuku), the bespectacled appearance of a silvereye or the golden frowns of Fiordland penguins.

The most beautiful songbird is the tui, a nectar-eater with an inventive repertoire that includes clicks, grunts and chuckles. Notable for the white throat feathers that stand out against its dark plumage, the tui often feeds on flax flowers in suburban gardens but is most at home in densely tangled forest ('bush' to New Zealanders). The bellbird (korimako) is also musical; it's common in both native and exotic forests everywhere except Northland (though it is more likely to be heard than seen). Its call is a series of liquid bell notes, most often sounded at dawn or dusk. Fantails (pīwakawaka) are also common on forest trails, swooping and jinking to catch insects stirred up by passing hikers.

At ground level, the most famous native bird is of course the kiwi, NZ's national emblem, with a rounded body and a long, distinctive bill with nostrils at the tip for sniffing out food. Sightings in the wild require patience and luck, but numerous sanctuaries allow a peep of this iconic bird. Look out for other land birds like pukeko, elegant swamp-hens with blue plumage and bright-red beaks. They're readily seen along wetland margins and even on the sides of roads nearby – be warned, they have little road sense. Far rarer (though not dissimilar in appearance) is the takahe, a flightless bird thought to be extinct until a small colony was discovered in 1948. It's worth seeking them out at Te Anau's bird sanctuary (p196).

If you spend any time in the South Island high country, you are likely to spot the kea (unless it finds you first). A dark-green parrot with red underwings and a sense of mischief, its bold antics are a source of frustration and delight to New Zealanders. Kea are particularly common in car parks along the Milford Hwy, and in the West Coast's glacier country, where they hang out for food scraps or tear rubber from car windscreens (we've also seen them nibbling at ski bindings in winter sports resorts around Queenstown: consider yourself warned). Resist the urge to feed them, as it's hugely damaging to their health.

Volcanic New Zealand

There is far more evidence of volcanism in the North Island, tragically evident in the 2019 eruption of White Island/Whatakaari that killed 21 people, but the South Island of New Zealand also has ancient volcanoes to thank for its existence. Without what is now called the Banks Peninsula being there to repel the sea, the vast Canterbury Plains, built from alpine sediment washed down the rivers from the Alps, would have eroded long ago.

KUNGRAYFISH/SHUTTERSTOCK ©

Top The largest native reptile in New Zealand, the tuatara (p335) can live for up to a century.

Bottom The Pōhutukawa or New Zealand Christmas tree holds a prominent place in Māori mythology.

And what of the native bats? Populations of both short-tailed and long-tailed bats are declining at frightening speed, though Kahurangi National Park and Nelson are believed to be home to small populations. DOC (Department of Conservation) is hard at work protecting bats, including ambitious plans to resettle them on predator-free islands. If you spot a bat, count yourself lucky – and consider telling DOC.

Trees

No visitor to NZ (particularly Australians) can last long without hearing about the damage done to the bush by that bad-mannered Australian import, the brushtail possum. The long list of mammal pests introduced to NZ, whether accidentally or for a variety of misguided reasons, includes deer, rabbits, stoats, pigs and goats. But by far the most destructive is the possum. At their height, 70 million possums were chewing through millions of tonnes of foliage a year. Following efforts by DOC to control their numbers, the possum population has almost halved but they remain an enormous threat to native flora (and to bird life – possums prey on chicks and eggs).

Among favoured possum food are colourful kowhai, a small-leaved tree growing to 11m, which in spring has drooping clusters of bright-yellow flowers (informally considered NZ's national flower); the pōhutukawa, a beautiful coastal tree of the northern North Island that bursts into vivid red flower in December, earning the nickname 'Christmas tree'; and a similar crimson-flowered tree, the rātā.

Native timber trees include the distinctive rimu (red pine) and the long-lived tōtara (favoured for Māori war canoes). NZ's perfect pine-growing conditions encouraged one of the country's most successful imports, *Pinus radiata,* which grow to maturity in 35 years (sometimes less).

You won't get far into the bush without coming across tree ferns. NZ has an impressive 200 species of fern and almost half grow nowhere else on the planet. Most easily recognised are the mamaku (black tree fern) – which grows to 20m and can be seen in damp gullies throughout the country – and the 10m-high ponga (silver tree fern) with its distinctive white underside. The silver fern is a national symbol and adorns sporting and corporate logos, as well as shop signs, clothing and jewellery.

National Parks

More than 85,000 sq km of NZ – almost one-third of the country – is protected and managed within parks and reserves. Almost every conceivable landscape is found in this diminutive island nation, offering huge scope for wilderness experiences from climbing, skiing and mountain biking to hiking, kayaking and fishing.

Three places are World Heritage Areas: NZ's Sub-Antarctic Islands; Tongariro National Park (on the North Island); and Te Wāhipounamu (Southwest NZ), an amalgam of several national parks in southwest NZ that boasts the world's finest surviving Gondwanaland plants and animals in their natural habitats.

Access to the country's wild places is relatively straightforward, though huts on walking tracks require passes and may need to be booked in advance. In practical terms, there is little difference for travellers between a national park and a forest park, though pets are generally not allowed in national parks. Disability-assist dogs can be taken into dog-controlled areas without a permit. Camping is possible in all parks, but may be restricted to dedicated camping grounds – always check where camping is allowed via DOC websites and information leaflets before you pitch up.

Nature Guide to the New Zealand Forest (2000) by J Dawson and R Lucas is a beautifully photographed foray into NZ's forests, home to ancient species dating from the time of the dinosaurs.

ENVIRONMENT NATIONAL PARKS

B Heather and H Robertson's *Field Guide to the Birds of New Zealand* (2015) is a comprehensive guide for bird-watchers and a model of helpfulness for anyone even casually interested in the country's remarkable bird life. Another good guide, only available secondhand, is *Birds of New Zealand: Locality Guide* (2000) by Stuart Chambers.

Environmental Issues

New Zealand's reputation as an Eden, replete with pristine wilderness and eco-friendly practices, has been repeatedly placed under the microscope. The industry most visible to visitors, tourism, appears studded with green accolades, with environmental best practices employed in areas as broad as heating insulation in hotels to minimum-impact wildlife-watching. But mining, offshore oil and gas exploration, pollution, biodiversity loss, funding cuts and questionable urban planning have provided endless hooks for bad-news stories.

Travellers seeking sustainable tourism operators should look for businesses accredited with Qualmark (www.qualmark.co.nz) or those listed at Organic Explorer (www.organicexplorer.co.nz).

Water quality is arguably the most serious environmental issue faced by New Zealanders and one the government started to tackle seriously in 2019. Research from diverse sources suggests that the health of New Zealand's waterways has been in decline, the primary culprit: 'dirty dairying' – cow effluent leaching into freshwater ecosystems, carrying with it high levels of nitrates, as well as bacteria and parasites such as *E. coli* and giardia. A 2017 government push to make 90% of rivers and lakes swimmable by 2040 was met with initial scepticism about the metrics involved, but there's a strong impetus to make NZ's waterways worthy of the country's clean and green reputation.

Another ambitious initiative kicked off in 2016: Predator Free 2050. The aim is to rid NZ of introduced animals that prey on native flora and fauna. The worst offenders are possums, stoats and rats, which eat swathes of forest and kill wildlife, particularly birds. However, controversy rages at the Department of Conservation's (DOC) use of 1080 poison (sodium fluoroacetate) to control these pests, despite it being sanctioned by prominent environmental groups as well as the Parliamentary Commissioner for the Environment. Vehement opposition to 1080 is expressed by such diverse camps as hunters and animal-rights activists, who cite detriments such as by-kill and the potential for poison passing into waterways. Proponents of its use argue that it's biodegradable and that aerial distribution of 1080 is the only cost-effective way to target predators across vast, inaccessible parts of NZ. Still, 'Ban 1080' signs remain common in rural communities and the controversy is unlikely to end until the poison is banned.

As well as its damaging impact on waterways, the $12 billion dairy industry – the country's biggest export earner – generates 48% of NZ's greenhouse gas emissions. Some farmers are cleaning up their act, lowering emissions through improved management of fertilisers and higher-quality feed, and major players DairyNZ and Fonterra have pledged support. But when it comes to contributing to climate change, the dairy industry isn't NZ's only dirty habit. New Zealand might be a nation of avid recyclers and solar-panel enthusiasts, but it also has the world's fourth-highest ratio of motor vehicles to people.

The Department of Conservation website (www.doc.govt.nz) has useful information on the country's national parks, tracks and walkways. It also lists backcountry huts and campsites.

There have been fears about safeguarding the principal legislation governing the NZ environment, the 1991 *Resource Management Act,* in the face of proposed amendments. NGOs and community groups – ever-vigilant and already making major contributions to the welfare of NZ's environment – will find plenty to keep them occupied in coming years. But with an eco-conscious prime minister, Jacinda Ardern, leading a coalition government, New Zealanders are hopeful of a greener future – Ardern has pledged an ambitious goal of reducing net greenhouse gas emissions to zero by 2050.

With more trains, 100% renewable energy sources and planting 100 million trees per year, NZ could take a lead in the global response to our current climate emergency.

Māori Culture

Māori culture is as diverse as its people. Some are engaged with traditional cultural networks and pursuits; others are adapting traditions and placing these in dialogue with a globalised New Zealand culture. As a visitor you'll immediately notice the language and cultural understandings imbued in the everyday life of New Zealanders from its indigenous population, though areas where there's a larger proportion of Māori families living today are mainly in the North Island.

People of the Land

The indigenous Māori are New Zealand's *tangata whenua* (people of the land), and the Māori spiritual relationship with the land has grown over hundreds of years. Once a predominantly rural population many Māori people now live in urban centres, away from their traditional homelands, but it's still the practice in formal settings to introduce oneself by reference to 'home': an ancestral mountain, river, sea or lake, or an ancestor.

The Māori concept of *whanaungatanga* – family relationships – is central to the culture: families spread out from the *whānau* (extended family) to the *hapū* (subtribe) and *iwi* (tribe) and even, in a sense, beyond the human world and into the natural and spiritual worlds.

If you're looking for a Māori experience in NZ you'll find it – in conversations, galleries, gigs, cultural performances, on an organised tour...

The best way to learn about the relationship between the land and the *tangata whenua* (people of the land) is to get out there and start talking with Māori. Learn some language first via apps like Kupu (kupu. co.nz).

Māori Then

Some three millennia ago people began moving eastward into the Pacific, sailing against the prevailing winds and currents (hard to go out, easier to return safely). Some stopped at Tonga and Samoa, and others settled the small central East Polynesian tropical islands.

The Māori colonisation of Aotearoa began from an original homeland known to Māori as Hawaiki. Skilled navigators and sailors travelled across the Pacific, using many navigational tools – currents, winds, stars, birds and wave patterns – to guide their large, double-hulled ocean-going craft to a new land. The first of many was the great navigator Kupe, who arrived, the story goes, chasing a giant octopus named Muturangi. But the distinction of giving NZ its well-known Māori name – Aotearoa – goes to his wife, Kuramarotini, who cried out, '*He ao, he ao tea, he ao tea roa!*' (A cloud, a white cloud, a long white cloud!).

Kupe and his crew journeyed around the land, and many places around Cook Strait (between the North and South Islands) and the Hokianga in Northland still bear the names that the crew gave them and the marks of their passage. Kupe returned to Hawaiki, leaving from (and naming) Northland's Hokianga. He gave other seafarers valuable navigational information. And then the great *waka* (ocean-going craft) began to arrive.

The *waka* that the first settlers arrived on, and their landing places, are immortalised in tribal histories. Well-known *waka* include *Tākitimu, Kurahaupō, Te Arawa, Mataatua, Tainui, Aotea* and *Tokomaru*. There are many others. Māori trace their genealogies back to those who arrived on the *waka* (and further back as well).

Wikipedia has a good list of *iwi* websites and a map showing *iwi* distribution (www.wikipedia. org/wiki/ list_of_iwi).

What would it have been like, making the transition from small tropical islands to a much larger, cooler landmass? Goodbye breadfruit, coconuts, paper mulberry; hello moa, fernroot, flax – and immense space (relatively speaking). New Zealand has more than 15,000km of coastline. Rarotonga, by way of contrast, has a little over 30km. There was land, lots of it, and flora and fauna that had developed more or less separately from the rest of the world for 80 million years. There was an untouched,

VISITING MARAE (TRADITIONAL MEETING PLACES)

As you travel around NZ, you will see many *marae* complexes. Often *marae* are owned by a descent group. They are also owned by urban Māori groups, schools, universities and church groups, and they should only be visited by arrangement with the owners.

Marae complexes include a *wharenui* (meeting house), which often embodies an ancestor. Its ridge is the backbone, the rafters are ribs, and it shelters the descendants. There is a clear space in front of the *wharenui*, the *marae ātea*. Sometimes there are other buildings: a *wharekai* (dining hall); a toilet and shower block; perhaps even classrooms, play equipment and the like.

Hui (gatherings) are held at *marae*. Issues are discussed, classes conducted, milestones celebrated and the dead farewelled. Te reo Māori (the Māori language) is prominent, and sometimes the only language used.

Visitors sleep in the meeting house if a *hui* goes on for longer than a day. Mattresses are placed on the floor, someone may bring a guitar, and stories and jokes always go down well as the evening stretches out.

The Pōwhiri

If you visit a *marae* as part of an organised group, you'll be welcomed in a *pōwhiri* (welcoming ceremony).

Outside the *marae*, there may be a *wero* (challenge). Using *taiaha* (quarter-staff) moves, a warrior will approach the visitors and place a baton on the ground for a visitor to pick up, to demonstrate their peaceful intent.

There is a *karanga* (ceremonial call). A woman from the host group calls to the visitors and a woman from the visiting group responds. Their long, high, falling calls begin to overlap and interweave and the visiting group walks on to the *marae ātea* (meeting house courtyard). It is then time for *whaikōrero* (speech-making). The hosts welcome the visitors, the visitors respond. Speeches are capped off by a *waiata* (song), and the visitors' speakers present a *koha* (gift, usually an envelope of cash). The hosts then invite the visitors to *hariru* (shake hands) and *hongi*. Visitors and hosts are now united and will share light refreshments or a meal.

The Hongi

To perform the *hongi*, press forehead and nose together gently, shake hands, and perhaps offer a greeting such as *'Kia ora'* or *'Tēnā koe'*. Some prefer one press (for two or three seconds, or longer), others prefer two shorter (press, release, press). Men and women sometimes kiss on one cheek. The *hongi* symbolises the sharing of breath – or life – with the nose touch, followed with a metaphoric exchanging of knowledge by pressing foreheads together.

Tapu

Tapu (spiritual restrictions) and *mana* (power and prestige) are taken seriously in the Māori world. Sit on chairs or seating provided (never on tables), and walk around people, not over them. The *pōwhiri* has *tapu*, and mixing food and *tapu* is right up there on the offence-o-meter, so only eat and drink when invited to do so by your hosts. You needn't worry about going hungry, though: an important Māori value is *manaakitanga* (hospitality).

Depending on area, the *pōwhiri* has gender roles: women *karanga* (call), men *whaikōrero* (orate); women lead the way on to the *marae*, men sit on the *paepae* (the speakers' bench at the front). In a modern context, the debate around traditional roles continues.

massive fishery. There were great seaside mammalian convenience stores – seals and sea lions – as well as a fabulous array of birds.

The early settlers went on the move, pulled by love, trade opportunities and greater resources; pushed by disputes and threats to security. When they settled, Māori established *mana whenua* (regional authority), whether by military campaigns or by the peaceful methods of intermarriage and diplomacy. Looking over tribal history it's possible to see the many alliances, absorptions and extinctions that went on.

Histories were carried by the voice, in stories, songs and chants. Great stress was placed on accurate learning – after all, in an oral culture where people are the libraries, the past is always a generation or two away from oblivion.

Māori lived in *kainga* (small villages), which often had associated gardens. Housing was cosy by modern standards – often it was hard to stand upright while inside. From time to time people would leave their home base and go to harvest seasonal foods. When peaceful life was interrupted by conflict, people would withdraw to *pā* (fortified villages).

And then Europeans began to arrive.

Read Hirini Moko Mead's *Tikanga Māori* (2006; available on Kindle), Pat and Hiwi Tauroa's *Te Marae* (2009), and Anne Salmond's *Hui* (2009) for detailed insights into Māori knowledge and customs.

MĀORI CULTURE MĀORI TODAY

Māori Today

Today's culture is marked by new developments in the arts, business, sport and politics. Many historical grievances still stand, but some *iwi* (Ngāi Tahu and Tainui, for example) have settled major historical grievances and are significant forces in the NZ economy. Māori have also addressed the decline in Māori language use by establishing *kōhanga reo, kura kaupapa Māori* and *wānanga* (Māori-language preschools, schools and universities). There is now a generation of people who speak Māori as a first language. There is a network of Māori radio stations, and Māori TV attracts a committed viewership. A recently revived Māori event is becoming more and more prominent – Matariki (Māori New Year). The constellation Matariki is also known as the Pleiades. It begins to rise above the horizon in late May or early June and its appearance traditionally signals a time for learning, planning and preparing as well as singing, dancing and celebrating. Look out for talks and lectures, concerts, dinners and parties to celebrate and learn more.

Religion

Christian churches and denominations are prominent in the Māori world, including televangelists, mainstream churches for regular and occasional worship, and two major Māori churches (Ringatū and Rātana). But in the (non-Judeo-Christian) beginning there were the *atua Māori,* the Māori gods, and for many Māori the gods are a vital and relevant force still. It is common to greet the earth mother and sky father when speaking formally at a *marae* (meeting house). The gods are represented in art and carving, sung of in *waiata* (songs) and invoked through *karakia* (prayer and incantation) when a meeting house is opened, when a *waka* is launched, even (more simply) when a meal is served. They are spoken of in the *marae* and in wider Māori contexts. The traditional Māori creation story is well known and widely celebrated.

Kupe's passage is marked around NZ: he left his sails (Nga Ra o Kupe) near Cape Palliser as triangular landforms; he named the two islands in Wellington Harbour Matiu and Makoro after his daughters; his blood stains the red rocks of Wellington's south coast.

The Arts

There are many collections of Māori *taonga* (treasures) around the country. Canterbury Museum (p70) in Christchurch has a good collection, while Te Hikoi Southern Journey (p186) in Riverton has riveting displays on early interactions between Māori and Pākehā.

You can stay up to date with what's happening in the Māori arts by listening to *iwi* radio stations or tuning into Māori TV (www.maoritelevision.com) for regular features on the Māori arts. Māori TV first went to air in 2004, an emotional time for many Māori who could at last see their culture, their concerns and their language in a mass medium.

Over 90% of content is NZ made, and programs are in both Māori and English: they're subtitled and accessible to everyone. If you want to really get a feel for the rhythm and metre of spoken Māori from the comfort of your own chair, switch to Te Reo (www.maoritelevision.com/tv/te-reo-channel), a Māori-language-only channel.

E-Tangata (e-tangata.co.nz) is an online magazine run by the Mana Trust specialising in stories that reflect the experiences of Māori and Pasifika in Aotearoa.

Tā Moko

Tā moko is the Māori art of tattoo, traditionally worn by men on their faces, thighs and buttocks, and by women on their chins and lips. *Moko* were permanent grooves tapped into the skin using pigment (made from burnt caterpillar or kauri-gum soot) and bone chisels (fine, sharp combs for broad work, and straight blades for detailed work). Canterbury Museum (p70) in Christchurch has a display of traditional implements for *tā moko*.

The modern tattooist's gun is common now, but bone chisels are coming back into use for Māori who want to reconnect with tradition. Since the general renaissance in Māori culture in the 1960s, many artists have taken up *tā moko* and now many Māori wear *moko* with quiet pride and humility.

Can visitors get some work done? The art of *tā moko* is learned by, and inked upon, Māori people – but the term *kirituhi* (skin inscriptions) has arisen to describe Māori-motif-inspired modern tattoos that non-Māori can wear. *Kirituhi* can be profoundly meaningful and designed to fit the wearer's personal story, but there's an important distinction between *kirituhi* and *tā moko*.

Whakairo

Traditional Māori carving, with its intricate detailing and curved lines, can transport the viewer. It's quite amazing to consider that *whakairo* was done with stone tools, themselves painstakingly made, until the advent of iron (nails suddenly became very popular).

Some major traditional forms are *waka* (canoes), *pātaka* (storage buildings) and *wharenui* (meeting houses). Along the greenstone-rich West Coast, numerous workshop-boutiques double as galleries that showcase fine examples of modern *pounamu* carving (particularly in Hokitika). You can see sublime examples of traditional woodcarving at Dunedin's Otago Museum (p147), including an impressive *waka taua* (war canoe).

The apex of carving today is the *whare whakairo* (carved meeting house). A commissioning group relates its history and ancestral stories to a carver, who then draws (sometimes quite loosely) on traditional motifs to interpret or embody the stories and ancestors in wood or composite fibreboard.

The biggest change in carving (as with most traditional arts) has been in the use of new mediums and tools. Rangi Kipa uses a high-density plastic to make his *hei tiki* (traditional pendants). You can check out his gallery at www.rangikipa.com.

Weaving

Weaving was an essential art that provided clothing, nets and cordage, footwear for rough country travel, mats to cover earthen floors, and *kete* (bags) to carry stuff in. Many woven items are beautiful as well as practical. Some were major works – *korowai* (cloaks) could take years to finish. Woven predominantly with flax and feathers, they are worn now on ceremonial occasions – a stunning sight.

Arriving for the first time in NZ, two crew members of *Tainui* saw the red flowers of the pohutukawa tree, and they cast away their prized red feather ornaments, thinking that there were plenty to be had on shore.

The best route into culture is through language. Pick up some te reo Māori with apps Kupu (kupu.co.nz) and Drops (languagedrops.com). Another popular language app, Duolingo, plans to include a te reo Māori course for beginners in 2020. You can also fill your messages with EmoTikis (tepuia.com/emotiki).

HOW THE WORLD BEGAN

In the Māori story of creation, first there was the void, then the night, then Ranginui (sky father) and Papatūānuku (earth mother) came into being embracing, with their children nurtured between them. But nurturing became something else. Their children were stifled in the darkness of their embrace. Unable to stretch out to their full dimensions and struggling to see clearly in the darkness, their children tried to separate them. Tāwhirimātea, the god of winds, raged against them; Tūmatauenga, the god of war, assaulted them. Each god child in turn tried to separate them, but still Rangi and Papa pressed against each other. And then Tāne Mahuta, god of the great forests and of humanity, placed his feet against his father and his back against his mother and slowly began to move them apart. Then came the world of light, of demigods and humanity.

In this world of light Māui, the demigod ancestor, was cast out to sea at birth and was found floating in his mother's topknot. He was a shape-shifter, becoming a pigeon or a dog or an eel if it suited his purposes. He stole fire from the gods. Using his grandmother's jawbone, he bashed the sun so that it could only limp slowly across the sky, allowing people enough time during the day to get things done (if only he would do it again!). Using the South Island as a canoe, he used the jawbone as a hook to fish up Te Ika-a-Māui (the fish of Māui) – the North Island. And, finally, he met his end trying to defeat death itself. The goddess of death, Hine-nui-te-pō, had obsidian teeth in her vagina (obsidian is a volcanic glass that has a razor edge when chipped). Māui attempted to reverse birth (and hence defeat death) by crawling into her birth canal to reach her heart as she slept. A small bird – a fantail – laughed at the absurd sight. Hine-nui-te-pō awoke, and crushed Māui to death between her thighs. Death one, humanity nil.

Today, tradition is greatly respected, but not all traditions are necessarily followed. Flax was (and still is) the preferred medium for weaving. To get a strong fibre from flax leaves, weavers scraped away the leaves' flesh with a mussel shell, pounded it until it was soft, dyed it, then dried it. But contemporary weavers are using everything in their work: raffia, copper wire, rubber – even polar fleece and garden hoses!

The best way to experience weaving is to contact one of the many NZ weavers running workshops where you're visiting (see www.nztextileexperiences.com). By learning the techniques, you'll appreciate the examples of weaving in museums even more. And if you want to take a shortcut and buy something? Woven *kete* and backpacks have become fashion accessories and are on sale in most cities. Weavings are also sold in dealer art galleries around the country.

Haka

Adrenalising, awe-inspiring and uplifting, the *haka* is not only a war dance – it is used to welcome visitors, honour achievement, express identity or to put forth very strong opinions.

Haka involve chanted words, vigorous body movements and *pūkana* (when performers distort their faces, eyes bulging with the whites showing, perhaps with tongue extended).

The well-known *haka* 'Ka Mate', performed by the All Blacks before rugby test matches, is credited to the cunning fighting chief Te Rauparaha. It celebrates his escape from death. Chased by enemies, he hid himself in a food pit. After his pursuers had left, a friendly chief named Te Whareangi (the 'hairy man' referred to in the *haka*), let him out; he climbed out into the sunshine and performed 'Ka Mate'.

You can experience *haka* at various cultural performances, including Ko Tane (p80) at Willowbank in Christchurch. But the best displays of *haka* are at the bi-annual Te Matatini National Kapa Haka Festival (www.tematatini.co.nz), when NZ's top groups compete for honours.

Māori legends are all around you as you tour NZ: Māui's *waka* became today's Southern Alps; a *taniwha* (legendary water being) formed Lake Waikaremoana in its death throes; and a rejected Mt Taranaki walked into exile from the central North Island mountain group, carving the Whanganui River.

Contemporary Visual Art

A distinctive feature of Māori visual art is the tension between traditional Māori ideas and modern artistic mediums and trends. Shane Cotton has produced a series of works that conversed with 19th-century painted meeting houses, which themselves departed from Māori carved houses. Kelcy Taratoa uses sci-fi, superheroes and pop-art imagery.

Of course, Māori motifs aren't necessarily the dominant features of work by Māori artists. Major NZ artist Ralph Hotere (1931–2013) was wary about being assigned any cultural, ethnic or genre label and his work confronted a broad range of political and social issues.

Contemporary Māori art is by no means only about painting. Many other artists use installations or digital formats – look out for work by Jacqueline Fraser, Peter Robinson and Lisa Reihana.

There are some great permanent exhibitions of Māori visual arts in the major centres. The Christchurch Art Gallery (p69) holds a particularly strong collection.

See Ngahuia Te Awekotuku's book Mau Moko: The World of Māori Tattoo *(2007) for a close-up of Māori body art, including powerful, beautiful images and incisive commentary.*

Theatre

Powered by a wave of political activism, the 1970s saw the emergence of many Māori playwrights and plays, and theatre remains a prominent area of the Māori arts today. Māori theatre drew heavily on the traditions of the *marae*. Instead of dimming the lights and immediately beginning the performance, many Māori theatre groups began with a stylised *pōwhiri* (welcoming ceremony), had space for audience members to respond to the play, and ended with a *karakia* (prayer or incantation), or a farewell.

The Taki Rua company is an independent producer of Māori work for both children and adults and has been in existence for more than 30 years. As well as staging its shows in the major centres, it tours most of its work – check out its website (www.takirua.co.nz) for the current offerings. Māori drama is also often showcased at the professional theatres in the main centres. Look out for work by Hone Kouka, Briar Grace-Smith and Mitch Tawhi Thomas.

Could heavy metal be the newest form of expressing Māori identity? Singing (or screaming) in te reo Māori, Waipu guitar trio Alien Weaponry (alienweaponry. com) thrash out songs that narrate the battles of their ancestors.

Contemporary Dance

Contemporary Māori dance often takes its inspiration from *kapa haka* (cultural dance) and traditional Māori imagery. The exploration of pre-European life also provides inspiration.

New Zealand's leading specifically Māori dance company is the Atamira Dance Collective (www.atamiradance.co.nz), which has been producing critically acclaimed, beautiful and challenging work since 2000. If that sounds too highbrow, get acquainted with the work of musician

COMMON MĀORI GEOGRAPHICAL TERMS

The following words form part of many Māori place names in New Zealand, and help you understand the meaning of these place names. For example, Rotoroa is the Long (roa) Lake (roto) and Rotoiti is the Small (iti) Lake (roto).

a – of; **ara** – way, path or road; **awa** – river or valley; **iti** – small; **kai** – food; **kare** – rippling; **kati** – to shut or close; **makariri** – cold; **maunga** – mountain; **moana** – sea or lake; **motu** – island; **mutu** – finished, ended, over; **ngā** – the (plural); **nui** – big or great; **o** – of, place of...; **one** – beach, sand or mud; **pā** – fortified village; **poto** – short; **puke** – hill; **puna** – spring, hole, fountain; **rangi** – sky, heavens; **raro** – north; **roa** – long; **roto** – lake; **rua** – hole in the ground, two; **runga** – above; **tāhuna** – beach, sandbank; **tāne** – man; **tapu** – sacred, forbidden or taboo; **tata** – close to, dash against, twin islands; **te** – the (singular); **tonga** – south; **wāhine** – woman; **wai** – water; **waka** – canoe; **wera** – burnt or hot; **whanga** – harbour, bay or inlet; **whenua** – land or country

Māori man celebrating Waitangi Day

and visual artist Mika Torotoro, who blends *kapa haka*, drag, opera, ballet and disco. Check out clips of his work at www.mika.co.nz.

Cinema

Although there had already been successful Māori documentaries (*Patu!* and the *Tangata Whenua* series are brilliant), it wasn't until 1987 that NZ had its first fictional feature-length movie by a Māori writer and director, with Barry Barclay's *Ngati*. Mereta Mita was the first Māori woman to direct a fiction feature, with *Mauri* (1988). Both Mita and Barclay had highly political aims and ways of working, which involved a lengthy pre-production phase, when they would consult with and seek direction from their *kaumātua* (elders). Films with significant Māori participation or control include the harrowing *Once Were Warriors* and the uplifting *Whale Rider*. Oscar-nominated Taika Waititi, of Te Whānau-ā-Apanui descent, has dominated international screens in recent years after *Boy* (2010).

Literature

There are many novels and collections of short stories by Māori writers, and personal taste will govern your choices. Keri Hulme *(The Bone People, Stonefish)* and the South Island go together like a mass of whitebait bound in a frying pan by a single egg (ie very well). Other significant writers include Patricia Grace *(Potiki, Cousins, Dogside Story, Tu)*, Witi Ihimaera *(Pounamu, Pounamu; The Matriarch; Bulibasha; The Whale Rider)*, Alan Duff *(Once Were Warriors)*, James George *(Hummingbird, Ocean Roads)*, Paula Morris *(Rangatira, Queen of Beauty, Hibiscus Coast, Trendy but Casual)* and Kelly Ana Morey *(Bloom, Grace Is Gone)*. If poetry appeals, you can't go past the giant of Māori poetry in English, the late, lamented Hone Tuwhare *(Deep River Talk: Collected Poems)*, who famously sounds like he's at church and in the pub at the same time.

For information on Māori arts today, check out Toi Māori at www.maoriart.org.nz.

The first NZ hip-hop song to become a hit was Dalvanius Prime's 'Poi E', which was sung entirely in Māori by the Patea Māori Club. It was the highest-selling single of the mid-'80s in NZ.

The Arts

Music, storytelling, dance and visual arts have been a part of New Zealand's cultural identity since its precolonial days. Then European settlers imported their artistic sensibilities, and mixed with Māori modes and motifs, a distinctive postcolonial artistic identity has developed. Writers and visual artists led the way, but it has been music and cinema that has really catapulted NZ's unique creative worldview on to the world stage.

Literature

In 2013, 28-year-old Eleanor Catton became only the second NZ writer to win the Man Booker Prize, one of the world's most prestigious literary awards, for her epic historical novel *The Luminaries,* set on the West Coast. *Mister Pip* by Lloyd Jones was shortlisted in 2007, but the only other Kiwi to take the prize to date was Keri Hulme, in 1985, for her gritty magic-realist novel *The Bone People.*

Jane Campion was the first Kiwi nominated as Best Director at the Academy Awards and Peter Jackson the first to win. *The Return of the King* won a mighty 11 Oscars in 2004.

New Zealand has a proud lineage of female authors, beginning in the early 20th century with Katherine Mansfield, who was famous for her short fiction. The tradition was carried forward by Janet Frame, whose dramatic life was depicted in Jane Campion's film *An Angel at My Table* – which was based on an autobiographical trilogy including the much-loved novella *To the Is-land* (1983). Frame's *The Carpathians* won the Commonwealth Writers' Prize in 1989. Also on New Zealanders' must-read lists is Catherine Chidgey, whose heart-rending novel *The Wish Child* (2016) won the country's top fiction prize at 2017's NZ Book Awards.

Less recognised internationally, Maurice Gee gained the nation's annual top fiction gong six times, most recently with *Blindsight* in 2006. A landmark survey in 2018 voted Gee's *Plumb* as the best Kiwi book of the past 50 years. His children's novel *Under the Mountain* (1979) was made into a seminal NZ TV series in 1981, and then a motion picture in 2009. In 2004 the adaptation of another of his novels, *In My Father's Den* (1972), won major awards at international film festivals.

The late Maurice Shadbolt also achieved acclaim for his many novels, particularly those set during the New Zealand Wars. Try *Season of the Jew* (1987) or *The House of Strife* (1993).

For children's literature fans, the *Hairy Maclary* series by New Zealand author Lynley Dodd holds a special spot in all our hearts.

MĀORI VOICES IN PRINT

Some of the most interesting and enjoyable NZ fiction voices belong to Māori writers, with Booker-winner Keri Hulme the most well known. Witi Ihimaera's novels give a wonderful insight into small town life on the East Coast – especially *Bulibasha* (1994) and *The Whale Rider* (1987), which was made into the acclaimed film in 2002. Patricia Grace's work is filled with exquisitely told stories of rural life: try *Mutuwhenua* (1978), *Potiki* (1986), *Dogside Story* (2001) or *Tu* (2004). *Chappy* (2015) is Grace's expansive tale of a prodigal son returning to NZ to untangle his cross-cultural heritage.

MIDDLE-EARTH TOURISM

Did the scenery of the epic film trilogies *Lord of the Rings (LOTR)* and *The Hobbit* lure you to Aotearoa? The North Island has most of the big-ticket filming locations but both islands have knowledgeable operators that can take you set-jetting on foot, on horseback or by 4WD. Dedicated enthusiasts can buy a copy of Ian Brodie's *The Lord of the Rings: Location Guidebook* for detail on filming locations and their GPS coordinates. Online, DOC has a useful primer (www.doc.govt.nz/lordoftherings).

Southern Alps, aka Misty Mountains Peter Jackson made the most of this untamed landscape, choosing Mt Cook Village as the setting for Minas Tirith. Hassle Free Tours (p80) offers a trip from Christchurch to the site of Edoras.

Takaka Hill Used for various scenes in both trilogies.

Pelorus River, Marlborough Sounds The setting for the barrel scene in *The Hobbit: The Desolation of Smaug*. Experience it on a kayaking trip with Pelorus Eco Adventures (p313).

Twizel OneRing Tours (p126) allows you to play dress-up at the sites of Laketown and the Battle of the Pelennor Fields.

Queenstown & Glenorchy Nomad Safaris (p220) and Private Discovery Tours (p219) offer a range of 4WD tours out of Queenstown, complete with Middle-earth movie locations. Glenorchy-based Dart River Adventures (p228) runs horse treks along a LOTR theme.

Te Anau Fangorn Forest, Silverlode and Nen Hithoel were set in Mavora Lakes Conservation Park (www.doc.govt.nz), while the Upper Waiau River became the River Anduin.

Cinema & TV

If you first dreamt of visiting NZ when watching *The Lord of the Rings* and *The Hobbit* on the silver screen, you're in good company. Sir Peter Jackson's NZ-made trilogies have been the best thing to happen to NZ tourism since the *Endeavour* sailed past.

Yet NZ cinema is not always easy watching. In his BBC-funded documentary, *Cinema of Unease,* NZ actor Sam Neill examines the often bleak, haunted work of Kiwi filmmakers. One need only watch Lee Tamahori's harrowing *Once Were Warriors* (1994) to see what he means.

The uniting factor on its screens is its wild landscapes, which provide an unnerving backdrop to films such as Jane Campion's *The Piano* (1993); the BBC co-production TV series *Top of the Lake* (2013); Brad McGann's *In My Father's Den* (2004); and Jackson's *Heavenly Creatures* (1994). Each mixes lush scenery with disturbing violence, a land that is mystical and isolating all at once.

Even when Kiwis do humour, it is as resolutely black as their rugby jerseys. Check out Jackson's early splatter-fests, and Taika Waititi's *Boy* (2010) for some early examples. But NZ humour has found an international audience with Waititi and Jemaine Clement's *What We Do in the Shadows* (2014) and Waititi's *Hunt for the Wilderpeople* (2016), propelling the scriptwriter and director to critical acclaim. Then Marvel Studio's *Thor: Ragnarok* (2017) made him a household name, while some argue that the director's role voicing Thor's friend Krog was the film's accidental highlight. His Hitler comedy *Jojo Rabbit* (2019) was nominated for six Academy Awards, winning for Best Adapted Screenplay.

The HBO-produced TV musical parody *Flight of the Conchords* – featuring a mumbling, bumbling Kiwi folk-singing duo (Jemaine Clement and Bret McKenzie) trying to get a break in New York – also received international renown and a cult following.

Kiwis have won more Oscars for behind-the-scenes work than on camera. Acting awards go to Anna Paquin (for *The Piano*) and Russell Crowe (for *Gladiator*). Paquin was born in Canada but moved to NZ when she was four, while Crowe moved from NZ to Australia at the same age.

Visual Arts

The NZ 'can do' attitude extends to the visual arts. If you're visiting a local's home, don't be surprised to find one of the owner's paintings on the wall or one of their mate's sculptures in the back garden, pieced together out of bits of shell, driftwood and a length of the magical 'number 8 wire'.

This is symptomatic of a flourishing local art-and-crafts scene cultivated by lively tertiary courses churning out traditional carvers and weavers, jewellery-makers, and moulders of metal and glass. The larger cities have excellent dealer galleries representing interesting local artists working across all media.

Traditional Māori art has a distinctive visual style with important motifs that have been embraced by NZ artists of every background. In the painting medium, these include the cool modernism of Gordon Walters and the more controversial pop-art approach of Dick Frizzell's *Tiki* series. Likewise, Pacific Island themes are common, particularly in Auckland; look out for the intricate, collage-like paintings of Niuean-born, Auckland-raised John Pule.

Charles Frederick Goldie painted a series of compelling, realist portraits of Māori, who were feared to be a dying race. Debate over the political propriety of Goldie's work raged for years, but its value is widely accepted now: not least because Māori themselves generally acknowledge and value them as ancestral representations. In 2016 Goldie's last work became the first NZ painting to be sold for more than $1 million.

Recalibrating the ways in which Pacific Islander and Māori people are depicted in art, Lisa Reihana wowed the Venice Biennale in 2017 with her multimedia work *In Pursuit of Venus*.

Depicting the Land

It's no surprise that in a nation so defined by its natural environment, landscape painting constituted the first post-European body of art. In the late 19th century, John Gully and Petrus van der Velden were among those to arrive and capture the drama of the land in paintings.

Colin McCahon is widely regarded to have been NZ's most important artist. Even where McCahon lurched into Catholic mysticism, his spirituality was rooted in geography. His brooding landscapes evoke the land's power but also its vulnerability to colonialism. McCahon is widely quoted as describing his work as a depiction of NZ before its seas become cluttered with debris and the sky turns dark with soot.

Landscape photographers also capture the fierceness and fragility of NZ's terrain. It's worth detouring to a few of the country's resident photographers, many of whom have their own gallery (sometimes within or adjoining their own home). Westland is home to the gallery of exceptionally gifted photographer Andris Apse (www.andrisapse.com) and to the Petr Hlavacek Gallery (www.nzicescapes.com), which showcases some of NZ's finest landscape photography.

Music

New Zealand music began with the *waiata* (singing) developed by Māori following their arrival in the country. The main musical instruments were wind instruments made of bone or wood, the most well known of which is the *nguru* (also known as the 'nose flute'), while percussion was provided by chest- and thigh-slapping. These days, the liveliest place to see Māori music being performed is at *kapa haka* competitions in which groups compete with their own routines of traditional song and dance.

THE ARTS VISUAL ARTS

A wide range of cultural events are listed on www.eventfinda.co.nz. This is a good place to find out about gigs, classical-music recitals and *kapa haka* performances. For more specific information on the NZ classical-music scene, see www.sounz.org.nz.

Not all the best galleries are in Auckland, Wellington or Christchurch. Gore's Eastern Southland Gallery (p182) has an important and growing collection. Some of the most interesting galleries have a makeshift, multi-use vibe: part-gallery, part-museum of curios, part-cafe, designed for road-trippers to pull over and marvel, like the Catlins' Lost Gypsy Gallery (p180), which showcases a bamboozling collection inside a bus.

Classical

Early European immigrants brought their own styles of music that evolved into local variants during the early 1900s. In the 1950s Douglas Lilburn became one of the first internationally recognised NZ classical composers. More recently the country has produced a number of world-renowned musicians in this field, including legendary opera singer Dame Kiri Te Kanawa, million-selling classic-to-pop singer Hayley Westenra, composer John Psathas (who created music for the 2004 Olympic Games) and composer/percussionist Gareth Farr (who also performs in drag under the name Lilith LaCroix).

Rock

New Zealand's most acclaimed rock exports are the revered indie label Flying Nun and the music of the Finn Brothers.

Started in 1981 by Christchurch record-store owner Roger Shepherd, many of Flying Nun's early groups came from Dunedin, where local musicians took the DIY attitude of punk, but used it to produce a lo-fi indie-pop that received rave reviews from the likes of *NME* in the UK and *Rolling Stone* in the US. Many of the musicians from the Flying Nun scene still perform live to this day, including David Kilgour (from the Clean) and Shayne Carter (from the Straitjacket Fits, and subsequently Dimmer and the Adults).

Want something heavier? Hamilton heavy-metal act Devilskin's 2014 debut album hit the top spot on NZ's charts, as did their punchy 2016 follow-up *Be Like the River*. Beastwars, a rasping, trance-inducing sludge metal band from Wellington, is another stalwart of NZ's heavy-metal scene. Meanwhile, hitting the big leagues during tours of North America and Europe, technical death metal band Ulcerate have risen to prominence as NZ's best-known extreme metal act.

Reggae, Hip-Hop & Dance

The genres of music that have been adopted most enthusiastically by Māori and Polynesian New Zealanders have been reggae (in the 1970s) and hip-hop (in the 1980s), which has led to distinct local forms. In Wellington, a thriving jazz scene took on a reggae influence to create a host of groups that blended dub, roots and funky jazz – most famously: Fat Freddy's Drop.

The local hip-hop scene has its heart in the suburbs of South Auckland, which have a high concentration of Māori and Pacific Island residents. This area is home to one of New Zealand's foremost hip-hop

Tickets for most events can be bought at www.ticketek.co.nz, www.ticketmaster.co.nz or, for smaller gigs, www.undertheradar.co.nz.

The TV show *Popstars* originated in New Zealand, though the resulting group, TrueBliss, was short-lived. The series concept was then picked up in Australia, the UK and the US, inspiring the *Idols* series.

THE BROTHERS FINN

There are certain tunes that all Kiwis can sing along to, given a beer and the opportunity. A surprising proportion of these were written by Tim and Neil Finn, many of which have been international hits. Tim Finn first came to prominence in the 1970s group Split Enz, who amassed a solid following in Australia, NZ and Canada before disbanding in 1985. Neil then formed Crowded House with two Australian musicians (Paul Hester and Nick Seymour) and one of their early singles, 'Don't Dream It's Over', hit number two on the US charts. Tim later did a brief spell in the band, during which the brothers wrote 'Weather with You' – a song that reached number seven on the UK charts, pushing their album *Woodface* to gold sales. Neil has also remained busy, organising a set of shows/releases under the name 7 Worlds Collide – a collaboration with well-known musicians. Tim and Neil have both released a number of solo albums, as well as releasing material together as the Finn Brothers. Neil is now playing with rock stalwarts Fleetwood Mac.

labels, Dawn Raid, which takes its name from the infamous 1970s early-morning house raids that police performed on Pacific Islanders suspected of outstaying their visas. Dawn Raid's most successful artist is Savage, who sold a million copies of his single 'Swing' after it was featured in the movie *Knocked Up*. Within New Zealand, the most well-known hip-hop acts are Scribe, Che Fu and Smashproof (whose song 'Brother' held number one on the NZ singles charts for 11 weeks).

Dance music gained a foothold in Christchurch in the 1990s, spawning dub/electronica outfit Salmonella Dub and its offshoot act, Tiki Taane. Drum 'n' bass remains popular locally and has spawned internationally renowned acts such as Concord Dawn and Shapeshifter.

For a deep dive into NZ 's music scene:

Audio Culture (www.audio culture.co.nz)

NZ Musician (www.nzmusician.co.nz)

13th Floor (www.13thfloor.co.nz)

Movers & Shakers

Since 2000, the NZ music scene has hit its stride after the government convinced commercial radio stations to adopt a voluntary quota of 20% local music. Since then Kiwi bands have had enough commercial airplay to gain large folllowings, though social media, streaming and YouTube have all played their part in the rising popularity of many NZ artists.

The soul/dance/reggae fusion outfit Six60 are now playing at a level previously only international bands enjoyed in NZ, selling out 50,000-seat venues like Auckland's Western Springs.

Following in the foosteps of soulful Māori songstress Bic Runga, Troy Kingi won best Māori artist at the 2019 NZ Music Awards. Teeks (Te Karehana Gardiner-Toi) sings in te reo and English, and hip-hop artist Kings had the longest-running NZ single with 'Don't Worry 'Bout It' at number one for 33 weeks in 2017.

On the female solo artist front check out Benee, Bailey Wiley, Tammi Neilson and Holly Smith. New Zealand also produced internationally acclaimed pop electronica bands like Drax Project and Broods.

Good Lorde!

The biggest name in Kiwi music is Lorde, a singer-songwriter from Devonport on Auckland's North Shore. Known less regally to her friends as Ella Yelich-O'Connor, Lorde was 16 years old when she cracked the number-one spot on the US Billboard charts in 2013 with her hit 'Royals' – the first NZ solo artist to top the American charts. 'Royals' went on to win the Song of the Year Grammy in 2014. Her debut album *Pure Heroine* spawned a string of hits and sold millions of copies worldwide, while moody follow-up *Melodrama* instantly topped charts in NZ and the US upon its release in 2017.

Survival Guide

Directory A–Z

Accessible Travel

Kiwi accommodation generally caters fairly well for travellers with mobility issues, with most hostels, hotels and motels equipped with one or two wheelchair-accessible rooms. (B&Bs aren't required to have accessible rooms.) Many tourist attractions similarly provide wheelchair access, with wheelchairs often available. For advice on local attractions with maximum accessibility ask at i-SITE visitor centres.

Tour operators with accessible vehicles operate from most major centres. Key cities are also serviced by 'kneeling' buses (buses that hydraulically stoop down to kerb level to allow easy access), and many taxi companies offer wheelchair-accessible vans. Large car-hire firms (Avis, Hertz etc) provide cars with hand controls at no extra charge (but advance booking is required, of course). Air New Zealand accommodates travellers in wheelchairs.

Download Lonely Planet's free Accessible Travel guides from http://lptravel.to/AccessibleTravel.

Resources

Access4All (www.facebook.com/Access4all.Ltd) Now only a Facebook page, but a travel company with good links to accommodation and other accessible essentials.

Firstport (www.firstport.co.nz) Includes a high-level overview of transport in NZ, including mobility taxis and accessible public transport.

Mobility Parking (www.mobilityparking.org.nz) Apply for an overseas visitor mobility parking permit ($35 for 12 months) and have it posted to you before you even reach NZ (for a further $10).

Accommodation
B&Bs

Bed and breakfast (B&B) accommodation in NZ pops up in the middle of cities, in rural hamlets and on stretches of isolated coastline, with rooms offered in everything from suburban bungalows to stately manors.

Breakfast may be 'continental' (a standard offering of cereal, toast and tea or coffee); a heartier version with yoghurt, fruit, home-baked bread or muffins; or a stomach-loading cooked breakfast (eggs, bacon, sausages, though, with notice, vegetarians are increasingly well catered for). Some B&B hosts may also cook dinner for guests and advertise dinner, bed and breakfast (DB&B) packages.

Midrange B&B tariffs are typically in the $160 to $250 bracket (per double), though upwards of $350 per double is not unusual. Some hosts charge cheeky prices for what is, in essence, a bedroom in their home, though room-sharing websites like Airbnb have impacted this market in NZ too.

Camping & Holiday Parks

Campers and campervan drivers converge on NZ's hugely popular 'holiday parks', pitching up in powered and unpowered sites, cheap bunk rooms (dorm rooms), cabins (using the shared bathroom facilities) or fully self-contained units (often called motels or tourist flats). Features often include well-equipped communal kitchens, dining areas, games and TV rooms, and playgrounds for kids to run riot in. In cities, holiday parks are usually a fair way from the action, but in smaller towns they can be impressively central or near lakes, beaches, rivers and forests.

The nightly cost of holiday-park tent sites is usually $20 to $30 per adult, with children charged half price; powered campervan sites can be anything from $35 to around the $50 mark. Cabin/unit accommodation normally ranges from $90 to $150 per double.

The 'glamping' scene has not really taken hold in NZ as it has in other places, but expect to see more bell tents popping up over the next year or two as rural property owners look to diversify their incomes.

DOC & FREEDOM CAMPING

A fantastic option for those in campervans is the 200-plus vehicle-accessible 'Conservation Campsites' around the country run by the Department of Conservation (DOC; www.doc.govt. nz), with fees ranging from free (basic toilets and fresh water) to $23 per adult (flush toilets, showers and powered sites). DOC publishes free brochures with detailed descriptions and instructions to find every campsite (even GPS coordinates). Pick up copies from their offices before you hit the road, or visit the website.

DOC also looks after hundreds of 'Backcountry Huts' and 'Backcountry Campsites', which can only be reached by foot. Nearly 60 'Great Walk' huts and campsites are also managed by DOC, and can be found on all Great Walks.

Farmstays

Farmstays open the door to the agricultural side of NZ life, with visitors encouraged to get some dirt beneath their fingernails at orchards, and on dairy, sheep and cattle farms. Costs can vary widely, with bed and breakfast generally costing $90 to $150. Some farms have separate cottages where you can fix your own

food; others offer low-cost, shared, backpacker-style accommodation.

Farm Helpers in NZ (www. farmhelpers.co.nz) hosts an online database of hundreds of farms across the country providing lodging in exchange for four to six hours' work per day. Registration costs $40.

Hostels

New Zealand is packed to the rafters with backpacker hostels, both independent and part of large chains, ranging from small, homestay-style affairs with a handful of beds to refurbished hotels and towering modern structures in the big cities. Hostel bed prices listed by Lonely Planet are nonmember rates, usually $30 to $50 per night.

HOSTEL ORGANISATIONS

Budget Backpacker Hostels (www.bbh.co.nz) A network of more than 50 hostels across the South Island. Membership costs $35 for 12 months and entitles you to stay at member hostels at rates listed in the annual (free) BBH Backpacker Accommodation booklet. Non-members pay an extra $4 per night. Pick up a membership card from any member hostel or order one online ($50).

YHA New Zealand (www.yha. co.nz) Around 20 hostels in prime South Island locations. The YHA is part of the Hostelling

International network (www. hihostels.com), so if you're already an HI member in your own country, membership entitles you to a discount at its NZ hostels. If you don't have a home membership, you can join at major NZ YHA hostels or online for $25, valid for 12 months (it's free for under-18s). Non-members pay an extra $3 or more per night. Membership has other perks, such as discounts with some car-hire providers, travel insurers, DOC hut passes and more.

Base Backpackers (www. stayatbase.com) Chain with hostels in Wānaka, Queenstown, Dunedin and Christchurch. Expect clean dorms, women-only areas and party opportunities aplenty. Offers a flexible 10-night 'Base Jumping' accommodation package for $289, bookable online.

VIP Backpackers (www.vip backpackers.com) International organisation affiliated with around nine South Island hostels (not BBH or YHA), mainly in the tourist hot spots. For around $61 (including postage) you'll receive a 12-month membership entitling you to a $1 discount off nightly accommodation and discounts with affiliated activity and tour providers. Join online or at VIP hostels.

Haka Lodge (www.hakalodge. com) A local chain on the way up, with snazzy hostels in Queenstown and Christchurch. Rates

Climate

Christchurch

Queenstown

Nelson

are comparable to other hostels around NZ, and quality is high. Tours are also available.

Pubs, Hotels & Motels

The least expensive form of NZ hotel accommodation is the humble pub. Some are full of character (and characters); others are grotty, ramshackle places that are best avoided (especially if travelling solo). Check whether there's a band playing the night you're staying, or you could be in for a sleepless night. In the cheapest pubs, singles/doubles might cost as little as $50/80 (with a shared bathroom down the hall); $70/90 is more common.

At the top end of the hotel scale are five-star international chains, resort complexes and architec-

turally splendid boutique hotels, all of which charge a hefty premium for their mod cons, snappy service and/or historic opulence. We quote 'rack rates' (official advertised rates) for such places, but discounts and special deals often apply.

New Zealand's towns have a glut of often nondescript low-rise motels and 'motor lodges', charging $90 to $200 for double rooms. These tend to be squat structures skulking by highways on the edges of towns. The best ones have been thoroughly modernised, but some have been neglected with decor mired in the 1990s (or earlier). Expect basic facilities, namely tea- and coffee-making equipment, fridge and TV. Prices vary with standards.

Customs Regulations

For the low-down on what you can and can't bring into NZ, see the New Zealand Customs Service website (www. customs.govt.nz). Per-person duty-free allowances:

➡ Three 1125mL (max) bottles of spirits or liqueur

➡ 4.5L of wine or beer

➡ 50 cigarettes, or 50g of tobacco or cigars

➡ Dutiable goods up to the value of $700

It's a good idea to declare any unusual medicines. Hiking gear (boots, tents etc) will be checked and may need to be cleaned before being allowed in. You must declare any plant or animal products (including anything made of wood), and food of any kind. Weapons and firearms are either prohibited or require a permit and safety testing. Don't take these rules lightly – noncompliance penalties will really hurt your wallet.

Discount Cards

The internationally recognised **International Student Identity Card** is produced by the ISIC Association (www. isic.org), and issued to full-time students aged 12 and over. It provides over 150,000 discounts across more than 130 countries – on accommodation, transport, entertainment and attractions. The same folks also produce the **International Youth Travel Card**, available to travellers aged under 31 who are not full-time students, with equivalent benefits to the ISIC. Similar is the **International Teacher Identity Card**, available to teaching professionals. All three cards are $30 and can be bought online.

The **New Zealand Card** (www.newzealandcard.com) is a $35 discount pass that'll score you between 5% and 50% off a range of accommodation, tours, sights and activities. Browse participating businesses before you buy. A one-year **Budget Backpacker Hostels** (www.bbh.co.nz) membership card costs $35 and entitles you to discounts at BBH member hostels, usually snipping 10% off the price per night.

Travellers aged over 60 with some form of identification (eg an official seniors card from your home country) are often eligible for concession prices.

Electricity

To plug yourself into the electricity supply (230V AC, 50Hz), use a three-pin adaptor (the same as in Australia; different to British three-pin adaptors).

Type I
230V/50Hz

Health

New Zealand poses minimal health risks to travellers. Diseases such as malaria and typhoid are unheard of, poisonous snakes and other dangerous animals are absent, and there are currently no dangerous insect-borne diseases. The biggest risks to travellers involve exploring the great outdoors: hikers must be clued-up on rapidly changing weather and diligent about sharing any plans to visit remote areas. Drivers must be very careful on NZ's notoriously winding, often-narrow roads.

Before You Go
HEALTH INSURANCE

Health insurance is essential for all travellers, even to safe, wealthy countries such as New Zealand. While healthcare in NZ is of a high quality and not overly expensive by international standards, considerable costs can be built up, and repatriation is pricey.

If you don't have a health insurance plan that covers you for medical expenses incurred overseas, buy a travel insurance policy – see www.lonelyplanet.com/travel-insurance. Find out in advance if your insurance plan will make payments directly to providers or reimburse you later for overseas health expenditures. Check whether your policy covers the activities you're planning to do in NZ (eg rock climbing or winter sports) and whether there's a limit on the number of days of cover for the activity.

RECOMMENDED VACCINATIONS

New Zealand has no vaccination requirements for any traveller, but the World Health Organization recommends that all travellers should be covered for chickenpox, diphtheria, hepatitis B, measles, mumps, pertussis (whooping cough), polio, rubella, seasonal flu, tetanus and tuberculosis, regardless of their destination. Ask your doctor for an international certificate of vaccination (or 'the yellow booklet') in which they will list all the vaccinations you've received.

In New Zealand
AVAILABILITY & COST OF HEALTH CARE

New Zealand's public hospitals offer a high standard of care (free for residents). All travellers are covered for medical care resulting from accidents that occur while in NZ (eg motor-vehicle accidents or adventure-activity accidents) by the Accident Compensation Corporation (www.acc.co.nz). Costs incurred due to treatment of a medical illness that occurs while in NZ will only be covered by travel insurance. For more details, see www.health.govt.nz.

The 24-hour **Healthline** (☑0800 611 116; www.healthline.govt.nz) offers health advice throughout NZ (free from local mobile phones or landlines). Interpreters are available.

INFECTIOUS DISEASES

Aside from the same sexually transmitted infections that are found worldwide (take normal precautions), giardiasis and (following an outbreak in 2019) measles are the main infectious diseases to be aware of when travelling in NZ.

HYPOTHERMIA

Hypothermia, a dangerous drop in body temperature, is a significant risk to travellers in NZ, especially during winter and year-round at altitude. Mountain ranges and/or strong winds produce a high chill factor, which can cause hypothermia even in moderate temperatures. Early signs include the inability to perform fine movements (such as doing up buttons), shivering and a bad case of the 'umbles' (fumbles, mumbles, grumbles, stumbles).

To treat, minimise heat loss: remove wet clothing, add dry clothes with wind- and waterproof layers, and consume carbohydrates and water or warm liquids (not caffeine) to allow shivering to build the internal temperature. In severe hypothermia cases, shivering actually stops – this is a medical emergency requiring rapid evacuation in addition to the above measures.

BITING INSECTS

Wear long, loose clothing and use an insect repellent containing 20% or more DEET to ward off sandflies and mosquitoes, which are particularly common in lake areas and tree-lined clearings. Bites are intensely itchy, but fortunately don't spread disease.

TAP WATER

Tap water throughout New Zealand is generally safe to drink, and public taps with nondrinkable water tend to be labelled as such. However, water quality has faced pollution challenges in some places. Very occasionally, a warning may be issued that tap water must be boiled – your accommodation should inform you if this happens.

PHARMACEUTICALS

Over-the-counter medications are widely available in NZ through private chemists (pharmacies). These include painkillers, antihistamines, skincare products and sunscreen. Some medications, such as antibiotics, are only available via a prescription obtained from a general practitioner. If you take regular medications, bring an adequate supply and details of the generic name, as brand names differ from country to country.

Insurance

➡ A watertight travel-insurance policy covering theft, loss and medical problems is essential when travelling. Some policies specifically exclude designated 'dangerous activities', such as scuba diving, bungy jumping, whitewater rafting, skiing and even hiking. If you plan on doing any of these things (a distinct possibility in NZ!), make sure your policy covers you fully.

➡ It's worth mentioning that, under NZ law, you cannot sue for personal injury (other than exemplary damages). Instead, the country's Accident Compensation Corporation (www.acc.co.nz) administers an accident compensation scheme that provides accident insurance for NZ residents and visitors to the country, regardless of fault. This scheme, however, does not negate the necessity for your own comprehensive travel-insurance policy, as it doesn't cover you for such things as income loss, treatment at home or ongoing illness.

➡ Consider a policy that pays doctors or hospitals directly, rather than you paying on the spot and claiming later. If you have to claim later, keep all documentation. Some policies ask you to call a centre in your home country where an immediate assessment of your problem is made. Check that the policy covers ambulances and emergency medical evacuations by air.

➡ Worldwide travel insurance is available at www.lonelyplanet.com/travel-insurance. You can buy, extend and claim online anytime – even if you're already on the road.

Internet Access

Getting online in NZ is easy in all but remote locales. Expect abundant wi-fi in cafes and accommodation in big towns and cities, but thrifty download limits elsewhere.

Wi-fi You'll be able to find wi-fi access around the country, from hotel rooms and pub beer gardens to hostel dorms. Usually you have to be a guest or customer to log in, and you should be issued with an access code. Sometimes it's free, sometimes there's a charge, and often there's a limit on time or data.

Hotspots The country's main telecommunications company is Spark New Zealand (www.spark.co.nz), which has more than 1000 wireless hotspots around the country, recognisable by the company's pink-and-white phone boxes and wi-fi signs. You can purchase prepaid access cards or a prepaid number from the login page at any wireless hotspot using your credit card, while all Spark mobile and broadband plans come with up to 1GB of free daily data. See the website for hotspot listings.

Equipment and ISPs If you've brought your tablet or laptop, consider buying a prepay USB modem (aka a 'dongle') with a local SIM card: both Spark and Vodafone (www.vodafone.co.nz) sell these from $65.

Legal Matters

If you are questioned or arrested by police, it's your right to ask why, to refrain from making a statement, and to consult a lawyer in private.

A binding referendum on the decriminalisation of marijuana will be held in New Zealand in 2020, but for the time being it remains illegal, with the threshold for presumption of supply standing at 28g, or 100 joints. Anyone caught carrying this or other illicit drugs will have the book thrown at them.

Drink-driving is a serious offence and remains a significant problem in NZ. The legal blood alcohol limit is 0.05% for drivers aged 20 years and over, and zero for those under 20.

LGBT+ Travellers

The gay tourism industry in NZ isn't as high profile as it is in some other developed nations, but LGBTQI+ communities are happily established in Christchurch and Dunedin, and myriad support organisations work across both islands. New Zealand has progressive laws protecting human rights: same-sex marriage and adoption by same-sex couples were legalised in 2013 (ahead of anywhere else in the region), while the legal minimum age for sex between consenting people is 16. Generally speaking, Kiwis are fairly relaxed and accepting about same-sex relations and gender fluidity, but that's not to say that homophobia and/or transphobia don't exist. Rural communities tend to be more conservative, and public displays of affection may attract unwelcome attention.

Resources

There are loads of websites dedicated to gay and lesbian travel in NZ. Gay Tourism New Zealand (www.gaytourismnewzealand.com) is a starting point, with links to various sites. Other worthwhile websites include the following:

➡ www.gaynz.net.nz

➡ www.lesbian.net.nz

➡ www.gaystay.co.nz

Check out the nationwide monthly magazine *express* (www.gayexpress.co.nz) for the latest happenings, reviews and listings on the NZ gay scene. RainbowYOUTH (www.ry.org.nz) supports queer and gender-diverse people between 13 and 28, and New Zealand Awaits (www.newzealandawaits.com) is a local operator specialising in tours serving LGBTQI+ travellers.

Maps

New Zealand's **Automobile Association** (AA; ☑0800 500 222; www.aa.co.nz/travel) sells maps. Scan the larger bookshops, or try the nearest Department of Conservation (DOC) office or visitor information centre for topo maps.

Map geeks will also love www.topomap.co.nz.

Online, log onto AA Maps (www.aamaps.co.nz) to pinpoint exact NZ addresses.

Money

Bank cards are used for most purchases, and are accepted in most hotels and restaurants. ATMs are widely available in cities and larger towns.

ATMs & eftpos

Branches of the country's major banks provide ATMs (cashpoints) across the island, but you may not find them in the very smallest towns. It's generally better to decline the on-the-spot conversion rate ATMs will offer, although this depends on your home bank's rates and market movements.

Many NZ businesses use Eftpos (electronic funds transfer at point of sale), allowing you to use your bank card (credit or debit) to make direct purchases and often withdraw cash as well. With over 52,500 devices connected to its New Zealand network, the system is close to universal.

Bank Accounts

You'll need to open a bank account if you want to work in NZ in any capacity (including working holidays) and it's best to arrange this in advance. Some banks, such as ANZ, allow you to

apply before you arrive and activate the account at a branch when you get here (armed with the requisite ID, usually a passport, certified translation if applicable, and proof of NZ residence). Proof of address might involve using an identity verification service. All interest earned on accounts is taxed at 33% (the highest rate) for those without an Inland Revenue (IRD) number.

Credit Cards

Credit cards are widely accepted for everything from a hostel bed to a bungy jump, and are pretty much essential for car hire. Credit cards can also be used for over-the-counter cash advances at banks and from ATMs, but be aware that such transactions incur charges. Diners Club and American Express cards are not as widely accepted as Visa and MasterCard.

Debit Cards

Debit cards enable you to draw money directly from your home bank account using ATMs, banks or Eftpos facilities. Any card connected to the international banking network (Cirrus, Maestro, Visa Plus and Eurocard) should work with your PIN. Fees will vary depending on your home bank; check before you leave. Alternatively, companies such as Travelex offer prepaid currency cards with set withdrawal fees and a balance you can top up from your personal bank account while on the road.

Money Changers

Changing foreign currency (and to a lesser extent travellers cheques) is usually no problem at NZ banks or at licensed money changers (eg Travelex) in major tourist areas, cities and airports. However, withdrawing directly from ATMs usually secures the most favourable rates.

Tipping

Tipping is completely optional in NZ.

Guides Your kayaking guide or tour-group leader would happily accept tips; and $10 is kind.

Restaurants The total on your bill is all you need to pay. If you like, reward good service with 5% to 10%.

Taxis If you round up your fare, don't be surprised if the driver hands back your change.

Opening Hours

Opening hours vary seasonally depending on where you are. Most places close on Christmas Day and Good Friday.

Banks 9am to 4.30pm Monday to Friday, some also 9am to noon Saturday

Cafes 7am or 8am to 3pm or 4pm

Post offices 8.30am to 5pm Monday to Friday; larger

branches also 9.30am to 1pm Saturday

Pubs and bars noon to late ('late' varies by region, and by day)

Restaurants noon to 2.30pm and 6pm to 9pm

Shops and businesses 9am to 5.30pm Monday to Friday and 9am to noon or 5pm Saturday

Supermarkets 7am to 9pm

Public Holidays

New Zealand's main public holidays are as follows:

New Year 1 and 2 January

Waitangi Day 6 February

Easter Good Friday and Easter Monday; March/April

Anzac Day 25 April

Queen's Birthday First Monday in June

Labour Day Fourth Monday in October

Christmas Day 25 December

Boxing Day 26 December

For an up-to-date list of provincial anniversaries, see www.govt.nz/browse/work/public-holidays-and-work/public-holidays-and-anniversary-dates.

Safe Travel

New Zealand is no more dangerous than other developed countries, but take normal safety precautions, especially after dark on city streets and in remote areas.

➡ Kiwi roads are often made hazardous by map-

distracted tourists, wide-cornering campervans and traffic-ignorant sheep.

➡ Avoid leaving valuables in vehicles: theft is a problem, even in remote areas.

➡ New Zealand's climate is unpredictable: hypothermia is a risk in high-altitude areas.

➡ At the beach, beware of rips and undertows, which can drag swimmers out to sea.

Telephone

New Zealand uses regional two-digit area codes for long-distance calls, which can be made from any landline or mobile. If you're making a local call (ie to someone else in the same town), you don't need to dial the area code. But if you're dialling within a region (even if it's to a nearby town with the same area code), you do.

To make international calls from NZ, the international access code is ⌨00. So for a London number, for example, you'd dial ⌨00-44-20, then the number. If dialling NZ from overseas, the country code is 64, followed by the appropriate area code minus the initial '0'.

Mobile Phones

It's simple to buy a local SIM card and prepaid account at outlets in airports and large towns (provided your mobile is unlocked).

Mobile coverage is good in built-up areas, but can be patchy in places on the South Island.

Local carriers can set you up with a NZ Travel SIM and phone number from around $20.

Payphones

Local calls from payphones cost $1 for the first 15 minutes, and 20c per minute thereafter, though coin-operated machines are scarce (and if you do find one, chances are the coin

---

SURF BEACHES

New Zealand has exceptional surf beaches across its 15,000km coastline. The power of the surf can fluctuate as a result of the varying slope of the seabed: rips and undertows are common, and drownings do happen. Check with local surf lifesaving organisations before jumping in the sea, always heed warning signs at beaches, and be realistic about your own limitations and expertise.

slot will be gummed up). You're better off relying on a phonecard. Calls to mobile phones or numbers outside the locality attract higher rates.

Phonecards

New Zealand has a wide range of phonecards available, which can be bought at hostels, newsagents and post offices for a fixed-dollar value (usually $5, $10, $20 and $50). These can be used with any public or private phone by dialling a toll-free access number and then the PIN number on the card. Shop around – rates vary from company to company.

Premium-Rate & Toll-Free Calls

➡ Numbers starting with 0900 sometimes charge nearly $2 per minute (more from mobiles). These numbers cannot be dialled from payphones, and sometimes not from prepaid mobile phones.

➡ Toll-free numbers in NZ have the prefix 0800 or 0508, and can be called from anywhere in the country, though they may not be accessible from certain areas or from mobile phones.

➡ Numbers beginning with 0508, 0800 or 0900 cannot be dialled from outside NZ.

Time

➡ New Zealand is 12 hours ahead of GMT/UTC and two hours ahead of Australian Eastern Standard Time (AEST).

➡ The Chathams are 45 minutes ahead of NZ's main islands.

➡ In summer, NZ observes daylight saving time: clocks are wound forward by one hour on the last Sunday in September; clocks are wound back on the first Sunday of April.

Tourist Information

Almost every Kiwi city or town seems to have a visitor information centre. The bigger centres stand united within the outstanding i-SITE network (www.newzealand.com/travel/i-sites) – more than 80 info centres affiliated with Tourism New Zealand. The i-SITE centres have trained staff, information on local activities, itineraries and attractions, and free brochures and maps. Staff can also book activities, transport and accommodation.

Bear in mind that some information centres only promote accommodation and tour operators who are paying members of the local tourist association, and that staff shouldn't recommend any providers over others.

There's also a network of 19 Department of Conservation (DOC; www.doc.govt.nz) visitor centres to help you plan outdoor activities and make bookings (particularly for hiking tracks and huts). The visitor centres – in national parks, regional centres and major cities – usually also have displays on local flora and fauna.

Visas

Visa application forms are available from NZ diplomatic missions overseas, travel agents and **Immigration New Zealand** (☑0508 558 855, 09-914 4100; www.immigration.govt.nz). Immigration New Zealand has more than 25 offices overseas, including the US, UK and Australia – consult the website for exact requirements and the list of nationals entitled to a visa waiver. Such entrants to NZ must still obtain a NZeTA (New Zealand Electronic Travel Authority), unless they're NZ nationals or Australians travelling on Australian passports. NZeTAs take from 10 minutes to three

days to come through, and cost $9 through the Immigration Department's app, or $12 through its website.

Visitor Visa

Citizens of Australia don't need a visa to visit NZ and can stay indefinitely (provided they have no criminal convictions). UK citizens don't need a visa either and can stay for up to six months.

Citizens of another 58 countries that have visa-waiver agreements with NZ don't need a visa for stays of up to three months, for no more than six months within any 12-month period, provided they have an onward ticket and sufficient funds to support their stay: see the website for details. Nations in this group include Canada, France, Germany, Ireland, Japan, the Netherlands, South Africa and the USA.

Citizens of other countries must obtain a visa before entering NZ. Visitor visas allow stays of up to nine months within an 18-month period, and cost $170 to $220, depending on where in the world the application is processed.

A visitor's visa can be extended from nine to 12 months, but if you get this extension you'll have to leave NZ after your 12-month stay has expired and wait another 12 months before you can come back. Applications are assessed on a case-by-case basis; you may need to provide proof of adequate funds to sustain you during your visit ($1000 per month) plus an onward ticket establishing your intent to leave. Apply for extensions at any Immigration New Zealand office – see the website (www.immigration.govt.nz) for locations.

Work Visa

It's illegal for foreign nationals to work in NZ on a visitor visa, except for Australian citizens or permanent residents, who can legally gain work without a visa or permit. If you're visiting NZ to find work, or you already have an employment offer, you'll need to apply for a work visa, which can be valid for up to three years, depending on the type in question and your particular circumstances. You can apply for a work permit after you're in NZ, but its validity will be backdated to when you entered the country. The fee for a work visa can be anything upwards of $495, depending on where and how it's processed (paper or online) and the type of application.

Working Holiday Scheme

Eligible travellers looking for short-term and seasonal employment to supplement their travels can take part in one of NZ's working-holiday schemes (WHS). Under these, citizens aged 18 to 30 (occasionally 35) from 45 countries – including France, Germany, Ireland, Japan, Malaysia, the Netherlands, Scandinavian countries and the USA – can apply for a working-holiday visa. For most nationalities the visa is valid for 12 months, but citizens of Canada and the UK can extend theirs for up to 23 months. It's only issued to those seeking a genuine working holiday, not permanent work, so you're not supposed to work for one employer for more than three months.

Eligible nationals must apply for a WHS visa from within their own country. Applicants must have an onward ticket, a passport valid for at least three months from the date they will leave NZ and evidence of at least $350 in accessible funds for each month of their stay. The application fee is $280 and isn't refunded if your application is declined.

The rules vary for different nationalities, so make sure you read up on the specifics of your country's agreement with NZ at www.immigration. govt.nz.

Volunteering

New Zealand presents an array of active, outdoorsy volunteer opportunities for travellers to get some dirt under their fingernails and participate in conservation and other programs. These can include anything from tree planting and weed removal to track construction, habitat conservation and fencing. Ask about local opportunities at any regional i-SITE visitor information centre, join one of the programs run by DOC (www.doc.govt.nz/get-involved), or check out these online resources:

➡ www.conservation volunteers.org.nz

➡ www.helpx.net

➡ www.nature.org

➡ www.volunteeringnz.rg.nz

➡ www.wwf.org.nz

Women Travellers

New Zealand is generally a very safe place for female travellers, and the South Island is no exception. The usual sensible precautions apply (for both sexes): avoid walking alone at night; never hitch-hike alone; and if you're out on the town, have a plan for how to get back to your accommodation safely. Sexual harassment isn't frequently reported, but does of course still occur. See www.womentravel.co.nz for tours aimed at solo women.

Work

If you have been approved for a working holiday scheme (WHS) visa, there are a number of possibilities for temporary employment in NZ. Pay rates start at the minimum wage ($17.70 per hour, at the time of writing), but depend on the work. There's plenty of casual work around, mainly in agriculture (fruit picking, farming, wineries), hospitality

(bar work, waiting tables) or at ski resorts. Office-based work can be found in IT, banking, finance and telemarketing. Register with a local office-work agency to get started.

Seasonal fruit picking, pruning and harvesting is prime short-term work for visitors. Fruit picking is physically-taxing toil, working in the dirt under the hot sun – turnover of workers is high. You're usually paid by how much you pick: if you stick with it for a while, you'll get faster and fitter and can actually make some reasonable cash. Prime South Island picking locations include Nelson (Golden Bay), Marlborough (around Blenheim) and Central Otago (Cromwell, Alexandra and Roxburgh).

Winter work at ski resorts and their service towns includes bartending, waiting, cleaning, ski-tow operation and, if you're properly qualified, ski or snowboard instructing.

Resources

Backpacker publications, hostel managers and other travellers are often good sources of info on local work possibilities. Base Backpackers (www.stayatbase.com/work) runs an employment service via its website, while the Notice Boards page on the Budget Backpacker Hostels website (www.bbh.co.nz) lists job vacancies in BBH hostels and a few other possibilities.

Kiwi Careers (www.careers.govt.nz) lists professional opportunities in various fields (agriculture, creative, health, teaching, volunteer work and recruitment), while Seek (www.seek.co.nz) is one of the biggest NZ job-search networks, with thousands of jobs listed.

Try the following websites for seasonal work:

➡ www.backpackerboard. co.nz

➡ www.seasonalwork.co.nz

➡ www.seasonaljobs.co.nz

➡ www.picknz.co.nz

➡ www.pickingjobs.com

➡ www.picktheworld.org

Income Tax

For most visitors, Kiwi dollars earned in NZ will be subject to income tax, which is deducted from payments by employers – a process called PAYE (Pay As You Earn).

Income tax rates are 10.5% for annual salaries up to $14,000, then 17.5% up to $48,000, 30% up to $70,000, and 33% for higher incomes. The national

Accident Compensation Corporation (ACC) scheme levy (around 1.2%, but fluctuating each year) will also be deducted from your pay packet.

If you visit NZ and work for a short time (eg on a working-holiday scheme), you may qualify for a tax refund when you leave. Lodging a tax return before you leave NZ is the best way of securing a refund. For more info, see the Inland Revenue Department website (www.ird.govt.nz), or call ☎0800 775 247.

IRD Number

Travellers undertaking paid work in NZ (including working holidays) must first open a New Zealand bank account, then obtain an Inland Revenue Department (IRD) number. Download the *IRD number application – non-resident/offshore individual IR742* form from the IRD website (www.ird.govt. nz). IRD numbers normally take eight to 10 working days to be issued.

Transport

GETTING THERE & AWAY

Christchurch Airport is the primary international gateway to the South Island, with flights to/from Australia, Singapore, Fiji, China (Guangzhou and Hong Kong) and Los Angeles (commencing October 2020). Plenty of domestic airports are also connected. Queenstown Airport is becoming increasingly popular as Australian and local carriers bring visitors directly into the South Island's premier resort town. The only other airport servicing international arrivals is Dunedin, with five weekly flights to and from Brisbane.

Christchurch is also the South Island's biggest domestic air travel hub, particularly for Air New Zealand flights connecting with Nelson, Hokitika, Queenstown, Dunedin, Invercargill and a range of North Island centres. A host of little regional airlines reach smaller destinations such as Westport and Stewart Island/Rakiura, while Sounds Air connects Wellington and

DEPARTURE TAX

Border clearance levies are paid on arrival ($15.79) and departure ($2.94) and are included in your ticket price.

Blenheim with several centres at the top of the Island, plus Christchurch and a few North Island centres. Jetstar services Christchurch, Dunedin, Queenstown and Nelson, mainly flying to North Island and Australian cities.

Crossing Cook Strait between the North and South Islands is possible with Bluebridge and Interislander ferry services, both offering several sailings daily between Wellington and Picton. The ferries carry cars and campervans, although it is generally cheaper to pick up a new hire vehicle on each island.

Flights, cars and tours can be booked online at lonely planet.com/bookings.

Entering the Country

Entering NZ is a fairly straightforward affair and customs officials are relatively friendly, provided you have all your paperwork in order and follow the rules around what you need to declare to maintain NZ's biosecurity. Most airlines will not let you check in to your flight to NZ without your 90-day NZeTA (New Zealand Electronic Travel Authority) pre-approved.

Passport

There are no restrictions when it comes to foreign citizens entering NZ. If you

have a current passport and visa (or don't require one), you should be fine.

Air

New Zealand's abundance of seasonal activities and attractions means that airports here are busy most of the year. If you want to fly at a particularly popular time (eg over the Christmas period), book well in advance.

The high season for flights into NZ is during summer (December to February), with slightly less of a premium on fares over the shoulder months (October/November and March/April). The low season generally tallies with the winter months (June to August), though this is still a busy time for airlines servicing the ski fields.

Airports & Airlines

While **Auckland Airport** (AKL; ☏09-275 0789; www.aucklandairport.co.nz; Ray Emery Dr, Māngere) is the main international gateway to NZ, the South Island has limited, direct international services to the following airports, which otherwise mostly handle domestic traffic:

Christchurch Airport (CHC; ☏03-358 5029; www.christchurchairport.co.nz; 30 Durey Rd)

Dunedin Airport (DUD; ☏03-486 2879; www.dunedin airport.co.nz; 25 Miller Rd, Momona; ☏)

CLIMATE CHANGE & TRAVEL

Every form of transport that relies on carbon-based fuel generates CO_2, the main cause of human-induced climate change. Modern travel is dependent on aeroplanes, which might use less fuel per kilometre per person than most cars but travel much greater distances. The altitude at which aircraft emit gases (including CO_2) and particles also contributes to their climate change impact. Many websites offer 'carbon calculators' that allow people to estimate the carbon emissions generated by their journey and, for those who wish to do so, to offset the impact of the greenhouse gases emitted with contributions to portfolios of climate-friendly initiatives throughout the world. Lonely Planet offsets the carbon footprint of all staff and author travel.

Queenstown Airport (ZQN; Map p211; ☑03-450 9031; www. queenstownairport.co.nz; Sir Henry Wrigley Dr, Frankton)

New Zealand's international carrier is **Air New Zealand** (☑0800 737 000; www. airnewzealand.co.nz). Air New Zealand, **Jetstar** (☑0800 800 995; www.jetstar.com) and **Virgin Australia** (☑0800 670 000; www.virginaustralia. com) fly into all three airports, while Qantas flies into only Christchurch and Queenstown. Christchurch also welcomes year-round flights on Cathay Pacific, China Southern Airlines, Emirates, Fiji Airways and Singapore Airlines.

Sea

Ferry Regular ferry services between Wellington and Picton link the North and South Islands.

Cruise ship If you're travelling from Australia and content with a slow pace, big names like P&O (www.pocruises.com.au) and Princess (www.princess.com) cruise to New Zealand.

Yacht It is possible (though by no means straightforward) to make your way between NZ, Australia and the Pacific islands by crewing on a yacht.

GETTING AROUND

New Zealand is long and skinny, and many roads are two-lane country byways: getting from A to B requires some planning.

Car Travel at your own tempo, explore remote areas and visit regions with no public transport. Hire cars in major towns. Drive on the left; the steering wheel is on the right (...in case you can't find it).

Bus Reliable, frequent services to most destinations around the country (usually cheaper than flying), though services thin out in rural areas. To get further than main cities, you'll need to rely on tours.

Plane Fast-track your visit with affordable, frequent, fast internal flights.

Train Reliable, regular services (if not fast or cheap) along specific routes on both islands.

Air

Those who have limited time to get between NZ's attractions can make the most of a widespread (and very reliable and safe) network of intra- and inter-island flights.

Domestic Airlines

The country's major domestic carrier, Air New Zealand, has a network covering most of the country, often operating under the Air New Zealand Link moniker on less popular routes. Australia-based Jetstar also flies between main urban areas. Between them, these two carry the vast majority of domestic passengers in NZ. Beyond this, several small-scale regional operators provide essential transport services to outlying islands and smaller centres. There

are also plenty of scenic- and charter-flight operators around NZ, not listed here. Operators running scheduled flights include the following:

Air New Zealand (☑0800 737 000; www.airnewzealand.co.nz) Offers flights between eight South Island destinations, plus myriad overseas hubs.

Golden Bay Air (☑0800 588 885; www.goldenbayair.co.nz) Flies regularly to Takaka in Golden Bay from Nelson. Also connects to Karamea for Heaphy Track hikers.

Jetstar (☑0800 800 995; www. jetstar.com) Joins the dots between key centres: Christchurch, Dunedin, Queenstown and Nelson.

Soundsair (☑0800 505 005; www.soundsair.co.nz) Numerous flights daily between Wellington and Blenheim, Nelson, Picton, Westport and Taupo, plus flights from Blenheim to Paraparaumu, Napier and Christchurch, and Nelson to Paraparaumu.

Stewart Island Flights (☑03-218 9129; www.stewartisland flights.co.nz) Flies between Invercargill and Stewart Island/ Rakiura three times daily.

Bicycle

Touring cyclists proliferate in NZ, particularly over summer. The country is clean, green and relatively uncrowded, and has lots of cheap accommodation (including camping) and abundant fresh water. The roads are generally in good nick, and the climate is typically mild. Road traffic is the biggest danger: trucks overtaking too close to cyclists are a particular threat. Bikes and cycling gear are readily available to hire or buy in the main centres, and bicycle-repair shops are common.

By law all cyclists must wear an approved safety helmet (or risk a $55 fine); it's also vital to have good reflective safety clothing. Cyclists who use public transport will find two- and three-tier exterior racks on all Christchurch buses (and many elsewhere) where bikes can be secured for free. Some of the smaller shuttle-bus companies also have storage space for bikes, but may impose a surcharge.

If importing your own bike or transporting it by plane within NZ, check with the relevant airline for costs and the degree of dismantling and packing required.

See www.nzta.govt.nz/walking-cycling-and-public-transport for more bike safety and legal tips, and check out the New Zealand Cycle Trail (p54) – a network of 22 'Great Rides' across NZ.

Hire

Rates offered by most outfits for hiring road or mountain bikes are usually around $25 for a short hire to $60 per day. Longer-term hire is usually available, at reduced rates. Hire basic bikes from your accommodation (hostels, holiday parks etc), or better machines from bike shops in the larger towns.

Buying a Bike

Bicycles can be readily bought in NZ's larger cities, but prices for newer models are high. For a decent hybrid bike or rigid mountain bike you'll pay anywhere from $800 to $1800, though you can get a cheap one for around $500 (factor in panniers, helmet, lock etc,

and the cost quickly climbs). Other options include the post-Christmas sales and mid-year stocktakes, when newish cycles can be heavily discounted.

Boat

New Zealand may be an island nation but there's virtually no long-distance water transport around the country. Obvious exceptions include the passenger ferry across Foveaux Strait between Bluff and Oban on Stewart Island/Rakiura and the Interislander service across Cook Strait, between Wellington and Picton.

If you're cashed-up, consider the cruise liners that chug around the NZ coastline as part of broader South Pacific itineraries.

Bus

Bus travel in NZ is easy-going and well organised, with services transporting you to the far reaches of both islands (including the start/end of various walking tracks)...but it can be expensive, tedious and time-consuming.

New Zealand's main bus company is **InterCity** (www.intercity.co.nz), which can drive you to just about anywhere on the North and South Islands and offers fares as low as $1 (!). InterCity also has a sightseeing arm called **GreatSights New Zealand** (www.greatsights.co.nz) handling scenic routes such as Queenstown to Mt Cook and Milford Sound.

The low-fare bus company **Skip** (www.skip.travel) only operates on the North Island at present.

Privately run shuttle buses can transport travellers to some trailheads or collect them from the end point of a hike; advance booking essential.

Seat Classes & Smoking

There are no allocated economy or luxury seat classes on NZ buses (very democratic), and smoking on the bus is a definite no-no.

Reservations

Over summer (December to February), school holidays and public holidays, book a week or two ahead for seats on popular routes. At other times, a day or two ahead is usually fine. The best prices are generally available online, and in advance.

Bus Passes

If you're covering a lot of ground, InterCity offers a range of passes, priced according to your proposed itinerary and length of journey. If the itineraries and fare schemes offered suit you, this can be cheaper than paying as you go, but do the maths before buying and note that you'll be locked into using one network. Passes are usually valid for 12 months.

InterCity offers a discount of around 10% on standard fares for students and YHA, ISIC, HI, Nomads, BBH or VIP backpacker card holders, on selected services. Senior discounts only apply to NZ citizens.

FlexiPass A hop-on/hop-off InterCity pass, allowing travel to pretty much anywhere in NZ, in any direction, including the Interislander ferry across Cook Strait. The pass is purchased in blocks of travel time: the minimum is 15 hours ($132) and the maximum 60 ($459). The average cost of each block becomes cheaper the more hours you buy. You can top up the pass if you need more time.

TravelPass Hop-on/hop-off, fixed-itinerary nationwide passes offered by InterCity. With names like Aotearoa Explorer and Island Loop, these passes link tourist hotspots across either or both islands, and range from simple regional itineraries costing as little as $125 to grand, country-wide circuits worth $1045. See www.intercity.co.nz/bus-pass/travelpass for details.

Shuttle Buses

Beyond InterCity's network, regional shuttle buses fill in the gaps between smaller towns. Operators include the following (see www.tourism.net.nz/transport/bus-and-coach-services for a complete list), offering regular scheduled services and/or bus tours and charters:

Abel Tasman Travel (www.abeltasmantravel.co.nz) Traverses the roads between Nelson and Marahau, on the fringe of Abel Tasman National Park.

Atomic Shuttles (www.atomictravel.co.nz) Has services from Christchurch to Dunedin and Greymouth, stopping at points of interest along the way.

Catch-a-Bus South (www.catchabussouth.co.nz) Invercargill and Bluff to Dunedin and Queenstown.

Cook Connection (www.cookconnect.co.nz) Triangulates between Mt Cook, Twizel and Lake Tekapo.

East West Coaches (www.eastwestcoaches.co.nz) Offers a service between Christchurch and Westport via Lewis Pass, and Greymouth via Arthur's Pass.

Hanmer Connection (www.hanmerconnection.co.nz) Daily services between Hanmer Springs and Christchurch.

Tracknet (www.tracknet.net) Track transport (Milford, Hollyford, Routeburn, Kepler) with Queenstown, Te Anau and Invercargill connections. Services are sparser in winter.

Trek Express (www.trekexpress.co.nz) Shuttle services to all hiking tracks in the top half of the South Island (eg Heaphy, Abel Tasman, the Ghost Trail).

Bus Tours

Clock up some kilometres with like-minded fellow travellers. The following operators run fixed-itinerary bus tours, nationwide or on the North or South Islands.

Accommodation, meals and hop-on/hop-off flexibility are often included. Styles vary from activity-focused itineraries through to hang-over-mandatory backpacker buses.

Bottom Bus (www.travelheadfirst.com/local-legends/bottom-bus) Three-day tours of the South Island's nether regions: Dunedin, Invercargill, Queenstown, Milford Sound and the Catlins.

Flying Kiwi (www.flyingkiwi.com) Good fun, activity-based trips around NZ with camping and cabin accommodation from a few days to a few weeks.

Haka Tours (www.hakatours.com) Three- to 24-day tours with adventure, snow or mountain-biking themes.

Kirra Tours (www.kirratours.co.nz) Eight- to 20-day upmarket coach tours (graded 'Classic' or 'Platinum' by price) from an operator with 50 years in the business.

Kiwi Experience (www.kiwiexperience.com) A major hop-on/hop-off player with ecofriendly credentials. Myriad tours cover the length and breadth of the South Island.

Stray Travel (www.straytravel.com) A wide range of flexible hop-on/hop-off passes and tours.

Car & Motorcycle

The best way to explore NZ in depth is to have your own wheels. It's easy to hire cars and campervans, though it's worth noting that fuel costs can be eye-watering. Alternatively, if you're in NZ for a few months, you might consider buying your own vehicle.

Automobile Association

New Zealand's **Automobile Association** (AA; ☎0800 500 222; www.aa.co.nz/travel) provides emergency breakdown services, distance calculators and accommodation guides (from holiday parks to motels and B&Bs).

Members of overseas automobile associations should bring their membership cards – many of these bodies have reciprocal agreements with the AA.

Driving Licences

International visitors to NZ can use their home-country driving licence – if your licence isn't in English, it's a good idea to carry a certified translation with you. Alternatively, use an International Driving Permit (IDP), which will usually be issued on the spot (valid for 12 months) by your home country's automobile association.

Fuel

Fuel (petrol, aka gasoline) is available from service stations across NZ: unless you're cruising around in something from the 1970s, you'll be filling up with 'unleaded', or LPG (gas). LPG is not always stocked by rural suppliers – if you're on gas, it's safer to have dual-fuel capability. Aside from remote locations like Milford Sound and Mt Cook, petrol prices don't vary much from place to place: per-litre costs at the time of research were hovering around $2.40.

Hire
CAMPERVAN

Check your rear-view mirror on any far-flung NZ road and you'll probably see a shiny white campervan (aka mobile home, motorhome, RV), packed with liberated travellers, mountain bikes and portable barbecues, cruising along beside you.

Most towns of any size have a campsite or holiday park with powered pitches (where you can plug your vehicle in) for around $50 per night. There are 90-plus vehicle-accessible Department of Conservation (DOC; www.doc.govt.nz) campsites around the South Island, priced at up to $23 per adult. Weekly Campsite Passes for hired campervans slice up to 50% off the price of stays in some of these campsites; check the DOC website for info, and make sure your intended site(s) offer the discount.

You can hire campervans from dozens of companies. Prices vary with season, vehicle size and length of hire, and it pays to book months in advance.

A small van for two people typically has a mini kitchen and foldout dining table; the latter transforming into a double bed when dinner is done and dusted. Larger, 'superior' two-berth vans include shower and toilet. Four- to six-berth campervans are the size of trucks (and similarly sluggish) and, besides the extra space, usually contain a toilet and shower.

Over summer, rates offered by the main firms for two-/four-/six-berth vans booked three months in advance start at around $120/150/230 per day (though they rise much higher, depending on model) for hire for two weeks or more. Rates drop to $60/75/100 per day during winter.

Major operators include the following:

Apollo (☑0800 113 131, 09-889 2976; www.apollocamper.co.nz)

Britz (☑09-255 3910, 0800 081 032; www.britz.co.nz) Also does electric campervans.

Maui (☑09-255 3910, 0800 688 558; www.maui-rentals.com)

Wilderness Motorhomes (☑09-282 3606; www.wilderness.co.nz)

CAR

Competition between car-hire companies in NZ is fierce, particularly in the big cities and Picton. Remember that if you want to travel far, you need to specify unlimited kilometres. Some (but not all) companies require drivers to be at least 21 years old – ask around.

International car-hire firms don't generally allow you to take their vehicles between islands on the Cook Strait ferries. Instead, you leave your car at either Wellington or Picton terminal and pick up another car once you've crossed the strait. This saves you paying to transport a vehicle on the ferries, and is a pain-free exercise. However, some local car-hire firms (such as Apex) are fine with you taking your rental vehicle on the ferry and will even book your ferry ticket for you.

INTERNATIONAL HIRE COMPANIES

The big multinational companies have offices in most major cities, towns and airports. Firms sometimes offer one-way hire (eg collect a car in Christchurch, leave it in Queenstown), but there are usually restrictions and fees.

The major companies offer a choice of either unlimited kilometres, or 100km (or so) per day free, plus so many cents per subsequent kilometre. Daily rates in main cities typically start at around $50 per day for a compact, late-model Japanese car, and from $80 for medium-sized cars (including GST, unlimited kilometres and insurance).

Avis (☑09-526 2847, 0800 655 111; www.avis.co.nz)

Budget (☑09-529 7788, 0800 283 438; www.budget.co.nz)

Europcar (☑0800 800 115; www.europcar.co.nz)

Hertz (☑0800 654 321; www.hertz.co.nz)

Thrifty (☑0800 737 070, 03-359 2721; www.thrifty.co.nz)

LOCAL HIRE COMPANIES

Local hire firms proliferate. These are almost always cheaper than the big boys – sometimes half the price – but the cheap rates obviously have strings attached: vehicles are often older,

depots might be further away from airports/city centres, and with less formality sometimes comes a less-protective legal structure for renters.

Rentals from local firms start at around $30 or $40 per day for the smallest option. It's cheaper if you hire for a week or more, and there are often low-season and weekend discounts.

Affordable, independent operators with national networks include the following:

Ace Rental Cars (☑0800 502 277, 09-303 3112; www.acerentalcars.co.nz)

Apex Rentals (☑03-595 2315, 0800 500 660; www.apexrentals.co.nz)

Ezi Car Rental (☑0800 545 000, 09-254 4397; www.ezicarrental.co.nz)

Go Rentals (☑0800 467 368, 09-974 1598; www.gorentals.co.nz)

Omega Rental Cars (☑09-377 5573, 0800 525 210; www.omegarentalcars.com)

Pegasus Rental Cars (☑0800 803 580; www.rentalcars.co.nz)

Transfercar (☑09-630 7533; www.transfercar.co.nz) Relocation specialists with massive money-saving deals on one-way car hire.

MOTORCYCLE

Born to be wild? NZ has great terrain for motorcycle touring, despite the fickle weather in some regions. Most of the South Island's motorcycle-hire shops are in Christchurch, where you can hire anything from a little 50cc moped (aka nifty-fifty) to a throbbing 750cc touring motorcycle and beyond. Recommended operators (who also run guided tours) offer opening rates of around $100 per day, rising steeply with the quality of the machines:

New Zealand Motorcycle Rentals & Tours (☑09-486 2472; www.nzbike.com)

Te Waipounamu Motorcycle Tours (☑03-372 3537; www.motorcycle-hire.co.nz)

Insurance

Rather than risk paying out wads of cash if you have an accident, you can take out your own comprehensive insurance policy, or (the usual option) pay an additional fee per day to the hire company to reduce your excess. This brings the amount you must pay in the event of an accident down from around $1500 or $2000 to around $200 or $300. Smaller operators offering cheap rates often have a compulsory insurance excess, taken as a credit-card bond, of around $900.

Many insurance agreements won't cover the cost of damage to glass (including the windscreen) or tyres, and insurance coverage is often invalidated on beaches and certain rough (4WD) unsealed roads – read the fine print.

See www.acc.co.nz for info on NZ's Accident Compensation Corporation (ACC) insurance scheme (fault-free personal injury insurance).

Purchase

Planning a long trip? Buying a car then selling it at the end of your travels can be one of the cheapest and best ways to see the South Island. Christchurch is the easiest place to buy a car: scour the hostel noticeboards or see what comes up at Turners Auctions (www.turners.co.nz), NZ's biggest car-auction operator.

LEGALITIES

Make sure your prospective vehicle has a Warrant of Fitness (WoF) and registration valid for a reasonable period: see the New Zealand Transport Agency website (www.nzta.govt.nz) for details.

Buyers should also take out third-party insurance, covering the cost of repairs to another vehicle in an accident that is your fault: try the **Automobile Association** (AA; ☑0800 500 222; www.aa.co.nz/travel). New Zealand's no-fault Accident Compensation Corporation (www.acc.co.nz) scheme covers personal injury, but make sure you have travel insurance, too.

If you're considering buying a car and want someone to check it out for you, various companies inspect cars for around $150; find them at car auctions, or they will come to you. Try **Vehicle Inspection New Zealand** (%09-573 3230, 0800 468 469; www.vinz.co.nz) or the AA.

Before you buy it's wise to confirm ownership of the vehicle, and find out if there's anything dodgy about it (eg stolen, or outstanding debts). The AA's **LemonCheck** (%09-420 3090; www.lemoncheck.co.nz) offers this service.

BUY-BACK DEALS

You can avoid the hassle of buying/selling a vehicle privately by entering into a buy-back arrangement with a dealer. Predictably, dealers often find sneaky ways of knocking down the return-sale price, which may be 50% less than what you paid, so hiring or buying and selling a vehicle yourself (if you have the time) is usually a better bet.

Road Hazards

A higher percentage of international drivers are involved in road accidents in NZ – suggesting something about the challenges its roads pose. Kiwi traffic is usually pretty light, but it's easy to get stuck behind a slow-moving truck or campervan – pack plenty of patience, and know your road rules before you get behind the wheel. There are also lots of slow wiggly roads, one-way bridges and plenty of gravel roads, all of which require a more cautious driving approach. And watch out for sheep!

To check road conditions, call ☑0800 444 449 or see www.nzta.govt.nz/traffic.

Road Rules

➜ Kiwis drive on the left-hand side of the road; cars are right-hand drive. Give way to the right at intersections.

➜ All vehicle occupants must wear a seatbelt or risk a $150 fine. Small children must be belted into approved safety seats.

➜ Always carry your licence when driving.

➜ Drink-driving is a serious offence and remains a significant problem in NZ, despite widespread campaigns and severe penalties. The legal blood-alcohol limit is 0.05% for drivers aged over 20, and zero for those under 20.

➜ At single-lane bridges (of which there are a surprisingly large number), a smaller red arrow pointing in your direction of travel means that you give way.

➜ Speed limits on the open road are generally 100km/h; in built-up areas the limit is usually 50km/h. Speed cameras and radars are used extensively.

➜ Be aware that not all rail crossings have barriers or alarms. Approach slowly and look both ways.

➜ Don't pass other cars when the centre line is yellow.

➜ It's illegal to drive while using a mobile phone.

Hitching

Hitchhiking is never entirely safe, and we don't recommend it. Travellers who hitch should understand that they are taking a small but potentially serious risk. That said, it's not unusual to see hitchhikers along NZ country roads.

Alternatively, check hostel noticeboards for ride-share opportunities.

Local Transport

Bus & Tram

The South Island's larger centres have extensive bus services but, with a few honourable exceptions, they are mainly daytime, weekday operations; weekend services can be infrequent or nonexistent. Christchurch has city buses and a historic tramway. Don't expect local bus services in more remote areas.

Taxi

The main cities have plenty of taxis and even small towns may have a local service. Taxis are licensed, metered, and generally reliable and trustworthy.

Ride-Sharing

With the global explosion of ride-sharing apps, there are plenty of hungrily-circling alternatives to traditional taxis in Kiwi cities. They're still principally a city-based convenience, you can expect surge pricing at busy times, and fares are usually similar across the different providers. Here are a few of the most common:

Uber (www.uber.com) The original, and still easily the biggest. Covers Christchurch, Dunedin and Queenstown.

Ola (www.ola.co.nz) Trades on more equitable profit-sharing; currently servicing Christchurch on the South Island but we expect more SI cities soon.

Zoomy (www.zoomy.co.nz) Kiwi-owned, serving Christchurch so far.

Train

New Zealand train travel is all about the journey, not about getting anywhere in a hurry. **Great Journeys of New Zealand** (☑04-495 0775, 0800 872 467; www.greatjourneysofnz.co.nz), operated by KiwiRail, runs two routes on the South Island, listed below. It's best to reserve ahead, either online or by phone through Great Journeys of New Zealand, or in person at most train stations, travel agents and visitor information centres. Cheaper fares appear if you book online within NZ. All services are for day travel (there are no sleeper services).

Coastal Pacific This scenic route traces the east coast from Christchurch to Picton, closing annually in winter.

TranzAlpine Traversing the Southern Alps between Christchurch and Greymouth, this spectacular train journey is deservedly world famous.

Train Passes

Great Journeys of New Zealand's **Flexi** and **Flexi Plus** passes allow you to break your journey and change bookings up to 24 hours before departure. Both types of pass require you to book your seats a minimum of 24 hours before you want to travel, and have discounts for early birds and kids.

Language

New Zealand has three official languages: English, Māori and NZ sign language. Although English is what you'll usually hear, Māori has been making a comeback. You can use English to speak to anyone in New Zealand, but there are some occasions when knowing a small amount of Māori is useful, such as when visiting a *marae*, where often only Māori is spoken. Some knowledge of Māori will also help you interpret the many Māori place names you'll come across.

KIWI ENGLISH

Like the people of other English-speaking countries in the world, New Zealanders have their own, unique way of speaking the language. The flattening of vowels is the most distinctive feature of Kiwi pronunciation. For example, in Kiwi English, 'fish and chips' sounds more like 'fush and chups'. On the North Island sentences often have 'eh!' attached to the end. In the far south a rolled 'r' is common, which is a holdover from that region's Scottish heritage – it's especially noticeable in Southland.

MĀORI

The Māori have a vividly chronicled history, recorded in songs and chants that dramatically recall the migration to New Zealand from Polynesia as well as other important events. Early missionaries were the first to record the language in a written form using only 15 letters of the English alphabet.

Māori is closely related to other Polynesian languages such as Hawaiian, Tahitian and Cook Islands Māori. In fact, New Zealand Māori and Hawaiian are quite similar, even though more than 7000km separates Honolulu and Auckland.

The Māori language was never dead – it was always used in Māori ceremonies – but over time familiarity with it was definitely on the decline. Fortunately, recent years have seen a revival of interest in it, and this forms an integral part of the renaissance of *Māoritanga* (Māori culture). Many Māori people who had heard the language spoken on the *marae* for years but had not used it in their day-to-day lives, are now studying it and speaking it fluently. Māori is taught in schools throughout New Zealand, some TV programs and news reports are broadcast in it, and many English place names are being renamed in Māori. Even government departments have been given Māori names: for example, the Inland Revenue Department is also known as Te Tari Taake (the last word is actually *tāke*, which means 'levy', but the department has chosen to stress the long 'a' by spelling it 'aa').

In many places, Māori have come together to provide instruction in their language and culture to young children; the idea is for them to grow up speaking both Māori and English, and to develop a familiarity with Māori tradition. It's a matter of some pride to have fluency in the language. On some *marae* only Māori can be spoken.

Pronunciation

Māori is a fluid, poetic language and surprisingly easy to pronounce once you remember to split each word (some can be amazingly long) into separate syllables. Each syllable ends in a vowel. There are no 'silent' letters.

Most consonants in Māori – h, k, m, n, p, t and w – are pronounced much the same as in English. The Māori r is a flapped sound (not rolled) with the tongue near the front of the mouth. It's closer to the English 'l' in pronunciation.

The ng is pronounced as in the English words 'singing' or 'running', and can be used at the beginning of words as well as at the end. To practise, just say 'ing' over and over, then isolate the 'ng' part of it.

The letters wh, when occuring together, are generally pronounced as a soft English 'f'. This pronunciation is used in many place names in New Zealand, such as Whakatane, Whangaroa and Whakapapa (all pronounced as if they begin with a soft 'f'). There is some local variation: in the region around the Whanganui River, for example, *wh* is pronounced as in the English word 'when'.

The correct pronunciation of the vowels is very important. The examples below are a rough guideline – it helps to listen carefully to someone who speaks the language well. Each vowel has both a long and a short sound, with long vowels often denoted by a line over the letter or a double vowel.

Vowels

a	as in 'large', with no 'r' sound
e	as in 'get'
i	as in 'marine'
o	as in 'pork'
u	as the 'oo' in 'moon'

Vowel Combinations

ae, ai	as the 'y' in 'sky'
ao, au	as the 'ow' in 'how'
ea	as in 'bear'
ei	as in 'vein'
eo	as 'eh-oh'
eu	as 'eh-oo'
ia	as in the name 'Ian'
ie	as the 'ye' in 'yet'
io	as the 'ye o' in 'ye old'
iu	as the 'ue' in 'cue'
oa	as in 'roar'
oe	as in 'toe'
oi	as in 'toil'
ou	as the 'ow' in 'how'
ua	as the 'ewe' in 'fewer'

Greetings & Small Talk

Māori greetings are becoming increasingly popular – don't be surprised if you're greeted with *Kia ora*.

Welcome!	*Haere mai!*
Hello./Good luck./ Good health.	*Kia ora.*
Hello. (to one person)	*Tēnā koe.*
Hello. (to two people)	*Tēnā kōrua.*
Hello. (to three or more people)	*Tēnā koutou.*
Goodbye. (to person staying)	*E noho rā.*
Goodbye. (to person leaving)	*Haere rā.*

How are you? (to one person)	*Kei te pēhea koe?*
How are you? (to two people)	*Kei te pēhea kōrua?*
How are you? (to three or more people)	*Kei te pēhea koutou?*
Very well, thanks./ That's fine.	*Kei te pai.*

Māori Geographical Terms

The following words form part of many Māori place names in New Zealand, and help you understand the meaning of these place names. For example: Waikaremoana is the Sea (*moana*) of Rippling (*kare*) Waters (*wai*), and Rotorua means the Second (*rua*) Lake (*roto*).

a – of
ana – cave
ara – way, path or road
awa – river or valley
heke – descend
hiku – end; tail
hine – girl; daughter
ika – fish
iti – small
kahurangi – treasured possession; special greenstone
kai – food
kāinga – village
kākā – parrot
kare – rippling
kati – shut or close
kōura – crayfish
makariri – cold
manga – stream or tributary
manu – bird
maunga – mountain
moana – sea or lake
moko – tattoo
motu – island
mutu – finished; ended; over
ngā – the (plural)
noa – ordinary; not *tapu*
nui – big or great
nuku – distance
o – of, place of...
one – beach, sand or mud
pā – fortified village
papa – large blue-grey mudstone
pipi – common edible bivalve
pōhatu – stone
poto – short
pōuri – sad; dark; gloomy
puke – hill

puna – spring; hole; fountain
rangi – sky; heavens
raro – north
rei – cherished possession
roa – long
roto – lake
rua – hole in the ground; two
runga – above
tāhuna – beach; sandbank
tāne – man
tangata – people
tapu – sacred, forbidden or taboo
tata – close to; dash against; twin islands
tāwaha – entrance or opening
tāwāhi – the other side (of a river or lake)
te – the (singular)
tonga – south
ure – male genitals
uru – west
waha – broken
wāhine – woman
wai – water
waingaro – lost; waters that disappear in certain seasons
waka – canoe

wera – burnt or warm; floating
wero – challenge
whaka... – to act as ...
whānau – family
whanga – harbour, bay or inlet
whare – house
whenua – land or country
whiti – east

Here are some more place names composed of words in the list:

Aramoana – Sea (*moana*) Path (*ara*)
Awaroa – Long (*roa*) River (*awa*)
Kaitangata – Eat (*kai*) People (*tangata*)
Maunganui – Great (*nui*) Mountain (*maunga*)
Opouri – Place of (*o*) Sadness (*pouri*)
Te Araroa – The (*te*) Long (*roa*) Path (*ara*)
Te Puke – The (*te*) Hill (*puke*)
Urewera – Burnt (*wera*) Penis (*ure*)
Waimakariri – Cold (*makariri*) Water (*wai*)
Wainui – Great (*nui*) Waters (*wai*)
Whakatāne – To Act (*whaka*) as a Man (*tane*)
Whangarei – Cherished (*rei*) Harbour (*whanga*)

GLOSSARY

Following is a list of abbreviations, 'Kiwi English', Māori and slang terms used in this book and which you may hear in New Zealand.

All Blacks – NZ's revered national rugby union team
Anzac – Australia and New Zealand Army Corps
Aoraki – Māori name for Mt Cook, meaning 'Cloud Piercer'
Aotearoa – Māori name for NZ, most often translated as 'Land of the Long White Cloud'
aroha – love

B&B – bed and breakfast accommodation
bach – holiday home (pronounced 'batch'); see also crib
black-water rafting – rafting or tubing underground in a cave
boozer – public bar
bro – literally 'brother'; usually meaning mate

BYO – 'bring your own' (usually applies to alcohol at a restaurant or cafe)

choice/chur – fantastic; great
crib – the name for a bach in Otago and Southland

DB&B – bed and breakfast accommodation including dinner
DOC – Department of Conservation (or Te Papa Atawhai); government department that administers national parks, tracks and huts

eh? – roughly translates as 'don't you agree?'

farmstay – accommodation on a Kiwi farm
football – rugby, either union or league; occasionally soccer

Great Walks – set of nine popular tramping tracks within NZ

greenstone – jade; *pounamu*
gumboots – rubber boots or Wellingtons; originated from diggers on the gum-fields

haka – any dance, but usually a war dance
hāngī – oven whereby food is steamed in baskets over embers in a hole; a Māori feast
hapū – subtribe or smaller tribal grouping
Hawaiki – original homeland of the Māori
hei tiki – carved, stylised human figure worn around the neck; also called a *tiki*
homestay – accommodation in a family house
hongi – Māori greeting; the pressing of foreheads and noses, and sharing of life breath
hui – gathering; meeting

i-SITE – information centre

iwi – large tribal grouping with common lineage back to the original migration from *Hawaiki*; people; tribe

jandals – contraction of 'Japanese sandals'; flip-flops; thongs; usually rubber footwear

jersey – jumper, usually woollen; the shirt worn by rugby players

kauri – native pine

kia ora – hello

Kiwi – New Zealander; an adjective to mean anything relating to NZ

kiwi – flightless, nocturnal brown bird with a long beak

Kiwiana – things uniquely connected to NZ life and culture, especially from bygone years

kiwifruit – small, succulent fruit with fuzzy brown skin and juicy green flesh; aka Chinese gooseberry or zespri

kumara – Polynesian sweet potato, a Māori staple food

Kupe – early Polynesian navigator from *Hawaiki*, credited with the discovery of the islands that are now NZ

mana – spiritual quality of a person or object; authority or prestige

Māori – indigenous people of NZ

Māoritanga – things Māori, ie Māori culture

marae – sacred ground in front of the Māori meeting house;

more commonly used to refer to the entire complex of buildings

Māui – figure in Māori (Polynesian) mythology

mauri – life force/principle

moa – large, extinct flightless bird

moko – tattoo; usually refers to facial tattoos

ngā – the (plural); see also *te*

ngāi/ngāti – literally, 'the people of' or 'the descendants of'; tribe (pronounced 'kai' on the South Island)

NZ – universal term for New Zealand; pronounced 'en zed'

pā – fortified Māori village, usually on a hilltop

Pacific Rim – modern NZ cuisine; local produce cooked with imported styles

Pākehā – Māori for a white or European person

Pasifika – Pacific Island culture

paua – abalone; iridescent paua shell is often used in jewellery

pavlova – meringue cake topped with cream and kiwifruit

PI – Pacific Islander

poi – ball of woven flax

pounamu – Māori name for *greenstone*

pōwhiri – traditional Māori welcome onto a *marae*

rip – dangerously strong current running away from the shore at a beach

Roaring Forties – the ocean between 40° and 50° south, known for very strong winds

silver fern – symbol worn by the *All Blacks* and other national sportsfolk on their jerseys; the national netball team is called the Silver Ferns

sweet, sweet as – all-purpose term like *choice*; fantastic, great

tapu – strong force in Māori life, with numerous meanings; in its simplest form it means sacred, forbidden, taboo

te – the (singular); see also *nga*

te reo – literally 'the language'; the Māori language

tiki – short for *hei tiki*

tiki tour – scenic tour

tramp – bushwalk; trek; hike

tuatara – prehistoric reptile dating back to the age of dinosaurs

tui – native parson bird

wāhine – woman

wai – water

wairua – spirit

Waitangi – short way of referring to the Treaty of Waitangi

waka – canoe

Warriors – NZ's popular rugby league club, affiliated with Australia's NRL

Wellywood – Wellington, because of its thriving film industry

zorbing – rolling down a hill inside an inflatable plastic ball

Behind the Scenes

SEND US YOUR FEEDBACK

We love to hear from travellers – your comments keep us on our toes and help make our books better. Our well-travelled team reads every word on what you loved or loathed about this book. Although we cannot reply individually to your submissions, we always guarantee that your feedback goes straight to the appropriate authors, in time for the next edition. Each person who sends us information is thanked in the next edition – the most useful submissions are rewarded with a selection of digital PDF chapters.

Visit **lonelyplanet.com/contact** to submit your updates and suggestions or to ask for help. Our award-winning website also features inspirational travel stories, news and discussions.

Note: We may edit, reproduce and incorporate your comments in Lonely Planet products such as guidebooks, websites and digital products, so let us know if you don't want your comments reproduced or your name acknowledged. For a copy of our privacy policy visit lonelyplanet.com/privacy.

WRITER THANKS

Brett Atkinson

It's always a privilege to explore my own country. Cheers to Cate and Riwai Grace in Christchurch for tips and friendship, and Mum and Dad provided invaluable support during a busy time. Thanks to my co-authors: Peter, Tasmin and Monique; and to Kat and Angela in Melbourne for answering all my questions.

Peter Dragicevich

Many thanks to all the people that make working on the *New Zealand's South Island* guidebook such a joy. Special thanks goes to Hamish Blennerhassett for his outstanding hospitality in Wanaka and Queenstown, and to Liam Beattie for making my Glenorchy and Arrowtown stays so pleasurable. Thanks to my fellow authors, too, for tips and advice along the way – particularly Brett Atkinson, my hometown colleague, for being a sensible sounding board on many matters.

Monique Perrin

Thanks so much to Tasmin Waby for trusting me with this gig. Big kisses to Bob Scott for flying 36 hours to join me on the bike trail and to Matt Drake-Brockman for tramping with me through the snow. Enormous

thanks to Peter Dragicevich for the patient pro tips. And a huge bouquet of gratitude to Sonnet Curé, Acey Teasdale and Zyra McAuliffe – without your generosity and flexibility I simply could not have hit the road.

Tasmin Waby

Thanks to my co-writers, especially Brett and Peter for the mentoring on the road and back at my desk. Cheers, too, to Clare Loudon and Dave Tucker for putting up with me in Auckland. Thanks to my gorgeous family: Hugh, Willa and Maisie, for all the love and support this year. And finally my huge gratitude to ALL the Lonely Planeteers who made this excellent title (you know who you are). Your quest for excellence in publishing, and travel advice, continues to inspire me on every single trip.

ACKNOWLEDGEMENTS

Climate map data adapted from Peel MC, Finlayson BL & McMahon TA (2007) 'Updated World Map of the Köppen-Geiger Climate Classification', *Hydrology and Earth System Sciences*, 11, 1633–44.

Cover photograph: Moeraki Boulders, Otago, travellinglight/Shutterstock ©

THIS BOOK

This 7th edition of Lonely Planet's *New Zealand's South Island* guidebook was researched and written by Brett Atkinson, Peter Dragicevich, Monique Perrin and Tasmin Waby. The previous edition was curated by Peter Dragicevich, and researched and written by Brett Atkinson, Andrew Bain, Samantha Forge and Anita Isalska. The 5th

edition was written by Charles Rawlings-Way, Sarah Bennett, Peter Dragicevich and Lee Slater. This guidebook was produced by the following:

Destination Editor Tasmin Waby

Senior Product Editors Kate Chapman, Kathryn Rowan

Regional Senior Cartographer Diana Von Holdt

Product Editor Kate Kiely

Book Designers Virginia Moreno, Catalina Aragón

Assisting Editors Michelle Coxall, Gemma Graham, Rosie Nicholson, Kristin Odijk, Charlotte Orr, Mani Ramaswamy, Alison Ridgway, Gabrielle Stefanos, Fionnuala Twomey, Anna Tyler, Simon Williamson

Cartographer Mick Garrett

Cover Researcher Brendan Dempsey-Spencer

Thanks to Janet Dixon, Sasha Drew, Marcus Feaver, Mel Hutchinson, Angela Tinson

Index

Map Legend

Sights

- Beach
- Bird Sanctuary
- Buddhist
- Castle/Palace
- Christian
- Confucian
- Hindu
- Islamic
- Jain
- Jewish
- Monument
- Museum/Gallery/Historic Building
- Ruin
- Shinto
- Sikh
- Taoist
- Winery/Vineyard
- Zoo/Wildlife Sanctuary
- Other Sight

Activities, Courses & Tours

- Bodysurfing
- Diving
- Canoeing/Kayaking
- Course/Tour
- Sento Hot Baths/Onsen
- Skiing
- Snorkelling
- Surfing
- Swimming/Pool
- Walking
- Windsurfing
- Other Activity

Sleeping

- Sleeping
- Camping
- Hut/Shelter

Eating

- Eating

Drinking & Nightlife

- Drinking & Nightlife
- Cafe

Entertainment

- Entertainment

Shopping

- Shopping

Information

- Bank
- Embassy/Consulate
- Hospital/Medical
- Internet
- Police
- Post Office
- Telephone
- Toilet
- Tourist Information
- Other Information

Geographic

- Beach
- Gate
- Hut/Shelter
- Lighthouse
- Lookout
- Mountain/Volcano
- Oasis
- Park
- Pass
- Picnic Area
- Waterfall

Population

- Capital (National)
- Capital (State/Province)
- City/Large Town
- Town/Village

Transport

- Airport
- Border crossing
- Bus
- Cable car/Funicular
- Cycling
- Ferry
- Metro station
- Monorail
- Parking
- Petrol station
- Subway station
- Taxi
- Train station/Railway
- Tram
- Underground station
- Other Transport

Routes

- Tollway
- Freeway
- Primary
- Secondary
- Tertiary
- Lane
- Unsealed road
- Road under construction
- Plaza/Mall
- Steps
- Tunnel
- Pedestrian overpass
- Walking Tour
- Walking Tour detour
- Path/Walking Trail

Boundaries

- International
- State/Province
- Disputed
- Regional/Suburb
- Marine Park
- Cliff
- Wall

Hydrography

- River, Creek
- Intermittent River
- Canal
- Water
- Dry/Salt/Intermittent Lake
- Reef

Areas

- Airport/Runway
- Beach/Desert
- Cemetery (Christian)
- Cemetery (Other)
- Glacier
- Mudflat
- Park/Forest
- Sight (Building)
- Sportsground
- Swamp/Mangrove

Note: Not all symbols displayed above appear on the maps in this book

OUR STORY

A beat-up old car, a few dollars in the pocket and a sense of adventure. In 1972 that's all Tony and Maureen Wheeler needed for the trip of a lifetime – across Europe and Asia overland to Australia. It took several months, and at the end – broke but inspired – they sat at their kitchen table writing and stapling together their first travel guide, *Across Asia on the Cheap*. Within a week they'd sold 1500 copies. Lonely Planet was born.

Today, Lonely Planet has offices in Tennessee, Dublin, Beijing and Delhi, with a network of over 2000 contributors in every corner of the globe. We share Tony's belief that 'a great guidebook should do three things: inform, educate and amuse'.

OUR WRITERS

Brett Atkinson

Christchurch & Canterbury Brett is based in Auckland, New Zealand, but is frequently on the road for Lonely Planet. He's a full-time travel and food writer specialising in adventure travel, unusual destinations, and surprising angles on more well-known destinations. Craft beer and street food are Brett's favourite reasons to explore places, and he is featured regularly on the Lonely Planet website, and in newspapers, magazines and websites across New Zealand and Australia. Since becoming a Lonely Planet author in 2005, Brett has covered areas as diverse as Vietnam, Sri Lanka, the Czech Republic, New Zealand, Morocco, California and the South Pacific.

Peter Dragicevich

Queenstown & Wanaka, Marlborough & Nelson, the West Coast After a successful career in niche newspaper and magazine publishing, both in his native New Zealand and in Australia, Peter finally gave in to Kiwi wanderlust, giving up staff jobs to chase his diverse roots around much of Europe. Over the last 15 years he's written over 100 books for Lonely Planet on an oddly disparate collection of countries, all of which he's come to love. He once again calls Auckland, New Zealand his home – although his current nomadic existence means he's often elsewhere.

Monique Perrin

Dunedin & Otago, Fiordland & Southland Monique is a freelance writer, organic gardener, keen bushwalker and wannabe singer-songwriter. She's written on Tibet, the Philippines, Australia, India and travelling with kids for Lonely Planet, and she's worked across the world, including for the United Nations in Sri Lanka and as a journalist in Hong Kong. But her secret love is unearthing the hidden highlights of her awesome home town, Sydney.

Tasmin Waby

London-born to Kiwi parents, Tasmin was raised in Australia, for which she is incredibly grateful. As well as travelling, learning and writing, Tasmin is madly in love with cartography, wild swimming and starry skies. When not on assignment she lives on a narrowboat in England, with two hilariously funny school-aged children and a fat Russian Blue cat called Millie. Tasmin wrote the Plan, Understand and Survival Guide chapters.

Published by Lonely Planet Global Limited
CRN 554153
7th edition – Mar 2021
ISBN 978 1 78701 606 4
© Lonely Planet 2020   Photographs © as indicated 2020
10 9 8 7 6 5 4 3 2 1
Printed in China